Also by Kenneth M. Pollack

ARABS AT WAR: MILITARY EFFECTIVENESS,
1948–1991

The Threatening Storm

THE THREATENING
STORM

The Case for Invading Iraq

KENNETH M. POLLACK

RANDOM HOUSE / NEW YORK

Founded in 1921, the Council on Foreign Relations is a nonpartisan membership organization, research center, and publisher. It is dedicated to increasing America's understanding of the world and contributing ideas to U.S. foreign policy. The Council accomplishes this mainly by promoting constructive discussions and by publishing *Foreign Affairs,* the leading journal on global issues. The Council is host to the widest possible range of views, but an advocate of none, though its research fellows and Independent Task Forces do take policy stands. From time to time, books and reports written by members of the Council's research staff or others are published as a "Council on Foreign Relations Book."

Library of Congress Cataloging-in-Publication Data

Pollack, Kenneth M. (Kenneth Michael).
The threatening storm : the case for invading Iraq / Kenneth M. Pollack.
p. cm.
Includes bibliographical references and index.
ISBN 0-375-50928-3
1. Iraq—Politics and government—1991– 2. National security—United States. 3. United States—Relations—Middle East. 4. Middle East—Relations—United States. I. Title.

DS79.75 .P65 2002
956.7044'3—dc21   2002031619

Random House website address: www.atrandom.com
Printed in the United States of America on acid-free paper

24689753

First Edition

Book design by Casey Hampton

FOR ANDREA,
my wife, my everything.

THE SECOND COMING

Turning and turning in the widening gyre
The falcon cannot hear the falconer;
Things fall apart; the centre cannot hold;
Mere anarchy is loosed upon the world,
The blood-dimmed tide is loosed, and everywhere
The ceremony of innocence is drowned;
The best lack all conviction, while the worst
Are full of passionate intensity.

Surely some revelation is at hand;
Surely the Second Coming is at hand.
The Second Coming! Hardly are those words out
When a vast image out of Spiritus Mundi
Troubles my sight: somewhere in sands of the desert
A shape with lion body and the head of a man,
A gaze blank and pitiless as the sun,
Is moving its slow thighs, while all about it
Reel shadows of the indignant desert birds.
The darkness drops again; but now I know
That twenty centuries of stony sleep
Were vexed to nightmare by a rocking cradle,
And what rough beast, its hour come round at last,
Slouches towards Bethlehem to be born?

—W. B. YEATS

PREFACE

The first time I really smacked my head against U.S. policy toward Iraq was in July 1990. At that time, I was the junior military analyst on the Iran-Iraq account at the Central Intelligence Agency. Ever since the end of the Iran-Iraq War in 1988, my colleagues and I had had a series of scrapes with the policy makers on the other side of the Potomac. We kept raising Saddam's increasing military capabilities, his bellicose rhetoric, and his pursuit of all manner of weapons of mass destruction, and the State Department in particular kept accusing us of exaggerating the threat. But in July 1990, everything came to a head.

On July 17, U.S. satellites began to detect the lead elements of the Hammurabi Republican Guard Armored Division—the most powerful division in all of Iraq—arriving near Safwan, just north of Iraq's border with Kuwait. The previous day, Iraq's then foreign minister, Tariq Aziz, had accused Kuwait of trying to undermine the Iraqi economy by producing oil beyond its OPEC quota, and that same day, Saddam had himself delivered a speech attacking Kuwait for waging economic warfare against Iraq. Over the next couple of days the Iraqis continued their rhetorical attacks while information continued to mount that Baghdad was moving the entire Republican Guard—120,000 men and almost 1,000 tanks, the elite of the Iraqi armed forces—to the border with Kuwait in an unprecedented deployment.

By July 19, I was pretty certain that Iraq was building up for an all-out invasion of Kuwait, so I wrote an intelligence memo laying out my argument. But that memo went nowhere. Many of my colleagues at the CIA and elsewhere in the government disagreed, arguing that Saddam would not be so foolish or so crazy as to invade Kuwait, especially given the poor state of his economy. Many argued that he was only bluffing or, at worst, intending to seize two disputed islands and the southern half of the ar-Rumaylah oilfield, which straddled the Iraq-Kuwait border.

But the information kept pouring in, and I became increasingly convinced that Saddam intended a full invasion and nothing less—and increasingly alarmed that the U.S. government wasn't doing anything about it. Although Bush administration officials had become somewhat disenchanted with Saddam by the summer of 1990, they remained committed to a policy of constructive engagement with Iraq and didn't particularly want to hear a junior CIA analyst telling them that their policy was about to go up in smoke. Our Arab allies reassured Washington in its preferred course of action by promising us that Saddam was just bluffing. Moreover, many American policy makers continued to operate on the assumption that Saddam was a pragmatist who thought more or less like themselves and so would not do anything so rash as to conquer Kuwait.

In the end, I did get my analysis out, at least in part. My division chief, Winston Wiley, and deputy division chief, Bruce Riedel, recognized the importance of the argument I was making and fought to get my work a hearing—albeit in somewhat watered down form—in a piece that was sent to senior policy makers on July 25. This piece stated that Iraq was not bluffing about attacking Kuwait; its exact intentions were unclear, but it had the forces to conduct a full-scale invasion. The administration was hearing what it wanted to hear from other sources and dismissed our warning. That day I wrote a longer report, again trying to make the case that Iraq was going to invade, but it took me, Bruce, and Winston until August 1 to fight our way through the bureaucratic resistance and get it cleared. By then there was only time for Bruce to brief the report directly to Deputy Director for Central Intelligence Richard Kerr, who presented the conclusions to the National Security Council in a session that afternoon. That night, the Iraqis invaded Kuwait.

Unfortunately, July 1990 was not the last time I would witness U.S. policy makers assuming that if they did nothing, Saddam would act reasonably and we would not have to exert ourselves to bring him to heel or eliminate him as a threat to the stability of the vital Persian Gulf region. Unfortunately, it also was not the last time that U.S. policy toward Iraq was dangerously behind the power curve and operating on assumptions that were no longer valid. Nor was it the last time that U.S. policy makers (and intelligence officers) would indulge in mirror-imaging—assuming that Saddam would think as they would if they were in his shoes. All of these mistakes caused us to make poor policy choices toward Iraq on several occasions over the last twenty years.

Today, we face possibly the most important policy decision regarding Iraq we have ever had to make, and we cannot afford to make such mistakes. It is hard to pick up a newspaper or a magazine without finding some article or opinion piece arguing for one strategic direction toward Iraq or another. We are at a fork in the road of our policy toward Iraq, and the path we choose to take will have enormous repercussions. We are part of the world's most vibrant democracy; our choice must be a collective one. We cannot simply leave it to the government to decide what is best, because the choice we make could affect us all in profound ways—and because the Congress and the White House are going to need the support of the American people on whichever path they take. Consequently, it is critical that we engage in a comprehensive and informed public debate and make a choice that the American people can strongly support.

I wrote this book to try to help those trying to understand the problems we face with Iraq and the options available to the United States. It is intended for many different readers: the reader who knows very little about Iraq, the reader who knows a great deal about Iraq, and everyone in between, will, I hope, find things of interest here. The book begins by describing the history of U.S.-Iraqi relations over the last twenty years as a way of understanding how the United States and Iraq reached the unhappy stand-off that currently prevails. It then describes the state of Iraq today: its economy, its political system, the state of its people after three decades of Saddam's misrule and a decade of sanctions, the state of its weapons of mass destruction as best we understand them, Saddam's terrifying security apparatus and how it keeps him in power, Iraq's support for terrorism, and the state of its armed forces. It also describes how Iraq is perceived by its various neighbors and how those states would like to see the United States handle Saddam. Finally, it lays out a range of U.S. policy options and considers each one in turn: its advantages, its disadvantages, its strengths and weaknesses.

However, this book is not entirely neutral. While I have tried hard to be fair to each of the policy options and to make the strongest case for them that I could, there is a strong central argument running through the book: through our own mistakes, the perfidy of others, and Saddam's cunning, the United States is left with few good policy options toward Iraq, and increasingly, the option that makes the most sense is for the United States to launch a full-scale invasion of Iraq to topple Saddam, eradicate his weapons of mass destruction, and rebuild Iraq as a prosperous and stable society for the good of the United States, Iraq's own people, and the entire region.

I do not advocate such a policy lightly. Indeed, having spent my entire career in government wrestling with the problem of Iraq—as an Iran-Iraq military analyst at the CIA, as a senior research professor at the National Defense University (where I spent much of my time writing on Persian Gulf matters for the Joint Chiefs of Staff), and as director for Persian Gulf Affairs at the National Security Council—I embrace it only grudgingly. As I try to demonstrate in this book, a new war with Iraq definitely won't be cheap and might not be easy. I recognize full well that such a war could result in the deaths of thousands of people—Americans, Iraqis, and others—and destroy the lives of many more. It would cost tens of billions of dollars. And it would likely be the highest U.S. foreign policy priority for many years, precluding other foreign policy initiatives as we turn our resources and attention to Iraq.

I believed for many years that the United States could prevent Saddam Hussein from threatening the stability of the Persian Gulf region and the world through the combination of sanctions and limited military operations referred to as the policy of "containment." I still believe that there were paths not taken that could have produced a stronger containment regime that could have done the job better for longer. Even so, containment served the United States very well for many years, and it is a testimony to the skill of the many American officials charged with implementing Iraq policy since 1990 that the United States was able to play a losing hand for so long. Unfortunately, I believe that containment is no longer a viable option. Nor are any of the other alternative policies discussed in this book more palatable or more realistic. It is often said that war should be employed only in the last resort. I reluctantly believe that in the case of the threat from Iraq, we have come to the last resort.

The fact that a war against Iraq could be potentially quite costly should make us think long and hard about whether or not we should embark upon such an endeavor, but it should never be an absolute impediment. Often, the costliest wars are the ones that are the most important to fight. Still more often, fighting sooner is frequently far less costly than fighting later. In the case of Iraq, if we do not act soon to topple Saddam Hussein's regime, we are likely to face a much worse conflict with him down the road after he has acquired nuclear weapons and advanced conventional weapons. An invasion of Iraq in the near term, when Saddam has only a limited stockpile of weapons of mass destruction and his conventional forces remain weak, is likely to seem effortless and cost-free compared to a war with Saddam after he has crossed the nuclear threshold. Given Saddam's propensity to miscalculate, his penchant for aggression, and his willingness to absorb horrific punishment, it would be a terrible mistake for the United States to allow him to acquire such capabilities and risk war with a nuclear-armed Iraq.

The moment we face is reminiscent of another in early 1938. At that time, Britain and France were unquestionably stronger than Nazi Germany. They looked out across the Rhine and they saw a Germany they knew would trouble them in the future. They saw in Adolf Hitler a leader who was aggressive, willing to use force, and rapidly rebuilding Germany's strength. Winston Churchill and others argued for making war on Germany then and there to end German belligerence and head off a greater threat before it could develop. The leaders of Britain and France believed that if they did launch such a preventive war against Germany, they would probably win, but after the carnage of the First World War, they feared that any war against Germany would be too bloody. Instead, they decided to try to find some other way of dealing with Hitler. In the end, this was a terrible mistake. Bloody though a war in 1938 might have been, it would have paled in comparison to the actual savagery and slaughter of the war that Hitler unleashed in the fall of 1939. Britain and France almost certainly would have defeated Germany in 1938. By waiting until 1939, France was crushed and Britain came very close to following. In retrospect, there are few who doubt that Britain, France, and the entire world would have been much better off had England and France steeled themselves and resolved on war in 1938.

Just as France and Britain should have taken up arms in 1938, I believe that the United States should take up arms against Iraq to end the threat from Saddam Hussein's regime once and for all. This is not to insinuate that those who wish to contain or deter Saddam are somehow equivalent to those who opposed a war with Hitler—that they are appeasers. That would be a vicious slander, undeserved by intelligent and patriotic men and women who simply have a different point of view. Nor is it to suggest that the threat posed by Saddam Hussein is of the same magnitude as that posed by Hitler's Germany. It is only to argue that the choices we face are closely akin to those faced in London and Paris in 1938—a potentially costly war now or a far worse war in the near future. This book argues that war with Saddam's Iraq is well nigh inevitable and that it would be far, far better for the United States to face this challenge sooner rather than later.

CONTENTS

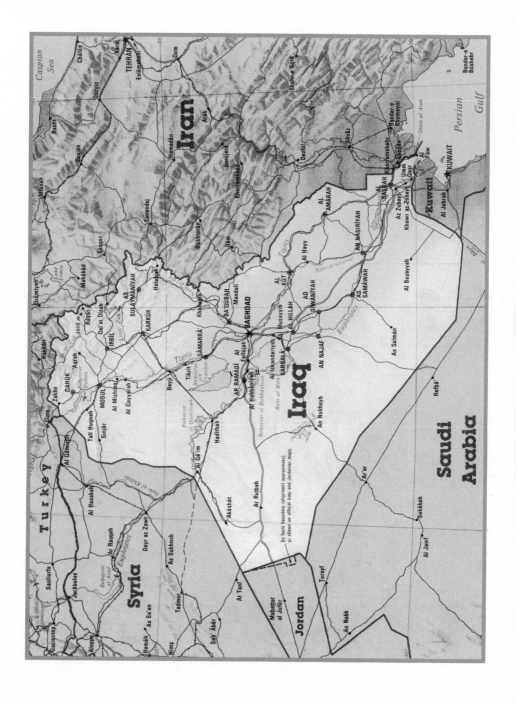

The Problem of Iraq

As best we can tell, Iraq was not involved in the terrorist attacks of September 11, 2001. American intelligence officials have repeatedly affirmed that they can't connect Baghdad to the attacks despite Herculean labors to do so. "There's not a drop of evidence" linking Iraq to the attacks, one senior intelligence official told the *Los Angeles Times*.[1] Iraq's ties to Usama bin Ladin's al-Qa'eda terrorist network were always fairly limited. Saddam generally saw bin Ladin as a wild card he could not control and so mostly shied away from al-Qa'eda for fear that a relationship could drag him into a war with the United States that was not of his making.[2] Likewise, bin Ladin detested Saddam for his lack of piety, his cynical support for Islam only when it was politically convenient, and his brutal suppression of Islamic leaders who challenged his control over Iraq.

So far, the evidence that has been produced to claim an Iraqi link to the 9/11 attacks has failed to measure up. The claimed "smoking gun" was a reputed meeting between the 9/11 mastermind, Muhammad Atta, and an Iraqi intelligence official in Prague during April 2001. However, the Czechs have changed their story on this meeting several times, and U.S. intelligence officials are skeptical that the meeting took place.[3] Even if they did meet, since no one knows what they said and there is no other evidence to implicate Iraq, the fact of a meeting itself doesn't allow us to make the case that Saddam was behind 9/11. Likewise, stories have emerged that Iraq has supported an Iraqi Kurdish group with strong ties to al-Qa'eda, initially called Jund al-Islam but later called Ansar i-Islam, as a proxy against the Patriotic Union of Kurdistan (PUK)—one of the two main Iraqi Kurdish factions. Although the claims come from prisoners of the PUK and therefore should be treated with caution, they may be valid. Nevertheless, even if it does turn out to be true that Saddam has supported a small faction of pro-al-Qa'eda Iraqi Kurds against the other Kurdish militias, this is still a far step from demonstrating that he was behind al-Qa'eda terrorist operations against the United States. Both the United States and Iran supported the Bosnian Muslims during the 1990s, but that doesn't mean the United States was behind Iranian terrorist operations.[4]

U.S., British, Israeli, and Arab intelligence services generally agree that the links between Iraq and al-Qa'eda were fairly tenuous. Iraq does support terrorist groups, and Iraq's main intelligence service, the Mukhabbarat, engages in terrorist actions itself. As such it is involved in the terrorist underworld and at times Mukhabbarat agents have made contact with al-Qa'eda operatives. It also seems likely that Iraq and al-Qa'eda have probably exchanged services at various times (Iraq selling al-Qa'eda forged passports or al-Qa'eda providing Iraq with intelligence). Finally, there are some rumors that over the years members of both groups have tried to explore ways to cooperate against their common foes, including the United States. However, none of the Western agencies has found any evidence of sustained contact or cooperation. Instead, whenever information has been available, it has demonstrated that neither side wanted to have too much to do with the other and they mostly went their separate ways. After all, Saddam Hussein is an avowed secularist who has killed far more Muslim clerics than he has American soldiers, and this puts him high on bin Ladin's list of enemies. As a more general point, Paul Pillar, the national intelligence officer for the Near East and South Asia and the former deputy director of the CIA's Counterterrorism Center, has written that "terrorism is by no means the main U.S. concern regarding Iraq."[5]

Even though it appears doubtful that Iraq was involved in the September 11 attacks, the question of U.S. policy toward Iraq is still very relevant in the post-9/11 world. The tragedy of September 11 was a wake-up call to the American people. After the victories of the Cold War and the Persian Gulf War, many Americans felt safe. Threats to U.S. national interests, let alone to American civilians themselves, seemed small and distant. The U.S. public grew complacent about its security. September 11 shattered that sense of complacency. It drove home to many Americans the realization that there are still deadly threats in the world and that there are people who are looking to inflict terrible destruction on the United States. September 11 convinced many Americans that we needed to be more engaged in the world, to actively seek out threats and destroy them before they can strike at us.

Iraq is clearly one of these threats. In the months after the September 11 attacks, polls consistently showed large majorities of Americans desirous of using force against Iraq. For example, in a poll conducted six months after 9/11 by the Pew Research Center, the Council on Foreign Relations, and the *International Herald Tribune,* 69 percent of Americans favored military action against Iraq to end Saddam Hussein's regime.[6] As September 11 recedes into history, these numbers have begun to decline—another poll conducted by Gallup in June 2002 found that those supporting a military campaign to topple Saddam had fallen to 59 percent of those polled.[7] It is also unclear from the polls to what extent the public understands how much force would likely be required to oust Saddam or the potential costs of doing so. Nevertheless, these numbers are still remarkably high. The combination of popular willingness both to use force against Iraq and to make sacrifices to safeguard the nation open up the possibility of new policy options toward Iraq—policy options previously considered unfeasible because of an assumed absence of public support. For instance, before September 11, the notion of mounting a full-scale invasion of Iraq was thought politically impossible because no Washington decision maker believed that the U.S. public would be willing to shoulder the potentially heavy costs of such an endeavor. As a result, those who favored regime change had to argue for policies based on covert action or limited uses of military force. Today, a full-scale invasion is considered a highly plausible course of action because Washington believes that the American people would support it.

Moreover, the rest of the world also recognizes that the United States has been galvanized into action by the September 11 attacks, and this suggests that the United States may encounter less diplomatic opposition to more ambitious Iraq policies than in the past. Many nations are willing to give the United States a wider berth than in the past. No one wants to cross the wounded superpower. Others are genuinely sympathetic, recognizing that in the wake of the death of three thousand innocent American citizens, the United States has the right to take action to protect American lives. Others simply respect American power. They see that the U.S. public is willing to make sacrifices to achieve greater security, which means that Washington can tackle much greater challenges than before 9/11. Given that the United States is more willing to exert itself, there are nations that are simply more willing to follow our lead.

In addition, there are potential risks if the United States does not address its policy toward Iraq at this time. The global war against terrorism could also prove a distraction from Iraq. Baghdad, and many of its advocates, may believe that they can bargain with the United States, offering greater cooperation in the war on terrorism in return for U.S. concessions on Iraq. On the other hand, through its aggressive rhetoric, the Bush administration has convinced many people around the world that it intends to use force against Iraq, and this conviction has given Iraq and its advocates pause. Should the United States not make good on those threats, international opinion is likely to be more convinced than ever that there are no penalties for noncompliance with the U.N. resolutions on Iraq and that the United States will never be willing to incur the costs necessary to actually overthrow Saddam's regime. At the very least, the United States needs to seize the opportunities of this moment to put in place a new policy that can address the problem of Saddam Hussein's Iraq beyond tomorrow.

THE EROSION OF CONTAINMENT

Perhaps the single most important reason why the United States must act soon to adopt a new policy toward Iraq is that our old policy, the policy of containment, is eroding. Containment served the United States well after 1991, much better than most ever thought it could. But it is failing. The United States missed opportunities throughout the post–Gulf War era, first to build a better containment policy and later to reform it so that it could last over the long term. The fault, however, was not entirely our own. Many of our allies proved perfidious, feckless, or outright duplicitous. Moreover, in the end, Saddam devised a strategy that took advantage of our own missteps and the shortcomings of our allies to undermine the policy and help speed its demise. Containment is not going to disappear tomorrow. We could cling to it for a few years more even in its current ailing state, but it is not long for this world.

Containment of Iraq was always a subtly different strategy from that which the United States had successfully employed against the Soviet Union throughout the Cold War. With the Soviets, U.S. strategy was simply to deter or prevent them from pushing out beyond the borders of their "bloc"—the USSR itself and its satellite states in Eastern Europe and Northeast Asia. What the Soviets did within the confines of the Iron Curtain was their business. From the start, containment of Iraq was intended to be different. It proceeded from the central premise that Saddam Hussein was too dangerous a leader to allow to develop weapons of mass destruction (WMD), particularly nuclear weapons. Thus, containment of Iraq was intended not just to prevent Iraq from conducting new aggression beyond its borders but to prevent Iraq from rebuilding the military power to be able to even entertain the *idea* of new aggression. The United States did not want to have to deter or defeat another Iraqi invasion. Instead, the goal was to deny Saddam the capability to mount a threat in the first place. Consequently, containment of Iraq was always a much more ambitious undertaking than containment of the USSR had ever been.

When originally conceived during 1991–92, containment consisted of four central elements designed both to prevent Iraq from rearming and to keep it from making trouble in the vital Persian Gulf region. The linchpin of the effort was a U.N. disarmament program intended to strip Iraq of its extant WMD and ballistic missile arsenal as well as its capability to produce new such weapons. Although it was assumed that the actual disarmament would be over quickly, the United Nations also created a mechanism for long-term monitoring intended to prevent Iraq from ever reconstituting these programs. To ensure Iraq's compliance with the disarmament provisions, the draconian sanctions first imposed on Baghdad in 1990 to try to force Saddam to rescind his conquest of Kuwait were kept in place. Strangely, although no one believed the sanctions would have been adequate to force Saddam to give up Kuwait by themselves, great confidence was placed in them to force Saddam's full compliance with the United Nations' disarmament provisions. Later, the sanctions took on a larger role within the containment policy as another means of preventing Iraq from rebuilding its military, especially when it became clear that Saddam had no intention of complying with the United Nations' disarmament program.

Meanwhile, U.S. military forces would remain in the Gulf to deal with the much reduced military threat Iraq presented after the devastation of the Gulf War. In addition, at least among the U.S. government's Iraq experts, it was always recognized that U.S. forces would also be required to periodically punish Iraq when Saddam inevitably cheated on his international obligations. Saddam was not one to go gentle into that good night; he was always going to have to be dragged forcibly, and a U.S. military presence would be needed for that onerous task. Unfortunately, the United States gave up its greatest leverage to enforce Iraqi compliance when it precipitously withdrew its forces from southern Iraq, leaving us to do it the hard way, from outside the country. Eventually, the United States, the United Kingdom, and France would add two large no-fly zones (NFZs), in which Iraqi aircraft were prohibited. Although principally intended to limit Saddam's ability to repress Iraq's Shi'ite and Kurdish populations, in practice they were more useful as elements of containment in maintaining pressure on the regime and preventing an Iraqi threat to Kuwait, Jordan, or the Kurdish-held lands of northern Iraq.

The problem the United States faces today is that all of these elements of containment are foundering. The U.N. disarmament effort died when Saddam evicted the weapons inspectors in the fall of 1998. Even at that time, the U.N. inspectors believed that Saddam was preserving a hidden cache of chemical and biological weapons (CW and BW) and ballistic missiles.[8] They were also convinced that the Iraqis had retained the know-how and probably much of the equipment they needed to rebuild their WMD and ballistic missile arsenals and to get back to work building nuclear weapons. Since then, defectors have revealed that Saddam had concealed quite a bit more than even the inspectors realized and that soon after ousting them he resumed his WMD programs to regain and surpass the capabilities he had amassed before the Gulf War.

The American military presence in the Persian Gulf is under pressure. The people of the region are generally unhappy with the presence of U.S. military forces in their countries. Some see it as a necessary evil; others condemn it as a form of imperialist occupation. Painfully few welcome it. The governments of the region continue to want our presence, but they recognize the popular discontent and increasingly bend to it. Although there is no sign that U.S. forces will be asked to leave soon, it appears ever more clear that the days of our current force levels in the Gulf are numbered. Perhaps we could maintain the same presence for five years, perhaps longer. Few people believe that we can maintain the current force posture in the region—with major bases in five of the six Gulf Cooperation Council (GCC) states—for another decade or more.[9]

Of greater importance still, the ability of the United States to employ limited military operations to compel Iraqi compliance with U.N. resolutions is effectively gone. This is a critical point with which few Americans have yet come to terms. Starting in 1996, the GCC states began to grow uncomfortable with American air strikes against Iraq. Over time, these problems have worsened. On some occasions, the Saudis and other regional allies have indicated that they simply would not support a U.S. military operation against Iraq. More often, they have restricted how the United States was able to operate. In particular, the Saudis now forbid us to fly strike missions from their air bases, insisting that they be launched instead from Kuwait, Bahrain, or carriers in the Gulf. Today, the GCC states and Turkey are dead set against new, limited military operations (Chapter 5 discusses the reasons for this state of affairs). They have made very clear that while they would support one last, massive operation to remove Saddam from power once and for all, they are not interested in waging an open-ended war against Iraq. Thus the coercive military operations that were an essential part of containment have largely been taken out of our hands.

The no-fly zones themselves are becoming hard to hold on to. As part of their overall distaste for limited U.S. military operations, many of the moderate Arab states would like to see the no-fly zones eliminated. Since early 1999, Iraqi air defense forces have been shooting at coalition planes patrolling the no-fly zones on an almost daily basis, provoking the coalition pilots to respond in self-defense from time to time. Iraqi propaganda has successfully convinced much of the Arab world that the no-fly zones are illegal and that the U.S. and U.K. response strikes are killing large numbers of innocent Iraqi civilians. Although most of the Arab governments know that this is untrue, they also hate the anger that these responsive strikes create among their publics. Kuwait and Saudi Arabia continue to support the NFZs only because the southern zone provides vital warning of an Iraqi attack, and Turkey puts up with the northern zone out of deference to its American allies and fear that Washington would retaliate regarding other key Turkish interests (Cyprus, its application for European Union membership, and so on) if it did not. However, none of them cares for the NFZs and they would prefer that we find another way to protect Shi'ites and Kurds and provide warnings of Iraqi moves. Even our British allies are tiring of the commitment to the NFZs (the French bailed out several years ago) and would like to see us drastically scale back our sorties. London dislikes the constant conflict with the Iraqi air defense forces, fears that it might lose a plane (and have a pilot captured by Iraq), and worries that the anger of Arab publics against the allied responses is undermining both their standing in the region and other aspects of containment.

Worst of all, however, is the rapid increase in smuggling to Iraq and the concomitant erosion of the sanctions. In 1999, Iraqi oil smuggling amounted to about $350 million, or roughly 5 percent of its total revenue. Today, oil smuggling amounts to $2.5 billion to $3 billion, representing 15 to 22 percent of Iraqi revenue. And these numbers are climbing. Jordan, Syria, Lebanon, and Turkey are all working to try to increase the amount of illegal Iraqi oil they can handle.[10] Meanwhile, all manner of goods are flowing into Iraq. Throughout the period of sanctions there have been countries and companies that have been willing to sell Iraq anything it wants. For example, in 1995, Jordanian officials (acting on information provided by the U.N. inspectors) intercepted a shipment of illegal Russian missile gyroscopes headed for Iraq.[11] However, the liberalization of the oil-for-food program over the last three to four years has made it easier for Baghdad to sneak illegal goods in and seems to have made many countries more willing to flout the remaining sanctions. For example, in 2000, the United States discovered that China was building a nationwide fiber-optic communications system that was to have been employed by Baghdad's military and internal security infrastructures, including its air defense command. Such a massive project demonstrated a shocking disregard for the sanctions by a member of the U.N. Security Council's five permanent members.[12] Saddam has ever greater control of Iraq's resources and is more and more able to get hold of prohibited items for his military.

Finally, there is the problem of Saddam's nuclear program. Iraq knows how to build a nuclear weapon and did so in 1990; the only thing it was missing was the fissile material, the uranium. Because Iraq has natural uranium deposits, all the Iraqis need to do is build a process to enrich that uranium to weapons grade and then enrich enough to make one or more Hiroshima-sized weapons. Today, we have information from key defectors and a consensus among knowledgeable experts that the Iraqis are hard at work on such a program and that they have all the know-how and the technology to do it. The only question is how long it is going to take them. Given the opportunity to deal with the Iraq problem created by 9/11, it would behoove us to decide now how the United States will deal with that eventuality.

THE MENU OF DECISION

Containment may not yet be at a crisis point, but the ground beneath our feet is fast crumbling. Moreover, because of the window of opportunity created by the tragedy of September 11, we have reached a fork in the road. The path we are currently on leads to a particular destination; that destination is a policy called "deterrence." Many intelligent Americans are perfectly comfortable with deterrence, but many others are not, and there is no question that deterrence, as understood in the Iraqi context, is a different policy from containment, and has different risks. Indeed, we would do well to examine those risks and decide whether that is the policy we wish to adopt rather than simply stumbling into it (as we stumbled into containment) for lack of a better alternative. Probably for the last time, the United States now has the chance to make a major change in its Iraq policy. At the very least, we should look hard at deterrence and the other policy options, decide what is best for this country, and pursue that policy with conviction.

The problem is deciding what that new policy should be. Today, the United States essentially has five options:

1. **Rebuild containment** so that it can last for the long term. This would require dramatically altering the sanctions to choke off the smuggling to Iraq, finding a way to restore the inspectors to Iraq and allow them to do their job for as long as it takes, restructuring the U.S. force presence to reduce the strain on our regional allies, and rebuilding an international consensus to make it possible for the United States to employ limited force to coerce Saddam when he (inevitably) challenges the system.

2. Rely on pure **deterrence** to keep Iraq from again threatening the stability of the region. The key difference between the policy of deterrence and that of containment in the Iraq context is that deterrence would effectively give up on both inspections and sanctions and allow Saddam to build WMD, counting on the military power of the United States—and, ultimately, our own nuclear arsenal—to deter him from new aggressions.

3. Try to topple Saddam's regime by relying on traditional **covert action** methods to create or empower forces inside Iraq, probably from within Saddam's inner circle, to move against him in a coup d'état.

4. Employ the **"Afghan Approach"** of support to indigenous opposition forces backed by U.S. air power and special forces to overthrow the Iraqi regime. Although the focus would be on ousting the regime without committing a heavy U.S. presence, as in Afghanistan, the

United States would still likely find itself committed to rebuilding Iraq after Saddam's fall.

5. Mount a full-scale **invasion** of Iraq to remove the Iraqi regime, scour the country for WMD, and rebuild a stable, prosperous Iraq.

As I will explain over the course of this book, I believe that the last option, a full-scale invasion, has unfortunately become our best option—or at least our "least bad" option. However, I am equally convinced that an invasion of Iraq must be done right. We must commit ourselves fully to the effort, employ all the forces necessary to secure victory quickly and with the least loss of life, and be ready to lead an international effort to rebuild Iraq afterward, to ensure that we do not simply trade the threat of a nuclear-armed Saddam for the threat of an Iraq in chaos and civil war.

The place to start thinking about a new U.S. policy toward Iraq is in the lessons of the recent past. It is important to understand Iraq's history, our own policies toward the Persian Gulf region, and the history of U.S.-Iraqi relations, because the choices available to the United States today are largely a product of this history. What's more, the history of U.S.-Iraqi relations furnishes a great deal of important evidence that is critical to evaluating the policy options we now face. To decide where we should go from here, it is important to know how we got to where we are.

Part I

IRAQ AND THE UNITED STATES

ONE

From Sumer to Saddam

For many long years, Iraq and the United States had little to do with each other. The days of Iraq's greatest glory occurred long before there ever was a United States, and in recent centuries, while America was still a young and relatively isolated nation, the Iraqis were ruled by the Ottoman Turks, whose relationship with the United States barely existed. Even after the fall of the Ottoman Empire in World War I and the formation of the modern state of Iraq, it was Britain, not America, that dominated Iraqi politics for decades. Indeed, as for many Arabs, until only the last few decades, the United States was little more than a strange name of a distant land for most Iraqis. Before the Second World War, the United States had only commercial relationships in the Persian Gulf, and it carefully avoided any involvement in the region's politics. In the decades after the war, Washington did take an increasing interest in the Gulf but mostly focused its attentions on Saudi Arabia and Iran. Iraq was a weak radical Arab state with ties to Russia but did not pose enough of a threat to take seriously. It was not until the 1980s that the two countries came into meaningful contact, and then the limits of their prior relations bred ignorance, miscalculation, and suspicion, leading to regular misreadings of each other's intentions.

THE SHADOW OF IRAQ'S PAST

In the popular imagination, Iraq is a vast desert, interrupted by occasional oases and cut by the two great rivers of ancient Mesopotamia, the Tigris and Euphrates. While much of Iraq is desert, especially in the south and west, the Kurdish north is heavily mountainous and great swathes of the country are fertile farmland. Indeed, in ancient times, Iraq was one of the lushest regions on earth. The biblical Garden of Eden was set in Iraqi Mesopotamia. More than 5,000 years ago, that verdant soil produced the world's earliest known civilization, that of Sumer in southern Meso- potamia, which developed writing, divisions of labor, complex social hier- archies, and an elaborate political and religious system. Out of ancient Sumer came Abraham, the father of Jews and Arabs, the founder of Ju- daism, the first monotheist. The Sumerians were also the first pyramid builders, although their massive ziggurats were great temples like those of the Mayans and Aztecs, rather than tombs like the Egyptians. Sargon I of Akkad conquered Sumer and spread its culture to the Mediterranean by adding northern Mesopotamia, Syria, and southern Turkey to his demesne. After the Sumerians, two of the ancient world's great empires ruled the lands that would become Iraq. First Babylon, whose Hanging Gardens were a wonder of the ancient world and whose people bequeathed us the Code of Hammurabi, perhaps the world's first written legal system and the origin of "an eye for an eye, a tooth for a tooth." After that came Assyria, whose fearsome armies are credited with the first systematic application of the science of military logistics. Later Assyrian and Babylonian kings ruled all of modern Iraq, Syria, Jordan, Lebanon, and Israel. Indeed, it was the Babylonian king Nebuchadnezzar II who sacked Jerusalem and took the Jews into captivity in Babylon.

For more than a millennium after the fall of Babylon and Assyria, the lands of Iraq would be ruled by empires out of what would become Iran. First the Medes, then the Persians, and finally the Parthians would rule Mesopotamia, both north and south. Throughout that time, Babylon re- mained an important center of culture and political administration. Alexan- der passed through on his campaigns, fighting a mighty battle at Arbela (present day Arbil in northern Iraq). However, it was not until the Islamic conquest of the seventh century A.D. that Iraq again resumed prominence. Mesopotamia was among the first of the conquests of the caliphs who suc- ceeded the prophet Muhammad, and it enjoyed temporary glory again when 'Ali ibn Abi Talib, the fourth caliph and the husband of Muhammad's beloved daughter, Fatima, moved the Islamic capital to Kufa in southern Mesopotamia. But 'Ali was murdered after only a brief reign. His follow-ers became the Shi'ah (from *Shi'at* 'Ali, the Party of 'Ali), while his rival, Mu'awiyah of Damascus, became caliph and leader of the majority Sunni branch of Islam, transferring the capital to Syria.

Less than a hundred years later, in A.D. 762, a new dynasty of caliphs, the Abbasids, built a new capital at Baghdad that would remain the center of the Islamic empire for nearly five hundred years. During that time, Baghdad was arguably the greatest center of art, learning, and culture in the world and was ruled by storied caliphs such as Harun al-Rashid, famous for his role in the epic *Thousand and One Nights*. In the midst of this golden age, barbarian warriors (at least the Arabs considered them such) from Christian Europe invaded the Levant to seize Jerusalem and other sites con-sidered holy by all three of the great monotheistic faiths. In the long war against these Crusaders, it was another Iraqi—Salah ad-Din, or Saladin, a Kurd from the city of Tikrit—who would turn the tide in favor of the Islamic armies, recapturing Jerusalem and setting in motion the inevitable destruction of the Crusader kingdoms. These glory days ended in the thir-teenth century, when Mongol hordes under Hulagu Khan smashed the caliph's armies and sacked Baghdad in 1258, ending the reign of the Ab-basids. Although the Mongol conquest was brief, it was terrible, and it broke the power of the Islamic Arabs, paving the way for the rise of the Turkish empires, first of the Seljuks and later of the Ottomans, who would rule Iraq for nearly four hundred years, until the First World War.[1]

During the Ottoman era, the territory of Iraq was administered by three separate provinces (*vilayet*s). In the north was Mosul *vilayet,* including the cities of Mosul, Kirkuk, Arbil, and as-Sulaymaniyyah and dominated by Sunni Kurds.[2] In the center was Baghdad *vilayet,* comprising the former Islamic capital, its environs, and the lands to the west that were primarily Sunni Arab. Finally, al-Basrah *vilayet* administered most of the old lands of southern Mesopotamia. It was heavily Shi'ite Arab and included the Shi'ite holy cities of Karbala and an-Najaf.[3]

After the defeat of the Ottomans during the First World War, their terri-tory was divided up by the British and French, who established mandates over much of the former Ottoman Empire. Britain coveted Baghdad and al-Basrah (what it called "the Mesopotamian provinces") in part for its sus-pected oil and agricultural wealth, but mostly because London wanted a contiguous land bridge from the Persian Gulf to the Mediterranean across which it could move forces to defend British India. The British secured the Mediterranean end of this route by acquiring Palestine and Trans-Jordan (later renamed "Jordan"). The eastern end would be the new mandatory territory of Iraq, at first intended to comprise only the Baghdad and al-Basrah provinces. Eventually, London would add Mosul province, not only because it was believed to be rich in oil (later proven by the finding of the massive Kirkuk oil fields in the 1920s) but also to create a buffer zone against Turkey and Russia. As for Iraq's western boundary, it was determined largely by simple geography: the great urban centers of Baghdad and the Mesopotamian valley were divided from those of the Levant by the Syrian desert, and the main transportation artery stretching across it was the Baghdad-Amman road. The British essentially divided that road in half and gave the administration of territory to the west of that midpoint to Jordan, while that to the east went to Iraq. In 1921, the British decided to make Faysal ibn Hussein al-Hashim, the third son of their World War I ally (and Lawrence of Arabia's principal confederate) Sharif Hussein of Mecca, the new king of Iraq.[4]

The Hashimites would rule Iraq for thirty-seven years. It was a turbulent reign because the kings were foreigners installed by the British, whom the Iraqi people quickly learned to hate. Of the three Hashimite kings, only Ghazi, who ruled from 1933 to 1939, had any degree of popularity, because he was anti-British. When he died in an automobile accident in 1939, it was widely believed that London was responsible. In 1936, Iraq was the first Arab nation to experience a military coup, although the generals were seeking only to replace the pro-British cabinet and not the popular King Ghazi. In 1941, with German armored columns driving toward the Middle East from both the west (Rommel's Afrika Corps) and the north (from Russia), a pro-Axis military cabal took power and attempted to evict the British from Iraq with German support. But the British quickly deployed forces from Palestine and India and crushed the revolt. The monarchy was then restored to its full authority and would rule with British approval for another seventeen years.

SADDAM HUSSEIN AND THE BA'TH

Saddam Hussein was born in the small village of al-'Awja outside of the backwater town of Tikrit in northwest Iraq, probably on April 28, 1937.[5] He was born into the Bayjat clan of the al Bu Nasir tribe, a modest-sized Sunni tribe. His name, a somewhat unusual one, means "he who confronts." His father, Hussein 'Abd al-Majid, died before Saddam was even born. His mother, Subhah Talfah, remarried quickly, to a man named Hassan Ibrahim, who was known locally as "Hassan the Liar." Hassan and his family reportedly made their living as local bullies and petty thieves.[6]

What little we know about Saddam's early life indicates that it was unpleasant for all involved. Various sources claim that Hassan Ibrahim often beat Saddam with an asphalt-coated stick and kept him busy stealing with his own sons and their cousins. For his part, Saddam was something of a loner, famous for carrying an iron bar wherever he went that he would heat until it was white hot and then use to impale unwary animals—dogs, cats, whatever made the mistake of coming within his reach. When he was ten years old, he was sent off to live with his uncle Khayrallah Talfah, a former army officer who had briefly been jailed for his role in the 1941 pro-Nazi coup attempt. In later years, Khayrallah regaled the world with his philosophy in the book *Three Whom God Should Not Have Created: Persians, Jews and Flies*. Saddam's closest friend from childhood was Khayrallah Talfah's son, Adnan, who convinced Saddam to go to school to learn to read and write. Adnan eventually passed the entrance exam to Iraq's military academy, thereby earning a career in the army, but Saddam failed the exam—to his enduring resentment.

As a young man, Saddam got caught up in the maelstrom of Arab politics during the 1950s. In those days, Communists, socialists, Nasserists, Pan-Arabists, and nationalists of every stripe actively vied for power throughout the Middle East. Saddam soaked up the politics of his uncle Khayrallah and Khayrallah's cronies, who included a kinsman and army officer named Ahmed Hassan al-Bakr, an important member of the Iraqi Ba'th Party. The Ba'th (Renaissance) Party had started in Syria in the 1930s as one of many Pan-Arabist parties but later sprouted offshoots in Iraq and several other Arab countries. Like numerous other political parties then in vogue, the Ba'th combined socialism and Pan-Arabism in a nebulous and often contradictory philosophy that showed little real erudition or practical knowledge. Its treatises were mostly rhetorical gobbledygook that provided little basis for concrete action. But in this respect too, the Ba'th was not unlike many of its competitors. Saddam himself began carrying a gun and drifted among various groups of Nasserists and Pan-Arabists before eventually falling in with Bakr and the Ba'th. The early Ba'thists were mostly intellectuals, army officers, students, and lawyers; Saddam stood out for his limited education, money, and manners. His only virtues were his ambition and penchant for violence. He was relegated to a low position within the small Iraqi branch of the Ba'th Party.

In 1958, the monarchy was finally overthrown by General 'Abd al-Karim Qasim, who capitalized on the widespread popular unhappiness with the government because of its failure to provide any support to Nasser's Egypt when it had fought the Israelis, British, and French in the 1956 Sinai-Suez War. When Qasim overthrew the monarchy, Saddam and the Ba'thists rejoiced, only to become quickly disillusioned with the new dictator. The key to Pan-Arabism was the notion of uniting all of the Arab states into one great Arab nation, powerful enough to stand up to the Western powers as an equal. Qasim refused to join the Pan-Arabist vehicle, the new United Arab Republic, which Syria and Egypt had formed under Gamal 'Abd al-Nasser. In addition, Qasim began relying heavily on the Iraqi Communists and increasingly regarded the nationalist and Pan-Arabist parties as enemies. Saddam and the Ba'th's other toughs began mixing it up with their opposites from the Communist Party in bloody gang wars. In 1959, Saddam participated in an assassination attempt against Qasim. He was the seventh member of a seven-man hit team, and his job was to provide covering fire against Qasim's bodyguards to allow the rest of the team to kill the dictator. But Qasim was late on the day of the hit. When he finally arrived, Saddam was so keyed up that he forgot his assignment and instead fired at Qasim too. Thanks to Saddam's impatience, the hit failed: Qasim was seriously wounded but not killed because his bodyguards were able to kill one of the assassins and drive the rest off, wounding Saddam. Eventually, Saddam managed to flee to Syria and from there to Egypt, where he spent three years lying low, debating politics, and waiting to return to Iraq.

The Ba'th finally managed to overthrow Qasim in 1963, but only by combining forces with a group of army officers including Qasim's former accomplice in the 1958 coup, Colonel 'Abd as-Salim Arif. With the Ba'th in the driver's seat, Saddam returned home as a follower of Hassan al-Bakr. However, the Ba'th was ill suited to rule Iraq and no sooner had it taken power in Baghdad than the left and right wings of the party fell to fighting among themselves, leaving Bakr to try to moderate—unsuccessfully. The divisions within the Ba'th then allowed Colonel Arif to turn on them and purge them the next year. While a traumatic event for the party, its ouster proved to be to Saddam's advantage. The radical wings of the party were purged, and Bakr emerged as the leader of the new Ba'th with Saddam as his right-hand man—a ruthless thug whom Bakr could count on to work tirelessly and do *anything*. Saddam spent two years in prison as a result of his work for Bakr.

'Abd as-Salim Arif ruled Iraq for less than three years before dying in a helicopter crash in 1966. He was succeeded by his less crafty brother, 'Abd ar-Rahman Arif, who managed to hold power for only two years. On July 17, 1968, a combination of the reformed Ba'th Party and another group of high-ranking military officers again overthrew the dictator. Official Iraqi accounts notwithstanding, Saddam played little part in the July 1968 coup that returned the Ba'th to power. However, he was Hassan al-Bakr's right-hand man and quickly became the central cog in the party machine. He was the head of the party's internal security force, the Jihaz Hunin, and was named the deputy secretary-general of the Revolutionary Command Council (RCC), the highest policy-making body, akin to the Soviet Politburo. The Ba'th numbered only about 2,500 members at that time, but they had learned the lesson of their previous experience in power and were not going to be shunted aside by their military compatriots again.[7] Saddam enforced discipline within the party's ranks and took the offensive against the senior military officers who had helped bring the Ba'th back to power.[8] He outmaneuvered each of the various groups of officers and then set his sights on potential rivals within the Ba'th, pursuing each in turn until only he and Bakr were left as the unchallenged power brokers of the regime.

By the early 1970s, Saddam had emerged as the regime's *eminence grise*. In 1970, it was Saddam who negotiated the famous "March Manifesto" that granted the Kurds considerable autonomy as a way of ending the nine-year guerrilla war they had been waging against successive Baghdad regimes. In 1974, it was Saddam who decided to renege on the March Manifesto and attack the Kurds. And it was Saddam who negotiated the humiliating Algiers Accord with the shah of Iran in 1975, when the Second Kurdish War blew up in his face. By that point, Saddam had eclipsed Bakr as the de facto ruler of the country, although it was not until 1977, when Saddam convinced Bakr to give up his secondary position as defense minister, that Saddam's position truly became unassailable. Without the defense portfolio, Bakr lost his long-standing ties to the military, and when he handed the position over to Saddam's cousin Adnan Khayrallah (promoted from colonel to major general) this ensured that Bakr could not use the military against Saddam. At that point it was simply a matter of time, and in 1979, Bakr was forced to step down. On July 16, 1979, Saddam Hussein assumed the presidency of Iraq.

Like his idol, Josef Stalin, Saddam Hussein quickly set about purging the party and government of any but his most devoted and nonthreatening adherents. In the most famous of the events of this first purge, Saddam convened a meeting of the senior members of the party on July 22. He produced Muhyi 'Abd al-Hussein Mashadi, secretary-general of the RCC. Mashadi had openly opposed Saddam's succession, and when he appeared on the twenty-second, it was physically apparent that he had paid a terrible price for his opposition. In a broken voice, Mashadi read a long, contrived confession regarding a Syrian-backed plot against the nation he had led. Saddam then took the podium and named fifty-four additional conspirators—all of them sitting in the room. As each one's name was read out, armed guards walked down to him and led him out of the auditorium to meet his fate. Many broke down in tears and had to be dragged out by the guards. Many of those who remained began to sob uncontrollably as Saddam read the list of names. That same day, Saddam convened a kangaroo court of high-level officials to try and sentence the guilty. In the coup de grâce of this macabre production, Saddam then ordered all of the other high party officials whose names had not been called to participate in the firing squads that dispatched the victims. In the words of the Iraqi dissident Kanan Makiya, "Neither Stalin nor Hitler would have thought up a detail like that. What Eichmann-like refuge in 'orders from above' could these men dig up in the future if they were ever to marshal the courage to try and depose their Leader? . . . With this act, the party leadership was being forced to invest its future in Saddam."[9]

With this act, Saddam would cement his image as the most ruthless and thorough of Iraq's dictators, a reputation that was already well established from the brutal purges he had conducted as Bakr's second-in-command. During his years waiting in the wings he had developed a host of methods to maintain his power, and these he now deployed to their fullest extent. He had carefully studied the methods of Stalin (and to a lesser extent Hitler) and learned how to apply them to Iraq, and even how to improve on them. He placed only the most trusted personnel in the highest internal security positions. He shifted personnel in lower-level positions constantly to prevent them from building up any kind of a loyal following that could be used in a coup plot. He built multiple agencies with redundant missions and responsibilities to ensure that nothing would be missed, and to create rivalries that would allow him to play one group off against another. He centralized all power and information in his own hands so that no one else fully understood everything that was going on in the Iraqi state. And he created an atmosphere of merciless cruelty that kept all Iraq in line out of sheer terror.

THE UNITED STATES AND THE PERSIAN GULF, 1800–1980

For America, the lure of the Persian Gulf has long been the lure of commerce. Soon after the end of the Revolutionary War, American merchantmen began venturing into the Indian Ocean to trade with the Arabs of the southern Arabian peninsula. The Sultanate of Muscat, the antecedent of modern Oman, was the first of the states of the region to emerge as an important trade partner for the United States, and on September 21, 1833, representatives of the United States and the sultanate signed a treaty of commerce and friendship. American merchants continued to expand their contacts in the Persian Gulf region throughout the century.

At that time, the region was under the dominance of the British Empire, which tolerated the American trading presence if only because the British had too many other problems in the area. It was an unstable region even then, with religious, ethnic, dynastic, and all manner of political disputes, and the British generally had their hands full. Moreover, this was the era of the "Great Game," when Britain and Russia fought fiercely over the southern half of the Eurasian landmass. At that time, Persia (modern Iran) was a key piece on the board of the Great Game. As U.S. trade expanded, the Persian shah tried on occasion to entangle Washington in an alliance to help him fend off both the British and Russians. But the United States was content to remain a purely mercantile power in the region and carefully sidestepped the shah's entreaties.[10]

Then, in 1908, William K. D'Arcy, an Englishman, struck oil near Masjid-i-Sulayman in Persia and changed the world forever. At that time, petroleum was just beginning to become an important industrial fuel, and alone among the great powers of the world, only the United States and czarist Russia were major producers. The rest relied on imports, primarily from America. The opening of the Persian Gulf oil fields now promised a new—and neutral—supply. In 1909, the Anglo-Persian Oil Company (APOC) began work on a pipeline to transport the oil from their wells to nearby ports on the Persian Gulf. In 1913, the first APOC refinery at

Abadan began production, purifying the oil for use even before it left the shores of the Gulf. The next year, the outbreak of the First World War increased demand for oil, in part because the Royal Navy began converting from coal-burning ships to more efficient oil-burning vessels, and in part because armies soon began adding gasoline-fueled trucks, tanks, and airplanes to their orders of battle.

After the war, the demand for oil continued to grow, and with it so too did the hunt for new oil fields in the Persian Gulf region. In 1927, the British discovered oil near Kirkuk in their mandatory territory of Iraq. Although Britain granted Iraq nominal independence in 1932, it continued to run the country behind the scenes and effectively did the same in Persia, allowing it to monopolize the production of Iraqi and Iranian oil. Meanwhile, shut out from oil exploration in Persia, Iraq, and the British protectorate of Kuwait (where oil was discovered in 1938), American oil companies set their sights farther south. In March 1938, only weeks after the discovery in Kuwait, Standard Oil of California (what would later become Chevron) struck oil in eastern Saudi Arabia. By the outbreak of the Second World War, oil production in the Persian Gulf had increased by 900 percent over the previous twenty years, and the region was already recognized as a future oil giant.[11]

It was World War II that gave the United States its first great geostrategic tug into the Persian Gulf region, and it was the region's oil potential that supplied the pull. Inadequate supplies of oil were critical elements in the eventual collapse of both German and Japanese power. Moreover, the vast logistical efforts of the Allies had been possible only because of the enormous supplies of oil available to them. Although 80 percent of that oil came from the United States, ever larger quantities came from the Persian Gulf states. Saudi Arabia in particular increased production from 580,000 barrels in 1938 to 21 million barrels in 1945 to support the Allied war effort.[12] By 1944, a U.S. government technical report had labeled the Persian Gulf "the center of gravity" of future oil development.[13] Moreover, the growing realization of the importance of Persian Gulf oil was coupled with a newfound concern about the limits of British military power. During the war, the United States had been compelled to move military forces to defend the region because the British were stretched too thin.

After the war, Britain's weakness in the region increasingly concerned American strategic thinkers, who suffered a further scare when Soviet forces briefly tried to occupy Persia in violation of Stalin's agreements with

Churchill and Roosevelt. Although the United States convinced Moscow to leave Persia in peace, the threat demonstrated that someone would have to see to the defense of the region to protect it against future Soviet challenges. Secretary of the Navy James Forrestal recounted a conversation he had with Senator Owen Brewster in May 1947:

> I said that Middle East oil was going to be necessary for this country not merely in wartime but in peacetime, because if we are going to make the contribution that it seems we have to make to the rest of the world in manufactured goods, we shall probably need very greatly increased supplies of fuel. Brewster said that . . . Europe in the next ten years may shift from coal to an oil economy and therefore whoever sits on the valve of Middle East oil may control the destiny of Europe.[14]

Indeed, the Persian Gulf was fast becoming a principal source of global energy. In 1940, 70 percent of the world's oil production came from the United States, while the Persian Gulf region contributed only 5 percent. By 1955, U.S. oil production had fallen to 43 percent of global production, while that of the Persian Gulf region had climbed to 20 percent.[15] The world needed Persian Gulf oil, and because of its power and its interest in seeing a stable, prosperous world, the United States had to take a hand in ensuring that the oil continued to flow freely. After the war, the United States maintained a small naval task force in the area based in Bahrain in support of the lingering British military presence.

Because the postwar rush to demobilize meant that America could not keep large forces in the Gulf, Washington started to use other methods to secure the region. In 1953, the CIA helped the shah of Iran (now independent and with its modern name) overthrow his socialist prime minister, Muhammad Mossadeq, whom Washington and London feared would nationalize the Iranian oil industry and cast Iran's lot with Moscow. Later the Eisenhower administration would try to defend the Persian Gulf with the same solution it had preferred for the defense of Europe: a regional alliance. The Baghdad Pact, signed by Iraq and Turkey in 1954 and later joined by Great Britain (1954), Pakistan (1955), and Iran (1955), was the fruit of these efforts. Although the United States was not a formal adherent to the treaty, Americans sat on its key committees and were an unmistakable presence in all of its deliberations. But then in 1958, when the pro-British monarchy was overthrown by Qasim, the new dictator pulled Iraq out of the Baghdad Pact, allied himself with the Iraqi Communist Party, and opened a new relationship with the USSR. In response, Washington ordered the CIA to oust Qasim, although the 1963 coup that succeeded in doing so probably did not have CIA assistance.

For twenty-three years after World War II, the United States was able to play this background role in securing the Persian Gulf because the British remained willing to deploy military forces when other methods would not suffice. Throughout the 1950s and 1960s, it had been Britain that had done the heavy lifting when military intervention was required in the Gulf—such as sending troops to Kuwait to block an Iraqi invasion in 1961 and crushing insurgents in Aden. However, the U.S. position suddenly became far more complicated in January 1968, when Britain announced that it lacked the strength to maintain its traditional global commitments and so would be withdrawing from "East of Suez" by 1971. To make matters worse, in 1968 the Russians began deploying their own naval forces to the Indian Ocean while the United States was deeply mired in the conflict in Vietnam and could not spare the forces to take over Britain's role as protector of the Gulf. The United States was in a fix. The solution the Nixon administration devised was to rely on proxies to serve as regional strongmen as a substitute for the commitment of U.S. forces. As Michael A. Palmer has pointed out in his excellent study of U.S. involvement in the Persian Gulf region, this was a natural extension of the "Nixon Doctrine," which called on Asian nations (by which Nixon principally meant Vietnam) to take a greater role in their security and alleviate the military responsibilities of the United States.[16] In the Persian Gulf region, the administration turned to the shah of Iran to be its main enforcer. Almost as an afterthought, Washington also designated Saudi Arabia as a second American proxy, despite the fact that the Kingdom then lacked the economic and political clout it has today and had virtually no military capability. But the Saudis were rich and cooperative, and unlike the Persian Iranians, they were Arabs whom the United States hoped could prevail upon their Arab brothers.

Through much of the 1970s, U.S. policy toward the Persian Gulf region rested on these "Twin Pillars," as the strategy was called. For the shah in particular, it was a bonanza. The United States gave him carte blanche to purchase whatever weapons he wanted—including state-of-the-art F-14 Tomcat fighters and Phoenix long-range air-to-air missiles, which the United States would not sell to anyone else. Iranian defense spending grew at a torrid pace, roughly quintupling between 1969 and 1978.[17] The United

States looked the other way at Tehran's misdeeds—such as instigating the 1973 oil embargo that caused the first oil crisis in the United States and Europe after the 1973 Arab-Israeli War. Puffed up with his new weaponry, the shah also began throwing his weight around, intimidating the smaller Gulf states. But he also did act in a manner helpful to the United States. He sent troops to help the pro-U.S. sultan of Oman fight Dhofari rebels backed by Marxist South Yemen. He backed Iraqi Kurdish separatists against the Ba'thist regime in Iraq in conjunction with CIA and Mossad support.[18] And he fought Soviet influence in the Gulf region as fiercely as any U.S. administration could have asked. The Twin Pillars policy seemed so successful that even after the United States pulled out of Vietnam, Washington stuck with it as a way of economizing on U.S. military commitments around the world.

In 1977, the Carter administration took the first tentative steps toward a resumption of direct U.S. responsibility for the security of the Persian Gulf region by inaugurating the formation of a Rapid Deployment Force (RDF), largely for contingencies in the region. However, the RDF was little more than a name on a piece of paper, and the Twin Pillars approach continued to be the guiding force of U.S. policy toward the region. Nevertheless, as part of the development of the RDF concept, Washington took a fresh look at its policies toward the Middle East and the Persian Gulf region and finally articulated the American interests in the region that have guided U.S. policy ever since. In September 1978, the Joint Chiefs of Staff set down three primary U.S. goals:

1. To assure continuous access to petroleum resources.
2. To prevent an inimical power or combination of powers from establishing hegemony.
3. To assure the survival of Israel as an independent state in a stable relationship with contiguous Arab states.[19]

For a few more months, the Twin Pillars policy would serve those goals.

THE IRANIAN REVOLUTION, THE IRAN-IRAQ WAR, AND THE TILT TOWARD IRAQ, 1980-1988

Twin Pillars collapsed in January 1979 as revolution swept the shah of Iran from his throne. Without the shah, the stronger of the Twin Pillars was gone, and in his place came the fiery Ayatollah Ruhollah Khomeini, spewing bile against the "Great Satan" (the United States) and the "Little Satan" (Israel), backing a variety of (mostly Shi'ite) Islamic terrorist groups, and calling for Islamic revolutions to uproot the other governments of the region. Things only got worse when in November of that year the Iranians seized the U.S. Embassy in Tehran, taking fifty-two American diplomats and Marine guards hostage and tossing the United States into a 444-day nightmare of paralysis and frustration. In less than twelve months, Iran had gone from the United States' principal ally in the region to its bitterest foe.

The wheel of fate turned again in the fall of 1980, when Saddam Hussein, newly anointed as president of Iraq, invaded Iran. Saddam was motivated by a combination of opportunity and fear. On the one hand, he had chafed under the military domination of the shah, who had supported Iraq's Kurdish insurgents and so overawed Iraq militarily that Baghdad had been forced to sign the humiliating Algiers Accord, which had demarcated its border and the Shatt al-Arab waterway to Iran's liking. But Saddam also had his eyes on a bigger prize: Iran's southwestern province of Khuzestan, populated mostly by ethnic Arabs and containing the vast bulk of Iran's oil reserves. In 1980, Iraq was producing 6 million barrels of oil per day and Iran 5 million barrels, almost all from Khuzestan. The combined 11 million barrels per day would have amounted to 20 percent of global oil consumption and given Saddam economic wealth and power greater than that of Saudi Arabia.[20] Meanwhile, the Iranian armed forces had been ravaged by the revolution, purged by the ayatollahs for their prior close ties to the United States, and their equipment had been sabotaged by many of the shah's loyalists (not to mention departing U.S. military advisers). To Saddam, Iran looked weak and Khuzestan looked vulnerable.

Saddam was also driven by fear, however. The majority of Iraq's population was (and still is) Shi'ite Arab, although the Baghdad regime was overwhelmingly Sunni Arab. Iran's population is mostly Shi'ite, and Saddam feared that the ayatollah's revolution would light a fire among Iraq's own Shi'ah. His fears weren't entirely baseless. Prior to the invasion, Shi'ite clerics in Iraq had organized some of the most important resistance to his regime. Moreover, Khomeini had lived in Iraq for a number of years while in exile (until the shah had insisted that Baghdad kick him out in 1977), and the Shi'ah of southern Iraq still remembered the charismatic ayatollah and his mesmerizing sermons. Thus, Saddam attacked Iran in the hope not only of reversing the terms of the Algiers Accord and conquering

Khuzestan but also of toppling the new Iranian regime and preventing it from igniting a revolution in Iraq.[21]

The initial invasion of Iran was not the blitzkrieg Saddam had envisioned. Between September and December 1980, Iraqi forces lumbered clumsily into southwestern Iran against little opposition. The Iranians were paralyzed and distracted by their own internal problems but quickly began to recall military personnel dismissed by the revolution, form local bands of Revolutionary Guards, and buy up weapons wherever they could. The Iraqi invasion was one of the most inept military operations of the twentieth century: it failed to occupy any of the major cities in Khuzestan except one, it failed to reach the (undefended) Iranian oil fields, and it failed to block the mountain passes through which Iranian reinforcements had to flow. By January 1981, the Iraqis had been stopped by meager Iranian opposition with virtually nothing to show for their efforts. That month, the Iranians launched the first of a series of counteroffensives that mauled the Iraqi Army and, by the end of May 1982, had expelled Iraqi troops from Iran altogether. In mid-1982, Ayatollah Khomeini decided to make good on his promise to spread the Islamic revolution and liberate the Shi'ite holy sites of an-Najaf and Karbala in southern Iraq. In July, he launched Operation Blessed Ramadan, a massive offensive to conquer al-Basrah, Iraq's second largest city and the "capital" of Shi'ite southern Iraq. After six weeks of horrific fighting, the Iraqis stopped Iran, but just barely. Turned away at al-Basrah, Iran still would not relent in its invasion of Iraq, and for the next five years Tehran pounded on Iraq's defenses, trying to overthrow Saddam and reach the oil kingdoms beyond Iraq's borders.[22]

In the meantime, Iraq had suffered another humiliating defeat. On June 7, 1981, fourteen Israeli warplanes flew across the Arabian desert undetected and obliterated Iraq's Osiraq reactor at Tuwaitha, just outside Baghdad.[23] At the time, Osiraq was the key to Saddam's nuclear weapons program and the French-built reactor was due to go online within a matter of weeks. The daring Israeli raid single-handedly set Iraq's nuclear bomb program back by several years. However, it taught the Iraqis an important lesson. Thereafter, Saddam ordered a redoubling of the Iraqi program but this time he ordered multiple, redundant facilities, heavily defended, hardened against attack, and camouflaged against detection. These practices would eventually allow Iraq to keep most of its vast WMD programs hidden from the United States during Operation Desert Storm, preserving far more of these facilities than the United States had ever dreamt the Iraqis possessed.

For the United States in the 1980s, the prospect of an Iranian victory over Iraq was so terrifying that the Reagan administration decided it had to shore up Iraq against the ayatollah's legions. Washington had never cared much for the Ba'thist regime or Saddam Hussein. They were brutal thugs, and he was a first-class tyrant. What's more, Iraq under the Ba'th had continued to flirt with the Soviet Union, signing a treaty of friendship in 1972 and purchasing large amounts of weapons. Iraq had also sent large armored forces to fight against Israel in the 1973 Arab-Israeli War, was a key supporter of several Palestinian terrorist groups, and had led the condemnation of Egypt for signing the Camp David Peace Accords with Israel in 1978.[24] Nevertheless, Saddam and Iraq suddenly took on a rosier hue when they became the only thing standing between revolutionary Iran and the Persian Gulf oil fields.

The first signal of what would become a U.S. "tilt" in favor of Iraq came in February 1982, when the Reagan administration removed Iraq from its list of terrorism-supporting states (where it had been a charter member). Washington claimed that this was in recognition of diminished Iraqi support for terrorism, but at that time, the evidence of such a diminution was scanty at best. In fact, only a few months later, in June 1982, Iraq would instigate the assassination of Israel's ambassador to Great Britain to try to spark the long-expected Israeli invasion of Lebanon that Saddam hoped would create a new Arab-Israeli war that would somehow convince Iran to cease combat operations against Iraq in order to concentrate its forces against Israel. (This hare-brained scheme did cause the Israeli invasion of Lebanon but had no impact on the ayatollah, who continued to proclaim that the road to Jerusalem ran through Baghdad.)[25] Nevertheless, taking Iraq off the terrorism list—no matter how cynical the reasoning—removed a number of hurdles that would have hindered U.S. support for Iraq. Soon thereafter, Washington began passing high-value military intelligence to Iraq to help it fight the war, including information from U.S. satellites that helped Iraq fix key flaws in the fortifications protecting al-Basrah that proved important in Iran's defeat the next month.[26]

U.S. support for Iraq blossomed throughout the war. Starting in 1983, the United States provided economic aid to Iraq in the form of Commodities Credit Corporation guarantees to purchase U.S. agricultural products—$400 million in 1983, $513 million in 1984, and climbing to $652 million in 1987. This allowed Iraq to use money it otherwise would have spent on food to buy weapons and other military supplies. With Iraq off the terrorism list, the U.S. could also provide quasi-military aid. For example, Washington sold Baghdad ten Bell UH-1 Huey and sixty Hughes MD-500 Defender helicopters that were ostensibly in "civilian configurations" but that Iraq very quickly converted to military use. Iraq was also able to purchase large numbers of trucks that Washington knew would go to its war effort. Then, in March 1985, the United States began issuing Baghdad high-tech export licenses that previously had been denied. The sophisticated equipment Iraq bought with these licenses proved crucial to its weapons of mass destruction programs. In addition, the Reagan administration kept ratcheting up its level of intelligence cooperation with Baghdad, eventually authorizing a liaison relationship between U.S. intelligence agencies and their Iraqi counterparts. Perhaps more than anything else, the high-quality intelligence the U.S. regularly furnished Baghdad regarding Iranian forces and operations proved vital to Iraq's conduct of the war.[27]

Finally, Washington encouraged its allies to similarly support Iraq against Iran. Britain extended agricultural products, and sold high-tech goods and even some weaponry. France had a strong relationship with Iraq that predated the war—it was France that had sold Iraq a nuclear reactor in 1976 that was ostensibly for energy production but that the French knew was intended to produce nuclear weaponry. Consequently, it did not take much encouragement for France to deepen its ties to Iraq. By 1982, Iraq accounted for 40 percent of French arms exports. Paris sold Baghdad a wide range of weapons, including armored vehicles, air defense radars, surface-to-air missiles, Mirage fighters, and Exocet antiship missiles.[28] German firms also rushed in without much compunction, not only selling Iraq large numbers of trucks and automobiles but also building vast complexes for Iraq's chemical warfare (CW), biological warfare (BW), and ballistic missile programs. Although Iraq did pretend that it was purchasing the German equipment and expertise for civilian purposes, the disguise was ridiculously thin and no perceptive German scientist could have bought the ruse.[29] But in the 1980s, no one in the West asked too many questions about what Saddam was being allowed to purchase as long as it would help defeat the Iranians.

The United States also tolerated a great deal from Iraq. Washington chose not to raise a diplomatic ruckus when an Iraqi Mirage pilot inadvertently put his Exocet missiles into the side of an American frigate, the USS *Stark,* killing thirty-seven sailors.[30] The Reagan administration largely turned a blind eye when Iraq started employing the WMD capabilities the

Germans (among others) were helping them to acquire. In its desperate efforts to convince Iran to make peace, Iraq dumped chemical warfare agents
on Iranian troops, hit Iranian cities with missiles and air strikes, and attacked Iranian tankers and oil facilities—each of which prompted Iran
(sooner or later) to respond in kind. Iraq first used chemical warfare to try
to defeat Iranian human-wave attacks in late 1983. In March 1984, a U.N.
report documented Iraq's usage, at which point the United States issued a
formal denunciation. Washington did press the Europeans—especially
Germany—to tighten their export controls. However, the Reagan administration refused to further censure Iraq or even reduce its own support and
blocked a congressional resolution that would have imposed sanctions on
Iraq. Moreover, the protests to the European countries were little more than
slaps on the wrist and did not have any discernible impact.[31]

In retrospect, the most reprehensible of Saddam's actions that the
United States and Europe chose to overlook was his campaign against
Iraq's own Kurds known as al-Anfal, a twisted reference to a verse in the
Quran. When the Iranians counterattacked in 1982, they opened a front in
Kurdistan. Seeing an opportunity to be rid of Saddam's rule, the Kurds
joined the Iranians in fighting the Iraqi Army. In March 1987, Saddam appointed his murderous cousin 'Ali Hassan al-Majid governor of northern
Iraq. It was superfluous to give him orders to get control of the Kurds any
way he could—'Ali Hassan only knew one way. Less than six weeks after
his appointment, 'Ali Hassan had employed chemical warfare to wipe out
several towns in the Balisan valley, where the PUK's main headquarters
was located. The following year, with Iranian troops threatening key Iraqi
positions, 'Ali Hassan unleashed the al-Anfal campaign, an operation of biblical brutality. Iraqi forces began clearing areas of Kurdish residence with
massive bombardments of chemical weapons and high explosives, followed by army sweeps that often killed anyone left alive and razed to the
ground anything left standing. On March 15, 1988, 'Ali Hassan conducted
his most famous attack, swamping the Kurdish town of Halabja with several varieties of CW and killing at least five thousand Kurdish civilians.
When the campaign finally ended in 1989, some two hundred thousand
Kurds were dead, roughly 1.5 million had been forcibly resettled, huge
swaths of Kurdistan had been scorched by chemical warfare, and four thousand towns had been razed.[32] The U.S. Senate passed a bill to impose sanctions on Iraq, but the Reagan administration prevailed upon the Congress to
drop the matter.[33]

Of course, Washington did get something from its support for Saddam. First, Iraq was able, just barely, to hold the Iranians at bay. Indeed, by 1986, the war seemed mired in a World War I–like stalemate with little expectation of a breakthrough by either side. Second, Iraq made sure that the United States was well compensated, paying off all of its loans to the United States on time and, in 1987, offering the United States $1 off the world price on each barrel of Iraqi oil. As a result, American consumption of Iraqi oil quadrupled, from 30 million barrels in 1987 to 126 million in 1988.[34] Saddam also responded to White House entreaties on other issues of importance to America, evicting many members of the notorious Palestinian terrorist organization Abu Nidal from Baghdad and mostly preventing Abu Abbas's Palestine Liberation Front from conducting operations.

In addition, Saddam adopted the cause of a negotiated settlement between Israel and the Arabs, supporting virtually every effort toward peace during the 1980s, although it is clear that this was only a tactical move intended to secure the American support he needed. In a 1982 interview in *Time* magazine, Saddam was asked about the recent peace initiative of Saudi King Fahd, and he responded, "We favor it with minor adjustments. . . . We favor what the Palestinians accept."[35] This was a monumental turnabout for Iraq, which previously had been a leading Arab hard-line state. That same year, Saddam told King Hussein of Jordan that he would back the Jordanians if they moved forward on peace negotiations based on the Reagan peace plan of September 1982. In November 1984, Saddam's foreign minister, Tariq Aziz, went to Washington to normalize ties with the United States and announced that Iraq would accept "a just, honorable, and lasting settlement" to the Arab-Israeli conflict. At the time, this was an extremely propeace position and was seen as a betrayal by Saddam's erstwhile allies among the Arab radicals—Syria and Libya.[36] The next month, Saddam himself took another step, stating publicly that "No Arab leader looks forward to the destruction of Israel" and that peace would have to include "the existence of a secure state for the Israelis."[37] In the mid-1980s, this was about as far in favor of peace as any Arab government would go, basically putting Iraq in the propeace camp with Egypt. And Iraq would maintain this propeace posture throughout the war. In fact, in December 1988, four months after the end of the war with Iran, the PLO publicly recognized Israel's right to exist, and Iraq, along with Egypt, supported PLO Chairman Yasir Arafat in taking this dramatic step. In the end, Iraqi and Egyptian support shielded the PLO from Syria's wrath and made it possible for Arafat to do so.[38]

Nevertheless, Saddam was never fully comfortable with his relationship with the United States. High-ranking Iraqi defectors report that Saddam was always suspicious of America's motives, given Washington's previous dislike of Iraq. In addition, Saddam continued to believe that the U.S. and Israeli governments were virtually inseparable and that Israel had aggressively been helping Iran throughout the war. Saddam saw his suspicions confirmed with the 1986 revelation that the Reagan administration had secretly been selling weapons to Iran in what later came to be known as the Iran-*contra* scandal. The United States had sold Iran weapons via Israel, including thousands of sophisticated tube-launched optical-tracking wire-guided (TOW) antitank missiles and Homing-All-the-Way-Killer (HAWK) surface-to-air missiles, in a bid to get Iran to release American hostages held by Iran's Lebanese ally, Hizballah. Although Saddam never forgot this American perfidy, Iraq was too desperate for America's assistance for Saddam to complain.

The prevailing stalemate along the Iran-Iraq front was shattered in February 1986, when Iran launched a sudden amphibious assault across the Shatt al-Arab and caught the Iraqi defenders by surprise. Picked Revolutionary Guards swarmed over the Iraqi lines, capturing the al-Faw peninsula—the southernmost tip of the country and Iraq's only coastline—and threatening al-Basrah from the south. Saddam responded with a vast counterattack accompanied by air strikes and massive doses of chemical warfare, but it failed miserably. Stymied on the ground, Saddam reacted by ratcheting up his attacks on Iranian cities and Iran's oil exports. The Iranians responded in kind. They deployed Chinese Silkworm antiship missiles on the al-Faw peninsula and used them to shoot at oil tankers loading at Kuwaiti oil terminals, across the Persian Gulf. (Kuwait and the other oil kingdoms had banded together to form the Gulf Cooperation Council in 1981, and all of them were providing Iraq with huge loans and other support to fight the Iranians. Hence, Iran considered them allies of Iraq.) In addition, Iran stepped up its attacks on Iraqi and GCC tankers in the Persian Gulf and began setting up Silkworm launch sites along the Strait of Hormuz.

Although in the short term these developments were advantageous for Iran, they set into motion a train of events that led to Tehran's eventual defeat. First, the humiliating defeat at al-Faw allowed Iraq's generals to convince Saddam that he had to completely reform his army to be able to defeat the Iranians on the ground. Throughout the war, Saddam had been forced to relinquish ever greater control over operations to his professional military officers, and now he removed the last remaining shackles. In response, the Iraqi General Staff took the Republican Guard, previously the regime's palace guard, expanded it, retrained it, re-equipped it, and turned it into the elite of the Iraqi armed forces. When the Iranians launched another massive offensive against al-Basrah in 1987, it was the reformed Republican Guard that ultimately defeated them in bloody combat at the gates of the city. Meanwhile, Kuwait had approached the United States about protecting its oil exports by reflagging its tankers under American colors, which would then be escorted by the U.S. Navy. Initially, Washington balked at the idea, but when Kuwait then turned to the Russians, the United States quickly changed its mind. Finally, with European assistance, Iraq had achieved an important technological breakthrough, modifying its old Russian-made Scud ballistic missiles to more than double their normal range of three hundred kilometers, albeit with less accuracy and a lighter warhead. Previously, Iraq had been at a distinct disadvantage in that Baghdad was only about a hundred kilometers from the Iranian border—putting it within easy range not only of Iranian air strikes but even of Iran's own Scuds—while Tehran was nearly six hundred kilometers from the Iraqi border, well beyond the range of Iraq's Scuds and far enough that Iraqi air strikes were difficult and vulnerable to the Iranian air defenses. With their new, modified Scuds (which they called "al-Husseins"), the Iraqis could rain down missiles on Tehran unimpeded.

These changes set the stage for the climactic battles of 1988. In February, Iraq fired the first al-Husseins at Tehran, and over the next six months launched nearly two hundred at Iranian cities, mostly Tehran and Iran's spiritual center at Qom. When rumors spread in Iran that Iraq was loading the missiles with chemical warheads, nearly a million people fled the Iranian capital. Then, on April 17, 1988, Iraq launched its first major ground offensive since 1980, employing the Republican Guard as the spearhead of an armored assault on the Iranian positions on al-Faw. In a single day, the Guard and several army formations swept aside the Iranians after a terrifying preliminary bombardment of artillery and chemical warfare. The next day, the United States conducted Operation Praying Mantis. In response to Iran's mining of the Strait of Hormuz (and the damage to a U.S. naval vessel that had struck an Iranian mine while escorting reflagged Kuwaiti tankers), the U.S. Navy engaged the Iranian Navy in the Gulf, sunk two of Iran's biggest surface ships and crippled a third. Over the next three months, Iraq staged four more ground offensives, each of which was led by the Republican Guard, featured punishing artillery and chemical warfare bombardments, and smashed important elements of the Iranian armed forces. By the end of July, the Iranian Army was down to about two hundred operable tanks while Iraq was routinely deploying two thousand or more for a single operation.[39] As a kind of coup de grâce, on July 3, U.S. forces engaged some of the remnants of the Iranian Navy in the Strait of Hormuz and an Iranian civilian jet strayed over the battle area. The USS *Vincennes* mistook the airliner for an Iranian fighter and shot it down. Although it was a mistake, in Tehran it was viewed as a sign that the United States was now actively allied with Iraq and would take any action—including deliberately killing Iranian civilians—to defeat Tehran.[40] In August, even the Ayatollah Khomeini, who had resisted all previous pleas to end the war, was forced to concede that Iran could not fight both Iraq and the United States any longer. Tehran accepted a cease-fire with Iraq that brought the war to an end.

After eight long years of war with Iran, Iraq had won—but at a terrible price. Iraq had had roughly 200,000 men killed in battle and another 400,000 to 500,000 wounded. With its population of only 18 million, that would be the equivalent of having nearly 10 million Americans killed or wounded in a war. Baghdad had borrowed heavily to finance the war and by 1988 owed $86 billion, of which about $40 billion was owed to the GCC states and the rest to Western powers.[41] No one really expected Iraq to pay off the money owed to the other Arab states, but as long as the loans remained on the books they hurt Iraq's credit rating, hindering it from borrowing more. The damage from the war had been heavy, and estimates of the cost to rebuild the country ranged from $200 billion to $230 billion.[42] What's more, Saddam had little to show for his effort. He had not conquered Khuzestan and ended up with only a few small scraps of Iranian territory with no real strategic value. Nor had the Islamic republic fallen as Saddam had hoped. The only tangible asset Iraq took away from the war with Iran was its newfound military might. With roughly 1.2 million men under arms, Iraq had the largest military in the Middle East and the fourth largest in the world. Iraq had a range of weapons of mass destruction and considerable experience using them in battle. What's more, Iraq was building a gigantic military-industrial infrastructure to further expand its military capabilities.

It was this end to the Iran-Iraq War that set the stage for the next phase of U.S.-Iraqi relations. Iraq had paid a terrible price for its meager victory and had little to show for its efforts except a vast military machine. However, to win the war, Iraq had distorted its economy and virtually bankrupted itself. These unsatisfying results would soon set Saddam looking for new prizes that would afford him the glory he felt he deserved but had been denied. Meanwhile, Washington had worked so hard to ignore Saddam's obvious flaws that it had essentially convinced itself that Saddam was little different from other brutal dictators with whom the United States had developed long and profitable relationships. Many saw Saddam as little worse than Ferdinand Marcos, Augusto Pinochet, or the shah of Iran and began to think that he might actually take the place of the shah in a revival of the Twin Pillars policy. These misperceptions set Baghdad and Washington on the road to the long confrontation that has dominated U.S.-Iraqi relations ever since.

The Worm Turns

Between 1988 and 1992, during the George H. W. Bush administration, Iraqi-U.S. relations reached their apogee, only to quickly plummet into war. The Reagan administration's groundbreaking efforts to open up relations with Iraq had been uneven, but the new Bush administration saw them as promising. The ignorance and miscalculations on both sides created by the lack of any real relationship before 1982 persisted. In some ways, they made possible the rapprochement between Baghdad and Washington by disguising the stark differences in the goals and tactics of the two sides. The United States mistakenly assumed Saddam to be conservative and reasonable, someone it could work with as it had a long litany of other brutal tyrants. Saddam assumed, perhaps only briefly, that the United States would continue to condone his pursuit of a wide range of weapons of mass destruction and his aspirations to become the dominant power in the Persian Gulf region. It did not take long for both sides to realize how badly mistaken they were. Nevertheless, even after the denouement of the Persian Gulf War, each side continued to misunderstand the other and the course of events in the months following the Gulf War proved a disappointment to both the Bush administration and Saddam Hussein.

CONSTRUCTIVE ENGAGEMENT, 1988–1990[1]

After the Iran-Iraq War, Saddam recognized that he had to take action to address the political and economic distortion it had caused. However, his initial moves did not help matters. He started to demobilize the army to reduce defense expenditures, releasing as many as 350,000 men from service. However, Iraq had imported roughly 1.5 million foreign workers and had brought many women into the workforce to compensate for the men at the front, so there were no jobs. Rising unemployment led to domestic disturbances between out-of-work veterans and foreign guest workers. The regime ended most of its wartime food subsidies to reduce government spending, causing inflation to rise to 25 percent in 1989 without any corresponding increase in salaries. Living standards sagged, and people began to grumble. Iraqi GNP declined in 1989, and per capita income fell to half of what it had been in 1980. Meanwhile, defense spending and corruption among the regime's elite—which had exploded during the war—continued to grow, devouring ever greater shares of revenue.[2]

In what would become a frequent cycle in Iraq, economic problems created security threats for the regime. The poor economy caused public discontent and diminished the perks that Saddam used to reward his loyalists. The result was unrest and coup attempts. In November 1988, a coup plot was discovered among military officers who hoped to shoot down Saddam's plane as it returned from Egypt. In January 1989, the regime uncovered another plot among military officers that led to the purging of dozens, possibly hundreds, of officers from the army and air force. Another cabal was discovered in the military in September 1989, while on January 4, 1990, the regime crushed a coup attempt by military personnel from northern Iraq, including members of the Jubbur tribe in the army and Republican Guard. The January 1990 plot was especially disconcerting for Saddam because the Jubbur were one of the key Sunni tribes he relied on to maintain his power and they represented the largest group in the Republican Guard and Iraq's security services.[3]

Initially, Saddam believed that the way to dig himself out of his economic hole was to continue to court the West, and the United States in particular. Baghdad believed it had generally profited from the relationship and was eager to preserve its access to Western technology, credit, and other assistance. Iraq scrupulously paid its interest on American loans. In January 1990, Iraq increased the discount at which it sold oil to the United

States to $1.24 below market rate.[4] Saddam moved closer to the moderate Arab states aligned with the United States, creating the Arab Cooperation Council of Iraq, Egypt, Jordan, and North Yemen (ACC) in February 1989. And in May 1989, Iraq engineered Egypt's readmittance to an Arab League summit for the first time in ten years.

In the United States, Iraq was the subject of much debate. On the one hand, there were those who believed that with Iran defeated there was no need to look the other way at Saddam's human rights abuses, his continued (if reduced) support for international terrorist organizations, and his ravenous appetite for weapons of mass destruction. Members of the U.S. Congress repeatedly attempted to sanction Iraq for its various misdeeds. On the other hand, numerous voices both inside and outside government had been arguing since the end of the Iran-Iraq War that although Saddam was not perfect, he was pragmatic and broadly shared U.S. goals in the region, and so Washington should pursue a policy of engagement to wean him from some of his more egregious sins and allow him to take the vacant seat of the shah as America's proxy in the Persian Gulf. For example, one American academic writing in the summer of 1988 argued for accommodation with Baghdad on the grounds that "Iraq's foreign policy and internal situation have, since 1982, led to a rough and unrecognized congruence in American and Iraqi interests" and that Saddam's ever greater power was actually beneficial for the United States because "Centralization of power permits the regime to deviate from unworkable principles and pursue its interests. Indeed, whatever else one thinks of the Iraqi president, he has shown a capacity to make strategic decisions and abide by them."[5] Most of the U.S. intelligence community held the view that Iraq was war-weary and Saddam would refrain from foreign adventures to concentrate on rebuilding his devastated economy and society.[6]

The new administration of George H. W. Bush agreed with those who argued that the United States should engage Saddam to try to turn him into a regional ally. During the administration's first year in office, on October 2, 1989, the president signed a new National Security Directive, NSD-26, which directed that "The United States should propose economic and political incentives for Iraq to moderate its behavior and to increase our influence with Iraq." In theory, the policy was intended to be a carrot-and-stick approach, in which carrots (political and economic incentives) would be used to entice the Iraqis into ending their pursuit of WMD and human rights abuses, while holding out the stick of sanctions if they did not mend their ways.[7] In practice, however, the policy was more carrot than stick. A month later, after press revelations that the Atlanta branch of the Italian Banco Nazionale del Lavoro had helped Iraq divert massive amounts of U.S. agricultural credits to purchase weapons and prohibited technology, Washington still extended another $1 billion in credits to Iraq, plus $200 million in development loan credits from the Export-Import Bank.[8] Thus, initially, Iraq and the United States appeared to be on course toward better relations: Baghdad was looking to continue its good relations with the United States, and the Bush administration was looking for an accommodation with Saddam's regime and was willing to overlook a lot of Iraqi misbehavior to achieve it.

However, these policies soon began to hit snags over Iraq's pursuit of weapons of mass destruction. The problem was that victory in the Iran-Iraq War had given Saddam a taste of his dreams. Since his earliest days in power, Saddam had made it clear that he wanted to be the leader of the Arab world.[9] After the war, Saddam's decision to invade Iran and the Iraqi Army's disastrous early performance were forgotten, and instead he basked in the adulation of Arab leaders and masses alike for his victory. In particular, the Arabs praised him for his creation of a powerful arsenal of ballistic missiles and WMD, which they hoped would allow Baghdad to champion Arab causes against Israel. Indeed, Saddam was determined to match Israel's strategic arsenal, a feat he believed would be essential if he were to realize his dreams. As a result, Iraq's military industrialization, illicit procurement activities, and WMD production programs proceeded at breakneck pace.

Not everyone in the U.S. government was wholly comfortable with the administration's policy of engagement with Iraq. At the time, I was the junior analyst in the CIA's Iran-Iraq military analytic cell. My colleagues and I were deeply suspicious of Saddam's WMD programs and his designs on the rest of the region. Indeed, in briefings, we went to great lengths to point out that the devastation of Iranian military power meant that, for the first time, Iraq was effectively unrestrained in how it could pursue its regional ambitions. My division chief, Winston Wiley, and his deputy, Bruce Riedel, fought constant battles with other intelligence agencies to sound more ominous warnings about Iraq's WMD programs, particularly its nuclear weapons program. Others at the Department of Defense shared our concerns. Still others in the government recognized that regardless of administration policy, there were U.S. laws on the books that Iraq was violating and it was their job to prosecute such violations. Thus, despite the administration's determination to overlook Iraqi transgressions, there were some things that could not be suppressed, and these led to sensational cases such as the revelation of the Banco Nazionale del Lavoro scandal, FBI sting operations to catch the Iraqis illegally acquiring sensitive U.S. technology, and a steady stream of media reports raising alarms about Iraq's domestic repression and WMD acquisitions.

As best we understand it today, for Saddam, the split between the positive messages he was receiving from the higher levels of the U.S. government and the negative messages he was getting from the American media and lower levels of the U.S. government were only a minor part of his problem. The bigger problem he faced was Israel. Soon after the end of the Iran-Iraq War, Israeli officials began to voice their concerns about Iraq's budding strategic capabilities.[10] In December 1989, Iraq test-launched the first stage of its al-Abid space-launch vehicle, consisting of a cluster of Scud missiles. It was obvious that the al-Abid could easily be converted to a ballistic missile with a much longer range than Iraq's current inventory of Scuds and al-Husseins, and Baghdad boasted that such a missile, called the al-Tammuz, was already being developed. The test launch of the al-Abid started a war of words between Baghdad and Jerusalem.[11]

In February 1990, the situation worsened. Iraq inaugurated its first uranium enrichment facility at Tarmiyah to supply the fissile material for Iraqi nuclear weapons. Tariq Aziz later said that from this point on, Iraq's leaders became terrified of a repeat of Israel's 1981 air strike against the Osiraq nuclear reactor—Baghdad's first bid at a nuclear weapon.[12] On the fifteenth, the Voice of America news service broadcast an editorial warning that the fall of the dictatorships in Eastern Europe should be seen as a sign of things to come by other dictatorships—including Iraq. Saddam was deeply concerned by these developments (he reportedly had his security services study the fall of Romanian dictator Nicolae Ceaușescu in minute detail to learn how to prevent it happening to him), and he was incensed by such remarks coming from an official organ of the U.S. government.[13] On the twenty-fourth, at a meeting in Amman to commemorate the first anniversary of the ACC, Saddam gave a long speech in which he said that as a result of the decline of the USSR, the Arab world needed to band together to oppose American and Israeli machinations. He demanded the withdrawal of the U.S. Navy from the Gulf and called on Arab states to withdraw their capital from American financial institutions. He also reminded his audience of the hardships Iraq had endured while fighting Iran, calling for a debt moratorium to alleviate Iraq's burden. Finally, in February, the American press learned that the CIA had discovered five sites in western Iraq where Baghdad had built fixed Scud launchers aimed at Israel.[14] Israeli officials sounded increasingly concerned by the Iraqi threat, and American commentators regularly discussed the likelihood of a preemptive Israeli strike to disarm Baghdad.

Once again, these actions appeared to confirm Saddam's belief that Israel and the United States were effectively indistinguishable and seemed to resurrect his old convictions that they were working to undermine him. In March, there seemed to be a joint Western response to Iraq that reinforced this conviction. The notorious artillery designer Gerald Bull—who was helping Iraq build a supergun that could fire WMD-tipped rockets at Israel—was assassinated, almost certainly by the Mossad. A few days later, U.S. and U.K. customs agents intercepted a shipment destined for Iraq with ninety-five krytrons, capacitors that could be used to trigger a nuclear explosion. Saddam seems to have taken these moves as warnings of more lethal actions to come. In typical fashion, he overreacted. On April 2, in a speech to army officers, Saddam lashed out at the United States, boasted of having binary chemical munitions, and threatened, "We will make the fire eat up half of Israel if it tries to do anything against Iraq."[15] Although this was clearly intended as a deterrent threat (he made it clear that he intended only to respond to an Israeli attack with chemical weapons), the ferocity of his remarks and the angry tone in which they were delivered escalated the situation to near-crisis levels. Somewhat grudgingly, the U.S. administration condemned Saddam's remarks. Behind the scenes, Iraq made clear its fear of Israel. Saddam called in Prince Bandar bin Sultan, the Saudi ambassador to Washington, and asked him to convey a message to Israel through the U.S. government that he had no intention of attacking Israel. He also requested that Bandar seek a similar guarantee from Jerusalem. Ultimately, Israel did pass back a similar assurance, but it also warned Saddam that it would retaliate massively for any Iraqi aggression.[16]

The April 2 speech may have been a watershed for Saddam. In the West, he was being denounced as "the most dangerous man on earth" for what (in his eyes) was merely a deterrent statement. As if to convince him that America and its allies had turned against him, on April 10, British customs agents seized components of Gerald Bull's supergun as they were being shipped out to Iraq. Although only two days later he met with a delegation of five U.S. senators led by Bob Dole, who assured him that the United States wanted good relations with Iraq, the evidence appears to be that Saddam had already decided that the United States was playing a two-faced game with him: claiming to want good relations while secretly working to undermine him and lay the foundation for a new Israeli strike. Later, Saddam learned that the administration was debating whether to cease extending agricultural credits to Iraq as a result of the Banco Nazionale del Lavoro scandal, the April 2 speech, and the various revelations of Iraq's massive WMD development projects. As if in response, on April 19, in a meeting with Yasir Arafat, Saddam warned that if there were any attack on Iraq, Baghdad's response would "sweep away U.S. influence in the region." He threatened British and American warships in the Gulf and urged Arafat to ratchet up the violence of the first Palestinian *intifadah,* then taking place in Gaza and the West Bank, and to reject all peace negotiations with Israel.[17] From then on Saddam seemed to have concluded that he was on a collision course with the United States and Israel. Meanwhile, Arab public opinion loved Saddam's tough talk. Arabs heaped praise on him as the first Arab leader to publicly stand up to Israel since Nasser.[18]

Saddam's conclusion that the United States was determined to oppose him and his sense that the Arab world was solidly behind him appear to have been important contributing factors in determining his future course. Saddam concluded that he had to take action to head off the challenge from Israel and the United States—now unrestrained by the demise of the Soviet Union—and strengthen his position for a coming showdown.[19] Sometime that April, Saddam apparently decided to invade and annex Kuwait. In May, the Republican Guard began intensive training in secret for a full-scale invasion of Kuwait, although for security's sake they were told it was for an operation against Israel.[20]

Of course, Saddam's problems with the United States and Israel were only part of his motivation in attacking Kuwait. The other important element was financial: Iraq continued to founder economically, far outspending its revenues. In 1990, inflation rose to 45 percent. Civilian imports, which Iraqis had come to expect as a right of their oil wealth, grew to $12 billion for the year, added on to $5 billion in military imports. Servicing Iraq's debt to non-Arab countries was costing Baghdad another $6 billion to $7 billion annually. Expatriates living in Iraq were sending home $1 billion. Meanwhile, new sources of oil in Alaska, the North Sea, and the former Soviet Union were driving down the price of oil, which fell from

$22 per barrel in January to $16 per barrel in June. Part of the drop in oil prices was a result of overproduction by OPEC countries, such as Kuwait and the United Arab Emirates (UAE), which not only profited from their overproduction but were pursuing a long-term economic policy of trying to increase global dependence on oil by depressing prices. Saddam would claim that each $1 drop in the price of oil cost Iraq $1 billion in revenue, and he was basically right. As a result of all of these factors, by the spring of 1990, Baghdad was facing a serious financial crunch.[21]

Saddam's solution was as simple as it was misguided: raid the treasure chest next door. Kuwait was small, weak, and fabulously wealthy. Kuwait's oil reserves were nearly as large as Iraq's, and combined would have given Iraq economic power to rival Saudi Arabia. Of greater importance still, Kuwait's financial assets amounted to $208 billion, and Saddam believed that by invading Kuwait, he not only would get his hands on Kuwait's oil wealth, and so improve Iraq's economic prospects over the long term, but would be able to get his hands on Kuwait's financial assets, which he could use to solve his short-term budgetary needs. Indeed, the Iraqi invasion of Kuwait opened with a daring heliborne assault by two brigades of Republican Guard Special Forces personnel who moved immediately to secure the amir's palace and the central bank of Kuwait in the belief that they would find vast reserves of gold there. Unfortunately for the Iraqis, most of Kuwait's assets were invested overseas, so Saddam was only able to get his hands on about $4 billion in Kuwaiti gold bullion.[22]

The first inkling of what Saddam had in mind came at the end of May, at a meeting of the Arab League in Baghdad, where he excoriated the United States and Israel and accused Kuwait of waging economic warfare against Iraq. Saddam also demanded an Arab summit to compel the GCC states to forgive Iraq's war debts and provide it with $30 billion in economic aid.[23] Roughly six weeks later, on July 16, 1990, Iraqi Foreign Minister Tariq Aziz wrote a long letter to the Arab League accusing the GCC states of conspiring with the United States to undermine the Iraqi economy. The previous day, all eight of Iraq's Republican Guard divisions had begun preparing to move to the border with Kuwait.[24] Saddam followed Aziz's letter with a diatribe of his own on the seventeenth, the anniversary of the Ba'thist coup that had brought him to power. He again lashed out at Kuwait and the UAE and claimed they were scheming with the United States to wage economic warfare against Iraq. Saddam warned that "If words fail to afford us protection, then we will have no choice but to resort to effective action to put things right and ensure the restitution of our rights." That same day, U.S. satellites began to detect the lead elements of the Hammurabi Republican Guard Armored Division arriving near Safwan, just north of Iraq's border with Kuwait.

When the Republican Guard began showing up on the Kuwaiti border in mid-July, it created a dilemma for the Bush administration. Washington had become ever more unhappy with Saddam's behavior during the spring and summer, and his threats against Kuwait certainly weren't redeeming him in the administration's eyes.[25] On the other hand, they continued to believe that he was ultimately a pragmatist who would not act rashly and that the United States' best interests would be served by finding a way to work with him. The moderate Arabs, who claimed to understand Saddam as only brother Arabs could, reinforced this stance by advising the United States that Saddam was just bluffing, urged the administration to steer clear of the dispute and let them handle it. Meanwhile, the administration was receiving mixed signals from its own intelligence community. Most U.S. intelligence analysts did not believe that Saddam intended to invade, and some did not believe he would attack Kuwait at all. As I described in the preface to this book, I recognized early on that Saddam intended to invade and occupy all of Kuwait but had difficulty convincing my colleagues or getting my analysis out to the policy-making community.

In the midst of the debates in Washington over Saddam's intentions, we received a now-infamous cable from the U.S. ambassador to Baghdad, April Glaspie. On July 25, Glaspie had gone to the Iraqi Foreign Ministry to deliver a diplomatic message from the administration. Unexpectedly, she was shown in to see Saddam. Ambassador Glaspie's cable back to Washington reporting on the meeting was subtitled "Saddam's Message of Peace." I remember reading it the very morning that my first memo (the watered-down version) arguing that Iraq was not bluffing and had the capability to overrun all of Kuwait was finally being sent out to the highest levels of the government. As I read her transcript of what Saddam had said to her and how she had replied, I thought to myself that she had completely misread the importance of what Saddam was telling her.

The text of that cable has since been declassified and it recounts their conversation, with Saddam essentially telling Ambassador Glaspie that Iraq was being strangled by Kuwait and the UAE with U.S. encouragement, that he intended to deal with this problem by whatever means were necessary, and that the United States should stay out because America did not have the stomach for a fight with Iraq. Perhaps it was the atmospherics or Saddam's body language, but Ambassador Glaspie missed these key points. She assured Saddam that the United States did not intend to intercede in Iraq's dispute with Kuwait, while urging him to find a peaceful solution.[26] Glaspie has rightly pointed out that she stuck to the talking points that she had been given. This is somewhat disingenuous, however. Glaspie knew very well that Washington strongly opposed an Iraqi invasion of Kuwait, and had she picked up on the import of Saddam's words she could easily have stressed that the United States wanted to see a peaceful resolution of the dispute without exceeding her brief, and could have done so in a tone and manner that made America's position clear to Saddam. The fact that she misunderstood the implications of his statement was revealed not only in the subtitle of her cable and her own commentary—which indicated that she believed Iraq intended to settle the dispute with Kuwait through negotiations—but also by her final comment to Saddam that she was reassured by his words and so intended to go ahead with her vacation plans. A respected academic who has gone over the cable likewise commented that the "July 25 telegram does not give one the impression that the warning was stressed or delivered in a particularly forceful manner."[27]

Reinforced by Ambassador Glaspie's misguidedly optimistic cable, the Bush administration decided to try to ride out what it was being told was only a "passing summer cloud."[28] Washington continued to take a hands-off approach, and both the State Department spokesman and the assistant secretary of state for the Near East emphasized publicly that the United States did not have any treaty obligations to defend Kuwait. Both Kuwait and the UAE did get somewhat nervous, and the UAE requested a joint American military exercise for reassurance. Kuwait even mobilized its military near the end of July, but so few Kuwaiti reservists actually showed up—and then so many went AWOL only days later—that the call-up became something of a joke. The Kuwaitis canceled it and claimed that they were doing so as a gesture of goodwill to Iraq. In addition, when the United States suggested a port call by U.S. Navy ships to demonstrate America's commitment to Kuwait, the Kuwaitis turned down the offer. Meanwhile, all eyes focused on a high-level meeting set for August 1 in Jeddah, Saudi Arabia, between Iraq and Kuwait to try to resolve the crisis. The Iraqis sent a delegation led by 'Izzat Ibrahim ad-Duri, one of Saddam's longtime Ba'thist flunkies, and accompanied by none other than 'Ali Hassan al-Majid, whose treatment of the Kurds had earned him the sobriquet

"Chemical 'Ali." Back at the CIA, when we heard the composition of the delegation, we immediately realized that the Iraqis had no intention of seriously bargaining with Kuwait—if so, they would have sent their negotiators, Tariq Aziz or former ambassador to the United States Nizar Hamdun. This was a delegation intended to provoke the Kuwaitis. Our suspicions were confirmed when satellite imagery revealed that the Republican Guard's Madinah Munawrah Armored Division had moved south along the Iraqi-Kuwaiti border and was now ready to sweep in along the left flank of Kuwait's meager defensive positions along the Matlah Ridge. There was no question an invasion was coming, and nothing the Kuwaitis in Jeddah could do could have stopped it.[29]

The August 1 meeting in Jeddah went according to Saddam's script. The Iraqis demanded that Kuwait wipe clean Iraq's debt and pay Baghdad what amounted to $27 billion for war reparations. This was a demand clearly intended to elicit an angry Kuwaiti rejection—which it did—and so justify an Iraqi attack. The meeting broke up after less than two hours, and that night, at 1:00 A.M. local time, 120,000 Republican Guards poured across the border. Within thirty-six hours, Kuwait was conquered, its military was swept away, and its leadership had fled.[30]

THE PERSIAN GULF WAR, 1990–1991

The Iraqi invasion was a nasty shock for the Bush administration. It represented a serious threat to America's principal objectives in the Persian Gulf region, to ensure the free flow of oil and prevent an inimical power from establishing hegemony over the region. If Saddam were allowed to retain possession of Kuwait, leaving him with roughly 9 percent of global oil production, his economic clout would rival that of Saudi Arabia, which accounted for about 11 percent of global production. In addition, his military force, if left intact and occupying Kuwait, would allow him to so threaten the Saudis themselves that they would be effectively "Finlandized"— forced to follow foreign and oil-pricing policies dictated by Baghdad. This combination could effectively allow Saddam to control the global price of oil. In time of crisis, Baghdad could threaten to undermine the global economy by withholding Iraqi oil, thereby sending oil prices soaring. Even if Saddam chose to follow a policy of high production and low oil prices, the enormous revenues he would be collecting would allow him almost limitless spending on his WMD programs, terrorism, and other pet projects. It was simply a matter of time before the world would have to confront a nuclear-armed Saddam (and not very much time, as the U.N. inspectors discovered after the war). Moreover, the invasion of Kuwait demonstrated that the U.S. administration's policy of constructive engagement and its assessment that Saddam was "pragmatic" and "moderate" in his aims were mistaken.

These fears were driven home on Sunday, August 5, three days after the Iraqi invasion. That morning I was at the CIA bright and early when we began to receive ominous intelligence reports. The vast logistical tail that had supported the Iraqi invasion of Kuwait (and contained supplies for more than a month of high-intensity combat) had been discovered deep in southern Kuwait, where it had no business being if it was only supporting an occupation of Kuwait, but where it was perfectly placed for an invasion of Saudi Arabia. Likewise, we found Iraqi artillery pieces deployed far forward, close to the Saudi border. During the night there had been an incursion by Iraqi tanks from western Kuwait into Saudi Arabia. Meanwhile, other reports provided unmistakable evidence that the Iraqis were loading CW munitions onto strike aircraft at several of their airfields in southern Kuwait. Four of the best heavy divisions of the regular army were reinforcing the eight Republican Guard divisions in Kuwait as fast as they could. And several brigades of Republican Guard armor were reported heading south toward the Saudi border from their previous positions in southern Kuwait. Although it would later turn out that these last reports were exaggerated— the Iraqi units were battalions, not brigades—the combination of these reports set off alarm bells all over Washington.[31] I wrote up a report warning that these events could be signs of an imminent Iraqi attack on Saudi Arabia, and Bruce Riedel took it along with him when he joined Director of Central Intelligence William Webster at a meeting of the National Security Council (NSC) that afternoon. Judge Webster convinced the NSC that the Iraqi threat to the kingdom was very real (if not imminent) and would be disastrous to U.S. interests. Although no one could be sure that this was the start of an Iraqi invasion of Saudi Arabia, the NSC agreed that it could not afford to be wrong again. At the meeting, they decided to send Secretary of Defense Richard Cheney to Saudi Arabia immediately to convince Saudi King Fahd to let the United States defend the kingdom.[32] The next day, President Bush declared to the world that Iraq's invasion of Kuwait "would not stand," and after meeting with Cheney, King Fahd agreed to Operation Desert Shield, bringing 250,000 American troops in to defend Saudi Arabia.

As best we can tell, Saddam did not intend to invade Saudi Arabia on August 5. Instead, it now appears that his actions were meant to deter an American counterattack—like a blowfish, he was puffing himself up to look big and tough, to try to convince Washington that if we wanted to retake Kuwait from him we were going to have a terrific fight on our hands. Other events, such as the forward positioning of Iraq's artillery and logistics, were accidental, caused by the dislocation that had accompanied the invasion. That said, there is no question that Saddam would have used his dominant military position in Kuwait to blackmail the Saudis on various scores and, given how easy his invasion of Kuwait had been, might at some point have chosen to simply achieve his long-cherished goal of making himself the Gulf's hegemon by invading the kingdom and seizing its oil fields outright. Indeed, Saddam's then chief of intelligence, Wafiq al-Samarra'i, told an interviewer, "I believe that Saddam did not, and would not have been satisfied with only Kuwait. Had his invasion of Kuwait been without reprisals, he would have continued to take the Eastern part of Saudi Arabia."[33]

Over time, however, when it became clear that Saddam did not intend to attack Saudi Arabia immediately, Washington began to see the invasion as an opportunity. Saddam had now been revealed as an extremely dangerous leader, and the administration recognized that the past revelations regarding Iraq's unshakable pursuit of weapons of mass destruction and outrageous violations of human rights were further proof that the Baghdad regime was a force for real instability in the vital Persian Gulf region. Increasingly in the months after the Iraqi invasion, Bush administration officials saw the crisis as an opportunity to smash Iraq's military power, eliminate its WMD programs, and reduce or eliminate it as a threat to the region.

The evolution of Washington's strategy for dealing with the crisis demonstrated this shift. Initially, the Bush administration had only one thought: defend Saudi Arabia. After obtaining Riyadh's agreement, U.S. Central Command (CENTCOM)—the military command with responsibility for the Persian Gulf—began pouring forces into Saudi Arabia and the Gulf to defend it against a subsequent Iraqi attack. By early September, enough American forces had arrived that Washington could breathe a sigh of relief. Meanwhile, the Bush administration had played its diplomatic hand skillfully and—with some help from Iraq's aggressiveness and diplomatic bungling—had persuaded the U.N. Security Council to pass a series of resolutions condemning the Iraqi invasion, demanding that Iraq withdraw, and imposing severe sanctions on Iraq for failing to comply. This in turn made possible the fashioning of a coalition of Western and Arab states willing to defend Saudi Arabia. When Saddam proved that the sanctions alone were not going to convince him to withdraw from Kuwait, the Bush administration resolved to do the job militarily and in so doing destroy Iraq's conventional forces and WMD. The United States doubled the size of the American military force in the Gulf and elicited additional contributions from the coalition members to build an offensive capability to enforce the U.N. resolutions against Saddam's will.

———

Regardless of any illusions he had held before the invasion of Kuwait, afterward Saddam discerned fairly quickly that the United States was not going to accept his conquest. Initially, Baghdad tried to cover up its actions by inventing the excuse that Iraq had simply been responding to a request for intervention by "popular forces" in Kuwait. But for reasons of secrecy, Iraq had not taken any steps to contact Kuwaiti oppositionists before the invasion, so that after the fact, Baghdad could not find any Kuwaiti leader willing to serve as a quisling. By August 8, Saddam simply announced that he was annexing Kuwait as Iraq's nineteenth province. At roughly the same time, the first American ground and air forces began arriving in the Persian Gulf as part of Operation Desert Shield. Baghdad recognized that it was locked in a confrontation with the United States, and Saddam and his advisers refashioned their grand strategy around four critical assumptions:

1. Iraq believed that the multinational coalition the United States had put together was politically fragile and would collapse if pressure were applied to its weakest links, primarily the Arab members of the coalition. Baghdad believed that many of the Arab states were ambivalent about the fate of Kuwait, unhappy with U.S. support for Israel, and sensitive to charges of allowing "imperialist" forces to regain a foothold in the Middle East.[34]

2. Saddam took it as an article of faith that the United States would be unwilling to tolerate high costs, and particularly heavy casualties, to liberate Kuwait. He believed that Kuwait was not very important to the West—especially if he promised to keep the oil flowing—and believed that the lessons of U.S. experience in Vietnam and Lebanon were that America would throw in the towel if American units began to suffer heavy casualties.[35]

3. Saddam was also certain that in a war with Iraqi forces for Kuwait, the United States would take serious losses. Saddam failed to appreciate the vast disparity in the quality of equipment, tactics, and personnel between the Iraqi and Western militaries. Thus, he was certain that if he could not prevent a war by fracturing the political cohesion of the coalition, his army would be able to inflict a bloody stalemate on the coalition in battle that would force them to the bargaining table. What's more, Saddam was counting on the threat of this scenario to convince the Americans not to go to war in the first place.[36]

4. Last, Saddam believed that air power would play only a minimal role in a war with the coalition. In a radio address on August 30, Saddam reassured his people that "The United States depends on the air force. The air force has never decided a war in the history of wars. In the early days of the war between us and Iran, the Iranians had an edge in the air. They had approximately 600 aircraft, all U.S.-made and whose pilots received training in the United States. They flew to Baghdad like black clouds, but they did not determine the outcome of the battle. In later years, our air force gained supremacy, and yet it was not our air force that settled the war. The United States may be able to destroy cities, factories, and to kill, but it will not be able to decide the war with the air force."[37]

Iraq's strategy followed logically from these assumptions. Baghdad launched a public relations offensive to undermine the coalition's political will. Iraq threatened that a war with Iraq would be the "Mother of All Battles" in which thousands of troops would be killed. It threatened to destroy Kuwait's oil infrastructure, as well as that of Saudi Arabia, hoping this would convince oil-dependent Western nations to avoid a military showdown. Tariq Aziz, among others, stated that Iraq would drag Israel into the conflict to turn it into a new Arab-Israeli war that would force the Arab members of the coalition to choose between fighting their Iraqi Arab brothers or their Zionist enemy. Iraq called on the Arab masses to revolt against their corrupt regimes who were handing over Islam's sacred lands to armies of infidels from the West.

Meanwhile, the Iraqi armed forces remained on the defensive and prepared for a knock-down, drag-out fight. Iraq chose not to attack Saudi Arabia or the coalition forces building up there because Saddam felt that doing so would simply ensure the war that he preferred to deter. Instead, Baghdad stuffed as many units as it possibly could into the Kuwaiti Theater of Operations (KTO) to try to convince the coalition that a war would be long and bloody. By the start of Operation Desert Storm in January 1991, Iraq had deployed fifty-one of its sixty-six divisions to the KTO, a force that probably numbered somewhere around 550,000 men at its peak, and fielded 3,475 tanks, 3,080 armored personnel carriers (APCs), and 2,475 artillery pieces.[38] Iraq built extensive defensive fortifications to defend those troops, like the defenses it had constructed to stymie the Iranian offensives throughout the Iran-Iraq War. It dispersed the components of its WMD programs and heavily bunkered and reinforced what could not be hidden.

Saddam was so confident that his strategy would work that he never really took seriously the international efforts to negotiate a settlement to the crisis. Throughout the fall of 1990, a procession of officials—from the United Nations, the Arab League, France, Russia, and many other countries and organizations—came to Baghdad to try to resolve the dispute short of war. However, right up to the start of Operation Desert Shield (and for a month after it), Baghdad refused to accept any of the U.N. Security Council resolutions or to negotiate except on its own terms. Instead, the Iraqis attempted to turn each effort to negotiate a solution into an opportunity to score propaganda points. Moreover, by the end of August, Baghdad had concluded a sort of rapprochement with Tehran at the price of conceding virtually all of Iran's demands, including giving up the remaining Iranian land under Iraqi control and agreeing to some of the terms of the old Algiers Accord. The deal secured Iraq's eastern flank, allowing Baghdad to concentrate virtually all of its forces on the defense of Kuwait, but meant that Saddam now had absolutely nothing to show for the eight years of war against Iran. It meant that he was staking everything on winning the war for Kuwait.

The problem for Saddam was that the four assumptions underpinning his grand strategy all turned out to be wrong. The coalition never fell apart. It is an open debate just how close to collapse it ever came or how long it might have held together if Washington had had to delay the start of the war, but this is now a question for scholars: for Iraq it was a decisive failure. Similarly, who knows how many casualties the United States and its allies would have been willing to tolerate—although before the war, polls showed strong support even if a war resulted in 10,000 American casualties, and the administration never wavered. However, Iraq's armed forces found themselves hopelessly outmatched against the full might of the United States' armed forces and inflicted pitifully little damage on the coalition's Western militaries.

Starting on January 17, 1991, the U.S.-led coalition unleashed the forty-three days of Operation Desert Storm. The coalition air forces quickly disrupted Iraq's command and control network and tore up its extensive air defenses. American fighters quickly found that Iraqi pilots were poor dogfighters (many could barely fly, let alone fight) and shot down nearly three dozen Iraqi jets with only one coalition loss. Coalition strike aircraft shut down much of the country's electricity, water, and oil production, as well as destroying bridges and railroads, impeding movement on Iraq's roads, and hammering Iraq's military forces themselves. In addition, the coalition mounted a fierce campaign on Saddam's known WMD and arms production factories. Iraq did fight back, launching volleys of al-Hussein modified Scud missiles at Israel, Saudi Arabia, and Bahrain, but U.S. diplomacy (and the reassuring—if ultimately ineffective—presence of American Patriot surface-to-air missiles in Israel and Saudi Arabia) succeeded in keeping the Israelis out of the war and the Saudis in.[39] When the Scuds failed to do the trick, Saddam tried other approaches. He threatened the international oil market by setting Kuwait's oil wells on fire. He tried to create an ecological catastrophe by dumping Kuwaiti oil into the Persian Gulf. He tried to mount several terrorist operations against the coalition, but these were easily thwarted by Western intelligence services.[40] Finally, he mounted a surprise offensive by two of Iraq's best regular army divisions to maul some of the coalition Arab units in the hope that this would force the coalition high command to cut short the air campaign and get on with the ground campaign (in which, Saddam still believed, Iraq would be able to inflict heavy casualties on the coalition). But the attack had to be called off on its second day when the two divisions came under murderous fire from coalition air forces.

Very shortly, the Iraqis began to realize that things were not going according to their plan. As the weeks passed, Saddam concluded that many of his assumptions had been badly off base. Saddam's military advisers had expected that the coalition's air campaign would last three to seven days at most; even the most pessimistic among them had not believed it could go on more than ten days.[41] It never occurred to the Iraqi leadership that the coalition would sit back and bomb them for thirty-nine days before making a move on the ground. By mid-February, Saddam had become very concerned, in particular because the coalition air campaign was doing more damage to his army in the KTO than he had ever expected. As best we understand it, Saddam's concern was not that the air strikes themselves would destroy the Iraqi Army or drive it out of Kuwait, but that they were so weakening his army in the Kuwaiti Theater that it would not be able to stand up to the coalition ground forces when they finally did attack.[42] Coalition air strikes probably destroyed around 1,200 Iraqi armored vehicles.[43] Of far greater importance, the coalition air campaign had effectively shut down Iraq's logistical system in the KTO and was demolishing the morale of the army, leading to widespread desertions. Indeed, by the time the coalition ground offensive did kick off on February 24, Iraqi forces in the Kuwaiti Theater had fallen from their high of around 550,000 to about 350,000 because of these morale and logistical problems.[44]

At that point, Saddam finally began to try to negotiate his way out of Kuwait, using the Russians as intermediaries. Although initially Saddam may simply have been trying to trick the coalition into suspending its military operations, within a week he had become so desperate that he was genuinely trying to get his army out of Kuwait intact. By then he appears to have become convinced that his army was melting away and the coalition ground offensive could destroy it altogether—a catastrophe that would almost certainly produce challenges to his rule, perhaps even a full-scale revolution—and he calculated that if the army and Republican Guard were destroyed, he might not have the strength to defend himself. In mid-February, there were demonstrations in the southern Iraqi cities of al-Basrah and ad-Diwaniyyah in which the protesters shouted anti-Saddam slogans and killed several Ba'th Party officials, and Saddam may have seen this as a portent of things to come if he could not rescue the army in Kuwait.[45] Although Baghdad's first offers were little more than propaganda positions it had trotted out before the onset of Desert Storm (such as making one condition for Iraqi withdrawal from Kuwait a simultaneous Israeli withdrawal from the West Bank, the Gaza Strip, and the Golan Heights), by February 22 Iraq had agreed to begin withdrawing from Kuwait in twenty-four hours if the coalition would agree to suspend its military operations immediately and lift the U.N. sanctions. To the coalition, this Iraqi offer was just another hoax—what incentive would Saddam have to comply if the coalition ceased its military operations and lifted the sanctions? But from Saddam's perspective this was tantamount to surrender.[46] As Saddam's previous discussion with Soviet envoy Yevgeny Primakov had indicated, his greatest fear was that as Iraqi forces pulled out of their fortifications and withdrew from Kuwait, the coalition would launch its ground offensive and catch the Iraqis when they were most vulnerable. He was asking only that his army be allowed to survive and the status quo ante be restored in return for his withdrawing from Kuwait.[47]

Having rejected Saddam's final offer, the coalition launched its long-awaited ground campaign on February 24.[48] When it came, Iraq's frontline infantry divisions disintegrated in a mass of surrenders and flight. The coalition strategy consisted of a diversionary attack by U.S. Marines into southeastern Kuwait, coupled with a vast outflanking maneuver to the west of the Iraqi lines (the famed "Left Hook") by the U.S. VII Corps, the most powerful armored concentration in history. On the second day of the ground war Baghdad realized two important facts. First, that morning they had counterattacked the Marines with one of their best regular army mechanized divisions, only to have it wiped out in a few hours of fighting, having done virtually no damage to the Marines. This let Baghdad know that even its best formations could not hope to defeat the coalition army. Second, after several Iraqi units were destroyed by huge American armored formations in the far west of the Kuwaiti Theater, Baghdad recognized the Left Hook. It must have been a terrible shock to the Iraqis to realize that powerful U.S. armored forces were moving to cut off the entire Iraqi Army in Kuwait. In response, Saddam issued a general retreat order to try to get as much of his army out as fast as he could. Meanwhile, the Iraqi General Staff shifted five Republican Guard divisions and three armored and mechanized divisions of the regular army to form up defensive screens to the west and south, behind which the army was supposed to retreat. They also pulled several other Republican Guard and regular army heavy divisions back to defend Baghdad and al-Basrah against a possible coalition move to overthrow the regime.

On the third and fourth days of the ground campaign, coalition forces smashed into the Iraqi defensive screen and fought the hardest battles of the war. In southeastern Kuwait, the Iraqi First Mechanized and Third Armored Divisions put up a desultory fight around Kuwait International Airport and the Matlah Pass that kept the Marines occupied but never endangered them. However, in the west of the Kuwaiti Theater, the Republican Guards fought to the death. On February 26, three U.S. armored and mechanized divisions and one armored cavalry regiment (a combined force of more than one thousand M-1A1 tanks) plowed into the lines of the Iraqi Tawakalnah 'alla

Allah Mechanized Division of the Republican Guard. In roughly twelve hours of vicious combat, the Americans obliterated the Tawakalnah—destroying nearly every one of the division's three hundred operable tanks and APCs—but the Americans came away with a great deal of respect for the Republican Guards, who fought on despite being outnumbered, outgunned, and outmatched in every way. The story was the same on February 27, when other American armored units crushed a brigade of the Madinah Munawrah Armored Division and the Adnan and Nebuchadnezzar Infantry Divisions. The Guards did not fight well and inflicted minimal damage on the Americans, but they fought hard.[49]

Meanwhile, the fog of war had descended over the American political and military leadership, prompting the most controversial decision of the war. By the end of February 27, the U.S. Central Command believed that the Republican Guard had largely been destroyed. This was based on reports from American combat units claiming to have engaged with and wiped out Iraqi Republican Guard formations, reports that U.S. troops were already at the outskirts of al-Basrah, and the assumption that coalition air forces had sealed all the lines of retreat out of the Kuwaiti Theater. Added to this were reports of a massacre by coalition aircraft of Iraqi soldiers fleeing Kuwait (mostly in stolen Kuwaiti vehicles and piled high with loot). The president was already feeling domestic pressure to end the war and the "slaughter" of Iraqi forces. Consequently, with the advice of the Pentagon and CENTCOM, President Bush ordered a halt to the ground offensive during the morning of February 28.[50]

The reality was somewhat different. Of the eight Republican Guard divisions deployed to the Kuwaiti Theater, only three (Nebuchadnezzar, Adnan, and Tawakalnah) had been destroyed, and a fourth (Madinah) had lost about half of its strength. CENTCOM actually did not know where many American units were, believing them to be farther forward than was actually the case. Nor were the exits from the Kuwaiti Theater cut off: at least two Republican Guard divisions—the Baghdad Infantry and the Special Forces Divisions—had already escaped across the Euphrates River and were moving to defend the capital.[51] Finally, the Hammurabi Armored Division and al-Faw Infantry Division remained largely intact and, along with the remnants of the Madinah, were taking up positions to defend al-Basrah. Even the reported "slaughter" on what was becoming called the "Highway of Death" turned out to have been wrong: in fact, the vast majority of the Iraqis fled their vehicles when the first aircraft appeared, and only a few dozen bodies were found among the hundreds of wrecked vehicles. As a result, it was a rude surprise for the administration in the first days of March when we at the CIA began to write about the 842 Iraqi tanks that had survived Desert Storm (about 400 of which were Republican Guard T-72s) and the steps that the surviving Republican Guard divisions were taking to put down the revolts against Saddam's regime.[52]

1991, THE YEAR OF MISSED OPPORTUNITIES

During the fall of 1990, Saddam Hussein had badly miscalculated his chances of success because his key assumptions about a war with the U.S.-led coalition had proved wrong. In the spring and summer of 1991, it was the Bush administration's turn to miscalculate. On February 28, 1991, the Iraqi Army was disintegrating and little more than five Republican Guard divisions stood between the coalition forces and Baghdad. (Another Guard division and ten infantry divisions of the regular army were deployed along Iraq's borders with Turkey and Iran but probably could not have moved fast enough to intercept a coalition drive on Baghdad.) Given the ease with which American forces had dispatched twenty to thirty Iraqi Army divisions and four other Guard divisions in the preceding two days, there was little question that coalition forces could have taken Baghdad, and done so quickly. But the Bush administration chose not to. In fact, as President Bush and his national security adviser, Brent Scowcroft, have written, they never believed it was an option: the mandate from the United Nations was to liberate Kuwait. Neither the coalition nor the American people were prepared to change the government of Iraq by force.[53] It is also true that the United States had not done any planning or made preparations for the conquest of Iraq, which would have required massive logistical support and additional military personnel to administer the country after Saddam's regime had fallen. It would have been easy to take Baghdad in March 1991, but it would have been difficult to feed the Iraqi people or run Iraqi society, given our inadequate preparations.

However, this is not the whole story. In fact, the National Security Directive the president had signed laying out the strategy for Operation Desert Storm had called for a march on Baghdad in the event Saddam employed weapons of mass destruction against U.S. forces or if he set the Kuwaiti oil wells on fire. However, as the war unfolded, and Saddam did

set the Kuwaiti oil fields on fire, the administration chose not to implement this element of the plan. This decision derived from several other
important notions. First, the administration believed that Saddam could
not hold on to power much longer and therefore it was probably unnecessary to march on Baghdad and incur the problems of occupying and rebuilding an Arab state. This assumption seemed confirmed when revolts
broke out in southern Iraq on March 2, followed two days later by a mass
rising of the Kurds of northern Iraq. Second, the Bush administration remained captive to the old geopolitical thinking of the 1980s, which assumed that a strong, cohesive Iraqi state was necessary to balance Iran.
The threat that a U.S. drive on Baghdad would cause the country to fragment was also an important element in the administration's decision to
stop the war. The president and his chief advisers assumed that Iraq's
generals would "take care of" Saddam for them, if left to their own devices, and this would deliver what the United States wanted—a cohesive
Iraq without Saddam—at no additional cost. Last, the Bush administration had already set its sights on the Madrid Conference, where it would
begin a process of negotiations intended to bring peace to the Middle
East. It concluded that a long-drawn-out U.S. military occupation of Iraq
would divert attention from that goal.[54]

No sooner had Washington decided not to take action to bring about
Saddam's downfall than Iraqis were deciding it was time they did so. The
Iraqi *intifadah* (uprising) began in al-Basrah on March 1 with tired, hungry,
and angry Iraqi soldiers who turned on the regime and convinced many of
the Shi'ah who lived there to join them. The first act of the *intifadah* came
from a nameless Iraqi soldier who fired a long burst from his AK-47 at a
mural of Saddam in Sa'd Square in al-Basrah, sparking the huge number of
demoralized soldiers collected in the square to rebel against the dictator.[55]
Within twenty-four hours the city was in chaos as small units of rebels bat-
tled street to street with units loyal to the regime. Within just a few days,
similar revolts had erupted in two dozen other towns in southern Iraq, including the cities of an-Nasiriyah, as-Samawah, Karbala, an-Najaf, al-
Amarah, al-Hillah, and ad-Diwaniyyah. Iran tried to fuel the rebellion by
dispatching members of its at-Tawwabin Division (Iraqi prisoners of war
who had remained in Iran) and Badr Corps (Iraqi Shi'ah who had fled to
Iran).[56] The revolt in the south was a signal to the Iraqi Kurds, who had
been looking for an opportunity to rise up again and reassert their independence since the Anfal campaign. Although the Shi'ite revolt was almost en-

tirely spontaneous and uncoordinated, the Kurds had been planning their offensive since the invasion of Kuwait, sensing that they might have an opportunity if Saddam's army were defeated in battle. By March 19, the Iraqi Kurds were in control of virtually all of their ancient homeland, including the major cities of Arbil, Dahuk, Kirkuk, and as-Sulaymaniyyah.

The Iraqi *intifadah* provided another opportunity for the Bush administration to take action to try to bring about Saddam's demise. To a great extent, Washington was responsible for the uprisings. The United States had incited the Iraqi people to overthrow the regime, and this implied a commitment to back such a revolt if it materialized. For instance, on February 15, the president had given two speeches that were broadcast into Iraq in which he called on "The Iraqi military and the Iraqi people to take matters into their own hands and force Saddam Hussein the dictator to step aside."[57] Likewise, one of the leaflets that coalition aircraft dropped during the war declared, "O you soldier and civilian, young man and old, O you women and men, let's fill the streets and the alleys and bring down Saddam Hussein and his aides."[58] The Kuwaitis and Saudis supported intervention in the *intifadah* to aid the rebels and ensure Saddam's demise.[59] Some in the administration argued for providing weapons and other assistance to the Shi'ah and Kurds in fulfillment of America's implicit pledge and in pursuit of the goal of regime change. Others recommended that the United States intervene directly, at least with air strikes against units loyal to the regime. Still others suggested that the United States should simply revoke what had clearly been a mistake: at the cease-fire talks after Desert Storm was halted, the Iraqis asked for permission to fly their helicopters to move personnel and supplies around, and General Norman Schwarzkopf, the commander of the U.S. forces—acting without any instructions but trying to show magnanimity—permitted Iraq to use all of its helicopters, including armed gunships. As should have been expected, the Iraqis began using their gunships to attack the rebels, and the United States could have prohibited the Iraqis from doing so.

Once again, the president and his chief advisers demurred. At this point the administration was terrified that Iraq would fall into chaos or fragment along ethnic and religious lines, leaving a power vacuum in the region and no state to balance Iran. In Secretary of State James Baker's words, the United States did not assist the rebels "primarily out of fear of hastening the fragmentation of Iraq and plunging the region into a new cycle of instability. The Shia were quite naturally perceived as being aligned with Iran, and the Kurds, who had demanded an independent state of Kurdistan for decades, were very fragmented in their leadership and were a constant source of concern to Turkey."[60] What's more, since they were convinced that Saddam would be overthrown in a nice, clean military coup, they saw no need to aid the rebels. In fact, they feared that doing so would preclude the military coup that they were hoping for by causing the officer corps (much of which was Sunni) to rally around Saddam as the only alternative to the Shi'ah and Kurds taking over.[61] To some extent, many in the U.S. intelligence community encouraged the Bush administration to remain aloof by insisting that Saddam could not survive the loss of the Gulf War. However, my fellow military analysts at the CIA and I were busy reporting on how much strength Saddam had left, and our judgment was that while Saddam was facing the greatest challenge to his rule in a dozen years, he had extricated considerable force from Kuwait and would probably survive. This assessment was echoed both by our counterparts in the Pentagon and by CENTCOM's own intelligence personnel.[62]

The administration may have been right in suggesting that the *intifadah* had saved Saddam. It is true that the Sunnis rallied around Saddam, seeing him as a bulwark against the Shi'ah and the Kurds, and the military force that the Sunnis still controlled was too much for the rebels, whose numbers proved disappointingly small.[63] Although there is considerable evidence that millions of Iraqis welcomed the revolt and wished it success, far fewer were willing to actually fight the Republican Guard when the time came. Many simply used the occasion to loot and ransack stores and warehouses for desperately needed supplies that the regime had been hoarding.[64] In Kurdistan, the two main Kurdish groups were able to field 40,000 to 50,000 *peshmerga* fighters and perhaps an equal number of Iraqi Army defectors (most of them Kurds who served in special units in the Iraqi Army called *fursan* battalions—but known as *jash,* or donkeys, to the other Kurds). In the south it is harder to know how many actually took up arms against the regime, but it was probably fewer than 100,000. Even in the cities where the revolts were most popular, such as an-Najaf and Karbala, fewer than about 10,000 took up arms. Israel's great scholar of Iraq, Amatzia Baram, has noted the important fact that few of the main Shi'ite tribes participated in the revolt (although some of their clans did), and some even assisted the regime.[65] The simple fact was that Saddam had survived so many challenges to his rule and the Iraqi people were so terrified of his revenge if they joined in and the revolt failed that the vast majority decided to wait to see who would win before taking action that could invite the regime's retribution. As a result, the military forces that remained loyal to Saddam, particularly the Republican Guard, crushed the *intifadah* in a few weeks.

The regime's counterattack began on March 6 where the *intifadah* had been born, in al-Basrah. There, the Republican Guard's Hammurabi Armored and al-Faw Infantry Divisions, and the army's Fifty-first Mechanized Division—all of which had survived the war relatively intact—led the regime's forces in a bloody two-day offensive that crushed the rebels in tough street battles. Saddam had placed 'Ali Hassan al-Majid, "Chemical 'Ali," in charge of pacifying the south, and he did so in his usual fashion. The Republican Guards were ordered to act with a savagery that many observers claimed was more appalling than even the Anfal campaign against the Kurds. The Guards maimed and slaughtered thousands of people, and 'Ali Hassan insisted that the piles of bodies and severed limbs be left unburied throughout al-Basrah and its surrounding villages. On one occasion, 'Ali Hassan demanded that residents of the city turn out in Sa'd Square to show their support for the regime, but when he arrived he pulled out an AK-47 and he and his bodyguards began firing into the crowd, mowing down scores of innocent men, women, and children. He executed some captured rebels by running over them with tanks, while others were drawn and quartered by trucks.[66]

With al-Basrah brutally subdued, the Hammurabi spearheaded a drive north along the Shatt al-Arab to clear the key roads up into central Iraq. As they moved north, the Hammurabi not only killed large numbers of rebels but razed any village that offered any resistance, massacring the inhabitants and burning their crops for good measure. On March 15, the Hammurabi captured the key town of al-Qurnah, where the Tigris and Euphrates rivers unite to form the Shatt. There the regime's forces split, with the Hammurabi and several other units pushing north along the Tigris, clearing pockets of rebellion and retaking the city of al-Amarah, while the Guard's al-Faw Infantry Division and other units branched off along the Euphrates to join up with other loyal formations that had been reasserting the regime's control over central Iraq.

Saddam appointed another of his murderous relatives, his cousin and son-in-law Hussein Kamel al-Majid, the minister of industry and military industrialization, to suppress the rebellion in central Iraq. During the second week of March Hussein Kamel led the Republican Guard's al-Nida Armored Division and the regular Army's Fourth Infantry Division (both of which had been on the Turkish border during the war), along with elements of the Special Republican Guard (SRG) in crushing the revolt in Iraq's holy Shi'ite cities of Karbala and an-Najaf. In both places, Hussein Kamel's forces displayed the same purposeful cruelty as 'Ali Hassan's had in the south. They turned the cities into abattoirs, going so far as to slaughter hundreds (perhaps thousands) of people within the sacred tombs of the martyrs 'Ali, Hussein, and Adnan, punching holes in the mosques themselves with tank fire. Altogether, anywhere from 30,000 to 60,000 Shi'ah were killed in the suppression of the *intifadah* in the south.[67] Meanwhile the Hammurabi, supported by remnants of other Guard divisions, continued on its destructive anabasis northward along the length of Iraq. By March 27, the Hammurabi had arrived at the great oil city of Kirkuk in northern Iraq and led an assault that recaptured the city for the regime in about thirty-six hours of fighting. After that, Kurdish resistance largely collapsed and Republican Guard task forces were able to push out along the main roads quickly and without significant casualties, overrunning even the distant city of as-Sulaymaniyyah in northeastern Iraq just a few days later.[68]

In Kurdistan as in the south, the regime's forces acted with great brutality, slaughtering roughly 20,000 Kurds—many of them civilians—and prompting up to 2 million others to flee their homes for fear of another Anfal.[69] The scale of the diaspora threatened a humanitarian disaster. So on April 3, the U.N. Security Council passed Resolution 688, which demanded that the Iraqi regime cease the repression of its people—specifically mentioning both the Shi'ah of southern Iraq and the Kurds. Although the resolution was not adopted under Chapter VII of the U.N. Charter and therefore did not imply that member states could enforce its terms militarily, on April 16 the United States, Britain, and France created a safe haven in northern Iraq to protect Kurdish refugees from the regime's forces. As part of what was called Operation Provide Comfort, the three countries undertook to feed and care for more than 500,000 Kurdish refugees in an area of northern Iraq and announced the establishment of a no-fly zone (NFZ) north of the Thirty-sixth Parallel, in which Iraqi aircraft would be forbidden to fly and that would be patrolled by coalition fighters. The establishment of Operation Provide Comfort and the northern NFZ convinced Baghdad to keep its distance, and so regime forces were pulled out of Kurdistan in October to avoid inadvertant skirmishes between Iraqi and coalition forces that could trigger larger coalition military responses.

The other critical event of 1991 was the definition of the United Nations' postwar treatment of Iraq. Here too, the United States acted on several badly mistaken assumptions. The first of these was that the Operation Desert Storm air campaign had destroyed most, if not all, of Iraq's WMD facilities. Second, that in the wake of the colossal defeat of Operation Desert Storm, the Iraqis would cooperate readily with the United Nations to meet its conditions for the lifting of sanctions. And last, again, that Saddam Hussein's regime was not long for this world.

These assumptions formed the backdrop to the creation of U.N. Security Council Resolution 687, the cease-fire resolution, which codified the post–Gulf War U.N. approach to Iraq. It established the conditions for Iraq's eventual return to the community of nations and was adopted under Chapter VII of the U.N. Charter, which meant that it was binding upon all member states. It demanded that Iraq make restitution to Kuwait and other countries harmed by the war, free Kuwaiti citizens detained during the occupation, return Kuwaiti property stolen during the war, recognize Kuwaiti sovereignty, and demonstrate that it could live in peace with its neighbors. UNSCR 687 also established the U.N. inspection regime intended to strip Iraq of the last vestiges of its WMD programs. The resolution laid out a ninety-day timetable for the establishment of the U.N. inspection system. Although in theory the inspectors' work was open-ended, because everyone including the United States believed that Iraq's WMD facilities were largely destroyed, the ninety days were considered roughly the amount of time needed to do the job—180 days at most. Finally, it declared that the draconian sanctions imposed on Iraq after the invasion would remain in place as conditions for Baghdad's cooperation with the resolution, although it specifically exempted food, medicine, and other essential civilian supplies. The sanctions quickly became a bone of contention because the United States interpreted the relevant passage (paragraph 22 of the resolution) as requiring that the sanctions remain in place until Iraq had met all of the conditions in the resolution, whereas most states interpreted the same paragraph to mean that the sanctions would be lifted when Iraq had fulfilled only the terms of the disarmament clauses.

The problems with the resolution again lay in its underlying assumptions. In actuality, the coalition air campaign had eliminated only a fraction of Iraq's WMD program, as the inspectors quickly learned.[70] For example, only three of Iraq's seven major nuclear sites were destroyed during the war.[71] The programs were far bigger than Western intelligence had realized before the war and consisted of numerous hidden and redundant facilities, most of which the West did not even know existed. Iraq had dispersed and hidden many of the key components of these programs, so that even when a facility was located, the equipment, personnel, and documents that had been at the facility often were nowhere to be found. Moreover, it did not take long for the Iraqis to get over their fear that the coalition would continue its military campaign to Baghdad and overthrow the regime (U.S. forces withdrew from Iraq in April and May 1991). Once the gun was removed from Saddam's head, he began backtracking and obstructing the inspectors as fast as he could. Because none of these things proceeded as quickly as the United Nations had envisioned, the sanctions remained in place long after they were expected to have been lifted. As a result, over time the Iraqi people felt a real impact from the sanctions—an impact never intended by the Security Council. And finally, Saddam survived. He put down the *intifadah* and hung on to power.

This was the fatal flaw in the Bush administration's Iraq policy at the end of the Gulf War: its actions were predicted on the certainty that Saddam would fall from power. When he did not fall, it was left up to a group of working-level officials in Washington to cobble together a containment strategy to keep Iraq under control and apply enough pressure to topple him. Thus the administration stuck with the comprehensive sanctions designed to force Saddam out of Kuwait, started up a covert action program to encourage opposition efforts to remove him, and employed limited doses of force to further undermine his support inside Iraq. Again, these were high-risk gambits, which, if they did not succeed in the short term, carried long-term costs. But the administration opted for them because they believed Saddam's grip on power was weak and a few good shoves would knock him out. When he defied the odds and stayed in power, the United States was left with an unstable containment regime that would require great skill and attention, and the repeated application of military force, to keep in place. The sanctions could have been better designed so that they focused more on Saddam and his military and had less of an impact on the Iraqi people. The United States could have built in elements that could have made it easier to employ limited military operations against Iraq when it reneged on its commitments to the United Nations. Likewise, the inspection regime could have been set up to ensure greater Security Council unity over the long term and to make it harder for Iraq to exploit ambiguities in U.N. resolutions and differences among the five permanent members of the Security Council—the United States, Britain, France, Russia, and China, known as the P-5. Knowing what we know today—that the early post–Gulf War efforts to remove Saddam would fail—there is little doubt that Washington would have played its hand differently in 1991.

THREE

Containment and Beyond

In 1991, the United States lost its best opportunity to remove the regime of Saddam Hussein from power. Whether one believes that the Bush administration could or should have taken advantage of that opportunity is a matter of opinion, but the fact that the opening existed and was let pass is not. Of greater importance for the course of U.S.-Iraqi relations, however, is that many in the Bush administration did not recognize the passing of that moment. They continued to believe that Saddam's demise was a certainty and that all they needed to do was to hold on for just a little while longer until he was gone. As a result, many of the critical decisions of 1991—decisions that would establish the course of the entire postwar confrontation with Iraq—were made with these short-term considerations in mind. Because the administration did not envision a long-term need, long-term considerations were essentially never considered. Nevertheless, at lower levels of the federal bureaucracy there was a growing recognition over time that Saddam might not fall in a postwar coup and due consideration needed to be given to a policy that could last more than a few months.

Indeed, throughout the post–Gulf War period, there were important differences of opinion over how to handle Iraq, differences that took full form during the Clinton administration. In marked contrast to popular perceptions, the U.S. government debated Iraq policy constantly, with different schools of thought arguing for very different approaches. Often, it was these contending views that produced Washington's seemingly peripatetic approach to Iraq. In the media and in Congress, the debate over Iraq was frequently portrayed as a difference over values, character, and spine. However, among the professionals within the government (and to some extent in the policy community beyond it), the real debate was about making tough choices over how much priority and how many resources—political, diplomatic, and military—should be devoted to dealing with Saddam.[1]

The debate over Iraq policy focused largely on priorities and the resources necessary to execute different policy options. On the one hand were the "doves" who favored a less confrontational approach with Iraq. The term "doves" does something of a disservice to this group, because few of them ever espoused a policy of engagement or reconciliation with Iraq. There was a consensus in the U.S. government that Saddam was evil; the differences were simply over how best to handle his odious regime. The key to the dovish position on Iraq was in its priorities. The doves had a very ambitious international agenda they hoped to pursue. They saw the end of the Cold War as an opportunity to create a better world, and they knew that doing so would require tremendous effort. However, they saw Iraq as a small, relatively weak third-world country. They believed that Saddam could be prevented from causing trouble in the world through a strategy of containment and that because of his weakness (especially after the devastation of Desert Storm), the United States did not need to devote a great deal of time or resources to make containment work—time and resources they were determined to spend on issues such as NATO expansion, transforming the Soviet Union, rebuilding Eastern Europe, engagement with China, and the opening to India. They argued that these policy issues were of far greater importance to the long-term safety and prosperity of the United States.

Set against the doves were two different groups of hawks. The more extreme group of hawks favored an all-out policy of regime change right from the start. In the beginning, this was a very small group of people. Once it became clear that Saddam was not likely to fall in the wake of the Gulf War, even senior members of the Bush administration largely moved into the dovish position, wishing to leave Saddam to stew in Baghdad while they turned to addressing more important concerns such as Russia after communism, building better relations with China, starting a new Arab-Israeli peace process, and saving the hungry of Somalia. During the early Clinton administration only small numbers of people in two agencies believed that regime change was America's only option. Some uniformed military officers charged with keeping the peace in the Persian Gulf region believed a military showdown with Saddam was inevitable, and they were determined to finish the job. In addition, some within the arms control community believed that Saddam would never give up his WMD programs and inevitably would be able to build a nuclear weapon. Therefore regime change was necessary.

The center-right position was initially (and for many years) the more mainstream hawkish position. This group consisted primarily of the government's specialists on the Middle East and Iraq. These moderate hawks proceeded from the assumption that Saddam would never accept containment gracefully and that the only language he spoke fluently was that of force. They believed that containment was going to be a fight all the way and for it to succeed, the United States was going to have to be willing to make Iraq a high priority and use force to meet Saddam's more threatening challenges. Consequently, they favored an aggressive form of containment that would require the United States to play an active role in maintaining the diplomatic consensus to keep Saddam tightly contained, the regular use of military force to smack Saddam down whenever he mounted a serious challenge to some element of containment, and a program of regime change as well. The moderate hawks favored deliberate but prudent efforts at regime change (in the form of both direct covert action and support to Iraqi opposition groups) because, over the long term, they recognized that it would be better to get rid of Saddam than to have to sustain an effort to contain him. In addition, they argued that even if efforts at regime change did not succeed in removing Saddam from power, they would invariably keep pressure on him—and as long as he was preoccupied with his own internal security, he would be less able to challenge containment. Ultimately, the only real difference between the two groups of hawks was that the moderates believed that a policy of determined regime change would be so difficult and costly that senior policy makers (President Clinton in particular) would never agree to it—so they advocated an aggressive form of containment with accompanying efforts toward regime change as the best policy that was politically possible. Because both wings of the hawkish faction favored pressing ahead with regime change while maintaining a confrontational approach on containment, for most of the Bush, Sr., and Clinton administrations the two groups were virtually indistinguishable.

It is important to recognize that the debate within the Clinton administration over Iraq—which virtually paralleled similar debates both at the end of the Bush, Sr., administration and the beginning of the Bush, Jr., administration—was to some extent a debate between Middle East regionalists and senior policy generalists. Many of the hawks of both varieties were specialists on Iraq and the Middle East.[2] I myself fell into this category. Because we focused on Saddam and the problems he created for the larger Middle East, it was easier not only to recognize that it would take force to keep him in place and that we needed to be thinking about getting rid of him, but also to argue that the United States should devote considerable resources to those efforts. In truth, senior policy makers hear this sort of thing from their regional specialists all the time—every regionalist wants his or her region to get the most resources to solve its problems. And it is up to the men and women at the top of the national security hierarchy to prioritize among them. The doves never apologized for Saddam or argued that he was not a problem; they simply believed that Saddam could be handled in a less confrontational manner that would free up resources for what they considered higher priority issues. The most difficult questions I was always asked by my bosses were those such as, "Why should we devote all of these resources to Iraq to head off a problem that we *may* have in the future, rather than using them to solve the crises we have right now in Somalia, Bosnia, Haiti, Kosovo, etc.?" Especially early on in the Bush, Sr., and Clinton administrations, when Iraq was weak and the sanctions were strong, there was little evidence that regionalists could use to make a case.

THE PRODUCTS OF IMPATIENCE, 1991–1994

After the failure of the *intifadah* in 1991, the Bush administration wasted little time in making clear its policy toward Iraq. On May 7, 1991, Deputy National Security Adviser Robert Gates announced that "Saddam is discredited and cannot be redeemed. His leadership will never be accepted by the world community. Therefore, Iraqis will pay the price while he remains in power. All possible sanctions will be maintained until he is gone. . . . Any easing of sanctions will be considered only when there is a new government."[3] The sanctions were themselves seen as a form of pressure on the regime, hence Gates's statement that they would remain in place regardless of the effects on the Iraqi people, until Saddam was gone. But Washington was not going to rely on the sanctions alone. Later that month, President Bush signed a presidential finding authorizing a covert action campaign to "create the conditions for the removal of Saddam Hussein from power."[4] Five months later, the administration increased the funding of this program from $15 million to $40 million.[5] The CIA was encouraged to do whatever it could to give Saddam the last shove that the administration believed was all that was needed to knock him from power.

Not surprisingly, Saddam was not going to go without a fight, and unfortunately, the Bush administration had chosen to play the game on Saddam's turf. If there was one battle Saddam could win against the United States, it was a covert battle to stay in power in Iraq. With the Gulf War and the *intifadah* behind him, Saddam's greatest concern was his internal security position, where he faced numerous problems. Many of the Shi'ite rebels and army deserters who had been defeated during the *intifadah* fled to Iran or the marshes of southern Iraq and launched a guerrilla war against the regime. Iraqi society suffered considerable damage during both, feeding popular unrest. And while the Sunni "center" had rallied around him to oppose the Kurds and Shi'ah during the *intifadah,* Saddam knew that there were many who felt that with the danger past, his regime should also end. In May 1991, Saddam's intelligence services snuffed out a coup plot led by General Bariq Abdallah, a onetime commander of the Republican Guard.[6] Then, in June 1992, the regime crushed another, this one led by Saad Jabr (the son of former Prime Minister Salih Jabr), that included General Bashir Talib, the original commander of the Republican Guard in 1963, and former Ambassador Jassim Mukhlis. Saddam had 300 military officers and civilians (reportedly 150 of whom were officers in the Republican Guard) arrested for involvement in the plot, and many of them were executed.[7] Meanwhile, once the Iraqi military had been reformed and reconstituted after the trauma of Desert Storm, several divisions were sent south to conduct counterinsurgency operations in the Hawizeh and an-Nasiriyah marshes to root out the guerrillas nesting there.[8] So troublesome were the guerrillas, however, that in 1992, the regime's forces began a massive program to drain the southern marshes altogether to simply eliminate the sanctuary of the insurgents. The regime's counterinsurgency operations were so brutal that in August 1992, the United States, Britain, and France declared a second no-fly zone, this one over southern Iraq below the Thirty-second Parallel, to provide some protection for the Shi'ah from attacks by Iraqi aircraft and helicopter gunships.

Iraq's economic problems were an important contributing factor to the internal security threats Saddam faced. In some ways, these were relatively mild, especially compared to the deprivations to follow. Between the huge amounts looted from Kuwait and the regime's massive stockpiles, shortages immediately after the war were episodic and confined to certain categories. Nuha al-Radi, a Baghdadi civilian, wrote in her diary on March 14, 1991, "What a way to raid a country! Apparently we denuded Kuwait of everything plus the kitchen sink. Aeroplanes, buses, traffic lights, appliances, everything. Shops all over the country are full of their consumer goods. Imagine!"[9] Indeed, Iraq plundered as many as fifty thousand cars alone from Kuwait, glutting the Iraqi auto market. However, in other areas, problems arose immediately. For instance, on March 22, 1990, U.N. Undersecretary General Martti Ahtissari commented, "Nothing we had seen or read [about Iraq] had quite prepared us for the particular form of devastation which had befallen the country. The recent conflict has wrought near-apocalyptic results on the economic infrastructure of what was until recently a highly urban and mechanized society."

So great were Iraq's humanitarian problems that the United States and the United Nations quickly recognized that allowances had to be made so that the Iraqi people would not starve. It was Ahtissari's report that prompted the American drafters of Resolution 687 to exempt food from the embargo, ease restrictions on essential civilian needs, and unfreeze many of Iraq's foreign assets for the purchase of food and medicine.[10] In a similar fashion, a July 1991 report by the Aga Khan estimated the cost of restoring Iraq's oil, electricity, water, sanitation, agriculture, and public health systems to prewar levels at $22 billion, and roughly $7 billion in the first year. This led to the passage on August 15 of U.N. Security Council Resolution 706, which authorized Iraq to sell up to $1.6 billion in oil over six months using an escrow account, from which 30 percent would go to compensate victims of Iraq's aggression, the rest to buy humanitarian supplies.

The U.N. actions posed a danger to Saddam's strategy because they threatened to decouple the economic sanctions and the military sanctions, and because they created a mechanism by which Iraq's revenues would be administered by the United Nations to feed and heal the Iraqi people. This challenged Saddam's authority as the undisputed ruler of Iraq; if the United Nations were seen as an alternative source of authority and dispenser of benefits (even basic food rations), then Saddam's position would not be unrivaled. If the United Nations, not Saddam, controlled the revenues from Iraq's greatest resource, oil, Saddam's power would be greatly diminished. Consequently, Iraq rejected the resolution as an infringement of its sovereignty. Nevertheless, Baghdad recognized that it had to respond to its troubles and launched a domestic self-sufficiency campaign. The regime worked diligently to repair basic services and infrastructure and did so in a matter of months, albeit largely by a policy of cannibalization that it could not sustain.[11] Moreover, it encouraged Iraqis to feed themselves by turning to agriculture, triggering a large-scale flow of urbanites back out to the countryside. However, since Baghdad was unwilling to avail itself of the U.N. mechanisms, its economic problems deepened. By August 1991, Iraq's inflation rate reached 2,000 percent and earnings had fallen to one tenth of the prewar figures.[12]

The other battle Iraq geared up to wage was the long fight over its disarmament. Saddam had no choice but to accept all of the United Nations' terms simply because he lacked the military power to resist the U.S.-led coalition if it chose to enforce any of them. But Saddam had no intention of actually abiding by any of the U.N. diktats. As the former head of Iraq's nuclear weapons program, Khidhir Hamza, described it, Saddam did not accept the right of the United Nations to impose any conditions on Iraq, Iraq's signature on the U.N. Charter notwithstanding.[13] Thus, he would abide by anything the United Nations forced upon him, but he felt no obligation to comply except under threat of force. In particular, Saddam wanted the economic and military sanctions lifted as fast as possible, and he never had any intention of surrendering Iraq's WMD assets to the newly established U.N. Special Commission for the Disarmament of Iraq (UNSCOM). Of critical importance, Saddam assumed that the U.N. sanctions, the inspection regime, and the other U.N. constraints on Iraq would be short-lived. Saddam believed that the United States and its coalition allies would have little stomach for a protracted struggle with him and would soon be distracted by other matters. He also assumed that he could either fool or bribe the U.N. weapons inspectors into declaring Iraq disarmed, which would trigger the lifting of the sanctions. Consequently, at least at first, it never occurred to Saddam that he had a choice between having the sanctions lifted and retaining his WMD. To coordinate this strategy, on June 30, 1991, he secretly formed a Concealment Operations Committee, chaired by his younger son, Qusayy Saddam, and including Hussein Kamel and Tariq Aziz, now elevated to deputy prime minister.[14] This committee's sole purpose was to deceive the inspectors, hinder their work, and find ways to continue to pursue WMD development covertly.

On the inspections front, UNSCOM and its counterpart for nuclear inspections, the International Atomic Energy Agency (IAEA), proved not to be the pushovers Baghdad had expected. The inspectors took their jobs seriously, and although Iraqi intelligence was able to recruit some members of the inspection teams, by and large they resisted Baghdad's enticements and bullying.[15] In June, inspection teams led by the resourceful David Kay succeeded in unmasking Iraq's undeclared program to enrich uranium using gigantic magnets, called calutrons. In July, the IAEA discovered several kilograms of highly enriched uranium and large stocks of natural, unenriched uranium. The discoveries of the uranium and the calutrons created such ill will toward Iraq in the United Nations that Qusayy's concealment committee decided to admit that Iraq had a nuclear weapons program and to change its strategy to focus on retaining only the most essential elements of the WMD programs. The Iraqis grudgingly turned over to the inspectors huge amounts of WMD-filled bombs and artillery shells, many of their Scud missiles, and major chunks of their nuclear program in hopes that this would satisfy the inspectors. They held back considerable documentation, key equipment that would be difficult to replace, and a residual force of Scuds and WMD munitions as a final deterrent. These were then turned over to the Special Republican Guard (SRG)—a 25,000-man palace guard, heavily armed and deeply loyal to Saddam—and the Special Security Organization (SSO)—the central coordinating body of all Saddam's internal security services, including the SRG—to hide and disperse as necessary.[16] In addition, the Iraqis kept most of their key personnel away from the inspectors. They kept their scientists and engineers together in their preexisting teams, still working on WMD projects but dispersed and attached to bland government agencies where Baghdad assumed the inspectors would never think to look.

But the inspectors would not give up. Aided by national intelligence agencies, they kept turning up new Iraqi WMD caches that Baghdad had hoped to retain. In August 1991, the inspectors found Gerald Bull's supergun, which Iraq had not declared. Shortly thereafter, they discovered a huge quantity of heavy water for use in nuclear reactors. In September, another team (again led by David Kay) uncovered a treasure trove of sixty thousand documents detailing Iraq's nuclear weapons development program hidden away as part of the harmless-sounding Petro-Chemical 3 project outside of Baghdad. The Iraqis were so unnerved that the IAEA had found this collection that they physically prevented the inspectors from leaving with the documents, leading to a four-day standoff in the parking lot of the facility until Iraq finally allowed the inspectors to photocopy the key documents and take them out. In May 1992, Iraq was forced to confess that it had a biological warfare program, although it would admit to only a "defensive" program to protect itself against the use of biological agents by other countries.

While the inspectors were proving more effective than expected, the Bush administration's efforts at regime change were coming up empty. In truth, few at the CIA thought it likely that they would succeed. The most promising avenue the CIA found was with a group of exiles calling themselves the Iraqi National Accord (INA), or al-Wifaq. This group consisted mostly of former Iraqi military officers and other officials, many of whom had contacts still within the regime's armed forces and security services, which made them the perfect candidates to instigate a palace coup against Saddam. Nevertheless, the CIA pursued other approaches as well. In particular, during the summer of 1991, Langley had reached out to an Iraqi exile named Ahmed Chalabi, a former banker, to serve as the coordinator of an effort to create a more cohesive and effective external opposition under a single umbrella organization. But all of the opposition groups were weak and fractious, and Chalabi had been chosen because he was wealthy and had good organizational skills, *and* because he had no base of support inside Iraq nor any standing with any of the exile groups. In the words of one U.S. official, Chalabi "was acceptable as an office manager," which is all he was supposed to be. They thought he would be easily controlled and, because he was a *tabula rasa,* would not provoke objections from any of the more established groups. However, Chalabi's lack of support either inside or outside Iraq also meant that he would have an uphill battle helping the CIA to build a unified Iraqi opposition. Consequently, even when Chalabi's group, the Iraqi National Congress (INC), finally moved into northern Iraq in October 1992 with CIA funds, equipment, and assistance, they had great difficulty attracting recruits to their cause and other groups to their banner.[17]

In marked contrast to the regime change program, the containment strategy that the administration had been forced into adopting while it waited anxiously for Saddam's fall was working well: the inspectors were destroying huge chunks of Iraq's WMD programs (far more than Desert

Storm had), the sanctions were keeping Saddam weak and focused on his internal problems, and the Iraqi military was running to stand still. The key to the early success of containment was the broad international support it enjoyed. This became apparent in later years, when that international support dissipated and the impact on containment was profound. But in the immediate aftermath of the Gulf War, the international community remained united in its view that Saddam Hussein was a detestable tyrant, a war criminal, and a dangerous threat to the stability of the Persian Gulf region and its vital oil supplies. The memories of Iraq's unprovoked aggression against Kuwait were fresh in people's minds, as was the spirit of international cooperation and collective security that the Bush administration had sounded when it had built the Desert Storm coalition. Many countries saw the success of the U.N. effort to disarm Iraq and ensure that it comply with the will of the international community as critical to the future of the global order. Consequently, whenever Iraq refused to cooperate with the inspectors or accept a UNSC resolution, it was met by a solid diplomatic front.

Containment was working so well that by the end of 1992, Saddam was beginning to get impatient. He had expected to have been rid of both the inspectors and the sanctions by then and decided to take action to try to speed their departure. In addition, George Bush had lost in the U.S. presidential elections in November, and Saddam decided to find out whether the lame duck still had any fight left in him. In late December, he began harassing coalition air forces patrolling the southern no-fly zones, but all this achieved was angry warnings from the United States, France, Britain, and Russia and the loss of an Iraqi MiG in combat with a U.S. fighter. Stymied in the NFZs, Saddam shifted in early January 1993 to impeding the U.N. weapons inspectors and illegally sending personnel into Kuwait to reclaim equipment they had abandoned there at the end of the Gulf War. On January 11, the Security Council declared Iraq to be in "material breach" of the cease-fire resolution, setting up air strikes by 110 American, British, and French jets against Iraqi air defense targets in southern Iraq two days later. When Iraq still would not back down, on January 18, two days before the Clinton administration took office, the United States fired forty-five Tomahawk land attack missiles (TLAMs, the most common form of cruise missile) at the Zafaraniyah manufacturing complex outside Baghdad, which had been an important part of Iraq's nuclear weapons program. The next day, seventy-five coalition fighters restruck the targets missed in the January 13 strikes and Baghdad finally announced a "ceasefire."[18]

The new Clinton administration took office without the baggage of President Bush's failed efforts to oust Saddam and with little desire to focus on Iraq. From the start, the administration was dominated by the dovish position on Iraq. This group was led primarily by National Security Adviser Anthony Lake, Secretary of State Warren Christopher, and Deputy Secretary of State Strobe Talbott. The Clinton team recognized that the containment policy that their predecessors had stumbled onto remained effective and offered an opportunity to pursue a different agenda. The Clinton White House was not about to make the battle of wills with Saddam Hussein a primary focus—it had seen George Bush lose that battle and it was not going to allow it to happen again. During the campaign, its well-known mantra had been "It's the economy, stupid," and when it came to power, revitalizing the U.S. economy was its first priority in both domestic and foreign policy matters. The most clearly I ever heard this spelled out was in a discussion over Iraq policy with a high-ranking administration official, who argued that as long as the U.S. economy was prospering, the United States would be safe from most threats because we would simply be too strong for the majority of international actors to confront, while at the same time we would assure ourselves of the power to deal with any threat that become truly dangerous. Consequently, the first principle of Clinton administration foreign policy was to ensure the economic well-being of the country.

Moreover, in the foreign policy field, the Clinton administration (especially during its first term, under the direction of Lake, the high-minded national security adviser) was seeking to create a new paradigm of international relations—a true New World Order. The goals of this new paradigm were a world of global economic development, cooperation, collective security, and the use of force only to aid the oppressed and defeat aggression. It found expression in Washington's determined efforts to broker peace deals in the Middle East and Northern Ireland; the U.S. interventions in Somalia, Haiti, and Bosnia; and President Clinton's later remarks that he regretted not having intervened to prevent the Rwandan genocide. Actively confronting Saddam did not fit neatly into that brave new world. To the administration's doves, containment of Iraq therefore offered the opportunity to prevent Saddam from making trouble at a relatively low cost, with the hope that this would allow them to pursue the rest of their policy agenda. On May 18, 1993, Dr. Martin Indyk, the special assistant to the president for the Near East and South Asia, argued that the fall of the Soviet Union and the victory of the Gulf War created the opportunity to try to forge an Arab-Israeli peace, and the administration's new policy of "dual containment" of Iraq and Iran was vital if such a peace were to be achieved.[19] As Indyk would later describe the administration's thinking, "There was a window of opportunity to negotiate a comprehensive peace in the Middle East. If the negotiations were successful, that outcome would have a profound effect on the region. . . . The United States should therefore focus its energies on peacemaking, while containing the radical opponents of peace (Iraq, Iran, and Libya)."[20]

Nevertheless, there was still real debate regarding Iraq within the administration. At lower levels, there were a number of more hawkish officials who believed that the United States should be trying not just to contain Saddam but to bring him down. At the start of the administration, these officials had proposed a more aggressive version of containment that would employ a ramped-up covert action program and limited air strikes to press Baghdad and possibly create the circumstances in which Saddam might be overthrown. Indeed, little noticed at the time or since, Indyk's May 18 speech called for increased assistance to the Iraqi opposition. Others within the administration simply recognized that Saddam would work tirelessly to tear down containment and that the United States would have to push back hard whenever he challenged the inspections, the sanctions, the no-fly zones, the Maritime Interception Force (which prevented smuggling to Iraq in the Persian Gulf), and other elements of the policy. Both groups agreed that force would be necessary to check Saddam, and therefore simply keeping containment in place and intact would require the willingness of the United States to employ military operations from time to time in response to particularly dangerous Iraqi threats. A core of Iraq hardliners formed around Indyk himself, Bruce Riedel (initially Indyk's director for Persian Gulf affairs and later the deputy assistant secretary of defense for the Middle East), and Mark Parris (the principal deputy assistant secretary of state for the Near East). However, the regionalists who carried on the fight day to day were backed by some of the administration's heavyweights, including Vice President Al Gore; his national security adviser, Leon Fuerth; and U.N. Ambassador Madeleine Albright, all of whom were very hawkish on Iraq.[21]

The hawks in the Clinton administration got their chance in the spring of 1993. Former President Bush traveled to Kuwait for a ceremony commemorating the victory of the Gulf War, and the day before he arrived the

Kuwaitis announced that they had arrested fourteen men for conspiring to assassinate Bush and the amir of Kuwait. What's more, one of the defendants—an Iraqi—testified in his trial that Iraqi intelligence had orchestrated the plot. Indyk ordered a full-scale investigation into the claims, and within just a few months the CIA and FBI reported that the evidence of Iraqi involvement was overwhelming. Indyk, Parris, and Riedel seized on the assassination plot to make their case for a more robust approach, and, with strong backing from Fuerth and Albright, they convinced the Principals (the National Security Council meeting without the president is referred to as the Principals' Committee, or PC) that the United States had to respond to this act of Iraqi terrorism with force. On June 26, 1993, American warships fired twenty-three TLAMs at the Iraqi intelligence service headquarters in Baghdad—the service that had organized the hit—and flattened it.[22] The ultimate impact of the attack on Iraq's intelligence operations was probably modest, because it was launched in the middle of the night, when the building was effectively deserted, and so destroyed files and equipment but killed few Mukhabbarat officers. Nevertheless, the strike was considered an important victory by the hard-liners within the U.S. government. Moreover, they were able to use the assassination attempt against President Bush to remind the administration doves that Saddam remained dangerous and bent on vengeance and therefore the United States needed to be working harder to topple him.[23]

After the June 1993 cruise missile strike, Saddam, appearing to have decided that discretion was the better part of valor, lowered his level of confrontation with the United States and the United Nations. The Iraqis continued to look for ways to hamstring the inspectors, but their obstructionism and harassment were more an annoyance than an impediment. As the inspectors would later learn, during this period Iraq was having great success fooling the inspectors into believing that they had uncovered all of Iraq's WMD programs. Moreover, because Qusayy's committee reported to Saddam that their deception scheme was working and UNSCOM and the IAEA began to make noises about "transitioning to long-term monitoring," code for ending the phase of active inspections, Saddam was willing to bide his time. For its part, the Clinton administration was distracted by other projects, particularly its interventions in Somalia and Haiti. Although the hard-liners in the U.S. government continued to press for a more forceful response, they had little ammunition with which to fight the battle. About the best they could do was to see that the covert action programs moved forward—both the insurgency or popular revolt option and the coup option.

This situation of mutual waiting came apart in 1994, when Saddam finally decided that he had endured the U.N. inspections and sanctions long enough. For the first few years after the invasion, Iraqis had lived with deprivation, but the situation had not been calamitous. Initially, the edge of the sanctions was blunted by the regime's stockpiled supplies, the loot they had stolen from Kuwait, and their ability to cannibalize parts and equipment from other sources. But by late 1993 and early 1994, all of these partial solutions were wearing thin. The United Nations and aid agencies began to report increasing electrical outages. Especially when coupled with the shortages of tires and spare parts for vehicles, these problems began to badly affect hospitals, water, and sanitation facilities. In addition, the regime's hidden reserves of hard currency seemed to be running dry, and since Saddam refused to accept the United Nations' provision to sell oil to buy food and other humanitarian supplies, Baghdad had to print money to pay its expenses, further driving up inflation.

Once again, the worsening economic situation and popular unrest translated into security problems for Saddam. In 1993, elements of the al-'Ubayd tribe—one of the key Sunni tribes the regime relies on for support—revolted against Saddam's rule, forcing Baghdad to crack down on them and reassign many 'Ubaydi officers within the military and security services. On December 28, 1993, assassins hid a large explosive device in a broken tractor by the side of a road and detonated it while Saddam's motorcade was driving by. Saddam survived the explosion by sheer luck. The next month, a lone Republican Guard officer opened fire on him but was cut down before he could kill the dictator. Starting in 1994, bomb blasts started going off around Baghdad, the work of the CIA-backed al-Wifaq.[24]

These economic and security problems frightened Saddam, so he decided to act to remove the source of the problems. In May 1994, during the regular review of sanctions, Baghdad pressed hard for a relaxation of the sanctions but made no progress. Domestic confidence in the regime dipped even further, and the dinar slid lower. In July, UNSCOM Chairman Rolf Ekeus reported to the Security Council that the inspectors believed they were making good progress toward Iraq's disarmament. At Iraq's urging, Russia proposed that the Security Council set a deadline after which it would consider lifting the sanctions if it was satisfied with Iraq's progress toward disarmament. However, the United States countered that such a deadline was not part of Resolution 687 and would introduce artificial constraints into the inspections, something the Security Council had studiously avoided. With each setback the dinar slid lower, and by September 1994, Iraq's problems became so acute that the regime was forced to cut the monthly food ration by one-third.[25] Meanwhile, Iraq's deception efforts had worked so well that UNSCOM Chairman Ekeus and other inspectors began saying privately that they believed that disarmament of Iraq was effectively complete. Rumor spread quickly to Iraq that UNSCOM, however, would not oppose the United States and suggest transitioning to long-term monitoring (which would have triggered the lifting of sanctions), even though the inspectors believed Iraq to be fundamentally disarmed.

This appears to have been the last straw for Saddam. Faced with mounting internal threats, a deteriorating economic situation, and no relief in sight, Saddam decided to try to force the issue. At the beginning of October, Iraq issued a number of ominous warnings, promising unspecified consequences if the United Nations did not lift the sanctions at the next periodic review meeting scheduled for October 10. To back up these threats, Saddam began mobilizing Republican Guard divisions on October 2 and sending them south to the border with Kuwait. Days later, U.S. intelligence located elements of the Hammurabi and al-Nida Armored Divisions in place north of the Kuwaiti border (the same area from which the Republican Guard had launched the August 1990 invasion) and other units on the way. Along with the regular army divisions permanently deployed near Kuwait, this amounted to roughly 80,000 troops either in the area or headed there.[26] To this day, we do not know what Saddam's intentions were. It may be that he was trying to use the threat of force to goad the United Nations into action on the sanctions. He may have believed the United States to be so distracted by problems in Haiti, Bosnia, and North Korea that it would not be able to respond effectively. However, there is also strong evidence that Saddam actually intended to invade Kuwait again, to try to force the United Nations to agree to a lifting of the sanctions.[27]

Regardless of Saddam's intentions, this time, there was no disagreement in Washington that the United States had to respond. No American administration was going to countenance a repeat of the 1990 invasion. The United States commenced Operation Vigilant Warrior, a massive reinforcement of the American military presence in the region, to bring the 13,000

U.S. troops spread throughout the Persian Gulf up to a force of roughly 60,000, including an 18,000-man Marine Expeditionary Force, 16,000 troops of the Twenty-fourth Mechanized Infantry Division, a carrier battle group, and 350 additional aircraft, including B-52s and F-117 Stealth fighters. Britain also sent more aircraft and warships, and even the French dispatched a frigate in a show of solidarity. Within about ten days it had become clear that, unlike in 1990, the United States could now reinforce its presence in Kuwait far faster than Iraq could build up the forces to threaten it. To cap off Iraq's humiliation, on October 15 the Security Council passed Resolution 949 under Chapter VII of the U.N. Charter, demanding that Baghdad remove the forces it had moved into southern Iraq and refrain from further such deployments south of the Thirty-second Parallel. The United States and Britain let Iraq know that if Baghdad did not immediately begin withdrawing the Republican Guards from the Kuwaiti border, the coalition would begin striking them. Not only did Iraq comply with the coalition and Security Council demands, but to stave off an American retaliatory attack and try to get back into the good graces of the Security Council, on November 10 the Iraqi National Assembly endorsed the new, U.N.-delineated borders with Kuwait, and Saddam himself signed the decree.[28]

Nevertheless, there had still been an important debate in Washington over how to respond to Saddam's provocation. The administration's hawks wanted to exploit Saddam's misstep to try to topple him, or at least justify additional measures that could have further weakened his grasp on power. In particular, they had argued for demanding that Saddam agree to withdraw all of his forces from southern Iraq, thereby creating a sanctuary for the Shi'ite insurgents and relieving some of the pressure on the Marsh Arabs of southern Iraq, whose entire society was being destroyed by the massive campaign to drain Iraq's marshlands, where Shi'ite guerrillas were hiding from Saddam's forces. The doves had pushed back with a new variant on the old geopolitical thinking that had led the Bush administration to refrain from supporting the Iraqi *intifadah*. They had argued that forcing Saddam to withdraw his forces from the south would create a power vacuum that Iran would exploit to take control. Once again, the threat of the Iranian bugbear, coupled with the strong sense that the administration's approach to containment was working (if it ain't broke, don't fix it) quashed the efforts of the hard-liners to push U.S. policy in a more aggressive direction.[29]

THE TIDE TURNS, 1995–1996

Saddam's humiliating retreat in October 1994 apparently taught him an important lesson. It convinced him that in his current circumstances, an outright military threat to one of Iraq's neighbors would rally the international community against him and give the Americans the opportunity to mount a major military operation, one that might not stop short of Baghdad this time. If he were to find a way out of his conundrum, he could not do so in a way that would give the United States an excuse to hit him that hard. Nevertheless, he still had all of the same problems to juggle, and his latest confrontation with the United States had only made them worse. In December 1994, the dinar fell to 700 to the dollar, compared to 140 to the dollar at the beginning of the year (and three dollars to the dinar before the Gulf War).[30]

The economy was not Saddam's only problem. Beginning in late 1994, evidence began to emerge that the U.N. inspectors were being hoodwinked. In December 1994, the head of the Iraqi Intelligence Service (IIS, or Mukhabbarat), Wafiq al-Samarra'i, fled to Kurdistan, where he made contact with U.S. intelligence. In extensive debriefings, Samarra'i told UNSCOM that despite what it had been led to believe, Iraq had developed VX nerve agent (one of the most lethal forms of chemical warfare) and loaded it onto missiles during the Gulf War for use if the coalition had marched on Baghdad or used nuclear weapons; it had a far more advanced and extensive biological warfare program than the inspectors knew, and this program was largely intact and operating; and Iraq had held on to a secret stash of chemical and biological munitions along with more than forty modified Scud ballistic missiles.[31] In part due to Samarra'i's revelations, in April and May 1995, conferences of international experts convened by UNSCOM to examine the data regarding Iraq's various WMD programs found that Iraq had still not complied with the U.N. resolutions in fully disclosing its biological, chemical, and missile programs.

The debate within the Clinton administration between the hawks and the doves resurfaced in January 1995. A high-level meeting was held in Washington to address the question "How long can the U.S. hold containment of Iraq in place?" The doves, led by Undersecretary of State Peter Tarnoff, argued that containment could not last and that the best thing the United States could do would be to bow out gracefully before it collapsed around us. The doves pointed to the changing attitude of the French, who were increasingly anxious to ease sanctions on Iraq, and the new Russian leadership, which was uncomfortably close to Saddam.[32] The hawks, led by Indyk and Parris, countered that the United States could hold the line for as long as it wanted if the administration was willing to make Iraq a priority and push back hard whenever Iraq or one of its advocates challenged the sanctions, inspections, or other elements of containment. The upshot of the meeting was that Ambassador Albright was dispatched on a trip to a half-dozen key Security Council members and Arab allies, along with Parris and Riedel, to make the case for staying the course on containment and gauge the reaction of her audiences. Armed with the latest intelligence about Iraq's WMD programs, obstruction of the inspections, and human rights abuses, Albright got a strong endorsement for a hard line on Iraq from all of the countries she visited. This proved decisive in keeping the administration committed not only to containment but also to the covert action program working toward regime change.[33]

The hard-liners' victory proved short-lived, however. In early March 1995, part of the covert action program got out of hand. With the encouragement and assistance of several CIA officers, Wafiq Samarra'i, both Kurdish militias, and Ahmed Chalabi's INC cooked up a scheme to try to topple Saddam. With help from U.S. intelligence, they had established that the Iraqi Thirty-eighth Infantry Division holding the line south of the city of Arbil was ready to collapse. The Thirty-eighth Infantry was easily the worst formation in the Iraqi Army at the time, and as such it was last in line for spare parts, ammunition, replacement soldiers and equipment, fuel, medicine, and even food. Its soldiers were tired and unhappy. The Kurds made contact with one battalion commander who told them that his entire unit was ready to defect. Their hope was that a large force of Kurds could overrun the Thirty-eighth Infantry Division and then begin pushing to Baghdad behind American power; the Iranians would help by pinning Iraqi forces along the border while Samarra'i's contacts convinced other units to join the revolt and perhaps even execute a coup in the capital. But the plan had several problems. First, there were few indications that the rest of the Iraqi Army was ready to defect to the rebels. A Kurdish-led revolution would probably rally the most loyal (and mostly Sunni) formations to the regime, just as in 1991. Second, although it is unclear who back at CIA headquarters knew what the CIA officers in the field were up to, no one in the administration had been aware of the operation. National Security Adviser Anthony Lake and Secretary of State Warren Christopher were furious when they found out about it. Lake and Christopher both saw the operation as a second Bay of Pigs waiting to happen—an inadequate force of oppositionists was about to try to start a revolution and was counting on U.S. military power to bail them out if things soured. Worse than that, because only CIA had been aware of the operation, the U.S. military forces in the region were insufficient to support the operation even had the White House wanted to do so. Finally, the reason the administration suddenly became aware of it was that Washington had learned that Saddam's intelligence services were onto Samarra'i's part of the plan.[34]

The American NSC immediately cabled the members of the cabal that Iraqi intelligence was aware of the operation and the United States would provide them no support.[35] This prompted Masud Barzani's Kurdish Democratic Party (KDP) to back out of the operation. The others decided to proceed anyway, and on March 6 a force of roughly 10,000 PUK *peshmerga* and a few hundred INC personnel launched a surprise attack on the 130th and 847th Infantry Brigades of the Thirty-eighth Infantry Division. The operation was well planned and well executed, and the Kurdish troops handled themselves reasonably well, leading to initial success. As hoped, the disaffected battalion surrendered virtually en masse, and the two brigades were routed. Clinging to their original assumptions (and encouraged by some of their CIA handlers), the opposition still hoped that the United States would provide air power to allow the Kurdish and INC forces to keep pushing forward, while Samarra'i tried to convince other Iraqi Army units to defect and so create the snowballing march on Baghdad they hoped would lead to Saddam's ouster. But Saddam's agents rounded up Samarra'i's accomplices and the United States immediately detected other, better-supplied and -armed Republican Guard and army units deploying to crush the small Kurdish penetration, and the U.S. military had only a handful of aircraft in Turkey, a woefully inadequate force to try to stop Republican Guard divisions. Washington warned the Kurds to halt and dig in quickly because the Guard was closing in and the cavalry would not be coming to the rescue. The Kurds wisely chose to follow this advice, but they, the INC, and their CIA liaison officers all felt that Washington had scuttled what they believed might have turned into the fall of Saddam.[36]

The stillborn Kurdish offensive reinforced the dovish instincts of key administration officials. The Kurds, Chalabi's INC, and their CIA minders had greatly exceeded their brief and launched an operation that almost certainly would have resulted in disaster had they not stopped when they did. It confirmed to Lake, Christopher, and others that the regime change programs had to be kept on a tight leash. In the meantime, however, they had other priorities.

The one discordant note that Albright had heard on her tour of key U.S. allies had been a growing concern for the plight of the Iraqi people. The United Nations and international aid agencies were reporting on the declining economic and health situations in Iraq that were creating Saddam's internal security troubles. In addition, Iraq had launched an aggressive propaganda campaign to broadcast and exaggerate Iraq's humanitarian problems and to blame them entirely on the sanctions. Washington took these reports seriously and requested confirmation from the U.S. intelligence community, which consistently reported three basic points: (1) there was unquestionable malnutrition and disease in Iraq, (2) the Iraqi government was also unquestionably manipulating and distorting the numbers, and (3) the Iraqi government had the funds to address these humanitarian problems. The intelligence agencies could point to the slew of new palaces and military facilities Saddam was busily constructing as proof of the resources still available to the regime. Consequently, the administration's sentiment was that whatever additional suffering was occurring in Iraq was largely the result of Saddam's machinations, as it had been since 1979.[37]

Nevertheless, the administration recognized it had a problem. Even if the United States and its allies did not believe that it was the sanctions that were depriving the Iraqi people, the noise from the Arab world and within the United Nations was getting too loud. In response, on April 14, the United States proposed and the Security Council passed Resolution 986, which created what was called the "oil-for-food deal." Building on Resolution 706's offer to allow Iraq to sell some oil to buy food and medicine, UNSCR 986 set up a comprehensive system by which Iraq could sell $2 billion worth of oil every six months to buy food, medicine, and other humanitarian supplies. It created a U.N. escrow account into which all proceeds from Iraqi oil sales would be delivered and a U.N. system to approve all of Iraq's contracts for purchases with those funds. Furthermore, it allocated 30 percent of the funds to compensate the victims of Iraq's aggression and 4 percent to pay for the costs of the United Nations' various Iraq programs. In addition, it allocated 13 percent of the funds directly to the Kurds in northern Iraq, where the program would be administered by the United Nations—not the regime—leaving 53 percent of the funds for the rest of the Iraqi population. The resolution passed unanimously and was widely hailed as an important step toward alleviating the suffering of the Iraqi people.

Throughout 1995, Saddam's situation deteriorated. Although the Kurds and the opposition were smarting over Washington's rebuff in March, the defeat of the Thirty-eighth Infantry Division had been a humiliation for him as well. The morale of the Iraqi armed forces was a critical concern to him; an Iraqi unit had not suffered such a defeat at the hands of the Kurds since the Mount Handrin debacle in 1966, when poor Iraqi leadership had led to the death of 2,000 soldiers. Resolution 986 was another problem for Saddam. The international acclaim it enjoyed threatened to undermine his efforts to get the sanctions lifted, but if he accepted it, he would be giving up his control of Iraq's revenues to the United Nations—and he knew that the United Nations would force him to spend that money on humanitarian supplies for the Iraqi people rather than weapons and perks for his loyalists. As a result, Iraq rejected the resolution, which caused the dinar to lose an additional 47 percent of its value in May and June.[38] Saddam uncovered another dangerous coup plot in May, this one including General Muhammad Madhlum ad-Dulaymi. Later that month, when the general's remains were returned to his family with obvious marks of torture, elements of the ad-Dulaym tribe revolted against Saddam. The ad-Dulaym were another of the key Sunni tribes Saddam relied on to keep himself in power, and the riots that broke out in their main town of ar-Ramadi took the regime several weeks to put down.[39] Saddam was also encountering problems within his family itself, which he had increasingly relied on to help him maintain control since the end of the Gulf War, the *intifadah,* and the mounting coup attempts against him. In particular, Saddam's unstable elder son, Udayy Saddam, was increasingly feuding with other members of the family.

Saddam again began to feel that the pressure was unbearable, especially as the value of the dinar continued to erode in June and July. On July 17, the anniversary of the Ba'thist coup that had brought him to power, Saddam announced that Iraq would cease all cooperation with UNSCOM unless sanctions were lifted by August 31. Senior Iraqi personnel warned Rolf Ekeus that if the United States responded with military strikes, they would tie U.N. inspectors to the machinery they expected the United States to attack. Later, Saddam's vice president and one of his chief cronies, Taha Yasin Ramadan, boasted to an interviewer that Saddam had intended to start a final crisis with the United Nations at this time to bring the situation to a head once and for all. But fate intervened. Udayy Saddam had been fighting two running battles throughout the spring—one against his uncle Watban Ibrahim, whom Udayy detested and had succeeded in having sacked as interior minister after the revolt of the ad-Dulaym, the other with his cousin and brother-in-law, Hussein Kamel, for control of the massive smuggling operations that richly rewarded Saddam's inner circle at the expense of the Iraqi people. In early August, Hussein Kamel and Udayy had several nasty altercations. During the night of August 6–7, Udayy arrived at a party with an AK-47 and fired a long burst at his uncle Watban, killing several others and wounding Watban in the leg. Hussein Kamel decided Udayy was coming after him next and took the precipitous step of packing up his brother, Saddam Kamel (himself an important officer in Iraq's security services), their wives (both of them Saddam's daughters), and their children, and defecting to Jordan.[40]

Hussein Kamel's defection threw a wrench into Saddam's plans to provoke a crisis with the United Nations. He did not know what Hussein Kamel intended or what schemes he planned to spring. Saddam's first concern was that Hussein Kamel had secretly built a network of supporters to start a coup from within the regime's innermost circle. Indeed, on August 8, Hussein Kamel went on television and called on the army, the Republican Guard, and the internal security services to rise up against Saddam. King Hussein of Jordan, who previously had done everything he could to stay on Saddam's good side for fear of provoking his pro-Saddam Palestinian majority, suddenly declared his willingness to oust Saddam. Baghdad reacted immediately, mobilizing the Republican Guard and Special Republican Guard, dispersing the army, and implementing emergency security measures across the country. (The United States saw these widespread military moves but did not know what Saddam intended, so Washington launched Operation Vigilant Sentinel, a virtual replay of 1994's Vigilant Warrior, sending major reinforcements to defend Kuwait, Saudi Arabia, and Jordan against a possible Iraqi attack.)[41]

As the moving force behind Iraq's WMD programs since the end of the Iran-Iraq War and a member of Qusayy's concealment committee, Hussein Kamel also knew all about Saddam's shell game with the U.N. inspectors. The regime decided to try to deflect blame onto Hussein Kamel himself and suddenly told Rolf Ekeus that it had "discovered" that Hussein Kamel had been secretly hiding vast amounts of information about Iraq's WMD programs on his chicken farm near Habbaniyah. When UNSCOM officials were taken there, they found 650,000 pages of text, photos, videos, microfilm, and microfiche relating to Iraq's WMD program in forty crates that had unmistakably been moved there within the last few days. Later, Hussein Kamel would himself provide considerable information to the inspectors. As a result, the inspectors realized for the first time that they had been duped. Iraq had been much further along in all of its WMD programs than they had realized, and it still possessed considerable equipment, documentation, and even weapons. For instance, the inspectors learned not only that Iraq had an offensive BW program, but also that it had weaponized biological agents and had loaded them into 166 bombs and 25 missile warheads for use during the Gulf War if the coalition marched on Baghdad. They also learned that in August 1990, Saddam had ordered a crash program to enrich enough uranium to produce one nuclear weapon, which he planned to load onto a missile and fire at Tel Aviv if the coalition moved to depose him. (The program failed to produce either the uranium or a device that could be mounted on a missile.)[42] For the inspectors, and for Ekeus personally, the information provided by Hussein Kamel and contained in the documents that Iraq hastily surrendered were a revelation. Before, Ekeus and most of the inspectors had believed their job was essentially done, and they had resented American pressure and claims that Iraq was still hiding proscribed materials. Ekeus and the inspectors would never trust the Iraqis again.[43]

Hussein Kamel's defections also hurt Saddam by displaying to the entire world the perfidy of his regime and its determination to flout the will of the Security Council. In the aftermath of the defections even Iraq's most ardent defenders kept quiet. The dinar continued to slide, and economic and health conditions continued to deteriorate. In December, the government announced that its international telephone lines were being disconnected because it could not pay the bill. Finally Saddam tried drastic measures. He announced that the government would cease printing money, reduce subsidies, increase the price of government services, impose new taxes, and begin selling off government cars and equipment to raise capital. None of it worked. In January 1996, the dinar fell to 3,000 to the dollar.[44]

The situation was so bad that Saddam was forced to make a major concession. On January 20 he announced he was willing to discuss implementation of UNSCR 986, the hated oil-for-food deal. In typical fashion, the regime tried hard to warp the resolution to suit its purposes. On May 20, only after much haggling, Iraq signed a memorandum of understanding with the United Nations regarding the implementation of Resolution 986. In yet another unexpected turnabout, no sooner was the agreement signed than Iraq announced that it was no longer willing to implement it unless several trivial technical matters were resolved in its favor. The reason for this sudden reversal was that Saddam's mere acceptance of Resolution 986 and the negotiations with the United Nations over implementation had produced euphoria among the Iraqi people, whose mood was soaring in the expectation that goods would soon start flowing into Iraq again. The dinar surged, rising to less than 2,000 to the dollar. The regime experienced a rush of income, and Iraqi financial markets stabilized. Suddenly Saddam no longer needed Resolution 986, so once again he balked.

Back in Washington in early 1996, the debate between the hawks and doves within the administration had flared again. Mark Parris had succeeded Indyk as special assistant to the president for the Near East and South Asia, and he had brought in Stephen Grummon as his director for the Persian Gulf. Supported by Riedel at the Pentagon, Parris and Grummon argued strenuously that the United States had to press forward on regime change. After months of memo writing and interagency disputes, Parris, Grummon, and Riedel succeeded in having a meeting of the Principals' Committee called to sort out the debate. Parris made the case for ratcheting up the pressure by noting that the United States now had many things going for it: Saddam's internal security situation was precarious, UNSCR 986 had lifted all of the pressure on the United States in the Security Council, UNSCOM now realized that Saddam had been deceiving it all along, Jordan had come out in favor of regime change, and the March 1995 Kurdish offensive had demonstrated the demoralization of much of Saddam's armed forces. Parris also argued that other trends were emerging that in several years could seriously undermine the U.S. position: the oil-for-food deal would eventually alleviate Saddam's domestic situation; if the United States did not make a push on regime change, Jordan would inevitably reconcile with Saddam; several GCC states were becoming more worried about Iran than Iraq; and the Kurds had begun fighting among themselves again. The hard-liners concluded that the United States was at a critical juncture: the administration could adopt a policy of aggressive regime change in the hope of capitalizing on Saddam's current weakness, or else its position would inevitably weaken and it would find itself fighting a long rearguard action in defense of containment.

Secretary of State Christopher led the counterattack. Christopher argued that the Iraq policy was doing exactly what the administration had wanted: it was preventing Saddam from threatening the stability of the region at a very low cost.[45] This made possible the administration's other foreign policy efforts—from keeping the peace in the Balkans to engagement with China to the Middle East peace negotiations, which had entered a critical phase after the assassination of Israeli Prime Minister Yitzhak Rabin in 1995. Christopher's bottom line was that a more aggressive policy against Saddam would interfere with the administration's higher-priority initiatives. Many of the doves, including National Security Adviser Tony Lake, pointed to the March 1995 Kurdish fiasco. For many, this terrible experience ruled out the notion of pursuing regime change more aggressively. The doves' bottom line was "Now is not the time to rock the boat." The meeting ended in near-total defeat for the hard-liners. The one concession they secured—and it was CIA Director John Deutch who won this victory—was an agreement for continued support for the coup attempt the Agency was cooking up with the Iraqi opposition al-Wifaq, which they believed had a high likelihood of success.[46]

In February 1996, Hussein Kamel packed up his family and returned to Iraq, where he and his brother were immediately divorced from their wives and killed by their family in a bloody shoot-out at their home. U.S. intelligence had concluded that he was a megalomaniac, a thug, and a dullard—unworthy of U.S. support once he had spilled everything he knew about Iraq's WMD programs and security apparatus.[47] Thus Hussein Kamel was no longer a threat to Saddam. But the information he had provided UNSCOM had convinced the inspectors that they had to crack Iraq's concealment mechanism if they were going to succeed in disarming Saddam. The problem was that Iraq's concealment mechanism was deeply bound up with Saddam's security because the Special Republican Guard and Special Security Organization were ultimately responsible for both. During the spring of 1996, UNSCOM had been probing deeper into these organizations and inspecting sites more closely connected with Saddam himself to try to get at Iraq's hidden WMD. Iraq was well aware of the CIA covert action campaign and assumed that American inspectors were feeding information regarding the Iraqi security services to the CIA (which turned out to be largely true, although UNSCOM itself was unaware of it).[48] Meanwhile, Saddam remained determined to halt the inspections before the inspectors uncovered his clandestine programs and stockpiles, and he was still looking to provoke a crisis with the United Nations to speed the lifting of sanctions. So in June, Iraq blocked the weapons inspectors from entering several sensitive sites.

The hard-liners within the U.S. government saw this as a key challenge requiring an immediate and forceful U.S. response. It was the most flagrant

Iraqi obstructionism in four years. Washington intended to take the matter to the Security Council, and it expected to be able to get a resolution condemning the Iraqi actions as a "material breach" of the cease-fire, thereby justifying the use of military force. The hope of Washington's hard-liners was to convince the administration to respond with force to help further destabilize Saddam's regime. However, before the Security Council could act, UNSCOM Chairman Ekeus flew to Baghdad and negotiated a new agreement on inspections with Iraq that infuriated the U.S. administration. The Ekeus agreement listed sixty "sensitive sites" that UNSCOM would be able to inspect with only four people, escorted by a senior Iraqi official (and UNSCOM would have to wait until the senior official arrived).[49] In Washington's eyes, Ekeus had made major concessions to Iraq that compromised both UNSCOM's integrity and the Security Council mandate that the inspectors should have immediate and unconditional access to any site in Iraq.

During that summer of 1996, Saddam hit rock bottom and began to climb back up, while key elements of U.S. policy deteriorated. First, the CIA's coup attempt went up in smoke. The Agency had been working for some time with al-Wifaq, the opposition group made up mainly of former Iraqi military officers. As a result of al-Wifaq's contacts, they had carefully assembled a far-reaching cabal that included well-placed officers in Iraq's security services, army, air force, Republican Guard, and even the Special Republican Guard. But at some point, Saddam's Mukhabbarat had become aware of the plot. It strung along the operation for a little while to uncover its full extent and in June 1996 sprung its trap. Within a few days hundreds of the conspirators had been arrested, and the CIA teams supporting the operation had fled the region.[50] As with the March 1995 Kurdish attack, the elimination of the June 1996 coup was a major problem for both sides. For the United States, it meant the defeat of the most promising coup attempt the CIA would ever mount. For Saddam, it was another close escape. The regime was badly shaken by the extent of the cabal, by the participation of officers in even the Special Republican Guard, and by the CIA's ability to penetrate so deeply into the regime's inner circle.

The scene shifted quickly to Kurdistan. Since the 1970s, the two main Kurdish militias had probably spent as much time fighting each other as they had fighting the Ba'thist regime. In 1994, they had again come to blows and since then had fought off and on. The issue was money. As part of the regime's efforts to circumvent the U.N. sanctions, Baghdad opened a major smuggling route across the Habur River into Turkey. Petroleum products were smuggled out, and goods were smuggled in—and all of it had to pass through territory controlled by the Kurds, specifically by Masud Barzani's KDP. As part of their power-sharing agreement, Jalal Talabani's PUK and the KDP had agreed to a fifty-fifty split of the smuggling revenues, but the KDP consistently stiffed the PUK. By the summer of 1996, as many as six hundred tanker trucks were lining up at the Habur crossing each day, meaning a daily take of $500,000 for the KDP.[51] The PUK demanded that the KDP give it its share and called on the United States to press the KDP to live up to its agreement. The KDP made countercharges that the PUK had also reneged on the deal, specifically by taking over the city of Arbil, the largest in Kurdish hands. In Washington, the hard-liners pressed for the United States to mediate actively, fearing that inter-Kurdish warfare would further weaken the U.S. position. However, the doves saw the Kurds as hopeless and, especially after the debacles of March 1995 and June 1996, had no desire to entangle the United States more deeply in the Iraqi mess.[52]

Convinced that the United States was not going to press the KDP to keep up its side of the bargain, Jalal Talabani decided to take matters into his own hands. His PUK struck a deal with Iran for weapons, supplies, and even some advisers from Iran's Revolutionary Guard. Then, on August 17, it launched a major offensive that tore into KDP territory. It was now Barzani's turn to beg the United States to pressure his adversary, but once again, Washington demurred. Barzani then did what he considered his only alternative: he turned to Saddam. The two sides quickly worked out a deal, and Baghdad began moving forces north. The Kurdish infighting was like manna from heaven for Saddam. Desperate to restore the flagging morale of his armed forces (and particularly the Republican Guard) after the March 1995 humiliation, the recent coup attempt, and the inevitable purges that had followed, smashing the PUK offered Saddam the opportunity to give the Guard a victory. It also gave him the chance to drive the CIA and its oppositionist allies out of northern Iraq, reassert the regime's authority over its wayward northern provinces, and demonstrate his strength to the people of Iraq.

Nevertheless, Saddam moved warily. He did not know what the American response would be and feared a U.S. military attack. The United States had clearly defined its no-fly zone as being north of the Thirty-sixth Parallel, and virtually all of the PUK territory lay south of that, but Saddam could not be certain that Washington would not invoke Resolution 688's prohibition against the Iraqi regime repressing its own people to justify a strike against him. His internal political situation remained fragile, and he did not want to risk another drubbing at the hands of the United States, for fear of the impact it might have on the armed forces and his loyalists. Under the cover of an exercise, he concentrated two Republican Guard divisions and three regular army divisions around the city of Arbil, where both the PUK and the INC had their headquarters.[53] Meanwhile, Baghdad also concentrated another force near the Kurdish town of Chamchamal, where it could drive on the PUK's other principal city, as-Sulaymaniyyah. During the night of August 31, the Iraqis struck, overrunning Arbil in a few hours with the help of KDP forces. The Iraqis captured more than two hundred INC personnel, who were executed before the regime forces began pulling out the next day, leaving the city in the hands of the KDP. Baghdad kept its forces concentrated opposite Arbil and Chamchamal, poised to sweep over the rest of the PUK territory if Saddam gave the word, but first Saddam wanted to see how the United States would react.

Once again a blatant act of Iraqi aggression united the Clinton administration in its thinking. There would have to be a military response. Saddam had again violated UNSCR 688, which forbade him to repress his people, and had attacked the PUK and INC, which, no matter how wayward, were still Washington's clients. The United States had established Operation Provide Comfort to protect the Kurds and was maintaining the northern NFZ to prevent Saddam from attacking them with his air force. The immediate problem for the United States was that the disposition of Iraqi forces on the ground made it clear that Saddam was considering a larger move if the United States did nothing, but as in 1995, the U.S. military had few forces near northern Iraq capable of striking the regime's units there or preventing them from overrunning the rest of the PUK territory. Instead, the administration opted to mount a sizable air campaign against a range of targets, mostly in southern Iraq—where they were within reach of U.S. aircraft in Saudi Arabia—to demonstrate to Saddam that he would pay a price for any aggression. Secretary of Defense William Perry went to the region to build support for a strike. For the first time, however, the United States ran into a major snag: the Saudis and the Turks said no to Perry. The Turks wanted nothing to do with helping the PUK. The Saudis had never cared much for the Kurds and considered Saddam's actions in Arbil a positive step to counter Kurdish separatism. What's more, the Saudi people were increasingly unhappy about the suffering of the Iraqi people and the U.S. military presence in the Kingdom. Riyadh declined to allow the U.S. Air Force to fly strike missions from Saudi bases—as did the Turks and the Jordanians. Unable to find bases in the region but determined to do "something" to show Saddam he could not attack the Kurds with impunity, the United States and Great Britain settled for raising the northern boundary of the southern no-fly zone to the Thirty-third Parallel, just south of Baghdad, and launching forty-four cruise missiles at Iraqi air defense targets in the newly expanded NFZ on September 3 and 4.[54]

Although American commentators would later castigate the attack as a "cruise missile pinprick"—and in truth it did little damage to Saddam's forces—the strike had the desired effect on Saddam. He decided to quit with his limited victory at Arbil rather than try to drive the PUK out of Kurdistan altogether and risk a heavier American response. For him, this was good enough. Amatzia Baram has summed up Saddam's gains concisely:

> Iraq paid a price for the attack on Irbil, mainly by having to succumb to the US decision to expand the no-fly zone over southern Iraq. Yet, on the whole, the operation strengthened Saddam. If nothing else, it elevated his standing with the Guard and probably with the Army as well. Furthermore, the victory in Irbil freed his hands to accept Resolution 986. Having proved his mettle, having humiliated Talabani and the United States, having eliminated the Iraqi opposition and US intelligence personnel in Kurdistan, and having secured a victory, however small, for the Guard, he could afford the limited humiliation involved in accepting a UN resolution that he had previously rejected as incompatible with Iraq's sovereignty.[55]

Indeed, in November, Iraq declared that it was now ready to implement the oil-for-food deal and therefore would be increasing the monthly food ration by 35 percent. On this news, the dinar rose from 3,000 to the dollar after the attack on Arbil to less than 1,000 to the dollar.[56] Back in Kurdistan, the KDP pressed its advantage, taking many PUK towns, only to be stopped at as-Sulaymaniyyah by strong defenses and then evicted from its territory altogether in a counteroffensive that October after the PUK had regrouped and rearmed with weapons from Iran. By contrast, the opposition INC fled northern Iraq. More than six hundred of its people joined six thousand other Iraqis who had worked with U.S.-supported humanitarian programs and were airlifted out of the north by the United States and taken to Guam. The hasty departure of the INC infuriated the PUK, creating the first split between these two groups.[57]

Although few realized the magnitude at the time, for the United States, the Arbil crisis was a disaster. It was probably the beginning of the long deterioration in America's Iraq policy, providing the crucial first step Saddam needed to solve his problems.[58] He demonstrated his own strength, crippled the Kurds, and drove the CIA-backed opposition out of the country. He restored the morale of the Republican Guard—not completely, but to a point far better than it had been over the past five years—and as a result he was able to solidify his domestic political position enough to accept Resolution 986, which in turn boosted Iraq's economy, further improving Saddam's internal posture. Meanwhile, the United States ended up looking weak and isolated. The break with the Saudis, Turks, and Jordanians over the conduct of limited military operations against Iraq for violating U.N. resolutions was a sign of deeper problems to come. Saddam's reassertion of his power over northern Iraq would deprive the United States of the use of Kurdistan as a base for clandestine operations against the regime. Saddam's acceptance of Resolution 986 was a positive good for the Iraqi people, at least in theory, but it also meant that Baghdad would suddenly have considerable economic clout in terms of contracts for oil sales and food purchases that Saddam could manipulate to his political advantage. What's more, because Arbil appeared to confirm that Saddam probably would not be toppled anytime soon, King Hussein of Jordan retracted his previous declarations of support for regime change and instead reconciled with Saddam. Jordanian intelligence went so far as to inform Iraqi oppositionists that their safety was no longer guaranteed if they continued to work against Saddam from Amman.[59]

There was one last climactic event to finish out the ups and downs of 1996. On December 12, Saddam's sadistic eldest son, Udayy, was driving to a party when his car was surrounded by armed men and riddled with bullets. Although he survived the attack, he was hit eight times and several of the bullets lodged in his spine, leaving him paralyzed for many months. Remarkably, the assassins escaped altogether. The list of people with a motive to kill Udayy was almost endless, beginning with his closest relatives and extending to the thousands of fathers, sons, brothers, cousins, and friends of all of the women he had raped and murdered, and all of the men he had tortured and executed. As best we understand it today, the hit was conducted by a highly secretive resistance group of well-educated young Iraqis called an-Nahdah ("The Awakening"), working with Ra'd al-Hazaa, a former member of the SRG. Ra'd's uncle, General Omar al-Hazaa, had been arrested, tortured, and killed along with his son in 1986 for publicly criticizing Saddam after the defeat at al-Faw in 1986. Ra'd remained friendly with one of Udayy's closest friends and provided the information to allow an-Nahdah to conduct the hit.[60]

SADDAM ON THE OFFENSIVE, 1997–1998

Over the next two years, the momentum in the U.S.-Iraq confrontation seemed to slowly but inexorably swing in Iraq's direction. This was the result of both a change in Iraq's strategy and the maturation of several trends that had begun years before. As a result of the experiences of 1995 and 1996, Saddam had learned some lessons. He no longer suffered under the illusion that UNSCOM could be easily deceived and that sanctions would be quickly lifted; he now understood that the task of retaining his WMD programs and either undermining the sanctions or having them lifted would be a lengthy process and he would have to be patient. He had also learned that it was possible to challenge the United Nations in ways that would make it difficult for the United States to respond with force. Over time, he would also figure out that there were issues on which Security Council opinion was divided and that by pressing on those issues, he could deepen the rifts among the members and particularly the P-5. Finally, Baghdad began using oil-for-food to its advantage, doling out contracts for oil sales and goods purchases in return for political support, rewarding those who toed Baghdad's line and punishing those who did not.

Probably Saddam's greatest advantage was that after six years of sanctions and regular crises with Iraq, many nations had grown weary of the whole affair. Saddam could not afford to let his people starve altogether because domestic problems quickly translated into challenges to his rule, but he could keep the Iraqi people at a low level of health and could keep some pockets of the population (particularly among the Shi'ah of the south) in picture-perfect misery. As the United Nations continuously refined and expanded the oil-for-food program, the sanctions themselves diminished as the cause of suffering within Iraq, while the regime's deliberate callousness grew.[61] But because of the increasing sanctions fatigue, Iraqi propaganda actually enjoyed greater success after the passage of the oil-for-food deal than before. The United Nations (and the United States) churned out reams of statistics to demonstrate that there was no reason for any Iraqi to be malnourished or ill because the funds and the range of products available to Iraq should have been more than adequate to cover its needs. The United Nations repeatedly chastised Iraq for not buying enough of the humanitarian goods it claimed to lack. Kuwait caught ships smuggling food and medicine out of Iraq for resale on the black market. Baby milk sold to Iraq under the oil-for-food program turned up in markets throughout the Gulf region. Indeed, there was so much smuggled medicine from Iraq available in Jordan that by the late 1990s, Jordanian pharmacists asked customers whether they wanted "name-brand" or "Iraqi" versions, rather than "generic." None of it had any impact.

Likewise, Iraq proved devastatingly effective in manipulating the international media. For instance, Western journalists were refused interviews with Iraqi officials until they had filed at least one story on how the Iraqi people were suffering under the sanctions—and the Iraqi government always seemed to have ready crowds of starving children and hospital wards full of dying infants for these stories. Whenever the United States or United Nations published new statistics disputing Iraq's claims, the Iraqis would show more photographs of miserable children. It was crude, but it worked. All the statistics in the world paled next to the picture of an emaciated child on someone's television set.

In the United States, 1997 saw the second Clinton administration take office with a different cast of characters from the first. In particular, Samuel R. "Sandy" Berger moved up from the deputy slot to become the new national security adviser, and Madeleine Albright took over as secretary of state. Albright had made her reputation as a hawk on Iraq and promised to be a change from the dovish Warren Christopher, but Berger—who had a close relationship with President Clinton—was the key. Over time, he would emerge as the principal policy maker on foreign affairs. And Sandy Berger had a problem—he saw both sides of the Iraq issue.[62] As Tony Lake's deputy, he had participated in all of the policy debates of the first Clinton administration. Berger was much more sympathetic to the hard-line position than Lake had been and believed that ratcheting up the pressure on Saddam was probably the right course from purely the perspective of Washington's Iraq strategy. In particular, he believed that the United States should have turned up the heat on Saddam in early 1996, before the collapse of the al-Wifaq coup and the Arbil debacle. However, like Lake, he did not want to make Iraq the lodestone of the administration's foreign policy. His foreign policy team also had many other objectives, and an aggressive Iraq policy would make it difficult if not impossible to attain them. Moreover, Berger served a president who disliked the whole issue of Iraq and by his second term wanted to have as little to do with it as possible. Bill Clinton was certainly not looking to make Iraq the centerpiece of his foreign policy. And when the president found himself in domestic political turmoil as a result of the Monica Lewinsky affair, avoiding foreign policy crises became an even higher priority.

The upshot of all this was that, at least initially, the administration continued to debate fiercely how best to handle Iraq—determined to react strongly to Iraq's provocations but hoping to not have to react so strongly that it would prove a distraction from the president's other priorities. Reflecting these crosscurrents, in March 1997, Secretary of State Albright delivered a speech on Iraq at Georgetown University. Originally, the speech had been the brainchild of the administration hard-liners and was intended to focus on the need for regime change in Iraq. In particular, it would lay out the future the United States envisioned for Iraq post Saddam and all of the things the United States would be willing to do for Iraq once he was gone. But the speech became a political football, and when Albright finally delivered it, it fell short of expectations. It promised only vague economic benefits for Iraq after Saddam's fall and said little about how the United States planned to bring about such an event. No one was particularly happy with it.

———

Saddam had been planning a showdown with the U.N. inspectors in 1995, only to abort it when Hussein Kamel fled to Jordan. In 1997, he got this effort back on track. His goals were to impede UNSCOM's progress, exacerbate the growing differences within the Security Council, and antagonize the United States without presenting enough of a provocation to justify a major military response. However, he was also looking to fight back against the inspectors' efforts to penetrate the security of his regime. In particular, in early 1997, the soft-spoken Rolf Ekeus had stepped down as UNSCOM's chairman and been replaced by Richard Butler, a far more aggressive diplomat. Although the Iraqis had hoped that they would be able to charm a new UNSCOM chairman as they had initially fooled Ekeus (until the revelations of Hussein Kamel's defection), they soon realized that, if anything, Butler was going to be tougher than Ekeus. They concluded that under Butler, UNSCOM's efforts to penetrate their concealment mechanism would likely intensify. The first major change in Iraq's approach was to step up the level of their harassment of UNSCOM personnel. The Iraqis had always tried to intimidate or trip up the inspectors, but in 1997 their bullying reached new heights. For example, in June, in two separate incidents, Iraqi personnel interfered with UNSCOM helicopter flights, and in one of these instances an Iraqi tried to seize control of the helicopter while in flight, nearly causing it to crash. In early January 1998, someone fired a rocket-propelled grenade into UNSCOM headquarters in Baghdad, although luckily no one was injured.[63]

The real crisis, however, began in the fall. The Iraqis blocked a surprise inspection and resumed hindering the inspectors in other ways. The United States and Britain were finally able to convince the Security Council to send a message to Iraq that further recalcitrance would have serious repercussions. On October 23, the Council passed Resolution 1134, which threatened to impose travel restrictions on Iraqi officials if Iraq continued to hinder the inspectors. However, this only served to underscore the divisions on the Council because it passed with five abstentions, including France, Russia, and China. Iraq was emboldened and in November announced that no more Americans would be allowed on the inspection teams, demanded that American inspectors already in Iraq leave, and threatened to shoot down American U-2 spy planes overflying Iraq in support of the inspections. The Security Council reacted by passing another resolution that did impose the travel restrictions and threatened additional actions if Iraq did not shape up. Iraq's response was to declare that it would no longer participate in the oil-for-food program unless the United Nations agreed to set a firm date for the lifting of sanctions.

In response to Iraq's continued defiance, the United States and Britain began massing forces in the region, but almost immediately Arab and European governments began to distance themselves from Washington and London. The Saudis and other U.S. allies signaled that they would not support an attack because the issues seemed too minor, their people were increasingly unhappy about the plight of the Iraqi populace, and they felt that the United States had not given negotiations enough of a chance.[64] At this point, Russian President Boris Yeltsin offered to have his notoriously pro-

Iraqi foreign minister, Yevgeny Primakov, mediate the dispute. Without a realistic option to use force, the United States agreed to allow the Primakov mission to go forward. Ultimately, the deal Primakov struck met U.S. demands—Iraq agreed to allow all of the inspectors back in, in return for Russian promises to work to speed UNSCOM's progress and to convince the United Nations to set a timetable for the lifting of sanctions. On one level, this was a clear-cut victory for the United States: Saddam had agreed to Washington's terms, and the United States had given up nothing. In fact, Saddam too seems to have realized this, hence his decision to start another crisis only weeks later, when he may have realized that the Russian promises had hardly been a victory. However, by exposing the splits within the Security Council and among the coalition allies, the crisis had further weakened the U.S. position.[65]

Two months later, in January 1998, the game began all over again. UNSCOM sent in an inspection team whose mission was to pursue the Iraqi concealment mechanism, and the Iraqis immediately prevented them from doing any work. On the seventeenth of that month, Saddam himself issued another ultimatum to the United Nations: lift sanctions by May 20 or Iraq would cease all cooperation with the inspectors. Butler went to Baghdad to try to resolve the impasse but got nowhere. Exasperated by Iraq's flagrant violations of the Security Council resolutions and its unwillingness to abide by its own agreements, the administration again began building up its forces in the region. But again Washington found itself isolated. Russia and China condemned the threat of force immediately. Secretary Albright traveled to the region to build support but found little. The Saudis refused to allow the United States to use their bases, and only Kuwait was willing to do so.[66] Even in the United States itself, polls showed declining public support for military action and increasing confusion over the nature of the crisis. This time it was Secretary-General Kofi Annan who volunteered to go to Baghdad to resolve the deadlock. Washington feared that Annan would agree to concessions that would weaken the inspection regime and tried to convince him not to go. But he was determined. On February 23, Annan signed a new agreement with Tariq Aziz in which the Iraqis yet again promised "immediate, unconditional, and unrestricted access," while Annan promised that U.N. personnel (including UNSCOM) would "respect the legitimate concerns of Iraq relating to national security, sovereignty and dignity." Annan also agreed to new, restricted procedures for the inspection of eight huge "presidential" sites where the inspectors believed that Iraq was storing materials related to its clandestine WMD programs.

Once again, the outcome was another small victory for Saddam. He met with Kofi Annan in person and demonstrated that the United Nations had to negotiate with Iraq—it could not simply give orders. He succeeded in placing limits on how the inspectors could do their job. Once again he proved that few countries were willing to support the use of force and that the United States and Britain were virtually alone in their determination to see Iraq comply with its international obligations.[67] With this win under his belt and the new constraints on UNSCOM operations, things were quiet for several months. What started them up again was the inspectors' discovery of VX nerve gas on the fragments of missile warheads that Iraq had cleaned and then unilaterally destroyed. Baghdad categorically denied that it had ever loaded VX in a missile—this after first having categorically denied producing VX and then categorically denying having produced large quantities of it when the first lie was exposed.[68] After several months of wrangling over the VX issue, on August 4 the Iraqi National Assembly "voted" to end cooperation with the inspections. Saddam then ordered cooperation suspended, although he allowed UNSCOM to continue its long-term monitoring presence. He demanded a slate of changes to UNSCOM's leadership, personnel, and operations to reduce the American and British roles in the commission.

It is unclear what Saddam's thinking was at this point. He may have seen the VX incident as proof that the United States was never going to lift the sanctions and would "use" UNSCOM to justify their continuation— and if this was the case, why continue to cooperate with the inspectors? On the other hand, he may have been feeling confident and, after the muted reaction in the Security Council to the VX discovery, decided that the time was now ripe to bring his strategy to a head and end the inspections altogether. Whatever Saddam's motivation, the U.S. government was incensed, and the countdown to military action might have begun then but other events intervened. On August 7, Usama bin Ladin's al-Qa'eda organization detonated car bombs outside the U.S. Embassies in Kenya and Tanzania. By coincidence, this was also the day after Monica Lewinsky testified before a grand jury. The administration found itself caught up in these other issues and was wary of threatening to use force against Iraq given its previous experiences. Instead, Washington and London persuaded the Security Council to pass a resolution condemning Iraq's decision and calling it a "totally unacceptable contravention of Iraq's obligations." But the United States could not get a declaration that Iraq was in "material breach" of the cease-fire resolution and so left matters to the United Nations to resolve, at least for the moment.

Having gotten so mild a response from the United States, Saddam decided to press harder. In October, he expelled ten Americans on an inspection team, and then, on the last day of the month, Baghdad announced that it was no longer going to cooperate with UNSCOM at all. Instead, the Iraqis demanded a comprehensive review of their compliance and a timetable for lifting the sanctions. On November 7, the United Nations passed another resolution condemning the Iraqi decision but again refused to include the critical "material breach" language. This time the United States was ready to act anyway. The administration carefully canvassed its key allies, pointing out that Washington had refrained from using force at least twice, in November 1997 and February 1998, and that the Security Council had given diplomacy every opportunity to succeed but that it was clear that Saddam would listen only to force. The administration also made it clear that the American people—and particularly the Republican-led Congress—expected a forceful response. In September, Congress had passed the Iraq Liberation Act, calling for the overthrow of the Iraqi regime and authorizing $97 million worth of Pentagon goods and services for the effort.

In the end, the administration secured agreement from Riyadh to fly support missions from Saudi bases, agreement from Kuwait and other GCC states to fly strike missions from their bases, and agreement from Great Britain to participate. On November 14, with American and British planes in the air and headed toward Iraq, however, Tariq Aziz appeared on CNN and announced that Iraq would allow inspectors back in. Secretary General Annan immediately accepted the overture on behalf of the U.N. Under heavy British pressure, the administration agreed to abort the operation rather than appear to be attacking a nation that had already surrendered.

Saddam had won again. He had staved off an American attack at the last minute and made Washington look foolish in the process. In the United States, the administration was viciously attacked by the Republicans for being weak-willed and for handing over American policy to the United Nations. Vice President Gore, who had been one of the most vocal supporters of using military force against Saddam, was livid. Senior members of the administration were becoming ever more frustrated with Iraqi intransigence but had few answers to the dilemma they faced: use force and risk splitting the Security Council (which would undermine the inspections, sanctions, and the rest of containment), or refrain from using force and allow Saddam to undermine the inspections himself, flout the authority of the Security Council, and make the United States look impotent. Nevertheless, the administration had effectively backed itself into a corner: if Saddam blocked the inspections again, the administration couldn't *not* use force, having come so close three times in the past.[69]

At that time, the hawks in the administration again attempted to shift U.S. strategy toward a more aggressive posture. Led by Martin Indyk, now back as assistant secretary of state for Near Eastern Affairs, and Bruce Riedel, who had moved into Indyk's old slot as special assistant to the president for the Near East and South Asia, the hawks argued for a coercive air campaign against Iraq. From my perch as a senior research professor at National Defense University, I supplied some ammunition for this argument, writing several pieces contending that an air campaign aimed at Saddam's regime protection forces—the Republican Guard, SRG, SSO, etc.—would likely compel him to back down.[70] Indyk, Riedel, and others argued that when Saddam reneged, the U.S. response should not be punitive but coercive—a lengthy, punishing air campaign directed at his internal security forces that would threaten to loosen his grip on the country. However, other administration officials objected to an open-ended air campaign that, they argued, would be exactly like the mess the United States had created in Vietnam (and that it would soon nearly re-create in Kosovo). In the end, the Principals decided in favor of a punitive response rather than a coercive campaign.[71]

Naturally, Saddam reneged right away. On December 8, UNSCOM Chairman Richard Butler informed the Security Council that Iraq was continuing to impede the inspectors. On the fifteenth, after having withdrawn his staff from Iraq in expectation of an Anglo-American military operation, Butler delivered a formal report to the United Nations stating that Iraq was continuing to engage in a repeated pattern of obstruction and deception. The next day, the United States and Great Britain launched Operation Desert Fox, the mission they had halted in November, a limited punitive operation uncoupled from any coercive demands on Saddam.

Desert Fox consisted of four days of air and cruise missile strikes. Altogether, the United States and Britain flew 650 aircraft sorties and fired 415 cruise missiles at Iraq. The ostensible goal of the attack was to "degrade" Iraq's WMD programs and "its ability to threaten its neighbors." However, the fact was that only eleven of the ninety-seven targets attacked were WMD facilities because the administration generally did not know where Iraq was concealing its WMD programs.[72] This, of course, was why UNSCOM still had a job to do. Instead, for the first time, the United States principally struck a set of targets related to Saddam's control over the country, including eighteen command-and-control facilities, eight Republican Guard barracks, six airfields, and nineteen sites related to the concealment mechanism—which actually consisted largely of Special Republican Guard garrisons, internal security facilities, and other sites that were key components of Saddam's police state.[73]

The targets the United States struck in Desert Fox were mostly the regime protection and control targets that the administration hawks and several outside the administration, myself included, had been arguing should be the focus of a coercive campaign. The idea was that the way to coerce Saddam into doing something he otherwise would not do was to threaten his control over Iraq, always his principal concern.[74] In this, Desert Fox actually exceeded expectations. Saddam panicked during the strikes. Fearing that his control was threatened, he ordered large-scale arrests and executions, which backfired and destabilized his regime for months afterward. In January, the regime uncovered a coup plot by Lieutenant General Kamel Sajit and General Yelechin Omar and five other senior Sunni officers. Desert Fox also seemed to give new heart to opposition inside the country. Grand Ayatollah Sadiq al-Sadr began preaching subtle acts of defiance against the regime, and his sermons attracted tens of thousands of disaffected Shi'ah. In February, Saddam had al-Sadr and his two sons killed as they were leaving a mosque in an-Najaf. This sparked rioting in a number of Iraqi cities—including the Shi'ite ghettoes of Baghdad—that Saddam was forced to put down with Republican Guard and SRG units. The Shi'ite insurgency flared again in southern Iraq, and for a time it became dangerous for regime officials to travel in rural areas of the south. Eventually the regime was able to snuff out all of these threats, and none ever really threatened its control. However, these events raised the question of what might have happened if the Desert Fox strikes had gone on longer than just four days.[75]

The main reason that Desert Fox was cut short after an arbitrary four days was that Washington had backed into the raids. The administration pointed to the start of the Muslim holy month of Ramadan as its justification for cutting off the attacks, but this was an excuse, not a reason. Muslim states had never ceased military operations for Ramadan; many had launched attacks during the month and, given how unhappy Arab popular opinion was with the strikes as they were, it was unclear how much more unhappy they would have been had the strikes continued into Ramadan. The truth was that Washington had convinced itself that Saddam would not be persuaded by any amount of military force (a conclusion that flew in the face of twenty years of history) and therefore had set no political goals for the operation. There were no demands placed upon Saddam. He was never told that if he allowed the inspectors back in the operation would cease. Although the targets were the right ones (as witnessed by the impact of the operation in Iraq) the strikes were punitive, intended merely to make Iraq pay a price for its defiance of the United Nations and the United States. Consequently, after four days, the administration seized on Ramadan as a good excuse to justify ending the operation before it could become an open-ended air campaign.

REGIME CHANGE AND CONTAINMENT, 1999–2002

The painful eighteen months of repeated crises with Saddam that culminated in Desert Fox had brought about an important change in the administration's thinking toward Iraq. The Clinton foreign policy team had concluded that the only solution to the problem posed by Saddam Hussein was to topple his regime. On December 19, the last day of the Desert Fox strikes, President Clinton delivered a radio address announcing that the policy of the U.S. government was now to replace Saddam Hussein's regime, which clearly would never abide by its obligations to the United Nations or be able to live in peace with its neighbors.

This is where and how I re-entered the Iraq story. A few weeks after Desert Fox I got a phone call from my old boss from the CIA, Bruce Riedel, who had succeeded Mark Parris as the special assistant to the president for Near East and South Asian Affairs. Bruce wanted to know if I was interested in coming back to the NSC to be his director for Persian Gulf affairs. (I had served there under Mark Parris and Steve Grummon in 1995–96.) I was well known inside the government for favoring a hard line on Iraq. In addition, during the two and a half years between my NSC tours, I had written unclassified pieces arguing that limited military force could be used to compel Saddam to respect his U.N. obligations; that the United

States needed to revise containment to focus on the military sanctions, giving up the economic sanctions to rebuild a consensus among key U.S. allies to be able to employ force against Iraq whenever Saddam tried to subvert the inspections or sanctions; and that a sustained air campaign along the lines finally adopted (albeit too briefly) during Desert Fox should be launched to strike at Saddam's control over Iraq whenever he violated the UNSC resolutions. However, I had also coauthored an article in the journal *Foreign Affairs* arguing that the pet idea of several important Republicans—creating a small army under the leadership of Ahmed Chalabi's INC and then trying to use it to overthrow Saddam—was badly misguided and would likely result in disaster. This seemed to convince others in the administration that while my views were hawkish (and therefore accorded with their new interest in regime change), I was also realistic about how to accomplish regime change. Shortly after Bruce's call, I found myself in Sandy Berger's office interviewing for the job. For a half hour, Sandy explained to me that he and the other Principals had concluded that they could not keep playing cat-and-mouse games with Saddam and they had decided that the only solution was to topple his regime. Sandy told me flat out that he wanted me to come back to help the administration devise a realistic regime change policy. I accepted.

Thus, starting in early 1999, the Clinton administration began to develop options to overthrow Saddam's regime. We had several things in our favor at that point. First, after the frustrations of 1997–98 and the president's pronouncement that the United States was serious about regime change, the rest of the world was willing to see if this time we meant it. For the next six months, a parade of foreign dignitaries made their way to Washington to try to gauge whether the United States was willing to make the sacrifices necessary to get rid of Saddam. Some came with offers of help, others with warnings. But for the first time since 1991, the world suspected that the United States actually intended to try to get rid of Saddam. Second, Desert Fox had knocked Saddam off balance, and for much of 1999 he was forced to turn inward and deal with the problems that the strikes and his overreactions had created. Finally, Saddam had unwittingly opened another avenue of attack for the United States. In late December, in an effort to show his loyalists that Desert Fox had not affected him or the regime, he had ordered Iraq's air defense forces to start harassing U.S. and British jets patrolling the two no-fly zones. Between the poverty of Iraq's equipment and tactics on the one hand and the skills of U.S. and British pilots on the other, there was little likelihood that Iraq would score a hit (although a lucky shot was a constant concern for Washington). However, by constantly firing at U.S. aircraft, Baghdad gave the administration the option to respond militarily on a fairly regular basis. Initially, American field commanders asked for, and were granted, permission to take action to eliminate threats to their aircraft, but the administration began to think about how the responses might be used to serve the goal of regime change.

Nevertheless, we also faced serious hurdles. The most obvious external obstacle was that it was going to be very hard to overthrow Saddam's government without mounting a full-scale invasion, and at that point in time, no one thought that the U.S. public would support an invasion. Many of the other problems were internal. For example, the CIA had become gun-shy after its unpleasant experiences in 1995 and 1996. The Agency essentially wanted a guarantee that if it tried to mount a coup against Saddam, the administration would back it to the hilt, even if the operation failed completely—which it realized was a high probability, given how oppressive Saddam's security services were. The CIA developed an extremely conservative new covert action plan that, above all else, ensured that an operation would not blow up in its face, and it resisted efforts to do anything else.[76] The Agency wanted nothing to do with the Iraqi National Congress after having watched it fail to generate any significant support after four years inside Iraq—let alone produce mass defections from the Iraqi military or even spark a popular revolt—coupled with a series of unpleasant experiences with Ahmed Chalabi. Similarly, the uniformed military services had decided that the only sensible way to deal with Saddam was to mount a full-scale invasion. They saw Saddam as a serious threat and were fully willing to mount an invasion but believed nothing else likely to work. What's more, they generally believed that the administration's efforts to find a path to regime change short of a full-scale invasion was a sign that the Principals weren't serious at all. The Pentagon was less than enthusiastic about contributing to other, longer-shot efforts at regime change under those circumstances.

Finally, there was the Iraqi opposition. By 1999, the external Iraqi opposition was a mess. The Kurds continued to fight each other after the fall of Arbil in 1996, and although Secretary of State Albright arranged a reconciliation in Washington in September 1997, the KDP continued to deny the PUK a cut from its smuggling revenues and the PUK continued to plot against it—first with the Iranians and later with the Turks—to get that share. The Wifaq had been devastated by the failure of the 1996 coup attempt and was slowly attempting to rebuild its ties to Iraqi military officers still serving. The INC had been devastated by the fall of Arbil and its hasty departure from northern Iraq and then took a turn for the worse by trying to gain a monopoly over the rest of the opposition. When the CIA had created the INC after the Gulf War, it had been intended to be only a coordinating body, which was why Ahmed Chalabi, with his money and organizational skills but no base of support inside or outside the country, had been perfect to run it. However, over time, Chalabi came to believe that he could be something more than the "office manager" the CIA had originally envisioned and that the other opposition groups had been willing to accept. By 1997–98, Chalabi wanted to head a consolidated opposition and adopted somewhat ruthless methods to try to bend other groups to his will. Increasingly, Chalabi developed a network of supporters among the right wing of the Republican Party and used these powerful friends to wage an internal war within the Iraqi diaspora for control of the opposition. Many Iraqi oppositionists found this particularly galling since Chalabi did not "bring anything to the table" other than his friends in the U.S. Congress. Chalabi's politically astute but militarily ludicrous scheme to train 5,000 to 10,000 INC fighters (fighters he had never been able to produce when the INC had actually been in Iraq with U.S. backing in 1992–96) and then take over 60 percent of the country with support from U.S. air power was one aspect of this game and only further alienated other Iraqi opposition groups, who recognized it as a recipe for disaster. The result was the fragmentation of the INC as an umbrella organization. The Kurds, the Wifaq, and the Supreme Assembly for the Islamic Revolution in Iraq (SAIRI, the main Shi'ite opposition group, which controlled many of the guerrillas battling Saddam's forces in southern Iraq) all told the Clinton administration that they would remain a part of the INC in name but refused to take orders from Ahmed Chalabi.

Nonetheless, in recognition of the role that the Iraqi opposition would have to play in any regime change scheme, Secretary Albright named Frank Ricciardone to be the special coordinator for transition in Iraq. He was an excellent choice. Ricciardone spoke fluent Arabic and had seen long service in the region, including a tour at the embassy in Baghdad before the Gulf War. He got on extremely well with the Iraqis and had tremendous reserves of energy and optimism. Ricciardone's tasks were twofold: to convince the various opposition factions to stop fighting and work together, and to help them become a force capable of making a meaningful contribution to a regime change effort.

Getting the different opposition groups, with all of their rivalries and old hatreds, to work together was like herding cats. As one measure of just how bad it got for Ricciardone, Chalabi and the INC turned against him because it became his task—delegated by the Principals' Committee—that Chalabi set aside his dominating role and instead become part of a collective leadership that the administration hoped would meld the opposition into a more cohesive whole. This jeopardized Chalabi's preeminent position, so the INC worked tirelessly to undercut Frank. It was painfully ironic because Frank (along with myself and Martin Indyk) was one of the only people who was willing to argue in interagency meetings that the INC could play a role in a regime change strategy—albeit not the lead role it envisioned for itself.[77] Unfortunately, the fact that Ricciardone, Indyk, and I were all singled out for special venom by the INC despite the fact that we were essentially their lone supporters within the government was not lost on other administration officials, who concluded that the INC was a dog determined to bite the hand that was feeding it. As a result, the INC's standing in the administration declined even further.

Nevertheless, we set to work with what we had. Bruce Riedel and I had our marching orders to develop realistic options for regime change, and we had every intention of doing so. We began calling interagency meetings to discuss tactics and produce the necessary staff work for the Principals to make a decision. I began meeting with my counterparts throughout the government to get a better sense of what options and new ideas might be out there. In particular, I had a series of meetings with former CIA personnel who had worked on the Iraq program during the early and mid-1990s, all of whom had felt frustrated by some aspects of the Agency's program and were willing to share their ideas with me. It was a difficult process because none of the other agencies wanted to have anything to do with Chalabi's INC, the CIA wanted to stick with its conservative covert action program, and the Pentagon balked at the idea of responding to Iraqi attacks in the no-fly zones by targeting assets of higher value to the regime. But we were able to begin putting together a reasonable, coherent plan.

All of the preexisting problems might have doomed the regime change plan anyway, but what clearly sunk it was the Kosovo war. At the end of March 1999, NATO began an air campaign to force the Serbians to cease their ethnic cleansing of the Kosovar Albanians. This was a war the administration had never wanted to fight. Its expectation had been that if NATO demonstrated its willingness to use force, Serbian strongman Slobodan Milŏsević would back down as he had in Bosnia four years earlier. When Milŏsević did not, Washington found itself in an air campaign that lasted for nearly three months. Toward the end, there was real concern that air strikes alone would not do the job and ground troops would be required. Although Milŏsević did eventually cave in, Washington saw the whole campaign as a very narrow escape.[78] This was critical for U.S. policy toward Iraq because none of the Principals wanted to live through another Kosovo.

The impact of the Kosovo experience was brought home later that year, when we began to roll out the regime change options on Iraq that the Principals had requested. Everyone agreed it was a good, realistic course of action, and Martin Indyk, Bruce, and I began pressing for the Principals to consider it. Almost immediately, however, many senior administration officials began to express unease with the more aggressive options, if not the entire concept. The more we discussed the issue with our various superiors, the more I heard the echo of Kosovo in their voices: they (and the president) were not looking to back into a war with Saddam the way they had backed into one with Milŏsević. Sandy Berger and Leon Fuerth were virtually alone in expressing even a willingness to consider the regime change plan—although they too bore some scars from Kosovo—but given the administration's recent traumatic experience, they were not going to try to force a potentially risky course of action on their resolutely opposed colleagues.

The final element determining the fate of the regime change bid was the long-standing position of the doves that Iraq simply was not worth the candle. During a conversation about the regime change plan in early 2000, one senior administration official told me that "The President wants to finish his term by making peace between the Arabs and the Israelis, he doesn't want to start a war between us and the Iraqis." There were other things on the administration's plate that also had a higher priority, such as the opening to India and a new initiative toward Africa. We were proposing a potentially risky policy that even the most optimistic of its backers felt had no better than a one-in-three chance of succeeding, even if the United States pressed it to the hilt. It was a strategy designed to try to solve a long-term problem for the country at a time when the administration was thinking about wrapping up the projects it had been working on for the last seven years and then turning things over to its successor. Not surprisingly, it was Vice President Gore and his staff who remained most interested in the regime change plan, or at least an aggressive containment policy, to head off the possibility of future Iraq crises if they inherited the White House in the 2000 elections.

Instead, the administration decided to pursue a different track, crafting a new, comprehensive U.N. resolution on Iraq to try to restore the consensus within the Security Council. Originally, this approach had been designed to run in parallel with regime change, but increasingly it came to supersede it. Throughout the summer and fall of 1999, Washington negotiated over a new resolution that the Security Council would eventually pass on December 17 as UNSCR 1284. Resolution 1284 covered most of the waterfront of Iraq-U.N. issues. It lifted the cap on the amount of oil Baghdad could sell to pay for humanitarian goods and greatly expanded the types of goods it could import. After Resolution 1284, we began referring to "oil-for-stuff" rather than "oil-for-food" because the resolution freed the Iraqi economy of most of the remaining constraints so that there would be no reason for any Iraqi to suffer from malnutrition or inadequate medicine. At the same time, Resolution 1284 preserved the military embargo and the United Nations' control over Iraq's finances, which was essential to enforcing the arms ban. Since UNSCOM had effectively died in the fall of 1998 when Iraq had thrown out the inspectors, Resolution 1284 established a new inspection regime. On this point, the United States made a major compromise to try to rebuild Security Council consensus. Washington agreed to suspend the remaining economic sanctions if Iraq made significant progress on key remaining disarmament tasks—those tasks and the nature of the progress to be determined by a new inspection team named the U.N. Monitoring and Verification Commission (UNMOVIC).[79] Although the French had told the United States and Britain that they would vote for the new resolution if we agreed to this compromise, at the last minute, when Paris learned that Moscow planned to abstain rather than vote in favor, the French went back on their word and abstained as well. The resolution was passed 11–0 with four abstentions (China and Malaysia also abstained). As a result, the United States had made key compromises that weakened the inspection regime but still had not resurrected the U.N. consensus it had sought.

The French betrayal was symptomatic of Baghdad's momentum. By 2000, Iraq's trade was worth roughly $17 billion, and other countries were determined to get a piece of it. Iraq carefully awarded contracts to those who echoed its propaganda and voted its way in the Security Council. The French switched their vote on Resolution 1284 at the last minute for fear that if they did not match Russia's abstention, the Iraqis would take contracts away from French firms and award them to the Russians. In 2000, when Saddam decided to try to break the U.N. ban on air travel into Iraq, Baghdad made it clear that participation was a prerequisite for oil-for-food contracts. Not surprisingly, the Russians were the first ones in the door, followed quickly by the French. In contrast, the Chinese refused because Beijing agreed with Washington on the legality of the flight ban and wanted to preserve the authority of the Security Council (an important aspect of China's own international influence). Iraq retaliated by diverting contracts away from China. Beyond this, there simply was no downside for countries cooperating with Iraq, either legally or illegally. Many cases of illegal activity were referred to the U.N. Sanctions Committee, which did nothing about them. Certainly no member was willing to impose new sanctions on Iraq or those countries helping them to violate the sanctions.

When foreign nations finally recognized that the Clinton administration would not, in the end, make a determined effort to topple Saddam, this reinforced the rush to be on Baghdad's good side. If Saddam was going to be around for some time and there were no real penalties for supporting his policies or even violating the sanctions outright, why not take advantage of the bribes and profits he was doling out? As a result, smuggling with Iraq mushroomed. In 1999, the United States estimated that only about 5 percent of Iraq's oil revenues were skirting the U.N. system and ending up in Saddam's hands. By 2001, that number had grown to roughly 20 percent. Syria, Iraq's longtime enemy, opened the Iraqi-Syrian pipeline, which had been closed since 1982, and began pumping as much as 200,000 barrels of oil per day in flagrant violation of the U.N. sanctions. The Syrians also opened their border to goods headed into Iraq, and no one but the Syrians and the Iraqis knows what gets in through that route. Iraq began demanding illegal surcharges on each barrel of oil it sold, payable to private accounts outside the U.N. system—and companies paid them. Although Iran helped cut down on the smuggling through the Persian Gulf, the Emirate of Dubayy in the UAE shrugged off pressure both from the United States and from its federal government in Abu Dhabi and routinely accepted huge cargoes of smuggled Iraqi oil. Jordan and Turkey likewise began working to increase their ability to smuggle oil out of Iraq and goods into it. By the end of 2000, Washington found itself virtually powerless to stop the rapid erosion of the sanctions.

Meanwhile, the Iraqi opposition fell apart. Frank Ricciardone had done yeoman's work. Through constant explaining, cajoling, bargaining, and begging, he had gotten a large number of Iraqi opposition groups to agree to try to work together, and the State Department had set up a conference in October 1999 to create a new organizational structure and select personnel for the new opposition umbrella grouping. Frank even believed that he had convinced Ahmed Chalabi that this was the best route available. But at the conference, the opposition fell to infighting, in large part because Chalabi purposely alienated some groups and tried to undermine the standing of others. This brought out all of the differences among them, and the conference collapsed in squabbling and recriminations.[80] When Chalabi then tried to force the administration's hand—by going to the Senate and having the Senate support an INC scheme to begin sending personnel into Iraq with American surveillance equipment and propaganda materials, a plan the administration had already told them it was unwilling to condone—even Frank and I stopped trying to convince anyone that the INC was worth assisting.

By the summer of 2000, the Clinton administration was just looking to play defense on Iraq. The vice president was campaigning full-time, the president was investing ever more of his time in trying to secure a Palestinian-Israeli peace agreement before he left office, and the rest of the government was just trying to prevent its position on Iraq from deteriorating further. Martin Indyk's departure as assistant secretary (he returned to Israel, where he had previously served, as the U.S. ambassador) left only Bruce Riedel and myself to push for a more activist policy, and we could not fight the rest of the bureaucracy alone. The situation got even worse after the failure of the Camp David peace talks prompted the Palestinians to launch the "al-Aqsa *intifadah*," a popular uprising against Israel that would eventually turn into a vicious terrorist campaign. As Israeli-Palestinian violence soared, America's Arab allies refused to support further action against Saddam. Nevertheless, as Sandy Berger regularly reminded me, we had a responsibility to leave the next administration with a viable Iraq policy, not a mess. It would be up to that administration to decide what to do, but we had to leave our successors enough to have a reasonable set of choices.

One of the last memos I wrote for the Clinton team described the policy options on Iraq that would be available to the next administration. By this time, containment was losing most of its support within the U.S. bureaucracy as we watched it whither. Given that containment increasingly was not an option, the question then became whether one supported determined regime change or a retreat to deterrence. Some, mostly the old "doves," began to move increasingly toward pure deterrence of Iraq. Most of the hawks moved in the opposite direction. Since I considered deterrence extremely dangerous, I too began to feel that determined regime change was more and more the only realistic option.[81] In this last memo, I argued that because of the erosion of containment, the next administration would be left with two choices: to adopt an aggressive policy of regime change to try to get rid of Saddam quickly or undertake a major revamping of the sanctions to try to choke off the smuggling and prevent Saddam from reconstituting his military, particularly his hidden WMD programs. I noted that the steps that would be necessary for the latter option would be far more onerous than they first appeared because of the unwillingness of any country other than the United States to confront Iraq or impose penalties on states violating the sanctions.

There was one last confrontation between Iraq and the Clinton administration before it left office, this one spurred by the al-Aqsa *intifadah*. Saddam had been biding his time, relying on the strategy of eroding the sanctions that had been working for him since 1996 and avoiding anything but the low-level confrontations in the NFZs. However, the outbreak of the al-Aqsa *intifadah* in the early autumn of 2000 after the failure of the Camp David peace talks presented him with an opportunity to try to speed the end of containment that he could not resist. This *intifadah* had begun as the last had ended, with Palestinian boys throwing rocks at Israeli soldiers, but quickly escalated as Palestinian Authority security personnel joined in with small arms. Moreover, in 2000, new sources of media inflamed Arab sentiment throughout the region, particularly satellite television networks such as the notorious al-Jazeera, which broadcast incendiary content around the clock. Within weeks, the al-Aqsa *intifadah* had set the whole Middle East on edge.

Saddam realized that the Arab-Israeli violence was working to his advantage. It stirred up the Arab "street" against Israel and its American allies, making it harder for the Arab governments to support U.S. policy. Indeed, it appears that Saddam calculated that a full-blown Arab-Israeli war would be a tremendous opportunity for him because it probably would split the United States and the moderate Arab states, compel the GCC countries to evict the U.S. military forces based there, and possibly trigger the wholesale collapse of containment. Accordingly, Iraq began talks with the new Syrian regime of Bashar al-Asad. Bashar's father, Hafiz, had hated Saddam and was too cautious to allow himself to be used by the Iraqis. Bashar, on the other hand, was callow and rash and saw in the *intifadah* an opportunity to demonstrate to Israel and the other Arab states that he was not someone to be trifled with. Although we do not know the details, Baghdad and Damascus struck some kind of deal regarding Iraqi military cooperation with Syria—even permitting Iraqi troops to be deployed in Syria to demonstrate Arab solidarity and put pressure on Israel. In October, Iraq began moving divisions to the Syrian border. It first moved the Hammurabi Republican Guard Armored Division west of Baghdad and then began moving the Third Armored Division and three infantry divisions of the regular army out to Haditha, near the Syrian border.[82]

Washington recognized the danger immediately: Israel would likely see any movement of Iraqi troops into Syria as a *casus belli*. But Bashar did not understand that. Indeed, Bashar and some of the people around him were assuring other Arab leaders that they knew what they were doing with Saddam. The United States mounted a full-court press on Syria, bringing in Egypt, Jordan, and Saudi Arabia to add Arab weight to our argument. Saudi Crown Prince 'Abdallah summoned Bashar to Riyadh, where he was upbraided by 'Abdallah and then warned by Secretary of State Albright, who made a quick detour through the Kingdom. The message to Bashar was simple: you may think you are using Saddam, but he is using you. 'Abdallah and Albright told Bashar that either he abrogated his deal with Saddam or he would find himself out in the cold with no one but the Iraqis for friends. Bashar seemed to get the message, but we cannot be certain. In late October the Iraqis reversed the process and brought the forces headed to Haditha back to their garrisons, but it is unclear whether this was because Bashar had canceled their agreement or because Saddam found that the Iraqi military just couldn't handle the operation. Either way, the Iraqis went home and the threat of a wider Arab-Israeli war was averted.

ANOTHER BUSH CONFRONTS SADDAM

When the administration of George W. Bush took office in January 2001, many believed that if there were one topic on which the Bush team had already decided its policy, it was Iraq. It was widely believed that the administration would make regime change in Iraq one of its first and highest priorities. This seemed confirmed when the administration announced that the first comprehensive foreign policy review it would conduct would be on Iraq. However, prior to September 11, 2001, the Bush administration turned out to be not too dissimilar to the Clinton administration in its final days. Like their predecessors, the Bush officials broke down into the same three camps of "doves," "moderate hawks," and "extreme hawks." A group of doves including, most notably, Secretary of State Colin Powell approached Iraq with the same skepticism as had the early Clinton administration. They too believed that Iraq was a small, weak country that should not be allowed to monopolize U.S. foreign policy. This group had much bigger items on its agenda: Russia, China, Europe, perhaps Africa, and taking advantage of the Clinton opening to India. They saw the world in terms of traditional great-power politics, and Iraq simply did not measure up. They believed that Saddam could be kept contained at minimum cost, which would allow them to pursue other, more important foreign policy initiatives.

At the other extreme was a group led by Deputy Secretary of Defense Paul Wolfowitz and a number of others in the offices of the Secretary of Defense and the Vice President. This band had an almost obsessive fixation on getting rid of Saddam's regime. Interestingly, the Bush administration's extreme hawks saw Iraq as both highly (and immediately) threatening but also highly vulnerable. From day one, they urged an aggressive regime change strategy relying on the INC and U.S. air power to topple Saddam. Their dogma was that the Iraqi regime was the root cause of nearly every evil to befall the United States (from Arab-Israeli violence to international terrorism), while the Iraqi people were waiting to rise up against Saddam and would do so if the United States demonstrated that it was serious about overthrowing him.

Finally, there was again a group at the center, including Vice President Dick Cheney, that favored a more aggressive approach to containment and was willing to explore options for regime change but recognized that toppling Saddam was going to be difficult, potentially costly, and risky. Most of these officials thought that regime change in Iraq would be beneficial but wanted to look hard at what it would take to do so.

The administration's policy review exposed these differences and also drove home to the administration just how complicated the Iraq issue had become since Republicans had last been in office. Initially, the Bush team wanted to have its Iraq policy review completed in a matter of weeks, but it quickly became clear that it would need a much better understanding of the multiplicity of issues involved and much more staff work to develop new options. The first deadline for the review came and went, as did a later one, and another and another. By the summer of 2001 it had become clear that the administration was not going to pursue a radically new approach to Iraq. It was simply too difficult to reconcile the costs and risks of regime change with the administration's other foreign and domestic policy priorities.[83] Instead the administration announced that while it would continue to study options for regime change, it would move ahead with an overhaul of the U.N. system known as "smart sanctions."[84]

The concept behind smart sanctions had been batted around during the last years of the Clinton administration and at its core consisted of lifting the remaining economic sanctions in return for Security Council agreement to shut down the smuggling. The version that the Bush team embraced consisted of (1) a reduced list of dual-use items, including basically only those for which the Iraqis would have a hard time claiming another legitimate purpose; (2) an expanded list of goods that could use the streamlined review process created by Resolution 1284; and (3) a package of positive and negative incentives to convince Iraq's neighbors (Jordan, Syria, Iran, Turkey, and the GCC states) to stop the smuggling. The smart sanctions were a reasonable approach to a hard problem, but in truth, the Bush administration's version was never going to succeed, at least not the part that tried to restrict the smuggling. Iraq could be expected to resist this part with everything in its arsenal, and the smart sanctions never envisioned using carrots or sticks big enough to convince any of Iraq's neighbors to cease the highly lucrative (and in some cases economically essential) smuggling. As a result, the administration tried twice to have the Security Council adopt the smart sanctions, only to fail both times. In the end, in May 2002, the administration decided to cut its losses: it repackaged parts 1 and 2 of the original smart sanctions as a "goods review list" and got it through the Security Council. While this was useful because it made it harder for Iraq to blame the suffering of its people on the sanctions, because it did nothing to address the smuggling, it was less than half a loaf.

The problems the Bush administration encountered with the smart sanctions highlighted the contradictions in all post–Gulf War American policy toward Iraq. As the doves argued, Iraq truly was a small, weak state and the threat it represented was always a longer-term one. But Iraq was not so weak and inconsequential that it could not make a great deal of trouble for the United States. Thus, since the Gulf War, "doves" have focused on Iraq's weakness and inconsequentiality to the international order and have opted to try to keep it contained so that they could pursue other, more important foreign policy initiatives. However, keeping Iraq contained required much more than a minimal effort on the part of the United States. Sustaining containment required a willingness to make Iraq a priority and confront Saddam when he challenged it—in other words, a willingness to make Iraq a fairly high priority, thereby defeating the doves' goal in adopting containment.

By the same token, neither of the hawkish positions had much luck in gaining traction, at least not for very long. The extreme hawkish view always appeared unnecessary, given that the threat from Iraq was a relatively distant one and could be greatly reduced (perhaps even eliminated) if containment were kept strong enough that Saddam's ability to smuggle equipment for his WMD programs was kept to a minimum. In other words, because of Saddam's success in controlling Iraq, pursuing regime change was always going to be either very risky or very costly or both, and this option never seemed politically attractive as long as containment was a viable alternative.

The moderate "hawkish" position suffered from its own contradictions. The idea behind this policy was that since there was no political will to do what was necessary to actually bring about regime change, the United States would take the aggressive actions necessary to keep Saddam contained and also pursue some aspects of regime change in hope of getting lucky or at least keeping Saddam on the defensive. This meant making Iraq something of a foreign policy priority—just enough of a priority to complicate the rest of U.S. diplomacy but not enough of one to make it worth devoting the resources and political capital necessary to actually solve the problem. In addition, it was a policy that was derived from the absence of the political will to do what was necessary to remove Saddam (i.e., go to war), but that nonetheless ran the risk of war with Iraq on a fairly regular basis.[85]

In short, all of the different post–Gulf War U.S. policy options were fraught with contradictions. This is why the United States never had a great, obvious course of action toward Iraq. In truth, every administration chose what it believed was the "least bad" option, and interestingly, before September 11, 2001, every administration ended up with the dovish version of containment even though three of the four (Bush, Sr., second Clinton administration, and Bush, Jr.) all started off wanting to pursue one of the harder-line options. Thus, what is important about September 11 is that it has made Americans think twice about the risks inherent in the purely dovish position on Iraq that has so far predominated in U.S. policy. Simultaneously, the popular response to the terrorist attacks has made the strategies inherent in the more hawkish positions feasible in a way that they never were before, because the American people were never willing to make the sacrifices necessary to devote serious resources and political capital to the toppling of Saddam.

Part II

IRAQ TODAY

FOUR

Iraqi State and Society

In the wake of the Iran-Iraq War, the Gulf War, and the ongoing confrontation with the United States, Iraq today is a shadow of its former self. For the Iraqi people, the confrontation with the United States and the United Nations has been a disaster. Before the Gulf War, they lived in a Stalinist hell, but they were well fed, reasonably well educated, mostly healthy, and, by regional standards, relatively prosperous. Today, humiliation, economic woes, and health care problems have been added to the burden of Saddam's terror. Worse, the sanctions have, in many ways, strengthened Saddam's iron grip, making the Iraqi people even more vulnerable to his thugs and the predations of his family and flunkies. The oil-for-food deal is helping the people to recover their health, but this is only just beginning and the damage to Iraq's economic and social fabric persists. The augmentation of the regime's control may never be undone.

Saddam's position today is, paradoxically, both weaker and stronger than it was before he invaded Kuwait. Weaker because he has been deprived of most of the military strength that made him a regional power; because persistent coups, domestic unrest, and insurgent attacks have demonstrated the extent of his unpopularity and given heart to his opponents; because he still does not control the Kurdish lands, nor is he fully sovereign elsewhere since U.N. personnel monitor the oil-for-food system and coalition warplanes roam freely across 60 percent of Iraqi airspace. Moreover, Saddam's power base—the tribes and towns that have faithfully supported him throughout his reign and furnish most of the manpower for his security apparatus and key military units—has seen Iraqi power and prestige brought very low, and they chafe at this abasement. But Saddam is stronger too. So many have tried to overthrow him and failed—and suffered execution or banishment for their troubles—that there are virtually no leaders of any stature inside Iraq who might rally Iraqis against Saddam. Stronger also because the mechanisms devised by the U.N. sanctions and the oil-for-food deal have given Saddam strangleholds over aspects of Iraqi society that he never possessed in the past. And stronger because despite everything America has thrown at him, he has survived and now looks as if he will win it all at some point soon, when the sanctions are lifted or simply disintegrate.

Any new U.S. policy toward Iraq needs to proceed from an understanding of current Iraqi political, economic, and social realities. Just as the history of the U.S.-Iraqi relationship is critical to understanding the paths already followed and why they failed, so too is it critical to understand the circumstances of the country today. The reason that some courses of action are available and others are not is often a function of what is possible—or imaginable—with Iraq, its people, and its regime under the current state of affairs.

SADDAM'S POWER BASE

Any discussion of Iraq today should begin with an explanation of how Saddam keeps himself in power. This is the driving force behind the regime and all of its policies and so is the principal determinant of nearly every other aspect of Iraqi policy and society. Regis Matlak, a government official with wide expertise on the Middle East, has written that "No one individual has devoted more resources and spent more energy and time thinking about Saddam's grip on power than Saddam himself. His intense interest in and knowledge of intelligence and security issues is not episodic. His is a persistent and powerful personal engagement."[1] A critical element of Saddam's success in holding power since 1979 has been his ability to develop a network of groups that support his regime. Saddam has had to find groups of people willing to carry out his gruesome orders, and his ability to do so has been the key to the longevity of his regime. An old Arabic saying goes, "I and my brother against our cousin; I and my cousin against the stranger." In other words, there are rings of loyalty within traditional Arab society that Saddam has been able to count on: he can count on his near relatives to defend him against all challengers, and he can count on more distant relatives (as well as clansmen, tribesmen, and fellow Tikritis) to defend him against those who fall outside those groupings.

Saddam's first rule is to place only those he considers to have impeccable loyalty to himself in the highest positions, the inner ring of his regime. Relying on the powerful loyalties attached to close blood ties in Iraqi tribal society, he tends to fill the most sensitive jobs with family members. Upon Saddam's taking power, his cousin and closest friend, Adnan Khayrallah, remained as defense minister, his half brother Barzan Ibrahim ran the crucial Intelligence Service, and his uncle Khayrallah Talfah became mayor of Baghdad. Later, Saddam would invest other members of his family with other key positions. His half brothers Watban and Sabawi would be made interior minister and director of the al-Amn al-'Amm (General Security), two of the most important internal security positions. His cousin 'Ali Hassan al-Majid would serve in a number of important positions, including governor of occupied Kuwait and minister of defense. 'Ali Hassan's nephew, Hussein Kamel, would supervise Iraq's WMD programs and then be named minister of industry and military industrialization. Other cousins would be placed in other various sensitive positions, including Saddam's cousin Kamal Mustafa, who was put in charge of the Special Republican Guard. Finally, Saddam's elder sons, Udayy and Qusayy, have also been given important responsibilities. The unstable Udayy has rotated through a variety of positions and today runs several newspapers, is head of Iraq's Olympic Committee (and de facto "minister of youth"), and heads the Fidayin Saddam paramilitary organization. Qusayy has emerged as the star of the family. Quiet, dependable, and ruthless, he heads the Special Security Organization, which has become Iraq's preeminent internal security organization, with far greater responsibilities than Saddam had previously allowed any other security agency to possess.

As large as Saddam's family is, it is still not big enough to furnish the personnel necessary to control a nation of 23 million people. Thus, Saddam has sought personnel who have other ties to him for the rank-and-file positions throughout Iraq's government and security structure. Members of his Bayjat clan, his al Bu Nasir tribe, and his hometown of Tikrit are heavily recruited because Iraq's tribal traditions ensure a high degree of loyalty to their most famous native son. Beyond this, Saddam is seen as the champion of the Sunni Arabs in their struggle to dominate the more numerous Shi'ah, Kurds, and other nationalities. He has cultivated close ties with a number of large Sunni tribes and tribal confederations, such as the Jubbur, ad-Dulaym, al-'Ubayd, Khazraj, Shammar, al-Mushahada, 'Aqaydat, and Sa'dun.[2] He has even been able to coopt the support of several Shi'ite tribes, including the Banu Hasan and the Shi'ite branches of the Jubbur and Shammar.[3] Members of these tribes fill the ranks of the Republican Guard, the security services, and other key regime protection forces. Saddam can also count on the support of Iraq's core Sunni cities, mostly in western Iraq. Large numbers of men from Tikrit, ar-Ramadi, Haditha, ad-Dur, Samarra, Bayji, and the "right" parts of Baghdad are well represented in the Republican Guard and other regime protection forces because they too can be counted on to support Saddam's regime against his opponents—and particularly against the Shi'ah and Kurds.

Another source of support for Saddam is the Ba'th Party, which now boasts roughly 1.5 million members.[4] Saddam was never particularly ideological, and since his accession to power, Ba'thist ideology has been essentially relegated to a propaganda device. But the Ba'th Party is another matter. For better or worse (usually worse), Ba'thists have hitched their wagon to Saddam's star. They benefit from their party membership but are also culpable for the regime's crimes and damned to obey its orders. Consequently, they are a ready pool of manpower for the regime. Saddam has learned not to put too much faith in Ba'th Party ties after the cowardly performance of Ba'thists in the Iran-Iraq War and during the *intifadah,* and as a result, their prestige and prominence has declined over the years. But they still serve a purpose. They can be counted on to assist the secret police in ferreting out dissent, they can be mobilized for street demonstrations and to spread the regime's propaganda, and they can be armed and put on the streets to help keep order in time of crisis.

Saddam works assiduously to reinforce the bonds of loyalty that tie him to each of these groups. He rewards them in accordance with their degree of support and importance to him. His family, friends, and other high-ranking officials get limitless perks. Officials of the security services and the Republican Guard get better pay, cars, and other material benefits. Even the rank and file are ensured better living standards than their counterparts in the regular armed forces or in civilian life. On the negative side, Saddam provides constant reminders of the punishments that await traitors—and those from the inner circles who turn against him are usually treated much worse than outsiders. Moreover, as he first started doing in 1979, Saddam systematically includes his followers in his crimes. Torture, killing, rape, genocide, and other cruelties are parceled out as assignments to as many of the regime's personnel as possible (and many of them take to these tasks all too willingly). The regime is also fond of filming or videotaping its crimes and then distributing the tapes widely, both as a way of warning its enemies of what happens to those who oppose Saddam and as a means of implicating as many people in his monstrous behavior as possible. What's more, Saddam plays these different groups off against one another in his usual efforts to build redundancy and divide and conquer. For example, after the Gulf War and the *intifadah,* Saddam initially relied heavily on his family, only to be disappointed when the family began to misbehave (Udayy shooting Watban, Hussein Kamel's defection, and so on). He then turned to the Ba'thists, who found themselves in greater favor than they had enjoyed in twenty years. But soon the Ba'thists were once again eclipsed by the Sunni tribesmen.[5] In the future, these various groups will undoubtedly continue to rise and fall in Saddam's favor as his needs dictate.

THE INTERNAL SECURITY FORCES

If the loyal Sunni tribes, the Tikritis and other Sunni townsmen, the Ba'th, and his family are the foundation of Saddam's totalitarian edifice, it is the multiplicity of internal security and intelligence services that make up its iron walls. With good reason, Saddam suspects everyone and moves to arrest, remove, maim, or kill anyone who demonstrates the slightest inkling of opposition to him. In a famous story, Saddam once told a guest, "I know there are scores of people plotting to kill me, and this is not difficult to understand. After all, did we not seize power by plotting against our predecessors? However, I am far cleverer than they are. I know they are conspiring to kill me long before they actually start planning to do it. This enables me to get them before they have the faintest chance of striking at me."[6]

Early in his political career, Saddam recognized the importance of the security services in gaining and maintaining power. One of his first jobs of any importance in the Ba'th Party was building its security apparatus. To this day, internal security remains his first priority. Saddam has consciously studied the methods of Nazi Germany and Stalinist Russia in building

Iraq's internal security structure, and his work may very well surpass those prior archetypes.[7] Amatzia Baram has nicely described Saddam's emphasis on his own security even at the expense of other priorities: "Throughout his career as chief of internal security, then president, whenever Iraq's foreign interests clashed with perceived domestic security interests, the latter always prevailed. Insofar as internal security is concerned, Saddam Hussein has never taken any chances. The result was that while Iraq's relations with the world's superpowers often suffered, Saddam's control over the domestic scene remained near total."[8]

The security services are manned by personnel specially selected for their loyalty. Senior officers invariably have some deep tie to Saddam by blood or tribe. He recruits heavily from his own al Bu Nasir tribe for the security services, although there are also many Ubaydis, Jubburis, Dulaymis, and others from the most loyal Sunni tribes, especially in lower-ranking positions. Likewise, many of the rank and file are from Iraq's Sunni heartland—Tikrit, ar-Ramadi, Samarra, Bayji, and other towns west of Baghdad—where Saddam is seen as their champion. Saddam then works tirelessly to further weld these men to his side. They are subjected to relentless propaganda (in effect, brainwashing) to ensure that they see the world through his eyes. Their loyalty is constantly tested, and those who fail these tests do not live to tell the tale. Reportedly, a favorite regime trick is to have groups of armed men burst into the rooms of sleeping presidential guards or bodyguards as if they were conducting a coup d'état, place guns to the heads of the startled guards, and demand, "Are you with us or against us?" Those who give the wrong answer are executed on the spot. Saddam provides his security service personnel with lavish rewards far beyond what most of these boys from the slums or the sticks could ever have imagined. He also systematically incriminates security service personnel in brutal crimes to make them his accomplices and instill in them a fear that if he goes down, they will go down with him.[9] Thus the hatred and fear that Iraq's internal security services inspire serve two purposes: it makes it easier for them to control the country and makes them more determined to protect the regime for fear of the retribution they would face if the Iraqi people were ever free to take their revenge.

There are roughly a dozen Iraqi intelligence and security services. All told, Iraq may employ as many as 500,000 people in its various intelligence, security, and police organizations. When the armed forces and paramilitary units are added in, the number probably reaches close to 1.3

million—in a population of 23 million. Iraqis themselves believe that another 2 million to 4 million people serve as informants of the security services.

Although all of the security services have slightly different formal missions, they also have overlapping and redundant responsibilities, and all of them have at least some internal security functions. This ensures that it is highly unlikely that a threat will go unnoticed because at least one of Saddam's security organs is likely to find out about it. In addition, it minimizes the threat from any of the security services themselves. They are all watching one another, they have little ability to coordinate, and since no one knows the full picture except Saddam, every member of the internal security services and every one of its organizations must assume that it is being watched by multiple sources. The result is the pervasive and all-encompassing fear that has turned Iraq into a self-policing totalitarian state. A former member of the Himaya (bodyguards) described it thus: "Security for the president is very tight. It is quite fierce and rigorous, and it is merciless. . . . Everyone is afraid of everybody else. Everyone in the protective detail informs on everybody else. The president's security is more like a terrorist organization whose members will do anything to please the president."[10] Indeed, everyone in Iraq must assume that he or she is surrounded by security agents, informants, surveillance devices, and would-be snitches. The result is that few Iraqis can summon the courage to take even the first steps toward opposition, and most live their lives in constant fear.

The most important of the regime's security services include:[11]

Special Security Organization (SSO; al-Amn al-Khas). Created in 1982 as part of General Security (al-Amn al-'Amm), the SSO became a separate agency in 1984 and has emerged as the most important of Iraq's internal security forces. It is currently headed by Qusayy Saddam, who replaced Hussein Kamel after his defection and execution. The SSO has many responsibilities related to guarding Saddam himself. High-level SSO personnel are assigned as "bodyguards" to many important people, including all senior military commanders—whom they protect but whose obedience to the regime's orders they also ensure. There are roughly 5,000 members of the SSO. However, it is both an internal security agency in itself and an umbrella organization controlling several other important security forces, including the Presidential Guard, the Palace Guard, the Special Republican Guard, and the Republican Guard, all of which report to Qusayy in his capacity as head of the SSO. For the Republican Guard units, orders for field operations are formulated by the Iraqi General Staff but then must be approved by the SSO and transmitted down both the SSO and normal military chains of command to the RG corps and division command staffs.

The Companions (Murafiqin). These are Saddam's personal bodyguards. There are forty of them, all from Saddam's Bayjat clan of the al Bu Nasir tribe. The senior Murafiqin are some of the most feared men in Iraq and are responsible for supervising all of the security precautions for Saddam's physical safety. The Murafiqin are headed by Abid Hamid Humud, Saddam's personal secretary and the third most powerful man in Iraq after Saddam and Qusayy. Although the Murafiqin are not part of the SSO, they work closely with it, and the senior Murafiqin supervise the SSO personnel from the Presidential Guard and Palace Guard.

The Bodyguards (al-Himaya). This is the next ring around Saddam beyond the Murafiqin. Also sometimes referred to as the Presidential Guard, they number about 2,000 (nearly all from Saddam's al Bu Nasir tribe) and are broken up into at least three groups. First is a Mobile Group, which is responsible for Saddam's movements and secures Saddam's routes and destinations. Second is the Special Location Group, which handles or supervises security for Saddam at a number of his palaces as well as other places where he spends the night. The larger Palace Guard appears largely to follow the orders of the Special Location Group, especially when Saddam is present at a palace. The last is the Kulyab, a group of miscellaneous people with intimate access to Saddam, including his cook, butcher, food taster, and swimming companions.

Palace Guard (al-Amn al-Qasr). This provides the uniformed personnel who guard Saddam's palaces and a few other sensitive sites. It reports to the SSO and probably is part of the Himaya. Indeed, Palace Guard may be another name for the Special Location Group of the Himaya.

Special Republican Guard (SRG; al-Haras al-Jumhuri al-Khas). The SRG consists of four brigades and numbers as many as 30,000 troops, mostly from Tikrit and its outlying villages. It is heavily armed with its own artillery and armored fighting vehicles, giving it the combat power to defeat a large-scale civilian uprising or a coup attempt by a military unit. It is the next ring of security beyond the Presidential Guard and reports to the SSO. In addition to its role in hiding Iraq's proscribed WMD programs, the SSO is responsible for defending the regime against popular unrest or a revolt by the armed forces (including even the Republican Guard). After Iraq had expanded the Republican Guard to play a greater role in conventional military operations against Iran in the late 1980s, Saddam took several of the RG units charged with purely internal security missions, added additional loyal personnel, and designated them the Special Republican Guard with the original mission of the RG. Today, the SRG is the garrison of the city of Baghdad (not the Baghdad Infantry Division of the RG, which some erroneously assumed had that mission). It has participated in numerous important internal security missions when large, well-armed, and highly devoted military formations were required to deal with widespread unrest, such as during the Iraqi *intifadah* and the riots after Operation Desert Fox.

Iraqi Intelligence Service or General Intelligence (IIS; Da'irat al-Mukhabbarat al-'Amma). The IIS, or Mukhabbarat, is the granddaddy of Iraq's intelligence agencies, and its responsibilities are all-inclusive. The Mukhabbarat has primary responsibility for foreign intelligence gathering, although this is only one of its missions. As such it has all of the intelligence, counterintelligence, and covert action responsibilities of other foreign intelligence agencies. It has also played a role in terrorist operations—it was the Mukhabbarat that tried to kill former President Bush and the amir of Kuwait in 1993. As with all of Iraq's security and intelligence services, however, the Mukhabbarat also has an important internal security mission. The Mukhabbarat's responsibilities for watching over the Iraqi populace overlap with those of the Amn (see below). The Mukhabbarat also spies on all of Saddam's other intelligence and security services, in addition to the armed forces, the Ba'th Party, and the rest of the government bureaucracy.

General Security (al-Amn al-'Amm). This is believed to be the largest of the security services with possibly tens of thousands of agents, although its actual numbers are unknown. The Amn is principally concerned with domestic security matters, although it has also been known to conduct overseas assignments. The Amn is the most pervasive security organ and the service that average Iraqis are most likely to encounter. Every neighborhood in Iraq's bigger cities, every town, and every rural district has a local

Amn office that keeps tabs on everything that happens in the area. Amn personnel are some of the regime's worst petty thugs and those responsible for the majority of the harassment, terrorizing, and brutalization of the Iraqi people.

Military Intelligence (al-Istikhbarat al-'Askariya). As with all of Iraq's security and intelligence services, this is not just the functional equivalent of Western, or even Soviet-style, military intelligence. The Istikhbarat is charged with gathering intelligence on foreign militaries. However, its main function is to watch over and ensure the loyalty of the armed forces. The Istikhbarat was originally responsible for the political commissars attached to army units down to battalion level and air force units down to squadron level, although it is unclear if it still has this mission. The Istikhbarat maintains a massive network of informants throughout Iraq's military services. It also controls all of the military attachés assigned to Iraqi embassies, whose jobs often extend beyond pure diplomacy and information gathering. Istikhbarat military attachés have been involved in the assassination of Iraqi dissidents abroad, and it was an Istikhbarat officer who was unmasked as the ringleader in the assassination of Shlomo Argov, the Israeli ambassador to Great Britain, in 1982.[12]

Military Security (al-Amn al-'Askiriya). In 1992, after the Gulf War, the *intifadah,* and the immediate spate of coup attempts, Saddam felt the need for additional controls over the Iraqi armed forces, so he created Military Security. The division of responsibilities between Military Security and the Istikhbarat is unclear. There is clearly a great deal of redundancy, which fits with Saddam's predilection for overlapping authority and competing agencies. Military Security appears to have taken over control of the political commissars, themselves reinstituted after the Gulf War, with SSO officers added to the headquarters staffs for good measure.

Ba'th Party Security (al-Amn al-Hizb). The Ba'th Party has its own security apparatus. While Ba'th Party officials are enjoined to keep watch on their fellow citizens, the party's security branch keeps watch on them. Little is known about the size or activities of Ba'th Party security other than that its principal concern is with the behavior of its own members. It is reasonable to believe that it assists, backstops, and watches both the Amn and the Mukhabbarat in their various internal security responsibilities.

Fidayin Saddam. In late 1994, after coming to the brink of war with coalition forces once again after Saddam foolishly threatened Kuwait, Saddam formed the Fidayin Saddam under the control of his eldest son, Udayy. Initially, the Fidayin were laughable—they possessed no heavy weaponry and appeared to be a strange cross between a goon squad and a kamikaze brigade whose claim to fame was their constant public assurances that they were ready to die for Saddam. After the June 1996 coup plot was discovered within the RG and the SRG (both of which report to Qusayy, it is worth pointing out), Udayy's Fidayin suddenly got much better treatment. The force was greatly expanded and may now number as many as 100,000 men. Fidayin recruitment became more selective, its training was made more rigorous and professional, and it was given more advanced and powerful equipment. Although not on a par with the RG or the SRG, it is now a force to be reckoned with inside Iraq and is clearly intended as yet another counterweight in Saddam's game of checks and balances.

This list does not include all of the different police, border guards, customs inspectors, and other elements of Iraqi law enforcement. In addition, there are also the various elements of the armed forces, which have important internal security functions. The mission of the regular armed forces—the army, air force, and navy—is not only to defend the country against external foes but to defend the regime against internal foes. In this capacity, army and air force units participated in the suppression of the *intifadah* in 1991 and have fought major wars against Iraq's Kurds in every decade since the 1960s. The Republican Guard began its existence as a palace guard, and although its massive expansion during the 1990s (so that it could fight more effectively as a conventional military force) has diluted its loyalty somewhat, it has still demonstrated far greater loyalty to the regime than have regular army units. During the *intifadah,* very few Guards defected to the rebels, and it was because the Guard remained cohesive and loyal that Saddam was able to defeat the revolts. Beyond the armed forces and the Guard is the Ba'th Party's Popular Army, a militia with several hundred thousand men. During the Iran-Iraq War, Popular Army units were committed to combat against the Iranians—with disastrous consequences. However, during times of domestic crisis, Saddam has been able to call out the Popular Army to help exert an armed security presence throughout the country, and it has proved quite useful in this role.

The secret of Saddam's success is the police state he has built. His internal security apparatus is probably the most formidable institution inside Iraq. This is not to say that it is necessarily skillful or intelligent. Although there are some very sophisticated and savvy Iraqi intelligence personnel (particularly in the Mukhabbarat), this is not the rule. Many who have encountered Iraq's security services have found them surprisingly crude, clumsy, and ignorant, even stupid. But the genius is in their organization and their all-encompassing writ. If you have every organization in Iraq penetrated, if you have every Iraqi citizen so terrified that he or she believes that every word he or she utters is heard by the security services, and if you are willing to kill or torture every member of Iraqi society to find the information you seek, you can be just as effective as if you had brilliant agents, outstanding tradecraft, and ultrasophisticated technology.

THE RULE OF TERROR

The numerous security services have been the principal instrument that Saddam has used to create a pervasive climate of terror throughout the country, which is the linchpin of Iraqi totalitarianism. Unfortunately, it is difficult to convey a full sense of this terror in only a little space.[13] In April 2002, the U.N. Commission on Human Rights adopted a resolution condemning "the systematic, widespread and extremely grave violations of human rights and of international humanitarian law by the Government of Iraq, resulting in an all-pervasive repression and oppression sustained by broad-based discrimination and widespread terror; the repression faced by any kind of opposition, in particular the harassment and intimidation of and threats against Iraqi opponents living abroad and members of their families; summary and arbitrary executions, including political killings and the continued so-called clean-out of prisons, the use of rape as a political tool, as well as enforced or involuntary disappearances, routinely practised arbitrary arrests and detention, and consistent and routine failure to respect due process and the rule of law; [and] widespread, systematic torture and the maintaining of decrees prescribing cruel and inhuman punishment as a penalty for offences."[14] A more tactile sense is provided by John Sweeney, a veteran foreign correspondent for the BBC, who had this to say: "I have been to Baghdad a number of times. Being in Iraq is like creeping around inside someone else's migraine. The fear is so omnipresent you could almost eat it. No one talks."[15]

Max Van der Stoel, the former United Nations special rapporteur for human rights in Iraq, told the United Nations that the brutality of the Iraqi regime was "of an exceptionally grave character—so grave that it has few parallels in the years that have passed since the Second World War."[16] Indeed, it is to comparisons with the obscenity of the Holocaust and Stalin's mass murders that observers are inevitably drawn when confronted with the horrors of Saddam's Iraq. Saddamist Iraq is a state that employs arbitrary execution, imprisonment, and torture on a comprehensive and routine basis. A full catalogue of the regime's methods of torture is not available. Suffice to say that based on voluminous accounts of witnesses and victims, the list is very, very long. In some ways, to try to name all of its practices would detract from the regime's monstrosity.[17] A few examples, however, are useful.

This is a regime that will gouge out the eyes of children to force confessions from their parents and grandparents. This is a regime that will crush all of the bones in the feet of a two-year old-girl to force her mother to divulge her father's whereabouts. This is a regime that will hold a nursing baby at arm's length from its mother and allow the child to starve to death to force the mother to confess. This is a regime that will burn a person's limbs off to force him to confess or comply. This is a regime that will slowly lower its victims into huge vats of acid, either to break their will or simply as a means of execution. This is a regime that applies electric shocks to the bodies of its victims, particularly their genitals, with great creativity. This is a regime that in 2000 decreed that the crime of criticizing the regime (which can be as harmless as suggesting that Saddam's clothing does not match) would be punished by cutting out the offender's tongue. This is a regime that practices systematic rape against its female victims. This is a regime that will drag in a man's wife, daughter, or other female relative and repeatedly rape her in front of him. This is a regime that will force a white-hot metal rod into a person's anus or other orifices. This is a regime that employs thalium poisoning, widely considered one of the most excruciating ways to die. This is a regime that will behead a young mother in the street in front of her house and children because her husband was suspected of opposing the regime. This is a regime that used chemical warfare on its own Kurdish citizens—not just on the fifteen thousand killed and maimed at Halabja but on scores of other villages all across Kurdistan. This is a regime that tested chemical and biological warfare agents on Iranian prisoners of war, using the POWs in controlled experiments to determine the best ways to disperse the agents to inflict the greatest damage.

This is the fate that awaits thousands of Iraqis each year. The roughest estimates are that over the last twenty years more than two hundred thousand people have disappeared into Saddam's prison system, never to be heard from again. Hundreds of thousands of others were taken away and, after unforgettable bouts of torture that left them psychologically and often physically mangled, eventually were released or escaped.[18] To give a sense of scale, just the numbers of Iraqis never heard from again would be equivalent to about 2.5 million Americans suffering such a fate.

As terrifying as this is, so too is the ease with which an Iraqi can realize such a fate. It is not only the regime's political opponents who face these most terrifying measures. Torture is not a method of last resort in Iraq, it is often the method of first resort. When an Iraqi is brought in by one of the security services for a whole range of issues—many of them seemingly minor offenses such as accidentally defacing an image of the president—the regime's agents, particularly the Amn, often *start* by torturing the person before deciding what to do with him or her. Moreover, many people are brought in by the security services by mistake—their name was similar to that of someone the regime was looking for, they had an incidental conversation with someone the regime suspected, in a moment of anger or frustration they said something that was construed as anti-Saddam, they were at the wrong place at the wrong time—and it is only after lengthy torture and/or execution that the regime realizes its mistake. (It goes without saying that there is never an apology or restitution in such cases.) Two Iraqi soccer players who have defected since 1999 have reported that Udayy Saddam routinely had Iraqi athletes beaten and tortured for losing international matches.[19]

The regime is always watching. It has legions of regular informants who are rewarded for reporting suspicious activities. There are rewards for anyone who reports on someone else's antiregime activities and penalties for those who don't report such activity. Children are encouraged to inform on their parents and publicly rewarded for doing so. The regime bugs and listens to a wide range of communications media and locales. Most Iraqis, especially Baghdadis, automatically assume that everything they say in public will be heard by the regime. Even in private, many Iraqis are wary of expressing any political views for fear that the regime is listening or that a member of their household will inform on them. Iraqis have learned to adapt and survive in this Orwellian nightmare, but they live their lives on a tightrope, knowing that the slightest misstep could plunge them into a vat of acid—figuratively or literally.

As a final example of the lengths to which the regime is willing to go to ensure its control, beginning in 1992, Baghdad began a systematic effort to drain the Hawizeh, Hawr al-Hammar, and al-Amarah marshes in southern Iraq. These marshes had become a sanctuary for the army deserters and Shi'ite rebels who had mounted an insurgency against the regime after their defeat during the 1991 *intifadah*. Iraq built a massive system of canals to divert the waters of the Euphrates that feed these marshes. By late 1993, the regime had dried more than 4,500 square kilometers of wetlands, roughly 90 percent of the marshes. Iraqi soldiers were ordered to burn the villages and poison the water in what little remained. In so doing, they created an ecological catastrophe and destroyed the way of life of several hundred thousand Marsh Arabs who had made their homes among the rushes and reeds for more than a millennium.[20] Like the slaughter and forced deportation of hundreds of thousands of Kurds during the 1970s and '80s, this is just another example of the cruelty of the regime. Given Saddam's willingness to obliterate entire peoples and societies without a second thought, what chance does the average Iraqi have of happiness in what Kanan Makiya has aptly called "the Republic of Fear"?

THE SUFFERING OF THE IRAQI PEOPLE

Since the Gulf War, another misery has been added to those heaped on the Iraqi citizenry, that of disease and privation. There is no question that the Iraqi people are worse off today than they were before the Gulf War. Many innocent Iraqis, particularly children, have died since 1991. Many others have been crippled, malnourished, deprived of an education, a career, a family. Many Iraqis' lives have been twisted in innumerable ways over the last dozen years.

There is no single cause of this humanitarian disaster. The Iraqi regime is the principal culprit in that its actions and policy decisions caused much—probably most—of the dislocations that produced the disaster. However, the ill-designed U.N. sanctions are also culpable, if only indirectly, because they created the circumstances that allowed the Iraqi regime to make the decisions it did—decisions it was bound to make. When the sanctions were established in 1990, they were based on the flawed assumptions that either Saddam would be quickly overthrown or that the level of pressure they exerted would be so enormous that Baghdad would have to comply lest its economy and society collapse and its people perish. It never seems to have occurred to anyone at the time that the regime would simply choose to allow its people to perish.

When peering into these issues, there are several points to bear in mind. First, it is important to keep the scale of human suffering in Iraq in perspective. Although numerous groups and personages have constantly issued dire warnings, there has been no mass starvation such as that which wiped out 50 percent of Somalia's children in the single year of 1992, that killed one million Ethiopians in 1984–85, or that has killed as many as 2.8 million North Koreans since 1995.[21] There has been no catastrophic outbreak of disease, such as that which has killed more than 2 million people in the Congo in the last four years. Indeed, far, far more people have died as a result of AIDS in Kenya and Ethiopia since 1991 than have died of disease or starvation in Iraq.[22] Nevertheless, Iraq is also not the country it once was. Before the Gulf War, the Iraqi people were, by regional standards, well educated, well fed, and reasonably healthy. During the early 1990s, Iraq fell from the ranks of a moderately well developed third-world nation to a relatively poor third-world nation, and that sudden fall has had a profound impact on the Iraqi people. What's more, unlike AIDS or famine in Africa, the humanitarian crisis in Iraq was entirely man-made, the result of actions taken by the government of Iraq and the United Nations, which knew that its actions could have an adverse impact on the Iraqi people.

The second point to keep in mind is that our information about problems in Iraq is very sketchy. The only entity that can get, or allow others to get, accurate information about the status of the Iraqi people is the Iraqi regime, and it isn't interested. Baghdad has allowed a small number of international groups to conduct limited surveys, but even these cannot claim to present an accurate portrait of the whole population. The Iraqi government doesn't much like even sympathetic aid groups conducting studies because Baghdad is simply making up numbers to suit its political needs and it doesn't like being contradicted by outside sources. As just one example of Iraq's cavalier manipulation of the facts, Baghdad keeps changing the numbers of children it claims are dying on a monthly basis with little rhyme or reason: in late 1997, it was claiming that 12,000 children were dying per month, but when UNICEF published a lower number (itself based on Iraqi government figures), it cut its claim to 5,000 per month in 1998, only to suddenly up the number again to 7,000 per month in 1999 (which was after the oil-for-food program had begun to ameliorate the health problems in the country).[23] None of these numbers has any basis in fact. They are simply made up by the Iraqi government. What's more, many international organizations and aid groups, including the World Health Organization and the U.N. Food and Agriculture Organization, regurgitate these Iraqi numbers or make up their own by applying an arbitrary discount to the fabricated Iraqi numbers.

A third point is that the humanitarian disaster in Iraq in the 1990s was not unprecedented. Similar problems, albeit not so severe or widespread, occurred toward the end of the Iran-Iraq War. A study conducted by UNICEF and Tufts University immediately after the Gulf War found considerable evidence of preexisting malnutrition among Iraqi children as a result of that prior era of neglect.[24] One Iraqi who lived through that war wrote of the situation in 1987 that "The fact was that Saddam was incalculably cruel. Thousands of men were dying weekly at the front, but their widows were waiting a year or more for death certificates that would allow them to collect their benefits. Hospitals and pharmacies were running out of basic medicines, including those for heart ailments and diabetes, while no one could leave for medical care abroad. The quality and availability of basic foodstuffs were dramatically declining; at the same time, officials . . . were importing millions of dollars' worth of luxury furniture."[25] The main difference is that at that time Saddam was determined to keep these hardships hidden from the rest of the world (indeed, to a great extent, from the rest of the Iraqi people) because he was trying to project an image of a strong, prosperous Iraq, whereas today the regime is determined to exacerbate and exaggerate the extent of the problems.

The Course of the Humanitarian Disaster

When the comprehensive U.N. sanctions were imposed in August 1990, Iraq was in the curious position of being well equipped to withstand short-term deprivation but highly vulnerable to a longer-term disruption. The Iraqi regime was distrustful of foreigners and had suffered occasional embargoes by foreign suppliers. As a result, it had built up enormous stockpiles of all manner of goods, including food—far larger than was known at the time. In addition to its known overseas assets (all of which were frozen), Iraq also had as much as $30 billion in hidden assets held by Iraqi front companies in places the United States has not been able to locate even today.[26] On top of this, Iraq had systematically looted Kuwait of everything that wasn't nailed down, further increasing the supply of available goods.

However, Iraqi society could not subsist on these assets forever, and its economy had been badly mismanaged over the previous thirty years. Iraq had taken its windfall oil profits from the 1970s and 1980s and, rather than investing them in agriculture, commercial infrastructure, and basic manufacturing, had instead used them to build a massive military machine and import everything it needed from the outside world. As a result, Iraq's agriculture sector had withered because it could not compete with imported food. For instance, Iraq was self-sufficient in wheat production in the 1960s but by the 1980s was importing 2 million tons per year—four times domestic production.[27] There was no meaningful investment in industry, with the result that in 1990 the industrial sector accounted for only 10 percent of GDP.[28] These policies in turn prompted a major migration from rural areas to the cities, whose populations were heavily dependent on imported food, as well as government-supplied water, power, and sanitation. Likewise, the Iraqi medical system became heavily dependent on imported medical supplies and equipment and even Western medical personnel. Last, the government's policies made it the country's largest employer by far and the employer of last resort, producing a large class of civil servants dependent on government revenues for their livelihood.[29]

In the immediate aftermath of the Gulf War, the humanitarian situation was somewhat mixed. The war, and especially the *intifadah* that followed, had caused extensive damage—adding to the damage from the Iran-Iraq War that still had not been fully repaired. For instance, many schools suffered badly during the *intifadah* because the government was using them to store luxury items looted from Kuwait and the rebels took to burning them. Many hospitals in southern Iraq were also gutted during the *intifadah,* and then the sanctions made it difficult or impossible to replace the lost equipment. One source estimated at the time that Iraq would require $126 billion to repair all the damage from these three wars.[30] On the other hand, despite fears to the contrary, there was no large-scale starvation, as the preexisting stockpiles coupled with the food taken from Kuwait sufficed. In addition, the government made a determined effort to increase agricultural production, including giving out free fertilizer and diesel fuel for farm equipment and paying greatly inflated prices for food. This caused a rapid increase in farming (40 percent of the labor force by 1995) and food production (a 50 percent increase in wheat production).[31] The first surveys found that problems were being caused not by food shortages but by breakdowns in sanitation and power, which were producing dangerous hygienic conditions (including in hospitals), and a breakdown in water supplies and sanitation.

These in turn were producing outbreaks of disease, particularly diarrheal diseases and acute respiratory infections.[32] Even in these cases, the situation was serious but not yet disastrous, in large part because the government embarked on a massive program of repairs that succeeded in restoring many basic services, often by cannibalization.

Over time, however, the situation worsened. The government's stockpiles began to run out (and were increasingly hoarded for the regime's loyalists), as did the loot from Kuwait. The jury-rigged repairs began to give way, and there was less and less to cannibalize. Hospital care worsened because of power outages, a lack of medical supplies, poor sanitary conditions, and the fact that Iraq's Western-trained medical personnel were often inadequately prepared to help their patients without advanced drugs and medical equipment. Additional problems also began to crop up. Iraq's health care system was highly centralized and bureaucratized and lacked the flexibility to cope with sudden, large-scale problems. Furthermore, Iraq relied excessively on curative treatment and paid little attention to preventive care, creating additional problems when the medicines and equipment needed for cures disappeared. The regime insisted on trying to return to pre–Gulf War procedures rather than adapting to its new circumstances, with the result that the public suffered. For instance, there was no public education campaign to encourage people to boil water for drinking and cooking.[33]

By 1994–95, the situation in Iraq had become very serious, creating the internal problems that prompted Saddam to threaten Kuwait in 1994, provoke a showdown with UNSCOM in 1995, attack Arbil, and then accept UNSCR 986 in 1996. The United Nations reported that increased electrical outages, coupled with shortages of spare parts for vehicles, were having a severe impact on hospitals, water supply, and sanitation facilities. "From 1994 onwards, aid agencies noted a marked decline in overall health and welfare conditions," wrote Sarah Graham-Brown.[34] Nevertheless, the situation did largely begin to turn around with Iraq's acceptance of the oil-for-food deal, which has produced a significant improvement in the quality of life since 1997 (see below).

Health Problems

The best-known problems Iraq has encountered since 1990 have been health related. Although there has been no mass starvation, there has been widespread malnutrition. Even here it is hard to say how much worse the situation is beyond the preexisting levels of malnutrition found by the Tufts/UNICEF study, but there is general agreement that it is worse and probably considerably worse. Before the Gulf War, average kilocalorie consumption (the standard measure for the adequacy of a population's diet) in Iraq was 3,200. This is actually on the high side, and obesity in some parts of the population had become as much of a problem as malnutrition in others. During 1993–96, the worst period of Iraq's humanitarian crisis, this dropped to 2,250 kilocalories per day, which is just below the United Nations' target level of 2,400 kilocalories per day. But this does not tell the whole story. First, it represents a significant (25 percent) drop in average calorie consumption, and a sudden drop of this magnitude will invariably play havoc with any population. Second, this is the average across the entire population, and what it fails to reveal is that for some sectors of the Iraqi population the drop took them well below subsistence level, producing malnutrition and starvation. In particular, the Iraqi government provided food rations to the public that up until 1996 provided only about 1,300 kilocalories per day.[35] For many people, especially the very poor and especially the Shi'ah, the rations represented most, or even all, of the food they got each month because they simply did not have the money to pay for supplemental provisions.

Starvation was not more widespread in Iraq for a variety of reasons. The government was able to increase the amount of land under cultivation and the number of people engaged in farming, increasing agricultural production very quickly. In addition, Iraqis called on their families abroad to help, and the Iraqi diaspora responded generously, sending considerable sums of hard currency and goods to their relatives still in Iraq. In addition, from early in the post–Gulf War era Iraqis were able to smuggle food through Jordan, Turkey, Iran, Kuwait, and the GCC states. Although much of this went to line the pockets of smugglers, it meant that more goods were available than was otherwise the case, but they were largely in the hands of monopolies of one kind or another.[36] For many Iraqis, the impact was a badly distorted economy rather than complete collapse. As an example, in her diary of life in Baghdad during the embargo, Nuha al-Radi talks about a friend of hers who was forced to blow her nose on the old dress of one of her daughter's dolls, but the same friend "spends at least 200 dinars a day on cigarettes."[37]

By and large, disease has been a much bigger and more lethal problem than malnutrition. International organizations and aid agencies have consistently found that diarrheal and respiratory illnesses were the biggest killers in Iraq. Here the problems were the lack of medical supplies and working medical equipment, inadequate or unstable energy supplies, contaminated water, inadequate sanitation, inadequate transportation, and unsanitary medical conditions.[38] Moreover, these are categories in which the sanctions themselves were far more culpable, since they did specifically forbid the import of the transportation and heavy machinery necessary to keep sewage treatment plants, pumping stations, and the like functioning, which were only recently recognized as humanitarian needs. It is also the case, however, that the regime had considerable transportation assets available to it (certainly through 1995), which it chose to preserve for the armed forces and security services, rather than employing them to meet civilian needs.

The Breakdown of the Iraqi Economy

Since 1991, the Iraqi economy has not collapsed, but it has been severely damaged. The economy that Baghdad built in the 1970s and '80s was artificial and distorted. Over the long term, it would have encountered problems regardless of other factors. Nevertheless, this economy was functional and met the basic needs of most Iraqis, largely because the regime was able to keep feeding it petrodollars. As a result of the embargo and the regime's response to it, Iraq's artificial economy deflated.

Iraq's economy prior to the Gulf War was largely based on consumption—almost entirely of imports—and kept afloat by Iraq's massive oil revenues. When the sanctions shut off that oil revenue, the regime did not make much of an effort to change its ways.[39] Although defense spending dropped from $15 billion in 1989 to roughly $5 billion per year thereafter (and to about $2 billion by 1999), this was still an extremely high figure given both Iraq's circumstances and the funds available to the regime. In addition, Baghdad embarked upon a series of costly projects to build victory monuments and palaces for Saddam (fifty of them at last count), which cost Iraq as much as another $2.5 billion per year.[40] Much of this represented hard-currency expenditures, including illegal imports and payments to the regime's loyalists in dollars. In addition, the Iraqis were also spending about $1 billion on food imports each year,[41] this at a time when Iraq's export earnings were less than $300 million per year. Iraq's profligate spending spread into other areas as well. For example, the government paid exorbitant prices for locally grown cereals to try to encourage an increase in domestic agriculture. Because it no longer had oil revenues to pay for these expenditures, the government instead began printing money, creating the near hyperinflation of the mid-1990s.[42]

In many ways, this inflation was the real source of the problem in Iraq. Between the inflation, corruption, and monopolies, plus the dependence of so many Iraqis on government jobs (whose wages rarely kept pace with prices), it became difficult for average Iraqis to afford the food, medicine, and other basic supplies they needed. This, not the quantity of food available, was what created difficulties for most Iraqis. As Sarah Graham-Brown concluded in her outstanding study of the sanctions, "For ordinary Iraqis, prices, rather than shortages, have been the main problem since 1991. Most products—food, luxury goods, medications, even pumps and spare parts—have been available on the open market, but few can afford them."[43]

Another major difficulty was unemployment. Iraq had an unemployment problem before the Gulf War, which was one of the predicaments Saddam believed he could escape from by invading Kuwait. This situation was exacerbated by the embargo and the regime's response to it after the war. At the most basic level, the sanctions shut down large numbers of businesses for lack of any inputs—goods to be sold in stores, materials to be used in manufacturing. Those that still survived were forced to fire employees to cope with the general economic downturn. In addition, the government eventually recognized that it would have to rein in some of its spending. Initially, it did so by "releasing" about 500,000 soldiers who had deserted during Operation Desert Storm and the *intifadah*. However, since these men were not drawing salaries, the actual savings were minimal. Later, as the economic situation continued to deteriorate, rather than cut weapons programs and luxury construction spending, the regime began to demobilize military personnel and fire civil servants. Moreover, many of those who were demobilized were disabled or had no job skills, having been drafted before they could acquire them and then kept in the military for a decade or more. The result was even greater unemployment.[44]

Inflation, unemployment, the regime's foolish practices, and the sanctions themselves have produced other problems. Crime has increased dramatically—car theft for men and prostitution for women have become the illegal occupations of choice. The economy's deterioration has produced a significant widening of the income gap between rich and poor. The rich have done fine because they had significant amounts of wealth in hard currency, often outside the country, that actually increased their purchasing power in Iraq as a result of the inflation. Likewise, a class of fabulously wealthy *nouveaux riches* has arisen among those engaged in smuggling, virtually all of whom are connected to the regime. However, the middle class has been wiped out. Civil servants have been financially crippled because their salaries in particular have not kept pace with inflation. Professionals—engineers, doctors, and professors—cannot afford to live on their salaries. Most have been forced to liquidate their savings and sell whatever assets they had just to pay for groceries. Many have quit their jobs to become manual laborers or taxi drivers, or to take other blue-collar work that pays much better than their former white-collar jobs; taxi drivers were making roughly 130 times more than engineers in the mid-1990s.[45]

Another casualty of the post–Gulf War era has been Iraq's educational system. Many schools were destroyed during the *intifadah*. Although Iraq was never prohibited from importing school supplies under the sanctions, as with food and medicine, until December 1996, the regime chose not to take advantage of the mechanisms the United Nations created to import these items. As a result, there were few school supplies available. More problematic still, there were no teachers. Schoolteachers and professors were one of the largest sectors of the economy who found they simply could not survive on their salaries and so either tried to flee the country or found other employment. Those who remained in the schools mostly had to take second and even third jobs, with a corresponding decrease in their ability to teach. Likewise, many parents, especially in rural areas, stopped sending their children to school because they were needed to work or find food and because the costs of clothing, transportation, and school supplies were too high. As a result, the number of school-age children in school fell from 94 percent in 1991 to 75 percent in 1997—not catastrophic, but a marked decline.[46]

The Regime's Culpability

It is important to remember that Saddam and his cronies were the most important element in Iraq's humanitarian disaster. As the United States repeatedly intoned throughout the post–Gulf War era, Saddam always had it in his power to have the sanctions lifted by simply agreeing to give up his WMD programs. However, even beyond that, through a combination of purposeful cruelty, stupidity, shortsightedness, and depraved indifference, the regime played a major role in increasing the misery of its people.[47]

From the beginning, the regime has distributed the resources available to it selectively, rewarding its loyalists and depriving those it considers its opponents—and everyone in Iraq falls into one of those categories. The regime's security services, Ba'th Party members, and the regime's protection forces have gotten bigger and more frequent pay raises than other government employees. They have received larger rations and better-quality food, and have had their rations delivered rather than having to wait on very long lines. They have had access to state stores that sold nonration items at subsidized prices. Many, including the Special Republican Guard and the Republican Guard, have reportedly been paid in dollars to insulate them against inflation.[48] Indeed, similar perks were extended to some extent throughout Iraq's Sunni heartland. The United Nations has reported that "The central cities of Iraq, especially Tikrit, Samarra, and parts of Baghdad, continue to enjoy privileges in the distribution of limited resources. . . . Among social groups of Iraqi society, certain groups remain privileged by comparison with others, e.g., the military and Ba'th party elite."[49]

By the same token, specific segments of Iraq were deliberately kept in abject misery. This may have been strategically motivated, either to prevent revolts (revolutions are historically uncommon among populations living at subsistence levels) or to maintain large groups in desolation to aid Baghdad's propaganda efforts. Alternatively, it may simply have been a byproduct of the regime ruthlessly focusing Iraq's remaining resources on Saddam's loyalists. Probably all of these factors played some role. Whatever the reason, the impact was significant. Entire groups of people, such as the Marsh Arabs, were denied ration cards to try to starve them into submission. The regime deliberately closed hospitals and refused to rebuild others in parts of the country considered particularly resistant to its rule.[50] Overall, it was Iraq's Shi'ah that bore the worst of these measures, as reflected in a variety of statistical indicators, including the highest child mortality rates and the highest numbers of underweight children.[51] As the crowning indignity, during the drought of 1999, the regime diverted water from the Shi'ite south to the Sunni west.[52]

The regime further took advantage of the vulnerability of its people to make money. Smuggling and hoarding became commonplace. Even lower-level regime officials used their access and connections to buy goods that they could resell at a profit on the black market. The regime's highest officials took this corruption to unparalleled heights, using the sanctions as an opportunity to enrich themselves at the expense of the Iraqi people.[53] In July 1999, *Forbes* magazine estimated Saddam's personal wealth at $6 billion. Many of the fifty new palaces Saddam has built for himself since the Gulf War have gold-plated faucets and artificial rivers, lakes, and waterfalls that employ pumping equipment that could have been used to address the country's desperate water and sanitation problems.[54] UNSCOM inspectors came across military warehouses filled with medicine.[55] According to Khidhir Hamza, a senior Iraqi nuclear scientist who fled Iraq in 1994, "The shortages guaranteed corruption. Under Uday's direction, merchants began importing molding meat, eggs, and milk and repackaging them as fresh. Baklava was fried in automobile grease instead of oil. Tea was made from sawdust and coloring material. A new type of shortening distributed by the government stuck to the throat and made people sick. . . . Likewise, expired medicines were repackaged and sold as new. Since the price of most drugs was beyond the reach of ordinary Iraqis, however, it hardly mattered. Meanwhile, anesthesia was in such short supply that limbs were being reset and appendixes removed without it. Surgery, in any event, was a gamble: the operating rooms in government hospitals were so contaminated that infection was nearly guaranteed. Only the very rich had access to competent medical care."[56]

The regime also took advantage of the sanctions to extend its control over Iraqi society. Indeed, this is likely to be one of the longest-lasting effects of the sanctions. As a result of the rationing system and later the oil-for-food system, both of which placed distribution of essential supplies in the regime's hands, Baghdad now has far greater control over the lives of its citizens than it ever had before. The ration cards introduced in response to the imposition of sanctions are now vital to the livelihood of the vast majority of Iraqis, as the rations provide roughly three quarters of their monthly calories. The regime has been quick to use this new power to strengthen its grip over the people. The ration system, according to Graham-Brown, "is an effective way of keeping track of the population and its movements—there is now a computerized list of all beneficiaries—and binds people to the state to maintain a minimum level of life, giving them an incentive to conform and to do what they are told. As one refugee with family still in Iraq observed, 'The need to have a ration card is a form of pressure on families to do what the government wants—for example, to go on a demonstration or to vote.' The need to produce a ration card, along with other documents, to gain access to services is an additional form of

pressure."[57] Ration cards need to be approved by the local Ba'th Party official and can be denied for a whole variety of reasons—such as having a de-
serter or refugee in the family. The internal security services routinely
deprive people of ration cards as a means of punishment.[58]

The Impact of Oil-for-Food

The advent of the oil-for-food program in early 1997 has not eradicated all
of Iraq's problems, but it has helped considerably. This is evident in many
ways. By 2000, Iraqi oil exports were on a par with pre–Gulf War figures:
2.2 million barrels per day (compared with 2.6 million in 1989) and $17
billion in revenues (the same as in 1989). By 1997, Iraqi food imports were
higher than prewar levels in terms of dollars allocated.[59] The Iraqi food ration increased from 1,300 kilocalories per day in 1993–95 to 2,030 kilocalories in 1997–98, and then, in 2000, to more than the United Nations'
target level of 2,400 per day.[60] Similarly, by April 1999, UNICEF had
found that oil-for-food had halted the rise in malnutrition problems.[61] This
can also be seen anecdotally. Visitors to Iraq report a construction boom in
the capital as resources pour in. In the mid-1990s, one of Iraq's best-known
shortages was in tires. By 1998, UNSCOM Chairman Richard Butler reported seeing piles of brand-new tires, still in their factory wrapping, piled
up in warehouses along the roads.[62]

Oil-for-food has not been able to eliminate all of the regime's manipu-
lations of Iraqi suffering, but it has thrown some of them into bolder relief.
For example, a UNICEF field survey in July 1999 found that while the
child mortality rate had been allowed to double in the areas of the country
under the regime's control, in Kurdistan, where the oil-for-food program
was run by the United Nations, child mortality had actually been reduced
below pre–Gulf War levels.[63]

The United Nations has invariably had to fight with the regime to get it
to use all of the funds now available to it for food, medicine, and other
civilian supplies—supplies that Baghdad had previously claimed were the
difference between life and death for millions of Iraqis. Iraq has consistently contracted for only a fraction of the amount of humanitarian goods
the oil-for-food program has made available. For example, on January 18,
2001, Benon Sevan, the director of the U.N. Office of the Iraq Program,
complained "I am gravely concerned at the unacceptably slow rates of submission of applications, in particular under the health, education, water,
and sanitation, as well as the oil sectors." At that time, the value of applica-

tions for supplies submitted for the health sector was only $83.6 million, whereas $624 million had been allocated. For oil equipment and spare parts it was $22.7 million applied for versus $600 million allocated. For education, it was $21.58 million applied for versus $351.5 million allocated. For water and sanitation, the figures were $184.76 million applied for versus $551.16 million allocated.[64] Despite the regime's feigned concern for its dying children, the United Nations has constantly had to demand that Iraq buy more nutrient-rich products for young children and pregnant and nursing women.[65] For instance, by September 1999, Iraq had signed contracts worth only $1.7 million out of $25 million allocated for such nutritional supplements.[66] Even when the regime was forced to buy the supplies, it did not always distribute them; in May 1999, for example, Sevan complained that only 48 percent of the medical supplies that had been delivered to Iraq had been distributed and "The government warehouses are literally overflowing."[67] Baby formula sold to Iraq under oil-for-food is being smuggled out of Iraq by regime figures for major profits and now can be found throughout the Gulf region.[68]

How Many Iraqis Have Died Since 1991?

Unfortunately, the answer is: we just don't know. Whatever the answer, it is undoubtedly too many. That said, there are a number of things that we do know and that are worth saying.

First, however many people have died, the numbers that the Iraqi regime is disseminating—and that many well-meaning people and even U.N. agencies are recirculating—are clearly wrong.[69] Iraq's claims are grossly contradicted by the regime's own demographic data. In 1997, the Iraqi regime conducted a census, and two years later it released the data. The report stated that Iraq's population had increased from 16.5 million in 1987 to 22 million in 1997. Baghdad also claimed that had it not been for the U.N. sanctions, the population figure would have been 23.5 million but that 1.5 million people (1 million of them children) had died prematurely as a result of sanctions. Although this was the headline of the census, all of the other numbers in it controverted this lurid claim. The census figures indicate a population growth rate of 33 percent over ten years, a very high rate of population growth by itself. If one were to add back the 1.5 million people who Iraq claims died prematurely (and the 500,000 who fled the country during the same period), it would produce a ten-year growth rate of 45 percent—which is phenomenal and would have put Iraq among the fastest-growing populations in the world. However, Iraq was not known to be one of the fastest-growing populations in the world prior to the Gulf War. In fact, its population growth rate was about average for the region and was actually slowing down.

Amatzia Baram has demonstrated that the Iraqi figures themselves belie the assertions of the regime. For example, the census figures show Iraqi population growth rates remaining stable over the last thirty years, and the decrease in population growth rates the regime claims was produced by the sanctions would not have been big enough to create the actual population increase had 1.5 million people actually died. Thus, the census figures for population growth by themselves indicate that the Iraqi claims as to deaths from sanctions are significantly inflated.[70] To explain this discrepancy, Baghdad claims that there was a quantum leap in Iraq's birthrate in 1991–97, which not only offset the deaths but produced the growth. Interestingly, the census does not present any data to support this contention. Demographically, it is highly unlikely that there would have been such a sudden, massive increase in the birthrate. Moreover, in times of war and strife it is normal to see a *decrease* in the birthrate because men are not at home. Also, Iraq had achieved significant gains in the education of women prior to the Gulf War, which invariably produce lower birth and fertility rates.[71] In fact, previous data from the regime indicated that both the population growth rate and the birthrates had begun to decline in the 1980s, indicating that Iraq was not an exception to this rule. According to unofficial U.N. statistics, Iraq's birthrate continued to decline right through 1997. At the very least, the United Nations found no evidence of the enormous increase in birthrate that Baghdad claimed and that would have been necessary to account for such a large population growth despite so many claimed deaths.[72]

If the ludicrous assertions of the Iraqi regime are clearly false, it still leaves unanswered the question of how many Iraqis truly have died. Unfortunately, all that we have is a good guess. At present, the most comprehensive, thorough, and sensitive analysis has been conducted by Richard Garfield of Columbia University. Garfield's research was exhaustive, and his methodology is the current gold standard. Based on this work, Garfield concluded that between August 1990 and March 1998, anywhere from 106,000 to 227,000 Iraqi children under the age of five died as a result of the war, the *intifadah,* and its aftermath. Garfield suggests that the number is probably closer to the high end of that scale but that roughly 25 percent of those who died were killed during the Gulf War and the *intifadah.*[73]

Since Garfield also estimates that 1,000 to 5,000 Iraqi civilians died during the Gulf War, the vast majority of the children under the age of five killed in combat were therefore probably killed in the *intifadah*—an estimate that squares with the numerous accounts of the brutality of Saddam's forces and their slaughter of women and children in suppressing the revolts.[74]

So the best estimate we have is that roughly 135,000 to 150,000 Iraqi children died in the first seven years after the war. If the regime is right that children under the age of five constituted roughly two thirds of the total dead (which there is no particular reason to believe, given the regime's track record, but it looks at first blush to be a reasonable guess), then 200,000 to 225,000 Iraqis may have died prematurely during that period. Since that was the period of maximum hardship, the number today is probably not much higher. Regardless of whether one blames these deaths mostly on the sanctions or mostly on the regime's manipulation of and reaction to the sanctions, this is still a very heavy cost. Given that the Gulf War itself probably caused no more than 10,000 to 30,000 Iraqi military casualties and another 1,000 to 5,000 civilian casualties, it raises the question of whether full-scale combat is a more humane policy than draconian sanctions.

Might Things Have Been Different?

A government that cared about its people and placed the well-being of its citizens first, one that was less obsessed with its military capabilities and preserving the power and perks of a small number, might have handled the crisis differently. For example, after the Gulf War, a different government might have drastically cut military spending and eschewed palace building altogether. This might have reduced the roughly $7.5 billion Iraq spent annually on its military and Saddam's building projects to perhaps $1.5 billion. (After all, one cannot expect Iraq to have cut all such spending—it did go to providing jobs for hundreds of thousands of military personnel and construction workers.) Iraq might then have spent only half of the remaining $6 billion (to keep down inflation) on food, medicine, and other humanitarian supplies permitted by the U.N. sanctions. Since prior to the Gulf War Iraq imported $2 billion to $3 billion worth of food and $500 million worth of medicine, this extra $3 billion, when added to the $1 billion Iraq was already spending on food imports, should have been adequate to cover Iraq's basic humanitarian needs.[75] Iraq could have gone further and accepted the U.N. offer to sell oil under Resolutions 706 and 712, which, if made permanent (which seems highly likely if Iraq had asked for it), would have brought Iraq another $1.8 billion in annual revenues. Altogether, this would have meant that Baghdad would have had available close to $6 billion annually to meet its various humanitarian requirements. At least in theory, this should have been more than enough to provide basic subsistence for the Iraqi population and to make a modest beginning at rebuilding Iraq, starting with its education, water, power, and sanitation sectors—without triggering rampant inflation. Life would not have been pleasant in such a state—as noted above, there were still plenty of direct effects from the sanctions that would have persisted—but Iraq's circumstances would have been far better.

However, such a scenario presupposes an Iraqi regime that would place the well-being of its citizenry above all other considerations. Such an Iraq probably would never have invaded Kuwait in the first place. Such a state would almost certainly have been willing to give up its WMD programs in order to have the sanctions lifted. In short, such a state would never have found itself in the position of enduring twelve years of severe sanctions. Interestingly, this point has led critics of the sanctions to blame the United States and the United Nations for the problems Iraq has experienced since the Gulf War. Their argument is that we should have known that Saddam would never give up his WMD programs to avoid prolonged sanctions, let alone expend scarce resources on his populace rather than his military and his cronies, so that by drastically diminishing the resources available to the regime we were dooming the Iraqi people. It is a truly perverse argument—one that excuses Saddam for his cruelty the way that we would excuse a wolf for killing a sheep because that's just what wolves do and it was our fault for putting a sheep where it was vulnerable to the wolf.

Nevertheless, the argument should not be dismissed out of hand. The fact is that the United States has always held itself to a higher moral standard. In the end, no matter how willing you are to blame the Iraqi regime—and it does deserve the lion's share of the blame—there is still a kernel of truth to this perverse argument: even if only indirectly, the United States and the United Nations put a weapon in the hands of Saddam Hussein, who used it to slaughter another 200,000 of his people. Our guilt may be only indirect, but we cannot be absolved completely. Saddam is not a wolf that kills only for food and must kill to live. He is a murderer and a war criminal. But if you hand an ax to an ax murderer, can you consider yourself blameless when he plants it in someone's back?

THE SHI'AH

Iraq is a majority Shi'ah country, one of only three in the world (Bahrain and Iran are the other two). Roughly 60 percent of the Iraqi population are Shi'ite Arabs who live mainly in southern Iraq, in the heart of ancient Mesopotamia. Baghdad itself has a population that is majority Shi'ite, and the country is home to the most sacred shrines of the Shi'ite faith. Indeed, Shi'ism was born in Iraq. Nevertheless, the Shi'ites may be the most miserable of Iraq's people.

The Shi'ah, or Shi'at 'Ali (the Party of 'Ali), were the followers of 'Ali ibn Abi Talib, the fourth caliph. After the Prophet's death in A.D. 632, 'Ali claimed the mantle of his successor (caliph), but he was shunted aside. Only in 656, after three predecessors, was 'Ali made caliph, but he was assassinated in 661. After 'Ali, the caliphate was again disputed between his son Hassan and Mu'awiyah, the governor of Damascus. In the end, Hassan was persuaded to give up his claim in favor of Mu'awiyah, but the Shi'ah still took him to be the rightful successor. The main school of Shi'ism, "Twelver" Shi'ism, proclaimed 'Ali to be the first imam (prayer leader) and Hassan the second, then followed their lineage down through twelve generations. The Shi'ite imamate, in opposition to the Sunni caliphate, was only the most obvious difference between the two branches. Over time, Shi'ism would develop different interpretations of Islam from the Sunni mainstream.

The Shi'ah have been an underclass throughout Iraq's modern history. The Ottomans were Sunnis who treated the Iraqi Shi'ah with disdain but exercised little control over Baghdad and al-Basrah *vilayet*s by the early twentieth century and so were not an onerous presence for the Shi'ah. The problems began during the British mandate, especially after independence in 1932. The British-imposed king, Faysal, was a Sunni who surrounded himself with other Sunnis. In a pattern that would be repeated to this day, the Sunni Arabs saw the larger population of Shi'ah as a political threat and so monopolized the government. Moreover, they used their control over the levers of power to advance the economic and social interests of their community at the expense of the Shi'ah.

This practice continued with Saddam Hussein's Sunni regime. Although a handful of Shi'ah were given prominent positions as sops to their community, in truth all power was held by the Sunnis. What's more, with the exception of a small number of Shi'ite tribes who backed the regime,

Baghdad tended to see the Shi'ah as threats. As a result, the security services were more oppressive for the Shi'ah, the economic conditions more
stringent, the regime's largesse negligible, and punishments strictly enforced. Although during the Iran-Iraq War the regime conscripted millions
of Shi'ah, they were kept out of sensitive areas within the armed services
(such as military intelligence), and few Shi'ite officers made it to the higher
levels of command. Thus, even before the Gulf War, the Shi'ah had it
worst. Indeed, the situation became so tense that the word "Shi'ah" was effectively banned by the regime.[76]

The Shi'ite revolt during the *intifadah* that followed the Gulf War was
largely a product of Saddam's ruthless exploitation of the Shi'ah. But his
response afterward was simply to repress them even more. The Shi'ah got
the least of the rationed goods under the U.N. embargo. Whatever supplies
were available went to the south last. They were subjected to the worst pri-
vations. The security presence was most pervasive in the south and in the
Shi'ah neighborhoods of Baghdad. After the oil-for-food deal was finally
implemented, the Shi'ah still got the short end of the stick. They were the
groups least likely to receive their proper share of the humanitarian supplies. Their hospitals continued to have the worst shortages. Their infrastructure was the least likely to be repaired. It was the Shi'ah whom Saddam
kept in misery so that there would be plenty of material available for the TV
cameras to back his propaganda claims that the sanctions were creating a
humanitarian crisis. As the findings of the UNICEF survey of malnutrition
by the governorate in Iraq indicated, a disproportionate number of those
who have died or been disfigured since the Gulf War have been Shi'ah.[77]

———

It is a common mistake in the West to see Iraq's Shi'ah as an adjunct of
Shi'ite Iran, artificially attached to Iraq. In fact, the two communities are
very different. The most obvious difference is ethnic: the Iranians are
mostly Persians, and the Iraqis are largely Arab. Not only does this create
deep cultural differences, but the two ethnicities have millennia of distrust
and warfare between them. Nor should the unifying value of religion be exaggerated. The Shi'ism of southern Iraq is fundamentally different from
that of Iran in many respects. While Iran converted to Shi'ism starting in
the sixteenth century, in Iraq the growth of Shi'ism came as Iraq's nomadic
tribes became settled largely in the nineteenth century and so gave up their
primitive version of Islam for the more fully developed Shi'ism of an-Najaf

and Karbala. As a result, Iraqi Shi'ism bears the heavy stamp of Iraqi tribal society, while Iranian Shi'ism is typically Persian.

Some Iraqi Shi'ite opposition groups have looked to Iran for support. Any opposition group must have a patron, and Iran was always the obvious choice because of the religious ties and the implacable rivalry between Iran and Iraq. It is also true that some of these opposition groups have desired to establish a theocratic Shi'ite state in Iraq, possibly along the lines of Khomeini's regime in Iran. But the best estimates are that these represent a small minority (10 to 15 percent) of the Shi'ite population, and it is a far cry from that to suggest that this is what the Shi'ah of Iraq as a whole want. Even among the opposition groups, many have a very unhappy relationship with Tehran. The Supreme Assembly for the Islamic Revolution in Iraq (SAIRI), the largest and most important of the Iraqi Shi'ite opposition groups, has a very uneasy relationship with Tehran—it distrusts the Iranians and the Iranians distrust it. Tehran keeps it on a short leash, providing only enough resources to make it a nuisance to Saddam, never enough to launch a full-scale insurgency. Leaders within the SAIRI have actively tried to broker a better relationship with the United States as a counterweight to Iran.

The Shi'ah are not looking to split off from Iraq and form their own separate state, let along merge with Iran. Instead, what they want is fair representation in a new government in Iraq. Beginning in the 1920s and '30s, Iraq's Shi'ah have consistently agitated for a more equitable distribution of power. Indeed, today, the Shi'ah are probably the greatest advocates of democracy in Iraq. They do not want to split off from Iraq; they simply want their fair share of political power. This was made most clear during the Iran-Iraq War, when the Shi'ah made up the vast bulk of the Iraqi Army, particularly its frontline infantry formations. They fought with great determination against the Iranians—against the ayatollah and his aim of "liberating" Iraq's Shi'ah and creating a Shi'ite theocracy in Iraq. There were remarkably few cases of Iraqi Shi'ite soldiers refusing to fight or defecting to Iran because they sympathized with the Iranians. Several thousand Iraqi Shi'ite prisoners of war did eventually switch their allegiance to Iran, but this is another matter entirely that could have been the product of numerous other factors—having no desire to return to Saddam's police state, for example.[78] This is in marked contrast to the Kurds, who joined with the Iranians in opposing the Iraqi state during the Iran-Iraq War. In the words of Ofra Bengio, "The Shi'a have never challenged the territorial integrity of the state and their main demands have revolved around their inadequate representation in Iraq's political system. Further, not since the crushing of Shi'a tribal rebellions in the 1930s has a serious religious or political movement emerged among the Shi'a to press for such demands."[79]

Under the wrong set of circumstances, it is conceivable that this long-standing position might change and Iraq's Shi'ah might suddenly find that they prefer a separate state or even union with Iran. But this seems very unlikely. More likely, they will continue to fight on, accepting support from whatever quarter will provide it and hoping that at some point they will find an opportunity to install a new government in Baghdad that will not repress them but will instead give them their fair share in the governance of the country.

THE KURDS

The Kurds are a people originally of mixed Semitic and Central Asian ethnicity who primarily adhere to the Sunni Muslim faith. There are more than 25 million Kurds in the world today, the largest nation without a state. The Kurds live mostly in their ancestral lands in southeastern Turkey, northeastern Syria, northern Iraq, northwestern Iran, and parts of the former Soviet Union. The one thing all these lands have in common is mountains, which have always served the Kurds as a defense against the depredations of Syrian, Turkish, Iraqi, and Iranian regimes.[80]

In Iraq, the Kurds constitute roughly 20 percent of the population. Most Iraqi Kurds live in the northeast of the country, in the Zagros Mountains and the cities of Dahuk, Arbil, Mosul, Kirkuk, as-Sulaymaniyyah, and Khanaqin. Of course, several hundred thousand were forcibly resettled by the regime, mostly in southwestern Iraq, during the Anfal and other anti-Kurdish campaigns. In northern Iraq, the Kurds are mostly divided between the two great militia parties of the Kurdish Democratic Party, led by Masud Barzani, and its offshoot, the Patriotic Union of Kurdistan, led by Jalal Talabani.

Of all the people of Iraq, only the Kurds will say that they are better off today, after the Gulf War and the sanctions, than they were before.[81] There are many reasons for this. The first and most obvious one is that they are not being oppressed by Saddam's regime. Whether it is the threat of massive U.S. retaliation should he reoccupy Kurdistan or the realization that doing so will bog down the Iraqi Army in guerrilla warfare, as has been the case for the past four decades, or probably both, since 1991 Saddam has stayed out of the north and allowed the Kurds to govern themselves. After the genocidal campaigns of his regime in the 1980s, this absence alone constitutes an enormous advance in the situation of the Kurds.

Although the Kurds started worse off than many Iraqis as a result of three decades of war and oppression, they have done well under the oil-for-food system. The population of the three Kurdish governorates constitutes about 18 percent of the total Iraqi population, but the oil-for-food system grants them 13 percent of all Iraqi oil revenues. The other 82 percent of the population gets only 59 percent of this revenue (changed in December 2000 from 53 percent), because 3 percent goes to pay for the U.N. programs and 25 percent goes to compensate the victims of Saddam's aggression. Thus, Kurdistan gets slightly more per capita than the rest of the country. Of more importance, the Kurds have been able to develop extensive trading networks with Iran, Turkey, Syria, and central Iraq that have greatly benefited them. Barzani's KDP also makes about $500,000 per day from the smuggling it allows to cross its lands into Turkey. This is only likely to increase in the future, as the Turks are talking about opening a second crossing point to try to nearly double the amount of smuggling. Kurdistan's well-watered mountain valleys make ideal farmlands. Because of the regime's oppressive policies during the 1960s, '70s, and '80s, the Kurds were never able to rely on food imports like the rest of the country; thus agriculture remained an important element of the local Kurdish economy. Consequently, the sanctions did not have the same impact on the Kurds, who had a much larger agricultural sector they could rely on. Moreover, unlike the territories under the regime's control, the Kurds welcomed nongovernmental organizations, which brought in much needed food and medical supplies, especially during the worst moments of the early 1990s. Finally, unlike the areas under the regime's control, the Kurds have taken full advantage of the oil-for-food system, allowing the United Nations and international aid organizations to run the program and operate freely in their territory. Indeed, by 1998, the United Nations admitted that there was actually an oversupply of food in northern Iraq.[82] As a result, health standards among the Kurds have improved considerably since the Gulf War.

Today, Iraqi Kurdistan is thriving. Its economy is booming from trade, smuggling, agriculture, and even nascent industry. Politically, the region is also flourishing. Although the PUK and KDP have not patched up their differences, the experiences of 1994–96 have taught them that only Saddam can gain when they fight. As a result, a grudging "live and let live" sentiment prevails between them. Kurds are the freest residents of Iraq, with the greatest opportunities in education and work.

Nevertheless, they live beneath a Sword of Damocles. They know they lack the military strength to stop the Republican Guard should Saddam decide to invade, and they also know that Saddam is determined to regain control of Kurdistan once it becomes politically viable for him to do so. As a result, the Kurds are desperate to find allies to help them keep Saddam at bay. They cultivate the United States, Iran, and Turkey, the three powers that could potentially help them against Iraq. Even here they are caught in a bind: both Iran and Turkey have Kurdish "problems" of their own and are terrified by the notion of Kurdish independence. The Turks support them only insofar as the Kurds are willing to help Ankara against their brother Kurds—the Kurdish opposition in Turkey. And Iran supports them only to keep Saddam weak. Even the United States is not a perfect backer. Not only is it distant and often aloof (and has stood by while Baghdad massacred their people on at least four occasions since 1970), but the United States is Turkey's NATO ally and Washington is committed to a unified Iraq. Moreover, the United States is dependent on Saudi Arabia and other Gulf states that have shown themselves indifferent to the plight of the Kurds and refused to allow the use of their bases for American air strikes when Saddam attacked Kurdish Arbil in 1996.

These factors account for the Kurds' policies. They recognize that they may currently have the best possible world: de facto independence, relative prosperity, and international aid and support. But they also know that all of this could be swept away tomorrow if the political conditions change and Saddam decides that he can afford to invade. They are desperately working to guarantee that Washington will defend them against Saddam. Although President Clinton effectively declared this in December 1998, stating that any Iraqi attack on the Kurds would trigger the use of American military force, the Kurds cannot be sure. They thought they had guarantees of American military support in 1991 and 1996 as well and were deeply disappointed. For this reason, they also would like to see Saddam's regime gone, but only if it is replaced by a federal democracy that would guarantee Kurdish rights and freedom from oppression. Thus, it is not enough for the Kurds that Saddam be overthrown, because a successor regime could actually be worse for them—another brutal Sunni dictator who was smart enough to abide by all of the U.N. resolutions could have the sanctions quickly lifted and the Americans off his back, leaving him free to reassert control over Kurdistan and terrorize the population, destroying everything the Kurds have built since 1991.[83] For the Kurds, such a cure would be worse than the disease.

FIVE

The Threat

Although Saddam is a daily menace to the people of Iraq, for the United States and the rest of the world, he is a somewhat longer-term threat and probably several years away from being an irremediable danger. This is a matter of both capabilities and intentions. Iraq's conventional armed forces remain weak as a result of their drubbing in the Gulf War and the protracted period under sanctions. Although the oil-for-food deal has allowed Baghdad to begin to revive some parts of its conventional military, it would likely require about five years and the lifting of the military embargo for Iraq to regain even the level of capability it possessed before the Gulf War, let alone move beyond it. Iraq has retained ballistic missiles, as well as chemical and biological warfare munitions. Its current force, however, is probably small and intended principally as a deterrent against efforts to topple the regime by enemies foreign or domestic.

There is little doubt that the Iraqis are continuing to develop chemical, biological, and nuclear weapons, but on the nuclear front, they are still believed to be several years away from having the fissile material needed to make a nuclear weapon. In addition, as long as Iraq is under sanctions, its ability to use any of its WMD as an instrument of its foreign policy (as opposed to a deterrent against overthrow) is limited because their use would obliterate all of Iraq's political efforts to break free of containment. Finally,

Iraq is working to rebuild the terrorism capabilities it let atrophy in the late 1980s and early 1990s. However, Iraqi terrorist operations remain clumsy and unsophisticated so far. In addition, Saddam has shown no inclination to use terrorism against the United States directly—at least not since 1993. As with WMD, he seems to recognize that a terrorist attack on the United States under current circumstances would only give Washington a *casus belli* to employ military force to remove his regime.

Saddam is working assiduously to rebuild and even enhance his military capabilities and has been willing to cripple Iraq's economy and allow large numbers of Iraqi people to die to do so. He also realizes that in 1990 he made the mistake of attacking the United States before he was strong enough. He is determined not to repeat that mistake. He expects another showdown with the United States at some point in the future, and he intends to be much better prepared the next time.

Even in their current weakened state, Iraq's capabilities would pose a significant threat to regional stability if the United States were ever to pull its forces out of the region. Saddam is already supporting various regional terrorist groups against Israel, Iran, and Turkey. Saddam's conventional forces are probably still adequate to overrun Kuwait or Jordan if the United States were unable to intervene to prevent it. Saddam's WMD arsenal could cause great panic, and potentially great damage, if he chose to employ it— which for the moment, seems likely only to defend his regime or if he believes he is doomed. But in truth, it is the combination of Saddam's intentions and his ceaseless efforts to enhance Iraqi capabilities that is most frightening.

SADDAM'S GOALS

Saddam Hussein is a man of grand ambitions. "Saddam's pursuit of power for himself and Iraq is boundless. In fact, in his mind, the destiny of Saddam and Iraq are one and indistinguishable," in the words of Jerrold M. Post, a psychologist who formerly worked for the U.S. intelligence community and has written extensively on Saddam's personality and leadership.[1] Saddam calls himself *al-qa'id ad-darura,* which means "the indispensable leader." The connotation of the title is that he was "meant" to rule Iraq in some kind of eschatological sense.[2] Indeed, Saddam thinks of himself as a great man of history, someone marked to accomplish great deeds. In his vast personality cult he is constantly compared to great figures of Iraq's past. He is the new Nebuchadnezzar, the Babylonian king who conquered biblical Israel, sacked Jerusalem, and took the Jews into captivity. He is al-Mansur, the caliph who built Baghdad and conquered new lands for Islam. He is the new Saladin, the Islamic general who defeated the Crusaders and retook Jerusalem for Islam. In fact, in a book for children about Saladin, Saddam had his image used for the cover painting of the great general. Two thirds of the book is actually about the life of Saddam, whom the book refers to as "Saladin II."[3]

These historical references are crucial to Saddam, who is, by his own admission, obsessed with history and his role in it.[4] He continues to see Iraq as a manifestation of its glorious past, both pagan and Muslim. Thus Saddam regularly employs names and myths from Iraq's past to explain his actions and enrich Iraqi nationalism.[5] He is determined to restore and surpass this glorious past.

Two other of Saddam's self-bestowed appellations also provide clues to his ambitions. He is *al-qa'id al-umma*, "the leader of the Arab nation," and "the man of the long days," *al-ayyam al-tawila*, which, Ofra Bengio points out, really means "the leader of the days of Arab glory."[6] Saddam believes himself destined to be the new leader of the Arabs, and he makes it apparent that this role will be a political-military role, meaning that he will achieve this position through some combination of conquest and acclaim. Addressing a unit of the Republican Guard, Saddam proclaimed that the honor of the Arab nation could not be achieved unless "Iraq's arm reached out [beyond Iraqi territory] to every point in the Arab homeland."[7] He has worked assiduously to make Iraq strong so that it can dominate the region militarily, acquire new territorial prizes, and become the champion of the Arabs.

Saddam has said often and loudly that his goal is to create a new Arab union of some kind, headed by a powerful Iraq, that will be a new superpower.[8] In January 1980, within six months of assuming the presidency, Saddam explained, "We draw a large picture of Iraq. We want Iraq to possess a weight like that of China, a weight like the Soviet Union, a weight like the United States, and that is indeed the factual basis of our actions."[9] Likewise, he has made it clear that he believes that the only way for Iraq to achieve this stature is through the exercise of military power. No great power has ever reached security "without moving along the road of force."[10]

Although it does not appear that Saddam has the same kind of well-formulated plan as Adolf Hitler, it is clear that he does have a set of concrete goals that he has attempted to achieve opportunistically. First, he wants to increase Iraq's wealth and power. He has tried to do this both by building Iraq's industry and military and by attempting to conquer additional territory that will strengthen Iraq—i.e., oil-rich Kuwait and Khuzestan province in Iran. Second, he intends to make Iraq the hegemon of the Persian Gulf. His bids for territorial conquest and the development of Iraqi military power were part of that ambition, but so too was his desire to weaken Iran and to drive the United States out of the Gulf. He believes that if he can strengthen Iraq and make it the Gulf hegemon, this will make it possible for him to become the "leader of the Arab world." Here his goal is far more palpable than the nebulous influence that Gamal 'Abd al-Nasser held when he was president of Egypt. Nasser was adored and admired, but he was not obeyed. In Saddam's vision, Iraq might not rule a vast Arab nation, but it would certainly call the shots in a grand Arab coalition whose members would have to seek his permission before making any major moves and would stand behind Iraq against the rest of the world.

Saddam also nurtures the idea of someday liberating Jerusalem. This does not necessarily seem to be a burning goal—it is not his first priority. But it does seem to be what he believes will eventually be his crowning achievement. He dwells on the issue too frequently for it to be mere rhetoric. It has been a theme of his speeches, of Iraqi politics, and of Iraqi propaganda from the very beginning of his reign up to the present. He constantly justifies his actions based on this ultimate goal. And while it is clear that he often uses this as nothing more than a cover for other motives, it is also the case that whenever he discusses his place in history and the comparisons he makes between himself and great political figures of Iraq's past, the theme of the liberation of Jerusalem pervades his thinking. Indeed, it is perfectly in character that—as the U.N. inspectors learned after the Gulf War—Saddam had predelegated orders to Iraqi Scud units to launch missiles filled with biological and chemical agents at Tel Aviv if the coalition marched on Baghdad.[11] From a military perspective, this makes no sense. The right military approach would have been to use those missiles to threaten the Saudi oil fields or some other high-value target to try to convince the coalition to halt its offensive. But it does accord with his image of himself as an historical figure who will someday, even if it is his final act, use force to rid the Arab world of the Israeli presence.

If Saddam is able to achieve these goals, it will be disastrous for the United States. Indeed, even his pursuit of them has proven a grave threat to

American interests, raising the specter of nuclear exchanges with Israel. It threatens the stability of the vital Persian Gulf region. And it threatens the economic health of the world, because all of the evidence we have suggests that if Saddam controls the Gulf oil fields he will use this power to advance Iraq's political interests, even to the detriment of its economic interests and the world's.

People often ask the rhetorical question "He can't drink the oil, can he?" to suggest that even if a dangerous leader like Saddam were able to gain control of most or all of the Persian Gulf oil fields, he would still sell its oil and therefore the world would be fine. Setting aside the countervailing experience of Khomeini's Iran, the specific evidence we have regarding Saddam is that this is not necessarily the case. Saddam seeks political and military power, not wealth—except insofar as wealth brings political and military power. Iraq's oil wealth has always served his grander geostrategic ambitions. Saddam has repeatedly demonstrated that he is willing to sacrifice Iraq's economy, its society, and the lives of its people to achieve his political goals. Especially over the last five years, he has frequently halted Iraqi oil production to try to blackmail the U.N. Security Council. He has also been willing to sell oil at cut-rate prices to advance his political agenda, regardless of the cost to his economy or people. Likewise, Saddam seems to believe that the Arab oil embargo of 1973 was a great victory—contrary to the views of Saudi Arabia and the vast majority of other Arab states.[12] As recently as April 2002, Saddam shut off all legal Iraqi oil exports to protest Israel's Operation Defensive Shield.[13] If Saddam were ever to control the Gulf region's oil resources, his past record suggests that he would be willing to cut or even halt oil exports altogether whenever it suited him to force concessions from his fellow Arabs, Europe, the United States, or the world as a whole.

Finally, the Gulf War and the confrontation with the United States that followed have given Saddam a new motive and a new goal: vengeance. In the tribal society that made Saddam, revenge is a driving force; not taking revenge is a sign of weakness. Moreover, we have seen Saddam take some tentative steps toward revenge even at this delicate stage—by attempting to assassinate former President Bush and Amir Jabir al-Sabah of Kuwait in 1993. At a more dispassionate level, Saddam has concluded that the United States is the greatest obstacle to achieving his ambitions. He knows now that the United States will never allow him to become the hegemon of the Gulf region, to control its oil resources, or to destroy the state of Israel. This recognition adds to his determination to confront the United States again at some future point.

TERRORISM

Iraq is now, and has been throughout Saddam's reign, a state sponsor of terrorism. However, terrorism is the least of the threats posed by Iraq to the interests of the United States. If the only problem the United States had with Saddam Hussein's regime were its involvement in terrorism, our problems would be relatively mild. On the grand list of state sponsors of terrorism, Iraq is pretty far down—well below Iran, Syria, Pakistan, and others. Similarly, if one were to make a list of all of Saddam Hussein's crimes against humanity, his support for international terrorism would be far down the list, and almost beside the point when compared to his mass murders, horrific torture, use of WMD against civilians, and other atrocities.

Saddam's employment of terrorism stems from a combination of his desire to play a role in the Arab-Israeli conflict—a key to his leadership of the Arab world—and his willingness to use whatever methods are available to advance Iraq's interests. Iraqi support for terrorism has evolved over time. Early on, in the 1970s and early 1980s, Iraq was heavily involved in international terrorism, especially in support of Palestinian groups attacking Israel. From the start, the Ba'thist regime was a staunch backer of the Palestine Liberation Organization (PLO) in its terrorist campaign against Israel. Around 1974, Baghdad had a falling-out with Yasir Arafat after the PLO began to take a more restrained approach (largely at Anwar al-Sadat's insistence). In response, Iraq began supporting the Abu Nidal Organization (ANO) and other radical Palestinian rejectionist groups that were fighting Arafat as much as or more than they were fighting Israel. Indeed, it appears that for Saddam this was more a struggle with Egypt for control over the Palestinian movement than it was about policy toward Israel.[14]

In 1982, in one of its more famous terrorist operations, Iraq orchestrated the assassination of Shlomo Argov, the Israeli ambassador to Great Britain. Iraq's motives are illuminating. In late May 1982, Iran completed the series of counteroffensives that swept Iraqi forces out of the territory they had gained in their initial invasion. Iraq's army was demoralized and desperate, while Iran was building up for a massive invasion of Iraq intended to topple Saddam from power. Saddam was terrified. His troops had shown almost no ability to deal with the new Iranian human-wave attacks, and he believed his survival was at stake. He ordered the killing of Argov because the right-wing Israeli government of Menachem Begin (with Ariel Sharon as defense minister) had made it clear that another terrorist attack would prompt it to invade Lebanon to clear out the PLO presence there. Saddam believed that if he could get the Israelis to follow through on this threat, it would start a new Arab-Israeli war that would convince the Ayatollah Khomeini to call off his invasion and make common cause with Iraq against Israel.[15] This scheme succeeded in triggering the long-expected Israeli invasion of Lebanon but had no impact on Iran, which invaded Iraq the next month.

Saddam's increasing desperation as the Iran-Iraq War dragged on caused a major shift in his support for terrorism. As Iraq became increasingly dependent on the support of the moderate Arab states, the United States, and Europe, it began to distance itself from its former terrorist colleagues. Saad al-Bazzaz, a high-ranking Iraqi defector, claims that in the 1980s Saddam made a decision not to engage in terrorism against the West.[16] Saddam recognized (in large part because the United States and Europeans told him repeatedly) that his support for terrorism could scuttle Western assistance with the war effort.[17] Saddam got the message. He allowed the Abu Nidal Organization to remain in Baghdad but basically prevented it from conducting operations. Iraq became one of the most forward-leaning of the Arab governments on the issue of peace negotiations with Israel. In addition, Saddam appears to have concluded that terrorism was a dangerous game that could get him into trouble but was not of great value in accomplishing his goals. The 1986 State Department terrorism report applauded Iraq's shift: "Terrorism, which had been used by the more radical Iraq of the 1970s largely to intimidate Arab moderate governments and moderate elements within the PLO, had become less useful as an instrument of Iraqi policy by the early 1980s. Widespread use of terrorism against Arab targets was largely inconsistent with Iraq's pan-Arab leadership aspirations in the pre-war period. Later, the war and Iraq's accelerated drift toward the moderate Arab camp made terrorism an even less useful— indeed counterproductive—weapon."[18]

This is not to say that Iraq stopped all of its terrorist activities. Iraq continued to assassinate opposition figures overseas, such as former prime minister 'Abd al-Razzaq Sa'id al-Nayif in London. After the Arab Liberation Front of Abu Abbas hijacked the cruise ship *Achille Lauro,* murdering an American in the process, the killers were given sanctuary in Baghdad.

The two men who conducted the terrorist attack at the Rome airport in 1985 had arrived in Italy from Baghdad and had return tickets. Moreover, after Israeli warplanes struck PLO headquarters in Tunis in October 1985, Saddam allowed Arafat to move much of his operation to Baghdad. However, this support for Palestinian groups, and particularly the PLO, was driven largely by Saddam's rivalry with Hafiz al-Asad of Syria. Any Palestinian group on the outs with Damascus was given a warm welcome in Baghdad.[19]

Iraq suddenly rediscovered an interest in terrorism during the 1990–91 Persian Gulf War.[20] However, Saddam found he had two problems. First, having severed most of its ties to terrorist groups, having sat on the Abu Nidal Organization and others, and having backed the propeace movement through most of the 1980s, Iraq had great difficulty finding terrorist groups interested in collaborating with it. Second, Saddam still did not trust international terrorists. They were freelancers whose goals did not always coincide with his own. Since they operated beyond Iraq's borders, it was a great risk giving them weapons, explosives, money, and other paraphernalia, sending them out into the world, and then hoping they would destroy the targets he had agreed to and not something else that fit their own needs. In particular, during the Gulf War, Saddam was determined to try to destroy the political cohesiveness of the U.S.-led coalition. Therefore, any terrorist attacks had to be carefully chosen to ensure that they would not galvanize the coalition against Iraq. Nevertheless, Saddam did invite terrorists to Baghdad and provided some of them with arms and other supplies. In January 1991, Baghdad Radio called on all Muslims to attack Western interests throughout the world. But nothing came of this effort: there were no terrorist attacks against the West.[21] Recognizing that he could not count on the professional terrorists, Saddam had already turned to his own intelligence services to try to conduct terrorist operations against American, British, and Saudi targets. However, since Iraq's security services generally did not conduct hits (in the past, they usually had orchestrated the efforts of others) and were accustomed to operating in Iraq itself, where they were in complete control and had no need for stealth, their efforts proved to be astonishingly amateurish.[22] As Paul Pillar, the former deputy director of the CIA's Counterterrorism Center, has described it, Iraq "failed because U.S. counterterrorist efforts were able to exploit the weaknesses of Iraqi tradecraft, which was much more inept than what most established terrorist groups and state security services demonstrate."[23]

The same proved to be the case in 1993. Saddam apparently was desperate to demonstrate to his power base that he could strike out against Iraq's enemies despite the oppressive sanctions. When former President Bush traveled to Kuwait for a commemorative event with the amir, Saddam sent a Mukhabbarat hit team to kill them both. Once again, Iraqi tradecraft proved so incompetent and the Mukhabbarat's security so inadequate that the operation was quickly rolled up and Iraq's culpability was easily proven. U.S. and European intelligence services were again surprised by how unsophisticated and amateurish the Iraqis were.[24]

Another presumed link between Iraq and anti-U.S. terrorism is now looking like a red herring. In the aftermath of the first attack on the World Trade Center in February 1993, one of the attackers—an Iraqi American named Abdul Rahman Yasin—fled to Baghdad. Although the U.S. intelligence community concluded after repeated investigations that there was no evidence of Iraqi involvement in the 1993 attack, Yasin's presence in Baghdad appeared to indicate that something else might be going on. In particular, many American officials believed that while Baghdad might not have sent Yasin to conduct the World Trade Center attack, the Mukhabbarat might have been working with him on other anti-U.S. terrorist operations. However, in May 2002, journalist Lesley Stahl and a team from CBS News' *60 Minutes* were able to interview Yasin at length in Baghdad. It now seems that Yasin fled to Baghdad on his own and was then kept under house arrest by the Iraqis, who feared that he was an agent provocateur deliberately sent by the United States to create a pretext for military operations.

Today, Iraq continues to support terrorist groups, but it has not resumed the support for international terrorism it mounted in the 1970s. Iraq continues to provide a home for ANO, the Palestine Liberation Front, the May 15 Organization, and other old-time Palestinian rejectionists, but they have largely been prevented from conducting operations for more than fifteen years. Iraq's principal terrorist activity is supporting local groups against its regional adversaries. Iraq supports the Kurdistan Workers' Party (PKK) against Turkey. It supports the Mujahedin-e Khalq (MEK, or National Council of Resistance) against Iran. The MEK has its own Iraqi-equipped army, which Saddam has not only used to stage raids into Iran but has even employed to suppress unrest inside Iraq.[25] Since the outbreak of the al-Aqsa *intifadah* in the fall of 2000, Iraq has also begun providing support to Hamas and other Palestinian terrorist groups.[26] Saddam has recognized that the worse the violence between Arabs and Israelis, the more isolated the United States is in the Arab world and the more popular support he garners. Thus he has sought to stoke the violence between Israel and the Palestinians as a way of further eroding the sanctions and containment. However, he seems to recognize that he has to be careful: if Iraqi involvement is too obvious or too closely tied to any specific attack, he will invite retaliation by Israel or the United States and could undermine his political position with the United Nations. Consequently, he has tried to walk a fine line, giving moral and some material support but refraining from actual operational involvement.

Meanwhile, the U.S. intelligence and law enforcement communities have not found any credible evidence of Iraqi involvement in terrorism against the United States since the botched assassination attempt against former President Bush in 1993.[27] There is, however, a general suspicion that Iraq is working on a variety of terrorist contingency plans in case Saddam finds it necessary to strike the United States—essentially if Saddam believes that the United States is about to try to topple his regime. Some Iraqi defectors have claimed that Baghdad is operating terrorist training camps for this very purpose.[28] However, Iraq continues to have problems. "Iraqi terrorism has been limited more by capabilities than intentions," according to Pillar.[29]

As for its involvement with al-Qa'eda, there have been connections between the groups, but these have been (as best we can tell) tenuous and inconsequential.[30] Both Iraqi intelligence and al-Qa'eda's various subgroups move in the underworld of Middle Eastern terrorism. They undoubtedly encounter each other and probably have assisted each other in different ways—such as selling forged passports or know-how. It may be that they have also both supported some of the same terrorist groups, such as the Ansar i-Islam, now said to be holed up in Iraqi Kurdistan. Director of Central Intelligence George Tenet told a Senate committee in March 2000 that Iraq "has also had contacts with al Qaeda. Their ties may be limited by divergent ideologies, but the two sides' mutual antipathy toward the United States and the Saudi royal family suggests that tactical cooperation between them is possible, even though [Saddam] is well aware that such activity would carry serious consequences."[31]

It remains to be seen, however, whether Saddam would be willing to risk such serious consequences to provide more active support to al-Qa'eda and whether bin Ladin's Muslim fundamentalists would be willing to collaborate with a mullah-killing secularist like Saddam. Although there is no evidence that they have already done so, there is always a first time. Especially if Saddam and al-Qa'eda both find themselves desperate in the face of U.S. attacks, they might put aside their differences to make common cause against their common American enemy.

CONVENTIONAL MILITARY FORCES

Understanding Iraq's conventional military capabilities is a bit complicated. In some ways Iraq's military is quite weak, in other ways quite strong. By 1990, Iraq's military had developed a range of limited capabilities that made it a formidable force by regional standards, though still very poor by first-world standards. As a result of its catastrophic defeat during the Gulf War and the long period under U.N. sanctions, however, Iraq has lost many of the elements of this limited capability. Today Iraqi armed forces are no match for the U.S. military, but they still pose a significant threat to Iraq's smaller neighbors and could easily overwhelm any force that could realistically be mustered by any of the Iraqi opposition groups, either internal or external. Moreover, Iraq's military has begun to revive as a result of the progressive liberalization of the oil-for-food program. It is still a far cry from even the modest level of competence it reached in 1990, but it is on the mend.

Iraq's regular army consists of about 300,000 personnel organized into seventeen divisions—including three armored and three mechanized[32]— and commanded by five corps headquarters. The bulk of the army, eleven of its divisions, is deployed opposite the Kurds, while another three divisions conduct counterinsurgency operations against the Shi'ite guerrillas in southern Iraq. The remaining three divisions (two armored and one mechanized infantry) guard Iraq's southern border with Iran. The regular army was hit hardest by Operation Desert Storm, the *intifadah,* and the sanctions. Its morale remains relatively low, especially among the infantry divisions, which are largely manned by Shi'ite conscripts and have last call on supplies, training, and virtually everything else.[33] It was the regular army's Thirty-eighth Infantry Division that suffered the ignominy of being defeated in battle by Kurdish *peshmerga* near Arbil in March 1995. Nevertheless, the army's heavy divisions (its six armored and mechanized divisions) retain a strong sense of professionalism and a corresponding esprit de corps. It is noteworthy that the regular army's Third and Twelfth

Armored Divisions and its Fifth and First Mechanized Divisions fought just about as hard as the Republican Guards during the Gulf War, albeit with even less skill than the Guards.[34]

The Republican Guard remains Iraq's elite fighting force—a very relative term. At present, the Guard consists of 80,000 men in six divisions, commanded by two corps headquarters. The Guard's three armored divisions, the most powerful formations in Iraq, ring Baghdad, forming a cordon around the capital that would be extremely difficult for regular army units to break through in an attempt to overthrow the regime. The Guard's two infantry divisions and one mechanized division are in the north, where they act as a reserve for the army formations and also keep the army's guns pointed north toward the Kurds, not south toward the capital. The Guard is heavily Sunni and highly professional—in terms of attitude and discipline, not necessarily prowess. It was built up during the Iran-Iraq War by plucking all of the best officers and soldiers from the regular army and reassigning them to the Guard, whether they wanted to be or not. Thus, most of the Guard personnel were chosen based on performance in battle rather than support for the regime. For this reason it should not be surprising that since 1990 there have been a fair number of coup plots from within the Republican Guard. Saddam has tried to win their support by lavishing on them higher pay and all manner of privileges. The Guard also gets better equipment (including all of Iraq's remaining 600 T-72 tanks), better and more frequent training, better logistical support, and greater accolades. In addition, Guard personnel seem to revel in their elite status and the fact that they generally get the toughest assignments. As a result, the Guard has demonstrated very high esprit, as witnessed by its willingness to fight to the death in the battles of the Gulf War.[35]

Iraq's air force has about 30,000 personnel and 300 aircraft. At least, that's how many airframes it has. In actuality, probably no more than about 150 are operational at any given time. Iraq has only a few dozen operational MiG-29 and Mirage F-1 aircraft (its most advanced fighters), and its remaining strike aircraft are virtually all old planes that can do little more than drop dumb bombs on big targets. Because once a pilot is in the air it is difficult to stop him from defecting with his $10 million to $20 million airplane, or bombing the presidential palace if that is his preference, the regime has always meticulously screened pilots for their loyalty. The result is a very loyal (and pretty expensive) force that Saddam has traditionally been loath to risk getting destroyed. During the Iran-Iraq War, the Iraqis committed their air force sparingly, throwing it into the fray only when they were really desperate. Likewise, during the Gulf War, once it became clear that Iraqi fighters would have little ability to shoot down U.S. aircraft, the air force was grounded. And when Baghdad realized that the air force was not safe from coalition superpenetrator munitions in their hardened aircraft bunkers, they took the extraordinary step of flying planes to Iran (where they have since been assimilated into the Iranian air force, much to Baghdad's chagrin).[36]

As for Iraq's air defense forces, they are the least favored service, even though they have borne the brunt of confronting U.S. and British forces since 1991. They consist of about 15,000 personnel with 500 surface-to-air missile (SAM) launchers. (The army and Republican Guard also have about 1,500 shoulder-launched SAMs, such as the Russian-made SA-7, SA-14, and SA-16.) Most of the SAMs are badly outdated SA-2s, SA-3s, and SA-6s, which U.S. forces are well equipped to handle. At times, morale in the air defense forces has dipped very low. Saddam demands that they keep shooting at coalition aircraft even though they have very little chance of bringing down a plane, and whenever they do, U.S. and British planes go after them in response. Thus, many air defense personnel have been killed with little to show for their efforts.[37]

The Conventional Threat

A glance at the numerical balance of forces in the Persian Gulf region illustrates the most obvious dimension of the Iraqi military threat. Despite the devastation of the Gulf War and the sanctions, Iraqi forces remain large enough to give them an edge over any single Gulf state or any combination of them (in the unlikely event they could ever cooperate in a serious military fashion). These numbers demonstrate that absent the massive qualitative superiority the U.S. military brings to the Persian Gulf balance of power, the GCC would face a significant threat from Iraq. Moreover, Iraqi forces possess a qualitative edge over the Gulf states that magnifies their quantitative advantage. Large numbers of Iraqi military personnel have combat experience from the two Gulf wars, while the GCC militaries have never been able to take full advantage of the advanced Western weapons systems in their arsenals.

However, the numbers are also deceiving. Although Iraq would pose a threat to many of its neighbors in the absence of U.S. forces, in fact Iraq's military is much weaker than it appears on paper. Throughout its modern history, Iraq's armed forces have suffered from a range of debilitating

MILITARY FORCES IN THE PERSIAN GULF, 1999

	Manpower	Tanks	Artillery	Armed Helicopters	Combat Aircraft	Major Warships	Sub-marines
IRAQ	430,000	2,200	2,100	120	200–300	0	0
IRAN	500,000	1,500	2,500	100	300	3–7	3
GCC TOTAL	280,000	1,632	912	99	851	17	0
BAHRAIN	11,000	100	60	10	24	3	0
KUWAIT	16,500	220	40	15	75	0	0
OMAN	43,500	90	100	0	45	2	0
QATAR	11,000	24	40	20	12	0	0
SAUDI	105,000	1,055	500	12	350	8	0
UAE	70,000	133	172	42	95	4	0
U.S. DAY-TO-DAY	23,000	116	24	18	200	15–20	0–2
U.S. SURGE	60,000	450	150	65	400	20–30	0–4

SOURCES: Central Intelligence Agency, *The World Factbook, 2001* (Washington, D.C.: GPO, 2001); International Institute for Strategic Studies, *The Military Balance, 2001–2002* (London: Oxford University Press, 2002); Anthony H. Cordesman, "If We Fight Iraq: Iraq and the Conventional Military Balance," Center for Strategic and International Studies, February 27, 2002; author's estimates.

problems caused by a host of political, economic, cultural, educational, and other factors.[38] Since its early operations against Israel in 1948, Iraq's junior officers—lieutenants, captains, majors, and colonels—have demonstrated little ability to take initiative in battle, adapt to changing circumstances, devise creative solutions to battlefield problems, or seize fleeting opportunities. Iraqi forces have consistently had great difficulty performing combined arms operations. Their pilots demonstrate little situational awareness, are heavily dependent on direction from the ground, and are very poor in fluid dogfights. Iraq's soldiery has generally lacked the technical skills to employ all of the capabilities of their weaponry, and their maintenance practices are generally abysmal. Iraqi forces have also regularly experienced crippling problems with information management, both in terms of an inattention to reconnaissance and an unwillingness or inability to disseminate accurate information across their chain of command, either vertically or horizontally. As a result, Iraqi forces have fared exceptionally poorly in fluid combat operations, particularly large-scale air battles and ground maneuver warfare. Any time an opponent is able to surprise Iraqi units or force them to conduct unstructured operations—as the Israelis did in 1973 and the U.S.-led coalition did in 1991—the Iraqis have been crushed quickly and easily.[39]

Although these problems have persisted throughout modern Iraqi military history, their impact on Iraqi military fortunes has waxed and waned. During the latter half of the Iran-Iraq War, Iraq's military leadership recognized the problems and developed a system that allowed their tactical forces to largely avoid these weaknesses and instead take advantage of their more limited range of strengths. The key to this improvement was the depoliticization of the military during the war. The Iraqi Army began the Iran-Iraq War as one of the most heavily politicized forces in modern history but ended it as one of the most professional a modern Arab state has ever fielded.[40] Throughout the war, as Iraq's defeats mounted, Saddam was slowly convinced to release his political stranglehold on the military to allow competent, professional senior officers to increasingly direct its operations. By 1988, Iraq's senior field commanders, and in particular its General Staff, were an experienced group of officers who became very good at planning large, complex military operations.

The new General Staff recognized that Iraq's tactical forces were extremely weak, and in response they developed a system of heavily scripted set-piece offensives designed to secure limited objectives. Iraq's best forces—the Republican Guard and its best regular army armored and mechanized divisions—received detailed operational orders, which they practiced ad nauseum on full-scale mock-ups of the terrain. Then the General Staff would set up an offensive in which the Iraqi forces had overwhelming advantages in numbers and firepower (and against Iran, chemical warfare too) allowing its tactical forces to simply put into effect the operations they had learned by heart. In this way, Iraq defeated Iran in 1988 and overran Kuwait in 1990. The danger was that if an adversary had the skill to force the Iraqis to diverge from their plan, as U.S. forces did during the Gulf War, the Iraqi units quickly lost all of these hard-earned advantages.[41]

Iraqi forces had some other strengths as well. Iraq's operational security was outstanding. Iraq's armed forces practiced good communications discipline, camouflage, and deception. Not only did Iraq consistently fool Iran, but during the Gulf War, the Iraqis were able to move two heavy divisions into southern Kuwait and launch a corps-level offensive against coalition units around R'as al-Khafji that caught U.S. forces completely by surprise. Iraq's combat engineers also turned out to be quite good. They could quickly build roads and bridges, clear or lay minefields, and erect formidable defensive fortifications. Iraq's logistical capabilities also proved to be surprisingly good. Iraqi forces rarely ever suffered from shortages of ammunition or other supplies, and by the end of the Iran-Iraq War, their logisticians had gotten so good that they could pick up several divisions and move them the length of the country in just a few days with relative ease. Finally, Iraqi troops proved to be tenacious in static defensive operations. Anytime that all an Iraqi unit had to do was dig in and fight back, without doing any maneuvering or counterattacking, it could put up a hell of a fight. Indeed, even during the Gulf War, American soldiers were impressed by how hard the Republican Guards and a few of the regular army's divisions fought in defensive engagements.[42]

In contrast, Iraq's air and air defense forces never achieved even the limited capabilities of its ground forces. Iraqi pilots proved mediocre, if not awful, in every mission they were assigned. The French rejected 80 percent of all Iraqi pilots sent to France for training, and the Soviets estimated that less than half of the Iraqi pilots they trained would have been accepted for duty in Soviet line fighter regiments.[43] Iraqi pilots were never able to operate in large formations or execute more than the simplest tactics and missions. Iraq's air defenses were heavily reliant on centralized control, and its gunners and missileers were very poor at operating their weapons. In fact, during the Iran-Iraq War, Baghdad was so disappointed in its antiaircraft gunners that it largely stopped employing the tracking systems on their guns and instead simply used a barrage fire system in which every gun was assigned a sector of the sky. Gunners were told to fire at anything that came into it in the hope that the sheer volume of fire would keep enemy aircraft at bay.[44]

However, throughout the period of Iraq's greatest military power, its most important advantage was sheer size. By the end of the Iran-Iraq War, Baghdad's military had grown to as many as 1.4 million men under arms. During the Gulf War, Iraq mobilized a similar number (in truth, it had kept about 900,000 in service even after the cease-fire with Iran). These numbers alone gave Iraq the largest military in the region and the fourth largest in the world. What's more, Iraq's competent military planners were very good at concentrating huge numbers of men for key operations. As a result, against Iran, Iraqi forces often outnumbered their Iranian counterparts by five or even ten to one.[45]

The Long Fall

As a result of the Gulf War and the sanctions, Iraq has lost much of the modest military capability it possessed in 1988–90. It required a lot of money to maintain the Iraqi military before the Gulf War—about $15 bil-

lion in 1990, and such sums were no longer available. In 2000, Iraq is believed to have spent about $2 billion on defense. In part because of the de-
cline in spending and in part because of desertions and demoralization, Iraq
has also lost its great advantage in size. Today, Iraq's armed forces number
only about 430,000 troops. Across the board, their numbers are only about
30 to 40 percent of what they were at the time of the Gulf War.

Qualitatively, the Iraqi military is in even worse shape. Much of Iraq's
weaponry was a generation out of date before the Gulf War, and today it is
approaching block obsolescence. After 1991, Saddam tightened his control
over the armed forces by establishing new command-and-control procedures that distorted the chain of command, reintroduced "political commissars," and replaced many professional officers with his loyalists.
Training standards are well below pre–Gulf War levels. Brigade-level exercises are sporadic and divisional exercises almost nonexistent. Many units
lack the funds, equipment, and supplies to undertake rigorous training. Because of the higher cost and greater demands of air operations, the Iraqi Air
Force suffers from these problems to an even greater extent than the ground
forces. For example, senior Iraqi pilots get no more than 100 hours of flight
time per year, while junior pilots generally get no more than 20 hours per
year; by comparison, U.S. Air Force pilots average 220 flying hours per
year.[46]

Probably the most notable difference between the Iraqi armed forces
today and before the Gulf War is the precipitous decline of Iraqi logistics as
a result of the sanctions. What had been one of the greatest strengths of the
Iraqi military may now be one of its greatest limitations. As an example,
before the invasion of Kuwait, the Iraqis moved the entire Republican
Guard (eight divisions, 120,000 men, 1,800 armored vehicles) an average
of 600 kilometers to the Kuwaiti border in less than two weeks.[47] By contrast, in the fall of 2000, the Iraqis found it impossible to move five divisions (with approximately 50,000 men and 500 to 600 armored vehicles)
roughly 300 kilometers to the Syrian border. After six weeks of traffic jams
and breakdowns, they simply gave up and sent the units back to their garrisons.[48]

Finally, Iraq has lost at least some of the expertise it gained during the
Iran-Iraq War. Many of the competent professional officers driven out by
Saddam's effort to regain tight political control over the armed forces took
with them valuable skills in planning and leading large armored operations.
Iraq's outstanding General Staff is no longer the bastion of efficiency it

once was, and the professional military ethos Saddam had allowed to develop is vanishing. In addition, many of the troops and junior officers who fought the battles of the Iran-Iraq War have retired from active service or have been demobilized, and they have taken their valuable combat experience with them.[49]

The Lingering Threat

Iraqi forces are still adequate to defend the country against all of its neighbors except Turkey. In addition, since 1991, the military has demonstrated that it can manhandle any of the internal opposition forces. Iraq's ground forces, particularly the six divisions of the Republican Guard, also retain some theoretical power projection capability. As demonstrated by their swift operation at Arbil in 1996, Iraq's military planners can still organize complex multidivision armor operations, and some Iraqi units (mostly the Republican Guards) maintain a core of reasonably competent personnel with the combat experience to execute such operations. In the absence of U.S. forces, the Republican Guards could probably overrun Kuwait again as they did in 1990, albeit with greater difficulty because of the state of Iraqi logistics. Iraqi forces might be able to undertake similarly limited operations against Saudi Arabia, Jordan, and Iran—although they probably could not replicate the multicorps offensives they staged against Iran in 1988.

Iraq almost certainly has lost the ability (even in the abstract) to mount sustained ground offensives that could threaten GCC oil production beyond Kuwait and, perhaps, northernmost Saudi Arabia. In particular, Iraq almost certainly could not seize Dhahran or the Saudi oil fields east of Riyadh. Likewise, Iraq would probably have a tough time conquering Iran's Khuzestan province. Between the Gulf War and the U.N. sanctions, Iraq has lost the logistical capabilities to sustain large armored formations over the kinds of distances required to reach such objectives. Similarly, maintenance has become so problematic for Iraq's aging fleet of armored vehicles that few Iraqi tanks could be expected to physically reach an objective as far away as the Saudi ports of Dhahran or even Jubayl. If Baghdad were to attempt such an operation in the absence of U.S. forces, these logistical and maintenance shortcomings would likely bring such an offensive to an inglorious halt long before they reached the heart of the Saudi oil industry.

As long as U.S. forces maintain their current levels of readiness in the region and are able to reinforce whenever Baghdad attempts to build up its forces in southern Iraq, even these meager Iraqi capabilities lose real meaning. U.S. ground and air forces are vastly more capable than their Iraqi counterparts—a gap that has only grown since the Gulf War. Although standing U.S. forces in the region are inadequate to stop a full-scale Republican Guard invasion of Kuwait, Washington has demonstrated that it can surge reinforcements to Kuwait faster than Baghdad can muster an invasion force in southern Iraq. The forces Baghdad currently has in place in the south lack the combat skills and the mobility to be entrusted with such a mission. Consequently, as in 1990 and 1994, Saddam would undoubtedly rely on the Republican Guard. However, as proven by 1994's Operation Vigilant Warrior, in the time it would take Iraq to muster the Guard on Kuwait's border, the United States could move far greater military power to the region.

The threat from Iraq's air force is even lower. The Iraqi Air Force has been the hardest hit of the armed forces by the impact of sanctions. Iraqi aircraft were never properly maintained, and the depletion of Iraq's stockpiles of spare parts, lubricants, tools, and other consumables has seriously curtailed Baghdad's ability to generate sorties. Many Iraqi aircraft have been cannibalized to provide spare parts, while others are capable of only very short flights. Of those still flyable, few Iraqi aircraft could be considered fully mission capable. It is believed that all of the Mirage F-1EQ5s that Iraq employed to bomb Iranian oil facilities and sink Iranian tankers during the Iran-Iraq War are in captivity in Iran. Similarly, all of Iraq's Su-24 strike aircraft remain in Iran (not that Iraqi pilots ever developed any proficiency with this aircraft anyway). Baghdad still retains an inventory of more than 100 Su-17/20/22 attack aircraft, but these planes lack the range and avionics to pose more than a marginal threat. In the abstract, the Iraqi Air Force still retains the capabilities to mount a modest air campaign in support of an Iraqi ground offensive against one of its neighbors. However, in practice, this would quickly come to naught. Establishing air superiority and providing on-call air support to ground force operations were the greatest failings of Iraq's mediocre air force. Finally, as long as U.S. air and naval forces remain in the region, Iraq's air force is simply incapable of contending with them.

Signs of Life
The continuing liberalization of the oil-for-food program and the mounting erosion of the sanctions are threatening to breathe new life into Iraq's

armed forces, particularly its crippled logistical sector. Iraq has already been able to smuggle in some spare parts and combat consumables. But so far, this has not been a very significant amount, certainly not enough to compensate for the continued erosion of Iraq's training, leadership, combat experience, and logistical capabilities along with the growing obsolescence of its equipment.

Nevertheless, the United Nations continues to relax the sanctions on Iraq (to ease the humanitarian burden on the Iraqi people), and Iraq continues to enjoy ever greater success in eroding and evading what remains, with direct consequences for Iraqi military strength. For instance, the changes the United Nations agreed to in the spring of 2002, which greatly eased the economic sanctions on Baghdad but retained the military sanctions and financial controls, will probably allow Iraq to make a partial recovery of its pre–Desert Storm military strength. In particular, Baghdad will have unimpeded access to trucks, cars, tires, asphalt, rolling stock, locomotives, rail track, telecommunications gear, construction equipment, and all of the other supplies needed to make railroads and wheeled vehicles work.[50] This access will be a huge boon to Iraq's crippled logistics. Within a period of as little as three to five years, Iraq may be able to recover its former logistical prowess. In addition, the sense that Iraq's international isolation is ending will almost certainly improve Iraqi morale, as will the reviving of the Iraqi economy by making life easier on the families of soldiers and leaving the regime with greater resources to reward loyal officers.

Until the military embargo is lifted, however, Iraq's recovery will remain limited. Iraq already is able to smuggle small numbers of spare parts and new weapons into the country, but in such paltry numbers as to be militarily insignificant. Unchaining Iraq's civilian economy will expand the opportunities for smuggling prohibited military items, but as long as the military sanctions remain in place *and enforced,* Iraq will be unable to purchase the vast amounts of weapons, equipment, spare parts, ammunition, and other combat consumables it desperately needs. Iraq can smuggle in 1,000 spark plugs for T-72 tanks fairly easily; but it can't smuggle in 1,000 T-72 tanks, and it is the tanks that Iraq needs to rebuild its military power.

The one way Iraq could make significant gains to its conventional military capabilities in the short run would be by acquiring large numbers of advanced standoff attack systems. This would require either the lifting of the military embargo or the near total erosion of the sanctions—no longer an unimaginable set of circumstances. If Iraq could acquire several thousand advanced standoff weapons from Russia, Europe, or China, this could greatly enhance the Iraqi conventional military threat. In particular, it would allow Iraq to mount a surprise strike against the comparatively small U.S. forces in the region and hinder (possibly even prevent) U.S. reinforcements from moving into the region quickly. This could preclude a rapid American military buildup in the area, giving Iraq a window of opportunity during which it could employ its weakened, but still regionally potent, ground forces in a limited offensive operation. For example, if Iraq were to acquire several thousand advanced surface-to-air missiles, standoff antiarmor weapons, and highly accurate ground-attack missiles, it might be able to shut down many of the air bases in the GCC, fend off or shoot down whatever U.S. and GCC aircraft were able to get airborne, bombard the camps of the U.S. forces already in the region, and close off (or greatly slow the operations of) the main ports and airfields through which U.S. reinforcements must flow. Especially if Iraq's logistical capabilities were revived by this time, such circumstances would probably allow the Republican Guard and several of the regular army's heavy divisions to invade and defeat the Kuwaiti, Saudi, and possibly even Jordanian or Syrian militaries.

WEAPONS OF MASS DESTRUCTION

Because of the limited capabilities of Iraq's conventional military forces, its WMD programs loom even larger. Before the Gulf War, Saddam could believe that his conventional forces were powerful enough to achieve most of his ambitions. Today, he knows full well that they cannot and that instead he must lean more heavily on his WMD arsenal. In fact, Iraq's security is more than ever bound up with its WMD programs, to guarantee the regime against internal threats, deter hostile neighbors, and (Baghdad hopes) convince the United States that a war with Iraq would be too costly to fight.

Despite the valiant efforts of the U.N. inspectors—who destroyed far more of Iraq's WMD programs than Baghdad ever expected—Iraq was able to hang on to most of the knowledge and equipment it needed. As one high-level Iraqi defector put it, "It is impossible to completely destroy the chemical and biological weapons. They cannot destroy the know-how in our scientists' heads. Facilities for the production of chemical and biological weapons were dismantled already before the U.N. inspectors arrived.

They were taken to secret places and reassembled again. All documents have been hidden in such a way that strangers will never find them."[51]

Ballistic Missiles

Beginning in 1973, Iraq purchased 819 Scud-B ballistic missiles from the Soviet Union along with 11 transporter-erector launchers (TELs). UNSCOM concluded in 1996 that Iraq had been able to manufacture roughly 80 Scud-type missiles indigenously, although most of them were apparently inoperable.[52] Iraq also built 8 indigenous mobile erector launchers and 28 fixed erector-launchers to supplement the Soviet TELs. It was the Scud-B that Iraq modified and turned into the 650-kilometer range al-Hussein. Iraq launched 330 Scud-Bs and 203 al-Husseins against Iranian cities during the Iran-Iraq War and 88 al-Husseins at Israel, Saudi Arabia, and Bahrain during the Gulf War.[53] Many of Iraq's Scuds were expended in testing and research and were cannibalized to make the al-Husseins—Iraq needed the parts from three Scud-Bs to make two al-Husseins. After the Gulf War, Iraq admitted that it had built 50 CW missile warheads (filled with the nerve agent sarin) and 25 BW warheads (filled with botulinum toxin, anthrax, and aflatoxin).[54]

The U.S. intelligence community believes that Iraq retains a small, covert al-Hussein force, probably on the order of 12 to 40 missiles.[55] UNSCOM discovered a secret Iraqi Scud engine plant still in operation in 1995, leading it to conclude that Iraq may have been building new missiles even as UNSCOM destroyed its old ones. Consequently, UNSCOM personnel concluded that Iraq had at least a dozen al-Husseins when it ceased cooperation with the inspectors in 1998. Defectors have argued that the number is higher, probably closer to 30 or even 45.[56] Although virtually all of the Soviet-supplied Scuds have been accounted for, because Iraq was able to produce Scud-type missiles indigenously there is no way to know just what its actual Scud inventory consisted of or how many it now has left.

In another shortsighted mistake, UNSC Resolution 687 allowed Iraq to retain ballistic missiles with ranges under 150 kilometers and to continue to perform research and development on such missiles. Iraq had Russian-made FROG tactical missiles with a range of 90 kilometers, and the framers of UNSCR 687 believed that it was important to maintain a strong Iraq to keep Iran in check, so they thought Iraq should be allowed to keep its FROGs. As should have been anticipated, Iraq has used this loophole to maintain an active ballistic missile development program. At its heart is a system called the al-Samud missile, which is a surface-to-surface missile based on the SA-2 SAM but incorporating much that Iraq learned from its Scud program. Iraq claims that the al-Samud has a range of 150 kilometers, but U.S. intelligence believes that its actual range is closer to 200 kilometers.[57] Iraq is developing another missile, called the Ababil-100, which is a solid-fuel missile that serves as a test bed for more advanced projects and also probably has a greater range than its claimed 100 kilometers. Under cover of performing research on the al-Samud and Ababil-100, Iraq has been able to keep all of its ballistic missile programs going unimpeded, including those on longer-range systems. The U.S. intelligence community believes that if left to its own devices, Iraq is likely to acquire intercontinental ballistic missiles capable of striking the United States within the next fifteen years.[58]

Indeed, even while the inspectors were combing Iraq, Baghdad kept working on its prohibited missile systems. For example, Iraq built a facility for the production of ammonium perchlorate, a key ingredient in solid missile propellant, indicating that work continues on advanced solid-fuel multistage missiles. In December 1995, Jordan intercepted 115 missile gyroscopes and material for making chemical weapons being smuggled to Iraq.[59] Since the inspectors were evicted in 1998, experts on Iraq's WMD programs are convinced that Iraq has accelerated all of these programs. Iraq is probably working hard to overcome its remaining problems in ballistic missile development—warhead fusing (all of Iraq's missile warheads were impact fuses, which are the worst kind for dissemination of chemical or biological agents), guidance, engine production, and missile staging—to enable it to design larger multistage missiles with greater ranges.[60]

Chemical Warfare

Iraq began the development of chemical weapons in 1974, starting with mustard gas, followed in the 1980s by simple nerve gases such as sarin and tabun. At some point after the Iran-Iraq War, Iraqi scientists were able to develop the highly lethal nerve agent VX. Iraq began using chemical warfare against Iranian forces as early as 1983 and, by its own admission, expended more than 100,000 chemical munitions against Iran. During the Gulf War, Iraq is not known to have used any chemical munitions against coalition forces, but it did prepare to do so. Baghdad moved thousands of CW-filled artillery shells and 122 mm rockets to storage facilities, one of which was located in the Kuwaiti Theater of Operations. Most were left in depots about 100 kilometers back, however, where they could be moved quickly to the frontline troops if Saddam ordered it but where they were unlikely to be fired accidentally.[61]

The U.N. inspectors destroyed huge quantities of Iraqi chemical warfare munitions and agents.[62] Until the end of the inspection program, UNSCOM fought with Iraq to provide a full accounting of its CW munitions expenditure. In July 1988, the inspectors temporarily obtained a key document that contradicted Iraq's assertions about its chemical munitions expenditures during the Iran-Iraq War, but the Iraqis took it back and then refused to admit to its existence. The inspectors were unable to destroy any of Iraq's stockpile of VX agent and filled munitions.

The inspectors believe that Iraq has retained 6,000 or more chemical munitions (including missile warheads), large amounts of precursor chemicals, and chemical warfare production equipment and that it has the ability to manufacture additional agent, munitions, and production equipment.[63] Since the Gulf War, Iraq has built several major dual-use chemical facilities, most notably at Fallujah. These facilities are designed to produce chemical warfare agents, but they can be and probably are being used to meet civilian needs as well.[64] Since most chemical warfare agents deteriorate over time but can be produced reasonably quickly, Saddam has no particular need to have huge stockpiles of CW rounds but can start up production several months before an expected conflict and make all that he needs. Until then, the facilities function as legitimate civilian industries. If the United States were to strike them, Saddam would waste no time bringing in outside observers, who could truthfully say that the factories had been producing innocuous chemicals when they were destroyed. Iraq's key development need in the chemical warfare arena and where it is probably working hardest is with better munitions. The munitions Iraq employed in the past, particularly its aerial bombs and missile warheads, were poor devices for disseminating CW.[65]

Biological Warfare

Iraq began its biological warfare program in 1972. It was the program Iraq was least forthcoming about with the U.N. inspectors. Iraq admits to producing anthrax, botulinum toxin, and aflatoxin for weaponization. However, UNSCOM discovered that Iraq had also conducted research on *Clostridium perfringens* (which causes gangrene), ricin, and several viruses, including plague, as well. Iraq had also taken some tentative steps toward genetically engineering strains of these agents to make them more resistant to antibiotics. Some of Iraq's efforts mystified the inspectors. For example, Iraq put aflatoxin (which causes cancer over a period of years) into bombs, where it could hardly be expected to produce near-term tactical results.[66]

Although Iraq was not known to have employed biological warfare before the Gulf War, some experts suspect that it may have experimented with biological agents against the Kurds during the late 1980s. Baghdad was prepared to use them during the Gulf War and may have tried to do so. Iraq produced up to 10 billion doses of biological agent by 1991. In December 1990, just before Operation Desert Storm, Iraq launched a crash program to field artillery shells and 25 al-Hussein missile warheads filled with BW agents that the regime was prepared to use if the coalition marched on Baghdad.[67] According to a declassified, unconfirmed CIA agent report, in the fall of 1990 Iraq developed a plan to try to use an Su-22 with a spray tank (like a crop duster) to spray coalition forces with a biological agent. The idea was to use three MiG-21s as decoys for the Su-22, and during the air campaign phase of Desert Storm, Iraq had three MiG-21s conduct a dry run for the attack. If the MiGs could make it to their target, then the next day, they were supposed to head back out with the Su-22, which would fly much lower to try to sneak under coalition radar and conduct the BW strike. However, according to the report, all three MiGs were shot down during the test run, and Iraq aborted the effort.[68]

Iraq retains a residual biological warfare program and a stockpile of filled munitions, almost certainly including missile warheads. It has also converted a number of its L-29 jet trainers into unmanned aircraft that can disseminate both biological and chemical agents.[69] After repeatedly denying the very existence of a biological warfare program, Iraq eventually told the U.N. inspectors that it had unilaterally destroyed all of its agent and munitions stockpiles, although it offered no credible evidence of this. UNSCOM inspectors believe that Iraq possessed three or four times more biological agent than it declared, as well as large stocks of growth media and munitions.[70]

The biggest problem with tracking Iraq's biological warfare program is that it does not require large facilities to produce agents. Consequently, defectors report that Saddam has taken the entire Iraqi program on the road. Baghdad now has a number of mobile BW labs that can move around the country as needed, leaving no trace and having virtually no signature that Western intelligence can detect.[71] The Iraqis have all the equipment and all of the agent samples they require, and it is assumed that they are hard at work. Moreover, some of the biological agents Iraq was working on, such as wheat smut, are tools of economic warfare that are used to destroy crops. Charles Duelfer, the longtime deputy chairman of UNSCOM, told a congressional committee in 2002, "The types of research Iraq is known to have conducted points to their interest in BW not just as a battlefield weapon, but as a strategic weapon, an economic weapon, a terror weapon, and possibly a genocide weapon."[72]

Nuclear Weapons

Iraq's nuclear effort began in 1971, when Saddam enjoined a small group of physicists to start a nuclear energy program as the cover for a weapons program.[73] In 1976, Iraq signed a deal with France for a reactor that Paris knew was intended to be a bomb factory.[74] Israel soon became aware of the operation, and the Mossad launched a program to stop, delay, or disrupt it. By assassinating Iraqi scientists and sabotaging key elements of the program (including blowing up the reactor core in 1979), Israel was able to slow the program but not derail it all together. In 1981, soon before the reactor was set to come on line, the Israeli Air Force conducted a brilliant raid that destroyed it.

The Israeli raid turned out to be a watershed in Iraqi WMD development. Baghdad learned that its WMD facilities were highly vulnerable. The Iraqis immediately began rebuilding the reactor and the program, but thereafter, the regime began to duplicate its efforts, hide the facilities, bury them, bunker them, and defend them. By the time of the Gulf War, Iraq had numerous redundant facilities, all heavily guarded and bermed, some of them so secret that Western intelligence did not know of their existence.

By the time of the Gulf War, Iraq had essentially figured out how to build a nuclear weapon. Its greatest difficulty was acquiring the necessary fissile material. Iraq pursued a wide range of methods for enriching uranium for this purpose. It tried centrifuges, tried laser-isotope separation, gaseous diffusion, ion exchange, and electromagnetic isotope separation (EMIS), among other routes. In August 1990, Saddam ordered a crash program to build a single nuclear weapon that could be placed in a missile warhead and used against Tel Aviv if his regime were at risk. Iraq was able to build a crude device (although it was too big to fit on a missile and would have had to have been dropped from an airplane or carried by a truck or ship) but was not able to come up with the necessary fissile material. U.N. inspectors believe that Iraq could have achieved a fully workable nuclear weapon in another year, given the time.[75]

After the Gulf War, the International Atomic Energy Agency (IAEA), which was responsible for eliminating and monitoring Iraq's nuclear program just as UNSCOM was responsible for Iraq's chemical, biological, and missile programs, believed that it had accounted for most of the program. However, there is a consensus that Iraq has resumed work on nuclear weapons. Saddam broke his nuclear weapons program up into its component teams and then hid them in seemingly innocuous locations where they could continue their work. According to Khidhir Hamza, the longtime head of Iraq's weapons design program who defected to the West in 1994, Iraq's nuclear effort actually expanded after the Gulf War and in 1993–94 numbered 2,000 engineers and 12,000 other workers.[76] A recent defector who worked as a design engineer stated that Saddam had ordered the entire nuclear program reconstituted in August 1998, when he announced that he had ceased all cooperation with the U.N. inspectors.[77] Former U.N. inspectors and other experts on the Iraqi nuclear program unanimously agree that Iraq is probably now working to enrich uranium (probably via centrifuge separation) for nuclear weapons. Alternatively, Iraq still has the precision tools needed to build new EMIS magnets and could do so easily, or it could be employing gas diffusion using the "short-cascade" method, which would make it difficult for Western intelligence agencies to detect.[78] Indeed, there is a consensus on this within the U.S. intelligence community as well, with Director of Central Intelligence George Tenet testifying to the Senate Intelligence Committee that "We believe Saddam never abandoned his nuclear weapons program."[79]

Just to be clear about this: in 1990, Iraq built a workable nuclear weapon. All it lacked was the fissile material. Iraq has natural uranium deposits, so it does not need to import uranium (although acquiring already enriched uranium would be a huge bonus). It also has the technology and the know-how to build a system capable of enriching that uranium to weapons grade. Thus it is only a matter of time before Saddam's regime is able to acquire nuclear weapons if left to its own devices.

What no one knows is how much time it will take for Iraq to build the enrichment system and then process the uranium to build one or more nuclear weapons. Given the difficulties Iraq was having using any of its various methods before the Gulf War, the U.S. intelligence community has estimated that it would take Iraq five to ten years from the start of a crash program to enrich enough uranium to make one or more devices.[80] If such a crash program started in 1999, Iraq might be able to develop such weapons by 2004. On the other hand, the crash program might not have gotten started until 2000 or 2001, depending on how long it took to re-assemble the teams, rebuild the facilities and equipment, and resurrect the development process. The German intelligence service, using methods it won't divulge, estimated in 2001 that Iraq was three to six years from hav-ing a nuclear weapon.[81] Moreover, Iraq has been actively looking to buy black market enriched uranium from the former Soviet Union, North Korea, China, Pakistan, or anyone else who might be willing to sell it. So far, Iraq has had no luck, but if it is able to buy it ready-made, it could then probably build a workable device in a year or two. Again, as Duelfer con-cluded, "While precise estimates of the Iraqi nuclear program are impossi-ble, what is certain is that Baghdad has the desire, the talent, and the resources to build a nuclear weapon given the time to do so."[82]

Why Are Weapons of Mass Destruction So Important to Saddam?

As experts constantly like to point out, Saddam has given up anywhere from $130 billion to $180 billion worth of oil revenues to hang on to his WMD programs. Resolution 687, paragraph 22, stated that the prohibi-tions on Iraq's oil exports would be lifted as soon as the U.N. inspectors verified that Iraq had met its obligations to give up its WMD. Although the United States tried for years to hold to a different interpretation, the truth was that it would have been well nigh impossible for Washington to have won that battle if Iraq ever really had come clean. By refusing to give up its WMD programs, Iraq forfeited all of that money, year after year. Even today, most of it goes into the U.N. oil-for-food system rather than into Saddam's wallet. The prolongation of the sanctions regime has not only caused the deaths of several hundred thousand Iraqis (admit-tedly, a rather minor concern to Saddam), it has also meant the continued deterioration of his conventional military forces. In short, Saddam has demonstrated for more than a decade that his WMD arsenal is more im-portant to him than Iraq's oil wealth, its people, its economy, or even its conventional military power. This would seem to make it the most im-portant thing in the world to him.

The picture is even more intriguing because if Saddam had come clean in 1991 and fully cooperated, he could have had the sanctions lifted in a matter of months and within a few years could have completely reconstituted Iraq's WMD programs. By this point in time, he might have been able to develop nuclear weapons and long-range missiles. To some extent, the answer to this mystery may lie in the tyranny of incremental decisions. As noted in Chapter 2, Saddam never expected the sanctions to last or the inspectors to do much damage to his program. Thus, in 1991 he made the decision not to cooperate. Over time, his assumptions were proven false, but by then he had invested his prestige in this course of action. By 1994–95, when Iraq was in dire straits, Saddam may have concluded that he should have cooperated in 1991, but to change course—and especially to do so at that point—would have been to admit that he had been wrong and that this mistake had simply impoverished Iraq and destroyed its economy to no purpose. Saddam generally believes that such admissions could fatally weaken his grip on power. His former chief of intelligence Wafiq al-Samarra'i suggested as much in an interview, explaining that the reason Saddam would not cooperate was that "If he gave in, it would be tantamount to a fatal loss in authority, it would be a terrible humiliation for him."[83] By 1996–97, Saddam's situation had improved enough that he believed he could keep his WMD programs and still get the sanctions lifted, albeit over a longer period of time than he had originally envisioned. This meant that he did not have to suffer the dangerous humiliation of reversing course and cooperating with the inspectors.

Even this explanation suggests deeper, more important motives, however. First and foremost, Saddam's possession of WMD is bound up with his control over Iraq. At the most basic level, Saddam almost certainly believes that his possession of WMD awes many would-be opponents, convincing them that they lack the strength to challenge his control of the country. His WMD proved useful to his internal control during the Anfal campaign against the Kurds. Likewise, Saddam's legitimacy, at least as he sees it, derives from his promise to make Iraq great and powerful—a promise he believes he has so far kept. This is especially important to his power base, the Sunni tribes and townsmen who man the Republican Guard and security services and keep him in power. They want a strong, powerful Iraq, and an important element of their backing of Saddam is that he has made Iraq a powerful, important state, and Iraq's WMD has been a crucial role in its new power. Thus, for Saddam, giving up his WMD programs could create major threats to his regime by undermining its military power and its claims to legitimacy.

Moreover, Saddam apparently believes that WMD have already saved his regime from overthrow by foreign forces. UNSCOM inspectors discovered that the Iraqis were convinced that WMD had saved the regime on two occasions: during the Iran-Iraq War, when Iraq used chemical warfare to turn back Khomeini's hordes; and in 1991, to deter a U.S. drive on Baghdad. "Whether the Iraqi leadership believes this was the only reason the United States did not go to Baghdad in 1991 is unknown. However, clearly they are convinced that the possession of WMD contributed to keeping the Americans away and thus was vital to their survival."[84]

Finally, Iraq's WMD programs are of critical importance in achieving Saddam's foreign policy ambitions—of making Iraq a powerful state and the leader of the Arab world. This appears to have been a key incentive right from the start. Amatzia Baram points out that in 1971, when Iraq began its nuclear program, it was too poor and too weak to feel a great enough threat from Israel to require a nuclear deterrent—Saddam's ostensible explanation for the program. Instead, Baghdad's goals were to deter Iran, which was pursuing a nuclear capability of its own, and to make Iraq a great power. Joining "the nuclear club" has long been seen as a mark of great power status, and Saddam is fully cognizant of this. Saddam's speeches and interviews indicate that he also believes he can use WMD to extract concessions from other states that lack the same capabilities.[85] Saddam's half brother Barzan made this point in explaining that Iraq wanted a nuclear program because "we want a strong hand in order to redraw the map of the Middle East."[86] Likewise, in 1990, Iraq began to try to use its WMD arsenal to extend a deterrence umbrella over other Arab states, and as Timothy McCarthy and Jonathan Tucker have astutely observed, "To benefit from Iraqi extended deterrence, other Arab states would have to accept Iraqi leadership."[87]

Iraqi WMD Today and Tomorrow

As long as some form of sanctions remains on Iraq, Baghdad's ability to *use* any of its WMD as elements of Iraq's foreign policy will be constrained. Especially before Saddam has a nuclear weapon—which he knows would change everything—he has to be careful because even brandishing WMD would undermine his efforts to have the sanctions lifted. It is for this reason that Baghdad mostly views its current arsenal as a deterrent of last resort rather than another tool in its foreign policy kit.

If Saddam believes his regime is threatened, of course, all bets are off.

He will employ every weapon at his disposal to stave off his own downfall, regardless of any moral or even long-term political considerations. The survival of his regime in the short term is always his paramount concern. Moreover, given the revelations about his various orders regarding WMD during the Gulf War, we should expect that if Saddam cannot prevent his overthrow, he is highly likely to use whatever forces remain to him at the end to lash out in a final paroxysm toward Israel and possibly others as well. Even if it is his final act, we should assume that Saddam will not miss his opportunity to go down in history.

Like Iraq's conventional military, Baghdad's WMD programs will benefit somewhat from a suspension of the economic sanctions. WMD programs require much smaller amounts of resources and equipment than conventional forces. Although some equipment is so esoteric that it can have only one possible use, much of the equipment Iraq needs for its WMD programs falls into the notorious "dual-use" category, which Baghdad may get access to if the economic sanctions are suspended. Moreover, the vast increase in trade moving in and out of Iraq under these circumstances will make smuggling much easier, and WMD items will undoubtedly get in no matter how vigilant the new inspection regime. Because of the priority Baghdad is likely to attach to WMD items, and because comparatively few items are needed for these programs, smuggling could make a significant difference to Iraq's clandestine WMD programs.

Finally, if Saddam is able to acquire nuclear weapons, everything else will become meaningless. Between his own behavior and the statements of Iraqi defectors, it is clear that Saddam sees nuclear weapons as being in a category by themselves and that if he has a nuclear weapon the world will have to treat him differently. Once he has acquired a nuclear weapon, he believes that he will be able to deter the United States and Israel under all circumstances except if he were to launch his own nuclear strike against them. He also believes that with nuclear weapons he could largely disregard the United Nations' demands and bully most of the regional states to ignore the sanctions altogether.

Would Saddam Give WMD to Terrorists?

In some ways, this is the $64,000 question. Under present circumstances, Saddam's ability to employ his WMD to pursue foreign policy ends, let alone to do massive damage with them is fairly circumscribed. Until he develops a nuclear weapon—or proves that he can effectively employ advanced biological agents to kill massive numbers of people—it is likely to remain so. Although this is probably only a matter of time, there is a big difference between before and after. Moreover, in a military campaign, U.S. forces could take action that would further reduce Saddam's ability to do great damage with his current inventory of WMD (see Chapter 11 for a more detailed explanation). But if Saddam were willing to give WMD to terrorists to employ against cities in the region or the United States, he might be able to do far more damage. A successful attack with VX could kill thousands; with a BW agent, tens of thousands; and with a nuclear weapon, hundreds of thousands or even millions.

The threat of terrorist employment of WMD should not be blown out of proportion. It is actually quite difficult to use chemical or biological weapons to kill large numbers of people. The agents have to be properly prepared in a form that remains airborne for some time and can be disseminated in the right dosages to actually kill people. Atmospheric conditions have to be just right, or the agent may be dissipated or destroyed. The attackers have to know when and where to disseminate the agent and to do it in a way that will actually allow it to have its maximum effect. The agent also has to be stored properly so that it does not lose its potency before it can be used. For all of these reasons, previous terrorist attacks using CW and BW have not killed very many people. In fact, on just about every occasion when terrorists did employ WMD, they undoubtedly would have killed far more people if they had employed conventional explosives instead.

It is unlikely that Iraqi WMD could fall into the hands of terrorists by accident. Iraq has always kept tight control over its stockpiles. They are guarded by the Special Republican Guard and the Special Security Organization, the two most feared security organizations in Iraq. Only Saddam can authorize use of chemical weapons in battle. And when he does, the munitions are stored and moved by special Chemical Corps transportation detachments that report to the SSO and that see to it that the munitions are fired immediately upon delivery.[88] Also, Iraq is itself a virtual prison. Terrorists in Iraq—except those fighting the regime—are kept under strict control by Iraq's internal security services. Saddam does not trust them, making it very unlikely they could get their hands on WMD without his permission. As for opposition terrorist groups, it is conceivable that they could attack an Iraqi WMD bunker, penetrate its security, and make off with some materials, but that is highly unlikely. The opposition groups have great difficulty conducting operations against the regime because of

Saddam's draconian security measures. Moreover, both biological and chemical warfare agents and munitions are difficult to transport and store.

Saddam has never given WMD to terrorists (at least to our knowledge) for the same reasons he has distanced himself from international terrorist groups in general. If he is uncomfortable with foreign terrorist groups because he cannot be certain how they will act and how their actions will affect his own security, this point is ten times more salient when weapons of mass destruction are involved. If Saddam were ever tied to a WMD terrorist attack, the targeted country would look to extract a fearful vengeance from him. Even in the case of countries unable to retaliate, Saddam would likely pay an exorbitant cost. If the United States could tie Saddam to an act of terrorism conducted with WMD, it would be able to demonstrate not only that he was violating the U.N. resolutions by retaining prohibited weapons but that he remained a danger to the rest of the world based on his willingness to employ such weapons against innocent civilians. Under those circumstances the United States would be free to do to Saddam whatever it wanted, probably with the blessing of the entire international community.

This suggests that Saddam is not *likely* to give WMD to terrorists. Of course, the possibility should never be ruled out. If Saddam believes it highly improbable that the attack could be traced back to him and if the operation offers a high payoff, he might well decide to do so.

Moreover, if Saddam believes his regime is in danger, we cannot rule out that Saddam would give WMD to terrorists simply because we cannot rule out *anything* under those circumstances. Saddam is not necessarily apocalyptic, but he will do anything to stave off his own overthrow and has absolutely no moral constraints on his actions. If he believes that his overthrow is imminent and unavoidable, the evidence we have from his behavior during the Gulf War is that he will seek to do the maximum damage to Israel (to ensure his place in history) and to his other enemies. It is also worth remembering that Saddam's sense of threats to his regime include things such as the economic straits in which Iraq found itself in both 1990 and 1994—which prompted the invasion of Kuwait and the later threat to Kuwait, both of which were extremely risky gambits designed to stave off what he perceived to be dire threats, even though they hardly appeared as such to the rest of the world.

SIX

The Regional Perspective

The final pieces of the Iraq policy puzzle that remain to be discussed are the views of Iraq's neighbors and the other states of the Middle East, whose support will be critical to any new U.S. policy toward Iraq. No matter what course of action the United States opts for, we will need the active participation of at least some of Iraq's neighbors. If we decide to pursue military operations to topple Saddam's regime, we will need bases in the region from which to launch our air and ground forces and passage across other countries to get those forces into position on Iraq's borders. If we decide to try to mount a coup to overthrow his government, we will need friends in the region who can help us to contact dissident elements within the Iraqi elite and provide safe passage for personnel and equipment into Iraq. If we opt to continue to contain Iraq, we will need the support of Iraq's neighbors both in the United Nations and on the ground to help shut down the smuggling that has jeopardized the entire containment regime. Even if we opt for pure deterrence of Iraq, we will need access for U.S. military forces to prevent Saddam from striking out across Iraq's borders.[1]

Of course, some policies require more support than others, and all require different kinds of support from different regional actors. Consequently, it is useful to have a sense of the perspectives of different countries toward Iraq and their preferred courses of action. First, however, there are several regionwide concepts that affect the thinking of many countries on Iraq and will likely influence their reaction to any U.S. policy.

LINKAGE

One of the most heated debates among Middle East experts today is over the notion of "linkage" between the Arab-Israeli dispute and Iraq policy. Arabs contend that violence between Arabs and Israelis makes it hard, if not impossible, to support the United States in taking a hard-line position against Iraq. Many Americans counter that there is no logical reason why this should be the case—the Gulf region and U.S. policy toward Iraq have nothing to do with what is going on between the Israelis and Palestinians.

Unfortunately, as one senior U.S. official put it, "You can argue till you are blue in the face that there should not be any linkage, but the fact is that if the Arabs say that there is linkage, there is linkage." Arab populations hate Israel and care deeply about the fate of Arabs (particularly the Palestinians) locked in struggle with Israel. For many decades, Arab media and educational systems have been suffused with anti-Semitism, producing an almost pathological reaction to the Arab-Israeli dispute. They hate U.S. support for Israel and believe that for the last twenty-five years, while the United States has been claiming to act as an "honest broker" between the Israelis and Arabs, it has actually been heavily biased in Israel's favor. In fact, in many Arab minds the United States has become inseparable from Israel. Thus, just as many Arabs tend to blame their own political, social, and economic problems on Israel—thus heightening their emotions—so the United States is often tarred with the same brush. We don't have to like it or even believe it makes sense, but linkage is a reality and one we are not likely to be able to change in the near term.

Linkage actually has a very long history. U.S. policies toward the Persian Gulf region have been made to suffer because of seemingly unrelated events in the Arab-Israeli confrontation since the beginning of the state of Israel. In October 1947, the Joint Chiefs of Staff warned that "implementation of a decision to partition Palestine, if the decision were supported by the United States, would prejudice United States strategic interests in the Near and Middle East and United States influence in the area would be curtailed to that which could be maintained by force. Further, there is grave danger that such a decision would result in such serious disturbances throughout the Near and Middle East area as to dwarf any local Palestine disturbances resulting from the decision. As a consequence, the USSR might replace the United States and Great Britain in influence and power in the region."[2]

Before 1971, when Britain was the dominant power in the region, it too suffered from the effects of linkage. Britain's participation in the Sinai-Suez War against Egypt caused a crisis throughout the Middle East. In Michael Palmer's words:

> The reaction against Britain in the Middle East demonstrated the depth of Arab emotions, Arab willingness to use oil as a weapon against the West, and the possible repercussions events that took place elsewhere in the Middle East could have in the Gulf. The Saudis mobilized their armed forces, began training volunteers, broke off diplomatic relations with Britain and France, banned the refueling of their ships in Saudi ports, and embargoed oil shipments to both countries. . . . For nine days Bahrainis rioted in Manama and Muharraq, attacking British nationals, as well as a few unfortunate Americans, and destroying property. . . . In Kuwait, while the demonstrations were somewhat less violent, the repercussions of the Suez affair were longer lasting. Arabs sabotaged British-owned and -controlled oil fields and facilities and subjected British firms to a boycott that lasted for two months.[3]

There was also widespread rioting in Iraq, to protest the pro-British monarchy's passivity throughout the crisis.

Since then, virtually every time there has been a major upheaval in the Arab-Israeli dispute, it has adversely affected U.S. interests in the Gulf region. During the 1967 Arab-Israeli War, there was anti-American rioting in Bahrain and Saudi Arabia that caused considerable damage to many American businesses. After the 1973 Arab-Israeli War, the Arabs imposed an oil embargo on the United States and the Bahrainis terminated their lease agreement with the U.S. Navy (although they did not press the U.S. personnel to leave and in 1975 quietly agreed to a lease extension, which then became permanent).[4]

THE ARAB "STREET"

The issue of linkage has arisen because of the greater sensitivity of Arab governments to their own popular opinion—what is often referred to as the Arab "street."[5] In recent years, Arab publics have taken an increasing interest in regional affairs. In part, this is a result of growing literacy and the spread of new forms of media such as the Internet and satellite TV stations, which provide Arab populations with far more information than was ever the case in the days when their governments had a monopoly on sources of information. Moreover, many of these sources of information pander to the worst Arab prejudices and so delight in showing Israel and the United States as evil and aggressive (not that the United States and Israel do not provide ammunition for such charges). To some extent, the regimes are themselves to blame, having deflected criticism of their own political and economic inequities onto Israel and the United States.

Thus the Arab "street" is a byword for the increasing political consciousness of Arab publics across the region. Many experts, including in Europe and the United States, have exaggerated both the volatility and the influence of the Arab "street"—claiming that it was going to rise up and sweep away Arab governments as a result of U.S. actions during the Gulf War and in Afghanistan. Although ultimately the fear of the Arab "street" is that a chain of events could ultimately produce a revolution, in fact, the workings of public opinion on Arab policy are more subtle. Nevertheless, even though they may be more subtle, they can still have a very important impact on the policy decisions of the moderate Arab states.

Given that there are no true democracies in the Arab world (although some, such as Yemen, Lebanon, and Jordan, are making progress in that direction), it may be surprising that public opinion can have an impact on Arab governments. Perversely, it is precisely because these states are not democracies that their governments have become so sensitive to the public tenor. In past eras, the leaders and ruling families of the Arab world could claim legitimacy from divine right, military conquest, traditional societal structures, descent from the Prophet, or Pan-Arabism. However, in recent years, and particularly since the Gulf War and the rise of the new Middle Eastern media, these justifications have worn thin. There are increasing calls for greater popular participation in government. These have even led Kuwait, Bahrain, Qatar, Jordan, and Yemen, among others, to establish parliaments where the people at least have a forum to air their grievances, if not yet a mechanism to govern themselves. Coupled with this are more strident calls for the governments' policies to better reflect popular sentiments.

These are also increasingly fragile regimes. Their economies are broken. Corruption is rampant. Across the region, standards of living are stagnating, while unemployment is rising. Even in the oil emirates, the rising birthrate and the long-term decline in oil prices, coupled with the oversized welfare systems they put in place during the fat years of the 1970s, are straining their finances and in fact have driven Saudi Arabia into debt. Thus the moderate Arab states must deal with publics who are increasingly frustrated by their economic and political circumstances and who have been taught that Israel and the United States are the source of many (in some cases all) of their woes. Meanwhile, the confrontation between traditional Arab societies and modernity (embodied by the United States of America) provokes strange combinations of awe, anger, and envy toward America, while simultaneously producing volatile debates over how these societies should deal with the question of modernity.

In this climate, the Arab regimes feel they need to be very careful about their support for the United States, and particularly for American policies that are unpopular with their people. U.S. policy toward Iraq ranks first on that list. In some quarters, Saddam is genuinely considered a popular hero for standing up to the Americans and Israelis. In others, Saddam is recognized as a vicious thug, but U.S. policy—whether it be containment or military operations—is seen as hurting the Iraqi people without having any impact upon him personally. In short, there is widespread popular animosity to any confrontational U.S. policy toward Iraq.

What all of this means for the moderate Arab states is that trouble in the Arab-Israeli arena taps into the huge pool of Arab anger and resentment, which gets expressed not only against Israel but against the United States and its policies as well. In turn, the moderate Arab states have become skittish about being seen as being too close to the United States for fear that the popular anger will be turned on them as "puppets" of the United States. They have become reluctant to take action in support of other U.S. policies, particularly unpopular ones such as confronting Saddam. This does not necessarily make it impossible for the moderate Arab states to cooperate with the United States; ultimately, they can suppress their people as they have many times in the past. But none of the Arab states likes to suppress its people, and they worry that such heavy-handed actions might someday spark an outright revolt against the regime. So the questions become for them: How much can they be seen as aiding the United States before they suffer a popular backlash? How bad will that popular backlash be? How much would it take to suppress serious popular unrest? What are the chances that such unrest could turn into a popular uprising? And even if it does not turn into a revolution, what would the long-term impact be on the regime's legitimacy and stability? In other words, the Arab states perform a complex set of assessments about the risks involved to them in supporting the United States.

It was this concern about the potential for a domestic backlash when popular opinion is already highly agitated over Israeli-Palestinian violence that produced the mock rapprochement among Saudi Arabia, Kuwait, and Iraq at the March 2002 Arab summit in Beirut. There, Saudi Crown Prince 'Abdallah famously embraced Iraqi representative 'Izzat Ibrahim ad-Duri, and the Kuwaitis and Iraqis signed a vague joint statement of reconciliation. Although Arab officials were quick to downplay these developments—and in private Arab officials dismissed them entirely—they are important signals that the United States cannot afford to miss.[6] They should be read as a sign that if the violence between Israel and the Palestinians does not abate (or, more properly, if the United States does not cause it to abate) the moderate Arabs will find themselves being pushed down the path toward reconciliation with Saddam and find it very hard to back an American policy of regime change.

One last important note: all of the Arab states are extremely conservative, especially when it comes to threats to their internal security. Consequently, they often overreact to popular unhappiness and exaggerate the threats to them from taking action such as supporting U.S. policy on Iraq. Thus, when they perform the complex assessment of the risks of supporting the United States, they tend to err on the side of caution, so it often takes a disproportionate effort on the part of the United States to secure their help. This balancing act, which all of the Arab states are now playing, is an important element of their own positions on Iraq and their willingness to support U.S. policies toward Saddam Hussein's regime.

VICTIMS OF OUR OWN SUCCESS

Another important aspect of the regional perspective on Iraq and U.S. policy is the diminishing sense of threat from Saddam's regime. In the early 1990s, right after the Gulf War, the Arab states of the Gulf region feared Saddam. They were convinced he was going to rebuild his forces quickly and come after them for supporting the United States. A key element of this fear was the conviction that the United States would soon lose interest in defending the Gulf region. As a result, there were early efforts in private by some Arab states to reach out to Baghdad and try to reconcile with Saddam.

In response, the United States launched a determined campaign to head off an Arab initiative to rehabilitate Iraq. U.S. officials spent considerable time and energy persuading Arab governments that the United States was committed to the defense of the Gulf Cooperation Council states, that it would remain in the region in force, and that U.S. forces would be capable of deterring or defeating any Iraqi attack. The quick, purposeful U.S. responses to Iraqi threats to Kuwait and Jordan in Operations Vigilant Warrior and Vigilant Sentinel in 1994 and 1995 particularly impressed the Arab states. UNSCOM continued its work for far longer than anyone had expected and destroyed tens of thousands of Iraqi WMD munitions. Meanwhile, Saddam's military eroded under the impact of the sanctions.

By the late 1990s, the situation had reversed itself. Now the Arabs were convinced that Saddam posed no threat at all. There was a widespread impression (except in Kuwait and to some extent Saudi Arabia) that the beast had been defanged. This impression made the various Arab states increasingly uncomfortable with the sanctions (which seemed misdirected), the U.N. inspections (which seemed excessive), U.S. strikes against Iraq (which seemed gratuitous), and even the U.S. military presence in the region (which seemed unnecessary). In many Arab minds, these facets of containment were probably unneeded, and therefore distasteful.

SAUDI ARABIA

The Saudi government would love to be rid of Saddam Hussein. The events of August 1990 and since have proven to it that Saddam is an extremely dangerous character who directly threatens its interests. Now, after more than a decade of containment in which Saudi Arabia was clearly the linchpin—both politically and militarily—the Saudis know that given the opportunity, Saddam will seek revenge against them. In addition, the Saudis know that one of Saddam's own conclusions about the Gulf War was not that he should not have invaded Kuwait but that he should have waited until he had a nuclear weapon before doing so and should have continued on into Saudi Arabia rather than stopping in Kuwait.[7] Contrary to some claims, the Saudis urged the United States to support the Shi'ite and Kurdish rebels during the 1991 *intifadah*.[8]

Since then, Riyadh's preferred solution to the problem has been a nice, clean covert action campaign that will result in Saddam's overthrow by another member of the Sunni ruling class. However, the Saudis seem to have recognized that Saddam's formidable internal security measures would make such an operation difficult, if not impossible. (See Chapter 9 for a lengthier discussion of this issue.) Throughout the 1990s the Saudis were anxiously supportive of the U.S. policy of containment and its efforts at regime change. "Anxiously," because they were always concerned that regime change would fail and containment could not last. Coupled with increasing popular disgruntlement at U.S. Iraq policy and its military presence in the Kingdom, these fears drove the Saudis to take a more parsimonious approach to supporting the United States. Instead of automatically backing U.S. policy initiatives on Iraq, the Saudis often had to be convinced and at times demurred. The Saudis were most helpful in pushing for action from the U.N. Security Council, reflecting their own rhetoric that Saudi Arabia was simply implementing the UNSC resolutions, plus their belief that containment required broad international support to be successful.

By any measure, the Saudis have become less supportive of limited U.S. military operations against Iraq.[9] In 1996, they would not allow U.S. aircraft to strike Iraqi targets after Saddam's attack on the Kurdish-held city of Arbil, and in February 1998, they publicly distanced themselves from U.S. strikes on Iraq to compel Baghdad's cooperation with U.N. inspections. Prince Sultan, the Saudi defense minister and among the most pro-American of the senior princes, went so far as to tell one newspaper, "We are against striking Iraq as a people and as a nation."[10] Since then, the Saudis have consented to U.S. strikes when Washington has put tremendous pressure on Riyadh but have allowed the U.S. only to use Saudi airspace and to fly support missions from Saudi bases—which allows them to say that no air strikes have been flown against Iraq from Saudi soil.[11]

These changes reflect both the Saudis' disenchantment with U.S. policy and their growing concerns about popular opinion. The Saudis were repeatedly disappointed by American claims to be making a major effort at regime change—first under the Bush administration and then at least twice during the Clinton administration—only to find that the United States would not use all of its resources and clout to make the effort successful. At the same time, Saudi society has been buffeted, possibly more than any other Arab state, by the combinations of a rising educational level, increasing access to information, and declining living standards. There were terrorist attacks within the Kingdom in the mid-1990s and rioting against the regime in Buraydah, in the Al Sa'uds' tribal heartland. Unemployment and popular disaffection rose as Saudi revenues fell. The Saudi people became increasingly unhappy with U.S. policy toward Israel, with the basing of U.S. forces in the Kingdom (despite monumental efforts by U.S. Central Command to lower the visibility of the American presence), and ultimately with U.S. policy toward Iraq. The Saudi populace became deeply concerned about the plight of the Iraqi people (based on Baghdad's exaggerations and lies) and chafed that American air strikes were killing Iraqis without doing anything about Saddam himself. A poll of ten countries (eight of them Muslim countries) in spring 2000 by Zogby International found that only in Saudi Arabia did a majority of those polled (51 percent) express negative feelings toward the American people. The Zogby poll also found that Saudis had a strongly negative impression of U.S. policy toward the Arab world (88 percent), of the U.S. war on terrorism (57 percent), and even of U.S. involvement in the liberation of Kuwait in 1991 (59 percent).[12]

As Saudi officials explain strenuously in private, they will support a U.S. effort to topple Saddam if it is done properly, but if the United States is not willing to do it "properly," they want no part of it and will eventually move to reach an accommodation with Baghdad. Indeed, the Saudis have been liberalizing their trade relations with Iraq to the point that the Kingdom's trade with Iraq is now estimated at $1 billion per year, and the Saudis have allowed Baghdad to accredit an ambassador to the Organization of the Islamic Conference, which has its permanent home in Jeddah, Saudi Arabia.[13] Riyadh's sentiment is that containment has eroded too far and the political costs to Saudi Arabia of trying to keep shoring it up are too high, given where public sentiment lies. They are not seeking the removal of the U.S. military presence from the Kingdom, but they may look for its further reduction in line with a policy of deterrence and accommodation of Iraq, should they move in that direction. In addition, the Saudis have stressed that they will not be able to support a U.S. effort at regime change in Iraq while Israel and the Palestinians are engaged in weekly violence. Although they do not believe that a comprehensive Arab-Israeli peace would be necessary before they could support a campaign against Iraq, they feel there must be negotiations and a sense of progress—not violence and a sense of hopelessness.

But what does handling regime change "properly" mean to the Saudis? It means an invasion and nothing less. Countless Saudi princes, officials, and businessmen have asked me, "Why won't you just invade?" Their points are that Saddam's security is so formidable and Iraq's armed forces are still strong enough that only the U.S. military has a high likelihood of bringing him down. The Saudis are thoroughly disenchanted with the Iraqi opposition, particularly the U.S.-created INC, which they consider feckless, manipulative, and without any support inside Iraq. In addition, the Saudis know that supporting a major American operation to topple Saddam will be highly unpopular among their people. What they have told us is that they are willing to handle popular discontent and believe they can do so, but they are willing to do so only for the minimum time required, not one day longer. What they stress is that they are not willing to launch an open-ended military campaign or a military campaign that tries to topple Saddam on the cheap.[14] They dismiss the notion of trying to overthrow the regime through a combination of air power and support to Iraqi opposition groups because they believe that it is unlikely to work and will take too long even if it does work. As one very senior GCC official put it, "When you are ready to use all of your forces, we will be there for you, but we are not interested in letting you try out theories about air power." For them, an invasion is the only option that makes sense because it virtually guarantees that Saddam's regime will be overthrown, it promises to do so quickly (as fast as U.S. forces can drive on Baghdad), and it is the most likely way to minimize Saddam's ability to strike back at them. In addition, the Saudis are concerned that after Saddam, Iraq will be left stable and not fall into chaos or disintegrate. They believe that only an invasion will allow the kind of a reconstruction that would ensure that Iraq is not worse after Saddam.

KUWAIT

In some ways, the Kuwaitis' sentiments are very close to those of their Saudi neighbors; in others, they are worlds apart. Kuwaiti public opinion is not quite so anti–U.S. policy as Saudi public opinion. The Zogby International poll found that 63 percent of Kuwaiti citizens had a favorable impression of the American people. In addition, the Kuwaitis have not forgotten that it was the United States that gave them back their country in 1991, with 98 percent of Kuwaiti citizens expressing a favorable impression of the U.S.-led liberation.[15] But neither is Kuwait wholly immune to the popular currents of the Arab world. Kuwaitis too are deeply unhappy about U.S. policy toward the Israeli-Palestinian dispute, and there were demonstrations against Israel and the United States during Israel's Operation Defensive Shield in March 2002.

The Kuwaiti government has been more supportive of U.S. policy toward Iraq than any other. Throughout the 1990s, only Kuwait consistently backed U.S. military operations against Iraq to the extent of being willing to allow U.S. aircraft to fly strikes against Iraq from its bases on every occasion.[16] To some extent, this is a product of sheer desperation. Kuwait remains deeply concerned about Iraq's intentions—every time that Baghdad is forced to express its respect for Kuwait sovereignty officially, other Iraqi figures are quick to point out that they regard the eventual reconquest of Kuwait as simply a matter of time.[17] In 2001, the Kuwaitis were stunned when Iraq again accused them of stealing oil from the ar-Rumaylah oil field—the precise charge it leveled in 1990 to justify its invasion.[18] What's more, Kuwait is so small (in both size and population) and so exposed to Iraq that, absent U.S. intervention, it could be overrun by the Iraqi armed forces even in their current weakened state. The Kuwaitis are watching the slow revival of Iraqi logistics as a result of the liberalization of oil-for-food with great anxiety. For this reason too, Kuwaitis remain at least grudgingly supportive of the U.S. military presence there—though many Kuwaitis privately say that they wish that they could do without it.[19]

Similarly, more than any other country, the Kuwaitis would like to see the United States topple Saddam. However, they have the same set of concerns as the Saudis. They too believe that taking covert action or backing any of the Iraqi opposition groups is unlikely to succeed. Moreover, they are not interested in experimenting at this point. Given the direction that the rest of the Arab world is taking, the Kuwaitis are nervous about getting too far out of step with their Arab brethren. Because of their vulnerability to Iraq, they too are terrified by the notion of an open-ended campaign with an uncertain conclusion. Even more than the Saudis, the Kuwaitis insist on the need for a short, decisive operation in which the United States uses the full panoply of its forces to ensure Saddam's swift demise—in other words, an invasion.

The last point about Kuwait that needs to be kept in mind is its close relationship with Saudi Arabia. Kuwait must be mindful of the wishes of its large southern neighbor. Saudi Arabia too could pose a tremendous threat to Kuwait if it ever wanted to, and the Saudis have far more ways to put pressure on the Kuwaitis than do the Iraqis. Although the Saudi military is bigger than Kuwait's, that is beside the point. Economically, politically, and socially, Kuwait is dependent on the Saudis. The Kuwaitis remember full well that it was Saudi support that made possible the liberation of

Finally, only 33 percent of Emiratis had a favorable impression of the U.S. war on terrorism, while 48 percent had an unfavorable view.[20]

It should come as no surprise that the southern GCC states are also far less supportive of any kind of confrontational policy toward Iraq. Qatar, Oman, and the UAE were among the first Arab governments to publicly call for an easing of the sanctions, starting in March 1995. That October, Shaykh Zayid an-Nahyan, president of the UAE and the grand old man of the Arab world, called for a lifting of the sanctions and reconciliation with Saddam.[21] It was no coincidence that this came at a time when Iran was heavily involved in terrorist planning around the Gulf, including stirring up domestic opposition in Bahrain. Since then, the southern Gulf states, particularly the UAE and Qatar, have been most opposed to imposing new constraints on Iraq (almost regardless of Iraqi behavior), most in favor of lifting all of the U.N. resolutions, and least interested in actively trying to topple Saddam. Their leaders generally detest Saddam, with one high-ranking official recently commenting that "No one would be disappointed for a second if Saddam were gone," but even those southern Gulf officials most favorably disposed to the United States argue that regime change would be difficult (perhaps impossible) and containment should be liberalized if not dropped in favor of mere deterrence.

Nevertheless, the southern Gulf states should not be considered a lost cause should the United States wish to pursue a more robust version of containment or certain aspects of regime change. In the end, all of the southern Gulf states have larger, more important strategic issues than Iraq, which means that not only are they less concerned about the threat but they are also more willing to be flexible. In particular, like Kuwait, all of the southern GCC states follow the Saudi lead to some extent. If the Saudis press them to back a new Iraq policy, even an aggressive one, they are likely to go along. (By the same token, if the Saudis press them *not* to support a new U.S. policy on containment or regime change, we will have a tough time convincing them to break ranks with Riyadh.) Nor are the southern GCC states immune to American influence. For the foreseeable future, all rely on the American military presence to defend them against Iran, Iraq, and (the dirty little secret of the Gulf) one another. Certainly no one in the Gulf region would object to a covert effort to oust Saddam. If we and the Saudis press them to back an invasion, they will support that too—although, like the Saudis and Kuwaitis, they are unlikely to back an open-ended war with Iraq and will be loath to support limited military operations as part of a new containment strategy. That said, senior officials from the southern Gulf states have gone furthest among the GCC to stress that any U.S. military operation against Iraq should come only during a period of relative calm between Israelis and Palestinians, lest regime change pour fuel on the flames of popular discontent.

JORDAN

Of all the Middle Eastern states, none has the same Iraq dilemmas as Jordan. Jordan is among the most fragile of the Arab states. Its economy is foundering, with a growth rate of 2 percent and unemployment running at close to 30 percent. This will probably only get worse: three quarters of Jordan's population is under the age of thirty, and the economy is not creating new jobs fast enough to absorb all of Jordan's new workers. There is a deep ethnic split in Jordan. The country is ruled by Jordan's "East Bankers"—those whose families lived in the territory of Jordan when it was created by the British after the First World War—who generally support the Hashimite monarchy. However, roughly two thirds of the population are Palestinians—many of whom fled to Jordan after Israel's conquest of the West Bank during the 1967 Six-Day War—who detest the king's pro-peace, pro–United States, and anti-Saddam policies.[22]

To make matters worse, Jordan's economy is heavily dependent on Iraq. Iraq supplies all of Jordan's oil, about 100,000 barrels per day, half of it for free and the other half at a significant discount rate (which is paid directly to Baghdad, rather than into the U.N. escrow account). Iraq is also the largest consumer of Jordanian imports and the largest exporter to Jordan, representing 15 to 20 percent of all Jordanian trade.[23] If Iraq cut its oil sales and trade, the Jordanian economy would collapse. It simply cannot afford to pay for oil at market rates, nor could its economy make up for the loss of Iraqi markets. Tens of thousands of Jordanians would immediately be thrown out of work. Consequently, Iraq uses Jordan as one of its main conduits for smuggling. Large numbers of Iraqi front companies and businessmen operate out of Amman, and naturally, with them come large numbers of Mukhabbarat personnel. So powerful are the Iraqis in Jordan that the Mukhabbarat has gunned down dissidents and smugglers in the street without any repercussions.

All of this means that the Jordanian government must walk a fine line. It cannot afford to be too anti-Iraq for fear of sparking unrest among the

Palestinians or economic reprisals by Baghdad. In addition, the Jordanians must worry that Saddam might someday use his heavy intelligence presence and the sympathy of the Palestinians to actually try to overthrow the regime. Like the GCC states, the Jordanians at least want the United States to wait until the Arab-Israeli peace process is back on track, if Washington is determined to mount a military operation against Iraq.[24]

Nevertheless, Amman is under no illusions about the Iraqi regime. The Jordanians hate Saddam and chafe at their dependence on him. They would love to be rid of him, and in 1995, after the defection of Hussein Kamel seemed to indicate that Saddam was losing his grip on power, Amman publicly supported an effort to overthrow the Ba'thist regime. They would still applaud such an effort but would probably find it hard to participate because of the likely reaction by the Jordanian public. Jordan would condemn any limited use of force against Iraq and would find it difficult to support any effort to strengthen containment. Likewise, any effort to shut down the smuggling through Jordan is a nonstarter unless other countries are willing to make up for the losses to Jordan by providing cheap oil and trade—something the U.S. government has pitched to the Saudis and Kuwaitis numerous times, only to be rebuffed on every occasion. As a final point, because Jordan's position is so precarious and so dependent on Iraq, the United States must take care to ensure that whatever policy it adopts toward Iraq does not cause Saddam to respond by going after the Jordanians.

SYRIA

When Hafiz al-Asad was alive, he could be counted on to support virtually any initiative designed to hurt Saddam Hussein. But Hafiz is dead, and the new Syrian leadership, headed by his son Bashar, is quite different. First, Bashar does not seem to have inherited his father's vendetta against Saddam and in fact has become quite close to Saddam's sons—Qusayy in particular. Second, Bashar may not yet have all of the reins of power in his hands, and many of the other senior members of the government, such as Foreign Minister Faruq al-Shara and Defense Minister Mustafa Tlas, have long advocated a better relationship with Baghdad as a way of applying pressure on Israel (and Turkey). Third, the Syrian "street" has become more of a factor and, like elsewhere in the region, hates U.S. policies and supports Saddam if only as an act of defiance against the United States.

However, all of these reasons pale beside Syria's overriding interest in Iraq: money. Like so many of its neighbors, Syria's economy is weak and problems loom on the horizon. Syria has serious debt problems. Unemployment is hovering at around 20 percent, and Syria too has a quickly growing population that threatens to create ever greater problems. Syria's economy remains heavily dependent on its agriculture sector, which is backward and overly dependent on rainwater, making for potentially volatile economic swings.[25]

Iraq has skillfully capitalized on Syria's economic weakness. In 2000, the Syrians reopened the oil pipeline from Iraq that ran to their port of Baniyas, which Hafiz had closed during the Iran-Iraq War, when he allied Syria with Iran. This pipeline allows Iraq to pump 150,000 to 200,000 barrels of oil per day, outside the U.N. system. Baghdad sells the oil to Syria at 50 percent of market prices, the Syrians pay the Iraqis directly rather than into the U.N. escrow account, and they make a hefty profit by reselling the oil at market rate. In addition, there is now a tremendous volume of smuggling overland—in both oil and goods—across the Iraqi-Syrian border. Increasingly, Syria is the number one smuggling route into and out of Iraq, and this too is greatly profiting Damascus. The Clinton and Bush administrations repeatedly tried to get the Syrians to shut down the smuggling, but to no avail. The Syrians keep promising to do so, then simply ignore their pledges.[26] As a result, Syrian trade with Iraq climbed from $50 million in 1997 to $2 billion in 2001.[27] Damascus is falling all over itself to expand its trade with Iraq, signing an agreement in the spring of 2002 that would allow free transfer of capital between the two countries, unify their tariffs, and establish a joint telephone company.[28]

Syrian support for U.S. policy toward Iraq is likely to be dominated by these economic considerations. The Syrians will ferociously oppose (and inevitably ignore) any efforts to tighten the sanctions and cut back on smuggling as part of a reinforced containment policy. They probably could live with pure deterrence of Iraq, although Damascus might actually object if all sanctions were lifted because this could obviate Iraq's need to smuggle, eliminating the rents that Syria has been able to extract from Iraq. Kurdish sources that have met with Syrian senior officials claim that Damascus would not object to any form of regime change as long as it is quick and the post-Saddam regime continues to sell Syria discounted oil.[29] However, the Syrians would likely object to a protracted or open-ended campaign against Iraq for fear that this would hurt their business and rouse their people.

TURKEY

Turkey's concerns about Iraq are more complicated. Turkey does have a sense of threat from Iraq, although it is not a dominant consideration. The Turks remember 1990, when Iraq threatened to retaliate against them as well if they participated in the Gulf War coalition. Many Turkish politicians are well aware of the atrocities that take place daily inside Iraq and readily admit that both the world and the region would be better off without Saddam's regime. They also consider Saddam an aggressive, unstable leader whose foreign policy adventures have caused Turkey a great deal of harm.

Turkey's most pressing concerns, however, are economic. Turkey makes considerable money legally from Iraqi oil exports under the U.N. oil-for-food program through a pipeline from Iraq that terminates at the Turkish port of Ceyhan. However, like Syria and Jordan, Turkey also makes a huge amount of money from smuggling with Iraq. Although Turkish-Iraqi trade has suffered considerable fluctuations, on average, 450 to 500 tanker trucks carry oil illegally from Iraq into Turkey via the Habur River crossing per day. Many of them carry back goods for resale in Iraq. Overall, the trade is worth roughly $2 billion annually, and this money is critical to the economy of impoverished southeastern Turkey. Drivers of the tanker trucks, most of whom are Turks, earn thirty to forty times their investment from each trip. Ankara considers this trade not only vital but a partial compensation for what it claims to be billions of dollars lost to it in trade from Iraq as a result of the U.N. sanctions.[30]

Another issue of equal stature for the Turks is the question of Iraqi Kurdistan. Although Ankara has hammered out working relationships with both of the main Iraqi Kurdish groups and skillfully plays off one against the other, it is not wild about the status quo. The Turks fear that Iraqi Kurdistan's state of de facto independence is encouraging Turkey's own Kurdish minority to seek the same. More important still, the Turks worry about what the future might bring. They would much prefer to see a strong central government in Baghdad reassert control over northern Iraq and snuff out any Kurdish movement toward true independence—and they would be willing to live with Saddam or anyone else to get that result.

The final consideration for Turkey is its alliance with the United States through NATO, a commitment that the Turks value very highly. Turkey's alliance with the United States is still its most important foreign policy priority. The Turkish General Staff, which has final say in such matters, is often loath to break ranks with the United States on issues of great importance to

Washington. As a result, the Turks have grudgingly supported Operations Provide Comfort and Northern Watch since 1991, not out of any love for the Iraqi Kurds but purely because of the importance of the U.S. alliance.

Turkey's preference is for a lifting of the sanctions on Iraq and a dismantling of the no-fly zones to allow Baghdad to resume its previous trade with Turkey and reassert its sovereignty over the Kurdish north. They will press hard for this and will fight any U.S. policy that threatens to crack down on smuggling, prolong the sanctions, or split Kurdistan off from the rest of Iraq. They will also oppose any U.S. regime change schemes for fear of what would follow. They don't believe that the United States could organize a coup that would be likely to topple Saddam and fear that a more likely outcome would be chaos, which would destroy their trade and provide the Kurds with an opportunity to declare independence. They are distressed by U.S. notions of backing the Iraqi opposition against Saddam because they know full well that the Kurds are the best suited for that job and they fear that this too would be the prelude to Kurdish independence. They even oppose a U.S.-led invasion because they do not know what kind of government we might install afterward.[31]

All of this said, American experts on Turkey believe that if the United States is willing to mount a full-scale invasion and secures the support of the GCC states (making the operation a reality), the Turks can probably be brought around. Ankara will not want to disappoint the United States on such an important foreign policy issue. The Turks know that this could have repercussions for U.S. support for their own foreign policy interests in E.U. membership, Cyprus, and other matters. Turkey will also calculate that if Washington is willing to mount a full-scale invasion and the Saudis are on board, there is no question that Saddam is finished and there will be a new government in Baghdad. Under those circumstances, it will have an overwhelming incentive to join the operation as the best way to ensure that its interests are protected when the post-Saddam government is created.[32] Nevertheless, even then it is likely to place important restrictions on U.S. operations and might forbid American ground forces to operate out of its territory for fear of encouraging the Iraqi Kurds.

EGYPT

Egypt's position bears a great deal of similarity to Turkey's but with the critical addition that Egypt's physical distance from Iraq means that the country is much less of a problem for Cairo. Egypt's population, led by a bilious and irresponsible press, has a strong streak of anti-American sentiment. The Zogby International poll found that only 35 percent of Egyptians had a favorable impression of the American people, while 47 percent had an unfavorable view. Likewise, 86 percent of Egyptians had an unfavorable view of U.S. policy toward the Arab world, 52 percent had an unfavorable view of the U.S.-led liberation of Kuwait (only 23 percent had a favorable impression, despite Egypt's major contribution to the effort), and 67 percent had an unfavorable impression of America's war on terrorism.[33] Not surprisingly, Cairo is among the forefront of the Arab governments urging caution on the United States on Iraq policy for fear that it will boil over into domestic unrest in Egypt.

Iraq has also worked hard to give Egypt a stake in the erosion of sanctions by directing large numbers of expensive oil-for-food contracts to Egyptian firms such that Egypt has typically been among the top five countries in terms of contracts since the inception of the oil-for-food program. The Egyptian economy is weak, and unemployment is a concern for Cairo; thus it cannot dismiss its trade with Iraq lightly. Moreover, there are geopolitical considerations. Egypt is far more concerned with the Arab-Israeli dispute than with Persian Gulf stability and fears that U.S. preoccupation with Iraq will mean instability in the Arab-Israeli arena. Egyptian officials fiercely guard their leadership of the Arab world and believe that at times this requires them to oppose the United States on issues of importance to the Arab world. At present, the future of Iraq is an issue of great importance to the Arab world, and Egypt will, at least publicly, want to be seen as leading in this area as well.

However, there are countervailing pressures as well. President Hosni Mubarak detests Saddam for his brutality and aggressiveness, and for having personally lied to Mubarak before the Iraqi invasion of Kuwait. Cairo is angry with Baghdad's efforts to usurp Egypt's place as leader of the Arab world and with its support of Palestinian and other Arab radicals as a means to achieving this end. Indeed, the Egyptians know that Saddam believes a new Arab-Israeli war would be to his benefit and is trying to stir one up—something that would be catastrophic for their own interests. Finally, like Turkey, Egypt places too much value on its strategic partnership with the United States to break too openly over an issue of (ultimately) secondary importance.

Cairo's preferred solution to the Iraq problem is a revised form of containment, one that would eliminate all constraints on the Iraqi economy (and on Iraq's ability to use the paltry restraints still in place for propaganda value) but keep Saddam tightly in check so that he could not stir up or destabilize the Gulf region. The Egyptians would oppose efforts to tighten the sanctions as unfairly hurting the Iraqi people without hurting Saddam, as well as hurting other Arab countries, such as Jordan. If the United States opts for regime change, the Egyptians will prefer covert action, but if that is not possible, they will urge a full-scale invasion to ensure that the operation is over as quickly and surely as possible. Publicly, Egypt might oppose a U.S. invasion to stay in step with its domestic audience, but it will allow Washington to move ships through the Suez Canal and planes across its airspace—as it has in every single Iraq crisis since 1991, regardless of its feelings about U.S. policy—and that is the minimum the United States needs.

ISRAEL

Israel is well aware of the threat it faces from Iraq. After all, it was Israel that hindered the Iraqi nuclear program throughout the 1970s, eventually bombing the Osiraq reactor in 1981. It was Israel that Saddam threatened to "burn" half of in 1990 and that he lobbed thirty-nine Scuds at during the Gulf War. The Israelis have listened carefully to Saddam's rhetoric for thirty years and have watched carefully as he built up Iraq's strength, at least rhetorically, for an eventual confrontation with Israel. The Israelis also know that Saddam believes that a new Arab-Israeli war would serve his interests and he is actively trying to foment one, including by providing support to Palestinian rejectionist groups. For all of these reasons, the Israelis want Saddam gone.

There are two caveats that apply, however. The first is that many Israelis believe that Iran is the more immediate threat. Many in Jerusalem believe that Saddam is weak and currently contained by the United States. Iran is growing stronger, it does not have to go to the same lengths to conceal its WMD programs, and it continues to receive support from the Russians. What's more, Iran is a far more active and dangerous sponsor of Palestinian terrorism than is Iraq. Whereas Iraq provides money and some material assistance, Iran provides the bulk of the material assistance as well as intelligence support and in many cases operational guidance. Iran's Hizballah allies are among the most dangerous threats to Israel right now. Thus, some Israelis would prefer to see the United States concentrate first on Iran, since they tend to see Iraq as a longer-term threat and Iran as an immediate one. Second, the Israelis know that if the United States tries to topple Saddam in an overt fashion, he is certain to lash out at Israel as he did in 1991, and this time he will most likely try to do so with weapons of mass destruction.

But neither of these caveats appears to be critical to Jerusalem. One Israeli official told me, "We'd rather see you deal with Iran first, but if you choose to deal with Iraq first, we won't object." The Israelis recognize that Saddam is enough of a threat to them that whenever the United States believes it has the political and diplomatic backing to do the job, they should give Washington their wholehearted support.[34] They have also indicated that they are ready to deal with Iraq's efforts to strike them with WMD. Unlike in 1991, Israel now has the Arrow antiballistic missile system, and although it is unproven, it has done well in tests and Jerusalem hopes it can be relied on. In addition, the Israeli government has stressed that any American military operation will have to take maximum measures to prevent Saddam from launching Scuds and air strikes at Israel, and this means a large ground presence in western Iraq. Because of the limited range of Iraq's al-Husseins, the Iraqis have to launch them from west of Baghdad to be able to reach Israel. During the Gulf War, the United States tried to eliminate the Scud threat to Israel using only air power and special forces personnel on the ground. The Israelis wanted to put large numbers of ground troops in, but we convinced them to stay out. Today, although U.S. sensor and strike technologies have improved considerably, the Israelis do not want to take a chance and want us to deploy a big ground force in western Iraq to keep the number of Scud launches against them to the absolute minimum.

IRAN

If there is any country in the world with an incentive to want Saddam Hussein dead, it is the Islamic Republic of Iran. During the brutal eight-year war that he started, Saddam employed every weapon against Iran that he could get his hands on. He bombed its citizens and gassed its soldiers. In all, the war cost Iran roughly 400,000 dead and twice that number wounded. Since then, Iraq has supported anti-Iranian terrorist groups (most notably the Mujahedin-e Khalq, or National Council of Resistance). Of course this has not stopped the Iranians from engaging in massive oil smuggling with Iraq—after all, this is the Middle East. As much as $500 million worth of Iraqi oil is smuggled through Iranian waters to the UAE each year, and perhaps another $100 million to $200 million worth is trucked overland through Iran.[35] In addition, on several occasions since 1991 the Iranians have reached out to Iraq to see if they could not reach a *modus vivendi* to pursue their common antipathy to the United States. Each time, the Iraqis unexpectedly and bizarrely scuttled the deal.[36]

The Iranians would like to see Saddam gone. However, they are willing to settle for keeping him tightly contained. Although Tehran pays lip service to the suffering of the Iraqi people, in truth, Iranian officials have little sympathy for them. The Iranians might even be willing to shut down their contribution to Iraqi oil smuggling if every other outlet were also stoppered and Tehran were offered some form of compensation. Although the Iranians are contributing to the erosion of the sanctions, they recognize that the demise of containment (or its replacement by simple deterrence) would not be in their best interest because this would allow Saddam to rebuild his WMD programs. The Iranians are concerned that the West might not object so loudly if Saddam turned his WMD arsenal against Iran.

Iranian officials are equally concerned with the composition and structure of any future Iraqi government, and this shapes their views toward regime change. Iran would like very much to see the Shi'ites in power in Baghdad, believing that they will be more favorably inclined toward their coreligionists in Tehran than the Sunnis have been over the last seventy years. More than that, the Iranians are afraid of a pro-U.S. government coming to power in Baghdad. At present, there are U.S. military forces in Pakistan, Afghanistan, Uzbekistan, Georgia, Turkey, Kuwait, Saudi Arabia, Bahrain, Qatar, Oman, and the Persian Gulf. In addition, Turkey is a NATO ally and Turkmenistan a member of NATO's partnership for peace. A pro-U.S. government in Baghdad, particularly one that allowed a U.S. military presence, would just about literally complete the encirclement of Iran by American forces and allies.

Thus, Iran's preference is probably a return to the suffocating containment of the early 1990s. Perversely, it might also favor a U.S. military campaign to oust Saddam using only air power and the Iraqi opposition because this could bog the United States down in a protracted, enervating military campaign that, if it succeeded, would leave the U.S. little appetite to go after other countries—such as Iran. In addition, in any situation where opposition forces were playing a major role, Tehran's control over the main

Shi'ite groups would allow it the maximum opportunity to carve out a sphere of influence in post-Saddam Iraq and otherwise influence the shape of the next Iraqi government. The Iranians would prefer not to see a full-scale invasion of Iraq because this would ensure a swift American victory that would do most to preclude an Iranian role afterward. Nevertheless, they would likely play such a scenario as they did the U.S. military campaign in Afghanistan: initially they would mind their manners and try to be helpful, if only because with several hundred thousand American troops in the region they would not want to give us an excuse to come after them. But after the fall of Saddam, they would work as hard as they can to undermine our presence in Iraq, carve out buffer zones for themselves among the Shi'ah, hamstring our efforts to build a new government, and try to gain as much influence over the new government as they possibly can. In 1991, the Bush, Sr., administration made it clear to the Iranians that Operation Desert Storm was not aimed at them and that if they acted responsibly, the United States would not take action against them. This approach had the desired effect and was very important in removing a potentially serious problem for U.S. forces in the region—a threat from Iran on their eastern flank. If the United States plans a major military operation against Iraq in the future, it would behoove us again to ensure Tehran's neutrality as best we can because if not, they could cause us a great deal of pain and frustration.

BEYOND THE REGION

Of course, the countries of the Middle East are not the only ones that matter to America's Iraq policy. Other countries also play important roles because they are key to rebuilding consensus in the United Nations (itself critical to revamping containment), because they are key supporters of Iraq and therefore our greatest diplomatic adversaries, and/or because they are U.S. allies whose support Washington should try to secure for any Iraq policy.

Great Britain has always been the country closest to the United States in the U.N. Security Council. Its continued support is critical to any new policy of containment. After Operation Desert Fox, London concluded that containment was no longer workable and resolved to move to a policy of simple deterrence. Since then, the British have worked skillfully to bring the United States around to that position. Today, that probably would be

Britain's preferred option and still seems to be the choice of the Foreign Office. However, press reports and Prime Minister Tony Blair's own remarks have made clear that No. 10 Downing Street would be willing to support a U.S.-led invasion of Iraq to change the regime once and for all.[37] London is under no illusions about the problems Saddam's regime could cause if it is someday free to do as it likes, and since it is the United States that will have to bear the serious costs, Blair is willing to go along if we are serious enough to do it right. That said, the British are sticklers about international law and often have a much higher legal threshold for military action against Iraq than does the United States. Consequently, London would very much like to have a clear green light from the United Nations before launching into new military operations against Iraq.[38]

France is one of Iraq's chief advocates and, while still a NATO ally of the United States, believes that taking an "independent" line is critical to French stature and the good of the world. In addition, Iraq owes France $4.5 billion from pre–Gulf War sales.[39] France is also one of Iraq's largest trading partners. To be blunt, the French have not hesitated to compromise their principles if it meant a greater share of Iraqi trade. In 2000, when Iraq began demanding that countries fly commercial aircraft into Baghdad in violation of the U.N. flight ban in return for further oil-for-food contracts, Paris suddenly discovered a new "interpretation" of the U.N. resolutions that indicated that there was no such flight ban—even though it had voted for the original resolution and had respected the ban for the preceding ten years. As a result of this shameless pandering, the French have been the largest or second largest recipient of Iraqi oil-for-food contracts in every phase of the program.

France's preferred policy toward Iraq is one of deterrence. In their hearts, the French recognize that Saddam Hussein cannot be left to his own devices. However, they also know that in the end it is the United States—not France—that will be expected to deal with Saddam should he acquire nuclear weapons, and they are perfectly comfortable with that arrangement. In the meantime, they would like to see the sanctions liberalized if not lifted altogether, to maximize their profits from Iraqi trade. The French will likely oppose any effort to shore up containment, if only because Iraq will oppose it and will make future oil-for-food contracts contingent upon toeing its line. The French probably will oppose any U.S. effort at regime change because they are unlikely to receive the same preferential treatment from Saddam's successors, whoever they may be. That said, if France becomes convinced that the United States is absolutely determined to remove Saddam and is willing to use all of its power to do the job, they likely will flip and become supporters of the operation to try to secure some piece of post-Saddam Iraq's trade and reconstruction.

The **rest of Europe** tends to split into two camps over Iraq, largely upon geographic lines. Southern Europe, particularly Spain, Italy, and Greece, tends to line up with the French in favoring a lifting of virtually all sanctions and opposing efforts toward regime change. Northern Europe, particularly Germany, the Low Countries, and the Scandinavians, are closer to the British. They are wary of Saddam's efforts to acquire WMD and appalled at his human rights record. They would like to see more done for the Iraqi people but would prefer that this be done within a strengthened containment regime to keep Saddam under wraps. They are generally leery of a new military operation against Iraq but probably could be convinced that it was necessary. In this case, the northern European states would want a U.N. imprimatur on the campaign plan and a firm sense of U.S. plans not only for the "takedown" but also for rebuilding a stable Iraq afterward. This brings up a final concern of all the Europeans, which is that the United States will decide unilaterally on regime change but will then try to make reconstruction a multilateral project to spread the costs. For the Europeans, having a say in the decisions on regime change will be their price for helping to pay for the rebuilding of Iraq afterward.

Russia has been Iraq's strongest advocate since the Gulf War and has been rewarded with a healthy slice of Iraq's oil-for-food contracts, vying with France for the top slot during each round of contracting. Iraq owes Russia $8 billion from pre–Gulf War sales, mostly for military equipment.[40] The Russians have signed numerous long-term contracts with Iraq for the development of Iraqi oil fields, infrastructure, and other lucrative projects. Consequently, Russia has quite a bit at stake with Saddam Hussein's regime. What's more, post-Soviet Russia hates to see the United States throw its weight around the world and therefore tends to oppose American military moves for geopolitical reasons as well. Moscow will resist a tightening of the containment regime with all of its influence and do what it can to head off a U.S. military operation against Iraq.[41] In fact, the Russians would like to see *all* of the sanctions lifted because it would mean a bonanza for Russian firms, especially Russia's foundering military industries, which would find themselves flooded with Iraqi orders for tanks, MiGs, and everything else that can kill people.

That said, Washington need not consider Russia a lost cause if it opts for regime change. First, Moscow tends to grudgingly recognize that its relationship with the United States is still its most critical foreign policy concern. What's more, if the United States is willing to employ all of the military force necessary to ensure Saddam's ouster and Washington can assure the participation of the moderate Arab states, thereby making such a strategy feasible, the Russians are likely to recognize that Saddam is doomed and there will not be anything they can do to save him. Russia is not going to threaten to go to war on behalf of a client as the Soviet Union did over Cuba and Egypt during the Cold War. Moreover, if the United States makes it clear that it has the will and the regional support to get the job done, Moscow (like Paris) will have a huge incentive to try to secure its economic interests in the inevitable post-Saddam world. The Russians might not be willing to contribute an armored division to such an effort (and the U.S. military would not want it) but they might be willing to be helpful in other ways—perhaps even in the United Nations.[42]

China will probably end up opposing any U.S. policy on Iraq. Beijing vehemently opposes any use of American military force, and the idea of the United States forcibly overthrowing another regime is anathema to the Chinese—whose record on human rights and WMD is probably closer to Iraq's than to Sweden's. Like Russia's and France's, China's advocacy of Iraq over the years has paid off in large oil-for-food contracts as well as some hefty illegal contracts, such as the construction of a fiber-optic communications network for Iraqi military and internal security forces.[43] However, in some instances, the Chinese have rigidly adhered to the UNSC resolutions so as to preserve the Security Council's authority—one of China's principal sources of influence in the world. For these reasons, the Chinese will also likely oppose any efforts by the United States to create a new containment regime that will patch up the holes in the current sanctions.

America's **other core allies,** such as Canada, Australia, and Japan, can be expected to be as supportive as Britain and the northern European countries or more so in terms of a more robust policy. All of them would probably prefer a revamped form of containment, if only because they would all find regime change somewhat unpalatable for one reason or another. They would certainly be willing to accept pure deterrence if that were the United States' choice, recognizing that it would be up to Washington to make such a policy work. In the event that the United States decides to pursue regime change, these allies would prefer covert action as the "cleanest" way of removing Saddam. In the end, all would likely go along with a military campaign if the United States made clear its commitment and willingness to pay the costs and rebuild Iraq afterward. In addition, these other allies would be far more comfortable with an approach that first secured the United Nations' blessing for the operation. Under those circumstances, all would be likely to provide some support to the campaign itself and probably economic and political assistance in building the new Iraqi government afterward.

Part III

THE
OPTIONS

SEVEN

The Erosion of Containment

The first option to consider when thinking about future U.S. policy toward Iraq is the policy of containment—the current policy and one that has served the U.S. reasonably well since 1991. American foreign policies are inevitably the result of painful debates among competing strategic, diplomatic, economic, and domestic political interests. Consequently, any policy that is implemented usually was adopted because it best met those competing needs or, more often, was the lowest common denominator among them. Consequently, there are always powerful forces working in favor of the status quo and against any change in policy.

Containment of Iraq has been no exception. It was essentially the lowest common denominator—the one strategy that met America's minimum strategic requirements without creating undue political, diplomatic, or economic costs. For many years after the Gulf War, containment did meet Washington's minimum strategic requirement toward Iraq: preventing Saddam Hussein from reconstituting Iraq's military power so that he could again threaten the Persian Gulf region. Moreover, for many years, containment did this at minimal cost to other U.S. policies, to domestic political interests, and to the budget. Thus, there were few voices in favor of abandoning containment for the alternatives. Pure deterrence—lifting the sanctions, writing off the inspections, ending the NFZs, and drawing down the level of U.S. forces in the Gulf region—was even lower cost, but it was considered too risky to meet minimum U.S. strategic requirements. At the other end of the spectrum, the highest-probability approach to regime change, a full-scale invasion, was considered much too costly because no one believed that the American people would support such a policy. A number of other regime change options had a much lower probability of success (and in some cases entailed high risks). As discussed in Chapter 3, at times the United States was willing to try some of these other regime change options, but only as an adjunct to containment, never as a substitute for it. Given the low probability of success of these other options, no one wanted to jettison containment in pursuit of a will-o'-the-wisp.

In addition, containment had several other advantages. Of greatest importance in the aftermath of the Gulf War and the collapse of the Soviet Union, it promised to allow the United States to prevent Saddam from threatening the Gulf region at the minimum cost in resources and political exertion, thereby allowing the United States to concentrate on other foreign policy issues. At a moment when the whole world appeared to be in flux and senior U.S. policy makers felt it was crucial to seize that opportunity to fundamentally reshape the international system, containment of Iraq appeared to be tailor-made. It also had the huge advantage of being the policy of the United Nations. Containment was enshrined in the various resolutions of the Security Council that demanded Iraqi disarmament, imposed the sanctions to impel Iraqi compliance, insisted that Iraq cease repressing its people, prevented it from threatening Kuwait, and justified the no-fly zones. Containment is the multilateral approach that the international community embraced after the Gulf War to deal with the threat of Saddam Hussein and his pursuit of weapons of mass destruction and hegemony in the Persian Gulf region. In that sense, pursuing containment for the United States also meant working within the international system that we sought to bolster as part of the New World Order.

Given all of these advantages, even today containment is still the preferred option of many. If we could forgo the costs of a major invasion by relying on a revitalized containment program that we could be confident would last for many more years, there would be a strong case for doing so. As long as containment was working, it benefited everyone except the Iraqi people, who were forced to endure not only the cruelty of Saddam's regime but the effects of the sanctions as well. However, the plight of the Iraqi people can be ameliorated only by mounting a full-scale invasion to forcibly remove Saddam from power, and as long as the American people are unwilling to pay the costs of such a commitment, there is no policy the United States could embrace that would be more beneficial (or simply less harmful) to them than containment. Indeed, because the oil-for-food program ensures that the regime spends at least some of Iraq's revenues on food, medicine, and other humanitarian supplies, sticking with containment is probably the least bad of the other options for the Iraqi people as well.

The central problem with containment today is that the policy is no longer meeting our minimum strategic requirements. Moreover, the cost of restoring containment so that it could do so would be so exorbitant as to invalidate the essential premise of the policy.

TAKING ON WATER

When Iraq evicted the U.N. weapons inspectors in the fall of 1998, the sanctions became the critical element of containment. Originally, the sanctions and the inspections operated in tandem—with the burden of the sanctions pressing Iraq to comply with the inspections and the inspections helping to minimize Iraq's ability to skirt the sanctions and smuggle goods for its proscribed weapons of mass destruction programs.[1] In truth, the sanctions were always more important than the inspections, if only because it was clear from the start that Saddam never intended to cooperate with the inspectors and would probably be able to keep his WMD programs intact and functioning despite their best efforts. The inspectors themselves will tell anyone who asks them that there is only so much inspections can do if the Iraqi government refuses to cooperate. The sanctions were always the greatest impediment to Iraqi military reconstitution, particularly to rapid progress on Iraq's nuclear weapons program.

There was always some degree of leakage in the sanctions. Right from the start, the Security Council chose to ignore Iraq's illegal oil sales to Jordan. Jordan petitioned the Security Council for an exemption to the sanctions just after they were imposed, but the Council took no action. Until some other country was willing to furnish Jordan with the cheap oil and major import market its economy required, the Security Council was not going to enforce the sanctions against Amman for fear of wreaking havoc in the Hashimite Kingdom. Likewise, for many years, the illegal truck traffic between Iraq and Turkey grew and the United Nations did nothing about it. As a NATO ally and the key to the northern no-fly zone, Turkey largely got a bye from the United States, Britain, and France until Washington began to tackle all of the smuggling problems in 1999–2000. In addition, a fleet of rickety tanker ships was smuggling oil through the Gulf. The coalition deployed a Maritime Interception Force (MIF) to stop this trade, but the smugglers got around it by sailing in Iranian territorial waters (where they paid a toll to Tehran's Revolutionary Guards), and then darting across the Strait of Hormuz to sell their illicit cargo in Qatar or the UAE. The emirates of Dubayy and Fujayrah, in particular, were (and are) notorious for their disregard of the Iraq sanctions.

Up until about 1999, this trade was more an irritant than a threat. Through most of the 1990s, the truck trade with Turkey netted Iraq only about $100 million per year. The trade with Jordan ran to about $225 million and the smuggling in the Gulf $15 million to $50 million. Thus, the Iraqi regime made about $300 million to $350 million per year.[2] With this money, Saddam not only had to procure illegal items for his WMD programs but also had to provide perks to his loyalists, make some sops to the Iraqi armed forces, and provide for his family's (and his own) lavish lifestyle. There is no question that Saddam's WMD programs were able to survive and make some progress on this strict allowance, but they do not seem to have been able to thrive.

Today, the sanctions are hemorrhaging. Whereas as recently as 1999, Saddam's regime netted only about $350 million, in 2002 it will rake in $2.5 billion to $3 billion, representing 15 to 22 percent of all Iraqi revenue. The greatest problem is the Syrian trade. Iraq is pumping 180,000 to 200,000 barrels of oil per day (bpd) through the Iraqi-Syrian oil pipeline. Iraq and Syria are talking about boosting this figure to 250,000 bpd, and since the maximum capacity of the pipeline is 800,000 bpd, that figure may climb even higher. In addition, trucks are carrying another 30,000 to 40,000 bpd across the Syrian-Iraqi border. In return, the Syrians allow Iraq to import essentially whatever it wants. As a result, Saddam is making at least $1 billion and possibly as much as $2 billion per year just from the illegal trade with Syria.[3]

Not to be outdone, the Turks have ramped up their smuggling, with the central government now taking an active role in regulating (and taxing) the trade. In 2001, trucks carried about 150,000 bpd from Iraq to Turkey, netting another $340 million to $400 million for Saddam outside the oil-for-food system. Like the Syrians, the Turks also want to expand their capacity to smuggle Iraqi oil and have announced plans to increase smuggling by 50 percent.[4]

Jordan too has been increasing its oil imports from Iraq, since there have been no repercussions for Iraq's other neighbors. In 2001, Iraq made $450 million from the Jordanian trade, and although this year's numbers are expected to be lower, they will still be a lot higher than the 1990s average of $225 million.[5]

The tanker trade in the Gulf is more variable, in large part because of the unpredictability of the Iranian government, which at times has responded to U.N. (and U.S.) pleas to cut down on the smuggling. Nevertheless, it is still expected that Iraq will make somewhere between $500 million and $1 billion per year, depending on Tehran's mood. Iraq also smuggles oil by illegally "topping off" legal tankers—filling them with the legal amount of oil while U.N. monitors are present but then illegally adding hundreds of thousands of additional barrels after the monitors leave, which are paid for directly to Iraq rather than into the U.N. oil-for-food accounts.[6]

Of course, all of this oil has to come from somewhere. Iraq has been diverting oil from legitimate sales via oil-for-food to smuggling. According to the *Petroleum Intelligence Weekly,* in 2001, Iraq legally exported only 1.67 million bpd on average (down from about 2.1 million bpd in 2000) and illegally exported 365,000 bpd—or 18 percent of total oil exports.[7] In part because of this practice, Iraq's legal oil-for-food revenues fell from $17 billion in 2000 to about $11 billion in 2001, while its smuggling revenues increased from about $600 million in 2000 to more than $2 billion in 2001.[8] So much for the regime's concern for the Iraqi people.

Iraq has also managed to skim money from the oil sales that go through the U.N. system. Starting in 2000, Iraq began demanding surcharges of 20 to 70 cents on each barrel of oil sold. The buyers were forced to pay this surcharge to Iraqi bank accounts outside the oil-for-food program. To sweeten the deal, the Iraqi government began significantly underpricing its oil—enough to both compensate the buyer for the surcharge and still keep the price per barrel 35 to 65 cents per barrel below market rate to give companies the incentive to violate the sanctions by paying the surcharge. As a result, between November 2000 and May 2002, Iraq earned about $300 million from the surcharges. The United Nations fought back in a variety of ways to prevent the Iraqis from keeping their prices down (thereby making the surcharges uneconomical).[9] Its efforts have partially worked, but the main result is that Iraqi exports have fallen dramatically. In fact, in 2002, the situation got so bad that Iraq was forced to lower its surcharges to 15 cents per barrel to boost its market share again. Even this reduced rate will still net it about $100 million outside the U.N. system by year's end.[10] Of course, while the United Nations' efforts did cut the amount Iraq was able to skim off of the legal oil sales, it was the oil-for-food program—and thus the Iraqi people—that took the biggest hit, losing more than $2 billion in early 2002.[11]

While ever more illegal oil flows out of Iraq, ever more illegal goods flow into it. The real danger in the breakdown of the sanctions and the regime's growing control over Iraqi revenues is that Baghdad is using this money to import prohibited items for its conventional military and its WMD programs. With more cash available, Iraq can make breaking the embargo more worthwhile for unsavory arms dealers and struggling scientists. Baghdad can use the cash to bribe customs agents and other government officials to look the other way when shipments ostensibly destined for Jordan or Syria are obviously intended for Iraq. And because the value of Iraq's smuggling is so important to its neighbors, they are more than willing to turn a blind eye to the flow of illegal goods across their borders bound for Iraq.

Unfortunately, it is difficult to know exactly what is going into Iraq. This is the main problem; if the United States and United Nations knew, they might be able to stop it. As it is, we know only that between the smuggling and the surcharges Saddam is making $2 billion to $3 billion per year that he can spend as he likes. In addition, we have been able to intercept some shipments and get intelligence on others that give at least a sense of what Saddam is using his illegal revenues to import. For instance, in June 2002, the Indian government brought charges against the executives of an Indian company for selling atomized aluminum powder and titanium engine parts to Iraq in such quantity and of such quality that India's Defense and Research Development Organization concluded they could only have been intended for chemical warfare and ballistic missile production.[12] As another example, in 2000, the United States discovered that China was constructing a nationwide fiber-optic communication system for the Iraqi government that would have been employed by the Iraqi military and internal security forces. This in particular was a stunning sign of the erosion of containment: not only was China a member of the P-5 and therefore one of the countries most responsible for seeing the implementation of Security Council resolutions, but this was a massive project in terms of money, manpower, and geographic scope. It is hard to imagine that China really believed that it could keep so large a project secret from U.S. intelligence and therefore demonstrates the extent to which it was willing to flout the sanctions.[13]

As another indication of the loss of international respect for the Iraq sanctions, the ban on air travel to Iraq has simply disintegrated. In UNSC Resolution 670, passed unanimously on September 25, 1990, the Security Council decided that all states "shall deny permission to any aircraft to take off from their territory if the aircraft would carry any cargo to or from Iraq or Kuwait other than food in humanitarian circumstances subject to authorization by the Security Council." The Resolution also demanded that all member states deny overflight to such aircraft unless they were authorized by the Security Council or landed and were searched to ensure that there was no contraband on board.[14] At the time, this was considered by all member states as a ban on flights to Iraq except those specifically approved by the Security Council. This ban stood for ten years, until August 2000, when, on the eve of the U.S. presidential elections, the Russians flew a commercial aircraft into Baghdad without permission from the United Nations or an inspection.[15] This opened the floodgates. Iraq demanded that countries resume flying to Baghdad if they wanted a share of its oil-for-food contracts, and since the Security Council did nothing, Iraq's trade partners duly lined up. Jordan followed the Russian lead, followed by planes from Yemen, Morocco, Tunisia, Turkey, the UAE, Algeria, Libya, Egypt, Lebanon, Ireland, Iceland, Greece, and France. By May 2001, Jordan announced that it was resuming regular commercial flights to Iraq.[16]

As the breakdown of the flight ban demonstrates, a key problem with the sanctions today is the considerable economic influence Baghdad now wields as a result of its control over oil-for-food contracts.[17] This is another perverse impact of the sanctions and the oil-for-food program: the Iraqi regime now controls literally all legal trade between Iraq and the outside world, giving it a power and a degree of control over the Iraqi economy it never had before. Before the Gulf War, the Iraqi government simply regulated most of its trade, but Iraqi businesses imported and exported on their own initiative, as long as they complied with the government's regulations and paid its duties. Today, however, all legal Iraqi trade must be conducted by the regime through the oil-for-food program; it is illegal (according to the U.N. sanctions) for an Iraqi businessman to arrange for international deals outside of oil-for-food. Only the illegal smuggling takes place outside the government's hands, but even that is largely controlled by the regime's senior figures. Naturally, given this total control over trade, economic considerations (let alone what might be best for the Iraqi people) have taken a backseat to the regime's political goals. Thus Baghdad carefully doles out oil-for-food contracts only to its biggest supporters. It makes very clear what the political price is for these contracts, and it rewards those who toe its line and punishes those who do not. Since Iraq has anywhere from $11 billion to $17 billion in oil-for-food revenues to spend (depending on how much it plays with oil production for surcharges and smuggling), it has been able to buy plenty of political support to further erode the sanctions.

THE FALSE PROMISE OF THE "SMART SANCTIONS"

When the administration of George W. Bush took office in January 2001, its answer to the problem of the snowballing smuggling was what they called "smart sanctions." This idea had been percolating in the bureaucracy for a number of years during the Clinton administration, and if Vice President Gore had won the 2000 election, his administration might have adopted something similar.

The premise of the smart sanctions was certainly the right one. The idea was to focus the sanctions on those areas of greatest concern—Iraq's military and WMD programs—and eliminate the economic sanctions, which had become a terrible public relations burden on the entire containment regime. The smart sanctions would accomplish this shift by lifting the remaining U.N. economic sanctions on Iraq, streamlining the contracting process so that there would be fewer delays (from either national holds or simply the bureaucratic oversight of thousands of contracts), and tightening the sanctions by choking off the smuggling. The smart sanctions would effect the first two changes through a new, much reduced list of dual-use items that Iraq would be prohibited from importing. All other contracts would be handled by an expedited process that the United Nations had already been using for most contracts for foodstuffs and medical items.[18]

The kicker, however, was always in successfully tightening the sanctions to eliminate the smuggling, and here the smart sanctions got the answer wrong. The Bush administration wanted to shut down the smuggling by concentrating on Iraq's neighbors—the principal conduits for the smuggling. Its intent was to try to bring all of Iraq's illegal oil smuggling into the U.N. program by legalizing the pipeline through Syria; the truck traffic through Turkey, Jordan, Syria, and Iran; and the tanker traffic in the Gulf (efforts that had been begun during the previous administration). In addition,

Washington hoped to create a system of incentives for each of Iraq's neighbors to convince them not only to agree to bring their oil smuggling under oil-for-food but also to halt the flow of smuggled goods back into Iraq. Unfortunately, this was never going to work. Indeed, at the end of the Clinton administration, we had tried similar measures only to have them founder.

At the most basic level, the problem with going after Iraq's neighbors to cut down on the smuggling is that the smuggling is far too profitable and, in most cases, economically vital to the neighboring states. Iraq would undoubtedly retaliate against any neighboring state that agreed to legalize its share of the smuggling by cutting off all trade—legal and illegal—with it. The neighbors know this and have already made it clear that any program to cut off the smuggling will have to compensate them for the expected loss of both. Thus, in the case of Jordan, someone would to have to provide it with roughly $500 million in free and discounted oil, as well as make up for the loss of $900 million in trade, including $683 million worth of Jordanian exports to Iraq.[19] As noted in Chapter 5, the Clinton administration tried several times to get the Saudis and Kuwaitis to step in at least on the oil side but was rebuffed every time. Even then it is an open question whether Jordan would go along with such a plan because of the threat that Iraq might try to destabilize the Jordanian regime by stirring up its Palestinian population or employing its intelligence personnel in a covert action campaign against the king's government.

Syria would be even harder to convince. Not only would the United States and United Nations have to find a way to compensate Syria for the loss of $500 million in revenue from Iraq's smuggled oil and nearly $2 billion in trade, but we would probably have to bribe the Syrians to actually shut down the smuggling even after we had compensated them for it. Both the Clinton and Bush administrations have repeatedly pressured Syria to stop the smuggling or bring it under the U.N. program. Every time the Syrians have agreed to do so and then simply ignored their promise.[20] Since there has been no penalty for Syria, it is highly likely that Damascus would simply pocket whatever compensation the United Nations came up with and continue to smuggle on top of it. The United States and the United Nations would have to find a powerful disincentive for Syria (unlikely, given how the Arab world would react and the importance of Syria to the Middle East peace process) or else pay off the Syrians to actually shut down the smuggling. How many more billions of dollars would it take to convince the Syrians that the payoff from the United States/United Nations was greater than the payoff from continued Iraqi oil smuggling, and therefore make them willing to actually shut down the Iraqi smuggling? The world will probably never know.

Turkey would be equally difficult. The Turks make about $400 million from the Iraqi oil smuggling, and overall their trade with Iraq is worth about $2 billion.[21] Like the Jordanians, they see this commerce as a critical element of Turkey's overall economy, particularly for the economy of their politically fragile southeast. Hesar Hsimoglu of the Chamber of Drivers in Silopi, Turkey, summed up Turkey's perspective: "The life of the region is tied to this trade. We have lived through tough times. The traffic has brought peace to the region."[22] Moreover, like the Syrians, the Turks have ignored repeated efforts to get them to stop the smuggling or bring it under the U.N. program, indicating that it may take more than just dollar-for-dollar compensation to actually get the Turks to shut down the smuggling.

Iran makes less off of Iraq, about $250 million from smuggling and another $130 million in trade. However, the smuggling revenues are not part of the official Iranian budget. Instead, they go directly to the Revolutionary Guards and their hard-line masters in Tehran, making their value much greater to key regime figures than the actual dollar values might imply. Moreover, like Turkey and Syria, Iran has gotten away with this for years despite various efforts to convince them to stop.[23] Iran does not always take its international obligations seriously—it is a signatory to the Nuclear Non-Proliferation Treaty and the Chemical Weapons Convention and is taking an active role in the formulation of the Biological and Toxin Weapons Convention, yet it continues to have active programs in all of these areas.[24] Consequently, in this case as well, it might take a lot more than $400 million per year to convince Iran to actually stop the smuggling. There is an additional problem with Iran: it is U.S. government policy to deny Tehran hard currency to hinder its efforts to rearm and support terrorism. What U.S. government is going to be willing to pay Iran several hundred million dollars in hard currency to stop its illegal trade with Iraq?

As for the Gulf states—Qatar and some of the emirates, in particular—this is more of a straight business proposition for them. However, given their abject dismissal of U.N. sanctions and U.S. pressure in the past, there can be little doubt that it would take a lot of money to bribe them into shutting off the tanker smuggling in the Gulf—probably a lot more than they are actually making, given that they too would be glad to pocket U.N. "incentives" and keep on smuggling.

Just to make matters worse, for such a scheme to work, the United States would have to convince *all* of Iraq's neighbors to shut down the smuggling. If any one of them did not go along, the Iraqis would immediately divert as much of their smuggling and trade to that country as possible—both to utilize the open conduit and to reward that country for its noncompliance. Consequently, any of the neighboring states could demand compensation not just for what they had been making beforehand but for what they could make if they continued to smuggle after such a regime were put in place—when they could expect to see their Iraq-related revenues skyrocket.

As all of this suggests, concentrating on Iraq's neighbors, especially in isolation, was economically and politically misguided. And, in fact, the Bush administration tried for the first year of its term to get the smart sanctions adopted by the Security Council but was stymied by Iraq's advocates and by the neighbors themselves, who made it clear that they were not going to shut down the smuggling based on the terms of the administration's proposals.[25] In response, in May 2002, Washington decided to take what it could get. It sponsored a resolution that would only put in place a new "Goods Review List" to effectively lift the economic sanctions and streamline the contracting process—the parts of the smart sanctions that Iraq and its neighbors were prepared to accept—and gave up on the measures intended to stop the smuggling.[26] Thus, the United States has not yet found a way to halt the smuggling and save the sanctions.

REVISING THE SANCTIONS

There are two basic reasons for the erosion of the sanctions. First, when drafted, they had no teeth. There were no provisions for penalties either to Iraq or to other countries for violating the sanctions. Instead, each time the Security Council was faced with a violation, it had to devise a new means of dealing with the violation, which required an act of political will on its part. The second, related problem was the erosion of international will to punish the violators of sanctions. In most cases, Iraq was the violator that the Council failed to punish, but over time other countries joined in, to a great extent because the Council's inability to summon the political will to punish Iraq convinced them that there would be no repercussions for their lesser transgressions.

Ideally, a revised sanctions regime would be mandated by the Security Council itself because multilateral sanctions are always more effective than

unilateral sanctions, and sanctions decreed by the United Nations tend to be
the most effective of all. In addition, because it was the Security Council
that established the sanctions in the beginning, pursuing any other route to
try to restore the embargoes on Iraq would be seen as an obvious sign of
failure that would encourage noncompliance.

A new U.N. sanctions regime for Iraq would need to include the following elements to shore up the crumbling containment approach:

1. **Lift any remaining economic sanctions.** This is almost a nonsensi-
   cal point, since the approval of the Goods Review List in May 2002
   effectively removed the last remnants of the economic sanctions,
   leaving only the military sanctions and the financial controls that un-
   derpin them. Nevertheless, it would be important to state this and get
   rid of any lingering elements of the economic sanctions, if only for
   symbolic purposes. For example, revising the sanctions should include legalizing the de facto dissolution of the flight ban.

2. **Impose harsh secondary sanctions.** The key to a new sanctions
   regime that might have some hope of cutting off the smuggling
   would be to impose severe secondary sanctions on the countries and
   companies that are illegally buying oil from Iraq and selling goods
   to it. The buyers of Iraqi oil and the sellers of Iraqi contraband are
   generally much more dependent on international trade and much
   less dependent on trade with Iraq than are Iraq's neighbors, making
   them far more vulnerable to this kind of economic pressure. These
   secondary sanctions would have to be truly draconian to drive up the
   costs of smuggling so high that no oil company or arms maker, nor
   any country with such industries, would want to take the risk of
   being caught. After all, one of the problems with enforcing the sanctions against Iraq is the skill with which the Iraqis have camouflaged
   their nefarious activities. For example, the secondary sanctions
   could trigger the immediate seizure of all assets of any company
   caught buying smuggled Iraqi oil or paying the Iraqi surcharge. Alternatively, they could prohibit all international transactions with the
   company, effectively forcing it out of overseas trade. There would
   also have to be corresponding penalties for the country itself to provide an incentive for nations to police their own corporations lest the
   whole country be subjected to the penalties. Such punishments
   could include denying the country all assistance by international fi-

nancial institutions, prohibiting all foreign aid or investment, or, at the most extreme, prohibiting all trade with the country for a period of six, twelve, or twenty-four months.

3. **Bring all Iraqi oil outlets under U.N. auspices.** The new sanctions would have to legalize the Syrian oil pipeline; the truck traffic through Turkey, Jordan, Iran, and Syria; and the Gulf tanker traffic. In the last case, it would have to legalize the Iraqi oil terminal at Abu Flus, which is currently not regulated by the United Nations and so is where most of the oil smuggled in the Gulf comes from.

4. **Create incentives for Iraq's neighbors to comply.** If coupled with harsh secondary sanctions against Iraq's illegitimate trade partners, measures to compensate for the loss of revenue to Iraq's neighbors would be both essential and more feasible. Penalties would have to apply to these states as well if they continued to smuggle, perhaps even the same that would be applied to the sellers and buyers. However, accommodations might also be created as positive incentives. In particular, the neighbors could be offered special trade dispensations, greater support from international financial institutions, or even direct foreign aid. Certainly, they could all be provided with a generous cut of the (legalized) Iraqi oil flowing through their borders.

5. **Institute greater monitoring of Iraqi trade.** Right now, there are 150 U.N. monitors charged with overseeing the oil-for-food program for roughly 20 million Iraqis in the territory controlled by the regime. This is a laughable ratio. In addition, firms contracted by the United Nations to inspect cargo at Iraq's borders inspect those shipments only if the owners want to be paid via the oil-for-food system. In other words, inspections are purely voluntary and the monitors do not actively attempt to uncover smugglers. This too would need to change. The United Nations would have to install a much heavier monitoring presence both on Iraq's borders and inside the country. (This would require the consent of Iraq's neighbors, further necessitating the need for both penalties and inducements for them.) Inspections would have to become mandatory for all traffic flowing into or out of Iraq. This would not end the smuggling—Iraq's borders are simply too long and porous to stop it all—but it would further diminish the smuggling by driving up the cost and, when coupled with the secondary sanctions and incentives to the neighbors, could make a serious dent.

6. **Show a greater willingness to employ limited force against the Iraqi regime.** Iraq will find ways to circumvent even these sanctions. What's more, it will challenge them right from the start. The monitors in particular will be an obvious target. As everyone has known but few would admit, military force was always going to be needed to beat back Iraq's challenges to the U.N.-based containment regime from time to time. Baghdad simply does not respond to anything else. However, a mistake of the original sanctions was not to have stipulated this up front. This mistake would need to be corrected, ideally in a new resolution authorizing member states to enforce the new sanctions by all necessary means—the original language of UNSC Resolution 678, which authorized the use of force before the Gulf War. Although the United States has long maintained that UNSCR 678 provides adequate justification for all military action against Iraq since then (and this may well be correct from a legal standpoint), politically, few countries agree with us. Thus, for political and not necessarily legal reasons, if we are going to return to a multilateral effort to contain Iraq, it would behoove us to have a new resolution making such authorization plain in order to restore the international consensus on the use of force to compel Iraq's compliance with the new sanctions.

7. **Pursue Iraqi war crimes more aggressively.** The Iraqi leadership is guilty of vast crimes against humanity, so an international tribunal is well warranted. It would also be a very useful component of a new sanctions regime. Pursuing the Iraqi leadership for crimes against humanity by itself would delegitimize trade (especially illegal trade) with the regime, therefore making enforcement of the sanctions that much easier. Moreover, convicting Saddam and some of his cronies of crimes against humanity would make it easier to sustain international sanctions and justify military operations over the long term.

WHY NONE OF THIS WILL EVER HAPPEN

It would be wonderful if the United States could convince the United Nations to adopt such a revised approach to the Iraq sanctions. It is also essentially unthinkable. The Russians, French, and Chinese simply will not permit it. These three members of the P-5 lead a growing group of countries that are determined to see the Iraq sanctions lifted, not strengthened.

They will fight any U.S. effort to tighten the sanctions. Nor is there reason to believe that they would agree to actions designed only to maintain the military embargo. They publicly say that they recognize the need for the military sanctions, but their actions often speak otherwise. Chinese firms have violated the sanctions by selling equipment to Iraq that would enhance its military capabilities. The missile gyroscopes Iraq illegally acquired in 1995 came from Russian submarine-launched nuclear-armed ballistic missiles, which strongly suggests that the Russian government too has been at least cavalier about illegal arms exports to Iraq. In addition, Russia would benefit enormously from the repeal of the military embargo and has become so subservient to Baghdad's interests that it is hard to imagine that Moscow would not take Iraq's side in this debate as well. If anyone had any doubts about the depths to which Russia is willing to sink in arguing Iraq's case, in June 2002, Moscow criticized the Security Council's measures to control Iraq's oil prices and eliminate the Iraqi surcharges.[27] Likewise, the French are actively competing with the Russians for Baghdad's favor, and Paris appears to have decided that if Saddam is able to reconstitute its military capability, that will be Washington's problem, not theirs.[28] Certainly it has not raised a finger in the Security Council to punish those guilty of violating the military embargo and has excused the Iraqis whenever they have transgressed. Finally, there are many other countries that would like to see all of the sanctions on Iraq lifted because they dislike the idea of the United Nations imposing such strict sanctions on any country (because they might be next) and because they are weary of constant crises with Saddam. Indeed, there are only a handful of countries that would be willing to consider imposing new sanctions on Iraq—far too few to get such tough new sanctions through the Security Council.

The whole notion of going to the United Nations to strengthen the sanctions misses the crucial changes that have occurred in international opinion in the last ten years. There is no meaningful support for a tough containment policy toward Iraq. The vast majority of countries simply want the problem to go away. Ambassador Richard Butler, the former chairman of UNSCOM, relates an anecdote that sums up the problem. In 1999, former Brazilian foreign minister Celso Amorim was asked by the United Nations to conduct a series of reviews of Iraqi compliance, and before taking up this task he asked Butler whether "we really need to have the Iraq problem on our table every six months. . . . We've all become very tired of the Iraq problem. Isn't there some way of getting rid of it, once and for all?" When

Butler replied, "Certainly, by disarming Saddam," Amorim concluded, "Oh well, I'm afraid that's probably too much to ask."[29] In addition, this approach to revising sanctions overlooks the considerable political influence Baghdad now wields as a result of its deliberate manipulation of oil-for-food contracts and smuggling to reward its advocates. When added to the innate opposition of the Russians, French, Chinese, and others to the American exercise of power and their determination not to allow the Security Council to become a vehicle for the United States to punish rogue states, the approach unravels.

Some people have suggested that the United States could persuade the Security Council to tighten the sanctions despite all of the problems described above if Washington were to make it clear that the alternative was a U.S. invasion of Iraq. That is, if the United States were to threaten to invade Iraq unless the Security Council got serious about cutting down on the smuggling, the United Nations would go along with us. Probably not. First, the Russians, French, and Chinese would all see such an American ultimatum as an opportunity to start bargaining with the United States, to string us along and preclude the threatened invasion by delay. Second, the Russians, French, and Chinese probably would not ultimately agree to our demands anyway. In fact, they would likely see the United States coming to the Council with such an ultimatum as a sign that the United States was internally divided over the invasion and therefore unlikely to follow through regardless of what the Security Council did. Third, none of these states would want to set the precedent of giving in to such a U.S. ultimatum; what unites them in their diplomacy is their fear of and opposition to American unilateralism. Finally, even in the unlikely event that they agreed to some tightening, it would not last. As soon as the threat of invasion receded—and we could not remain poised to invade for more than a few months—Iraq and its partners would quickly return to their old ways. This is the greatest problem with any new U.N. measures designed to bolster containment: under present circumstances they simply cannot be sustained for the life of Saddam's regime.

There are some other problems with pursuing such measures via the United Nations, although they pale beside the basic problem of convincing a Security Council that abhors the Iraq sanctions to impose new sanctions that penalize other countries for violating the hated Iraq sanctions. The issue of deciding which countries and companies were actually violating the sanctions would be a nightmare. No matter how much evidence the

United States produced (and we would be loath to do so in the Security Council because this would jeopardize our intelligence sources and methods), the Russians, French, Chinese, and others would likely declare it inadequate to actually impose the mandated sanctions. Especially after the Milošević experience, few countries are interested in further war crimes tribunals for fear of the precedent they set (and the fear that someday a tribunal might be established to look into their own misdeeds). Few countries would be interested in coughing up the billions of dollars that would be needed to compensate/bribe Iraq's neighbors enough to get them to actually shut down the smuggling or even accept additional border monitors, given how violently Iraq would object. Finally, more limited American military operations against Iraq would only further inflame Arab popular sentiment against the United States, making the implementation of our Iraq policy—and the rest of our Middle East agenda—that much harder to accomplish.

The Unilateral Route

Given that the United Nations would be so unlikely to endorse such new sanctions, the United States might instead take matters into its own hands. The United States could lay down a new set of principles it would follow to enforce the military embargo even without additional United Nations measures. However, a unilateral approach would be much more difficult and much more costly for the United States. Moreover, a number of the items enumerated above would simply become impossible without the Security Council's imprimatur—such as additional monitors inside Iraq, additional border controls, and bringing the smuggling routes under U.N. control. Nevertheless, at least in theory, there are steps the United States could take on its own if we were willing to do so.

The United States could announce that it was imposing its own secondary sanctions on the countries and companies illegally buying Iraqi oil and selling prohibited items to Iraq. The U.S. intelligence community would have to determine such smuggling, and in any instance that the Director of Central Intelligence found a company or country guilty of smuggling, the sanctions would be applied immediately and automatically. There could be no waivers for any country under this policy. Because these secondary sanctions would be so draconian, every time the United States intelligence community found a country guilty of smuggling with Iraq, its advocates within the U.S. government, its lobbyists, and its allies would go to great lengths to get an exemption. Thus, we would have to inoculate ourselves against such pressure by eliminating all waiver provisions.

The secondary sanctions, like the U.N. sanctions proposed above, would have to be severe, perhaps even more so given that we would be attempting to regulate state behavior unilaterally—a much taller order than trying to do it through the Security Council. In the case of foreign companies, the United States could seize their assets in the United States, bar them from trading with the United States, and prohibit their employees from traveling to the United States. Once again, it would be crucial to penalize the countries as well, to give them an incentive to police their own corporations. Some foreign companies may have little or no trade with the United States, and in those cases the lure of smuggling with Iraq would greatly outweigh any potential risk of creating disfavor with the United States. The same cannot be said for most countries, for all of which trading with the world's single largest market is very important. Against the countries themselves, the United States could block international financial institutions from extending any assistance to the violating countries, we could impose tariffs on their goods, bar all of their companies from trading with the United States for a period of months or even years, or impose a range of other possible penalties. The main point would be for the sanctions to be so painful that any country would be faced with the choice of either smuggling to Iraq or trading with the world's only remaining superpower.

If it chose to do so, the United States could also try to unilaterally wean Iraq's neighbors from their dependence on Iraq and Iraqi smuggling. As described above, this would probably cost at least $6 billion annually and possibly much more, depending on how much the neighbors demanded to actually shut down the smuggling. On the other hand, at least some of this might be covered in the form of preferential trade accommodations, debt relief, commercial credits, loan guarantees, or agricultural donations. In the case of Syria, we might come up with some additional penalties to impose if it failed to shut down the smuggling, but even this would be difficult given the importance of Syria to the Arab-Israeli issue. It's hard to imagine the United States penalizing Jordan, the GCC states, or Turkey given our close ties with them, and it is hard to imagine what else we could do to Iran given that we have had comprehensive sanctions (and even secondary sanctions) against it since 1995.

The United States would also have to rely more heavily on limited military operations. These would have to serve two purposes: first, as always, to keep Saddam in check. Saddam would see the new U.S. sanctions as both a threat and an opportunity—a threat because the United States would be trying to fill the gap left by his destruction of the U.N. system, an opportunity because the mere fact that the United States could not get the United Nations on board for these new measures would be seen as a demonstration that international opinion now supported the lifting of all sanctions, allowing Iraq to paint the United States as isolated and unilateralist. Saddam would no doubt try hard to challenge the new U.S. initiative however he could to undermine it before it could take hold. As in the past, military operations would doubtless become necessary to deal with the more threatening of his challenges.

However, it would also be necessary to use military operations to enforce the military embargo. American secondary sanctions, no matter how heavy, would be unlikely to shut down all of the smuggling (especially given how unpopular the American sanctions are likely to be), and at that point, we would need some method of dealing with whatever Saddam is able to acquire. The only route available to us would be to try to destroy whatever items Iraq has been able to smuggle in—or, if we could not find the actual items, destroy a like amount that we could find. In other words, if the CIA were to determine that Iraq had smuggled in parts for twenty tanks, the U.S. Air Force would then destroy twenty Iraqi tanks.

Finally, pursuing the unilateral route would make it even more important to press for an international tribunal to investigate the Iraqi leadership for war crimes. Of course, it would also be much harder. With the United States imposing secondary sanctions on countries and using force more regularly against Iraq, there would be even fewer countries interested in bringing up Saddam on charges, as he would likely be seen as a victim of the "rogue superpower." Nevertheless, if Washington could do so—or could convince a friendly government to indict Saddam and other Iraqi leaders for crimes against their nationals—this would have a salutory effect on American efforts to maintain the embargo. It would again make it clear which was the outlaw state and which the state attempting to enforce international norms. It might also be possible to use such an indictment to impose further penalties on trade with Iraq.

Washington might be able to assemble a small coalition of like-minded states willing to join in such a new sanctions regime to prevent the further erosion of the military embargo and financial controls on Iraq. Saudi Arabia, Kuwait, Britain, Japan, the Netherlands, Australia, South Korea, and perhaps a few others might be willing to participate in such a coalition, but given what would be expected of them, none would be certain. If the United States were to pursue this approach, it would behoove us to try to bring as many countries as possible into it because of the greater international weight and the higher costs it would impose both on the smugglers and on Iraq's advocates, who no doubt would fight it every step of the way.

Why the Unilateral Approach Won't Work

This is what it would take for the United States alone, or with a small coalition of allies, to have some chance of putting the sanctions genie back into the bottle. If it were ever implemented, this approach would stand a good chance of working. However, it is almost unimaginable that this course would ever be adopted or, if adopted, would be fully implemented for more than a brief period of time. The problem is that this, and all schemes to revive the sanctions, place the United States in conflict with its allies and other third parties rather than with Iraq. In the past, the United States fought Iraq to keep the sanctions in place, and this was a conflict that everyone understood on a basic level. A revamped sanctions strategy, or any approach to revising the sanctions (including the Bush administration's smart sanctions), would force the United States to direct its energies not toward fighting Iraq but toward fighting other countries to keep the sanctions on Iraq in place. Most of those countries would be our trade partners. They might also be our allies or colleagues on the U.N. Security Council. This would be a dangerous direction in which to turn our Iraq policy.

The secondary sanctions would violate the United States' World Trade Organization (WTO) commitments and every principle of free trade. They would also enrage our European and Asian allies. In 1996, the United States passed the Iran-Libya Sanctions Act (ILSA), which imposed sanctions on foreign firms that invested in excess of $40 million in Iran's oil industry. That law has caused constant friction between the United States and its trading partners, despite its mild sanctions, which have hardly been enforced. The proposed secondary sanctions for Iraq would be far tougher, applied automatically, and without possibility of a waiver. Certainly Iraq's advocates would bring a suit against the United States in the WTO, and they would likely win it easily—and we might face multilateral sanctions in return. Some countries might choose to retaliate directly, levying their own unilateral sanctions or trade restrictions on the United States. The secondary sanctions would undermine U.S. efforts to convince other countries to engage in free-trade practices. Beyond the economic sphere, we would have to expect other countries to retaliate in other arenas—political, diplomatic, and cultural—wherever they thought they could hurt us most.

Limited military operations against Iraq, while essential if the new sanctions regime were to be able to resist Iraq's efforts to erode it as Baghdad eroded the old sanctions regime, would ultimately be self-defeating. The Arab world has become so disenchanted with limited U.S. military operations against Iraq that they cannot be sustained as a policy. As we learned from 1996 to 1998, each strike causes our regional allies to place additional restrictions on U.S. military operations and set the threshold for new military operations just a little higher. It took tremendous effort to get the Gulf states to agree to support Operation Desert Fox in 1998, and, having done so, it is virtually inconceivable that we could get them to do it again, given how events have unfolded since then. Moreover, Saudi Arabia relies strongly on the argument that the United States is simply enforcing the U.N. resolutions to justify supporting U.S. strikes against Iraq (and the patrols in the NFZs). If the United States were to adopt such a unilateral approach, this fig leaf would fall away and the Saudi reaction would likely be to restrain us from strikes except in extreme situations. Indeed, the entire concept may well be moot, given that the Saudis have generally signaled that they are no longer interested in limited military operations against Saddam—they want us either to invade or to move to pure deterrence.

Revising the sanctions and implementing them unilaterally would also be a costly policy in all senses of the word. First, there would be the billions of dollars it would take to buy off Iraq's neighbors. Second, the United States would still be paying the $1 billion–plus each year we currently spend to maintain current force levels in the Gulf region. If we opted to employ limited force more frequently against Iraq (and if the GCC states let us do so), this cost would increase. Desert Fox, for example, cost about $92 million.[30] Then there would be the costs of lost trade as a result of either retaliations for the secondary sanctions or similar unfair trade practices by other countries, which would use our actions to justify their own. On top of these financial costs, we would also face the diplomatic costs of fighting with our trade partners over the secondary sanctions, fighting constantly in the Security Council over Washington usurping the prerogatives of the United Nations, and resisting French, Russian, and Chinese efforts to make us pay a price for our unilateralism. Finally, there would be the domestic political costs of sustaining such a policy, including an Arab-American population that would grow increasingly more unhappy with seemingly endless U.S. military actions against Iraq; greater grumbling from the armed services about sustaining low-intensity warfare against Iraq; and the opportunity costs of not being able to pursue other foreign policy interests because of the need to concentrate on enforcement of the Iraq sanctions—not to mention how Congress and the administration could justify paying billions of dollars to Syria and hundreds of millions of dollars to Iran to bribe them not to smuggle with Iraq, despite the fact that both continue to support international terrorism and pursue WMD themselves. In fact, given current laws, it would be hard to imagine how that could be done—and if it could not, this would open huge holes for smuggling.

It simply is not realistic to believe that the United States would be willing to actually implement such a policy for the duration of Saddam's regime. It is hard to imagine that the United States would be willing to try this approach for even a year. In many ways, it runs counter to the original premise of containment, which was to prevent Saddam from threatening the Gulf region with the minimum commitment of resources to allow the United States to focus its diplomatic, economic, and military efforts on other issues that were considered more important. The sanctions regime has eroded to the point that it would be exceedingly costly to repair and maintain it over time—so costly that it would effectively undermine our ability to pursue many (if not all) of the other things that containment was supposed to allow us to pursue. Even if all the United States did was to adopt harsh secondary sanctions against the smugglers, is it feasible to believe that we could continue to build a new relationship with Europe at the same time? Or continue to bring Russia into the Western world? Or build coalitions to confront other aggressive states? If the United States were to adopt this course of action, it would dominate our foreign policy agenda for the foreseeable future. It would make Iraq our number one foreign policy issue for many years to come and destroy a great many of our other foreign policy initiatives—initiatives that were always considered far more important to our long-term security and the prosperity of the country.

THE INSPECTIONS TRAP

In the past, the U.N. weapons inspections were an important part of the containment of Iraq. Although the inspections have been dead since 1998, since the September 11 attacks, a number of people have begun talking

Kuwait in 1991 and know that if Riyadh ever wanted to, it could leave
the Kuwaitis to Saddam's tender mercies. The tribal connections between
the two states and the Saudi dominance of OPEC add further dimensions
to the relationship. What's more, although the Americans are defending
Kuwait right now, the Kuwaitis know that we will someday go home, while
Saudi Arabia and Iraq will always be their neighbors. Of those two, it is the
Kingdom that has Kuwait's best interests at heart. Thus, in the end, it would
be difficult for Kuwait to oppose Saudi wishes: if the Saudis reject a new
U.S. policy on Iraq, we should not expect the Kuwaitis to approve it.

THE SOUTHERN GULF STATES

Far more than in Saudi Arabia or Kuwait, the southern states of the GCC—
Bahrain, Qatar, the UAE, and Oman—suffer from the effects of linkage,
the discontent of the Arab "street," and the waning of a sense of threat from
Iraq. To a certain extent, the southern Gulf states never had the same fear of
Iraq as the Kuwaitis and Saudis. They do not share a land border and are at
least 500 kilometers away. Indeed, they have always been far more fearful
of Iran. Bahrain's population is majority Shi'ah, Iran has periodically attempted to incite the Shi'ites against the Sunni elites, and Tehran periodically reminds the world that it believes Bahrain should again be a part of
Iran, as it was at the height of the Persian Empire. The UAE has tussled
with Iran over the disputed islands of Abu Musa and the Tunbs, which the
shah occupied in 1971 even though they had previously been under UAE
administration. Oman looks out at Iran across the Strait of Hormuz and
Iran's major naval base at Bandar Abbas. Although Qatar is probably more
wary of the Saudis than either of its northern Gulf neighbors, Iran is closer
and more menacing to it than Iraq.

   The Zogby poll surveyed the UAE, but not the other three southern Gulf
states, yet its results are still interesting. Citizens of the UAE had the worst
impression of the American people (25 percent favorable, 61 percent unfavorable) of any of the countries surveyed. At least to some extent, this must
be attributed to linkage: 76 percent of Emirati citizens said that they would
have a more favorable view of the United States if it were to apply pressure
to ensure the creation of an independent Palestinian state. The UAE's very
low sense of threat from Iraq was also reflected in the poll, as just one third
of Emiratis had a favorable view of the U.S.-led liberation of Kuwait,
roughly the same number as those who had an unfavorable view of it.

about resurrecting them. There is still a great deal of affection for inspections, and many commentators continue to trot them out as a viable substitute for, or complement to, sanctions in a revived containment scheme.[31] Unfortunately, this would be a grave mistake. Inspections as an element of containment have become a trap for the United States, no matter how one conceives of them or of containment.[32]

The first problem is that the United States will almost certainly not get the kind of inspection regime it wants. UNSCOM had decent access for only a few years after the Gulf War, and even then it was hardly the full and unfettered access the Security Council had been promised. By 1995, in response to Iraqi threats and intimidation, Rolf Ekeus agreed to the first limitations on UNSCOM's access. By the time the inspectors were evicted from Iraq, a slew of additional restrictions, including those negotiated by Secretary General Kofi Annan, had given up key prerogatives, and resulted in a situation where the inspectors could see only facilities that Iraq wanted them to see. Former UNSCOM Deputy Chairman Charles Duelfer concedes that thanks to Iraq's dogged intelligence-gathering efforts and its willingness to block inspectors in a pinch (for which it rarely suffered any repercussions), UNSCOM itself was never able to conduct more than six or seven true surprise inspections. In every other instance, the Iraqis had sanitized the facility, although they were not always as fastidious as they should have been and their mistakes did provide crucial evidence of their larger deceptions.[33]

UNMOVIC, the new inspection regime established by UNSC Resolution 1284, promises to be weaker still. The United States was able to ensure that the new resolution stated that Iraq had to grant UNMOVIC "immediate, unconditional, and unrestricted access." We were also able to make sure that the timetable for any suspension of sanctions would be lengthy—at least nine months.[34] Nevertheless, UNMOVIC is not likely to prove as independent or aggressive as UNSCOM. The U.N. bureaucracy will have a say in deciding its personnel and planning, and the U.N. bureaucracy is outrageously pro-Iraqi and anti-inspections. In the past, whenever the United Nations or the member states (rather than the UNSCOM leadership) were allowed to determine personnel, they chose U.N. hacks and political flunkies. Indeed, former inspectors fear that UNMOVIC will never have the same caliber of inspectors that UNSCOM had. There are no performance criteria for the new inspection regime—it will not be asked to judge if Iraq is "complying," only if it is "cooperating," a lesser standard. In the case of

UNSCOM, the College of Commissioners—a group of twenty made up of either disarmament experts or political flunkies as chosen by their governments—had only an advisory role and even then were fairly disruptive. In the case of UNMOVIC, the new commissioners will have the added authority to review its work and reports. Resolution 1284 also demands that the inspectors abide by the prior agreements between Ekeus, Annan, and Iraq—a dangerous loophole that Iraq could again exploit to declare some sites off limits. Moreover, UNMOVIC was established as a lesser compromise on inspections: the consensus over aggressive inspections had broken down, and UNMOVIC was the compromise solution. Enshrining the notion of lesser compliance for a partial lifting of sanctions in the resolution is the monument to this simple fact. Thus, regardless of the words, everyone in the United Nations knows that UNMOVIC was never intended to live up to the same standards as UNSCOM.

Key aspects of Resolution 1284's disarmament program were purposely left ambiguous when the resolution was passed because the United States and Great Britain could not agree with the Russians, French, and Chinese, and so for the moment we agreed to disagree. This leaves the door open for further efforts by Iraq and its advocates to hamstring and water down UNMOVIC. At the very least, it means that additional negotiations will be necessary before the inspectors go in and probably afterward as well. For example, although UNMOVIC was charged with outlining the key remaining tasks on Iraqi disarmament, the Russians and French have indicated that they believe that the Security Council should be able to approve the list. The resolution states that as part of sanctions suspension appropriate financial controls will be put into place but leaves to further negotiations what those controls will consist of. At the time, the French proposed a ridiculously porous system that would have done nothing but scold Iraq for cheating after the fact. This too would likely have to be negotiated before the inspectors could return. There is a consensus that once the inspectors return to Iraq, they will first need to reestablish a baseline—that is, determine what has changed between UNSCOM's departure in 1998 and UNMOVIC's return—before the actual inspections could start, but the resolution does not set down a time limit. Numerous former inspectors have indicated that they believe an accurate baseline could require twelve to eighteen months to establish. There is little doubt that the French, Russians, and Chinese will press doggedly to cut the baselining process short, and if UNMOVIC resists, they will use that to discredit the new inspectors.

This raises a critical problem with any new inspection regime: the French, Russians, and Chinese are never going to allow it to come into conflict with Iraq. As proven by their past behavior, those governments made clear five or six years ago that they had ceased to be interested in aggressive inspections in Iraq. Since then, they have consistently attempted to shift the burden of proof from Iraq's having to prove that it has complied to the inspectors' having to prove that Iraq has *not* complied (an impossible task). French, Russian, and Chinese diplomats have actively colluded with Iraq to weaken and hinder the inspections. Russian diplomats, in particular, have outright lied during U.N. proceedings to defend Iraq and undermine the inspections. Finally, throughout the negotiations on Resolution 1284 and since then, the Russians, French, and Chinese have done little to hide their position that the inspections no longer served a useful purpose and thus they needed to be wrapped up quickly, regardless of the fact that Iraq unquestionably was not disarmed.[35]

We also need to recognize that, as our dealings with the French, Russians, and Chinese in the negotiations over Resolution 1284 indicated, they had no intention of ever allowing a new inspection regime to come into conflict with Iraq. This is one of the great problems with those who want to use a new inspection regime to justify war on Iraq—in the expectation that Iraq would block the inspectors and so furnish Washington with a legitimate *casus belli*. The problem with this is that the French, Russians, and Chinese figured out years ago (i.e., before Desert Fox) that Iraq's blocking inspections could become the pretext for U.S. military operations. So the approach they took to Resolution 1284 was that they would insert themselves into the process as much as possible to ensure one of two things: (1) that they would be able to so weaken the new inspection regime that there would be virtually no chance that it would come into conflict with Iraq after it began work, or (2) that there was enough ambiguity and Security Council involvement in the new resolution that they could insert themselves into any dispute so that the dispute would become one between them and the inspectors, rather than between Iraq and the inspectors. The United States will not be able to justify attacking Iraq if it is the French, Russians, and Chinese who are hindering the work of the inspectors and doing so in the United Nations—and Paris, Moscow, and Beijing all know this.

It is important to remember that as strong, independent, and aggressive as UNSCOM was, it was never able to eradicate Iraq's WMD programs. The Iraqi nuclear program continued to grow after the Gulf War and in

1994 was bigger than it had ever been. In the mid-1990s, the Iraqis were continuing to work on new biological and chemical agents and to refine their ballistic missile programs. All of this was done in complete secrecy. The only way we found out about it was from defectors such as Hussein Kamel and Khidhir Hamza. Thus, even if we could get a new inspection regime as good as the old one, we now know that it still would not be enough to stop Saddam from developing WMD. The inspectors definitely hindered Iraq's efforts and forced it to be more surreptitious than it otherwise would have been, but they could not stop the programs. Former Assistant Secretary of State Robert Einhorn, one of the architects of Resolution 1284, warns that "the UN inspectors cannot compel compliance and therefore cannot end the WMD threat posed by Iraq. At their very best, UN monitoring and inspections can complicate, constrain and slow Iraq's clandestine efforts and give us a better picture of what is going on in Iraq than we currently have. But that amounts to containing or managing the threat, not eliminating it."[36] Of greatest importance, very good inspections could probably delay Iraq's acquisition of nuclear weapons, but they would be unlikely to stop it.

Finally, a new inspections program would require reviving the sanctions to cut off the smuggling. It would not be possible for even a massive new inspections regime that was far bigger, more aggressive, and less constrained than UNSCOM ever was to eradicate Iraq's WMD programs as long as Saddam is making $3 billion per year outside the oil-for-food system and importing whatever he likes. Iraq is simply too big a country. The only way any inspection regime could succeed would be if sanctions were healthy enough to keep smuggling to minimal levels that the inspectors could handle. Thus, a return to inspections would also mean reviving the sanctions and shutting down the smuggling, meaning that pursuing the inspections route requires not only finding a way out of the inspections trap, but also solving all of the problems of fixing the sanctions and eradicating the smuggling.

Couldn't We Get Good Inspections If We Threatened to Invade?

As with reforming the sanctions, there is a school of thought that argues that if the United States were willing to threaten a full-scale invasion of Iraq, both the Iraqis and their advocates in the United Nations would be willing to accept a robust inspections regime as their only alternative. Indeed, I agree that it is highly likely that if faced with a quarter-million American troops on his border, Saddam would offer to resume the inspections immediately and provide them the full cooperation that we always sought. After all, Saddam is not suicidal. Throughout his history in power he has been willing to make significant concessions when faced with overwhelming force.

However, there is a big difference between Saddam being willing to accept inspectors when there is a gun to his head and actually complying with disarmament. The key problem is that we cannot hold the gun to Saddam's head for as long as it would take to actually disarm Iraq. First, Saddam will not believe that we actually intend to invade until the bulk of the forces have arrived. Again, this is his pattern—he usually does not wake up to threats until it is much too late, but in this case, given what he saw in 1991, it is reasonable to conclude that once he saw the troops in place he would assume we meant business. There is no way he will believe that or make meaningful concessions until the troops have arrived—he has heard the United States bluster and even move small forces to the region many times before, and he knows that they don't threaten him.

Once confronted with the invasion force itself, it seems very reasonable and entirely in keeping with Saddam's past behavior to believe that he would then suddenly make major concessions to try to derail the attack. What's more, as we saw in 1991, as long as U.S. troops are in place, he would probably comply mostly, if not fully, so as not to provide Washington with a pretext to attack. Instead, he would play for time. As he did with the Iranians in 1975 and the United Nations/United States in 1991, he would assume that he could outlast us, and he would be right. The problem is that the United States cannot keep an invasion force in the Gulf region for more than about six months—maybe twelve if the administration were absolutely determined and willing to bear enormous costs. Mounting such an operation would require huge call-ups from the reserve and the National Guard that would be politically unpopular. What's more, the invasion force would constitute the vast bulk of American combat power in terms of ground forces, air forces, and naval forces. Other commitments would inevitably force us to reduce this force over time. Such a deployment would compel all of the services to cancel and postpone normal leaves, retirements, training, maintenance, and replacements, and they would not be able to put such things off indefinitely. The forces themselves would be living in field conditions, on hair triggers, in the Arabian desert—one of the hardest environments in the world in which to live. Nor would the Gulf states themselves countenance such a prolonged deployment. As noted in Chapter 6, the reason they would be willing to support an invasion is its relative quickness: several months to build up, a month or two to attack, and all would be over. If we chose not to launch an invasion, they would want our forces gone very quickly.

Thus, all Saddam would need to do is wait until we were forced to start scaling back our forces in the region, and as the threat receded he would return to his past tactic of "cheat and retreat" with the inspectors that served him so well in 1991–98. The six (maybe twelve) months that we could keep an invasion force in place in the Gulf region would be laughably inadequate to disarm Iraq. As noted above, there is a consensus among American, British, Swedish, Dutch, and even French former inspectors that it would require twelve to eighteen months just to establish a baseline, let alone actually conduct inspections. And after that, we should never forget that once the inspections were completed we would need to transition to long-term monitoring to try to prevent Saddam from reconstituting the WMD programs.

Nor should we assume that we could build up for an invasion from time to time to keep Saddam on his best behavior. Such a massive deployment would be extremely costly for the United States economically, politically, and diplomatically. The military leadership itself would resist future feints because of the disruption to its normal training and operational cycles and the greater worries it would create over other threats. (Having seen us build up in the Gulf area once, would the North Koreans try to take advantage of us if they saw it again?) The administration and Congress would be loath to call up hundreds of thousands of reservists and National Guard personnel repeatedly. No one would like spending the billions of dollars each such threatened invasion would be likely to cost. And our allies in the Gulf region probably wouldn't let us do so anyway. If the United States were to build up a massive invasion force and the Gulf states did everything they would need to do to keep their populations under control to make such a deployment possible, and then at the last minute we backed down and agreed to new inspections, the Gulf states would wash their hands of us. They would undoubtedly have taken tremendous criticism for supporting the invasion in the first place and might be facing real popular unrest, and they would have done it all for nothing—Saddam would still be in power. This would be seen as the final proof of American perfidy. The Gulf states would likely conclude that we wanted to keep Saddam in power all along. They would never again support American military operations against Iraq and would bring their budding rapprochement with Iraq to fruition as their only alternative. Not only should we expect never to be able to return in such force (unless Saddam were to invade Saudi Arabia), but they might actually ask us to further scale back the preexisting force levels as a sop to their unhappy domestic constituencies.

And once we found ourselves in those circumstances, we could kiss any cooperation from Iraq on inspections good-bye.

THE NO-FLY ZONES

Of all the key elements of containment, the one under the least pressure right now is the Anglo-American patrols of the no-fly zones in northern and southern Iraq. The regular confrontations there between coalition aircraft and Iraqi air defenses do allow the Iraqis to make propaganda hay of them—and their absurdly exaggerated claims do continue to influence Arab populations throughout the Middle East. However, the Saudis and Kuwaitis continue to see the maintenance of the southern no-fly zone as vital to their security, and they have resisted all efforts to bring the NFZs to an end. As long as the southern NFZ remains, Washington can prevail on Ankara to allow the maintenance of the northern zone.

The southern NFZ is vital to the defense of Kuwait and Saudi Arabia for three reasons. First, British and American reconnaissance aircraft can overfly the area on a regular basis, providing valuable warning of any Iraqi military buildup that could threaten the Gulf states. Second, a strong Anglo-American air presence remains in the region, providing access to Iraqi airspace for strike missions in the event Iraqi military units begin heading south. Last, the enforcement of the no-fly zones prevents Iraq from fully reconstituting its air defenses in southern Iraq, which would make striking an Iraqi ground buildup near Kuwait or Saudi Arabia much easier. In other words, enforcement of the southern no-fly zone is now principally sustained by Resolution 949, which prohibits Iraq from reinforcing its units in southern Iraq and thus presenting a new threat to Saudi Arabia and Kuwait.

Because U.S. actions in the no-fly zones are so dependent on Saudi/ Kuwaiti and Turkish goodwill, it would be difficult to try to ratchet up the level or scope of Anglo-American operations. The Saudis are comfortable with the existing level of air activity in the zones, which consist of patrols roughly two out of every three days. If the United States felt that we could continue to guarantee Saudi security by flying on fewer days (which we probably could, if that were our only concern), they would be amenable to such a decrease. However, while the Saudis are willing to take the heat for sustaining the zones, they are not looking to make things harder on themselves. Consequently, there is no interest in the Kingdom in more aggressive enforcement, in using coalition responses to strike higher-value targets, or in otherwise trying to use the zones to bring greater pressure to bear on Saddam. They might have been willing to support such an initiative as part of a larger regime change campaign at another time, but today they are no longer interested in fighting a protracted war with Saddam. They want to keep the NFZ activity as far "under the radar" as they can without jeopardizing their security. Thus, while we could undoubtedly preserve the no-fly zones at their current level as part of a revived containment policy, we could not ratchet up our operations there to support more ambitious goals.

Why Can't We Just Bomb Iraqi WMD Facilities Whenever We Discover Them?

As a substitute for inspections, some have suggested that the United States simply launch air strikes against Iraqi WMD targets whenever the Iraqis begin to rebuild them.[37] In the abstract, this seems like a reasonable approach and one that avoids the trap of inspections and the high costs of regime change. Unfortunately, it is completely unfeasible.

The first problem is that we just don't know where most of Saddam's WMD facilities are. In some cases we probably never will unless we occupy the country. For example, he has taken his BW program mobile by breaking it up into small, self-contained units that fit into the back of generic tractor-trailers and can be driven all over the country. The chance that we will find out where any one of those units is in time to hit it from the air—let alone find all of them—is infinitesimally small. Likewise, we know of a few facilities associated with Iraq's missile programs, but we have no idea where its hidden Scud manufacturing plants are—although the former inspectors believe Iraq has them. Likewise, we just don't know where Iraq's hidden uranium enrichment plants or bomb-making factories are. We do know of several big chemical plants that are unquestionably dual-use, but right now they appear to be producing civilian chemicals. Destroying them would only further erode international support for our position.

This was the problem with the inspections: we knew the Iraqis were cheating but did not know where. If we had known, we would have bombed those facilities in 1998 during Operation Desert Fox. The fact that out of ninety-seven targets struck only eleven were WMD production facilities should give a good sense of the problem.[38]

Saddam would exploit such a policy to toy with us. He would build large numbers of facilities all over the country (something he learned to do after Israel's Osiraq strike). They would be big, well-protected facilities with lots of antiaircraft defenses that would take a major effort to destroy. Many of them would be decoys. We would have to send in large strike packages to destroy each facility, and the moment we were done, he would simply start rebuilding, as he has on every occasion that the United States has used force since the Gulf War. We could find ourselves launching hundreds of sorties every three to four months to deal with new Iraqi construction. We would also end up with a few tragic mistakes on our part—such as an errant bomb that hit a school or hospital, which Iraq will doubtless encourage. And at the end of the day, most of Saddam's WMD program would still probably remain untouched and working away.

Given the operational difficulties of this kind of approach, other considerations are essentially irrelevant, but it is worth noting that diplomatically, the idea of repeated, limited strikes against Iraq to prevent it from rebuilding suspected WMD sites is laughable. The Gulf states are simply not interested anymore. They supported Desert Fox and took a great deal of heat from their people and other Arab countries for doing so, and they know that it had little impact on Iraq's WMD programs. Today, they are not interested in an open-ended military campaign against Iraq. What they continue to tell us is that if we want to use force against Iraq, we had better finish the job this time.

A RISING PRICE FOR DIMINISHING RETURNS

The containment strategy that has endured since 1991 is eroding. Our control of Saddam's revenues is slipping, and his pursuit of weapons of mass destruction is becoming less and less constrained. Even under the remaining fetters, Iraq appears to have the necessary access to funds and material, just not as quickly or easily as it would like. The United States could build a new containment regime centered on a set of punishing secondary sanctions that imposed real costs on those who buy Iraqi oil illegally and sell

Baghdad prohibited military and dual-use items. If implemented in a determined fashion and sustained for the life of Saddam's regime, this could be an effective approach to the problem. However, the Russians, French, and Chinese have made it no secret that they will not allow any tightening of the sanctions in the Security Council, which leaves only the unilateral route. This would leave us fighting with many, if not all, of our allies and trade partners over actions that would clearly contravene our WTO commitments, important bilateral treaties, and our entire free-trade philosophy. Rather than allowing us to commit only minimal assets to ensure that Saddam cannot threaten the region again, thereby leaving us mostly free to pursue other foreign policy interests, a new containment policy would consume ever greater assets and make it harder for us to pursue other foreign policy interests by stirring up international opposition to the United States and its policies. It would turn the world against us in a fundamental way.

The United States has thrived for the last fifty years because we have had most of the world—and certainly most of the developed world—very much on our side. By usurping the prerogative of the Security Council because we could not get our way and threatening vicious secondary sanctions, the United States would create widespread ill will and provoke retaliation both directly, against our trade, and indirectly, against other American political interests. It is hard to capture on paper how damaging this would be for the United States. I cannot imagine that an administration would choose this route, in part because this was made clear to me during my years in the government. Indeed, it was the frustration of knowing that what it would take to save containment under the current circumstances would never be adopted (and sustained) by the United States that led me, and many of my colleagues within government, to conclude that containment was no longer an option and that the choice we faced was between deterrence and regime change.

EIGHT

The Dangers of Deterrence

The strategy of containment was designed to prevent Iraq from rebuilding its military strength without expending a vast amount of American resources (political, military, diplomatic, or financial). For many years it achieved its goals. Now, unfortunately, containment is falling apart, and so the United States is being forced to choose between its two distinct goals: either we can prevent Saddam Hussein's Iraq from reconstituting its conventional and unconventional military capabilities, or we can continue to make Iraq a relatively low priority in American policy. We cannot do both. Those who favor the first goal must now move decisively toward a policy of regime change, the variants of which are discussed in the next three chapters. Those who favor the second goal must accept the end of containment and fall back to a strategy of deterrence.

Deterrence means allowing the elements of containment mostly to lapse and instead relying on the threat of American military action to prevent Iraq from making mischief in the Persian Gulf region. For some, it is a continuation of the "dovish" approach to containment, in that it proceeds from the assumption that Iraq is a small, weak country that can easily be kept in check by the United States and should not become a preoccupation for Washington. In particular, deterrence derives from the principle that the United States should not draw off resources and political capital from other, more important foreign policy initiatives to try to "solve" the problem of Iraq but should instead treat it as a condition to be "managed." Others believe that deterrence is simply the only option available to us. While these proponents of deterrence recognize that containment cannot be sustained for much longer in its current form and that reviving it is not a realistic prospect, they are even less sanguine about any of the various regime change options. Many agree that a full-scale invasion is the only feasible way to overthrow Saddam, and they prefer the risks and costs of deterrence (potential wars with a nuclear-armed Saddam) to those of an invasion (combat deaths, WMD use, and the cost of rebuilding Iraq).

In practice, deterrence would be a relatively easy policy to adopt. First, the United States would effectively allow the Iraq sanctions, inspections, and even the no-fly zones to dissipate. We might or might not agree to their actual lifting by the U.N. Security Council. One reason to do so would be if there were some benefit we might accrue from going along with a U.N. move to repeal the sanctions. On the other hand, we might choose to leave the sanctions on the books but not enforce them in the hope that their continued existence would restrain at least some countries. Either way, the United States would not expend resources or political capital (let alone take military action) to prevent their erosion. The strategy explicitly recognizes that this would allow Saddam to rebuild his military and WMD capabilities, and eventually he would acquire nuclear weapons. The United States would make it clear to Saddam—and the entire world—that any military move beyond Iraq's borders would trigger an immediate American military response. The United States would try to retain a sizable military presence in the region and would ensure that it could reinforce its presence there quickly so that Iraq would be faced with both formidable American conventional forces and the ultimate threat of U.S. nuclear retaliation. The critical assumption of this policy is that Saddam would be deterred by such an American threat even if he possessed nuclear weapons himself.

In this sense, deterrence of Iraq would be reminiscent of the classic model of deterrence we employed against the Soviet Union. During the Cold War, the United States mostly abstained from interfering in the USSR's internal affairs. The Soviets were allowed to do whatever they wanted behind the Iron Curtain. However, the United States made it clear that a Russian military offensive beyond their borders—into Europe, Korea, or Japan—would be met by the full range of American military capabilities, and for forty-five years this held the Soviets at bay. Similarly, deterrence of Iraq would forfeit any effort to change Saddam's behavior within Iraq's borders. Especially after he acquired nuclear weapons, we would leave him to do whatever he wanted inside Iraq. Obviously, this option would mean leaving the Iraqi people to suffer continued misery at Saddam's hands. The core assumption of deterrence, however, is that Saddam would make the same calculation as the Soviets—that the risk of nuclear annihilation by the United States would be too great to risk any aggressive military moves beyond his borders.[1]

THE ADVANTAGES OF DETERRENCE

The advantages of a policy of deterrence are straightforward. First, and for many proponents of the policy, foremost, deterrence removes the need to embark upon a policy of regime change—all of the variants of which entail significant costs and risks. This is not to suggest that deterrence is either cost-free or risk-free. However, many of its advocates see it as the "Hippocratic oath option," in that it would have the United States "do no harm." Advocates of deterrence agree that neither covert action nor the "Afghan approach" is likely to succeed in ousting Saddam and therefore a full-scale invasion would be required. They point to the certain costs of such an operation—American and Iraqi deaths, rebuilding Iraq—and its potential risks—Iraqi WMD use and terrorism—and argue that it is not necessary for the United States to absorb such costs or run such risks. Instead, they argue that Saddam's Iraq can be prevented from new aggression, even after he acquires nuclear weapons, by a strategy of deterrence, just as the Soviet Union was for forty-five years. Indeed, in this sense, what we have come to call "deterrence" of Iraq is really the intellectual successor to what during the Cold War we called "containment" of the Soviet Union. And many of the most thoughtful advocates of deterrence of Iraq argue that just as the United States abjured rollback of the USSR during the Cold War because of the fear of the costs of doing so, we should abstain from regime change in Iraq for the same reasons.

However, there are also a range of other benefits of deterrence that would be realized by giving up the daily battle to shore up containment. By eliminating the constant fights over the sanctions, inspections, no-fly zones, and so on, we would eliminate a major drain on U.S. foreign policy. There would be no fierce debates with the Russians and French over whether Iraq is qualitatively disarmed. There would be no crisis with Saddam every six months. There would be no newspaper stories about smuggling and how Iraq was rebuilding its WMD programs right under the United Nations' nose. Instead, the United States could concentrate on other, reputedly more important issues. Many of the personnel and resources currently devoted to Iraq could be reassigned to other priorities. The Principals' Committee and other interagency groups would not have to spend hours every week debating our next move on Iraq or how best to respond to Saddam's latest challenge. There would be more time and energy available to develop options to solve other problems and advance other causes.

Since the goal of this strategy is to effectively eliminate the day-to-day confrontations between the United States and Iraq (and Iraq's advocates), the no-fly zones would follow the sanctions as an inevitable casualty of a shift to deterrence. The whole point of the strategy of deterrence is to refrain from interfering in Iraq's internal affairs and instead concentrate on Iraqi external aggression as the sole American concern. The no-fly zones run completely contrary to this: they are a form of interference in Iraq's internal affairs, they are a source of constant confrontation between the United States and Iraq, they hurt our public image (especially in the Arab world), and the need to maintain them is a constant drain on American diplomacy. Abandoning the no-fly zones would allow the U.S. military to reduce its presence in the region, slow its operational and personnel tempos, and send fewer soldiers, sailors, and airmen to unpopular destinations such as Camp Doha in Kuwait and Prince Sultan Air Base in Saudi Arabia.

A shift to deterrence would probably be met with a sigh of relief by many of our allies in Europe, Asia, and elsewhere, many of whom have been advocating such a change either privately or publicly for some time. It would remove Iraq as a priority in U.S. bilateral relations with many countries, meaning we could raise the profile of other issues. Since the Gulf War, it has frequently been the case that Iraq was one of the first items on the agenda in high-level meetings with foreign dignitaries, crowding out other issues. If the Iraq issue were no longer a priority, we could more vigorously pursue democratization in Russia, human rights in China, unfair trade practices in France, political and economic reform in Egypt and Saudi Arabia, and so on. Without the need to mind Arab sensibilities to try to keep them on board for our Iraq policy, we might more forcefully raise the issues of anti-Semitism and anti-Americanism in Arab school curricula and media. Alternatively, resources and diplomatic clout might now be available to try to combat AIDS in Africa, the destruction of the Amazon rain forest, or even global warming.

In the Gulf region, our allies would not be happy with this change, but they would probably be relieved that they no longer had to keep living in the limbo of containment. Saudi Arabia and the other GCC states would probably continue the rapprochement they have begun with Iraq. Kuwait would be alarmed, but given firm U.S. security guarantees, it would have no choice but to find a way to live with the monster next door. Elsewhere in the Arab region, we should not expect any great praise—the rest of the Arab world considers such a shift long overdue—but at least moving to deterrence would remove Iraq as a constant sore spot. It is unclear what effect a move to deterrence would have on the Arab-Israeli confrontation. It is conceivable that it would help, by removing Iraq as an issue that the Arab extremists can use to scuttle negotiations led by the United States and by diminishing the leverage of the moderate Arab states over Washington, since we would no longer need their support to maintain containment of Iraq. On the other hand, it could also hurt. Saddam would be free to do as he liked and would quickly regain control of his oil revenues—by either the lifting of sanctions or their collapse—and he could be expected to make mischief there. In addition, Israel is likely to feel a greater sense of threat from Saddam if he is unchained, so Jerusalem may be more reticent to take risks for peace.

The Kurds would pay the highest—or at least the most immediate—price for a U.S. shift to deterrence. Without the northern no-fly zone, and with the United States explicitly forswearing interference in Iraq's internal affairs, the Kurds would have no friends but the mountains, as their traditional saying bemoans. There are 4.5 million Kurds whose safety is largely dependent on the pledge of the United States. If that pledge were withdrawn, Saddam would undoubtedly move to reoccupy northern Iraq as soon as he was ready. His interest would be in crushing the Kurds completely, to stamp out the independent streak they have acquired during their years of freedom from his grip. He would undoubtedly arrest, torture, and execute large numbers of Kurdish leaders to break the spirit of the people and might even indulge in a second Anfal to convince the Kurds never to turn against him again. It certainly would not be the first time that the United States had abandoned the Kurds to Saddam's butchery, but we should understand very clearly that a shift to deterrence could mean condoning the resumption of Saddam's campaign of genocide against them.[2]

DETERRING SADDAM

The core of the argument in favor of the deterrence strategy is that Saddam can be deterred by the threat of American military force (including our own nuclear arsenal) even if he possesses nuclear weapons himself. If this is the case, deterrence is a viable policy option. If it is not the case, deterrence would be a terribly dangerous—and perhaps fatally flawed—course of action.

Saddam Hussein is not irrational. As best we understand his thinking, he does appear to construct means–ends chains by which he believes his actions will achieve his goals. If Saddam were irrational, this in and of itself would mean that he would be undeterrable because deterrence operates on the assumption that the target of the deterrence threat can understand "If I do this, my opponent will do that, and 'that' will be very, very bad for me." However, the fact that Saddam is not irrational is a necessary element of a successful deterrence strategy but hardly a sufficient one.

Neither is Saddam suicidal, as far as we can tell. Unlike Adolf Hitler, he does not have an apocalyptic conception of himself or of Iraq. This too is a necessary, but not sufficient, condition for establishing whether Saddam can be deterred. If Saddam did not care about his own survival or at some subconscious level was actually seeking his own destruction, there would be little reason to believe that the threat of his own possible extermination in an American nuclear retaliatory strike would give him pause.

Finally, there is some evidence that Saddam has a crude understanding of deterrence logic and has been successfully deterred in the past. In early 1990, Iraq and Israel traded threats, culminating in Saddam's lurid promise to "make the fire eat up half of Israel" if Israel should attack Iraq. This was clearly a deterrent threat on Saddam's part, a point reinforced in private communications between Iraq and Israel.[3] In 1991, during the Persian Gulf War, Iraq struck Israel with thirty-nine al-Hussein modified Scud missiles, hoping to provoke an Israeli conventional response. However, Baghdad refrained from striking Israel with WMD warheads (both chemical and biological were available) for fear that Israel would retaliate with nuclear weapons. Both of these actions demonstrate Saddam's understanding of basic deterrence. He recognized that by striking Israel, deterrence logic would compel Israel to strike him back (something he wanted to avoid in 1990 but wanted to provoke in 1991). Yet he was deterred from employing chemical and biological weapons against Israel for fear of the much heavier retaliation Israel could mount with its nuclear arsenal. Moreover, Saddam seems also to have put this into practice during the Gulf War, when he launched conventionally armed Scuds against Saudi Arabia (and Bahrain), but did not arm them with CW or BW warheads for fear of an American nuclear retaliation.[4]

These three simple facts have led a number of policy analysts and academics to conclude that a strategy of deterring Saddam, should he acquire nuclear weapons, is eminently feasible. They argue that Saddam respects deterrence and therefore is highly unlikely to use nuclear weapons or to act aggressively in the belief that his nuclear weapons would shield him from an American or Israeli response. Unfortunately, all of these analyses, many by highly intelligent and sensible people, are deeply flawed.

A number of these assessments base their conclusions on the experience between the United States and the Soviet Union during the latter half of the Cold War, when both superpowers recognized that there was no possible gain from aggression that was worth the risk of an escalation to nuclear warfare and so generally refrained from any provocative moves toward each other. Many supporters of deterrence against Iraq have taken this experience as conclusive that the terror inspired by nuclear weaponry is so overpowering that it trumps all other considerations and produces extremely conservative behavior that creates an uneasy, but durable, peace between the two sides of any nuclear standoff. However, as other, equally thoughtful academics have pointed out, "the early phase of the Cold War, before crises over Berlin and Cuba worked out the limits to probes and provocations, is a less reassuring model. Only with hindsight is it easy to assume that because the superpowers did not go over the edge it was foreordained by deterrence that they should not."[5] It is worth remembering that Soviet forces in Cuba were ordered to employ tactical nuclear weapons if the United States invaded during the 1962 missile crisis.[6] Had President John F. Kennedy proceeded with such an invasion rather than devising the clever solution of a blockade, the world might be a very different place today. Nor have other nuclear powers been quite so restrained, especially early on in their relationships. For example, in March 1969, thousands of Chinese and Russian troops clashed along the Ussuri and Amur Rivers, prompting the Russians to hint at using nuclear weapons and the Chinese to respond by alerting their nuclear forces.[7] Moreover, Britain's nuclear arsenal did not prevent Argentina from attacking the Falkland Islands in 1983, nor did Israel's purported nuclear arsenal prevent Egypt and Syria from attacking it in 1973, nor did the U.S. nuclear arsenal dissuade China from attacking American forces in Korea in 1950.[8]

One particularly dangerous method that many of the proponents of deterrence employ to make their argument is "mirror imaging." They essentially ask, "What would I do if I were in Saddam's shoes?" Similarly, they use their understanding of American decision makers (and to some extent, Soviet decision makers) to ask how Saddam is likely to behave based on how American and Soviet leaders behaved when faced with similar predicaments during the Cold War. While these are understandable approaches, they are also treacherous ones.[9] We may not have a perfect understanding of how Saddam Hussein thinks, but one thing we know for certain is that he does not think like an American president or even a Russian general secretary. This type of mirror imaging, or argument by analogy, has frequently gotten Americans into trouble when trying to predict Saddam Hussein's behavior in the past. Before the Gulf War, I regularly encountered U.S. policy makers who kept insisting that Saddam was not going to invade Kuwait because "I would never do this if I were in his situation" or because from their perspective "it makes no sense." In fact, John Helgerson, the deputy director for intelligence at the CIA at the time of the Gulf War, got so fed up with the constant mistakes produced by this kind of thinking that he decreed, "We will not predict what Saddam Hussein will not do." Assuming that Saddam Hussein will think and act like a Westerner—indeed, like anyone but himself—can only lead to disaster.

Some proponents of deterrence theory see in the notion that Saddam is not suicidal sufficient reassurance by itself. They assume that he would "know" that his use of nuclear weapons would trigger an Israeli or American nuclear response that would annihilate Iraq and himself as well and that since he is not suicidal, he would never embark on any action that could possibly lead to such an end. Although I agree that Saddam probably would not use nuclear weapons unprovoked (although even here I am not willing to bet my life, or the lives of other Americans or Middle Easterners, on it) because this probably would provoke an immediate retaliation that would risk his life for no particular purpose, this is not really the point. The real issue is whether Saddam would take other actions in the mistaken belief that he was *not* risking his own survival. In particular, would he act aggressively in the mistaken belief that his nuclear weapons would deter an American or Israeli nuclear response? Then the question might be whether we would be willing to risk sacrificing New York—or Tel Aviv, or the Saudi oil fields—to save Kuwait or Jordan or Syria. Of greater importance, what calculations would Saddam make about our willingness to do so? Here, even the experience of the Cold War is not reassuring. Nuclear threats are much easier to make than nuclear attacks, and you don't need to want to carry them out to be willing to make them—and make them as key elements of your most important policies. The United States threatened nuclear war on several occasions to compel the Soviets to cease actions it found threatening over Cuba and Berlin, and during the 1973 Arab-Israeli War. President Dwight D. Eisenhower used the threat of nuclear war to compel the Chinese to negotiate an end to the Korean War, and Israel did the same in 1973 to persuade the United States to come to its aid.

In addition, there is evidence that other countries believe that having acquired nuclear weapons, they can engage a more powerful country at a lower level of confrontation with relative impunity. The best example of this is the recent Indo-Pakistani experiences. At least since 1998, when both countries declared their possession of nuclear weapons, but arguably since the late 1980s, when Pakistan first acquired nuclear weapons and therefore eliminated India's nuclear advantage, Pakistan has waged an insurgent war against India in Kashmir, believing that India would not be able to respond effectively for fear of escalation to nuclear war. The Indo-Pakistani crises of 1990, 1999, and 2002 were all sparked by blatant Pakistani support for Kashmiri insurgents, and in every case India was restrained from responding as it would have liked by fear of escalation to nuclear war. Thus, Pakistan's possession of nuclear weapons has enabled it to mount lesser attacks on India for nearly a decade and a half. Indeed, a major study on nuclear weapons crises concluded that "a regional predator will find a small nuclear arsenal a powerful tool for collapsing regional military coalitions that the United States might craft to oppose such a future opponent."[10] There can be little doubt that Iraq is one of those potential regional "predators."

Other proponents of deterrence base their assessments on misreadings of Iraqi history. For example, some highly regarded scholars have argued that Iraq would be unlikely to employ nuclear weapons in a hypothetical crisis with the United States based on an inaccurate portrayal of Iraqi behavior during the Iran-Iraq War.[11] In at least one influential case, this assessment has been derived from the distorted history of Iraqi chemical weapons employment presented by Israeli analyst Aharon Levran, who mistakenly asserts that Iraq generally used these weapons only as a last resort—when the risk of an Iranian breakthrough was high—and generally only on Iraqi soil. Levran sees in this "selective" use of chemical warfare a sign of Iraqi restraint.[12] In fact, nothing could be further from the truth. The Iraqis used chemical munitions quite indiscriminately during the Iran-Iraq War after they had weaponized the agents and produced adequate stocks of munitions. The only "selectivity" they showed was that later in the war they realized that many of their earlier chemical attacks had been so cavalier that they had killed large numbers of their own troops. This realization did convince the Iraqis to take greater care in planning their chemical warfare attacks but had no impact on their willingness to employ them either offensively or defensively. They never diminished their use of CW either in frequency or magnitude. What's more, the Iraqis used CW in every battle on Iranian soil once they had the capability to do so (which they did not have during their invasion of Iran in 1980 and Iran's counteroffensives in 1980–81). When Iraqi forces again attacked into Iran in 1988, they employed massive chemical warfare barrages.

All of the arguments in favor of deterrence are flawed in that they overstate the certainty that any leader in possession of nuclear weapons can be deterred at all times. In some cases, it is because their assumptions are based on too narrow a view of history; in others, because they are based on a misreading of history. Nevertheless, even if all of the arguments about the strength of deterrence theory were right in the abstract, the question would still remain: Do we want to base our policy toward Iraq on theories? Iraq could always be the first of its kind. Theories about international relations never account for 100 percent of what happens in the world. In fact, a good academic theory might account for only about half of what goes on in the world. Unfortunately, policy making can't simply assume that since a theory is mostly right, it should apply in the case of Iraq and nuclear weapons as well. We have had more than thirty years of experience with Saddam in power in Iraq, and he has consistently defied all of the predictions of academic theory. Do we then want to bet that *this* theory will get him right? Indeed, because the cost of being wrong about Saddam Hussein and nuclear weapons is so high, we must look to the specifics of Iraq and Saddam's behavior to decide whether deterrence is a prudent course of action to adopt.

SADDAM THE DECISION MAKER

Nuclear deterrence is greatly facilitated by some key characteristics of a country's leadership and decision-making process. History has shown that deterrence works best when decision makers are conservative in their goals, avoid taking risky actions, are content with the status quo, have access to high-quality information about their adversary, and work within an effective decision-making process that considers a range of possibilities and reaches a decision only after each possibility has been subjected to careful scrutiny. There is still debate, however, over whether these traits are merely helpful to deterrence or actually indispensable. The problem is that we really have only the one case of the Cold War as evidence, and it is risky to draw conclusions from just one example. What's more, it just so happens that both the United States and the Soviet Union possessed all of those traits, so no one knows if deterrence worked during the Cold War because of those characteristics or because the logic of deterrence is so powerful that it would work even if none of those traits were present on one or both sides.

Nikita Khrushchev was the one Cold War leader who strayed most from the list of desirable leadership characteristics. He was a gambler, impetuous, and looking to change the status quo. It was also as a result of Khrushchev's actions that the United States and Russia experienced their most dangerous crises—those over Berlin and Cuba—and when the two superpowers probably came closest to nuclear war. In the end, however, Khrushchev was prevented from going over the edge by the conservative Soviet decision-making apparatus, which prevented him from acting too rashly and eventually decided that he was just too dangerous to lead the Soviet Union.[13]

Saddam Hussein and his regime are the polar opposite of every single one of the traits considered desirable, if not essential, for nuclear deterrence. The psychologist Jerrold Post, a longtime U.S. government expert on Saddam who has written extensively on him as a decision maker, says of Saddam that "while he is psychologically in touch with reality, he is often politically out of touch with reality. Saddam's worldview is narrow and distorted and he has scant experience outside of the Arab world."[14] Saddam is determined to overturn the status quo to make himself the hegemon of the Persian Gulf region and the leader of the Arab world, to evict the United States from the region, and eventually to destroy the state of Israel. Saddam is also one of the worst gamblers and risk takers in modern history. On the eve of the Gulf War, one of Israel's senior Iraq analysts in its Directorate of Military Intelligence concluded that "Saddam has a tendency to run risks; he takes surprising steps without considering all the inherent dangers. An example for this is the war against Iran. For that reason, his moves must be watched with care."[15] Saddam's behavior is also completely unrestrained by the Iraqi political structure.

I am always reluctant to draw comparisons between Saddam and Adolf Hitler because of the first Bush administration's effort to justify the Gulf War by claiming that Saddam was as dangerous as Hitler. For the most part, Saddam is not as dangerous as Hitler because he does not possess Germany's economic and military power, nor does he possess Hitler's apocalyptic vision of himself and his country. However, in terms of personality traits, Saddam does share some of Hitler's more dangerous traits, and one of them is his propensity to take colossal risks. Like Hitler, Saddam willfully distorts facts and probabilistic outcomes to suit what he wants to have happen. When Saddam looks at a situation, particularly an external situation, and determines his own actions, he invariably interprets all of the available data to conform to what would be best for him. Thus, Saddam plays very dangerous games, but, like Hitler, he plays them falsely confident that the game is not nearly as dangerous as everyone else around him believes.[16] This is probably Saddam's most dangerous trait and the one that makes him most difficult to deter, because it means that he downplays warnings and indicators of danger and plays up information and rationales that support what he wants to be true. It is this failing that has led him into his seemingly endless series of foreign policy fiascoes. It means he takes actions that he does not realize to be suicidal when he takes them and often does not realize that they are suicidal until it is too late to avert disaster.

There are no constraints on Saddam's thinking or his actions. Unlike in the case of Khrushchev, there is no Iraqi political structure that limits Saddam's conduct. In fact, the Iraqi state is designed to execute his orders without question, no matter how bizarre or dangerous, and to maximize his freedom of action. Saddam makes all decisions in Iraq based on what the former head of the U.S. Army Intelligence Agency's Middle East Division has euphemistically called his "unique role and vision."[17] There is little dissent or debate in Iraqi decision making. Saddam has few advisers, and those he turns to are sycophants who generally tell him exactly what he wants to hear.[18] Saddam has a history of shooting the messenger and seeing dissenting views as challenges to his authority—challenges usually met with dismissal or summary execution. "One criticizes a policy or decision of Saddam's at great peril for to criticize Saddam is to be disloyal, and to be disloyal is to lose one's job or one's life," as Post puts it.[19] Numerous stories are told by former members of Saddam's inner circle of his willingness to pull out a pistol and execute cabinet ministers who differed with his judgment.[20] Russian Prime Minister Yevgeny Primakov—a former Soviet ambassador to Baghdad and widely reputed to be a paid agent of the Iraqi regime[21]—has said that when he went to see Saddam during the Gulf War in 1991 to try to negotiate a solution, "I realized that it was possible Saddam did not have complete information. He gave priority to positive reports . . . and as for bad news, the bearer could pay a high price."[22]

The inputs into Saddam's decision making are also deeply suspect. Saddam himself is frighteningly ignorant of the outside world.[23] In a famous interview with Diane Sawyer in July 1990, Saddam was incredulous that the United States did not have laws forbidding criticism of its president and insisted that American Indians were forced to live on reservations.[24] As his American-educated former nuclear weapons chief has said of him, "Like most dictators, Saddam was bewildered by America. He didn't speak English, he had never visited the United States. He had traveled little, outside of his few years of exile as a young man in Cairo and then, much later, state visits to Moscow and Paris. He lived in a cocoon of yes-men, thugs, palace servants, and a harem. What Saddam knew of America came mostly from his spies and diplomats who tailored their reports to his prejudices."[25]

Iraq's intelligence services do not provide Saddam with anything like a comprehensive or objective picture of his strategic situation. Iraq's intelligence services are charged principally with enforcing internal security. Gathering information about the outside world is definitely a second-order priority. As a result, they have few assets overseas and little ability to gather information. Saddam has often gotten awful intelligence (and is rumored to rely on soothsayers more than his intelligence service) that has led him to make terrible decisions.[26] During the Gulf War, Iraqi officers were outraged by how little information they had about what the coalition was doing and were forced to listen to Radio Monte Carlo for news.[27] Since then Khidhir Hamza has related stories about the amateurishness of Iraqi intelligence in external affairs, including being constantly duped in its efforts to obtain fissile materials and other equipment for Iraq's nuclear program.[28] Moreover, its operatives tend to write their reports based on what they believe Saddam wants to hear. They too know that Saddam has frequently acted by punishing the bearers of ill tidings, and few are willing to run that risk.[29] Thus, before the Iran-Iraq War, Iraq had little information regarding developments in Tehran, the mood of the country, or the operational status of the armed forces and instead relied on the misinformation of former Iranian generals who had fled the Islamic Revolution and desperately wanted Iraq to attack to try to restore them to power.[30]

One of the most important aspects of Saddam's decision making is his obsession with internal security. Saddam gained power and has retained it for more than thirty years by mastering Iraqi domestic politics and devoting himself to them completely. He is paranoid about his internal security and invariably overreacts to internal threats. His preoccupation with internal threats, and his tendency to exaggerate their danger, leads him to believe that he can deal with them by taking action in the foreign policy arena, and his need and ignorance of the larger world lead him to underestimate the risks of these external actions. This has caused Saddam to engage in some of his most dangerous foreign policy gambits—the 1974 attack on the Kurds, the 1980 invasion of Iran, the 1990 invasion of Kuwait, the decision to fight for Kuwait in 1990–91, and the decision to attack Kuwait again in 1994—all of which were driven in large part by his fear of a threat to his internal position that he believed he could rectify by external aggression. His ignorance of the outside world, the poverty of the intelligence and advice he receives, and his tendency to calculate odds based on what he wants to be true all reinforce this willingness to embark on foreign policy adventures to solve his domestic political problems.

Finally, Saddam believes that most courses of action require sacrifice and conflict, and he generally is not discouraged by even heavy resistance. In Post's words, "When he pursues a course of action, he pursues it fully, and if he meets initial resistance he struggles all the harder, convinced of the correctness of his judgments."[31] Saddam regularly calculates that he (and Iraq) can absorb more damage than his adversary, and he is willing to do so in pursuit of his goals. This is echoed in countless statements since his accession to power, most famously in his cold-blooded assurance to U.S. Ambassador April Glaspie that "yours is a society that cannot accept 10,000 dead in one battle," implying that he and his society could.[32] Indeed, Amatzia Baram and others have argued that in Iraq's political culture, it is necessary to *suffer* damage before backing down—the *threat* of damage is not good enough. Backing down in the face of a threat brings shame and humiliation, which, if you are a leader, means that you lose the support of your loyalists against other challengers and may well be toppled by them. According to Baram, "In the Ba'thi political culture, it is far safer to look unnecessarily intransigent than weak. Only when all other options have been clearly exhausted and when Saddam has demonstrated beyond a shadow of a doubt that he is tougher than anyone else, will he risk making concessions."[33]

SADDAM'S DECISION MAKING IN PRACTICE

Saddam's foreign policy history is littered with bizarre decisions, poor judgment, and catastrophic miscalculations. When confronted with a problem, he has generally reacted with aggression and justified his offensives with distortions and convoluted logic. All too frequently, Saddam has reached conclusions that no Western leader would have reached; constructed scenarios that are fantastic when recounted; and taken risks that everyone around him (let alone outside observers) has found inexplicable.

The Ba'th Party returned to power in 1968 with Saddam as the deputy secretary general of the Revolutionary Command Council, the second highest position in the government. In October 1973, soon after the Ba'th Party had consolidated its position and Saddam had emerged as the strongman of the regime, Egypt and Syria launched a surprise attack on Israel that caught the Israelis, the Iraqis, and the rest of the Arab world by surprise. Most of the Arab states sent token forces (a brigade or an air force squadron) to fight in the October War, but Iraq sent an entire armored corps and about a hundred combat aircraft as quickly as it could. Although Iraq won considerable popular admiration for its contribution, the Iraqi forces were butchered by the Israelis when they eventually reached the Golan Heights area.

In 1974, Saddam made his first catastrophic foreign policy miscalculation: he decided to abrogate the March Manifesto, which had granted the Kurds limited autonomy and which he had negotiated in 1970. Instead, he chose to use force to restore Kurdistan to Baghdad's control. A key element of this decision was Saddam's belief that the shah of Iran would not intervene on the Kurds' side. It is not clear why Saddam believed this. Along with the United States and Israel, Iran had been backing the Kurds with money and weaponry since 1972 and had retrained Kurdish forces in conventional military operations. The shah's armed forces were far superior to Iraq's at that time, and there was nothing in particular to stop Tehran from intervening if the shah chose to do so. Nevertheless, Saddam simply assumed the shah would stay out and launched his attack. Initially, the Iraqi forces did quite well against the Kurds, but their successes prompted Iranian intervention. Iranian forces began clashing with the Iraqis along their border and moved into Iraqi Kurdistan to support the Kurds directly. Saddam panicked. He knew that Iraq did not have the power to stop the Iranian armed forces and feared that the shah intended to march on Baghdad and overthrow the regime. In response, Saddam was forced to sign the humiliating Algiers Accord in 1975 to prevent Iran from marching on Baghdad and further supporting the Kurds, which the shah did only when Saddam had recognized all of Tehran's territorial claims against Iraq, including along the vital Shatt al-Arab waterway. Taha Yasin Ramadan, Saddam's longtime vice president, later explained, "Our signing of the agreement came in circumstances under which we had to make calculations as to whether we would lose either Iraq or half the Shatt al-Arab. We chose what was in the best interests of Iraq."[34]

The next year Saddam was back at it again. In response to the Syrian invasion of Lebanon and Syrian threats to dam the Euphrates River (which supplies both Iraq and Syria), Saddam moved several Iraqi divisions to the Syrian border and threatened his hated rival, Hafiz al-Asad, with war. Once again, there was no assessment of risks or costs—nor were the Iraqi forces logistically prepared to mount an offensive across the breadth of the Syrian desert to reach Damascus or other Syrian population centers. Indeed, given the awful performance of Iraqi forces in battle in 1973 and 1980 (even worse than the Syrian performances in 1973 and 1976), the odds would have favored the Syrians had Iraq chosen to invade.[35] In the end, nothing came of this because the Syrians acquiesced to an Arab League plan that effectively granted them the suzerainty over Lebanon they had sought and provided Saddam with a face-saving means of backing down from his threats.[36]

Saddam's invasion of Iran in September 1980 was another colossal miscalculation that nearly cost him everything. Saddam feared that the Ayatollah Khomeini would spark an Islamic revolution among Iraq's majority Shi'ah population that would sweep his regime aside. Both at the time and since, outsiders have questioned the extent of the actual threat, but as usual, Saddam overreacted. He chose to try to solve his internal problem with an external adventure—invading Iran to eliminate the ayatollah's regime. Iraqi intelligence knew nothing about Iran or its armed forces. Instead, relying primarily on a group of former Iranian military officers who had fled the Iranian revolution, Saddam concluded that Iran was exceptionally weak and that one good shove would cause the regime to collapse. Saddam concocted a theory by which Iraqi forces would invade Iran and occupy its oil-rich Khuzestan province; somehow, this would produce either a military coup or a popular revolt against Khomeini. The sycophants around him applauded his decision, and he ordered the attack—without any real planning.

Iraqi divisions were moved to the border, given distant objectives, and told to move out—without any routes of march, logistical preparations, support plans, intelligence assessments, or any of the other rudiments of military planning.[37]

Of course, the Iraqi invasion did not go as Saddam had planned. The Iraqi forces ground to a halt about six weeks later, having failed to attain any of their objectives and having been stopped by paltry Iranian resistance. Then, beginning in January 1981, Iran put together a series of counteroffensives that smashed the Iraqi Army and drove it off Iranian soil. By the summer of 1982, the Iranian Army was preparing to invade Iraq and the ayatollah was daily proclaiming his intention to drive on Baghdad to overthrow Saddam. Once again Saddam panicked, fearing that Iran would be able to push into Iraq and oust his regime as easily as it had reoccupied its own territory. In response, Saddam ordered the production of chemical munitions to try to stem the Iranian onslaught. Iraq had first begun work on such weapons in 1971, but the effort had not had as high a priority as the Iraqi nuclear program and Baghdad had not produced enough munitions for use in battle. In 1983, Iraq employed a small amount of mustard gas to help beat back an Iranian attack in Kurdistan. By early 1984, Iraqi production was sufficient to allow Baghdad to employ chemical warfare in every major battle of the rest of the war and many minor ones—including skirmishes in Kurdistan that posed no threat to either the regime or the coherence of its defenses.[38]

At different points during the war when Iraq became especially concerned about Iranian battlefield advances, Saddam opted to launch air and missile strikes against Iranian cities—this despite the fact that the Iranians had a great advantage in that their most important cities—Tehran, Qom, Esfahan, Shiraz, Mashad—are much farther from the border than are the largest Iraqi cities, Baghdad and al-Basrah. As a result, it was relatively easy for Iran to hit Baghdad, and it could do so with Scud missiles, while Iraq could hit Tehran or other important Iranian cities only with small, difficult air raids that it could mount only sporadically. Consequently, until 1988, the pattern was the same: Saddam would react to a threatened Iranian ground advance by launching air and missile attacks against Iran's western cities, which would prompt Iran to retaliate against Baghdad. This would go on for a few weeks or months before Saddam would realize that he was taking more damage than the Iranians and so would halt his attacks. Despite the fact that there was no reason to expect a different result from the last time, Saddam tried this tactic repeatedly—in July–August 1982, October 1982, December 1982–January 1983, February 1984, March–June 1985, January–February 1987, and August–September 1987—each time with the same results.[39]

By 1987, Saddam was desperate and this desperation resulted in ever greater uses of chemical weapons and ballistic missiles. After Iran seized the al-Faw peninsula in 1986 and Iraq's massive counterattacks failed, Saddam kicked off a new campaign against Iranian shipping in the Gulf, removed the last political constraints on his generals, allowed the expansion and rebuilding of the Republican Guard as an elite offensive force, and ordered the development of longer-range missiles and WMD warheads so that he could strike Tehran and Iran's other major cities to try to force an end to the war. By 1988, he was ready. He employed the Republican Guards to evict the Iranians from al-Faw and then crush Tehran's armies in a series of ground offensives. These Iraqi offensives at al-Faw, Fish Lake, Mehran, the Majnun Islands, and Dehloran were preceded by artillery bombardments involving massive amounts of chemical warfare—this at a point in the war when the Iranians had developed their own chemical weapons and could, to some extent, respond in kind. Meanwhile, Saddam unleashed his new al-Hussein missile force on Tehran, firing about two hundred during 1988 and causing roughly one quarter of the population to flee the city for fear that Iraq planned to arm the missiles with CW warheads. That apparently was Saddam's intention. According to Wafiq al-Samarra'i, then head of the Mukhabbarat, Saddam was planning to employ CW-armed al-Husseins against Tehran as soon as they became available. Apparently this caused considerable consternation among members of the Iraqi elite, who realized that Iran would be able to retaliate with CW-filled bombs delivered by aircraft against Baghdad—a much more powerful delivery method. However, Iran accepted a cease-fire in August 1988, so the plan was never put to the test.[40]

Iraq then enjoyed peace for only two years before Saddam drove the country to war once again. As described in Chapter 2, Saddam became concerned over Iraq's economic problems, believing that they were creating a threat to his regime. He was also concerned because the collapse of the Soviet empire had left the United States unchecked, and he believed that Iraq needed to be stronger to be able to confront America. As Ofra Bengio has remarked, "The development that truly motivated Iraq to reappraise its policies was the collapse of the Communist bloc in Eastern Europe and the emergence of the US as the world's superpower. Rather than inducing Iraq to strengthen its ties with the US, the change in Eastern Europe encouraged Baghdad to challenge Washington."[41] In addition, Saddam was looking for greater glory and resources for Iraq, to realize his aspirations to dominate the Gulf region and make himself the leader of the Arab world. The course of action he chose was to invade Kuwait. To any outside observer, these explanations make little sense. There were much better courses of action available to Iraq to fix its economic problems. Attacking Kuwait could only bring a war-weary Iraq trouble. Indeed, this was the cornerstone of the erroneous judgment of the U.S. intelligence community (but not that of my fellow military analysts and myself) that Saddam would lick his wounds for a while after the Iran-Iraq War and would not engage in any new foreign aggression.[42] Apparently, Saddam's solution did not make much sense to other Iraqis. Saddam's then foreign minister, Tariq Aziz, claims even to have tried to subtly point out to Saddam the risks of this course of action, but to no avail.[43]

What is most disconcerting about Saddam's decision to attack Kuwait is that he apparently had concluded that there was a high probability that the United States would oppose an invasion of Kuwait militarily *and he believed that he could defeat the expected American response.* After the war, Tariq Aziz gave several interviews in which he said that Iraq had expected an immediate American military reaction to the invasion, probably by rapidly deployable American forces such as the ready brigade of the Eighty-second Airborne Division or a Marine Expeditionary Unit.[44] Iraqi military activity during the invasion of Kuwait fully supports the claims that Saddam expected a quick military response by Washington: Republican Guard infantry units moved to secure Kuwait's airfields and beaches, and immediately began building hasty defenses against either an air assault or an amphibious landing to repel a possible foreign intervention by air or sea. They did this to some extent at the expense of securing control over the Kuwaiti population.[45] Moreover, the size of the invasion force—all eight divisions of the Republican Guard—was far more than what was needed to overrun the small and ineffective Kuwaiti military and was almost certainly sized to deter or defeat any rapid U.S. military intervention in support of Kuwait.[46] As best we understand it, Saddam believed that if he could crush an immediate counterattack by the light forces Washington could quickly move to the region, the United States would be unwilling to suffer more casualties in a larger war (especially for something as insignificant as Saddam

believed Kuwait to be in American eyes) and so would grudgingly acquiesce to Kuwait's conquest.[47]

Many Americans have speculated that the United States failed to ade-
quately signal to Saddam that it would defend Kuwait if attacked and therefore this was not a good test of deterrence. The available evidence indicates
that this is untrue; Saddam had already made up his mind that he was willing to fight the world's only remaining superpower. The only thing that
seems to have surprised him is how the United States chose to fight—a
major military operation after a protracted buildup, rather than a quick intervention by light forces—and America's willingness to fight the war despite numerous predictions of heavy casualties. What this means is that,
especially given the difficulty of convincing Saddam beforehand that this
was the course the United States would take, it was probably impossible for
the United States to have deterred Saddam from invading Kuwait.[48]

As mystifying as this decision was, Saddam went one better by refusing
to withdraw from Kuwait even after the United States and its allies mustered a massive force of more than 700,000 troops, more than 3,500 tanks,
and 1,700 aircraft in the Gulf region to retake Kuwait.[49] Although all indications are that the Iraqi elite feared that the U.S.-led coalition would obliterate the Iraqi armed forces, Saddam convinced himself otherwise.[50] First,
he concluded that the coalition would be unlikely to muster the political
will to go to war. When Yevgeny Primakov was sent to Baghdad to try to
negotiate a way out of the war, he found that "evidently, tactical surprise of
the attack against Iraq was achieved. It seems that Saddam Hussein up to
the last moment still was operating on [the basis] that the 'multinational
forces' would not initiate military operations."[51] Second, Saddam convinced himself that even in the unlikely event that the coalition actually did
attack, it could not prevail over the Iraqi Army. According to General
Samarra'i, Saddam was dismissive of American military capabilities: "He
was very boastful. For instance, when we told him that they brought Stealth
jetfighters, the F117, he said, 'This—what you have read in the papers—
can be seen by our shepherds!' When we mentioned, for instance, a cruise
missile, he would say, 'A cruise missile on its way to its target. We will just
blind it. We will suppress its course. It will mislead, it will mis-hit its target.' We say, 'How do we do that?' He would say that 'We will fire mud and
water to the screen of these radars that are leading these cruise missiles.'
'Okay,' we would say. 'How do we do that when we are facing the Apache
helicopters, these machines can deal with six targets simultaneously at a

very long distance?' He said, 'Oh no, don't bother. This is just a myth.' "[52] Indeed, Primakov repeatedly tried to warn Saddam that when the coalition launched its ground offensive it would sweep away the Iraqi Army, but Saddam simply would not listen.[53]

As best we understand it, Saddam did harbor an exaggerated sense of coalition political and military weakness, as well as an excessively optimistic view of Iraqi military capabilities. However, the critical element apparently was that having invaded Kuwait to challenge the Americans for hegemony in the Gulf region and in expectation of fighting the United States, Saddam had engaged his own prestige in the retention of Kuwait. Withdrawing from Kuwait would have been a terrible humiliation for Saddam that he believed would have threatened his hold on power inside Iraq. Consequently, he believed he needed to stay in Kuwait to avoid a dire internal threat and interpreted events to provide a justification for doing so: the coalition would not summon the will to attack, and even if it did, Iraq would prevail.[54]

During the Gulf War, Saddam did refrain from employing weapons of mass destruction, and this appears to be (the only) unequivocal evidence of his having been deterred. However, even here the evidence actually isn't unequivocal. The best case is against Israel, where Iraqi sources have stated that Saddam chose not to arm the Scuds with WMD warheads for fear of Israeli nuclear retaliation.[55] However, this may also have been out of technical incapacity. The WMD missile warheads Iraq had then developed were extremely poor devices. The Iraqis themselves were not sure that the agents inside the warheads would survive the extreme heat of reentry into the earth's atmosphere. Moreover, Iraq had not been able to obtain or develop proximity fuses that would function in a ballistic missile to allow the warhead to detonate above the target (the ideal location for spreading chemical or biological agents), nor had it developed cluster submunitions or other ways to spray the agent when the warhead was detonated. Instead, all it had was contact fuses, which most experts, including the Iraqis, expected to destroy most of the agent, causing very few, if any, casualties.[56] In other words, Saddam may have fired only conventionally armed missiles at Israel because these were the only functional missiles he had.[57]

As for Iraqi restraint in using tactical WMD against the coalition armies, the evidence here is even more ambiguous. First of all, there is at least one unconfirmed CIA report that indicates that Saddam tried to use BW against coalition forces—an air strike involving three MiG-21s as decoys and an Su-22 fitted with a spray tank to spray coalition forces with a biological agent.[58] However, since this report was not further confirmed, the U.N. inspectors found no evidence of such an operation, and it runs counter to the few authoritative sources we have, it can probably be discounted.

Nevertheless, there is still a great deal of room for alarm regarding Saddam's intentions to employ WMD against coalition forces. On August 5, Saddam threatened the use of CW against American forces when he ordered the loading of Iraqi aircraft with chemical munitions to deter an American intervention in Kuwait. Thus Saddam was willing to threaten the use of CW to deter an American counteroffensive intended to deny Iraq the fruits of its conquest. Also, Saddam did order the movement of chemical munitions into the Kuwaiti Theater of Operations in August in preparation for a war with the newly formed coalition. However, as the U.N. inspectors discovered, he then ordered the withdrawal of these munitions later in the fall and instead had them deployed to several sites north of the Kuwaiti Theater, where they were more firmly under his control but could still be moved into the theater in a pinch.[59] This turnaround was probably in response to the U.S. threats that led Iraq to believe that Washington would retaliate with nuclear weapons. However, there is important additional evidence that complicates the picture. As noted, Saddam did not expect to fight the coalition, and, if there were a war, he did not expect to lose. Consequently, he believed it unlikely that he would require chemical munitions to stave off the destruction of his army. The fact that he still kept large stockpiles near the theater (and one stockpile at Khamisiyah, within what the United States had demarcated as the theater but that Iraq probably considered outside the likely combat zone) indicates that he did entertain the possibility of using them if the situation became grim.

As for why Saddam did not use WMD to prevent the rout during the ground phase of Desert Storm, it may be that he was deterred, but it seems at least as likely that he simply was unable to do so. The vast majority of Iraq's chemical munitions were not filled before the war because filled munitions begin to degrade fairly quickly.[60] Thus the Iraqis would have had to have filled large numbers of shells and then moved them into the theater and up to the frontline units for them to have been used. This process would have required several days for any tactically significant use of chemical warfare. However, U.S. forces moved so fast and overran Iraqi defensive lines so quickly that the special Iraqi units tasked with filling, moving, and ensuring the firing of the WMD munitions could not have done so in time. The few open roads between the theater and central Iraq were choked with Iraqi units fleeing Kuwait, and Iraq's artillery batteries in Kuwait were being quickly neutralized by U.S. counterbattery fire.[61] Even if we discount the unconfirmed CIA report of an attempted BW air strike, the evidence suggests that while Saddam may have been deterred at some level from using WMD tactically against coalition forces, this deterrence was actually quite conditional. It was predicated on the assumption that Iraq would not need to use chemicals, and it may well have been that Saddam would have employed CW had he been able to do so when that assumption was proven false.

Another point that is often overlooked is that the deterrence threat the United States made to Iraq before the Gulf War regarded not just Iraqi use of weapons of mass destruction, but also the destruction of the Kuwaiti oil wells and terrorist attacks. The letter from President Bush that James Baker handed Tariq Aziz in Geneva in January 1991 right before the onset of Desert Storm threatened Iraq with the severest consequences if it did any of those things. Although Iraq did not use (or was not able to use) its weapons of mass destruction, it certainly obliterated Kuwait's oil fields and tried to mount terrorist operations. Thus, at most, Saddam *chose* to be deterred only in the use of his weapons of mass destruction, which he did not believe necessary in any event.[62]

As with the Second Kurdish War of 1974–75 and the Iran-Iraq War, the Gulf War proved to be another catastrophic miscalculation by Saddam. Once again, he based his decisions on bizarrely overconfident judgments that were not shared by anyone around him but that conformed to his own wishes and then panicked when his assumptions were wrong. During the coalition ground offensive, Saddam suddenly realized that his army would not be able to stop the American-led forces. As Samarra'i describes it, "He did not think that the Americans and their allies would go as far as this. Except perhaps in the final stages, when the land assault took place. He asked me directly, 'Did you think that the allies would come as far as Baghdad?' And he was quite desperate, and he was quite frightened. I said, no, I did not think so."[63]

Nevertheless, Saddam clearly was not 100 percent certain of his own judgment. Of greatest importance, soon after the invasion of Kuwait and the start of Operation Desert Shield, he ordered a crash program to produce one nuclear weapon that he intended to fling at Tel Aviv in the event the coalition did attempt to topple his regime. Khidhir Hamza, the man responsible for building that weapon, recounts that "in August he'd ordered a crash program to produce enough fuel for at least one nuclear device, a warhead that he could mount on a missile and hurl at the Israelis if the Allies invaded. It was his doomsday weapon. If his own demise were imminent, he planned to take everybody down with him—no threats, no demonstration flash in the desert for diplomatic leverage. The crash program meant Saddam would use the bomb, once. And then we'd all go down with him when the Israeli missiles came whistling back."[64] Although the U.N. inspectors also concluded that this had been Saddam's intention, Wafiq al-Samarra'i argues that Saddam wanted the nuclear weapon to deter a U.S. attack to retake Kuwait altogether and that Baghdad's actions throughout the fall were designed to stall a coalition offensive until he could acquire a nuclear device, at which point he believed that the Americans would not dare to attack.[65] Finally, the U.N. inspectors learned that Saddam had equipped a special force of al-Husseins with WMD warheads and predelegated them launch authority to fire their missiles at Israel if communications with Baghdad were severed as a result of nuclear attack or a coalition drive on the capital.[66]

Here as well, Saddam's understanding of deterrence and willingness to be deterred appear dangerous. If Hamza is right and Saddam simply intended to atomize Tel Aviv if he had obtained a nuclear weapon and the coalition drove on to Baghdad, this was not deterrence, just sheer revenge. This was clearly the case with Saddam's WMD-armed missiles—which the West had no idea existed, and thus they could not have deterred any coalition actions. On the other hand, if Samarra'i is right that Saddam hoped to build a nuclear weapon to deter a coalition attack altogether, it suggests that Saddam believes that possession of nuclear weapons would inoculate him against American military action. Regardless as to which of them is right, none of this is very reassuring. Either way, it reinforces the conclusion that Saddam has bizarre and dangerous ideas about deterrence, nuclear weapons, and aggression.

The lessons that Saddam appears to have learned from the Gulf War, as best we understand them, are equally disquieting and indicate that he will not be easily deterred in the future. According to various Iraqi sources, in small meetings with the highest-ranking regime officials, Saddam has explicitly admitted to making five mistakes during the Gulf War. First and foremost, Saddam apparently believes that it was a mistake to have invaded

Kuwait before he had acquired nuclear weapons because he believes if he had, it would have deterred the United States from intervening. Second, he admitted that it was a mistake not to have continued the invasion to seize the Saudi oil fields and rig them for destruction, thereby holding them hostage to American behavior. Third, Saddam believes it was a mistake to have released his Western hostages in December 1990, rather than keeping them and placing them at high-value facilities that the regime did not want to have bombed. Fourth, he reportedly has concluded that it was a mistake not to have attacked U.S. troops when they first began deploying to the region and were vulnerable. Last, he admits that he put too much faith in French President François Mitterrand and Soviet General Secretary Mikhail Gorbachev to find a diplomatic solution to the crisis.[67] Assuming that this is true—and given the number of sources who have repeated some version of these reports and the fact that they conform closely to other elements of Saddam's thinking, there is good reason to believe that it is—the lessons Saddam seems to have taken away from the Gulf War are deeply disturbing. In particular, they indicate that Saddam has not concluded that it was a mistake to invade Kuwait and fight the world's only remaining superpower. Instead, he has concluded that invading Kuwait was the right idea; he simply did not do enough to deter the United States from mounting a counteroffensive, which would have required possession of nuclear weapons, a credible threat to Saudi oil fields, and/or the holding of Western hostages.

Nor has Saddam's behavior since the Gulf War indicated a break from this pattern. In 1994, faced with hyperinflation and mounting threats to his regime, Saddam took the inexplicable step of threatening another invasion of Kuwait—and the best evidence we have, from Hussein Kamel, was that Saddam was not bluffing but genuinely intended to attack.[68] Only when the United States started Operation Vigilant Warrior and the Security Council passed UNSC Resolution 949 demanding the withdrawal of Iraqi troops did Saddam realize that the international community would again rally around the Americans, who were prepared to employ massive force against his tattered divisions—something that should have been patently obvious to him beforehand. Even if Saddam intended only to threaten Kuwait, he should have recognized that such a demonstration of recidivist aggression would only ensure that the sanctions were maintained even longer, which is in fact what happened.

In 1998, in response to the well-targeted (if too brief) attacks of Operation Desert Fox, Saddam feared a domestic uprising and overreacted, arresting and killing many regime officials and Shi'ite religious leaders, which in turn prompted a series of riots and fed the insurgency waged by Shi'ite guerrillas in the south. Even in 2000, Saddam could not resist the opportunity to try to speed the collapse of containment by stoking an Arab-Israeli conflict and so began deploying divisions to the Syrian border. Both the United States and Israel drew up plans to pound Iraqi targets (basically the same types of targets as had been struck during Desert Fox) if Saddam ordered these divisions into Syria. Thus, even at this late stage, Saddam was still taking risks and courting military retaliation by the United States and/or Israel. Although we do not know exactly what Saddam's calculations were in 2000, he clearly had not learned to be patient or conservative in his diplomatic and military moves.

LESSONS FROM SADDAM'S EXPERIENCE WITH DETERRENCE

This closer examination of Saddam's historical record gives little reason to be sanguine that Saddam can be deterred in the future, especially after he acquires nuclear weapons. He has a twenty-eight-year pattern of aggression, violence, miscalculation, and purposeful underestimation of the consequences of his actions that should give real pause to anyone considering whether to allow him to acquire nuclear weapons. Saddam's first instinct when faced with a problem is to respond violently and aggressively, often with a cavalier disregard for the consequences. Dispatching an armored corps to the Golan Heights in 1973, threatening Syria with war in 1976, and sending five divisions to the Syrian border in 2000 were all rash acts that either were or could have been disastrous for Saddam.

Even when Saddam does consider a problem at length, his ignorance of the outside world, the poor intelligence and advice he receives, and his own determination to interpret geopolitical calculations to suit what he wants to believe anyway lead him to construct bizarre scenarios that he convinces himself are highly likely. His assumption that Iran would not intervene on the Kurds' behalf in 1974, his assumption that the Iranian regime would fall if he invaded Khuzestan in 1980, his belief that Iraqi forces could defeat the U.S.-led coalition in 1991, and his assumption that threatening (or attacking) Kuwait in October 1994 would somehow benefit his campaign to have the sanctions lifted all fall into this category. However, most mystifying of all was his thinking prior to the invasion of Kuwait. Given the mixed signals that the United States sent, it would have been reasonable for Saddam to conclude that the United States would not defend Kuwait. However, the actual scenario that Saddam concocted—that the United States probably would intervene in Kuwait, that it would do so rapidly and with light forces, that the Republican Guards would defeat the U.S. forces, and that afterward the United States would grudgingly accept Iraq's annexation of Kuwait—illustrates this very dangerous tendency to invent outlandish scenarios that allow him to do whatever it is he wants to do, no matter how dangerous.

Often, Saddam's foreign policy is driven by a combination of perceived domestic problems and the pursuit of opportunities to achieve his grandiose visions for himself and Iraq. In many cases, the domestic problems that prompt his actions do not seem to outsiders to be terribly grave, but to Saddam they appear dire. Most experts do not believe the Ayatollah Khomeini presented a serious threat of sparking a Shi'ite revolt in 1980, nor were Iraq's economic problems in 1990 so grave that they were worth a war with the United States. Even when his domestic problems are demonstrably acute, the courses of action he chooses to address them are often perplexing, such as the threat to Kuwait in 1994. Because Saddam is far more concerned with internal threats and understands Iraqi politics infinitely better than he does international relations, he often embarks on highly risky foreign policy adventures that make no sense to and are unexpected by outside observers, and which he insists have a higher likelihood of success than anyone else would expect.

Saddam is generally not deterred by the threat of sustaining severe damage. Although he is willing to reverse course and make substantial concessions, he has done so only after terrible damage was inflicted on Iraq. For example, he seriously offered to make peace with the Iranians only after the Iraqi military had been routed and the Iranians were threatening to drive on Baghdad. Likewise, during the Gulf War, not until a month into the coalition air war—when the Iraqi Army in the Kuwaiti Theater of Operations was hemorrhaging from desertions—would he begin serious negotiations to leave Kuwait. During the Iran-Iraq War he repeatedly ordered air and missile strikes against Iranian cities even though every time in the past the Iranians had demonstrated that they could do more damage to Iraq than he could to them. The notion that by the end of the war he was willing to launch CW-armed missiles at Tehran in full knowledge that the Iranians would do the same (with bombs) to Baghdad is particularly troubling.

To the extent that Saddam has been deterred, as best we can tell this has occurred only under a certain set of circumstances: his adversaries (the

United States and Israel) had nuclear weapons and he did not, his own WMD delivery capability was very weak, and he believed that use of WMD would not be necessary to accomplish his goals. The little we know about Saddam's thinking regarding nuclear weapons indicates that he believes that possession of them would deter the United States and Israel from interfering with Iraqi military operations as long as there was no direct threat to Israel or the United States itself. In other words, possession of nuclear weapons would deter his nuclear-armed adversaries from taking action against him, thereby enabling him to take actions that he otherwise could not. During the Cold War, we used to fear that the Soviets would come to this conclusion once they reached strategic parity with the United States and would employ their conventional forces to try to seize territory along the borders of the Iron Curtain. These fears were almost certainly misplaced because, as we now know, the Soviets were fundamentally conservative decision makers. Saddam is a fundamentally aggressive and risk-taking decision maker, and the available evidence indicates that he subscribes to this dangerous interpretation of the role of nuclear deterrence in enabling conventional offensives.

It is clear that Saddam has learned over time, but his pattern of learning is not something in which to take comfort. For instance, he has learned that by taking minor actions he can provoke the United States just enough to make us angry, but not enough to justify a large strike. But he still miscalculates how far he can push Washington: he clearly did not expect an operation as large as Desert Fox in 1998, as demonstrated by his overreaction to the air strikes. Likewise, had he persisted in his deployment of troops to Syria in October 2000, it is likely that again he would have faced a U.S. military operation that would have been very painful and probably would have outweighed whatever benefit he thought he could achieve by moving the forces into Syria.

Finally, there is a strong element of revenge in Saddam's behavior. In particular, his predelegation of launch authority to Scud missile units armed with WMD warheads to strike Tel Aviv in the event of a coalition nuclear attack or march on Baghdad served no deterrent purpose whatsoever. Had Saddam informed the coalition that he had such weapons and planned to use them in this fashion under those circumstances, this would have been an understandable deterrent threat. Instead, Saddam's orders could only have been driven by a desire for revenge and a determination to lash out at Israel as no other Arab leader has as his final act. Similarly, if Hamza is right about Saddam's intentions regarding the single nuclear weapon he had ordered built, this too reinforces both the sense that Saddam has no compunction about using these horrific weapons to kill millions and that he thinks more about revenge than deterrence.

These patterns of Saddam's behavior are well understood by the Kuwaitis, Saudis, Jordanians, and many of Iraq's other neighbors. It is why they are willing to countenance—and would prefer—a U.S.-led invasion of Iraq to a policy of deterrence. The Kuwaitis in particular fear that Saddam will acquire nuclear weapons that will enable him to overrun Kuwait without having to fear American retaliation. The Kuwaitis also worry that the United States will not be willing to sacrifice Tel Aviv or the Saudi oil fields (or an American city) to save Kuwait.

What the United States will or won't do is of much less importance than what Saddam believes it will or won't do. It is for this reason that sensible proponents of deterrence argue that the United States will have to convince a nuclear-armed Saddam that the United States will not be deterred by an Iraqi nuclear arsenal if he launches any attack beyond Iraq's borders.[69] However, on this point as well, the historical record is not good. In 1990–91, the United States and Israel do seem to have persuaded Saddam that they would use nuclear weapons if he employed chemical weapons, but Saddam was convinced that he did not need to use them. By the same token, the United States—and many of Iraq's advocates—also repeatedly warned Saddam that if he remained in Kuwait the coalition would annihilate his army, but Saddam chose to disregard these warnings until at least five weeks into the air campaign. Nor did our warnings not to employ terrorism or destroy the Kuwaiti oil fields—made in the same breath and with the same attendant threats as those regarding Iraqi WMD use—have any impact on Saddam. Similarly, throughout 1997 and 1998, Washington, the U.N. secretary general, and all of Iraq's backers warned Saddam that the United States would use force if Saddam did not comply with the inspections and that this operation would be bigger than the previous "cruise-missile pinpricks." Yet Saddam clearly was unprepared for the size and scope of Desert Fox when it came in December 1998. Thus, it is not clear just what it would take to convince Saddam of something that he does not want to believe.

CAN WE DETER A NUCLEAR-ARMED SADDAM?

Saddam Hussein is one of the most reckless, aggressive, violence-prone, risk-tolerant, and damage-tolerant leaders of modern history. While he may not be insane, he is often delusional in constructing fantastic conceptions of how his actions are likely to play out. He is driven by paranoia over his internal situation, which makes him insensitive and rash in his external actions. All of these traits have been boldly displayed throughout his years as Iraq's leader. They do not seem to make him impossible to deter, but they do appear to make him difficult to deter in most circumstances and impossible to deter in some. For example, given Saddam's concerns about his internal position and his incredible set of misconceptions about the United States, it is doubtful that he could have been deterred from invading Kuwait in 1990.[70]

Although it is unwise, as John Helgerson warned, to predict what Saddam Hussein will not do, it does seem unlikely that he would employ nuclear weapons as soon as he got them—to wipe out Tel Aviv, for example. Saddam generally uses violence instrumentally, rather than gratuitously—with the important exception being cases of revenge. Again, based on what we know of his thinking, he would likely understand that a nuclear attack on Tel Aviv would invite his own incineration. Some Israeli analysts have noted that the Iraqi regime has staged large-scale evacuations of Baghdad and that some Iraqi military officers have talked as if they believed they could survive a nuclear retaliation from Israel.[71] However, if nothing else, Saddam's behavior during the Gulf War indicates that he is wary enough of nuclear weapons that he probably will not deliberately court a nuclear attack on Baghdad by launching one of his own—at least not out of the blue. Instead, as his own thinking and actions demonstrate (as best we understand them), the much greater threat is that he will believe that his possession of nuclear weapons will allow him to carry out lesser acts of aggression because the United States, Israel, and anyone else would themselves be deterred from responding effectively.

If Saddam had nuclear weapons, especially weapons deliverable by ballistic missiles (which is his goal), Iraq's geographic location at the head of the Persian Gulf would allow him to threaten the destruction of a number of targets of great importance to the United States. Iraq's al-Hussein missiles can reach all of Israel, Jordan, and Syria; northeastern Saudi Arabia, including Riyadh, Dhahran, and virtually all of the Saudi oil fields; western Iran, including Tehran and the Iranian oil fields in Khuzestan; and eastern Turkey. The Saudi oil fields are a particularly worrisome target. A single well-placed nuclear weapon or several less well targeted nuclear weapons could wipe out 75 to 95 percent of all Saudi oil production. Moreover, because of the extent of both the immediate damage and the long-term radiation from a nuclear blast, it is entirely unclear when that capacity could be restored; it could take decades. At present, Saudi Arabia accounts for 15 percent of global oil production (and Iraq and Kuwait together account for another 7 percent).[72] The world has never experienced a supply shock anything like the instantaneous loss of 15 to 22 percent of global oil production. By way of comparison, the 1973 oil embargo withdrew only 2.75 percent of global oil production from the market, and the Iranian revolution withdrew 5.68 percent.[73] Although economists and oil experts caution that we cannot foresee all of the grievous ramifications of such an event, there is widespread agreement that it would cause a global recession probably on the scale of the Great Depression of the 1930s, if not worse.[74]

The problem is not so much U.S. dependence on Iraqi and Saudi oil (although both are now among the top five exporters to the United States) but global economic dependence on cheap oil. The loss of so much of the world's oil—and so much of the world's spare production capacity, most of which is in Saudi Arabia and Kuwait—would drive oil prices to astronomical levels in the short run, causing massive recessions in every nation's economy because oil is so critical both directly as an input into their transportation, heating, and manufacturing sectors, and also indirectly because of its importance to the advanced Western powers that dominate the world's trade. Nor could the strategic petroleum reserves of the United States, Europe, and Japan do more than cushion the blow for a brief period of time. The roughly 1 billion barrels in all of these reserve holdings would make up for the loss of Saudi, Kuwaiti, and Iraqi oil for only about two months at current production rates. Eventually, the global economy would find ways to adapt, conserve, and employ alternative fuels, but this would take years. In the meantime, the world would endure a nightmarish transition.

As Saddam's enumeration of his Gulf War mistakes makes clear, he is well aware of the importance of Persian Gulf oil production to the entire world, particularly the West. This knowledge, plus his ability to target so many other cities of important U.S. allies, would create opportunities for great mischief if he chose to hold the oil fields or those cities hostage to his designs. It is not hard to devise scenarios in which a future, nuclear-armed Iraq could pose terrible choices for the United States:

- At a future date when U.S. forces in the Gulf region have been drawn down (a likely outcome if the United States opts for deterrence because the Saudis will likely insist on it) and Gulf state politics are sensitive to charges of pandering to Washington, Saddam could again mass his forces near Kuwait, counting on the political climate to delay a GCC invitation to the United States to reinforce its presence in the region. Saddam could then invade Kuwait and perhaps continue driving on to the Saudi oil fields (assuming Iraqi logistics could handle the operation), threatening to wipe out the oil fields with one or more well-placed nuclear explosions if the United States intervened. This would certainly be in keeping with our understanding of his views regarding the mistakes he made during the Gulf War. The United States and its allies would be faced with the choice of intervening anyway and risking the loss of 22 percent of global oil production, possibly permanently, or giving Saddam control of that same share of the world's oil wealth.

- At some point, Saddam might try to take advantage of instability in the fragile Kingdom of Jordan—or manufacture it using his economic leverage and large intelligence presence—to topple the government in Amman. The new government might then invite in Iraqi troops to help it secure control. Who knows why Saddam might want to do such a thing—to gain a better position to influence the Arab-Israeli dispute, to reassert his bid to Arab leadership, or for some other reason known only to himself—but his invasions of Kuwait and Iran were equally mystifying at the time. The problem is that Jordan's current economic and political frailty creates the opportunity for him to do so. In the past, such an Iraqi move would have crossed an Israeli "red line" for the use of force and likely would have provoked an American military response as well. Saddam might again calculate that by threatening the Saudi oil fields, Tel Aviv, or other regional targets with nuclear weapons he could preclude such a response.

- Since the death of Hafiz al-Asad in 2000, the stability of the Syrian regime has also been a question mark. If the Alawis who rule in Damascus fell to feuding, Saddam might be tempted to intervene to install a government more to his liking. Alternatively, Iraq has nurtured a long-standing rivalry with its fellow Ba'thists in Syria, and it is plausible that the relationship could sour again in the future, prompting a resort to force as Saddam has done so many times in the past. Although neither the United States nor many of our allies would mourn the loss of the Syrian regime, no one would be pleased to have it replaced by a pro-Iraqi government that might move Iraqi troops to the borders of Jordan and Israel, and possibly into Lebanon. Once again, if Saddam possessed nuclear weapons, the available evidence indicates that he might believe he could deter Israel and/or the United States from intervening if he chose such a course of action.

· Finally, a nuclear-armed Saddam would also raise fears for NATO ally Turkey. Ankara and Baghdad have generally enjoyed good relations over the years, but with Saddam at the helm in Iraq there is no reason to believe this might not change overnight. After all, it was widely believed that Iraq enjoyed reasonably good relations with Kuwait until the spring of 1990. Differences could arise between them over water, the Kurds, Syria, Israel (with which Turkey has an informal alliance), or U.S.-Iraqi relations, to name only the most obvious. It is conceivable that in the future if Turkey chose to draw more water from the Tigris and Euphrates to meet its own needs, Saddam might decide to respond with force—by occupying the upper reaches of the rivers or destroying some of the Turkish dams—again believing that his own nuclear arsenal would not only limit the Turkish response but also deter the United States and Israel from intervening.

Saddam was born in 1937 or 1939 and is in distressingly good health as far as anyone outside himself and his doctor knows. He could easily live to be seventy-five, eighty, or even older. Consequently, we should not expect him to die before he can either acquire nuclear weapons or make further mischief in the region.

This raises another important question: What will happen at the end of Saddam's life if he has nuclear weapons? Let us imagine that we are able to successfully deter him for the remainder of his life because he does decide not to risk his own survival by starting down the path of nuclear confrontation with the United States or Israel (or Iran, once it acquires nuclear weapons). What bizarre notions would run through his mind as he confronted his own mortality without having achieved any of his grandiose visions? We could not rule out the possibility that he would decide to choose the time and place of his own demise by ordering a nuclear strike on Tel Aviv so that he could go down in history as the Arab leader who finally obliterated the state of Israel. Saddam's former Mukhabbarat chief, Wafiq al-Samarra'i, told PBS's *Frontline,* "Perhaps now, I'm seriously considering that Saddam might use this weapon when he's about to die. Perhaps he will use it before he dies. And perhaps he would say to himself that he will be immortalized in history textbooks."[75] Just because this makes little sense to a Westerner does not mean it would not make perfect sense to "the leader of the days of Arab glory."

Saddam is unpredictable, but this is not to suggest that he is inexplicable. It is usually possible to figure out why Saddam did something after the fact, but it is hard to predict ahead of time what he might do. What's more, because the most important catalyst in his thinking is often exaggerated internal threats that the world knows nothing about—since Iraq is such a heavily guarded police state—we do not always know when Saddam is even considering a momentous action. Consequently, the United States cannot always count on having time to bolster its deterrent posture to prepare for a challenge from Saddam. This is likely to be even more true in the future as Iraq takes advantage of the liberalization of the economic sanctions to restore its logistical capability, thereby enhancing Saddam's ability to deploy large conventional forces quickly.

Would Saddam be willing to employ nuclear weapons? Would he be willing to vaporize part or all of the Saudi oil fields in pursuit of an objective?[76] We don't know. To a Westerner, there might be little in such a course of action that would make sense. The risks might seem too great. But the key question is: Can we trust Saddam to reach the same conclusions? Given his track record, it would be foolhardy to do so. Saddam Hussein has repeatedly demonstrated that he thinks in strange and convoluted ways that often contradict what any Westerner—or even any other Iraqi—might think sensible. There is little in Saddam's personality or his history in power to suggest that he would feel a need for prudence or restraint once he acquired nuclear weapons. Instead, all of the evidence that we have indicates that he would feel emboldened by them to pursue his more grandiose objectives.

Would the United States be willing to intervene if Iraq possessed nuclear weapons and threatened one of its neighbors with a lesser degree of violence? And how would Saddam react if we did? Again, we don't know. The answers are probably irrelevant. Given Saddam's propensity to violence, constant miscalculations, willingness to accept terrible damage in pursuit of a goal, unwillingness to back down unless he has actually suffered terrible damage, and belief in his own messianic destiny, we could not and should not rule out any reaction from him. He would be the most dangerous leader in the world with whom to get into a nuclear confrontation.

What About His Biological and Chemical Arsenals?

This chapter has focused principally on the threat posed by Saddam's ultimate, and probably inevitable, acquisition of nuclear weapons. The obvious "elephant in the living room" that it has so far overlooked is the arsenal of deadly biological and chemical weapons that he is believed to possess already. And the obvious question lying out there unanswered is: Don't they create similar threats for the United States and our regional allies?

Biological and chemical warfare agents in Saddam's hands are unquestionably very dangerous. It would be much, much better for the region, the United States, and the whole world if he did not possess those weapons. If employed properly, VX gas could kill thousands of people, and some of Iraq's biological agents could kill millions. Many analysts fear that at some point in time, Saddam may be able to acquire biological agents (such as smallpox) that could potentially kill far more people than could a nuclear weapon.

However, there are some important differences between the threats posed by chemical and biological agents and those posed by nuclear weapons—differences that continue to place nuclear weapons in a category by themselves. First of all, it is much harder to kill huge numbers of people with CW and BW weapons. It is not impossible, but it requires a vulnerable population under the right set of conditions and with the right mechanism to deliver the agents. Introducing VX into the air-conditioning system of a large office building or spraying a small city with BW in a crop duster on a cool day with only a mild breeze can produce catastrophic results. In addition, because of the fear they produce, CW and BW can kill a lot of people just from overreactions due to panic.

By the same token, if a would-be mass murderer lacks those conditions and that access, chemical and biological agents can produce disappointing results. CW and BW agents are dangerous to handle. Chemical warfare agents degrade over time—and in ways very dangerous to those storing or handling them—while biological warfare agents can die if not stored properly. Chemical warfare agents can evaporate if it's too hot, and both can dissipate quickly if it is too windy. Countermeasures are often possible, in the form of protective clothing for chemical warfare and vaccines or antidotes for biological warfare. What's more, both are relatively tough to deliver promptly at strategic distances (i.e., hundreds of kilometers). This is hardest to do by missile, and, as noted, Iraq is not known to have solved its problems with missile delivery of CW and BW agents. The Iraqi Air Force is in pathetic shape at present and is likely to be the last of Iraq's military services to revive. Even then, U.S. air defenses so outmatch even potential Iraqi Air Force capabilities that Saddam could not have any real confidence that a CW- or BW-armed aircraft would reach its target. Terrorist methods are the best means of delivering CW and BW, and Saddam is leery of international terrorists, who are largely beyond his control, while his own intelligence services have thus far shown little ability to perform sophisticated terrorist operations. Again, this is not to suggest that we should ignore these threats, only that the risk is appreciably less than with a nuclear weapon, which only has to be near enough people when it is detonated to kill millions.

Second, the concept of thousands of civilian deaths from chemical warfare, let alone millions from biological warfare, remains in the realm of conjecture. No one has actually ever seen this happen. It is theoretically possible, but most people also recognize that there are means of defense—gas masks and inoculations or antidotes. Gruesome as it may sound, until a chemical or biological attack does cause mass casualties, these weapons will not provoke the same degree of fear as is caused by nuclear weapons—against which no defense is possible and for which we have the legacy of Hiroshima and Nagasaki to remind us of the scale of devastation they cause. This point is important because it makes chemical and biological weapons much less useful to Saddam as deterrents of his own. As long as the world believes that nuclear weapons trump chemical and biological weapons, Saddam will be more cautious about his foreign adventures.

Saddam himself recognizes this distinction. His order to start a crash program to build a single nuclear weapon in August 1990, and his admission after the war that it was a mistake to have invaded Kuwait until he had nuclear weapons, both speak clearly to this point. Whatever his own reasoning, Saddam understands that his existing arsenal lacks the deterrent power of nuclear weapons. This is critical to U.S. policy because it strongly suggests that Saddam will be less likely to undertake new foreign adventures while all he has are his extant capabilities. Thus the potential for a crisis with Saddam is much lower if all he has is chemical and biological weapons, as is the risk that such a crisis could result in the death of millions. There is no question that the world would be better off if Saddam did not have these weapons, but the danger is considerably less than if Saddam were allowed to acquire nuclear weapons, which he believes will deter the

United States and Israel and thereby would encourage him to engage in the kind of foreign aggression that would be likely to provoke a nuclear crisis.

GAMBLING WITH OUR FUTURE

Deterrence is a policy with terrible costs. It means condemning the Iraqi people to decades more terror and torture under Saddam's totalitarianism. Unlike containment, deterrence also means giving up our ability to protect the Kurds. Human Rights Watch argues that Saddam's Anfal campaign constituted genocide against the Kurds.[77] Certainly, it was horrific, with as many as 200,000 killed, 4,000 villages razed, and widespread and indiscriminate use of chemical warfare against Kurdish civilians. If we opt for deterrence, there will be no one to restrain Saddam should he decide to solve his Kurdish "problem" once and for all.

In addition, those who argue for deterrence for fear of the costs of an invasion, and, particularly, fear of Iraqi WMD use and terrorism, are setting a very dangerous precedent. They are, in effect, suggesting that the United States is already deterred by the weak arsenal of weapons of mass destruction Saddam already possesses and his similarly weak terrorist capabilities. In other words, a policy of deterrence toward Iraq not only is based on the belief that Saddam can be deterred but starts from the assumption that the United States already is. If the United States can be deterred from taking military action against Iraq given its current modest capabilities, every rogue state in the world will have little to do to ensure its security and will likely be emboldened to greater aggression. We would be allowing our hands to be tied with very weak string.

Deterrence also runs terrible risks. Although the alternatives are considerably more costly, deterrence is the riskiest of all the policy options available to the United States. We would be betting that we could deter a man who has proven to be hard (at times, impossible) to deter and who seems to believe that if he possessed nuclear weapons, it is the United States that would be deterred. If we were to make this bet and lose, the results would be catastrophic. Moreover, while deterrence is difficult enough, we would actually be trying to employ extended deterrence to Iraq's neighbors—deterring Iraq from attacking Kuwait, Jordan, or Saudi Arabia, rather than simply protecting ourselves. Patrick Morgan, one of the architects of Cold War deterrence theory, observes that "it is hard to make an extended deterrence threat to use WMD credible, particularly if the 'challenger' is also armed with them."[78]

The use of nuclear weapons anywhere in the world would be terrible. Their use on the Persian Gulf oil fields; against Tel Aviv, Ankara, Riyadh, or another regional city; or against U.S. military forces in the region is unimaginable. This would be no academic exercise or Pentagon war game to decide how many people one side could lose in the pursuit of victory; regardless of what else happened, such an event would be a tragedy and a disaster. Beyond this, Saddam Hussein with nuclear weapons has the potential to push the world into a second Great Depression while killing millions of people. His track record argues that if we allow him to acquire nuclear weapons, we are likely to find ourselves in a new crisis with him in which we will not be able to predict what he will do, and his personality and his history can only lead us to expect the worst. Leaving Saddam free to acquire nuclear weapons and then hoping that in spite of his track record he can be deterred would be a terrifically dangerous gamble.

NINE

The Difficulty of Covert Action

The most compelling reason for the United States to pursue a policy of regime change toward Iraq is that the alternatives are much worse. Containment is crumbling and is unlikely to prevent Saddam from acquiring nuclear weapons for more than a few more years. Reviving containment would require the United States to make Iraq the centerpiece of its foreign policy for the life of Saddam's regime, incurring heavy costs and jeopardizing trade and even alliance ties with other nations. Pure deterrence is an extremely risky—and potentially tragic—strategy to pursue, given Saddam's track record and what little we know about his thinking. It is because our less confrontational options are so weak that we have little choice but to consider the more confrontational ones.

Of course, there are actually some very good reasons to pursue regime change as well. If the United States were to remove Saddam's regime from power, there is little doubt that the Iraqi people would be much better off. Freeing the Iraqi people from Saddam Hussein's depredations would be justification enough for his overthrow if the American people were willing to pay the price of doing so. Ridding the other peoples of the Middle East of the threat of Saddam would be another. Creating an entirely new strategic landscape in the Middle East—and possibly jump-starting the moribund Arab-Israeli peace process—would be still another.

Regardless of the reason to embrace regime change, the place to start thinking about removing Saddam's regime is with covert action. Covert action—mounting an assassination attempt or a coup d'état or even sparking a popular uprising—is the obvious tool of choice because it carries a small price financially and diplomatically and requires no U.S. military presence—at least in theory. Covert action programs are comparatively cheap, especially in contrast to the cost of large military operations. Because covert action is conducted in secret, the United States could maintain "plausible deniability," meaning that we could deny having a hand in the regime's successful ouster. Although most states would know we were behind Saddam's demise, if it were done covertly they would be much happier because it would maintain the convenient façade that governments do not interfere in the internal affairs of other sovereign states—an important fiction in international diplomacy and the United Nations. If the CIA could help get rid of Saddam, that would also obviate the need for the Pentagon to do so. Military operations are not only big, loud, and expensive, they are also often quite bloody—both for us and for the country we are attacking. Moreover, in the case of Iraq, removing the regime covertly would theoretically eliminate the need for us to replace it with another. The Iraqis would themselves work out a new government, and the United States could avoid the problem of what to do with Iraq "the day after" Saddam is removed.

COULDN'T WE JUST KILL HIM?

Given that so many of our problems with Iraq derive from the peculiarities of Saddam individually, the obvious first question is whether the United States *could* eliminate Saddam himself. If the United States could assassinate Saddam or topple him in a palace coup, this would probably eliminate most of our problems with Iraq. At the very least, because most successors to Saddam would be unlikely to share the personality disorders that make him difficult and dangerous to try to deter, a policy of deterrence might then be more reasonable. At best, because most Iraqi elites seem to recognize that Saddam's policy of confrontation with the United States has gravely weakened Iraq, most potential successors would probably reverse Saddam's course and try hard to reach an accommodation with the United States to get the world's only remaining superpower off of its back. In fact, many of Saddam's potential successors would probably believe that a better relationship with the United States would be critical to their consolidation of power inside Iraq.

A Dearth of Legal Obstacles to Assassination

First of all, the legal restrictions on assassination are not as onerous as is commonly believed and are not the central problem with this policy option. There is no law prohibiting assassinations, only an executive order. In 1976, in response to revelations of CIA involvement in various assassination attempts (all of them ordered by the White House) during the 1960s and 1970s, President Gerald Ford signed Executive Order 11905, forbidding assassinations by U.S. government personnel. This executive order was carried over by the Carter administration. In 1981, the Reagan administration reissued the ban under Executive Order 12333, which has been adopted by every subsequent administration.

The operative paragraphs of E.O. 12333 read as follows:

2.11 Prohibition on Assassination. No person employed by or acting on behalf of the United States Government shall engage in, or conspire to engage in, assassination.

2.12 Indirect Participation. No agency of the Intelligence Community shall participate in or request any person to undertake activities forbidden by this order.

An executive order can easily be modified or rescinded by another executive order—which is not difficult for the White House to undertake. Of greater importance, the existence of E.O. 12333 has not prevented the U.S. government from attempting to kill foreign leaders. It has employed direct military strikes to try to kill Muammar Qadhafi in 1986, Mohammed Farah Aidid in 1993, Usama bin Ladin in 1998, and Saddam himself during the Persian Gulf War.[1] The government argues that it went after these leaders as legitimate "command-and-control" targets rather than individuals and so these were not, technically, assassination attempts, a legalism that was clearly lost on Saddam, Qadhafi, Aidid, and bin Ladin. For example, after the air strikes against Qadhafi, U.S. military lawyers argued that E.O. 12333 did not apply because it did not ban acts of self-defense against "legitimate threats to national security."

Second, the White House has still authorized "lethal" findings—directives to the CIA to undertake covert actions that could result in fatalities—specifically targeted against key individuals. The Reagan administration ordered the CIA to try to topple Qadhafi, knowing that his death would be a likely element of such an operation.[2] The Bush administration ordered the

CIA to oust Manuel Noriega of Panama, recognizing that he could be killed in the effort.[3] The Bush and Clinton administrations authorized the ouster of Saddam Hussein, again recognizing that his death would be a possible (in fact, a likely) outcome if such an effort were successful.[4] Finally, former President Clinton has publicly stated that "I authorized the arrest and if necessary, the killing of Osama bin Laden, and we actually made contact with a group inside Afghanistan to do it. They were unsuccessful. . . . We also trained commandos for a possible ground action, but we did not have the necessary intelligence to do it."[5] What this means is that in response to Executive Order 12333, the CIA steers clear of any action that could be construed as assassination unless it has the specific and explicit authorization of the president to do so.

Neither does international law strictly forbid assassinations. To some extent, international law is out of date in this area, since it recognizes only two situations: war and peace. The U.N. Charter says that "in peacetime, the citizens of a nation, whether they are political officials or private individuals, are entitled to immunity from intentional acts of violence by citizens, agents or military forces of another nation." However, in wartime, international law allows the targeted killing of a member of the enemy's chain of command, even the head of state—whether that person is a civilian or a military officer, and regardless of the means employed. Of course, one problem in the twenty-first century is that few wars are declared, making it difficult to know when the rules apply and when they don't. Since Iraq remains in flagrant violation of the terms of the U.N. cease-fire resolution, it would not be difficult for Washington to argue that Iraq is already in a state of war with the United States—and with all U.N. member states. Indeed, on many occasions the United States has justified other, military actions against Iraq by employing this same argument.

A Plethora of Practical Problems
Thus, the problem is not a legal one but a practical one. To be blunt, if the United States could have killed Saddam, it would have. And Washington could have found ample justification for its actions.

Assassinations are pretty hard to pull off. In the modern world, most rulers are protected by formidable security services, often with sophisticated methods and technologies for protecting their leaders. Despite numerous attempts, no U.S. president has been assassinated since Kennedy, no small feat given the liberality of U.S. gun laws and the number of attempts since 1963. By the same token, the United States did not enjoy a great deal of success on those few occasions early in the Cold War when it tried to assassinate a foreign leader. The most famous CIA assassination effort, ordered by President Kennedy against Fidel Castro, failed miserably after years of trying, despite numerous creative efforts to kill the Cuban leader, including poisoned cigars and a poisoned scuba-diving suit.

This is not to suggest that no intelligence service has had better luck. Israel has assassinated dozens of key Arab terrorists over the years, including systematically eliminating all of the Palestinian terrorists who massacred Israeli athletes at the 1972 Munich Olympics, and the 1996 killing of Yahya Ayyash, the notorious bomb designer known as "the Engineer" who was responsible for a series of deadly bus bombings. However, the Mossad's effort to assassinate Saddam was a failure.[6]

The Russians have certainly killed their fair share of Russian dissidents, most famously Leon Trotsky in Mexico City in 1940. However, they have not fared nearly as well with foreign leaders. The KGB twice failed to assassinate the shah of Iran. It is widely believed that the KGB, using its puppets in Bulgarian intelligence, tried to kill Pope John Paul II in 1983 because of his support for grassroots opposition movements in his native Poland. If they did, they again failed.

Beyond the general difficulty of conducting an assassination in the twenty-first century, anyone trying to kill Saddam Hussein in particular has his work cut out for him.[7] Saddam's security makes the Secret Service's wall around the president look like rice paper. Saddam is obsessed with his own security and spares no expense, including his own time and attention, to ensure his safety. He has surrounded himself with ring upon ring of bodyguards and security services. His palaces are fortresses with fences, walls, armed guards, attack dogs, and all manner of physical and electronic surveillance.

His innermost circle, the Murafiqin, are sworn to defend him to the death and have done so on occasion. They are all fellow members of his Bayjat clan, some are members of his close family, and all have tremendous ties of loyalty to him. Saddam usually carries a pistol and wears a bullet-proof vest, regardless of whatever else he has on. He employs doubles, who generally take his place whenever he is supposed to be at an event that could be conducive to an assassination attempt. He uses a food taster (currently the son of his personal chef, for good measure). He is also paranoid about germs and contact poisons. People being brought to see him are often forced to shower repeatedly and apply harsh disinfectants, and they are searched repeatedly with various instruments to detect foreign substances.

He travels in a large caravan of armored cars. He always uses duplicate caravans that travel to other destinations simultaneously or to the same destination by alternative routes to throw off assassins. Within the motorcade, he decides at the last moment which car he will be in and whether he will drive (which he usually does). Even then he may constantly shift the order of cars in the motorcade so that no would-be assassin can target a particular car. During Desert Storm, Saddam gave up even that, driving around in a recreational vehicle, a van, a truck, or even a taxicab.

Saddam rarely sleeps in the same place twice in a row. He frequently sends out advance teams to prepare five or six locations at which he might spend the night and decides only at the last minute where he will stay. During times of great trouble, such as during Desert Storm, Saddam stays away from his palaces and government buildings altogether, instead sleeping and holding meetings in civilian homes that are commandeered suddenly for the purpose.[8] For this reason, Wafiq al-Samarra'i, Saddam's former intelligence chief, estimates that coalition warplanes never struck within 10 kilometers of Saddam during the Gulf War.[9]

All of these measures make it virtually impossible for outsiders to assassinate Saddam by making it impossible to get timely and accurate information about Saddam's whereabouts. Not since before the Gulf War has Saddam's motorcade been ambushed. For this reason, an air strike against Saddam has never proven practicable. His security measures also make it impossible for gunmen to get near enough to establish that the target is Saddam and not one of his doubles, or to fight through the superior firepower of Saddam's guards. It is for this reason that the highly secretive and efficient an-Nahdah group decided that it was not possible for it to kill Saddam and so instead attempted to assassinate Udayy in December 1996.[10] And as for sending a foreign-trained assassin or military sniper, the person would have to be able to pass himself (or herself) off as a native Iraqi, with all the proper papers, fluent Iraqi Arabic, and a complete knowledge of Iraqi society and culture—because a mistake on any of these would likely get the assassin picked up by the security services for routine "questioning"—and would somehow need to hide a weapon while doing so. This is so tall an order that neither we, nor any of the other governments trying to kill Saddam, has been able to do it.

Finally, it is worth pointing out that there are reasons we might actually want to refrain from attempting an assassination even if we were in the unlikely position to actually be able to do so with some degree of confidence. First off, if Saddam were assassinated it would leave the rest of his regime intact and his most likely successor would be one of his two sons, or someone else from his inner circle—his personal secretary, Abid Hamid Humud; his cousin 'Ali Hassan al-Majid; or another brutal thug. Udayy and 'Ali Hassan would, unquestionably be just as dangerous, violent, and miscalculating as Saddam. Qusayy and Abid Hamid are believed to be more cautious and calculating, but both are also vicious killers and we should not expect the Iraqi regime to improve much with them at the helm.

In addition, we should never forget that engaging in assassinations means setting precedents we may not want to set. When Saddam attempted to assassinate former President Bush, we were righteously indignant and international opinion rallied around us. If we begin engaging in assassination, we will likely lose those advantages. In fact, we will probably only encourage Saddam (and others) to employ assassination themselves, and especially in the case of Iraq, engaging in such a competition with Saddam seems to violate the wise dictum "Never get into a pissing contest with a skunk."

The historian Franklin L. Ford concluded his comprehensive study of assassination from ancient history to the 1980s with the observation that "the history of countless assassinations, examined with an eye to comparing apparent motives with actual outcomes, contains almost none that produced results consonant with the aims of the doer, assuming those aims to have extended at all beyond the miserable taking of a life."[11]

WHAT ABOUT OVERTHROWING SADDAM IN A COUP?

Mounting a coup to topple Saddam would avoid many of the problems associated with an assassination. It would likely remove not only Saddam but virtually all of the top figures of the regime. The United States is impervious to a coup attempt, so Saddam could not retaliate in kind. A coup could be accomplished only by other Iraqi elites, so we would not have to worry about trying to get a foreign assassin into the insular Iraqi police state.

As with assassination, the problem is not the will but the way. The United States has tried to overthrow Saddam and failed. During the Gulf War, the United States hoped that the air campaign itself would produce either a military coup or a popular revolt.[12] Starting in 1992, the CIA supported the Iraqi National Congress to mobilize support for a popular revolt,

encourage defections from the armed forces, and otherwise instigate resistance to Saddam's regime. Although the INC operated out of Iraqi Kurdistan until 1996, with ample funding and with ostensible air cover from the
United States, it was never able to attract more than a few hundred full-time
followers and never garnered significant defections from the Iraqi armed
forces—let alone started a popular revolt. When the INC was driven out of
Kurdistan by the Republican Guards in August 1996, it had little to show
for its efforts. Similarly, the CIA worked with the Iraqi National Accord
(al-Wifaq), a group of mostly former Iraqi military and regime figures, to
try to spark a coup. Although the CIA's work with al-Wifaq produced one
of the more dangerous and far-reaching internal threats to Saddam's
regime, it too failed in the end. The cabal was betrayed to the Mukhabbarat,
and its key conspirators were rolled up in June 1996. In addition, the air
campaign of Operation Desert Storm had, as one of its purposes, to try to
trigger a military coup against Saddam. This effort too failed to produce
any results.[13]

The United States is not the only country that has tried to oust Saddam
only to fail. Iran, Syria, and Israel have all tried at different times to get rid
of Saddam via covert action, but they too have foundered on the rocks of
Saddam's police state.[14] Nor is there reason to be optimistic that a future effort might succeed.

In truth, the CIA does not have a great record in trying to topple foreign
leaders. The Agency succeeded in overthrowing Muhammad Mossadeq in
Iran, Ngo Dinh Diem in South Vietnam, and Jacobo Arbenz Guzmán in
Guatemala. In a few other cases, the United States got the result it wanted,
but it was not through the CIA's efforts that the ouster occurred. Thus
Patrice Lumumba of the Congo, Rafael Trujillo of the Dominican Republic, and Salvador Allende of Chile were overthrown as the United States
had hoped, albeit not by groups backed by the CIA. Conversely, the CIA
tried and failed to oust Enver Hoxa in Albania, Castro in Cuba, Qadhafi in
Libya, Noriega in Panama, and Saddam in Iraq.

This is not a knock against the CIA—few other intelligence services
have a better record, and most have fared much worse. Throughout the
Cold War, the Soviets were forced to use Red Army tanks to topple governments they did not like, even in their own satellites: Czechoslovakia in
1948 and 1968, Hungary in 1956, and Afghanistan in 1979. No one can
point to a single government overthrown by the KGB. The Mossad has
never overthrown any of the governments of Israel's Arab foes and was

forced to invade Lebanon to deal with the situation there when its covert action program to support the Maronite Christians could not produce results. The British have had a hand in their share of coups, although in most cases these came in former colonial possessions or other states under one form or another of British protectorship.

As with assassinations, however, Saddam's extensive security measures and his relentless attention to his own security make Iraq a far more difficult place to spark a coup than most. The rings of security make it very difficult to bring any military force to bear against Saddam. The rings are geographic as well as organizational. The Iraqi regular army, which is the least trusted, is kept farthest from the capital. Between the regular army and Baghdad are the six divisions of the Republican Guard, and the Guard's three armored divisions—the most powerful military formations in Iraq—ring the capital. Within Baghdad itself is the Special Republican Guard, 25,000 to 30,000 strong and probably capable of holding off at least one of the Guard's armored divisions in the urban terrain of Baghdad.

The biggest problem with a coup, however, is a catch-22: especially because of the size of Saddam's security forces, a coup will require a large number of people to have any chance of success, but the more people who are involved, the more likely it will be betrayed to the Mukhabbarat. The redundancy, overlapping responsibilities, wide-ranging writs, and fierce rivalries among the security services make it hard to conceal a coup for long, which is why the vast majority have failed. Similarly, when a coup is first hatched, it may be easy to keep the secret limited to a tiny group of people, all of whom know that they can trust one another. However, as it becomes necessary to bring more people into the cabal—people who control important levers of power and so are needed for the coup to be a success—the more likely it is that one of the coup plotters will misjudge someone and invite him to join the coup, only to have that person betray the plot to the regime.

Similarly, the greater the foreign involvement in any coup plot, the less likely it is to succeed because the more likely it is that the regime will become aware of it. At the CIA, we used to say that any coup plot we knew about, Saddam knew about. This has, unfortunately, turned out to be true. The Iraqi intelligence services aggressively scrutinize foreigners inside Iraq, and they generally don't try to be subtle. As a result, it is difficult for foreigners to move about in Iraq and meet with Iraqis without the regime being aware of it. Likewise, the regime tends to keep tabs on Iraqis who travel

abroad, for the very reason that they can more easily link up with foreign intelligence services. Finally, the Iraqis monitor all communications into and
out of the country very carefully, making it hard for foreigners to communi-
cate with people inside the country without the regime knowing about it.

It is for all these reasons that Director of Central Intelligence George
Tenet has reportedly told the White House that a new covert action program
to try to topple Saddam Hussein would have only about a 10 to 20 percent
chance of succeeding.[15] These odds might actually be too optimistic, reflecting the Agency's long-standing "can do" spirit that when the White
House gives it an assignment, it will try to find a way to make it happen.

This is not to say that Saddam might not be overthrown in a coup (or assassinated) tomorrow. Saddam has been the target of numerous coup and
assassination plots over the years, and there probably are cabals brewing
even today. One of them might succeed where all the others have failed.
This is not likely, but it can't be ruled out (and should obviously be hoped
for). However, it is highly unlikely that the United States could cause a
coup d'état or an assassination attempt against Saddam to succeed. Not
only are such operations inherently difficult, but in Iraq they are far more
difficult than virtually anywhere else because of Saddam's pervasive security establishment. Moreover, the fact of U.S. involvement would be more
likely to hurt the chances of a coup attempt—because of the regime's para-
noiac scrutiny of all foreign communications and interactions by its citizens—than it would be to help it.

The Wrong Policy for Right Now

There are some other problems with employing a covert action approach at
this point in time. The first is that the United States can't afford to fail at
regime change this time around. Our allies in the region have watched the
United States make halfhearted efforts at regime change for the last twelve
years. The most serious effort Washington ever made was in 1996, with the
Wifaq coup plot that Saddam rolled up in June. Both before and after there
was a series of less determined efforts that left the governments of the region wondering what we were doing and whether we actually wanted to
keep Saddam in power.

At this late date, and especially in the wake of the September 11
tragedy, we can only expect to get one more shot at regime change. If we
don't make it work this time, our allies in the region are likely to conclude
that we will never be serious about getting rid of Saddam. It is a big risk for

them to support any U.S. effort at regime change, even a covert action campaign. Even before Saddam learns about the coup plot itself, he will know which countries are helping us and he will wage war against them, in his own way, using all of the economic, political, and intelligence assets at his disposal. Thus there are real costs and risks for our allies in helping us—costs and risks they almost certainly will never be willing to pay again if we don't succeed this time. If we go to our allies in the region, having had so many previous efforts fail, in the aftermath of September 11, and after all of the Bush administration's rhetoric about regime change in Iraq, and we tell them that all we want to do is to start a new effort to mount a coup in Iraq, our allies are likely to conclude that we are still not serious and we never will be. They will wash their hands of our regime change efforts and try to figure out how they can live with Saddam.

Last, even if we could get allied support and we could afford another failure, trying to mount a coup would still not make sense at this point. To be done properly, this sort of operation requires a great deal of time, painstaking work, and enormous patience. To identify the right people in Iraq, make contact with them, convince them to trust us, help them to pull together a plot, provide them with whatever assistance they may need, and do all of this without the Iraqi intelligence services catching wind of it would take an enormous amount of time—several years, in all likelihood. Ultimately, the effort would still be likely to fail because of Saddam's formidable security apparatus. Given what we know about Saddam's capacity to build nuclear weapons and his desire to do so, and given what we don't know about how far along he is, we may not have several years to wait for a coup plot that isn't likely to succeed.

A POLICY OVERTAKEN BY EVENTS

The former director of central intelligence, Richard Helms, used to say that "covert action is frequently a substitute for policy."[16] Unfortunately, this is all too true. When an American administration has disliked a foreign government enough to want it gone but has not been willing to expend the resources to do so with certainty, it has often turned to the CIA and ordered it to try to do the job. We cannot afford to take that approach to Iraq today. If, in the wake of September 11, the United States is willing to remove Saddam's regime from power, it should not try to do so halfheartedly. Covert action is a useful tool, but it is not always effective.

TEN

The Risks of the Afghan Approach

Because covert action would take too long and would have only a slim chance of effecting Saddam's fall, a policy of regime change would require the United States to employ overt military force to get the job done. The question is, how much force and how should it be used? Since the success of Operation Enduring Freedom in 2001, a small but vocal group has argued that the United States should employ the same concept of operations that prevailed in Afghanistan to try to oust Saddam as well. This strategy is generally referred to as the "Afghan Approach."

In one shape or another, the Afghan Approach has been around for years. In about 1997, the Iraqi National Congress (INC) proposed the first version of the plan. At that time, the INC wanted U.S. funding to train an army of 5,000 to 10,000 men with small arms and antitank weapons that they would deploy into Iraq from Kuwait under U.S. air cover. They claimed that this force would have the capability to occupy all of Iraq south of the Euphrates and hem Saddam's regime in around Baghdad, where it would inevitably fall as the Iraqi people turned against it. Although the INC believed its ground forces could shoulder most of the burden of fighting those Iraqi units that remained loyal to the regime, particularly the Republican Guard, it did want U.S. air forces to provide air cover, close air support, and interdiction to hinder the movement of Iraqi ground forces. The

INC's plan envisioned ever larger numbers of Iraqis (particularly from the Iraqi Army) flocking to its small force. Indeed, this was the key to the scheme—that most Iraqis would rally to the INC's banner once it was raised with U.S. military backing on Iraqi soil. Aside from the inconvenient facts that during the four years the INC had been in northern Iraq with U.S. funding and ostensible air cover it had never been able to muster more than a few hundred fighters, large numbers of Iraqis had not rallied to its cause, and the Iraqi Army had not come over to its side, there was also the problem that 5,000 to 10,000 hastily trained Iraqis with nothing but small arms and antitank weapons and backed only by modest air power would never have a chance against Saddam's heavy divisions.[1] This early version was a ludicrous scheme that was effectively laughed out of town by the U.S. Central Command and the Pentagon.

But the idea did not die. The INC recognized that its original plan was easily dismissed because it relied too heavily on its own nonexistent combat capabilities and very little on U.S. military power. Over time, and with help from several American advisers, the INC refined the plan to include ever greater amounts of American military power. After the success of Operation Enduring Freedom, the INC and its American backers refined the plan further so that, in the latest version, they claim that most of the killing would be done by U.S. air power, while the INC ground forces would serve principally as bait. The concept is for the small INC forces to lure the Republican Guard divisions out into the open and get them to concentrate for counterattacks, which would leave them vulnerable to U.S. air power guided by American special forces operating with the INC. This view has gained a modest amount of currency because it fits the popular impression of how the United States won the war in Afghanistan and because there are those who assume that because Saddam is even more despicable than the Taliban, the Iraqis will be even quicker than the Afghans to throw off his yoke if they see the United States firmly committed to this course of action.[2]

Although the strategy was first conceived by the INC and its American supporters, since the fall of the Taliban, some of its advocates have divorced the idea from the need to back the INC as the primary opposition group. Indeed, a number of its adherents have shifted to the idea that other Iraqi opposition groups could better play the crucial role of the ground force element in the strategy—the anvil for the U.S. Air Force's hammer. Recognizing that the INC has not been able to muster several thousand troops and lacks the support inside Iraq to attract large numbers of defectors from the Iraqi armed forces, let alone spark a public revolt, some who favor the Afghan Approach now argue that the United States should rely on the two main Kurdish militias, which between them can field about 50,000 lightly armed *peshmerga*, and the Shi'ite resistance groups in southern Iraq, which can call on as many as 10,000 to 12,000 Iranian-trained insurgents.[3] Since the Kurds and Shi'ah do have some actual combat power, it is obviously more reasonable to believe that they could play the role of the Northern Alliance while U.S. air forces simply repeat their virtuoso performance from the Afghan war. By making this more realistic argument, some of the advocates of the Afghan Approach hope to save the plan by jettisoning its architects.

THE ADVANTAGES OF THE AFGHAN APPROACH

If the Afghan Approach could work, it would appear to offer a number of important advantages. Specifically, it would not require large numbers of American ground troops, only small numbers of American special forces personnel. Consequently, the probability of large numbers of U.S. casualties would be low. Since most of the fighting would, in theory, be left to the Iraqi opposition forces, there would be little danger that American troops would have to engage in urban warfare to root out Saddam's loyalists or endure chemical warfare attacks.

Second, because it would not involve American ground troops, the war might be less costly in pure dollar terms. Desert Storm cost the United States about $55 billion (although essentially all of that was actually paid by America's allies, particularly the Saudis, Kuwaitis, and Japanese, not U.S. taxpayers). As of early December 2001, when most of the major conventional military battles in Afghanistan were over, Operation Enduring Freedom had cost only about $4 billion.[4] In truth, this is not a fair comparison because the Iraqi armed forces in 1991 were more than two hundred times as large as the Taliban in 2001, so any military effort against Iraq would invariably have been much bigger and more costly, but proponents of the Afghan Approach still argue that the absence of large U.S. ground forces would keep costs down.

Third, the Afghan Approach holds out the tantalizing prospect that the United States could wage a war with Iraq at arm's length. Because we would have only a very limited presence on the ground, we would probably find it easier to disengage at war's end. In particular, the hope is that, as in Afghanistan, the United States would not have to establish a long-term occupation force in Iraq or engage in a process of nation building but could leave this to the Iraqi opposition (who would be responsible for the bulk of the political and economic cleanup and rebuilding after the invasion) and other members of the international community.

Some within the Bush administration find this approach particularly appealing because they believe it plays to America's strengths while minimizing the aspects of military operations that the American public finds least appealing. Their claim is that the operation would be low-cost in terms of U.S. casualties and resources, American involvement in the unpleasant business of ground combat (especially urban combat), and the need for postwar reconstruction. This also makes the strategy politically appealing to an administration that no doubt wants to go into the 2004 presidential election with a big victory over Iraq that would have cost the American people very little. Thus, the Afghan Approach seems to offer the administration exactly what it wants.

The problem with all of this is that the whole strategy is dangerous and antithetical to our strategic circumstances with Iraq. The Afghan Approach is unlikely to work in Iraq (not impossible, just unlikely) at a time when the United States has no reason to embark on a policy toward Iraq that has a low likelihood of success and every reason not to. If it were to fail, it could fail catastrophically both for the United States and for the region. Even if it were more likely to succeed, it would make no diplomatic or strategic sense for the United States to pursue it. In fact, all of the strategic and diplomatic issues argue resoundingly against trying it. Even if we did anyway, and even if it succeeded, it would be unlikely to achieve the advantages that its American advocates have held out for it. Referring to an earlier war, Eliot Cohen remarked that "the preference for aerial warfare seems a way to bypass the hazards of ground combat: in Kosovo, in fact, the American government went out of its way to deny itself that option. Thus the attractiveness of the scalpel seems to rule out the military equivalent of bone saws; but scalpels are not a solution to every surgical problem."[5]

In Iraq, the Afghan Approach means trying to overthrow Saddam on the cheap. In actuality, it would not be all that cheap, and if there is one thing we should have learned from our long confrontation with Saddam, it is that efforts to overthrow him on the cheap have never worked.

ESTABLISHING MY BONA FIDES

Those who advocate employment of the Afghan Approach in Iraq like to defend themselves against criticism by claiming that all of the "so-called experts" were wrong about such a strategy working in Afghanistan, and therefore any warnings that the same strategy would not work in Iraq should also be dismissed. For this reason, it's important for me to lay out my own record on this subject before describing the problems with the Afghan Approach.

From the first days after September 11, I argued that the best way to wage war against the Taliban and al-Qa'eda in Afghanistan was through the combination of air power, special forces operations, and support to the Northern Alliance that ultimately prevailed. In other words, I am not one of "those experts" who claimed that this strategy would never work in Afghanistan. On the contrary, I argued strenuously that it *would* work. On September 18, I wrote in *The Wall Street Journal,* "Assuming the Taliban chooses not to hand over bin Laden and his associates, the U.S. should conduct direct military operations against Afghanistan and Al Qaeda facilities there. . . . Ideally, a combination of manned aircraft, cruise missiles and special-forces operations would be used in a sustained campaign to destroy the Al Qaeda infrastructure in Afghanistan, hunt down Al Qaeda personnel there, and destroy Taliban military capabilities. Direct support should be provided to the military operations of the Northern Alliance. . . . [I]f [the United States is] committed and willing to make the sacrifice, the nebulous nature of its foe should not be an impediment to waging a successful war against Al Qaeda and its accomplices."[6] Two days later, in the *Los Angeles Times,* I coauthored a piece that began, "Sunday, the Northern Alliance, the main Afghan opposition force, announced that it would welcome U.S. aid in its fight against the Taliban. We should seize this opportunity because even without Ahmed Shah Masoud, their commander who was assassinated last week, the alliance can play a crucial role in compelling the Taliban to disgorge Osama bin Laden and his operatives." The piece went on to argue that the Northern Alliance, if backed by U.S. air power, could be a critical element in destroying the Taliban's military.[7]

In early November, after a month of air strikes against the Taliban, when many military analysts were warning of a quagmire in Afghanistan, I argued for staying the course. I felt we had the right strategy for victory, although I did argue for stepping up the intensity of the campaign and introducing additional dedicated ground attack aircraft such as the A-10 Thunderbolt—which the Pentagon announced it was doing soon afterward.[8] I confess that I did not expect the Taliban to collapse as suddenly as it did, but neither did anyone else, including the Pentagon, the intelligence community, and all of the people now claiming that we should employ the Afghan model in Iraq.[9] But I was convinced from start to finish that the Afghan Approach was the right strategy for the Afghan situation.[10]

WHAT REALLY HAPPENED IN AFGHANISTAN

Since the proponents of the Afghan Approach base their argument principally on the success of this strategy in Afghanistan, it is important to understand why Operation Enduring Freedom was so successful. In fact, the conditions that made for success in Afghanistan are not likely to obtain in Iraq.

The Taliban started out as a group of 2,000 to 3,000 young Pashtuns from Afghanistan and Pakistan educated in the madrassahs (Koranic schools) of Pakistan in the early 1990s. ("Talib" means "student" in Arabic.) By 1994, the Soviets were long gone from Afghanistan and the victorious Mujahedin had fallen to infighting. In that year, the Taliban entered the fray, determined to build a new, Islamic society in Afghanistan. Meanwhile, the Pakistanis wanted to get control over the chaos in their northern neighbor and install a friendly government in Kabul that could keep the peace. At the time, they were backing several different Afghan militias, but when the Taliban appeared and began to win battles, Islamabad was quick to embrace them as their new Afghan proxies. They armed and trained the Taliban and provided considerable support in the form of logistics, communications, intelligence, airlift, fire support, and combat advisers. Pakistan's direct aid was one of two crucial advantages the Taliban enjoyed early on.[11] The other was the combination of fierce devotion to the "Jihad" they believed they were waging and the discipline they had learned in the madrassahs. Indeed, even today, reporters in Afghanistan have noted the awe in which the other Afghan fighters hold the disciplined, zealous Taliban fighters.[12]

When the Taliban first entered Afghanistan in 1994, they were unlike anything the other Afghans had seen. After the defeat of the Soviets, the Afghan groups splintered into hundreds of different bands. Thus, a force of 2,000 to 3,000 men was a major power in Afghanistan.[13] However, the key for the Taliban right from the start was their willingness to fight battles to a decision. Afghan tribal battles were typically desultory affairs with the two sides trading fire until one side realized it was inferior and negotiated a withdrawal or surrender with the other. The Taliban did not play by these rules—its soldiers really fought, even to the death—and since most other Afghan bands were unwilling to fight so hard, it was not difficult for the Taliban to beat most of the other Afghan groups. Very quickly, many of the Mujahedin, especially the other Pashtuns, decided (again, in traditional Afghan fashion) that "if you can't beat 'em, join 'em," and cast their lot with the Taliban.[14]

The one group that the Taliban could neither convince to join them nor smash in battle was the Northern Alliance. The Northern Alliance had several unique qualities of its own. Of greatest importance was a cadre of highly competent, veteran commanders, led by the near-mythical Ahmed Shah Masud, the "Lion of the Panjshir," who was assassinated by al-Qa'eda on September 9, 2001. The Northern Alliance troops had tremendous loyalty to these commanders, who had led them to great victories against the Soviets and other Afghan factions. Second, the Northern Alliance was largely composed of ethnic Tajiks and Uzbeks, who did not expect to fare well in an Afghanistan run by the Pashtun zealots of the Taliban and their Pakistani backers. Finally, over time, Russia, India, and Iran all began providing degrees of support to the Northern Alliance, not on the level of Pakistani support to the Taliban, but to a degree that nonetheless helped them to stand up to the Taliban. All of these factors combined to make the Northern Alliance a far more formidable opponent for the Taliban than any other force in Afghanistan.

By the time of Operation Enduring Freedom, a rough stalemate had been achieved. The much larger Taliban (whose core of "true" Talibs had grown to about 6,000 to 8,000 men since 1994) fielded about 45,000 mostly Pashtun troops and had conquered roughly 85 percent of the country with this force. Against them stood 10,000 to 15,000 Northern Alliance fighters penned up in the traditional Tajik lands of northeastern Afghanistan. However, the Taliban was finding it harder and harder to grind down the Northern Alliance.[15]

The first blow the United States struck in Operation Enduring Freedom was diplomatic. Before the first bombs began to fall, Washington persuaded Pakistan's military leader, General Pervez Musharraf, to cut Pakistan's ties to the Taliban. Although these links were never fully severed, they were greatly attenuated. As a result, the Taliban lost an important source of supplies, airlift, ground transportation, intelligence, and even command and control. Thus, by the time the American attack began, the Taliban was already isolated, its mobility reduced, its command and con-

trol fragile, and its source of resupply largely gone. None of these losses
was crippling to the Taliban militarily, but they did diminish its capabilities.
The loss of Pakistani support was also the first blow to the Taliban's
morale. It appears to have dispirited many of the Taliban's allies, who now
realized they were alone and facing the world's only remaining superpower.[16]

It took some time for either the bombing or the loss of Pakistani support
to have any material impact. Initially, the United States could mount only
about twenty-five combat sorties per day against Afghan targets, although
that climbed to about ninety sorties per day within a week or two. The air
strikes did two things: they terrified many of the Afghan troops, and they
isolated the frontline troops from their rear area support. For all of the brag-
ging about the accuracy of U.S. precision-guided munitions (PGMs), the
bombing does not seem to have killed huge numbers of Afghan soldiers.
This is not to say that the use of PGMs was not important, just that they
generally did not work the way that the media have portrayed it. Instead,
the PGMs were important because they allowed U.S. aircraft to stay well
above the maximum altitude of Afghan surface-to-air missiles (SAMs) and
still hit their targets. But hitting targets—often well-fortified positions in
Afghanistan's mountainous terrain—did not always equate to causing
combat deaths. They certainly destroyed some of the Taliban's equipment,
but their effect on Taliban morale was much greater than any physical destruction. The Soviets had tried bombing too when they were occupying
Afghanistan but had had little luck because without precision-guided munitions their planes either had to fly at low levels, where they were vulnerable to Afghan SAMs (including U.S.-supplied Stingers), or else stay at
high levels that made their bombing inaccurate. With precision-guided munitions, U.S. planes could stay at safe altitudes and still plant their bombs
on Taliban defensive positions.[17]

The bombing did what bombing has always done: demoralized the
troops who were being targeted. Except for a small number of occasions
when Taliban troops were highly concentrated and the United States employed large numbers of air strikes, the bombing did not kill many of those
attacked—only 3,000 to 4,000 Taliban soldiers are believed to have been
killed in the entire war, the great majority of those in a handful of ground
battles.[18] However, the air strikes undermined the resolve of the Taliban's
less disciplined and less committed allies, who were already deeply concerned by Pakistan's abandonment of them. At the start of Operation En-

during Freedom, roughly 20,000 of the Taliban's 45,000 men belonged not to the Taliban proper but to allied "bands"—the private militias of Afghan warlords, tribal levies, or conscripts called up to help fight the Americans. None of these men had much loyalty to the Taliban. In addition, another 8,000 to 12,000 Taliban soldiers were volunteers from Uzbekistan, Pakistan, and elsewhere, whose commitment varied. After several weeks of bombing (including some disruption of their supplies and the flow of replacements and reinforcements), these units lost whatever tenuous desire to fight for the Taliban they might have had and, in typical Afghan tribal fashion, began looking for a way out. That left the 6,000 to 8,000 core Taliban and 2,000 to 3,000 equally fanatical al-Qa'eda fighters to try to hold the front together.[19]

The key event in the war was the fall of the northern city of Mazar-i-Sharif. At the beginning of November, the Northern Alliance mounted an attack on the city with heavy air support but was stopped cold by determined Taliban defenses. However, the concentrated U.S. bombing began to take its toll, convincing some Taliban allied commanders to give up the fight. These surrenders in turn began opening up gaps in the defensive lines that the Taliban and al-Qa'eda could not fill. The Taliban's fragile chain of command was under attack by U.S. air forces, disrupting their ability to control their forces. The loss of Pakistan's support, coupled with U.S. interdiction of Afghanistan's extremely limited road network, meant that the Taliban could not move reserves and reinforcements to plug the gaps as they were accustomed to doing. As a result, Northern Alliance units were able to push slowly into Taliban positions, prompting further surrenders by the Taliban's less committed allies. When the Northern Alliance launched a new attack on Mazar-i-Sharif during the second week of November, the Taliban lines began to crumble in a slow-motion offensive paved with negotiated surrenders.[20]

By then the Taliban forces along the front lines were in trouble. The negotiated surrenders were snowballing as more and more commanders saw their compatriots going over to the Northern Alliance to escape the incessant bombing—especially by the terrifying B-52 and B-1 heavy bombers—and they calculated that the Americans and the Northern Alliance were getting stronger and stronger. Once again they wanted to be on the winning side, and especially when they found that Northern Alliance advances were making their defensive positions untenable anyway, they started surrendering in ever greater numbers.[21]

Recognizing what was happening as their fair-weather allies deserted them, the core Taliban troops and their al-Qa'eda allies—who had not been broken by the bombing—attempted to fall back. They did not have enough manpower to cover the whole front without their former allies, so instead they tried to concentrate at strong defensive positions where they could collect enough combat power to put up a fight. Those that could not make it back to such strong points as Konduz, Taloqan, Khanabad, Tora Bora, Qandahar, and elsewhere, melted into the countryside. The withdrawal of the core Taliban and al-Qa'eda troops caused the final collapse of the Taliban's defensive lines, allowing the Northern Alliance to surge forward across the front and isolate the Taliban strong points. These pockets were then gradually reduced by concentrated U.S. air strikes, Northern Alliance bombardment, and more negotiated surrenders, but even then it took weeks to wear down most of them because the air strikes did not kill large numbers of the dug-in Taliban and al-Qa'eda fighters, nor did their morale break like that of their less disciplined and less committed allies. By the end of November, the battle was effectively over, with most of the remaining Taliban and al-Qa'eda personnel dispersing into the countryside to flee or try to wage a guerrilla campaign.[22]

THE KOSOVO EXPERIENCE

The United States had a very different experience waging a massive air campaign during the Kosovo War of 1999, and this campaign has additional lessons for U.S. policy toward Iraq. Operation Allied Force, as the campaign was called, was roughly similar to Operation Enduring Freedom. The United States and its NATO allies employed heavy air strikes, coupled with (and eventually in support of) local opposition forces, in this case the Kosovo Liberation Army (KLA), against the Serbs led by Slobodan Milošević.[23] Like the Northern Alliance and the Iraqi opposition groups, the KLA was much smaller than the Serbian army, was lightly armed, and largely relied on the NATO air forces to do most of the work in terms of breaking Serb formations. However, unlike in Operation Enduring Freedom, this combination failed in Kosovo.

There were three important differences between the Kosovo War and the Afghan War. First, the goal of Operation Allied Force was not to topple the Milošević government per se, though in fact many of its operations were designed to bring about exactly that result. Second, NATO did not employ large numbers of special forces personnel on the ground to serve as forward air controllers for NATO air strikes. In the latter half of the war, NATO did deploy extensive intelligence assets—including radars and signals intelligence collectors—to support KLA ground operations and relied on KLA personnel to direct air strikes, but they lacked the training and the technology (particularly laser designators) of Western military personnel.[24] Third, although both Afghanistan and Kosovo are heavily mountainous, Kosovo is carpeted by trees and heavily built up with towns and other inhabited areas, while Afghanistan is more sparsely vegetated and populated. This is important because throughout history it has been the case that trees and built-up areas have created the greatest problems for air power by providing natural cover for ground forces. As advanced as U.S. warplanes are, they (mostly) still cannot see through trees or buildings.

In the Kosovo War, destroying the Serbian army and preventing it from conducting further ethnic cleansing of Kosovar Albanians were two of the most important NATO goals—just as destroying the Iraqi Army and preventing it from crushing the opposition (and slaughtering the Kurds) would be in Iraq. In addition, as in Afghanistan, NATO sought to do this by striking Serb forces directly, interdicting their movements and supplies, and providing direct air support to the KLA forces—who were intended to be the anvil that would force the Serbs to concentrate, allowing them to be crushed by the hammer of NATO air strikes.[25] Again, these are the same roles that would be assigned to U.S. air forces and the Iraqi opposition if the Afghan Approach were employed against Iraq. Unlike in Afghanistan, however, in Kosovo the strategy did not work. NATO won the war, but the tactical air campaign against Serbian ground forces failed badly.[26]

During the seventy-eight days of Operation Allied Force, the NATO air forces barely scratched the Serbian units in Kosovo.[27] At the start of the war, there were 40,000 Serbian troops with 859 tanks, 672 other armored vehicles, and 1,163 artillery pieces in Kosovo.[28] By the end of the war, NATO believed it had hit only 93 tanks, 153 other armored vehicles, and 389 artillery pieces. By itself this is a distressing tally, given that NATO flew roughly five thousand attack sorties against the Serbian forces.[29] However, even these numbers for destroyed equipment are probably exaggerated. The Allied Force Munitions Effectiveness Assessment Team, a NATO contingent that went into Kosovo on the ground to assess the effectiveness of the air strikes after the war, found "very little evidence of damaged or destroyed equipment" and could confirm only 14 tanks, 12 self-propelled guns, 18 armored personnel carriers (APCs), and 20 towed artillery pieces destroyed by air strikes.[30] Similarly, NATO claims to have killed 10,000 Serbian troops in Kosovo, while the Serbians claim to have lost only about 500 soldiers.[31] Once again, the findings of the NATO investigative teams indicate that the correct casualty numbers are probably a lot closer to 500 than to 10,000. Indeed, even on those occasions when NATO believed that its air strikes killed thousands of Serbian troops, later evidence, including the findings of the NATO investigative teams, indicated that at most only a few hundred were killed.

Nor did NATO air strikes stop the ethnic cleansing. In fact, the Serbian military's ethnic cleansing campaign *increased* during the air strikes as Milošević tried to scour Kosovo to create new "facts on the ground." There was no loss of command and control of the Serbian forces doing the ethnic cleansing, nor any significant diminution of their ability to conduct the operations successfully. By the end of the war, roughly 90 percent of the Kosovar Albanian population had been killed or driven from their homes. Most of those that remained were purposely kept in place by the Serbs as shields against NATO air strikes.[32]

Nor did the air campaign allow the KLA to defeat the Serbian army. At the beginning of the war, the 40,000 Serbian troops in Kosovo were opposed by about 24,000 (much more lightly armed) KLA personnel. By the end of the war, far from being cut off by NATO air interdiction, the Serbs had reinforced their units in Kosovo to 47,000 troops, while the KLA had been beaten down to just 3,000 to 5,000 men remaining in Kosovo, and these largely in isolated pockets that eventually would have been reduced by the Serbs had Milošević not capitulated.[33] There is no evidence that the Serbs suffered from lack of supplies or even from demoralization—let alone heavy casualties. In fact, at the end of the war, the Serbian generals opposed Milošević's decision to pull out of Kosovo because the NATO air strikes had done so little damage to their forces.[34]

Neither did the NATO air strikes destroy Serbian forces or aid KLA forces when KLA operations forced the Serbs to concentrate for battle. From start to finish, the Serbs dominated the battlefield and manhandled the KLA. For example, on May 26, the KLA launched Operation Arrow, an offensive with 4,000 troops from its 137th and 138th Brigades designed to drive into Kosovo near Mount Pastrik and open up supply lines for some of the remaining KLA pockets trapped by the Serbian army. The KLA troops were trained and advised beforehand by American and British special forces, and the attack was preceded by heavy NATO air strikes and "intense" Albanian army artillery bombardments, but when the KLA finally attacked it was stopped cold by Serbian forces after advancing only a mile or two. For two weeks, the KLA fed in reinforcements, Albanian artillery provided fire support, and NATO warplanes hammered the Serbian positions—to no avail. The KLA forces were pinned down by the Serbs and could not make any additional progress.[35] Then, on June 1, the Serbs launched a multibattalion counterattack (in good weather), prompting the KLA to call in NATO air strikes, including by A-10s, AC-130s, F-16s, B-1s, and six B-52s. Although this was the perfect opportunity for NATO air power to show its ability to destroy Serb formations massed for attack, in the open, and in good weather, the results were again disappointing. The counterattack was stopped only after it had regained much of the lost territory, and although they took heavier casualties than in the past, far fewer Serbs were killed than NATO had expected. In the words of RAND air power expert Stephen T. Hosmer, "A subsequent examination of the battlefield around Mt. Pastrik, which had been subjected to heavy B-52 attacks, showed surprisingly little evidence of damage to [Serbian] forces or equipment. Indeed, the oft-cited claims that increased KLA ground activity during late May and early June had caused the [Serb] forces to mass and thereby become lucrative targets for NATO air attack generally were proven to be unsubstantiated."[36]

Overall, the experience of air power against the Serbian army in Kosovo was astonishingly poor. More than 1,200 NATO aircraft had flown 38,000 sorties, including more than 5,000 strike sorties against Serbian military forces in Kosovo, but had achieved very little.[37] They had killed few Serbian personnel and destroyed few heavy weapons. They had somewhat hindered but not prevented the Serbian army from conducting large-scale ethnic cleansing of Kosovo. They had somewhat hindered but had not prevented the Serbian army from mauling the KLA. They had been unable to smash Serbian forces when they concentrated for either offensive or defensive operations. The failure of the Afghan Approach in Kosovo is an important caution against its employment in Iraq.

LESSONS FROM THE GULF WAR

There is also important evidence from the Persian Gulf War of 1991 regarding the likely effectiveness of the Afghan Approach in a future war with Saddam. Interestingly, despite the increases in the effectiveness of U.S. air power since 1991, Operation Desert Storm was actually a far more devastating air campaign for the Iraqis than was Operation Allied Force for the Serbs or even Operation Enduring Freedom for the Taliban.

The principal impact of the air campaign on the Iraqi Army in the Kuwaiti Theater was psychological, not physical. By the time coalition forces finally launched their ground assault, the air campaign had already convinced the vast bulk of the army not to fight. Of the roughly 550,000 Iraqi troops deployed to the Kuwaiti Theater during the fall, more than 200,000 probably had deserted before the start of the ground campaign on February 24.[38] Then, when the coalition attacked, tens of thousands of Iraqi soldiers surrendered en masse, many without firing a shot, others after blowing off a single magazine for honor's sake. Still others readily retreated out of Kuwait when Saddam's order to withdraw finally came. Only the Republican Guard and several of the heavy divisions of the regular army stood and fought.

The most important factor in the disintegration of Iraqi morale during the Gulf War was the severing of Iraq's supply lines to its frontline divisions. Although coalition air strikes destroyed only a small percentage of the supplies Iraq had stockpiled inside the KTO, the coalition air campaign shut down Iraq's logistical distribution network within the theater. By mid-February, the Iraqis were virtually incapable of getting supplies to their frontline units: coalition fighter-bombers prevented their trucks from using the roads to the front, losses to air strikes had significantly reduced the size of the Iraqi truck fleet, and few Iraqi drivers were willing to make the trip. According to the commander of the Iraqi Twenty-seventh Infantry Division, his unit deployed with eighty trucks, but seventy were then destroyed by the coalition air campaign.[39] In postwar interrogations of Iraqi soldiers and officers, being without adequate food and water in the middle of the desert stood out as the first among various reasons that their frontline divisions collapsed in a mass of desertions, defections, and surrenders.[40]

Next in importance was the direct psychological effect on the troops themselves. The constant pounding by coalition air forces took a toll on Iraqi morale. The coalition did everything it could to reinforce this—by employing constant strikes, dropping enormous bombs such as the 15,000-pound BLU-82 "daisy cutter," using psychological warfare to heighten the fears of Iraqi troops, and conducting near-continuous raids (especially on key units) to prevent the Iraqis from sleeping or having any respite from the attacks. In postwar interrogations, Iraqi troops made clear that it was the B-52s that they feared most. The B-52s flew so high they were essentially unheard, and then, all of a sudden, the bombs would appear out of nowhere and it seemed as though the whole world was exploding. The thunder of the strikes could be heard from miles away. As a result, many Iraqis were psychologically unhinged by the strikes themselves or by the constant gnawing fear that they might suddenly be caught in the midst of an attack.[41]

Finally, the air campaign did destroy much of Iraq's weaponry. Before the air war began, Iraq had deployed 3,475 tanks and 3,080 armored personnel carriers to the Kuwaiti Theater. By the time of the coalition ground campaign, air strikes had probably destroyed about 1,200 of these 6,500 armored vehicles.[42] An equal number were probably put out of commission because of maintenance problems created by the air campaign. The Iraqis learned that being near an armored vehicle was life-threatening because that was what the coalition aircraft were trying to hit. As a result, they largely neglected maintaining their vehicles, and by the time the coalition ground war started, many were no longer operational.[43]

Geography and topography were key reasons for the success of the Desert Storm air campaign. Saddam sent more than 500,000 of his best troops (such as they were) to defend a line more than 400 kilometers long mostly stretched out across the featureless Arabian Desert. The Kuwaiti Theater presented the most ideal conditions imaginable for air power. There were virtually no trees in the theater, and certainly none for hundreds of kilometers along the front lines, nor were there any towns or other settlements. As a result, the Iraqi Army had zero cover from the air, which, as Kosovo and Vietnam have demonstrated, is probably the greatest impediment to air strikes. With the exception of the area around Kuwait City (which was not an important area for coalition air strikes) there were also effectively no civilians whom coalition air forces had to avoid. The Iraqi Army was laid out for the coalition as if on a tabletop, and all the coalition air forces had to do was to pound it. Moreover, the road network in the Kuwaiti Theater was woefully inadequate, and even before the air campaign commenced, Iraq's formidable logistical service had had difficulty keeping its forces supplied. Because of the absence of cover, the limited road network, and the long distances between Iraqi supply depots and the frontline troops, it was easy for coalition aircraft to sever Iraq's supply lines, creating the logistical problems that were the greatest cause of demoralization among Iraqi forces. Last, the fact that the Iraqis were deployed in a desert—one of the most inhospitable climates on earth—was a huge help to the coalition in that it meant that men did not have ready access to shade, shelter, food, water, or other provisions either from surrounding vegetation or from a local populace.

WHAT SMART BOMBS DO AND DON'T DO

Some advocates of the Afghan Approach claim that U.S. forces are now qualitatively different from those that fought even as recently as in the Gulf War. The improvements in U.S. command, control, communications, and intelligence capabilities and the greater availability (and in some cases, greater effectiveness) of precision-guided munitions have made U.S. forces far more lethal than in the past. U.S. air forces now generally require fewer munitions to destroy a given target, particularly a large stationary target such as a building or a bridge. U.S. aircraft can remain at higher altitudes, where it is harder for enemy air defenses to reach them, while still being able to put their bombs on or near the target. U.S. air forces can now detect threats and concentrate against them much faster and more easily than before.

These are important advantages for the United States, but they mostly have changed the amount of effort we need to put into an air campaign, not necessarily the impact of an air campaign on the adversary. In particular, there is no evidence that greater accuracy in bombing has a greater impact on the enemy ground forces being attacked. Thus, the greater percentage of PGMs employed in Afghanistan (56 percent) than in the Gulf War (9 percent) or the Kosovo War (29 percent) was meaningful mainly in terms of easing the logistical burden on U.S. forces and allowing us to operate in ways that minimized our own casualties, not in terms of the impact of the air campaign on the enemy's forces.

Having more accurate weapons does mean that it requires fewer sorties to destroy any given target, but there are a lot of important caveats to this. Air strikes have their greatest impact on ground forces by psychologically "breaking" ground units—causing them to desert, surrender, or run away— which historically has had nothing to do with the number of casualties a unit has suffered. In every war since World War II, studies have found that there is no correlation between the number of casualties a unit has suffered and when (or if) it breaks.[44] Instead, history has repeatedly demonstrated the commitment and discipline of the troops being attacked that are the key variables in determining whether ground units will break under repeated air strikes. Indeed, Afghanistan demonstrated this as much as did the Gulf War. In 1991, the Iraqi infantry divisions, which had the poorest morale and discipline, broke under six weeks of air strikes, while the more determined and disciplined Republican Guard and regular army heavy divisions did not. Likewise, in Afghanistan, the Taliban's allies and foreign volunteers broke under four weeks of bombing, but the more determined and disciplined core Taliban and al-Qa'eda units did not—and at Konduz, Qandahar, and Tora Bora, they fought hard, just as the Iraqi Republican Guard did. Thus the greater ability of PGMs to kill personnel and destroy weaponry does not necessarily translate into a greater ability to break enemy ground forces.

Aircraft equipped with PGMs do not necessarily do any better in breaking enemy formations than those equipped with "dumb" bombs because history has repeatedly demonstrated that the weight and duration of air strikes have a much greater impact on enemy morale than their accuracy and the casualties caused by them. In every war since World War II, the physical destruction caused by air strikes on ground forces has proven less than expected. Instead, the psychological impact of air strikes has always been far greater than expected, and far greater than their physical impact would suggest.[45] Thus, during the Gulf War, U.S. B-52 strikes killed few Iraqi troops, but they were the greatest source of demoralization for the Iraqis. In the Gulf War and in Afghanistan, our opponents do seem to have been impressed by the accuracy of U.S. air strikes, in which a single bomb would fall from the sky and take out a single tank or bunker. However, the evidence suggests that a massive B-52 strike that does not kill anyone or destroy anything is actually more powerful than a pinpoint attack that precisely obliterates a tank or bunker, because the terror of the former has a much greater impact on enemy morale than the impressiveness of the latter, and it is much easier and faster to eliminate a unit by causing its morale to break than by destroying all of its weaponry.[46]

During the Gulf War, the United States dropped 21,000 PGMs on Iraq. During the Afghan War, by the end of the conventional military campaign in December, the United States had employed only 8,000 PGMs. Those who argue that the greater percentage of PGMs employed in Operation Enduring Freedom than during the Gulf War were tactically decisive are somehow arguing that the 8,000 used on Afghanistan had a more devastating effect on the Taliban than the 21,000 dropped on the Iraqis *because* we also dropped another 200,000 "dumb" bombs on the Iraqis. Nor were the PGMs employed against Afghanistan meaningfully better than those used against Iraq.

The greatest impact of air power on ground forces has historically been its ability to choke off supplies to the front lines. Since the Second World War, whenever an air campaign has been able to cut off supplies to the frontline forces, this has had an enormous impact on enemy morale and has usually been the single most important factor causing enemy units to break. During the Gulf War, the shutdown of Iraq's logistical distribution system within the Kuwaiti Theater was the most important element of the air campaign in the collapse of Iraq's frontline formations, far outweighing the physical damage done. In contrast, the inability of NATO forces to cut Serbian supply lines in Kosovo was a primary reason that the air campaign did not break any Serbian formations. Although PGMs can certainly help an air campaign to cut logistical links, they are not as important as having enough aircraft with enough stamina to maintain a near-constant presence over the enemy's road network to dissuade enemy trucks from moving.

This is not to suggest that precision-guided munitions are worthless. Hardly. They are a huge asset to U.S. forces in a variety of ways. However, while they have revolutionized a number of aspects of air power, they have not revolutionized how air forces defeat ground forces. Instead, in all three of the major wars the United States has fought since 1990—the Gulf War, Kosovo, and Afghanistan—the pattern has been the same: sustained air strikes and the degradation of the enemy's logistical system broke poorly disciplined and committed troops but not the better-disciplined and committed (and better-supplied) troops. In the Gulf War, the largely Shi'ite conscript infantry divisions deployed along the front lines collapsed as a result of the psychological pounding and shutdown of Iraq's logistical system during the six-week air campaign, while the Republican Guards and the heavy divisions of the regular army did not. In Kosovo, the entire Serbian army was disciplined and committed, and NATO forces were unable to choke off their supply lines (despite the large number of PGMs employed); as a result, NATO had almost no impact on deployed Serb forces. In Afghanistan, the Taliban's poorly disciplined and motivated allies broke after about four weeks of bombing, while its hard core of Talibs and its fanatical al-Qa'eda allies did not.

IRAQ IS NOT AFGHANISTAN

This discussion of the lessons of America's most recent wars demonstrates that while air power is an effective instrument of policy, it is not omnipotent. In a future war against Iraq, air power alone could undoubtedly accomplish numerous missions. In particular, if we again wanted to coerce Saddam into respecting U.N. sanctions or U.S. red lines, a powerful air campaign would likely do the trick. A determined air campaign that focused on Saddam's key supporters—the Republican Guard, Special Republican Guard, Ba'th Party, Fidayin Saddam, and internal security services—would also have some potential to spark a coup resulting in his overthrow. In December 1998, Desert Fox struck at this target set and Saddam became so concerned that he overreacted, ordering emergency security measures that set off small uprisings throughout Iraq. However, coercing Saddam by threatening his overthrow is one thing; actually effecting it is another. Desert Fox did not result in a coup, and the unrest that Saddam created through his overreaction was easily suppressed. All of the available evidence indicates that we would have a much tougher time making this approach to regime change work in Iraq than we did in Afghanistan.

The Iraqi Opposition Can't Handle the Role of the Northern Alliance

The Iraqi opposition is much weaker relative to the Iraqi regime's forces than the Northern Alliance was relative to the Taliban's forces. The strongest of the Iraqi opposition groups, the two Kurdish militias, could muster as many as 50,000 lightly armed *peshmerga* if they could put aside their differences and fight together against Saddam, while the Shi'ite insurgents in the south might muster another 10,000 to 12,000 men. Against them, Baghdad has about 430,000 personnel in the Iraqi armed forces, Republican Guard, and Special Republican Guard (and that is not counting the armed forces' reserves, the Fidayin Saddam, the Ba'th Party militia, and other paramilitary groups). These forces are heavily armed, with more than 2,000 tanks and comparable numbers of armored personnel carriers and artillery. They have also repeatedly demonstrated that they are more than a match for the opposition forces. In 1991 and again in 1996, when the Kurds faced Saddam's Republican Guards, they were easily defeated. Their greatest victory against Iraqi forces came at the end of the Gulf War, when they panicked the handful of third-rate Iraqi brigades left to watch the north and were able to briefly seize control of their homelands until the remnants of the Republican Guard made their way back north. Likewise, in 1995, their success at Arbil was achieved by mounting a surprise attack by a much larger force against two demoralized brigades of the Iraqi Thirty-eighth Infantry Division. In this case as well, their success lasted only until Republican Guard units were brought in to halt the attack.

There is enough good raw material among the *peshmerga* that if the United States were to provide them with weapons, training, funds, and massive air support, at some point they probably would be able to hold Kurdistan against an Iraqi assault. However, even then there is little likelihood that they could translate such a defensive capability into the offensive power needed to overthrow Saddam. At the height of their military power in 1974–75, when they were being armed and funded by the United States and Israel, when they had Iranian Army units fighting with them, and when they were facing a much weaker Iraqi Army, the Kurds were still never able to move beyond Kurdistan to threaten Baghdad.

Taliban control over Afghanistan was much weaker than Saddam's control over Iraq. This meant that it was relatively easy for the United States and its allies to make contact with Afghan units inside Afghanistan and convince them to turn against the Taliban. In Saddam's Stalinist police state, our ability to contact potential oppositionists inside Iraq and encourage them to work against the government would be much more limited.

As for the INC, they have nothing in terms of military capabilities at present. No doubt they could quickly round up a few hundred people if they were offered U.S. money, training, and weapons, but they would still need to produce the thousands of fighters they have repeatedly promised but never delivered before they could be a credible part of an opposition force in an Afghan-style operation. Even then, it would take many months, if not years, to train such a force of INC soldiers, and we would still want the Kurds, Shi'ah, and any other opposition forces to try to assemble sufficient mass to take on the hundreds of thousands of much more heavily armed troops at the regime's disposal.

Nor should we count on the mass uprising of the Iraqi people that the INC insists will occur. There is no evidence to support such a claim and ample evidence to contradict it. As described in Chapter 2, Saddam's catastrophic defeat in the Gulf War sparked the two simultaneous revolts of the Iraqi *intifadah*. However, what was so interesting about those revolts was not how large they were but how relatively small. Perhaps as many as 100,000 Kurds joined the northern revolt, with an equal number of Shi'ah and disaffected soldiers joining the southern revolt—this in a population of 19 million. The vast majority of the populace were so scared of Saddam that they chose to wait to see how things would turn out rather than joining the rebellion and risking retribution if they lost. As a result, Saddam's battered Republican Guard crushed the *intifadah* in a matter of weeks. Similarly, when the INC was in northern Iraq trying to trigger such a revolt in 1992–96, and after Operation Desert Fox in 1998, when Saddam feared there might be such a revolt, nothing happened. The Iraqi people remained quiescent. Most of the Iraqi people are unlikely to move against Saddam until his doom is sealed.

Although the proponents of the Afghan Approach take it on faith that a regime change effort led by Iraqi opposition forces themselves would produce an outpouring of support, making the entire process easy, the opposite may actually be true—a regime change effort based largely on opposition forces could cause the Sunni center to rally around Saddam Hussein and make it harder to bring down the regime. Because the opposition groups with the greatest military strength are the Kurds and the Shi'ah, any Afghan Approach option would inevitably center on them. (It is also worth pointing out that Ahmed Chalabi, the head of the INC, is also a Shi'ah.) In 1991, the Shi'ite and Kurdish rebellions caused the Sunnis to decide to stick with Saddam rather than consign the country to their ethnic and religious rivals. The United States faced the same problem in Afghanistan with the mostly Tajik Northern Alliance, and we were able to overcome it there. However, we did so by working with Pashtun leaders in southern Afghanistan and bringing in well-known Pashtun leaders such as Hamid Qarzai, who still had considerable followings inside the country. It is unclear whether the United States could do the same in Iraq because few in the Iraqi diaspora have large followings among the Sunnis inside Iraq, while Saddam has effectively killed every person in the country with the kind of charisma and stature that would be needed. Thus, the problem is not just that we don't know who the "Hamid Qarzai of Iraq" is but that he might not even exist thanks to Saddam's relentless decapitation of Iraqi society.

Another reason that an opposition ground campaign would be more difficult in Iraq than it was in Afghanistan is that Iraq is a far more urbanized society (70 percent of Iraqis live in cities, compared to 21 percent of Afghans). Liberating Iraq's cities would be a tall order for any of the opposition groups. U.S. air power would be hampered in urban combat because of the difficulty of identifying and striking targets in cities and the risk of civilian casualties. None of the opposition groups would have the size, skill, or logistical capabilities to mask one or more large Iraqi cities and continue marching on Baghdad. At some point, even if the Iraqi opposition is unexpectedly successful in the field because U.S. air power is able to catch one or more Iraqi divisions in the open and break them, the opposition is going to come upon a large Iraqi city defended by one or more entrenched Republican Guard or loyal regular army divisions. Given that we will be highly reticent to try to flatten the city with air power (and one of the lessons of Stalingrad was that bombing a city actually helps its defenders by creating rubble for them to hide in), it is very, very hard to imagine that a lightly armed, semiprofessional force of Iraqi oppositionists (even the Kurds) could take an Iraqi city under such circumstances.

Finally, the opposition groups would likely face the threat of the regime's weapons of mass destruction. Since the goal of this campaign would be the destruction of Saddam's regime, he would have little incentive to exercise restraint. Since he has used weapons of mass destruction extensively against the Kurds already, it would be highly likely that he would do so against any opposition force that participated in an Afghan-style campaign. It is hard enough for well-trained and well-equipped troops to fight in a chemical warfare environment; for irregulars it borders on suicidal. Even if the United States provided opposition forces with some of the gear American military forces use to operate in a contaminated environment (and we probably could not fully equip all 50,000 Kurdish *peshmerga*), sending Iraqi oppositionists into battle to face chemical warfare barrages is a recipe for disaster.

A New Air Campaign Against Iraq Would Be Harder Than Operation Enduring Freedom

Unlike the Taliban, the Iraqi military has already been through a massive U.S. air campaign. The key to our victory in Afghanistan was that the withdrawal of Pakistani support combined with U.S. air strikes broke the morale of the Taliban's allies, reducing the remaining core of the Taliban and their al-Qa'eda allies—who had not been broken by the air attacks—to several isolated pockets. In Operation Desert Storm, the U.S. air campaign similarly broke Iraq's frontline infantry divisions. However, the air campaign never broke either the heavy divisions of Iraq's regular army or the Republican Guard divisions. The coalition flew more than a thousand sorties against several of these divisions, employing large numbers of PGMs and B-52 strikes against them, yet they did not break. In fact, these divisions fought extremely hard against the coalition forces during the subsequent ground campaign (though they did not fight well). U.S. veterans reported that the battles against the Republican Guard were harder than any firefight they had been through in Vietnam.[47] Then, after the war, these same divisions—battered by air strikes and in some cases eviscerated by U.S. ground forces—went on to crush the Shi'ite and Kurdish revolts.

As the Gulf, Kosovo, and Afghan campaigns all demonstrated, well-disciplined and -motivated troops that are not deprived of supplies are exceedingly hard to "break" by air strikes alone—no matter how punishing or accurate the strikes. In 1991, the Republican Guard and regular army heavy divisions made up only 17 of the 51 divisions Baghdad deployed to the Kuwaiti Theater. Today, they account for 12 of Iraq's 23 divisions; thus we should expect much less of the Iraqi Army to be vulnerable to breaking under air attack than was the case during the Gulf War and those that do not break to be more than adequate to deal with the opposition.

A key difference between a new air campaign against Iraq and Operation Desert Storm would be the terrain. This time, the Iraqis would be unlikely to deploy the vast bulk of their combat forces out in the desert, far from their supplies or population centers, served by a poor road network, and completely exposed to the skies. Instead, the Iraqis would likely deploy their troops to defend Iraq's key populated areas: central Iraq, the Mesopotamian River valleys, and the Sunni heartland northwest of Baghdad. Although there are large stretches of desert in these areas, especially northwest of Baghdad, and the land is mostly flat, much of the terrain is different from the Kuwaiti Theater. In these parts of Iraq there is far more vegetation; there are swamps, irrigated farmland, numerous towns, cities, and other built-up areas, and even some forests. The terrain of north-central Iraq and southern Kurdistan is hilly or mountainous, often with tree covering. All of this terrain would provide far better concealment for Iraqi forces than the Kuwaiti Theater, or Afghanistan, for that matter. It may not be as bad as the wooded mountains of Kosovo, but an air campaign against Iraqi forces in Mesopotamia and central Iraq would have a much tougher time than in 1991. Moreover, as with the Serbs, we should expect the Iraqis to try to make use of the urban areas and their civilian population to shield their forces, rendering units deployed in urban areas or near other settlements troublesome targets for air attack.

The different theater would also mean that it would be extremely difficult for U.S. air forces to cut the supply lines to the regime's ground forces, the single most effective instrument of air power against ground forces. The thicker vegetation and the urban areas will make it harder to detect Iraqi road movements and will provide greater cover for trucks, as was the case in Kosovo. In central Iraq, there will be more food, water, and other basic supplies (such as fuel) available near at hand than was the case in the uninhabited desert of the Kuwaiti Theater. The road network of central Iraq is very extensive, presenting a much greater challenge for U.S. air forces than was the case in the spartan Kuwaiti Theater. Finally, with the exception of the desert areas of northwest Iraq, the conditions of central Iraq are not as harsh and debilitating as those of the Kuwaiti Theater, meaning that Iraqi military personnel would likely feel any deprivations less immediately or powerfully than was the case in 1991.

Iraqi air defenses, which could be more troublesome than during Desert Storm, are roughly similar in composition and capability to Serbian air defenses. Most of the equipment is the same. The Iraqis have more of certain newer systems, but they have never employed their systems as well as the Serbs. However, the Iraqis and Serbs have had extensive discussions on air defense issues, and it is assumed that they have shared their experiences.[48] It may be that the Iraqis will be better prepared for U.S. forces next time around, although that is unlikely to have more than a marginal impact on the freedom of action of U.S. forces, if only because of the technical limitations on the Iraqi forces. Of greater importance will be the likely location of the air campaign. During the Gulf War, Iraqi air defenses in the Kuwaiti Theater were rather meager. The greatest problem was the short-range, shoulder-fired SA-14s and SA-16s, deployed mostly with the Republican Guard. Coalition aircraft avoided these by flying most missions above 10,000 feet. Because the Kuwaiti Theater was such a hospitable environment for air power, this was not terribly problematic. However, the air defenses of central Iraq are far more formidable—so much so that throughout the Gulf War only cruise missiles and F-117 Stealth fighters were used to attack Baghdad and the targets around it.[49] (The same was true in Kosovo, where only F-117s, B-2 Stealth bombers, and cruise missiles were used to attack targets in Belgrade).[50] In addition, the need to try to deal with both urban and natural concealment would undoubtedly make it harder to identify Iraqi military forces in central Iraq, which will mean one of two things: either U.S. aircraft would need to fly lower to get a better look, making them vulnerable to Iraq's SA-14s and SA-16s, or else they will do less damage, as in Kosovo.

If we were fortunate, the Iraqis would take the initiative and try to smash the opposition forces in counterattacks that would present the best opportunities for U.S. air power to break Republican Guard and other loyal divisions. In fact, this is virtually a requirement of the Afghan Approach. Since Iraqi opposition forces, even the Kurds, are unlikely to be able to slug it out with any but the smallest Iraqi military units, the hope is that U.S. air forces would do most of the killing when Iraqi forces concentrated for major counterattacks. To a great extent, American air power would have to "break" these counterattacks before they could do much damage to the opposition forces. However, even here, recent military history suggests that caution is in order. Although it is considered axiomatic that ground forces are far more vulnerable to air attack when they are massed and out in the open and moving for an attack, the results of air strikes against attacking armored forces in recent wars have not always met these expectations.

There are two examples from the Gulf War and one from Kosovo of enemy counterattacks hit by U.S. air strikes that provide some useful evidence:

- On the night of January 29, 1991, several battalions of the Iraqi Fifth Mechanized Division conducted a series of probing attacks against coalition lines during Desert Storm. These probes were preparatory to a corps-level counterattack the Iraqis put into action the next day after one of their battalions captured the abandoned Saudi town of R'as al-Khafji. The vast array of coalition sensors trained on Kuwait had failed to detect the preparations for the Iraqi attack even though it included the massing of the Iraqi Third Armored and Fifth Mechanized Divisions in southern Kuwait. Thus when the Iraqis attacked, it came as a complete surprise. On January 30, the coalition awakened to these developments and threw every available warplane into the fray. During the next twenty-four hours, the two Iraqi heavy divisions were hit by more than a thousand attack sorties, many by A-10 attack aircraft and Apache and Cobra helicopters, all of which employed the most lethal precision-guided munitions of all: Maverick, Hellfire, and TOW antitank missiles. This effort pummeled the two Iraqi divisions, sending them reeling back and forcing Baghdad to cancel the operation. Nevertheless, in the aftermath of the battle, the United States could find only several dozen destroyed Iraqi tanks and APCs, despite the intensity of the air effort. What's more, neither division was crippled—in fact, during the coalition ground campaign that followed, these two divisions fought among the hardest of any of the Iraqi divisions and deployed as many armored vehicles as any others U.S. forces encountered, indicating that they had not suffered unduly during the battle of R'as al-Khafji.[51]

- On the first day of the coalition ground campaign, February 24, 1991, the U.S. Second Marine Division breached the Iraqi lines in Kuwait near Manaqish and began driving toward Kuwait City. The nearby Iraqi Eighth Mechanized Brigade of the Third Armored Division launched a well-rehearsed counterattack to try to block the Second Marine Division's advance. The Marines immediately called for air support, which arrived in the form of several flights of A-10 attack aircraft that had been hovering overhead waiting for such a call. Within minutes, the A-10s had destroyed most of the Eighth Mechanized Brigade's tanks, causing the brigade commander to surrender to the Americans. However, the rest of his brigade, which had nearly all of its other armored vehicles intact, continued to attack. It was destroyed in ground combat by the Marines.[52]

- Finally, on June 1–7, 1999, several battalions of Serbian troops counterattacked the pinned-down KLA forces near Mount Pastrik in Kosovo. As described above, the KLA called in NATO air support, which responded immediately, including A-10s, AC-130s, F-16s, B-1s, and B-52s. Although NATO believed that it had killed 800 to 1,200 Serbs, postwar assessments indicated that very few had actually been killed. What's more, the Serb counterattack seems to have succeeded in pushing the KLA back in most places.[53]

These examples suggest that we should be wary of assuming that air power can always break counterattacks by itself. At R'as al-Khafji, Manaqish, and Mount Pastrik (and on another occasion during the Gulf War, when the Fifth Mechanized Division counterattacked the U.S. First Marine Division from the Burqan oil field on February 25), U.S. forces were unable to detect preparations for the counterattack before it started. At R'as al-Khafji, the massive coalition air effort did stop the counterattack in its tracks but did surprisingly little physical damage to the Iraqi forces. At Mount Pastrik, the NATO strikes also did little damage and largely failed to break the counterattack. At Manaqish, the air strikes did considerable damage to the Iraqi Eighth Mechanized Brigade but were unable to break its spirit or cause the unit to retreat. All in all a mixed bag. Only at R'as al-Khafji did U.S. air power actually stop the counterattack, and there it required an enormous air effort. If Kurdish forces (or worse still, a hastily scraped together INC force) had been attacked at Manaqish in 1991 rather than U.S. Marines, the remaining elements of the Eighth Mechanized Brigade probably would have made short work of them. This is essentially what happened to the KLA at Mount Pastrik: the air strikes failed to break the Serbs, who were more than able to defeat the lightly armed opposition.

It may well be the case, however, that the Iraqis would refuse to move out on the attack and instead would remain on the defensive and force the opposition and U.S. air power to dig them out of their fortified positions. Especially in the terrain of central Iraq, this could be problematic. As NATO's experience with dug-in Serbian defenders at Mount Pastrik demonstrated, even heavy air strikes employing large numbers of "smart" bombs can fail to soften up disciplined and well-protected defenders enough to allow lightly armed irregulars to win through. In Afghanistan as well, U.S. air strikes had considerable difficulty weakening the pockets of core Taliban and al-Qa'eda troops. It took weeks of constantly pummeling these cut-off units before they would surrender, and in every case there was little sign of heavy casualties from the air strikes, demonstrating once again that committed and disciplined troops can withstand even sustained air campaigns if they are properly dug in. Likewise, even in the exceptionally permissive conditions of the Kuwaiti Theater, coalition air forces had great difficulty actually killing Iraqi personnel in their trenches and bunkers, and it took considerable effort to destroy their well-protected tanks and armored vehicles, with or without PGMs. Under the likely circumstances in a future air war against Iraq, when the Iraqis would have better cover and concealment, as well as civilian populations nearby, we must expect air strikes to do worse than they did during Desert Storm, not better. This means that the Iraqi opposition forces would have to assault dug-in Iraqi defensive positions—a challenge for any light infantry and especially difficult because static defensive operations are one of the few things the Iraqi armed forces perform reasonably well.

Overall it is important to remember that in 1991, the United States hit Iraq with probably the most powerful preliminary air campaign in history. The coalition flew 118,000 sorties against Iraq, including 21,000 strike sorties against the Iraqi Army in the Kuwaiti Theater. Nor were these strikes harmless, as coalition air forces probably destroyed about 1,200 Iraqi armored vehicles. We then followed this air campaign with one of the most decisive ground operations of modern history. By the end of February

1991, the Iraqi armed forces were a pale shadow of their former selves. They were demoralized, disorganized, and deprived of much of their most powerful weaponry. In six weeks, the United States and its allies had smashed about 75 percent of Iraq's combat power. Yet in March 1991, the Iraqi regime still had enough military power (paltry though it was) to quickly crush the two largest simultaneous insurrections in Iraqi history and keep Saddam in power. By definition, employing the Afghan Approach would mean mounting a weaker military campaign against Iraq this time than we did in 1991 (if only because there would be no large ground attack by U.S. armored forces), yet its proponents would have us believe that this weaker campaign would somehow be more likely to accomplish what Desert Storm could not.

THE STRATEGIC AND DIPLOMATIC RISKS

For all of these military reasons, the Afghan Approach would have a low likelihood of toppling Saddam from power. On top of that, there are strategic and diplomatic considerations that make even trying this approach dangerous and misguided.

The United States cannot prosecute the Afghan Approach unilaterally. It would require considerable cooperation from regional states. It would take a lot of planes to mount the envisioned air campaign against Iraq. Because of the advances in command and control, surveillance, and precision-guided munitions, the United States probably wouldn't need the 1,700 aircraft it used during Desert Storm. We might not even need the 1,200 aircraft NATO employed against Kosovo. However, we would require a much larger force than the roughly 300 aircraft we used in Afghanistan because of (1) the size of the Iraqi armed forces, (2) the greater active and passive air defenses that Iraq employs compared to Afghanistan, (3) the need for U.S. aircraft to perform a much wider range of missions than was the case in Afghanistan (where the Taliban had so little ability to fight back and so rudimentary a military structure), and (4) the need to have far more U.S. aircraft available to deal promptly with Iraqi counterattacks against the opposition ground forces. In short, such an air campaign would probably necessitate anywhere from 700 to 1,200 aircraft. As was the case in the Gulf War, Afghanistan, and Kosovo, such a massive air presence would require bases in the region. We simply do not have enough aircraft carriers, tanker aircraft, and strategic bombers to be able to generate that much air power from the sea or distant bases outside the region. In fact to handle that many aircraft, we would probably need bases in Saudi Arabia, Kuwait, Qatar, Bahrain, Oman, and Turkey.

The Iraqi opposition forces would also need support and a sanctuary from which to operate. At the very least, the Afghan Approach would demand Turkish participation because only through Turkey can the United States realistically support opposition forces in Kurdistan. The INC or any other expatriate group would require a safe haven in Kuwait, Saudi Arabia, Jordan, or conceivably Syria in which to recruit, train, arm, resupply, rest, regroup, and heal, and to which to retreat if necessary. As for the Shi'ah, the most obvious candidate to play such a role would be Iran, but as long as the hard-line clerics continue to hold the reins of power in Tehran, it seems unlikely that Washington would be interested in mounting a major military operation from Iranian soil. After all, how could the United States provide such opposition groups with advanced antitank or antiaircraft weapons, knowing that many would probably find their way into the hands of the Revolutionary Guards—if not Hizballah or Hamas?

Regional allies would be critical for a number of other reasons, not least of them oil. If the United States attacked Iraq, Saddam would probably shut off Iraq's oil exports to put pressure on both his trading/smuggling partners and the entire oil-dependent world to urge the United States to stop. In response, we could release the Strategic Petroleum Reserve, which could compensate for the loss of Iraqi oil for about seven months. However, the likelihood that such a campaign would be long and uncertain would open us up to considerable problems if our reserves ran out before Saddam could be toppled. Even then, since there would be no U.S. ground forces to occupy the Iraqi oil fields at the start of a war, we would have little ability to prevent Saddam's loyalists from destroying those oil fields as a final act of vengeance, just as they destroyed Kuwait's in 1991. Since most of the excess oil production capacity in the world is located in Saudi Arabia, Kuwait, and the UAE, we would need our friends in the Gulf region to be willing to increase production to compensate for the loss of Iraqi oil for the duration of the campaign and however long afterward it would take to bring Iraq's oil back online.

Our Regional Allies Oppose the Idea
Thus, the Afghan Approach would depend completely on America's regional allies. This would be a serious obstacle because none of our allies in

the Middle East—let alone in Europe or Asia—are inclined to support employment of the Afghan Approach against Iraq. The catch-22 of the Afghan Approach is that we would need these allies (particularly the regional allies) to make this strategy work, but it is the one strategy they have made clear they would not support.

None of our allies has much enthusiasm for the external Iraqi opposition groups. In the region, most of these groups are considered laughable, and the idea that the United States wants them to be the main ground component in a campaign to oust Saddam Hussein would be viewed by many as confirmation that Washington was not serious about doing so. That leaves the Kurds and the Shi'ah. The Iranians would no doubt leap at the opportunity to serve as a conduit to the Shi'ah groups because this would allow them to divert much (perhaps all) of our aid to themselves, and what little was passed on would simply increase their control over their unhappy proxies.

For their part, we should expect the Turks to be apoplectic if we propose using the Kurds as our principal vehicle for overthrowing Saddam's regime. To begin with, they too would probably consider a U.S. proposal to employ the Afghan Approach as a sign that we were not serious and turn us down. Even if we could overcome that obstacle, it is difficult to imagine how the United States could convince the Turks to support Kurdish operations against Iraq without Turkish forces in Iraq participating and keeping an eye on the Kurds to prevent them from trying to assert their independence. Try as we might to convince the Turks that the Kurds have no intention of declaring their independence from Iraq—let alone that this would not be terrible for Turkey if they did—Ankara has never been persuaded by our arguments. And without use of Turkish territory and airspace, we could not logistically support Kurdish operations against the Iraqi regime. So getting Turkish permission to support Kurdish operations against Iraq, if we could secure it at all, would be likely to come at the price of agreeing to Turkish occupation of Iraqi Kurdistan. This would send the Kurds into equivalent paroxysms and, if it were possible at all, would doubtless require American ground forces in Kurdistan to reassure the Kurds. Even if we were willing to take such steps (which would take us far from the no-American-ground-troops claims of the Afghan Approach), it is still doubtful that the Turks and Kurds would go for it.

Iraq's Arab neighbors are dead set against launching what they consider a protracted, uncertain war against Saddam. If that were all we could offer them, they would probably balk. Our regional allies fear that a new U.S.-led war against Saddam would trigger unrest among their populations. Officials and royal family members from these countries continue to stress that they believe that Saddam is a great enough long-term threat to them that they are willing to keep control of their own populations for some period of time to make overthrowing him possible, but they do not want to have to do so for one day longer than is absolutely necessary. All believe that they could fend off revolution or other serious internal problems for some time, but they don't know exactly how long and they don't really want to find out. In addition, all of the governments of the region know that the moment the United States unleashed a new war against Saddam, he would strike back any way he could—overtly and covertly, by economic, political, and military means—and that they would be his most likely targets. For these reasons, the moderate Arabs continue to indicate that they would be willing to pay the price of a full-scale U.S. invasion, but not that of the Afghan Approach.

Their worry is that the Afghan Approach would not work and that in the time it would take to fail, they would be faced with an increasingly unhappy populace and ever greater threats from Saddam. Some of the Gulf states fear that if this state of affairs were to go on for too long, they might face a full-blown revolution.[54] Still others worry that they would pay a high price and then, at the end of the day, would still have to live with Saddam when the Afghan Approach failed to deliver. None of this looks the least bit enticing to the moderate Arab states.

Iraqi Counteroffensives

If the United States were to launch a major military operation with the expressed purpose of toppling him, Saddam would fight back with everything he has. Saddam would not go without a fight, and the closer his doom approached, the more he would lash out. Employing the Afghan Approach would not allow us to deal effectively with Saddam's inevitable counterattacks.

This is particularly true because the Afghan Approach would take quite some time to succeed—or, more likely, to fail. The impact of air strikes cumulates slowly in terms of both physical and psychological damage. It took weeks of bombing during Desert Storm and Enduring Freedom to break poorly disciplined, apathetic enemy formations despite their vulnerability to these operations. Who knows how long it would take to break the disciplined, committed Republican Guard divisions, especially when they are defending better terrain and enjoy a better logistical situation than in 1991? Thus, even if the Afghan Approach actually worked as advertised, it would still take time—at least weeks and probably months—and its failure would take even longer. During that time, Saddam could cause a great deal of damage.

Even if it were more likely to be successful, the Afghan Approach would still essentially cede the initiative to Saddam. While we were sitting back and pounding his forces, engaged in a form of aerial attrition warfare, Saddam would be relatively free to act as he wanted. It is a cardinal rule of military operations that an attacker should never voluntarily give up the initiative to the defender. It is a course that often leads to defeat.

Under the Afghan Approach, Saddam would have a great deal of latitude to fight back. Despite the claims of air power enthusiasts, it is extremely difficult to stop enemy ground movement from the air for a sustained period of time. We saw this in Desert Storm and Allied Force, where the Iraqis and Serbians were only hindered, never actually *prevented,* from moving and directing their forces. Even in the ideal conditions of the Kuwaiti Theater, the Iraqis were not prevented from moving forces on a grand scale—shifting six divisions in the west and three in the south to create screens against the coalition advance. Nor did air power prevent them from extracting divisions from the Kuwaiti Theater or launching Scud attacks. Like the Germans in World War II, the Iraqis did basically everything they wanted to; it just wasn't as easy. NATO air power could not prevent the Serbs from reinforcing their units in Kosovo or conducting a massive ethnic cleansing operation there. We should expect Saddam to use his freedom of action to strike back as hard as he can.

One obvious way Saddam could counterattack (and undoubtedly would if he believed his grip on power were seriously threatened) would be to employ his residual WMD and ballistic missile arsenal against U.S. allies in the region to try to persuade them to halt the attack. As Chapter 5 described, Saddam has retained roughly twelve to thirty-six Scud-type missiles, probably with WMD warheads. He may also have several dozen shorter-range al-Samud missiles, which may also have WMD warheads. He has the capability to produce anthrax and other biological agents, as well as VX nerve gas and other chemical agents. We would have to be prepared for Saddam to use those weapons either to stave off defeat, or simply as an act of final vengeance if our operations were successful.

During the Gulf War, the United States had no luck trying to find Iraq's Scud launchers in western and southern Iraq, even using large numbers of aircraft and special forces teams. Although the U.S. "Scud-hunting" efforts were not entirely fruitless, they were far from perfect. During the first two weeks of the war, Iraq launched fifty-one Scuds against Israel and Saudi Arabia, and in the last two weeks of the war, it launched twenty-eight. U.S. efforts seem to have diminished Iraq's launches by almost 50 percent, but far too many were still being launched. In a future war with Iraq in which Saddam might arm his missiles with WMD, such an accomplishment might be woefully inadequate. It is true that U.S. surveillance and precision-strike capabilities have improved since then, but no one in the U.S. military has high confidence that we could do much better today than we did in 1991 if we were to limit ourselves to air and special forces.[55] It is also true that as far as we know, Saddam does not yet possess missile warheads that can properly disperse chemical or biological agents. However, the more ballistic missiles with WMD warheads he is able to launch, the greater the chance that he will do real damage with them. He might also choose to deliver WMD using other methods; Iraqi intelligence operatives conducting terrorist attacks would be the most effective means.

Allowing Saddam repeated tries to get a WMD attack right would be reckless and potentially fatal. A successful WMD attack against a regional city (or a U.S. city via terrorist methods) could conceivably kill thousands, tens of thousands, or even hundreds of thousands of people. Biological agents delivered against Saudi and Kuwait oil production facilities could force the shutdown of the oil fields for weeks while the agents were being neutralized if the poorly paid oil field workers were unwilling to risk their lives before the machinery had been thoroughly decontaminated. This could cause a large drop in Gulf oil production that could send oil prices (and with them inflation and unemployment) soaring until the facilities could be brought back online. If such a disruption lasted long enough, it could spark economic recessions, including in the United States. Given these threats alone, regional governments might be deterred from ever participating in an Afghan-style campaign.

There is also the problem of Israel. Saddam would pull out all of the stops to try to hit Israel as hard as possible to bring Jerusalem into the war, in the hope that this would cause America's Arab allies to pull out (or not participate in the first place). Unlike in 1991, Israel now has its own anti-ballistic missile defense system, the Arrow, which has done well in tests. In addition, the United States could bolster Israeli defenses with the latest version of the Patriot surface-to-air missile, which, though less capable than the Arrow, would add some redundancy to Israeli defenses. Nevertheless, according to senior U.S. and Israeli officials, Jerusalem has told Washington bluntly that should the United States attack Iraq, the only thing that would prevent Israel from retaliating against Iraq—and thus creating a new Arab-Israeli war—would be the presence of large numbers of U.S. ground forces (basically a division) deployed in western Iraq to try to prevent Iraqi Scud launches. Israel's reaction to Iraqi attacks would likely be determined principally by the number of casualties the attack caused and how nervous the Israelis felt about signaling any weakness to the Palestinians. However, the United States would be in a much better position to convince Israel not to retaliate against Iraq if there were large U.S. ground forces driving on Baghdad and Saddam's end were just a few days away. It would be much harder if we were simply hitting Iraq from the air and relying on Iraqi opposition forces, which no one in the region believes can succeed against the regime. Under those circumstances, any Israeli government would likely see a need to take matters into its own hands to "help" the U.S. air campaign. We do not know how the Arabs would react to such a development. They certainly would not want to find themselves in such a situation, which is another reason it would be difficult to convince them to support the Afghan Approach.

Saddam has been reluctant to arm and employ international terrorist groups, in large part for fear that they cannot be controlled and that once they are abroad with Iraqi funds, training, and weaponry, any attack they conduct could become a pretext for the United States to come after his regime. That said, if the United States were to begin a massive military operation to topple his regime (even one that featured the Iraqi opposition as one of its main components), all bets would be off. Saddam would have nothing to lose and, given his past behavior, would likely try to hurt the United States and our allies in every way he could and convince us to halt the campaign. This could include giving WMD to terrorist groups, especially if his regime did begin to look doomed.

Although this would be a problem for the United States under any regime change scenario, it would be especially difficult if we employed the Afghan Approach. The long time that it would probably take for the Afghan Approach to have any chance of succeeding (and the likelihood that Saddam would know if it were actually working) would give him the ability to plan such operations and then conduct them according to his own schedule. He could attempt to tailor terrorist operations to specific goals, such as inflicting casualties on the United States or sowing dissension among already fractious allies. In particular, we should expect Saddam to do whatever he could to stoke the violence between Palestinians and Israelis in the hope that if he could coax Israel into a bloody overreaction, it would make it difficult if not impossible for the GCC states to continue to support a U.S. air campaign against him. The more time and freedom of action we gave Saddam, the more effective and destructive his terrorist operations would likely be.

The moment we began an Afghan-style air campaign, Saddam would have every incentive to crush the Kurds. The Kurds themselves recognize this and have repeatedly announced their opposition to the scheme for that reason. Given how important the Kurds would be to the Afghan Approach, this opposition is an important hurdle.[56] Our ability to defend Kurdistan without deploying large numbers of ground forces there is extremely limited. For that reason, we have in the past deterred Saddam by threatening a massive air campaign against targets in southern and central Iraq should he attack the Kurds. So far, this has worked, but if we were to start a massive air campaign anyway, he would have lost that disincentive and would have every reason to drive into Kurdistan to eliminate the threat on his northern flank. With air power alone, and especially if those aircraft were operating from bases as far away as even Incirlik in Turkey, the U.S. military is not sanguine about its ability to defend Iraqi Kurdistan. The terrain there is largely forested mountains, and the ability of U.S. air power to stop Iraqi ethnic cleansing operations there could turn out to be as ineffective as NATO's efforts to prevent Serbian ethnic cleansing in Kosovo in 1999. There are now 4.5 million Iraqi Kurds whose safety is at risk. How could we start an attack on Iraq that could lead to the death of hundreds of thousands of Kurds and drive millions more out of their homes to try to find refuge in Turkey or Iran? Indeed, the expectation that an attack on Kurdistan would create a massive refugee crisis for Turkey would make Saddam more willing to mount such an attack, and Turkey even less willing to support this strategy.

We should expect Saddam to lash out at his neighbors in any other ways possible, in particular by trying to stir up popular unrest, even revolutions, as best he could. All of Iraq's neighbors are somewhat vulnerable to such agitation, and their vulnerability would grow the longer an American military campaign against Iraq dragged on. Although we should not be blasé about the prospects for any of the moderate Arabs, the state that we must be most concerned about is Jordan, which is dependent on exports of Iraqi oil and Iraqi imports of Jordanian goods. Jordan is also infested with Iraqi intelligence agents, and its Palestinian population is enamored of Saddam. If the United States embarks on a military campaign against Iraq, Baghdad might very well decide to try to overthrow King Abdallah as a way of forestalling or derailing the campaign. Baghdad could cut all trade and oil exports to Jordan and direct its agents in Amman to try to assassinate King Abdallah or encourage his Palestinian population to overthrow him. The Israeli newspaper *Ha'aretz* reported that in June 2002, a high-level "war game" was conducted in Israel in which a U.S. war against Iraq provoked just such a response from Baghdad, and the game assumed that the Iraqi-inspired rebellion was successful—thus placing the United States and Israel in tenuous positions.[57] Before we embark on a war against Saddam, we need to make sure that the regime change it causes is not the fall of the Hashimites in Amman, rather than that of the Ba'thists in Baghdad.

A Difficult "Day After"

If we were to employ the Afghan Approach, our ability to determine who succeeded Saddam would be low, even if this approach succeeded in ousting him. Most of the Iraqi opposition groups do not speak for many people inside Iraq. Only the Kurdish militias can claim to speak for the Kurdish segment of the population. Even the Shi'ite groups in the south represent only a small segment of the Shi'ah—at most the 10 to 15 percent of Iraqi Shi'ah who favor the establishment of an Islamic regime in Iraq. Some of the groupings of Sunni exiles, particularly those organized around former military officers and regime officials, have important connections, but they do not have large constituencies. It is unclear who, if anyone, the INC speaks for inside Iraq, given how poorly it has fared in recruiting for its cause. As Iraq expert Andrew Parasiliti once remarked, "Support for the INC runs deeper along the Potomac than it does along the Tigris."[58] Consequently, without U.S. troops on the ground and relying only on nonrepresentative opposition groups, it would be difficult for the United States to determine the composition of a new Iraqi government. If we are resolved to dictate the shape of a future Iraqi regime, this is not the best way to do so.

Even if the United States does opt to employ the Afghan Approach, we defy the odds, and the strategy succeeds, we aren't likely to save much. As we have found in Afghanistan, the United States will not be able to simply pull down the government and walk away. Indeed, we are probably doing too much of that in Afghanistan. Regardless, we cannot afford to do so in Iraq. Iraq is too important a country in too fragile and important a part of the world to allow it to fall into chaos. (See Chapter 12 for a discussion of the necessity of and requirements for rebuilding Iraq.) What's more, under any regime change scenario, it is the reconstruction of Iraq that is likely to be the longest, most difficult, and most costly aspect of the operation. Imagine how much more difficult the rebuilding would be if we were to grant Saddam several (perhaps many) months to do mischief while we attempted to bomb his regime out of existence. As in Afghanistan, we would be likely to find ourselves deploying some kind of ground presence to help root out Iraq's WMD programs, restore order, and prevent Iraq's predatory neighbors from setting up buffer zones or conducting their own ethnic cleansing operations inside Iraq. We would still have to help build a new Iraqi government out of the chaos that would follow Saddam, a process that could be made far more difficult if we used opposition groups to overthrow him because they would want to create a new government that favored their own aspirations. The more reliant we were on them for the overthrow and the smaller our own ground presence, the harder it would be to prevent their doing so—or simply starting divisive battles in an effort to do so. Finally, the economic costs of rebuilding Iraq are going to remain the same regardless of how Saddam falls. As long as we are responsible for bringing about his downfall, we will also be responsible for paying those bills because we simply cannot allow a post-Saddam Iraq to fail. In short, we would actually save very little by trying to overthrow Saddam without large ground forces, while greatly increasing the odds of failure.

The Suffering Iraqi People

Unfortunately, too often in U.S. political discourse, the well-being of the Iraqi populace has been like the bark of the dog in the Sherlock Holmes story "Silver Blaze"—noteworthy only by its absence. For the Iraqi people, the Afghan Approach would be a nightmare. It would be another terrifying war with bombs falling on their country and great uncertainty as to what the Americans hoped to achieve by it. If they heard that no U.S. troops were on the way but the Iraqi opposition was, they would probably see this as further proof that Washington wanted to keep Saddam in power.

Of all the different groups that would be affected, the Iraqi people might suffer most. Saddam would know that we were looking to undermine his control of Iraq and so would ruthlessly suppress every hint of dissension. There would be large-scale purges of the officer corps, the Ba'th Party, the civil service, and other institutions, and the regime's iron fist would clamp down on the Iraqi people even more tightly than usual.

Saddam might go so far as to halt or cut food rations to his people. He could conveniently blame it on the U.S. air campaign or the machinations of the opposition and would count on the perfidy and cynicism of the U.N. bureaucracy and his advocates abroad to give these claims enough legitimacy to make them stick. He would hide his military forces among the civilian population, both to protect them and to entice the United States into striking civilian targets that would furnish him with innocent victims. He would exploit the international media to the hilt with photographs of Iraqis dying of starvation, disease, and U.S. bombs. Regardless of whether this would have any impact on the political cohesion of the coalition the United States would have to forge to fight the war (and this might simply consist of Turkey and the GCC states), Saddam would again inflict widespread misery on the Iraqi population for as long as the air campaign lasted.

WHY NOT TRY THE AFGHAN APPROACH AND INVADE ONLY IF IT DOESN'T WORK?

The more pragmatic advocates of the Afghan Approach recognize that it does not have a high likelihood of success and certainly does not come close to the level of certainty of a full-scale invasion. However, because they believe that it would be preferable for the United States to overthrow Saddam without using ground troops if at all possible, they argue for trying the Afghan Approach and then if, after a certain amount of time, it is not working, launching a full-scale invasion. They recognize that this would be a war that the United States could not afford to lose, so they concede that the United States must be willing to mount a full-scale invasion if that is what is necessary, but they would like to see if it couldn't be done with air power alone.

Under most circumstances, this might be a reasonable course of action. Unfortunately, in the case of Iraq, it does not make sense for many of the reasons described above. Of greatest importance, the allies we would require would object if we proposed such an approach. To reiterate: the GCC states are nervous about how their populations would react, they know that this would become a greater problem the longer a U.S. military campaign against Iraq went on, and for that reason they would not want it to go on any longer than absolutely necessary. If we went to them and said that we wanted to try an air campaign and mount an invasion only if that didn't succeed, the evidence indicates that they would tell us to forget it and come back when we were ready to go with the invasion from the start. They are rightfully concerned that they couldn't afford to grant us several months to try bombing before launching an invasion. They know that Saddam would fight back however he possibly could and that they would bear the brunt of it. For that reason, they want us to go on the offensive immediately, seize the initiative, use all of our capabilities to prevent Baghdad from lashing out, and bring the whole campaign to a speedy close. Meanwhile, the Israelis would demand that we put a division in western Iraq to preclude Scud launches against Israel. The Kurds too would want to know what we planned to do to protect them while we were trying out theories of air power on Saddam. If we decided to deploy a division in western Iraq and another in Kurdistan, it would make no sense to hold up the rest of the U.S. ground forces; once we had 40,000 ground troops inside Iraq, it would be foolish to restrain the other 150,000 when unleashing them would essentially guarantee a certain, swift victory.

In the end, this would be no way to fight a war. Wars are inherently unpredictable. Even the most confidently predicted victories can go badly awry when the shooting starts. Fighting Iraq in this fashion would mean starting the battle with one hand tied behind our back. Although beforehand it might seem easy to shift over to an invasion if, after several months of bombing, Saddam were still firmly in place, when the battle was actually joined it might not be so easy. We simply do not know what would happen; any number of events could intervene to preclude the invasion if we tried to hold it off until later. As Helmuth von Moltke warned, "No plan survives contact with the enemy." History is littered with the corpses of countries that thought they could win a war with only a partial effort. There are times when it is necessary to fight this way, but an effort to overthrow the regime in Iraq would not be one of them. Why court disaster to secure possible marginal savings when employing all of the forces at our disposal would cost little extra, secure considerable political and strategic benefit, and bring us as close to certain victory as we are likely to come?

A NONSENSICAL STRATEGY

The United States employed the strategy it did in Kosovo and Afghanistan because of the peculiar circumstances of those conflicts. In both cases, neither the Serbs nor the Taliban had any real ability to strike back. Neither had long-range weapons or weapons of mass destruction with which to retaliate against the United States or its allies. As a result, the United States could afford to keep them at arm's length and take the extra time needed to wear down their forces with air power and a limited contribution from opposition ground forces. In Kosovo, this was not just possible but necessary, because the Serbian army possessed considerable firepower that could have butchered the lightly armed KLA formations if the KLA had been forced to fight more pitched battles like the one at Mount Pastrik.

By the same token, in both Kosovo and Afghanistan, a ground invasion ran serious risks. In Kosovo, the United States was concerned that an invasion would tear NATO apart, and the preservation of alliance unity was vital. That said, by the end of the war, Washington was beginning to talk much more openly about the need for a ground invasion because the air campaign was having so little effect on the Serbian army. In Afghanistan, the United States was afraid that employing large numbers of ground troops would actually make the fighting much worse because it would trigger the traditional Afghan hatred of foreigners and so cause the Afghan people to rally around the Taliban. Although that could not have stopped a ground invasion, Washington feared that it could lead to a long, debilitating guerrilla war against U.S. forces afterward, just as it had for the Russians (and the British and Persians before them). Thus, a ground invasion was seen as being the worst course of action in Afghanistan.

In Iraq, all of these things would be reversed. Unlike the Serbs and the Taliban, Saddam can strike back hard at us and our allies in the region. Consequently, the United States cannot afford to try to beat Saddam from long range with only part of its forces. If we decide to topple him overtly, using U.S. military forces, we need to hit him as hard as we can and move as fast as we can to take down his regime before he can inflict significant damage. Unlike in Kosovo, the regional allies (and probably the extraregional ones too) don't fear an invasion—they are demanding it. Indeed, we are highly unlikely to secure their cooperation unless we are willing to mount a full-scale invasion that will go furthest to ensuring that Saddam's regime is gone as quickly as possible, while having done the least possible damage to them. Finally, unlike in Afghanistan, few experts fear that the

This is especially true for Iraq. Trying to wage a covert campaign against Saddam to infiltrate his security networks and convince other Iraqis to move against him is playing his game on his turf. If there is one arena where Saddam Hussein can stand toe-to-toe with the United States, it is in the world of Iraqi politics and intelligence operations. It is the one realm where he has most, if not all, of the advantages. If we are determined to remove Saddam Hussein, we should fight him where we have all of the advantages.

This is not to suggest that there is no role for covert action in any U.S. regime change policy. Quite the opposite. Although we have come to a point where we cannot rely on covert action alone, that should not rule out its use as a complement to a larger campaign encompassing economic and particularly military operations. In fact, should the United States wage war to bring down Saddam's regime, it will need all of the assets and capabilities of the CIA—in terms of intelligence gathering, sabotage, information warfare, secure communications, and liaison work. The CIA can help prepare the battlefield, ease U.S. military operations, disrupt Iraq's defensive efforts, and lay the foundation for a new government in Iraq. All of these missions will be vital to a future policy of regime change. But we should not look to the Agency to do the job alone.

There was a time when pursuing a strategy of covert action to try to spark a coup against Saddam Hussein made sense. When containment was strong and the risk that Saddam would be able to restart his WMD programs and acquire a nuclear weapon was distant, an aggressive covert action campaign to try to topple him without undermining containment or requiring more resources than America was willing to devote was entirely appropriate. Unfortunately, that time is past. Today, a covert action program alone would be tantamount to admitting that the United States is unwilling to make the sacrifices necessary to remove Saddam's regime before it acquires the weaponry to threaten the region and the world. If that is the case, we should opt for deterrence and save ourselves and our allies the bother.

Iraqi people would rise up against an American invasion and rally around Saddam's regime. Although it is unclear how many would fight for Saddam, the expectation is that the vast majority of Iraqis would probably sit on the fence and might even welcome an American invasion that would rid them of Saddam. (Strangely, it is the very people who most strongly support the Afghan Approach who are also the firmest believers that the Iraqis would welcome their liberation with open arms. If this is the case, why are they so afraid to use ground troops?)

Mounting a large U.S. ground effort would not be any more politically costly than using air power alone; indeed, it would be less so, given that the allies all oppose a regime change campaign without large numbers of ground troops. It might be somewhat more costly in financial terms, but since the reconstruction of Iraq is expected to dwarf the costs of any military campaign and we would have to pay for that regardless of how we handled the overthrow, these costs too are mostly irrelevant. We would certainly risk more American ground casualties, but as the next chapter explains, it is unlikely that their numbers would be catastrophic. On the other hand, the speed and decisiveness of an invasion over a pure air strategy offer the enormous advantages of minimizing civilian casualties among both Iraqis and our regional allies and providing the closest thing to certainty that Saddam's regime will be ousted quickly and definitively.

It is for all of these reasons that the U.S. military so staunchly opposes the Afghan Approach and believes that a full-scale invasion is the only realistic course of action if the United States is serious about regime change in Iraq. This is why the newspapers are full of stories about how the uniformed military leadership is fighting with the civilian advocates of the Afghan Approach in the Office of the Secretary of Defense.[59] One retired four-star general told me, "If you want me to get rid of Saddam, let me use the forces I need and I will get rid of him for you with no problem—but why are you going to tell me that I can only use some of my forces and not others?" A serving Marine colonel put it differently: "The way to win a war is to send a man to do a boy's job." Still another retired three-star general summed it up by saying, "No general tries to win a war 'just barely.' " It is also worth pointing out that both the Kurds and the main Shi'ite militia in southern Iraq oppose employment of the Afghan Approach as being unrealistic and leaving them open to Saddam's reprisals.[60]

This is not a war we should try to win "just barely." There is no reason to do so, and trying would be dangerous. We would get no prize for using the bare minimum of forces in ousting Saddam Hussein. If the circum-

stances were different—if we were desperate to oust Saddam and an invasion was impossible for some reason—it might be reasonable to try the
Afghan Approach simply because it would be better than doing nothing.
But we are not in such a situation. Instead, we would be seeking out this
war on our own terms—a war that we should and must win quickly and decisively. We cannot afford to fail, nor will our allies support a course of action that would run the risk of failure. Should the United States launch a
new war against Iraq to topple Saddam's government, it would be the most
important foreign policy initiative of the United States for the next decade
if not longer. That being the case, we should employ all of the capabilities
at our disposal to ensure that we prevail as quickly and painlessly as possible, and not try to win it "on the cheap." This is not the kind of operation in
which we should be trying to cut corners.

ELEVEN

The Case for an Invasion

I t is the inadequacy of all the other options toward Iraq that leads us to the last resort of a full-scale invasion. Containment is eroding, and it is no longer realistic to believe that it can be revived in a meaningful sense and sustained over time to prevent Saddam Hussein from acquiring nuclear weapons. Relying on pure deterrence to keep Saddam at bay once he has acquired a nuclear arsenal is terrifyingly dangerous. It is likely to find us confronting a Hobson's choice of either allowing Saddam to make himself the hegemon of the Gulf region (and in effect or actuality controlling global oil supplies) or else fighting a war with him that could escalate to nuclear warfare. Covert action would be unlikely to succeed and even less likely to beat the ticking clock of Iraq's nuclear program. The Afghan Approach would be only modestly more likely to succeed than covert action and probably would create more problems than it solved—if it were to solve any at all.

Unfortunately, the only prudent and realistic course of action left to the United States is to mount a full-scale invasion of Iraq to smash the Iraqi armed forces, depose Saddam's regime, and rid the country of weapons of mass destruction. Every time I say or write this, I find myself wondering whether it is truly necessary. It usually sets me off rehearsing in my mind all of the arguments for and against all of the other options in one last effort to devise some alternative to the costs of an invasion. Having spent much of my life since the Gulf War trying to find a way out of this conundrum, I cannot.

Every time I give a talk on our options toward Iraq to a group of people, someone always says, "There has to be another way. There has to be some middle option." There isn't. Sometimes history presents us with unpleasant choices. On those occasions, the worst thing we can do is to avoid making a choice in the hope that if we just think hard enough an unforeseen solution will materialize that will relieve us of the need to make the hard choice. In the case of Iraq, we need to recognize that we have run out of alternatives and our options truly have come down to a dangerous deterrence or a potentially costly invasion.

THE ADVANTAGES OF AN INVASION

The greatest advantage of an invasion is the near certainty of its outcome. Although nothing in war is truly certain, if the United States were to launch a full-scale war against Iraq, we can have high confidence in victory. Put differently, we can be as confident of victory as it is possible or prudent to be in war. The costs of that victory are unclear, but even the worst-case estimates are not catastrophic. These conclusions are also widely held within the U.S. military. From generals to privates, there is certitude that if they are allowed to fight a war with Iraq using all of their (conventional) capabilities, they will prevail, and will do so at a cost acceptable to the American people. At the end of an invasion, Saddam Hussein's regime would be destroyed, the United Nations would be able to cleanse the country thoroughly of his weapons of mass destruction programs (and would have several hundred thousand U.S. servicemen to help it in this effort), and the current threat to the region from Iraq would be eliminated. We would not have to worry about Saddam striking any of our regional allies, destroying or seizing their oil fields, supporting terrorism, or undermining the Arab-Israeli peace process and other initiatives to build a better Middle East.

At a more tactical level, an invasion would allow the United States to dictate the course of the war, limiting Saddam's ability to strike back and promising the quickest and probably least bloody route to his regime's demise. It would assure the moderate Arab states that we were serious about removing him and that we would do so as promptly as possible, thus minimizing the extent of the internal disruptions they would have to endure. It would allow us to reassure the Israelis and our other regional allies that we would be able to reduce Iraq's ability to launch WMD-armed missiles against them to the barest minimum. It is the regime change approach that is most likely to win the ready support of those among the Iraqi armed forces and populace who are looking to overthrow Saddam.

Although my principal reason for embracing an invasion is essentially that it is the only solution to the dilemma we face, there are actually more positive motives for supporting this course of action. The strategic benefits alone could justify the operation. Being rid of Saddam Hussein would be an enormous boon to U.S. foreign policy. We truly would be free to pursue other items on our foreign policy agenda. Every time there was a crisis elsewhere in the world, we would not have to think immediately of how Saddam might try to exploit it. Our efforts within the U.N. Security Council would not have to revolve around the questions of sanctions and inspections. And unlike the case with deterrence, we would not have to maintain combat-ready forces on Iraq's borders, work assiduously to maintain a coalition of states willing to stand up to Iraqi aggression, and spend resources and effort working to convince Saddam that we really would defend Kuwait with our own nuclear arsenal.

Invading Iraq would ultimately allow us to reduce our presence in the Gulf region and, in particular, pull our troops out of Saudi Arabia, where they don't want to be and the Saudi people don't want them. Similarly, we could end the two no-fly zones and the Maritime Interception Force, which patrols the Gulf for Iraqi smugglers. Our military personnel dislike the rigid regulations and inhospitable accommodations of the Kingdom, and our military presence there helps undermine the Saudi government's popularity. If we did not have to contain or deter Saddam (and instead had a friendly government in Baghdad) there would be no need for U.S. forces in Saudi Arabia. In general, we could significantly decrease the size of our forces in the region, the vast majority of which are there to deal with an Iraq contingency. Chances are we would retain a residual naval and air presence in Bahrain and Qatar, which are much less problematic because the people generally welcome U.S. forces (seeing them as a bulwark against threats from Iran or Saudi Arabia) and the facilities are more agreeable.

Removing Saddam from power would sever the "linkage" between the Iraq issue and the Arab-Israeli conflict. The rejectionists of the region could not play one issue off against the other, nor could governments or groups unhappy with developments between Israel and the Arabs vent their feelings against America's Iraq policy. Although an invasion might increase anti-American sentiments in the Arab world in the short term, over the long term it would remove an important source of anti-Americanism (the confrontation with Saddam) and potentially turn it into something positive, if the United States were to build a strong, prosperous, and inclusive new Iraqi state.

Indeed, this would be the final advantage of an invasion: it would offer the opportunity to build a new Iraq. Imagine how different the Middle East and the world would be if a new Iraqi state were stable, prosperous, and a force for progress in the region, not a source of violence and instability. Imagine if we could rebuild Iraq as a model of what a modern Arab state could be, showing the frustrated and disenfranchised of the Arab world what they should be trying to fashion. Imagine if there were a concrete symbol demonstrating that America seeks to help the Arab world rather than repress it. Invading Iraq might not just be our least bad alternative, it potentially could be our best course of action. If we are willing to accept the challenge and pay the price, we could end up creating a much better future for ourselves and all of the peoples of the Middle East.

THE MILITARY REQUIREMENTS

The military requirements of an invasion of Iraq would be considerable but not onerous. In terms of ground troops (Army and Marines), the United States should be prepared to commit four to six divisions plus additional supporting units, such as armored cavalry regiments (ACRs), independent aviation (helicopter) brigades, and possibly additional infantry brigades.[1] As for air forces, an invasion would probably necessitate 700 to 1,000 aircraft from the Air Force, Navy, and Marines. The more ground forces we bring, the fewer aircraft would be necessary.

Altogether, this force would probably number anywhere from 200,000 to 300,000 soldiers, sailors, and airmen. It would probably be closer to 300,000 (and might even exceed that number). During the Persian Gulf War, the 14 divisions and 1,700 aircraft the U.S.-led coalition mustered amounted to more than 700,000 personnel. A force with 30 to 50 percent of the combat forces of the Desert Storm contingent should be expected to amount to at least a similar proportion of its personnel commitment. Moreover, this time around we might need more troops for certain missions than was the case in 1991 because of the different objectives. For example, we would require tens of thousands of civil affairs personnel to immediately begin restoring basic services to the Iraqi people as our combat forces begin liberating Iraqi territory.[2]

In sizing the force, we should err on the side of deploying more rather than less. A force of four to six divisions along with a couple of ACRs and extra aviation brigades should have little difficulty overrunning the Iraqi armed forces and conquering the country, but it never hurts to be certain, and in this situation we need to be certain.

We would also want ground forces of this size to be able to handle a wide range of missions. The invasion would probably consist of a main advance on Baghdad and possibly one or more secondary thrusts—as diversions to support the main thrust, to secure secondary objectives, and/or to smash large Iraqi troop concentrations elsewhere in the country. Each of these thrusts should be built around one or more U.S. heavy divisions. (If we could get the British to commit an armored division as they did in 1991, it could also serve in such a role.) The main thrust should be built around two to four heavy divisions along with accompanying ACRs and other units. The main thrust in particular would need to have the power to be able to smash any Iraqi resistance in its way, mask heavily defended cities, and keep driving on Baghdad. So it would have to be strong enough to be able to overcome any resistance quickly and big enough to afford to detach subelements to mask cities, protect its logistical lines, and exploit any unforeseen opportunities for maneuver that present themselves along the way. Ideally, we would also deploy a light or air mobile division to western Iraq to try to prevent Saddam from launching Scuds at Israel and to pressure him from the west. We would probably also want a light division in Kurdistan to defend the Kurds, put pressure on Saddam from the north—and keep an eye on whatever Turkish forces Ankara inevitably would commit to the operation.

An invasion force would require substantial numbers of infantrymen to handle combat in Iraq's cities, which might necessitate deploying additional infantry formations if Central Command felt that there wasn't enough infantry in the heavy divisions themselves. Armor can help with certain missions in cities, but urban warfare is still very much an infantryman's job. Although the invasion force would want to bypass as many cities as possible, in some cases that would be impossible—the terrain might not permit us to bypass a city or town. We might feel it necessary to take and hold some large towns or cities to free up supply routes or to exert control if civil order began to break down. Moreover, at the end of it all, we would likely find Saddam barricaded in Baghdad with the Special Republican Guard and a half-dozen or more regular army and Republican Guard divisions dug in around him. If we chose to go in and dig him out, we would want high-quality infantry formations for the job.

Finally, we might want additional forces available for other missions. The invasion might include one or more brigades to quickly seize Iraq's largest oil fields. Additional units might be required to seize key movement choke points ahead of the armored thrusts. Other forces might be included to assault key WMD facilities, to the extent that we know where they are. Still other units could be tasked to try to prevent Saddam and his cronies from fleeing Baghdad or to trap them if they try to flee to his hometown of Tikrit or another bolt-hole. There are a lot of potential missions for U.S. forces, and because of the importance of winning fast and big, having enough forces available to conduct those missions would be the smart course of action.

Could We Do It with Less?
Could the United States mount such an operation with fewer than 200,000 men? Probably. We might be able to do it with only two to three divisions and accompanying air and ground forces, keeping the numbers down to 80,000 to 100,000 troops. But why would we want to?

Politically, once Washington is committed to sending more than about 10,000 to 20,000 troops, the additional forces become of diminishing cost. No one who opposes the invasion is going to oppose it any less if we use only 75,000 troops rather than 300,000 troops. In fact, to the extent that the larger force would make the victory swifter and less bloody, other nations and groups would probably be less unhappy. Certainly our allies in the Middle East would prefer a larger force because it would ensure them of both the certainty and speed of Saddam's demise.

There would be some economic savings from going with a smaller force. Likewise, a larger force would require a larger reserve call-up to support them. However, the additional economic costs would not be scaled entirely to the size of the invasion force. Much of the economic cost will be absorbed in creating an infrastructure for the invasion and paying for the forces needed to occupy and rebuild Iraq afterward. These two are likely to be roughly the same regardless of the size of the force. Many of the reservists would be needed for intelligence, communications, medical support, clerical work, combat engineering, air traffic control, base security, and other functions, the numbers of whom are roughly constant for any sizable overseas operation. For instance, the United States called up roughly 85,000 reservists to support the war on terrorism and Operation Enduring Freedom (with about 20,000 troops and 300 aircraft participating), compared to 245,000 reservists called up to support the much larger force employed during Desert Storm (540,000 U.S. troops and 1,500 aircraft).[3]

These additional costs would be more than outweighed by the potential risks of trying to conquer Iraq with a smaller force. The keys to a successful invasion would be speed, momentum, and initiative. The more U.S. forces could move fast, maintain momentum, and retain the initiative, the more certain the likelihood of victory, the sooner the campaign would be over, and the fewer the casualties that we or the Iraqi people would suffer. One of the great dangers of this campaign is that we would not bring enough force and then would find ourselves bogged down by unforeseen developments. For example, with a smaller contingent, we would run the risk of not having enough force to mask a city and move on. Instead, Central Command would have to stop the advance while it cleared the city. We might not have enough forces to envelop, bypass, or bound over strong Iraqi defensive positions, which could cost time and casualties to assault. We might not have enough forces to aggressively seek out and suppress Iraqi artillery and multiple-rocket launchers that Iraq would use to fire chemical and possibly biological weapons at our troops. In ground warfare, being small doesn't make you quick and nimble, it makes you tentative.

This is the paradox of an invasion: the bigger the ground force we bring, the faster we can move, the lower the casualties we and the Iraqi people are likely to sustain, and the less the risk to Iraq's neighbors who will have to support this operation. The smaller the force we employ, the slower we are likely to move, the greater the risk of casualties to U.S. forces and Iraqi civilians, and the greater the threat to our allies in the region. Moreover, the slower the advance, the more time the Iraqis will have to shift their forces, build new defenses, and devise traps and counterattacks for our troops. The longer the war goes on and the more cities the United States actually has to fight through, the more Iraqi civilians will undoubtedly die both in the fighting and at the hands of Iraqi regime forces attempting to maintain order. The longer the war goes on (and the higher the toll of Iraqi civilian casualties mounts), the more unhappy the populations of Iraq's neighbors are likely to grow and the more time there will be for Saddam to lash out at our allies in the region.

In 1990, during the Persian Gulf War, U.S. Central Command was initially asked to devise a ground offensive to liberate Kuwait using only the forces that had been deployed to the Gulf for Operation Desert Shield: two American heavy divisions, two American light divisions, a British armored brigade, a Marine brigade, and additional forces. Against a force of (at that time) roughly thirty Iraqi divisions, the coalition did not have the strength to execute the wide outflanking maneuver that eventually won the war, and instead the CENTCOM plan called for a thrust into the heart of the Iraqi defenses. Because this was what Iraq was expecting, it was the strategy that risked the greatest U.S. casualties. In response, General Brent Scowcroft, General Colin Powell, and Secretary of Defense Dick Cheney decided to deploy an additional ground corps with three more heavy divisions while building up the Marine force to two divisions, to give CENTCOM the force to fight more creatively and win faster.[4] The result was one of the most decisive victories of modern history.

The Air Campaign

Any invasion of Iraq should include a powerful air component. However, the importance of speed to the operation is also why an invasion probably should not be preceded by a lengthy air campaign. We don't need it. Although we tend to marvel at the new power of American air forces (and there is no question that they are in a league by themselves), we often forget how powerful U.S. ground forces have become.[5] A U.S. armored or mechanized division is without question the most powerful ground force on the planet, and nothing else comes close—certainly no Iraqi formation. In other words, if the United States is willing to deploy three to five American heavy divisions, those units will be more than capable of dealing with the Iraqi armed forces *by themselves* and will not need a great deal of help from our magnificent air forces—although every little bit counts. Professor Daryl Press makes an important point that during the Persian Gulf War, the more forces the Iraqis committed to a ground battle, the more forces they lost, without any impact on the course of the battle or U.S. casualties.[6] Even the best of Iraq's ground forces were hopelessly outmatched by American ground forces in 1991, and since then we have gotten stronger and they have gotten weaker. Consequently, we do not require a long preparatory air campaign to weaken Iraq's ground forces before we attack—they are already plenty weak compared to our own forces.

A long preparatory air campaign would actually be counterproductive. It would basically turn into the Afghan Approach, with all of the same problems: Saddam would have time to devise counters and strike back, the Iraqi people and the Kurds would be at risk (unless we deployed forces into Kurdistan ahead of time), Saddam could launch ballistic missiles at Israel (unless we deployed forces to western Iraq ahead of time) and our other allies, it would create political problems for the moderate Arab states, and so on. In addition, it would mean delaying what the U.S. military hopes to be one of the keys to the campaign: destroying the will of the Iraqi armed forces. The Republican Guard and the Iraqi Army's heavy divisions have shown they have the discipline and commitment to withstand a massive U.S. air campaign, but they lack the combat skills to withstand a massive U.S. ground campaign. Thus, the sooner U.S. ground forces get into Iraq, the sooner they will be able to engage and destroy Iraq's ground forces. This is expected to have two results. First, it should help persuade the Iraqi people that we are serious about removing Saddam and so convince them not to support the regime (or even to actively support U.S. forces). Second, it should help crack Iraqi military morale, including, hopefully, the morale of the Republican Guard. The sooner U.S. heavy divisions started crushing Iraqi heavy divisions, the sooner we would break the morale of the Iraqi armed forces. And the faster we broke the morale of the Iraqi armed forces, the less fighting we would have to do.

The United States might still want to precede the ground offensive with a brief air campaign. For instance, we might want to first neutralize Iraq's air defenses so that our air forces would be better able to support the ground operations, strike strategic targets deeper in Iraq, hinder the movement of Iraqi forces, and aid in the suppression of Iraq's WMD force. One particularly important operation that might precede any ground invasion would be air strikes against Iraqi air bases to shut them down and destroy the aircraft that Baghdad might want to use to deliver weapons of mass destruction against either U.S. ground forces or our allies in the region. Likewise, U.S. military planners might believe it worthwhile to begin the invasion by striking at Iraq's command-and-control network to try to cripple it, even though we had little luck doing so in 1991. Still, there is no particular reason that any of these operations has to precede the ground assault; in many cases they could start simultaneously with it. The bottom line is simply that the importance of speed to this campaign argues against a lengthy preparatory bombardment. It is unlikely that the United States would lose even if the invasion moved slowly, but the slower we moved, the higher the costs we, our allies, and the Iraqi people would have to pay.

DURATION AND CASUALTIES

As the previous discussion should make clear, there are considerable uncertainties surrounding an invasion, although not really in terms of its outcome. However, the time and the cost in casualties could vary considerably
based on three critical factors: how hard the Iraqi armed forces fight,
whether they are willing and able to defend Iraq's cities, and how able they
are to employ their weapons of mass destruction against U.S. forces. We
don't know the answers to any of these questions, but those answers will
likely determine the costs of the operation.

How Hard Will the Iraqi Armed Forces Fight?

As usual, there are a lot of people making grand prognostications about
how likely Iraq's military personnel are to fight to defend Saddam's regime
from a U.S. invasion. The far Right insists that with a few exceptions, the
Iraqi military will throw down its weapons after the opening shots. This is
based mostly on the assumption that all of the Iraqi people hate Saddam
and will take the first opportunity to throw off his yoke. The far Left insists
that after twelve years of sanctions and confrontation the Iraqi people
blame the United States for all of their ills, hate us with a passion, and so
can be expected to fight an invasion tooth and nail. Because Iraqi society is
largely cut off from the outside world, either of these positions might be
correct, but that seems unlikely. The limited evidence we have suggests
something in between.

During the *intifadah* of 1991, considerable numbers of Iraqi soldiers
joined the rebels. Kurdish troops joined the Kurdish revolt in the north. In
the south, the Shi'ite revolt attracted mostly Shi'ite soldiers and officers,
but some Sunnis joined as well. However, the Special Republican Guard,
the Republican Guard, and a handful of regular army divisions remained
both loyal and cohesive enough after the debacle of Desert Storm to suppress both of the revolts. This suggests that while some Iraqis do want to
get rid of Saddam and will try to seize the opportunity to do so, others—the
Guards and some regular army formations—were willing to fight hard for
the regime in a situation where they had the chance to oust Saddam if they
had wanted to. Of course, to some extent, we should ascribe the loyalty of
the Guards in 1991 to the fact that they were mostly Sunni and believed
they were fighting to preserve Sunni domination of Iraq as much as Saddam's regime itself.

The Gulf War provides additional evidence. After thirty-nine days of air strikes and without adequate food and water, sixteen Iraqi regular army infantry divisions ran or surrendered en masse to coalition ground troops. Many other formations had little fight left in them and fled pell-mell from Kuwait the moment they received Saddam's order to retreat. Although the deprivations of the coalition air campaign were the key to this collapse, the fact that few of the mostly Shi'ite conscript infantrymen believed Kuwait to be worth fighting for also appears to have contributed to their demoralization. Once again, the Republican Guards and several of the heavy divisions of the regular army fought ferociously. Unfortunately, even the debriefs of captured Republican Guards provide little insight into their motivations. It is likely that they were no more deeply committed to retaining Kuwait than were their compatriots in the infantry—certainly not enough to die for it. Many of the Guards also had ties of tribal loyalty to the regime that demanded that they fight hard—to the death if necessary. However, at that point in time, the Guard was not as heavily dominated by members of the Sunni tribes closest to Saddam as it is today. Most of the Guards were simply plucked from other units at the end of the Iran-Iraq War to create the new, elite Republican Guard, and the principal reasons they fought and died at the 73 Easting, Madinah Ridge, and other insignificant battlefields of the Gulf War seems to have been largely out of esprit and professionalism.

The Republican Guards and the soldiers assigned to the better divisions of the regular army (effectively, its heavy divisions) consider themselves professional soldiers. They take tremendous pride in this distinction. They are the elite of the Iraqi armed forces, they expect to get the toughest assignments, and they expect to satisfy the demands of honor and their profession by doing their duty. They were willing to fight and die in 1991 because that's what professional soldiers do: when called upon to make a last-ditch stand and cover the army's retreat, they do their duty and fight to the end.[7]

Finally, there is the evidence of the Iran-Iraq War. In that conflict, not only did the elite units of Iraq's armed forces fight fiercely, but so too did many other Iraqi formations, at least when they were defending Iraqi soil. Iraqi society has a powerful streak of nationalism, and against Iran, Saddam was able to tap into this reservoir. Thus there are at least three sources of motivation that have prompted Iraqi troops to fight hard in the past and could prompt them to do so again in the future: nationalism, professionalism, and tribalism.

Some other factors may also bear on this question. Today, the Republican Guard, and especially the Special Republican Guard, are more heavily composed of loyal Sunni tribesmen than was the case in 1991. If anything, this suggests that they will be even more willing to fight and die for this regime than was the case when the Tawakalnah, Nebuchadnezzar, and Madinah Divisions made their stands in the desert in 1991. Likewise, at least some among these units may fear the retribution that could follow Saddam's demise. During the 1991 *intifadah,* many Ba'th Party officials were killed by the Shi'ah even after they had surrendered.[8]

Nevertheless, there is also substantial evidence suggesting that the Iraqi armed forces will not fight to the death for Saddam's regime. Visitors to Iraq, relatives of those still in the country, and defectors fleeing Iraq all consistently report that many in the army remain deeply disaffected. To some extent, these sources are suspect because they all have reasons for telling us what they want to believe and what they want us to believe. That said, enough such reports, from a wide enough range of sources that have remained consistent over time, suggests that there may be some truth to them. As Operation Desert Storm rolled on, the United States began to get more and more Iraqi defectors crossing the line and describing how unhappy the other troops in their divisions were. Over time, we started getting concurring evidence from other sources, and many in the U.S. intelligence community began to believe that Iraqi morale really was suffering. In early February 1991, I tried to write a piece suggesting that Iraqi morale might be starting to erode across the board, but General Colin Powell himself shot it down with the angry rebuke that we should never write intelligence based on defector reporting because defectors can never be trusted. General Powell wasn't entirely wrong, but he also wasn't entirely right. In fact, the defectors were accurately reporting the state of Iraqi morale, and we had enough corroborating evidence from other sources to at least speculate.

The same appears to be true in this case. Enough different sources are reporting that the Iraqi armed forces are disaffected and would welcome an invasion that it is reasonable to believe that this is at least partially true. It seems most likely that we will probably encounter mixed reactions. A portion of the Iraqi armed forces—the Special Republican Guard, most if not all of the Republican Guard, and a small part of the regular army—will probably fight very hard. This could amount to one third of Iraq's forces. Another portion, possibly of equal size, will likely either surrender or desert immediately, or, if that is impossible, find other ways to avoid fighting. The rest will probably offer some desultory resistance until they are convinced that the United States is determined to remove Saddam and they have satisfied the demands of honor.

To What Extent Will the Iraqis Be Able to Use WMD Against U.S. Forces?

Another important unknown is the extent to which Iraqi forces will be able to employ tactical weapons of mass destruction against American forces. During the war with Iran, Iraq used chemical warfare liberally and got fairly good at conducting large-scale offensive and defensive operations employing chemical munitions. Since then, Iraq has also developed biological agents that it might try to employ against U.S. forces. Given that once our tanks start rolling, Saddam knows that they won't stop till they get to Baghdad, he will have zero incentive to refrain from using WMD and every incentive to do so in the hope of causing so many U.S. casualties that either our forces are incapacitated or Washington throws in the towel.

Iraq employed artillery, multiple-rocket launchers, aerial bombs, and aircraft with spray tanks (like crop dusters) to deliver weapons of mass destruction against Iranian troops. Against a U.S. invasion of Iraq, we should expect the same. If the Iraqis were able to catch U.S. forces unprepared for a WMD attack, they could do quite a bit of damage, inflicting scores if not hundreds of casualties in a single attack. U.S. forces tend to operate in dispersed formations and American armored vehicles can button up quickly to deal with such an attack, making it unlikely that Iraq could cause thousands of casualties. But it would not be impossible. Even if they are unable to kill large numbers of U.S. soldiers with WMD, if Iraqi forces can present a credible enough threat to do so, it will force our troops to operate for long periods of time in their cumbersome protective gear, which will reduce their effectiveness, increase mistakes, and cause casualties indirectly.

However, there are many important mitigating factors in the case of Iraqi tactical WMD use. A heavy air presence over Iraq coupled with a determined bombing campaign against Iraq's air bases would make it difficult for Iraq to deliver WMD by aircraft. This is not foolproof—Saddam could hide planes equipped with bombs or spray tanks around the country, near roads or other surfaces that could be used as ad hoc runways. However, if U.S. air forces kept a constant fighter presence over U.S. ground forces, between our surveillance systems and air combat capabilities, it would be hard for Iraq to conduct WMD air strikes that did serious damage.

With more than 2,000 artillery pieces and multiple-rocket launchers, Iraq's ground forces are the greatest threat for WMD attack. Here as well, the United States has excellent capabilities to deal with the problem. U.S. fixed-wing aircraft and helicopters would likely roam forward of most U.S. troop concentrations, looking to strike Iraqi artillery concentrations. U.S. Army and Marine units are highly skilled at counterbattery engagements—in which artillery fires at the enemy's artillery. Between the shell-tracking radars U.S. forces use to locate enemy guns, the precision of American artillery pieces, and the terrible firepower of our own multiple-rocket launchers, most Iraqi artillery batteries would be lucky to get off more than a few rounds before they were silenced by American guns. This was the case throughout the Gulf War, and today our capabilities are even better.

U.S. forces are also well equipped to deal with enemy chemical or biological attacks. Our troops have new, lighter-weight, and more effective protective suits. American ground units operate in protective gear whenever they operate in an environment where WMD might be used, and they regularly practice donning their gas masks in a matter of seconds. All U.S. armored vehicles are designed to block out chemical and biological agents, and since most U.S. soldiers ride into battle rather than walking, at most times the troops would be protected. Indeed, to cause numerous casualties to U.S. troops, the Iraqis would have to catch U.S. infantry dismounted and not wearing their protective gear, or a unit resting and unprepared for battle, or else find a way to attack American logistical columns (which are not as well equipped to deal with WMD). None of this would be impossible for the Iraqi forces, but it also would not be easy, especially if the invasion force possessed overwhelming strength, was moving fast, and retained the initiative so that the Iraqis were kept off balance and constantly reacting to our moves.

Finally, Iraqi troops would have to be *willing* to use their chemical and biological weapons. This is not guaranteed. Most Iraqis would probably suspect that any unit employing weapons of mass destruction would come under particularly heavy attack by U.S. forces. U.S. psychological warfare operations—including leafleting and constant radio broadcasts—would no doubt reinforce the message that those who used chemical or biological warfare against American troops would pay a terrible price. Few Iraqi units are as well prepared to operate in a WMD environment as U.S. forces are. Most Iraqi troops have no special protective gear to cover their entire bodies, instead carrying only gas masks into battle. Only a few of Iraq's most modern armored vehicles are equipped to block out WMD effectively, and then only if the systems have been properly maintained—which is less than likely, given Iraq's poor maintenance practices. During the Iran-Iraq War, Iraq suffered many casualties by misusing its own chemical munitions, and in a future war with the United States, Iraqi troops would have to ask themselves who would suffer more if they actually used their WMD—the well-equipped Americans or themselves? Even if they were convinced that they themselves would not be harmed by their own weapons, they might refrain for fear of killing large numbers of Iraqi civilians. For the many Iraqi troops who would recognize that Saddam's chances of withstanding a full-scale American invasion would be virtually nonexistent, they would also face the moral dilemma of unleashing horrible weapons in a losing cause and the legal threat of being prosecuted as war criminals after Saddam's inevitable defeat.

To What Extent Should We Expect Urban Combat?

With a big enough force, we could avoid most city fighting, but we would not be able to dodge it altogether. There would be some cities we simply could not bypass. In the end, we might have to fight through Baghdad to get to Saddam.

In part, the answer to the question of how much urban combat we would face depends on the answer to the question of how hard the Iraqi armed forces would fight. If masses of Iraqi soldiers were to remain loyal to the regime and fight hard in its defense, we could see considerable urban warfare. Our best chance of avoiding extensive combat in Iraq's cities, therefore, is to convince large numbers of Iraqis not to fight. For this reason as well, moving fast, getting the ground battles started (and won) quickly, and convincing the Iraqi armed forces that Saddam's days in power are over would be critical to minimizing U.S. casualties.

Some commentators like to insist that "no defended city has fallen in combat since the Second World War." This is not true, even in the Middle East. Jerusalem fell to the Israelis in 1967 and Beirut in 1982. Khorramshahr fell to the Iraqis in 1980 and was retaken by the Iranians in 1982. Port Said fell to the British and French in 1956. However, these examples do not contradict the fact that urban warfare is always ugly. The U.S. Marines have embraced the urban combat mission in recent years, and they have gotten better at it than most, but even for the best-trained and -equipped troops in the world it is extremely difficult. In a city, there are too

many places for an enemy to hide, too many possibilities for cover and concealment. There are too many ways to move around a city—through sew-
ers, across rooftops, through walls of buildings, through back alleys, let
alone through the main streets. There are too many opportunities for booby
traps and ambushes. There are too few long fields of fire and lines of sight
that allow units to keep the enemy at a distance. And for an army as concerned about noncombatant casualties as our own is, there are too many innocent civilians around.

For anyone who has seen the recent film *Black Hawk Down,* the perils
of city fighting are obvious. In a city, it is relatively easy for an untrained
man (or woman) with an assault rifle to surprise a superbly trained ranger
and gun him down. If the civilian population takes the enemy's side and
joins in the fight, the situation becomes even worse, because the attacker is
likely to find himself with enemies on all sides and unable to tell innocent
bystanders from would-be assassins. Moreover, as the Germans found at
Stalingrad, city fighting reduces advantages in long-range gunnery, maneuver, armored warfare, and air power—all advantages we would have over
the Iraqis but that would be diminished in their urban areas. Cities are great
"levelers" in that sense.

Nevertheless, urban warfare is not a hopeless mission. Superior tactics,
training, firepower, and leadership still create important advantages even in
city fighting. To return to *Black Hawk Down,* it is worth remembering that
a force of two hundred elite American soldiers took on several thousand
armed Somalis in the streets of Mogadishu in the actual battle that the film
depicts. In that battle, the Somalis killed eighteen American soldiers but
lost roughly a thousand of their own. If U.S. forces could achieve similar
results clearing Iraqi cities, they would do fine. If, as seems likely, the
Iraqis fought only as hard as the Somalis did in a few of Iraq's cities, U.S.
forces should come through without suffering catastrophic casualties.

The great question mark will be Baghdad. Saddam would likely keep
most of his loyal forces, including Republican Guard armored divisions,
the Special Republican Guard, elements of the Fidayin Saddam, and other
regime protection forces around Baghdad to try to turn it into a Mesopotamian Stalingrad. If so, the United States would have the option of attacking it or besieging it. If we chose the assault approach, we would
doubtless win, but at the risk of several hundred, if not several thousand,
casualties. On the other hand, a seige would be embarrassing and nerve-
wracking. Saddam might still have some weapons of mass destruction that
he could try to lob at our besieging forces from time to time. Of greater im-

portance still, he would hold hostage the citizenry of Baghdad (however many of its 4 million inhabitants had not already fled). Either way, a great many Baghdadis might die before we could get our hands on Saddam.

Tallying Up the Costs

These three variables are likely to be the principal determinants of both the length of the campaign and the number of casualties the United States would take. It is important to keep in mind that even if all three of these factors turn out as badly as possible for the United States, it is still highly unlikely that an invasion of Iraq would fail. The gap between U.S. and Iraqi forces in tactics, training, equipment, and leadership is so great that even if every Iraqi soldier fought to the death, Baghdad was able to employ WMD very effectively against U.S. forces, and Iraq made good use of its cities, the United States would still almost certainly win. The only question is at what cost.

If all of these questions worked out in the best possible way for the United States—few Iraqi soldiers were willing to fight for Saddam, the Iraqis were not able to use tactical WMD effectively, and there was little urban combat—the entire campaign could be over in a few weeks and could cost only a few hundred American combat deaths. If the worst-case scenario were to prevail—the entire Iraqi Army fought as hard as the Republican Guard did during the Gulf War, Iraq was able to employ considerable WMD, and there was large-scale city fighting—it is conceivable that the campaign could take three to six months and that the United States could suffer as many as 10,000 combat deaths. Probably the most likely scenario would be about one third of Iraq's armed forces fighting hard, limited use of tactical WMD, and some extensive combat in a few cities. In this most likely case, the campaign would probably last four to eight weeks and result in roughly 500 to 1,000 American combat deaths.

Obviously, a wide range of combinations and permutations is possible with these different variables, and it is impossible to break the figures down further without going into great detail about how each permutation would interact with the others. Even a few hundred American deaths would be deeply mourned, while 10,000 would be the most Americans killed in a war since Vietnam. That said, although we must prepare for the worst case, the best case is a more likely outcome. In other words, if the invasion did not go according to the most likely case laid out above (four to eight weeks, 500 to 1,000 combat deaths), it is more likely that the error would be positive (a faster campaign and fewer casualties) than negative (a longer campaign and greater casualties). This is because U.S. ground forces possess an enormous advantage over Iraq's military that has only grown since we last saw it tested in 1991, and it is hard to know precisely how much stronger than the Iraqis we are today compared to the time of the Gulf War. In addition, we need to keep in mind all of the circumstantial evidence suggesting that few Iraqis will fight to the death to save Saddam and the fact that there is very little evidence indicating the opposite. While it is prudent to take the claims of Iraqi defectors with more than a few grains of salt, given the frequency, consistency, and persistence of these reports, it is more likely that they will be proven at least partially correct than that they will be proven completely wrong.

In fact, many Middle East experts believe that it is not impossible that an invasion might make itself unnecessary. There is enough evidence to suspect that if the United States were to demonstrate that it was going to mount a full-scale invasion by drawing up several hundred thousand troops on Iraq's borders, this might prompt the Iraqi armed forces or even Saddam's power base to overthrow him. The Sunnis would actually have a strong incentive to do so: if they believed that the United States intended to install a democracy in Saddam's wake, it would mean the end of their eighty-year monopoly on power. Consequently, they might conclude that they should overthrow Saddam themselves to forestall the American invasion.

The bottom line is that the evidence coming out of Iraq provides enough of a sense that the armed forces are unlikely to fight that many experts suspect that if we prepare for all-out war, we might not have to fight one. This would certainly be welcome, but we should not embark on this course of action assuming that we won't have to mount the invasion. Instead, we should prepare for the worst, and if that produced the best, so much the better. It is certainly true that the coalition did not need all fourteen divisions to defeat Iraq in 1991. In particular, we almost certainly could have beaten the Iraqis with only six or seven of the nine American divisions we employed. But during the four-day ground war, we obliterated the Iraqi armed forces at the cost of fewer than 200 American lives (and probably no more than 10,000 to 30,000 Iraqi lives). Those are the kind of "mistakes" we should strive for.

THE DIPLOMATIC REQUIREMENTS

Many on the far right of the American political spectrum argue that the United States can and should overthrow Iraq entirely on its own. They are wrong. We can't, and we shouldn't. Since we do not share a land border with Iraq and Iraq's coastline is too small and difficult for a massive amphibious assault, we would have to get to Iraq through someone else's territory. That means having at least some allies in the region willing to allow the United States to use their territory to launch the invasion. Moreover, the United States is not some rogue superpower determined to do what it wants regardless of who it threatens or angers. If we behave in this fashion, we will alienate our allies and convince much of the rest of the world to band together against us to try to keep us under control. Rather than increasing our security and prosperity, such a development would drastically undermine it. For these reasons, an invasion of Iraq would require a new coalition to support it—one that could be as small as just the GCC states, Turkey, and Egypt but that would preferably be as large as we could make it.

The Gulf States

Based purely on logistical considerations, it would be possible to mount the invasion from Kuwait alone. That said, it would be enormously difficult and potentially costly. Kuwait lacks the bases to support the kind of air power we will want to employ, requiring us either to build new air bases (time-consuming, but well within our capabilities) or else anchor virtually our entire aircraft carrier fleet in the northern Persian Gulf—and realistically, this would not be an option except if the United States were faced with an imminent emergency. Kuwait has only three airfields and three ports, making the deployment of U.S. forces into the country difficult and probably stretching out the buildup for the invasion. Confining ourselves to Kuwait would further complicate air operations by forcing American tanker aircraft, command-and-control planes, and other important assets to operate either out over the Persian Gulf or over Iraq itself. In other words, either the planes would be in the wrong place or they would be vulnerable to Iraqi air defenses. Launching entirely from Kuwait would also constrain our ground movements, allowing Saddam to concentrate his troops and defenses against the limited axes of advance from Kuwait into southeastern Iraq.

If the United States could deploy only to Kuwait for an invasion, it would also make it effectively impossible to deploy large ground forces to western Iraq or Iraqi Kurdistan. We could still move the units themselves to those distant locales, but once there, it would be extremely difficult to resupply them by air from so far away—and with Iraqi air defenses lying along the route to Kurdistan. This would probably rule out deploying ground forces to prevent Baghdad from launching Scuds against Israel or from attacking the Kurds.

Thus, although we *could* mount an invasion only from Kuwait, we would not want to. Nor would the addition of Qatar, Bahrain, and/or Oman really solve these problems. The only difficulty that bringing in these other Gulf states would alleviate would be the amount of ramp space available for our aircraft at regional airfields.

Moreover, it is unlikely that Kuwait (or the other GCC states) would be willing to support a U.S. invasion if the Saudis told them not to do so. Indeed, for this among many reasons, it is unimaginable that the United States would embark on a major military campaign against Iraq without the Saudis on board. Given the importance of the issue to Saudi Arabia, it should not be that difficult to gain their support. With the Saudis on board, virtually all of our logistical problems would evaporate: we would have all of the airspace we needed, we would have many axes of advance (and supply routes) open to us, we would have all the bases we needed, and we would have little problem supporting large land forces in western Iraq. The only problem that would remain is defending the Kurds, which simply cannot be done from the GCC states. In short, Saudi participation in an invasion would be vital to its success. At the very least, we must convince the Saudis to allow us to use their airspace and base some of our aircraft in the Kingdom.

Saudi Arabia and the other Gulf states would probably want three things from the United States in return for supporting an invasion of Iraq:

1. They would want the violence between the Israelis and Palestinians to have died down enough that they felt able to deal with whatever unrest the invasion caused among their people. The Gulf states are legitimately concerned that as long as the Israelis and Palestinians are regularly trading blows, their own populations will remain so agitated that any additional unpopular event could spark serious domestic disturbances, even a popular uprising against the government, if the regime were seen as being on the "wrong" side of the event. This does not mean that Israel must have signed a comprehensive peace with all of its Arab neighbors before an invasion can get under way, only that there cannot be weekly terrorist attacks followed by Israeli security responses. Instead, both sides must have

the sense that they are moving toward an eventual settlement, and the United States must be actively involved and be seen as behaving in a reasonably evenhanded fashion. Because most of the Gulf elites want to see the United States invade Iraq, it is unlikely that they will set the bar very high in terms of the status of Palestinian-Israeli relations prior to an invasion.

2. They would want to make sure that we would bring enough force and conduct the campaign in such a way that they could be virtually certain that Saddam would be removed from power in the shortest possible amount of time.

3. They would want to see our plan for the rebuilding of Iraq. Especially after the way we are distancing ourselves from Afghanistan, making only the minimum effort to try to establish a solid political and economic structure there, the Gulf states would want proof that we do not intend to do the same in Iraq. They cannot afford to have Iraq fall into chaos. If Iraq after Saddam were to become like Lebanon in the 1970s, Sudan in the 1980s, or Afghanistan in the 1990s, it could destabilize their own countries. Although the GCC would probably be willing to make substantial contributions to ensure a stable Iraq and would also be willing to lobby the Europeans and East Asians to do the same, they know that only the United States could lead the effort and ensure that it succeeds. If the campaign plan we show them simply ends the day after Baghdad falls, the Gulf states probably would not let us start it.

Some on the far right complain that by agreeing to take actions on the Palestinian-Israeli dispute before moving against Iraq we are giving the moderate Arab states a veto over our actions. What this claim misses is that the Gulf states do have a veto over whether or not we invade Iraq. If the GCC states forbid us to use their territory to invade Iraq, we essentially cannot invade. Astonishingly, some on the far right go so far as to argue that if this is the case, we should invade Saudi Arabia and/or Kuwait, occupy those countries, and mount the invasion of Iraq from their (occupied) territory. The danger and foolishness of this idea brings to mind Oscar Wilde's remark "Sir, your argument does not deserve the compliment of rational discussion." Such actions would be the modern equivalent of the Vietnam-era absurdity of burning a village to save it. Setting aside the practical problems of launching our invasion amid 20 million very hostile Saudis and

Kuwaitis and the added costs of such a project, taking an action of such wanton lawlessness would make us, not Iraq, the international pariah. This is not how the United States behaves. The United States does not invade its allies.

Turkey

A number of proponents of attacking Iraq argue that the entire operation could be run out of Turkey. Unfortunately, this too is largely misguided. An invasion of Iraq would be very difficult to mount from Turkey alone, and if we proposed it, the Turks would probably turn us down. Having Turkey on board would be important, but would be neither necessary nor sufficient to enable an invasion of Iraq (or even a major air campaign).

Politically and militarily, operating out of Turkey presents major hurdles. Turkey does not want the United States to invade Iraq because of its deep-seated fears regarding the status of Iraqi Kurdistan in a new Iraqi government. Consequently, if the United States had no support in the Gulf region—if Saudi Arabia and Kuwait turned us down—so too would the Turks, because that would preclude the invasion they dread. Indeed, Turkish officials stress that they do not want any U.S. ground forces operating out of Turkey against Iraq under any circumstances. The only way the Turks would support an invasion is if the Saudis were already on board. In those circumstances, the Turks would know that the invasion was unstoppable regardless of what they did, so they would have an incentive to join to ensure that their views on northern Iraq were taken into account when the new Iraqi state was created after Saddam's demise. Once again, Saudi Arabia is the key.

Logistically, it would be even harder to stage an invasion solely out of Turkey than it would be to do so out of Kuwait alone. Kuwait at least has three sizable ports and three large airfields near Iraq. Incirlik, the nearest big Turkish air base, is on the Mediterranean. Even if we obtained overflight rights from Syria, strikes from Incirlik would have to fly more than 900 kilometers from Baghdad and other targets in central Iraq. Without overflight of Syria, the distances would virtually double. We certainly can (and do) fly strike missions from Incirlik against northern Iraq, but it is not ideal for strikes against the rest of the country. Moreover, Incirlik could not possibly handle all of the aircraft we would want to employ, requiring the use of even more distant Turkish air bases.

The nearest Turkish ports are on the Black Sea, at least 450 kilometers away, and these are too small to handle the logistical needs of a U.S. invasion.

This would necessitate using larger Turkish ports on the Mediterranean and/or Black Sea, which are all more than 550 kilometers away. From there, U.S. forces and their supplies would have to move over a bad road network through the mountainous terrain of southeastern Turkey to the Iraqi border, where the United States would have to build nearly all of the facilities needed to support an invasion because the infrastructure of the area is woefully inadequate. Could the United States do all of this? Sure, but it would probably add at least six months to the buildup for an invasion, and possibly a year or more.

Turkey's participation would be extremely helpful, and if Washington were to opt for an invasion, it should do everything it could to secure Ankara's support. We cannot defend Kurdistan without Turkey. It is simply too far to try to support a division or more in northern Iraq from Kuwait or Saudi Arabia. From Turkey, it is eminently feasible. Although the current infrastructure of southeastern Turkey could not support a 200,000-strong invasion force, it could support a 25,000-strong divisional force, maybe more. With such a force added to the Kurds' own defensive capabilities and some Turkish troops whom we probably could not prevent from moving into Iraqi Kurdistan if we wanted to, we should be able to block any Iraqi effort to attack the Kurds in response to the U.S. invasion. Similarly, although Incirlik is too far and too small to support the entire air effort, it certainly can handle several squadrons, and it is the airfield best placed for mounting strikes against northern Iraq.

Egypt

Americans have a bad habit of underestimating the importance of the strategic partnership between the United States and Egypt. A U.S. invasion of Iraq might be impossible without Cairo's blessing. U.S. air and naval forces must be able to fly through Egyptian airspace and pass through the Suez Canal to reach the Persian Gulf. We would also want to be able to use Egyptian ports and bases to rest, refuel, and possibly train some of our units. Given the absence of American bases between Guam in the Western Pacific and Diego Garcia or Oman in the western Indian Ocean, trying to fly squadrons of short-range Air Force fighters via the Pacific route in the event we did not have passage through Egypt might stretch our aerial refueling assets to the breaking point, even if we could secure basing privileges in Singapore or Thailand. In fact, it might not be possible at all.

One of the best things about the U.S.-Egyptian relationship is that we almost certainly would get Cairo's approval for all of these requests if we made the effort. In the past, even when Egypt has vociferously opposed U.S. policy in the region (including toward Iraq), not only has Cairo never turned down a U.S. request for passage by American warships or warplanes, but it has always approved it with speed, efficiency, and even courtesy. Although Egypt has a formal policy denying transit through the canal to nuclear-powered vessels, it routinely waives this regulation for American warships. During Operation Desert Storm, American aircraft flew 200,000 sorties across Egypt to the Gulf. During the October 1997 crisis with Iraq, Egypt granted the United States passage through the canal for the USS *George Washington* in an unprecedented twelve hours, even though Cairo publicly disagreed with the U.S. force buildup in the Gulf.[9] In this case, the Egyptians are likely to support a U.S. invasion of Iraq, if only because of Hosni Mubarak's hatred of Saddam. However, like the Gulf states, they too will probably want the United States to refrain from invading until we have quieted (not necessarily solved) the violence between Palestinians and Israelis.

Keeping Israel and Jordan Out of the Fray

If the United States were to embark on an invasion, Washington would need to keep both Jerusalem and Amman out of it. We do not know what Israeli attacks on Iraq would do to the coalition of moderate Arab states whose support we will need to mount the invasion. Israel's participation could cause some of the Arab states to bail out. More likely, the moderate Arab states would simply want guarantees from the United States that we would keep Israel out of the war before they agree to cooperate. Depending on who is in charge in Israel, that could be a tall order, but it is one that we should be ready to fill. The Israelis know that they would be Saddam's primary target once an invasion started, and we owe it to them and to our Arab allies to do everything we can (short of employing nuclear weapons) to prevent Iraqi attacks on Israel.

This means making a major air and ground effort in western Iraq, as the Israelis have requested. As much as our airborne surveillance and strike capabilities have improved since the Gulf War, without large numbers of ground troops in western Iraq to physically deny the area to Scud units, we cannot guarantee that we could prevent Baghdad from getting off several dozen missiles (quite possibly armed with weapons of mass destruction) at Tel Aviv, Haifa, and other Israeli targets. This would be especially threatening as U.S. military forces drew near Baghdad and Saddam realized that his end was approaching. At that point, given Saddam's personality and his actions during the Gulf War, we should expect him to order the launch of everything he has against Israel. If we had not occupied western Iraq with enough ground troops to physically prevent Scud units from moving out there, we could have little confidence that we would be able to stop such a final barrage.

We should probably keep Jordan out of the invasion coalition for different, but equally important, reasons. At present, it is too dangerous for Jordan to risk its political stability in joining a U.S.-led invasion of Iraq. It would be helpful to be able to use Azraq Air Base in eastern Jordan to support an invasion (and particularly to support U.S. ground forces deployed in western Iraq). However, if we had the use of Saudi bases and airspace, we could make do without it. Beyond this, we should accept any support from the Jordanian intelligence services that we can get because they can be very helpful in both providing information and contacting Sunni notables within Iraq—but this is as far as it should go. Jordan's population is too pro-Saddam, its economy is too dependent on Iraq, and its society is too heavily penetrated by Iraqi intelligence for Amman to be able to easily handle the risks of participating openly. The king and his government are too important to the peace and stability of the region to be risked for the relatively modest additional assistance Jordan could lend.

Instead, the United States would have to make arrangements with Saudi Arabia and the other GCC states to be ready to step in and compensate for Jordan's lost Iraqi oil, and possibly its lost trade revenue as well, since we must expect Saddam to cut all trade with Jordan in response to a U.S. military attack. Indeed, this is a step Saddam might take when U.S. forces were building up for the invasion, even before any shots had been fired. Convincing the Gulf states to provide Jordan with large amounts of heavily discounted oil, and possibly a market for Jordanian goods, is not going to be easy. The Saudis and Kuwaitis apparently still hold a deep grudge against Jordan arising from King Hussein's support of Saddam during the Gulf War, although the interdynastic rivalry between the Al Sa'ud and the Hashimites (who were driven out of western Saudi Arabia by the Al Sa'ud in the 1920s) may also play a role. Consequently, on every previous occasion when Washington has attempted to convince Riyadh to step in and wean Jordan from its dependence on Iraq, the Saudis have refused. Because neither we nor they can afford to have the Jordanian monarchy overthrown as a by-product of an invasion of Iraq, Riyadh must understand that this is part of the price for conducting a full-scale invasion—*something it wants*.

Syria

If the United States were to make it clear that it intended to invade Iraq—and if it was clear that Saudi Arabia and other Gulf states were on board—Syria would want to join in the enterprise. Syrian endorsement of an invasion would be useful. Syria prides itself on being the most nationalistic, the most Pan-Arabist, of the Arab states. Its support for a U.S. invasion would go a long way toward muting dissent among Arab populations. Even its acquiescence would have an important salutary effect. Consequently, it would be worthwile for the United States to bring Syria on board in some way. The Syrians have indicated that they are for sale on this issue: as long as we guarantee them discount oil sales after Saddam's fall, they will let us do whatever we want to their Ba'thist rivals.

Nevertheless, actual Syrian participation in an invasion would cause headaches. Syria uses the same old Soviet weaponry as the Iraqis, so Syrian divisions are hard to distinguish from Iraqi divisions, creating potential problems on the battlefield. Neither the U.S. military nor the U.S. intelligence community trusts the Syrians to be honest partners in such an operation. The Syrian regime has little love for the United States, and U.S. Central Command would likely feel it necessary to devote assets to watching the Syrians to make sure that they remained entirely on our side. Finally, Damascus would no doubt like to carve out a buffer state in northwestern Iraq to match its Lebanese vassal in the west. This would give Damascus a say in what happened in Baghdad, protect Syria's eastern border, and bring with it control of Iraq's uranium mines at Akkashat. For all of these reasons, Washington should try to secure Syria's acquiescence and rhetorical support while making it clear that its participation is not required.

Won't the Arab "Street" Rise Up?

We don't know, but it does not seem likely. Some experts predict widespread revolutions across the region if the United States so much as touches Iraq. Others claim that the Arab "street" is a myth that has never amounted to anything meaningful. My strong sense is that what commentators claim about the reaction of the Arab populations has more to do with their own feelings about U.S. policy toward Iraq than any meaningful evidence or analysis.

In the past, every time commentators have warned that the Arab "street" would rise up and overthrow their governments—specifically during the Gulf War and the recent Afghan campaign—the reaction has not lived up to the predictions. That said, there can always be a first time. Especially if the United States has done little to bring the Israeli-Palestinian violence under control, an American invasion of Iraq could spark the frequently predicted but never realized Arab revolts.

One reasonable barometer is the Arab governments themselves. Given that they continue to encourage American officials to believe that they would support an invasion of Iraq, this suggests that they believe a tidal wave of Arab popular unrest is unlikely and that they would be able to deal with whatever disturbances arose. However, the fact that these same governments vehemently oppose any lesser effort at regime change (specifically the Afghan Approach), in part because they are concerned about the length of time it would take, suggests that they are not 100 percent certain of their judgment and don't want to test it for too long.

Alternatively, it may be that the concern being expressed by the moderate Arab governments is principally the fear of being seen as out of step with their people for any length of time. The most immediate concerns of the Arab governments are not revolutions but undermining their own legitimacy by highlighting the fact that the regimes do not necessarily reflect the will of the ruled. This breeds popular resentment, which can create a variety of problems short of revolution. This would suggest that the Arab states are not worried that backing a U.S. invasion of Iraq could threaten their hold on power but that it could weaken their ability to govern easily and effectively.

There is also reason to believe that the reaction of the Arab populations would be determined more by what the United States does after the invasion than before or during. One of the principal complaints about U.S. policy toward Iraq in the Arab world is that it is wholly destructive and is punishing the Iraqi people without harming Saddam. These sentiments form part of a larger pool of anger at the United States for a variety of reasons, not least among them our unwillingness to take meaningful action to help bring democracy or economic development to the Arab world more generally. Regardless of the validity one attaches to these claims, an American invasion of Iraq would give us the opportunity to prove them wrong. If the United States were to remove Saddam from power quickly and with a minimum of casualties and then rebuild Iraq as a prosperous nation, with a government that represented the will of its people and governed for their benefit, this would send a powerful signal to the entire Arab world that the United States is not anti-Iraqi, anti-Arab, or anti-Muslim. It is possible that the result would burnish the image of the United States in the eyes of the Arab world, rather than tarnish it.

Building a Broader Coalition

The acquiescence of the Gulf states and Turkey, plus right of passage across Egyptian territory, constitutes the bare minimum the United States would require in terms of diplomatic support for an invasion of Iraq. Nevertheless, it would be very helpful if the United States could assemble a larger coalition of states to participate.

Militarily, several of our NATO allies could make useful contributions if they chose to do so, but allied contingents are a two-edged sword. A British armored division and strike aircraft would be of great help because British units are essentially as good as our own and their personnel work well with ours. The French also have a highly professional military, and if Paris could be convinced to keep politics out of its military participation, French forces could also play a useful role. In addition, the Germans, Dutch, and several of our other European allies have first-rate units, if they could be persuaded to send them. So too could the Canadians and Australians. Beyond that, few of America's allies have forces capable enough to add much to a U.S. invasion, except Japan, whose constitutional constraints might forbid it. Moreover, the more nationalities (and languages) we add to the operation, the more cumbersome its decision making will become. Indeed, a critical element in accepting forces from other countries is that they would accept an American chain of command and a carefully circumscribed role once the shooting starts. Beforehand, we would have to be willing to take our allies' views into account (in fact, some of their suggestions might well be helpful), but once the invasion started, there should be no second-guessing military tactics by the allied governments, as happened regularly during the war in Kosovo.

The political reasons for building a larger coalition far outweigh the military considerations for or against. The United States has all of the forces it needs to defeat Iraq militarily, but it needs to recognize that the military element of the operation would be only one part, and probably not the most difficult or important one. Diplomatically, a larger coalition would make the enterprise much easier. For the moderate Arab states, European and Asian participation would be important to legitimize the operation in the eyes of their people; the more the operation was seen as having broad international support, the more legitimate it would seem to Arab populations, while the less international support it had, the more it would be seen as an anti-Arab scheme cooked up by the United States, its Arab "puppets," and (they will insist) Israel. If the whole world were to oppose an invasion of Iraq, it would be much more difficult to convince the moderate Arab states to go along with it. Diplomatic support has a self-reinforcing quality. The more European and Asian countries we could convince to support the effort (and even send forces), the more comfortable and supportive the moderate Arab states would be—and the more supportive the moderate Arab states were, the more willing European and Asian states would be to participate. On the other hand, the reverse is also true: the more the European and Asian countries stood aloof or even condemned an invasion, the more skittish the Arab states would be, which would solidify the Europeans and Asians in their skepticism.

In addition, there is the difficult matter of rebuilding Iraq. Once Saddam has fallen and we have overrun the country, we will have to put the place back together again, hopefully better than it was before. The United States could probably do this alone, but it would be better to share the effort (and its costs) with our allies. Moreover, in this case, our allies might actually be better at this part than we are. Because the Europeans have devoted more attention to building democracy and civil society than we have, especially as a result of their efforts in Eastern Europe after the collapse of communism, they often have better ideas and more skill in doing so than we do. However, the only way we would be able to secure European help in rebuilding Iraq is if we were to bring them in and give them a say in the planning of the war in all of its aspects, even its military ones. It might be painful to bring the allies on board before and during the invasion, but afterward we would be glad that we did.

We should not assume that assembling such a coalition is impossible. The British government of Tony Blair has already indicated its willingness to participate. Other countries might too if addressed with respect and given an appropriate say in the planning process. The French know full well that if the Saudis went along with an invasion, Saddam's fate would be sealed, and under those circumstances they would be looking to safeguard French commercial interests in post-Saddam Iraq, meaning they too could be brought on board. Russia has similarly indicated it would not try to block an invasion of Iraq as long as Moscow was assured of the repayment of Iraq's $8 billion debt to the USSR plus a slice of the Iraqi reconstruction pie. If true, this would even open up the possibility of a new U.N. Security Council resolution, although China might be difficult to convince. A new resolution would change the nature of the endeavor completely, eliminating virtually all diplomatic problems.

A Smoking Gun

Assembling such a coalition would be infinitely easier if the United States could point to a smoking gun with Iraqi fingerprints on it—some new Iraqi outrage that would serve to galvanize international opinion and create the pretext for an invasion. Saddam's pursuit of nuclear weapons is the real reason for invading, but because estimates vary widely of how long it will take for Iraq to do so, and because some countries simply assert that Iraq is not doing so and dismiss all of the evidence to the contrary, that may not appear to be an imminent enough threat to justify the march to war, especially for those countries (such as France, Russia, and Turkey) which do not want to see Saddam overthrown.

Tying Saddam to some new terrorist attack would be a perfect smoking gun, but unfortunately, the evidence regarding the September 11 attacks continues to point entirely to al-Qa'eda. The anthrax-filled letters are now believed by the FBI to be the work of an American. Saddam is probably being careful not to get involved in a new terrorist operation for fear of providing the United States with just such a *casus belli*.

The U.N. weapons inspectors are another obvious source of such a pretext that many have been suggesting. Under this approach, the United States would give Iraq one more chance to cooperate with the weapons inspectors, and only if Iraq failed to do so (by refusing to cooperate with the new inspection regime or by blocking an inspection) would Washington launch the attack. Many U.S. allies in Europe are recommending this approach. As appealing as it may seem, it is a trap. We probably will never get to the point where Iraq has the opportunity to reject such a scheme or block an inspection because the French, Russians, and Chinese are determined not to let us use the U.N. inspectors to create a pretext. While they would go along with an invasion if we decided to mount one because they would have no choice, they would much prefer to keep Saddam's regime in place and would block us if we gave them the opportunity to do so. Moreover, if faced with the threat of an imminent invasion, Iraq would probably go along with a new inspection regime for some period of time, just to fore-stall the invasion and buy time in the expectation that the United States would eventually become distracted by other events, allowing Iraq to start cheating again. Pursuing the inspections route is a dead-end street.

There are probably other courses the United States could take that might prompt Saddam to make a foolish, aggressive move, that would then become the "smoking gun" justifying an invasion. An aggressive U.S. covert action campaign might provoke Saddam to retaliate overtly, provid-ing a *casus belli* (one of the many ways in which covert action could com-plement an invasion). Other means might also be devised. However, in the end, we will have to act regardless of whether we have a pretext or not. Under those circumstances, we will have to make our case as best we can based on the unique threat posed by Saddam Hussein—the serial aggressor and mass murderer—and his pursuit of nuclear weapons.

THE POLITICAL REQUIREMENTS

Just as the United States can, should, and to a certain extent must build a diplomatic coalition to support an invasion, so too must the U.S. govern-ment build domestic political support for this operation. Over the past fifty years, successive administrations from both parties have conducted mili-tary operations with less than full popular support. Sometimes this has been necessary and vindicated by subsequent developments. Sometimes there simply was not enough time and opportunity to muster the necessary sup-port. In the case of an invasion of Iraq, we have the time, the opportunity, and the need to do so.

As the discussion of the military requirements and potential casualties should make clear, an invasion of Iraq would be a big and potentially painful operation. Moreover, the costs of rebuilding Iraq and the commit-ment of time and resources necessary (discussed in Chapter 12) mean that this would not be a quick, painless operation even if the military campaign turned out as best we could hope. Before the U.S. government commits this country to so grand an endeavor, it needs to make sure that the country is both aware of what it is agreeing to and willing to make the commitment.

This means that the administration needs to do an honest job explaining to the American people—both directly, and through their representatives in Congress—why the United States needs to undertake this effort and what it might cost. Moreover, it will be incumbent upon the administration to allow the American people to participate in the debate over this course of action. Given the costs and the potential size and length of the commitment, it is crucial to have the American public firmly on board. The comparisons to World War II and Vietnam are again useful; as in those wars, the United States should not embark upon this one without the clear, expressed support of the American people. There are many polls that suggest that the American people support the use of force against Iraq, but it is not at all clear that the respondents understood the amount of force that would be required or the other costs of the operation.[10] Likewise, many in the Congress remain skeptical of the need for such an operation.[11]

Consequently, it is both practically and morally incumbent upon the administration to make the case to the American people and secure the approval of their representatives in Congress before launching an invasion of Iraq. And the United States has a powerful case to make. Saddam Hussein is developing weapons of mass destruction, including nuclear weapons. Twelve years of sanctions, the loss of as much as $180 billion in oil revenues, and the erosion of his conventional military capabilities have not been enough to dissuade him from that goal. He is a mass murderer, a repeat aggressor, and a serial miscalculator. His actions over thirty years in power and the limited evidence we have about his thinking leave us little reason to believe that he can be deterred once he acquires nuclear weapons. His acquisition of nuclear weapons could result in a new Great Depression and the death of millions of people, and the risks of such catastrophic outcomes demand action. Because Saddam now sees us as his implacable foe, because his dominance of the Gulf region and its oil supplies would constitute a dire threat to U.S. national security, and because the United States is the only country with the capability to block him from achieving those goals, another conflict with Saddam is virtually inevitable. The choice we have is to fight Saddam and remove him from power soon, before he has acquired nuclear weapons, or else fight him later once he has acquired nuclear weapons, when even the costs of victory could be devastating.

In addition, it would be helpful for the administration to present at least some of the evidence that supports this case. I am convinced because I have seen the evidence, and I have tried to muster at least the unclassified elements in this book. But I believe that there is more that could be shared. To some extent, the administration may be concerned that because we do not have a "smoking gun," a piece of paper in Saddam's handwriting that says, "As soon as my scientists finish making me a nuclear weapon, I am going to start attacking American allies in the region," the evidence we have will not be persuasive. I disagree. Certainly, any public prosecutor will note that the vast majority of cases are won on circumstantial evidence. We may not have a smoking gun (at least, not yet), but we have a very strong circumstantial case, and the administration would do well to start laying out that case to try to convince the American people, the Congress, and our allies to the greatest extent possible without jeopardizing the sources and methods of the intelligence community.

Finally, at the risk of seeming old-fashioned, I think that an invasion of Iraq would do well to have the endorsement of a congressional declaration of war. Nothing could make more explicit the full backing of the American people for the effort—or the president's authority to take all necessary actions. Aside from the long-standing dispute between the executive and legislative branches over the authority to use force, the most important difficulty with seeking a declaration of war would be purely practical; in order to keep Saddam guessing about our intentions and preserve some element of surprise, we will not want to betray the specific purpose of our buildup until the last moment. Consequently, a true declaration of war could be difficult for the president to secure before the start of hostilities. Nevertheless, it may still be possible for the Congress to pass a resolution authorizing him to use "all necessary means," including the use of large military forces, to preserve the peace and security of the vital Gulf region. At the very least, it is imperative for the administration to seek a congressional resolution backing the effort and committing the necessary resources. Again, the invasion and rebuilding of Iraq are going to be a long and potentially difficult effort, and it will behoove the administration to have the Congress's support made explicit up front.

INTERNATIONAL LAW

I am not a lawyer, nor am I steeped in the mysteries of international law. Consequently, I cannot offer a definitive answer regarding the legality of a U.S. invasion of Iraq. However, I believe that this is an important consideration when contemplating one.

There is no country on earth that benefits more from the system of international legal agreements than the United States. We are the great status quo power, and what is most threatening to the United States is the efforts of those looking to improve their status by circumventing international law.

International law is a bulwark against terrorists, rogue states, and others looking to cause mayhem and to undermine the power and prosperity of the United States. Even though international law may be honored more in the breach than in the observance, it is a valuable element of U.S. policy. It would make the support of the American people firmer and the participation of our foreign allies more likely. Consequently, it is important that U.S. actions conform to international law.

That said, international law is neither as black and white nor as restrictive as domestic law. In particular, the rights of collective security and self-defense enshrined in the U.N. Charter provide considerable leeway for military action against a murderous regime such as Saddam Hussein's, which has so frequently violated not only every tenet of international law but every moral code in existence. For example, Iraq has flagrantly violated the 1925 and 1949 Geneva Conventions regarding the treatment of prisoners of war, the use of weapons of mass destruction, and the purposeful targeting of civilians. It has violated the Vienna Conventions on diplomatic and consular relations. It has also violated the Nuclear Non-Proliferation Treaty of 1993. Many human rights groups argue that it has even violated the 1948 Genocide Convention. While these may not constitute *casus belli,* they certainly help us to build the case that Iraq is an outlaw state whose actions regularly violate international law and endanger its neighbors and other countries outside the region.

In addition, there is the international legal principle of "anticipatory self-defense," which allows for actions taken in self-defense before an opponent has actually struck but when it is reasonable for a country to believe that it will. There is a great deal of debate over the concept of anticipatory self-defense, with some scholars arguing that it is illegal because it contradicts long-standing criteria for self-defense established in 1837. Other experts argue that this need not always be the case, particularly when the issue is the opponent's development of nuclear weapons—a threat completely beyond the ken of those who framed the doctrine in 1837.

Perhaps of greater importance, accepted or not, anticipatory self-defense has been used by various nations many times over the past fifty years. The United States has justified the blockade of Cuba during the 1962 Cuban Missile Crisis, the 1998 cruise missile strikes on Afghanistan and Sudan, and Operation Enduring Freedom's war on Afghanistan as invocations of self-defense more consistent with the standards of anticipatory self-defense than with the 1837 standards. NATO invoked anticipatory self-defense to justify the 1999 war over Kosovo. Likewise, Great Britain's 1982 "exclusion zone" around the Falkland Islands after the war with Argentina and Sweden's declaration that it would use force against any foreign submarine found within twelve miles of its territorial seas were both exercises of anticipatory self-defense. Of particular relevance, Israel justified its strike against Iraq's Osiraq nuclear reactor in June 1981 as anticipatory self-defense; the Osiraq reactor was scheduled to go online in the near future, but it still would have taken many years for Iraq to have used it to build nuclear weapons. Israel argued that if it waited until the threat actually became imminent, it would be too late for it to take action, hence "imminence" had to be defined by when its ability to prevent Iraq from obtaining nuclear weapons would evaporate, not when the actual threat from Iraq would materialize. At the time, Israel's strike at Osiraq was condemned by many as a violation of international law based on the 1837 definition; today—especially given what we have since learned about Iraq's nuclear intentions after the Gulf War—the operation looks like eminent good sense and may have saved the lives of millions of people.[12] Thus, the narrow definition of self-defense is increasingly giving way both in practice and, more remarkable still, even in theory, because its nineteenth-century provisions are increasingly impractical in twenty-first-century circumstances.[13]

In addition, the United States could employ the same legal justification it has used for previous military action against Iraq. U.N. Security Council Resolution 678 authorizes member states to "use all necessary means to uphold and implement Security Council Resolution 660 and all subsequent relevant resolutions and to restore international peace and security in the area." Resolution 660 was the first UNSC resolution after the Iraqi invasion of Kuwait, condemning the invasion and demanding that Iraq withdraw immediately. Since the Gulf War, the United States has regularly justified the use of force against Iraq based on Resolution 678. Some nations argue that the resolution's reference to "all subsequent relevant resolutions" meant only those already on the books prior to the passage of 678. However, the United States has employed a more literal interpretation—namely any resolution regarding Iraq passed after, and derived from, its actions during and after the invasion of Kuwait. We are also not the only nation that subscribes to this interpretation.

In 1991, the Security Council passed Resolution 687, which laid down the terms for the termination of hostilities, established the inspection regime, and established the conditions under which the sanctions would be lifted. Moreover, this resolution was adopted under Chapter VII of the U.N. Charter, which invokes the rights to collective security and self-defense. Iraq has been in flagrant violation of the terms of the cease-fire since at least October 1998, when it threw out the U.N. inspectors. On numerous other occasions since 1991, the United States has justified taking military action against Iraq on the basis of Iraqi violations of the terms of the cease-fire resolution, although initially we preferred to have the Security Council recognize those Iraqi breaches before taking action.

It would not be a terrible stretch for Washington to make the legal argument that Iraq's constant, flagrant violations of UNSCR 687, among others, requires the United States to once again invoke UNSCR 678's authorization of "all means necessary" to remove the regime of Saddam Hussein as being the only way to ensure that Iraq will abide by the relevant resolutions. In addition, we can cite the Security Council's frequently expressed determination to see that Iraq demonstrate "peaceful intentions," to return all Kuwaiti personnel seized during the Iraqi invasion, to abide by the U.N. sanctions, to cease the repression of its own people, and to discontinue its nuclear programs, all of which Iraq has blatantly failed to do. Indeed, if international law cannot condone the invasion of Iraq to remove from power one of the most odious, aggressive, dangerous, and bloody dictators since Josef Stalin, then there is something wrong with international law.

Although the United States should be able to build the appropriate legal argument in support of an invasion of Iraq, we should also be mindful to avoid setting the wrong precedent. The case of Iraq is unique in many ways. Iraq's possession of nuclear weapons is infinitely more threatening than India's possession of nuclear weapons, for example, because of Saddam's consistent patterns of reckless and violent behavior. Likewise, the existence of a body of Security Council resolutions—and Iraq's failure to comply with them—clearly place the country well outside the bounds of international law. Iraq truly is an "outlaw" state in the literal sense of the word. It is upon these arguments that we should build our case for invasion, not just legally but politically as well. We should be wary of making facile arguments based on Iraq's support of terrorism or on its pursuit of weapons of mass destruction alone (i.e., uncoupled from Saddam's behavior and Iraq's clear violations of international law). Terrorism is often in the eye of the beholder, and one man's terrorist is another man's freedom fighter. Likewise, Washington has never raised concerns about the French nuclear arsenal because it does not believe that France's possession of nuclear weapons creates a threat to Europe.

In taking action against Iraq, we should not set a precedent that would allow other nations to make a similar claim enabling them to take preemptive action against countries they might not like. Invading Iraq is a unique case that can meet high standards for preemptive action. In arguing the case, we should make it clear how high we believe those standards should be and that we will hold ourselves and other nations to the same standards in the future. By arguing the uniqueness of the Iraq case—in terms both of the long history of Iraqi aggression and flagrant violations of international law and its refusal to comply with dozens of Security Council resolutions, many of them enacted under Chapter VII of the UN Charter—we would reassure other nations that Iraq will not simply be the first in a string of U.S. military actions against countries we don't like and minimize the ability of other states to justify their own preemptive attacks by recourse to our precedent.

WOULD SADDAM TRY TO ATTACK
U.S. FORCES BUILDING UP FOR AN INVASION?

This issue is not nearly as problematic as some have made it out to be. Although U.S. military personnel are very concerned about this eventuality because it would complicate their logistical and force protection tasks, it would make our political tasks infinitely easier and would run little risk of actually scuttling the invasion.

From a purely military-technical perspective, Saddam's capability to strike at U.S. forces building up in Saudi Arabia, Kuwait, Turkey, or elsewhere is quite limited. Given the capabilities of U.S. air defenses, it is inconceivable that Iraq could mount a sustained air campaign against the buildup for an invasion. At most, he might get lucky once or twice and sneak a few aircraft in for a WMD attack. If such an air strike actually hit anything, this might be painful and enraging, but it would not preclude the invasion.

Saddam might instead turn to his ballistic missile force. As noted, Iraq is believed to have only twelve to thirty-six Scud-type missiles right now, and perhaps several dozen shorter-range al-Samuds. While perfectly fine for terrorizing civilian populations, a force of this size is wholly inadequate to do significant damage to a large military contingent. Even if Saddam has secretly been able to produce many more missiles than we suspect, even as many as 300 to 400, this would fall far short of what he would need to significantly disrupt an American buildup. Every time Iraq fired a missile at a port, air base, warehouse, depot, or garrison that the U.S. invasion force was using for the buildup and that missile actually hit the facility, it might cause several dozen, possibly several hundred, casualties and require several days of cleanup to decontaminate the area. However, the United States would have scores of such facilities throughout the Gulf region, and the buildup for an invasion of this size would likely require three to five months anyway. Thus, at the absolute worst, such missile strikes would be a nuisance, not an impediment to the buildup. They might delay the buildup here and there, but they could not prevent it.

What's more, given the number of facilities and the number of troops and war machines the United States would be bringing in, if Baghdad tried to harass the buildup continuously, it would very quickly run out of missiles. Do some quick math: if the United States were using six ports in the region for the buildup and Iraq had to hit each port with just three WMD-equipped missiles every week to prevent any American ships from unloading troops or equipment at the port (an unrealistically low number, which I am using just to make a point), then in one month it would have expended seventy-two missiles just against the ports. This is the high end of the estimates of the number of missiles Iraq is believed to have right now. If Iraq were also to try to hit the air bases, garrisons, warehouses, and other mustering facilities we would be using in the region, it would expend several hundred missiles in just a few weeks—assuming that it had that many missiles to begin with.

Moreover, this calculation is wildly generous to the Iraqis, and in reality it would take them a lot more to shut down a port or airfield. Iraq's missiles are extremely inaccurate—so inaccurate that more than 50 percent of the time they don't even come within a mile of their target. In most cases, to do real damage to a military target, even with WMD, the missile has to strike within about 200 yards of a target. Iraq is not believed to have reliable missile warheads for WMD attacks, further diminishing the likelihood that its missile force could do significant damage. So if we redo the calculation and assume that only one out of three Iraqi missiles would actually hit the port (and this is still being very generous, given how inaccurate Iraqi missiles are) and that only one out of three of those would actually spread its agent in such a way as to affect people at the port (again a very generous assumption, given what we know about Iraqi missile warheads), Iraq would have to be able to fire 648 missiles per month just to prevent U.S. ships from unloading at Gulf ports. Even more realistic calculations make it clear that Iraq would have to expend thousands of missiles per month to really do the job. There is no one who believes that the Iraqis have anything close to that many missiles, and that still does not account for the airfields, garrisons, and other transshipment facilities we would be using.

Thus, in many ways, it would be great for the United States if Iraq did try to prevent the invasion buildup with a missile campaign because it likely would do little damage to U.S. forces, would delay the buildup only marginally, and would exhaust Iraq's ballistic missile force in short order. It would be much better for us if Baghdad chose to expend its WMD-equipped missiles against the buildup rather than against regional cities. From Iraq's perspective, about the best it could hope to do would be to occasionally lob a ballistic missile or two into one of the ports, airfields, garrisons, and other facilities at random intervals in the hope of doing some damage and causing American personnel to work under uncertain conditions. This would slow the pace of the buildup, but that's all.

In some ways, using terrorist methods would be a much better way to employ WMD against the invasion force. Terrorists, or Iraqi intelligence personnel, would be more likely to be able to disseminate the chemical or biological agents properly than Iraq's ballistic missiles (although even they might have a tough time doing it right). However, U.S. forces and the countries of the region would be expecting such attacks and so would make extensive efforts to protect U.S. forces and local facilities. There is no question that with a determined enough effort, a few such terrorist attacks might succeed, and if they were really lucky might kill a large number of people—for example, if they could find some way to introduce biological agents into the water supplies of a U.S. combat unit. This would be hard to do, and even if it were possible, it would raise the costs of the invasion but would not stop the buildup. In fact, it would undoubtedly make the American military and the American people even more determined to seek revenge.

Nor does Saddam have many other options to try to stop an invasion. In August 1990, the balance of forces in the region was such that if the Republican Guards had kept going into Saudi Arabia, we probably could not have gotten enough forces there in time to prevent them from overrunning Saudi Arabia's eastern ports and the oil fields. Today the situation is reversed: we are the ones who can bring the greatest force to the area the fastest. Given the forces we have in place already in Kuwait, Saudi Arabia, and elsewhere in the Gulf region and the reinforcements we could add within seven to fourteen days, Iraq would be foolish to try to invade Kuwait to deprive us of its airfields and ports. And that is largely the limit of Iraq's military capabilities.

If it would be militarily infeasible for Saddam to stop the U.S. buildup for an invasion, it would be diplomatically suicidal. Iraqi attacks on American forces in the region would be acts of unprovoked aggression and would galvanize international support for the invasion. It is important to remember the political circumstances that are likely to surround the buildup. Unless the government is being run by utter morons, the United States would not announce that it was planning to invade Iraq and then start the buildup. Instead, after discussing our plans with our allies and securing their consent and cooperation, we would start the buildup at low levels months in advance, moving over as many forces as we could without tipping our hand. At some point, several months before the invasion's planned start, we would need to start moving things that couldn't be kept hidden— armored divisions and Air Force wings. When we reached that point, the president would probably make a speech. In that speech he would say something to the effect that he remains deeply concerned about Iraq's continued pursuit of weapons of mass destruction, its ongoing ties to terrorist groups, and its flagrant violation of the various U.N. resolutions. For this reason, he would announce, he has decided to move large U.S. forces to the region to demonstrate to Iraq the seriousness of his intent to deal with its outlaw behavior and to give the United States a full range of options. He would assure the American people that while he has not made a decision to invade, he wants to have all options available. Other administration officials would assure the press that we have not yet made a decision to invade and that the buildup of forces is intended to give the president a range of options, from coercing Saddam to comply with a new containment regime up to and including an invasion if that became necessary. Only when the buildup was complete and the military operation was set to begin would the president announce to the world that after much painful reflection, he has concluded that an invasion is our only reasonable course of action.

In such circumstances, any Iraqi military campaign to try to prevent the United States from building up an invasion force in the region would be of tremendous benefit to Washington. If there is anything that would solidify American popular support for invading Iraq and rally international opinion in our favor, it would be an Iraqi preemptive attack on our forces in Kuwait and Saudi Arabia before a shot had been fired by the United States and after the American president had indicated that he was still considering other options. Especially if Iraq employed terrorist attacks or weapons of mass destruction against American forces, the American people would become incensed and would demand revenge. If Saddam used weapons of mass destruction, the rest of the world would have to admit that he had been hiding proscribed WMD all along, and so all of the claims by Saddam's apologists that Iraq was abiding by the U.N. resolutions and was no longer a threat would be revealed as lies and nonsense. Any such attacks would also demonstrate unequivocally that Saddam remained just as willing as ever to use the most horrific weapons against foreign countries. It would again reveal him to be an unrepentant aggressor. There is nothing that would make the task of building domestic and international support for an invasion easier for the United States.

Although we cannot be certain and should assume the worst, it is likely that Saddam recognizes all of these same points and so would be unlikely to try to attack U.S. forces directly during the buildup. Saddam apparently has told his close aides that it was a mistake not to have attacked the U.S. buildup in the Gulf region in 1990, prior to Desert Storm, and this should give us some pause. However, he probably understands that the opportunity he had to do so in 1990 is gone. It was clear that Saddam did not expect the United States to build up its forces in the Gulf as quickly as we did in 1994, when he threatened Kuwait again. Now, having seen the United States do so on at least four separate occasions—during Operations Vigilant Warrior in 1994, Vigilant Sentinel in 1995, Desert Fox in 1998, and Enduring Freedom in 2001—he is probably under no illusions about the ability of Iraqi forces to beat more powerful American units to the GCC ports and airfields. After the experience of the Gulf War, he also probably knows that it would be difficult for him to conduct air strikes in the face of coalition air defenses. Thus, he would likely want to retain his limited air and missile forces for use against the region's cities and oil fields after the United States has attacked and not waste them trying to hit U.S. military forces beforehand.

Saddam also probably understands that once American tanks cross Iraq's borders, his odds of survival plummet because of the imbalance between the U.S. and Iraqi forces. Therefore, we should expect that his principal effort would be directed at preventing the United States from ever launching the invasion, and the best way for him to do that would be to convince the states of the region not to cooperate with a U.S. invasion. Over the years, Saddam has learned that he garners more international support by playing the victim than the aggressor. He would be most able to stir Arab populations against their governments if he appeared harmless and reasonable. Once 200,000 or more American troops were lined up on his doorstep, he undoubtedly would signal a new willingness to accept the U.N. inspectors. He would do everything he could to show that an invasion was unnecessary and that the United States was a rogue superpower determined to crush any Muslim state that got out of line. This is likely to be a much bigger problem during the buildup than Scuds landing on ports in the region.

At the same time, Saddam would probably have an active component to his prewar strategy of deflecting a U.S. invasion. For instance, he would try to walk a fine line between not admitting that he had WMD while threatening dire consequences for Israel, the United States, and any states that supported the American invasion. Indeed, this would be another reason for him to hold back his remaining WMD; they would be far more useful as a threat than if they were actually used. As we prepared for an invasion, our airwaves would be filled with the voices of experts warning of the millions and millions of people who might die from an Iraqi WMD attack. Saddam probably understands (especially after Iraq's experiences during the Iran-Iraq War and the fact that Iraqi scientists recognized that the WMD warheads for their Scuds were awful) that it would be hard for Iraq actually to kill millions of people with the agents and delivery methods it currently possesses. Therefore, the deterrent effect of his WMD arsenal would be much greater if he did not try to use it, because if he were to do so and the attack were to fizzle, so too would his deterrent.

On top of all this, Saddam is still in the same position he was twelve years ago: the United States has nuclear weapons, and he does not. He almost certainly continues to believe that if he were to employ chemical or biological weapons against U.S. forces building up for the invasion, there would be a good chance that the United States would respond with nuclear weapons. Since the whole point of his strategy would be to prevent the destruction of his regime, why on earth would he do something that he has acknowledged could provoke the United States to wipe it out completely?

DEALING WITH SADDAM'S COUNTERATTACKS

Once the invasion started, however, we would be in a different situation. If the United States were to launch a full-scale invasion of Iraq with the goal of overthrowing his regime, Saddam would have no incentives for restraint and would undoubtedly lash out at us with everything he had. Thus, an invasion would have to deal with the same set of Iraqi counterattacks as the Afghan Approach. We would have to expect Iraq to launch WMD attacks against Israel, Turkey, and the moderate Arab states. We would have to expect Saddam to try to launch terrorist attacks on the United States itself, quite possibly with weapons of mass destruction. We would have to expect him to try to crush the Kurds and possibly to destabilize Jordan. We would have to expect him to try to disrupt the region's oil exports to the extent he could.

An important difference between the Afghan Approach and a full-scale invasion, however, is that if we opted for an invasion we would be far better positioned to handle Saddam's counterattacks. By deploying troops to western Iraq and Kurdistan, we would largely eliminate Saddam's ability to fire Scuds at Israel and attack the Kurds. As soon as large numbers of U.S. ground forces were in place in western Iraq, the most Saddam could do would be to sneak one or two launches at Israel, and even this would be difficult. Similarly, U.S. ground forces driving up from Saudi Arabia and down from Turkey and Kurdistan would quickly overrun the areas Iraq must use to launch Scuds at most Turkish and Saudi cities and the main Saudi oil fields and export terminals. Unfortunately, Kuwait is within range of Iraqi Scuds launched from as far away as the Baghdad area, and we would have to hope that the combination of our aerial Scud-hunting efforts and several batteries of the latest Patriot missiles deployed to Kuwait would take care of whatever Saddam tried to launch before he went down in defeat.

The speed of the ground offensive should also be a major impediment to Saddam's counterattack efforts. By hitting Iraq with overwhelming force and advancing as quickly as possible, U.S. forces should be able to deprive Saddam of many of his counterattack options before they could be executed, throw others out of kilter and off schedule, and create both enough of a "fog of war" and an expectation of Saddam's imminent fall that his subordinates would (hopefully) feel willing and able to avoid complying with his orders. The example of the Gulf War, during which Saddam was probably prevented from employing his tactical chemical weapons against coalition forces because of the dislocation caused by the speed of the coalition ground advance, should serve as a model of the salutary effects of a fast-moving ground campaign.

Likewise, because our allies would be comfortable that Saddam would be gone, and quickly, we should be able to convince all of them to take extraordinary security measures to defeat other Iraqi counterattacks in the expectation that those measures would not have to remain in place for very long. This is especially true with regard to terrorism, which would be the hardest Iraqi method of counterattack to handle. It would be much easier for us to convince our allies to bite the bullet and make an all-out counterterrorism effort if they knew it would be for a finite length of time. Our adversaries, other terrorist-supporting states, and Iraq's advocates would likely be less willing to support or condone an Iraqi-sponsored terrorist campaign if they knew that Saddam's fate was sealed. If the United States were to launch a massive invasion of Iraq, what country would come to Saddam's defense? Iran, Syria, North Korea, Libya, and the rest of the rogues' gallery might carp from the sidelines, but they would be unlikely to take any actions that could send them down along with him. Even many of the established terrorist groups would likely be wary of accepting a commission from Saddam if they knew he would not be around to protect them in the future.

The obvious exceptions to this rule are groups such as al-Qa'eda that do not want or need Saddam's protection (but would gladly accept his weapons of mass destruction if he were giving them away) and Saddam's own intelligence service personnel. It would be best to hold off on plans for an invasion until al-Qa'eda was more thoroughly eradicated. Since September 11, the United States and its allies have destroyed some elements of the al-Qa'eda network both in Afghanistan and abroad and have suppressed much of the rest of it. However, the network remains mostly intact and therefore dangerous. If al-Qa'eda elements were to acquire weapons of mass destruction from Saddam Hussein, they could still do a great deal of damage. The threat from Saddam's own intelligence services is probably the lesser of the two, because they lack al-Qa'eda's international network and have demonstrated such incompetence in recent years. Although waiting until al-Qa'eda has been further weakened would make a great deal of sense, we may never wipe it out entirely, and new terrorist groups with similar goals and capabilities might eventually emerge. Consequently, we would need to accept that, in the end, we would have to make a major counterterrorism effort as part of any U.S. regime change policy toward Iraq. For the reasons enumerated above, such a campaign would be easier if we were to invade than if we were to employ the Afghan Approach or another half measure, but either way it would be necessary.

To push the above point to its logical conclusion, we also should assume that Saddam might try to head off a U.S. invasion by encouraging terrorism against the United States by al-Qa'eda and other anti-U.S. groups *prior to a U.S. invasion.* In the aftermath of 9/11, the U.S. government must pay particular attention to any terrorist threat to Americans. Consequently, the greater the threat posed to the United States by international terrorism, the more Washington will concentrate its efforts and its resources on this threat and therefore the harder it would be to mount an invasion of Iraq. Saddam would have to be careful to cover his tracks, because if we ever could tie him to an al-Qa'eda terrorist act, we would have the smoking gun we sought and the international community would wash its hands of his regime for good. Nevertheless, this too argues for holding off on an invasion until the threat from al-Qa'eda in particular—the only international terrorist group that has demonstrated the ability to kill large numbers of Americans in the United States—has been further reduced.

Iraq almost certainly would strike back by trying to provoke ever greater violence between Palestinians and Israelis. So useful would this be for Saddam that we should expect him to pursue it during the buildup for an invasion as well as after its start. (Indeed, this, not ballistic missile attack, is both Saddam's most likely and most deadly means of trying to preclude the invasion.) Saddam has already demonstrated that he understands that the worse the violence between the Israelis and the Palestinians becomes, the more reluctant the moderate Arab states will be to allow the United States to launch an invasion from their territory. This is one of the reasons he is paying $25,000 apiece to the families of Palestinian suicide bombers, thereby encouraging more. As the threat of invasion drew closer, he would undoubtedly press harder, although even here his freedom of action would be somewhat constrained. He cannot allow the United States (or Israel) to catch him directly supporting terrorist attacks on Israel because this could furnish the *casus belli* that he knows we would be looking for. Nevertheless, the near certainty that Saddam would pursue this strategy should reinforce our determination to deal with the Arab-Israeli conflict and get it moving in the right direction, lest Saddam stir it to the point where the moderate Arab states really don't feel they can go along with an invasion.

Finally, the Iraqi threat to regional oil exports would also be considerably easier to meet in the context of an invasion. The United States could assault and capture many of Iraq's biggest oil fields early in the war, hopefully before Saddam could destroy them. As with the Afghan Approach, we would also have to expect Saddam to try to launch attacks against Kuwaiti or even Saudi oil fields. Again, between extensive aerial Scud hunting, the speed of an invasion, and our ability to occupy the areas from which Iraq would have to launch Scuds to hit most of the Saudi oil fields, we should be able to preclude most such efforts. Nevertheless, because of the extent of the Iraqi oil infrastructure and the proximity of the Kuwaiti and northern Saudi oil fields, some damage to the region's oil exports might be unavoidable under any circumstances. However, since it would be far more likely that the Gulf states would support an invasion as opposed to the Afghan Approach, it would be equally likely that we would be able to convince them to ratchet up their own production to compensate for any losses.

WILL THE IRAQI PEOPLE RESIST OR WELCOME AN INVASION?

I did not include this issue among the key variables likely to determine the cost and duration of a U.S. invasion of Iraq because it is not likely to have a decisive impact on the campaign. Certainly it would be better for the United States if the Iraqi people welcomed their liberation from Saddam, and it would create new difficulties if they fought us savagely. However, given the disparity between the capabilities of the two armies, a friendly Iraqi population would only marginally speed an American invasion and an unfriendly Iraqi population could do little to hinder U.S. forces in a meaningful sense. Unhappy Iraqis could certainly help their armed forces defend Iraq's cities, and this would add to the total of U.S. casualties; however, as the fighting in Somalia made clear, armed civilians can cause some deaths, but they are unlikely to be able to sway the tide of battle.

The perspective of the Iraqi people is still important for more than purely military reasons. First of all, the American people prefer to liberate others rather than to conquer them. In addition, the attitude of the Iraqi people would likely have a huge impact on other Arab populations and countries around the world. If the Iraqi people welcomed a U.S. invasion, it would help extinguish any discontent in the Arab "street," reassure the countries that joined us in the operation, and quiet those that opposed it. Who could seriously oppose an American invasion if the Iraqi people were ecstatic about it? However, the opposite would also be true. If the Iraqi people opposed an American invasion and fought it hard, it would greatly exacerbate the criticism of a U.S. invasion, prompting protests in Europe and Asia and possibly sparking unrest in the Arab world.

Unfortunately, the question of how the Iraqi people are likely to react is another great unknown. Saddam has so stifled free speech that it is impossible to know what the Iraqi people think and want. Nevertheless, a number of points can still be made. To start with, one of the things that we found throughout Eastern Europe after the Cold War was how much the Germans, Poles, Romanians, Czechs, and other East European peoples had despised their governments and wanted them gone. Even the Russians generally hated their totalitarian state. It seems reasonable to believe that the same oppressive security, arbitrary arrests and punishments, widespread use of torture, suppression of free speech, and pervasive climate of fear that spawned such deep antipathy among Eastern Europeans have also produced similar feelings among Iraqis.

The evidence we have from defectors and expatriates also supports this supposition. No one who leaves Iraq and feels free to speak his or her mind has anything good to say about the place. And lots of people, including very high ranking officials, do seem to want to leave. Nor have any expressed the sentiment that the Iraqi people would oppose a U.S. invasion. The former head of the Iraqi News Agency, Saad al-Bazzaz, has stated, "The majority of Iraqis feel that there was no need for Iraq to confront the United States. Nobody asked Iraq to fight the United States, just like nobody asked it to liberate Palestine. At the same time, nobody welcomes planes to bomb his town. But anger over that is minor compared to anger about getting into the wrong battle at the wrong time with the wrong enemy." When asked if he sensed any hatred toward the United States by most Iraqis, Bazzaz answered, "No, Iraqis see their future being connected to the United States, complete with good relations."[14] When Wafiq al-Samarra'i, Saddam's former Mukhabbarat chief, was asked in an interview how the Iraqi people would have responded if the United States had marched on Baghdad in 1991, he replied, "Had the US gone into Baghdad [in 1991], there would never have been a second Vietnam, and the people would have applauded the USA."[15]

The trickle of information from inside Iraq suggests a more complicated set of Iraqi feelings toward the United States. Three entries from the published diary of Nuha al-Radi, a Baghdadi who lived through the Gulf War and its aftermath, illustrate this complexity. On March 19, 1991, al-Radi wrote about the possibility of U.S. intervention in the Iraqi *intifadah:*

"In the coffee shops the talk is not of nationalism, but of the desire for the US to come in and take over—get it over with."[16] Several months later, in November 1991, al-Radi wrote, "Saw Faiza today. She said she'd like a catastrophe to envelop the US and swallow the whole continent. 'What about my two brothers who live there?' her husband Mahmood asked. 'They can go down with it,' she said. 'Serve them right for living there.' Hatred for the US is paramount here."[17] Finally, on March 6, 1995, al-Radi noted, "Umm Imad, the maid at Ma and Needles' house, said that if the US army marched into Baghdad they would be welcomed with open arms, adding that if she could smuggle her two boys out of the country she would. It would be worth the missing them. Ma calls her the voice of the people, the barometer of Iraq."[18]

As the various entries in al-Radi's diary suggest, most Iraqis seem to be of two minds regarding the United States. They blame us, at least in part, for their current suffering. There is still a pervasive belief in Iraq that the United States is both omniscient and omnipotent and that if they are living in misery it is because the United States wants them to. While they are well aware of the depredations of the regime, they believe that the sanctions are also to blame, if only for making those depredations possible. It seems that many Iraqis simply don't understand why we continue to pursue a policy that, from their viewpoint, inflicts so much hardship on them and seems to have so little impact on Saddam. However, the Iraqi people do seem to hold out the hope that the United States can and will deliver them from their misery. If al-Radi's mother's maid—the Umm Imad her mother calls "the barometer of Iraq"—truly reflects the sentiments of the nation, as al-Radi's mother believes, the Iraqi people would like to see the United States get rid of Saddam's regime.

Still, we need to be careful about translating what probably is a strong desire for liberation on the part of the Iraqi people into an assumption that they will pour out into the streets to welcome us. They may do that. But we must also factor in the experience of the Gulf War and the *intifadah,* when few Iraqis were willing to take action to try to bring about Saddam's downfall. Most Iraqis probably would be unwilling to show their true colors until they were certain that Saddam's regime was finished, and we don't know what it would take to convince them of that. Having had their expectations that the United States was coming to save them dashed so many times, most Iraqis are likely to be wary this time around. It is possible that we would have to be at the gates of Baghdad before the Iraqi people really believed that this time Saddam was not going to be allowed to remain in power. Since the Iraqi people watched U.S. ground forces advance to within about 225 kilometers of Baghdad in 1991, only to stop and turn around, just launching an invasion might not be enough to convince them that this time we meant it.

DON'T WE NEED TO GET SADDAM?

No. We really don't. The problem with Saddam is his control over the Iraqi state and his use of its resources to try to dominate the vital Persian Gulf region and build weapons of mass destruction. If Saddam is no longer in control of Iraq, he no longer presents the same threat. In this respect he is very different from Usama bin Ladin. The problem with bin Ladin is twofold: he controls a shadowy international terrorist network that cannot be physically conquered by the United States, and he inspires a cultlike following that is willing to conduct suicide attacks against the United States and his other enemies. Thus, there is nothing that the United States could "conquer" to take bin Ladin's power away from him. With Saddam, if we conquer Iraq, he is out of business. If he flees to Syria, Sudan, or Yemen, or even if he tries to hide in Iraq, he presents no threat to the United States.

Of course, if Saddam is not killed during the invasion, the United States, the new Iraqi government, and all of the countries that have suffered at his hands will want to bring him to trial for crimes against humanity. This might necessitate a manhunt for Saddam. Since Saddam does not have the same kind of international network of supporters, safe houses, and means of traveling in secrecy as Usama bin Ladin does, he should be easier to catch. Even if he weren't, it would be a nuisance but would hardly constitute a defeat for this course of action: even if we spend twenty years searching for Saddam Hussein around the world, if he were not in power in Iraq he could not threaten the Middle East with nuclear war.

However, the contours of Saddam's life and his personality as we understand it suggest that he is unlikely to outlive his regime. Saddam and his sons have been responsible for more murders, torture, and rapes than anyone can imagine. In a tribal society such as Iraq's, there will be hundreds of thousands of people (mostly men) who will want their revenge on this man and his family. Saddam himself recognizes this and has told people he has wronged that they should not expect they will ever get revenge on him, because if he falls, there are so many who want to kill him that by the time all of the others get done with him there will be nothing left but little pieces. In other words, Saddam believes that he cannot survive unless he is in power. In addition, there is also his obsession with his place in history to consider. It seems very unlikely that if his regime is collapsing around him, Saddam will run and try to live out the remainder of his life in hiding in South America or a friendly Islamic state. Unfortunately, it seems far more likely that he will play Sampson and try to pull the walls of the temple down around him in order to go down in the history books with a bang.

THE ROLE OF THE IRAQI OPPOSITION

Last, there is the question of what role the Iraqi opposition, both internal and external, should play in a U.S. invasion of Iraq. Whereas it would be foolish to rely on any of the opposition groups (even the Kurds) to bear the brunt of the ground effort as the Afghan Approach would have us do, as part of a ground invasion, Iraqi oppositionists could help in a wide range of activities.

- **By providing military forces:** Depending on the actual invasion plan developed by U.S. Central Command and the Joint Staff at the Pentagon, it might be helpful to have Iraqi opposition forces supporting the operations of U.S. (and allied) units. Unless the invasion were postponed for months if not several years, during which time an expatriate body of several thousand men could be trained, these forces would have to come from the Kurds and Shi'ite guerrillas, who are the only ones with existing military capabilities. Under some circumstances, U.S. military commanders might want the assistance of Iraqi opposition forces. However, there might be some concern that too great a reliance on Kurdish and Shi'ite military forces would cause the Sunnis to rally around Saddam. This might require limiting opposition forces to operations within the areas where their ethnic groups are dominant.
- **By collecting intelligence:** All of the Iraqi opposition groups could be useful in gathering information about the state of Saddam's armed forces, his preparations to defend the country, his intentions regarding WMD, and other issues. Although the opposition reports would undoubtedly be of varying accuracy and reliability, they would likely include considerable useful information.
- **By contacting Iraqi elites:** The United States would need ways to contact Iraqi military officers and regime officials as part of an inva-

sion. We would want them to understand our goal—to oust Saddam—
and assure them that we are not looking to destroy Iraq or the Iraqi
armed forces. The hope would be that we could convince Iraqi military units not to fight, or even to defect to our side. Iraqi oppositionists, particularly the former military officers and regime officials of
some of the external opposition groups, could be critical in these efforts. Not only might they know whom to contact and how, but if their
names were well known, it might be more reassuring to the Iraqi officers on the receiving end to hear from a known Iraqi commodity.

- **By reassuring the Iraqi people:** Since we don't know how the Iraqi
people will react to an invasion, it would undoubtedly be useful to
have Iraqis accompanying the invasion force to reassure the populace
that the United States is coming not to conquer and colonize Iraq but
to liberate it from Saddam. At the most basic level, the oppositionists
might serve as guides and interpreters. At a larger level, we could
hope the presence of Iraqis with the American forces would have the
same palliative effect as the presence of Free French units had during
the liberation of France during World War II.

When considering the role of the Iraqi opposition, it is crucial to bear in
mind that we have no idea how any of the expatriates would be received by
Iraqis inside Iraq. Many claim widespread support, but only when Iraq is
liberated would we know whose claims, if any, were true. There may be
some truly popular figures among the expatriates, but there are bound to be
many more who are hated or simply unknown. Our experience with Ahmed
Chalabi and his inability to stir up support inside Iraq when his Iraqi National Congress was operating from the Kurdish areas in 1992–96 should
be a cautionary example. This vital consideration raises two caveats regarding the support that the opposition could provide to an invasion. First,
it would be a mistake for the United States to designate a government-in-
exile to be brought into Iraq to run the country after the invasion, even if it
were merely a provisional government. Given our uncertainty about the
popularity of any of the expatriates, the biggest mistake we could make
would be to impose a government on the Iraqis that might be filled with
people they do not know or do not like. There are not many things the
United States could do that would be more likely to create the impression
that we intended to impose an American puppet regime on Iraq to "control"
the country as the British and Ottomans did. It would create immediate an-

imosity and resistance to the invasion and could cause many to rally around Saddam.

Second, we need to be prepared to adapt our operations with the Iraqi opposition if our assumptions going in are proven wrong. Because there are some important uncertainties, we should not try to adhere rigidly to a preinvasion plan but should be ready to adapt as circumstances dictate—militarily, politically, and diplomatically. But this is especially the case with the Iraqi opposition, whose viability is simply too unclear to have much confidence in predicting it. If we find that the Iraqi people are suspicious of the opposition, we should be ready to move them to lower-profile missions. If we find that the Iraqi people are reassured by the presence of Iraqi expatriates with the U.S. and allied units, we should be ready to highlight their participation. If, as the Iraqi oppositionists all maintain, their desire is simply to help free their own people, they should have no problem playing whatever role circumstances dictate for them.

TWELVE

Rebuilding Iraq

The rebuilding of Iraq cannot be an afterthought to a policy of regime change. Instead, it must be a central element in U.S. preparations. It is likely to be the most important and difficult part of the policy, and we would be living with the results or suffering from the consequences for many decades to come. Saddam's overthrow would remove an enormous threat to the vital interests of the United States. However, because Iraq is a pivotal state in one of the most important and fragile regions of the world, what will follow Saddam is of equal importance. It would be a tragic mistake if we were to remove the threat of Saddam only to create some new, perhaps equally challenging, threat in Iraq following his demise.

COMPETING APPROACHES TO IRAQ AFTER SADDAM

To the extent that any in the United States have contemplated the goals the United States should pursue in Iraq after the fall of Saddam's regime, two very different approaches have emerged. One is the course the United States followed toward Afghanistan after Operation Enduring Freedom, which focused on putting in place a minimally workable political arrangement that would allow for the early exit of U.S. forces and obviate the need for a long and costly effort to actually transform the country politically and economically. This "Pragmatic Approach" can be contrasted with a "Reconstruction Approach," which emphasizes the need to build a stable Iraqi political system that is unlikely to revert back to dictatorship, warlordism, or chaos but would require a much more significant investment of time, resources, and diplomatic capital. This was effectively the model that NATO employed in Bosnia during the mid-1990s and again in Kosovo (and that the United Nations adopted toward East Timor).

The Pragmatic Approach: Advantages and Disadvantages

The Pragmatic Approach proceeds from the fundamental assumption that building a new, stable Iraq is going to be a long and costly process—if it can succeed at all—and therefore that the United States should be looking for a practical short-term solution, rather than a Wilsonian long-term one. Essentially, once Saddam is gone, the United States would look to help establish a new political structure in Iraq that would be reasonably stable, regardless of whether it was equitable. The United States would work with the existing power bases in Iraq to fashion a new government, without trying to fashion a new Iraqi nation. The United States would engage the Kurdish militias, elements of the Iraqi armed forces (preferably those least tainted by Saddam's crimes against humanity), the Sunni tribes, and a palatable selection of Shi'ite leaders—religious, tribal, and military. Whether or not these groups truly represented the Iraqi people would be largely irrelevant. With the demise of Saddam's regime, these groups would quickly emerge as the only forces left in Iraq with some degree of power and would therefore be those best able to preserve the stability of the country.

Under a best-case scenario, the United States would help craft some sort of oligarchic government based on power-sharing arrangements among these groups. Thus there might be a "national unity government" of Kurdish, Shi'ite, and Sunni members from these different groups. Although they would not actually represent the will of the Iraqi people, they would at least resemble Iraq's ethnic and religious composition, and the various members could be expected to protect the most basic interests of their coreligionists and coethnicists.

Under a worst-case scenario, a new dictator would probably emerge who, while unappealing, would maintain order and who would likely be someone with whom the United States could work. We probably would not help in the creation of such a dictator, but we would probably accept him as long as his methods for consolidating power were mostly peaceful and he observed a "decent interval" after the withdrawal of U.S. forces before doing so. In effect, the United States would be acquiescing to the establishment of just one more Arab autocracy that, hopefully, would be no more problematic than Hosni Mubarak's Egypt—although it would be hard to prevent it from turning out like Asad's Syria, Qadhafi's Libya, or Saddam's Iraq all over again.

The greatest advantage of the Pragmatic Approach is that it would spare the United States the cost of attempting to rebuild Iraq and create a new Iraqi state and society. U.S. forces could probably be withdrawn quickly from Iraq, in a matter of months, giving way to whatever forces the new power brokers of the state had available. Since our goal would essentially be to remove Saddam and then disengage, we would have no reason to try to provide security or stability for all Iraqis and so would not need a large troop presence or a lengthy one. As in Afghanistan, an international force might take over from U.S. forces for some period of time to ease the transition, but we would mostly leave it up to whatever local military forces survived Saddam's fall (or quickly reemerged after it) to maintain stability for the country.

Similarly, the United States would be expected to pony up some economic assistance for the new Iraqi government for some period of time, but since our goals would be modest, so too could our aid. The United States would have to provide some level of financial assistance in the short term to prevent the economic collapse of the country; however, because all we would be doing would be turning over the country to the old, established Iraqi elites—either a coalition of groups or a single strongman—and we would not be trying to build a new Iraqi state, society, or economy, the resources we would need to provide would have to be adequate only to allow the successors to consolidate power—a low standard given where they would be starting.

In addition, the advocates of the Pragmatic Approach argue that their preferred course would allow Washington to avoid the tangle of Iraqi politics and the competing interests of Iraq's neighbors. The Saudis would probably want a new Sunni autocrat in charge in Baghdad. So too might the Egyptians, Syrians, Jordanians, and Kuwaitis, although each would probably have a different candidate. The Turks would insist on minimizing the influence and autonomy of the Kurds in any new government. The Iranians would be looking to maximize the influence of the Iraqi Shi'ah in any new government. Within Iraq, the creation of a new kind of state—especially one that had any of the trappings of democracy—would threaten the interests of many of the existing elites, including the Sunni tribes, the Sunni townsmen from the region west of Baghdad, and whatever is left of the Sunni-dominated military and security services. Employing the Pragmatic Approach would allow the United States to minimize the need to try to reconcile (or overcome) these competing interests.

Finally, some advocates of the Pragmatic Approach argue that a long-term U.S. presence in Iraq—no matter what it was actually doing—would be portrayed as an imperialist effort to subjugate Iraq and that this would cause popular unrest throughout the Arab world for as long as the United States remained there. They argue that undertaking an ambitious nation-building effort in Iraq not only might fail in Iraq but could produce instability or revolution among other U.S. allies in the region.

The disadvantages of the Pragmatic Approach, however, are also significant. In particular, critics of this notion believe that it would be unlikely to produce the kind of stability that its advocates seek. In his three decades in power, Saddam has destroyed all of the other centers of power in the state. Those that remain—the armed forces, the Sunni tribes, some of the Shi'ite militias and religious figures—are pygmies, lacking anything like the independent power needed to dominate the country. The armed forces (particularly the Republican Guard) obviously have the power and cohesiveness to rule the country, but a U.S. invasion would undoubtedly fracture and decimate their ranks, stripping them of that capability. The Kurds, the one group beyond Saddam's control since 1991, have little influence beyond their own homelands. All could dominate their parts of the country, at least in the short term, but would have little ability to control others—and no desire to be ruled by a new central government that they themselves did not dominate.

Thus the immediate result of pursuing the Pragmatic Approach would inevitably be a form of warlordism, whereby each of the power centers that emerged after Saddam's fall would move to consolidate its control over its home territory. Part of this effort would probably be the "cleansing" of other ethnic and religious groups from their territory and, in the Shi'ite south, large-scale reprisal killings against Sunnis as the Shi'ah vented their pent-up anger after eight decades of Sunni repression. To the extent that these groups did "cooperate" in a new federal structure set up by the United States before our troops (or those of a small multinational follow-on force) departed, their intent would be threefold: (1) to prevent their rivals from gaining control of the federal government, (2) to try to gain control of the federal government themselves to increase their own power, and (3) to use their participation in the federal government to secure as much of the country's resources for themselves as possible. This is precisely what is happening in Afghanistan as a result of the United States' pursuit of this strategy.

Our experience with warlord states in Afghanistan and Somalia in the 1990s and Lebanon in the 1970s and '80s should make us wary of accepting such a situation in Iraq in the future. These are not stable polities. They inevitably degenerate into civil war as different groups vie for power and resources. In Iraq, the Sunnis would no doubt attempt to reassert their prior dominance of the country and would be fiercely resisted by the Shi'ah and the Kurds. Again, as we saw in both Lebanon and Afghanistan, civil war tends to spill over into neighboring states, destabilizing them too. Civil wars tend to be the bloodiest of all conflicts, often far bloodier than interstate conflicts, especially given that some Iraqi groups might try to employ whatever weapons of mass destruction they could seize after the collapse of Saddam's regime. Civil war would preclude the effective distribution of humanitarian supplies, creating additional civilian deaths and the further destruction of the Iraqi economy. Warlordism and civil war also breed terrorism. It is no accident that Hizballah arose out of Lebanon and al-Qa'eda found a home in Afghanistan.

Indeed, critics argue that the *best* outcome we could hope for from the Pragmatic Approach might actually be the emergence of a new Sunni military dictator. If a new dictator did emerge, he would at least keep the peace. However, in this case, we might have great difficulty seeing Iraq comply with the disarmament terms of the U.N. resolutions because a new military dictator who was still trying to consolidate power would probably not want to give up his weapons of mass destruction. In addition, it would be unpalatable for the United States to mount a vast military effort against one Sunni dictator and his WMD arsenal (Saddam Hussein) only to have him replaced by another. Although a successor Sunni general almost certainly would not be as willing as Saddam to take risks, interpret reality to suit his needs, and pursue an expansive foreign policy based on aggression, it would still be tough to accept what would look like a Saddam clone. Moreover, if a Sunni general were to take power, we would have to expect large-scale repression of the Shi'ah and the Kurds as he consolidated his control over them. Last, even this best case is improbable. Given the likely state of the Iraqi armed forces after a U.S. invasion of Iraq, it would be difficult for any general to round up the forces needed to assert control over the entire country without considerable foreign assistance.

Instead, the most likely outcome of a Sunni effort to install a new military dictatorship would itself be civil war. Because it is unlikely that any Sunni general would have the force to gain control of the country without considerable foreign assistance, those who tried would provoke civil war when they attacked—but were unable to defeat—rival military forces. However, each group would no doubt reach out to friendly foreign governments to seek the assistance necessary to defend themselves and gain control over the country. Just as various Lebanese factions pleaded for (and eventually secured) first Syrian, then Israeli, then Iranian, and then Iraqi military assistance, and as various Afghan groups requested (and then secured) first Soviet, then Pakistani, then American, then Iranian, Central Asian, and eventually Russian assistance in Afghanistan, so too would the various Iraqi factions jostling for control inside of Iraq do the same. The result in Iraq would be just as horrendous as each of those foreign involvements proved to be in Lebanon and Afghanistan.

Finally, critics of the Pragmatic Approach argue that, at best, it would produce more of the same: more of the "bad old Middle East." It would leave in place all of the autocracy that has alienated Arab populations, the corruption and cronyism that have impoverished them, and the sectarianism and intrastate animosities that have destabilized them. In short, even if the Pragmatic Approach could somehow avoid a descent into chaos and civil war, the best it would deliver would be a restoration of the very unsatisfactory regional status quo.

The Reconstruction Approach:
Advantages and Disadvantages

The Reconstruction Approach starts from the belief that the current Iraqi political and social framework cannot produce a government that is stable or legitimate (and that the absence of legitimacy would inevitably contribute to its instability). This has been the pattern of Iraqi politics since independence in 1932. Only Saddam Hussein created a sort of stability, but he did so at the price of mass killing, totalitarianism, constant warfare, and genocide. In addition, the Reconstruction Approach assumes that after a major U.S. military campaign, it would be politically unpalatable for the United States to allow Iraq to slide back into dictatorship, civil war, or warlordism. It assumes instead that the American people would demand that the Iraqi people be better off when we leave than they were before we attacked. Along these lines, those who favor the Reconstruction Approach argue that the perception of the United States in the Arab world would be greatly enhanced by demonstrating a commitment to building a stable, prosperous Iraq with a government that represented its people rather than repressing them, because this would dispel the claims that the United States is interested only in installing autocrats and does not care about the average Arab—a view that would be greatly reinforced by pursuit of the Pragmatic Approach.

The broad outlines of the Reconstruction Approach are that the United States would commit the resources necessary to help transform Iraq both politically and economically. We, and our coalition allies, would commit to providing security for the entire country for a sustained period of time—at least until after a new Iraqi government could constitute a new national army. We would provide the resources to help build a functional Iraqi economy, one that is not distorted by ubiquitous corruption and overly dependent upon imports. And we would help create a new pluralist, inclusive political system that might not necessarily be a Western-style democracy but might be the first Arab-style democracy. At the very least, it would be far more democratic than any other in the Arab world.

The advantages of the Reconstruction Approach are that it offers the best (in fact, really the only) prospect to solve the problems of Iraq over the long term. It would allow for the reconciliation of Iraq's ethnic and religious groups or at least would create political mechanisms to handle them other than force. It would create a truly legitimate Iraqi government, one that did not repress any elements of the Iraqi people but instead worked for them. For the first time in modern Iraqi history, the government would be striving to enrich its citizenry, rather than enriching itself at the citizenry's expense. It would create a wholly new set of economic conditions in the country that would eliminate the worst aspects of the economic stagnation gripping the Arab world—and might create a vibrant Iraqi economy that could serve as a regional engine for development.

In the short term, only by taking the route of the Reconstruction Approach could the United States meet its objectives of stripping Iraq of weapons of mass destruction and preventing a humanitarian catastrophe in the wake of the invasion. Only with a U.S. security presence throughout the country could we be certain that U.S., and later U.N., humanitarian goods would be distributed to the Iraqi people rather than being seized and hoarded by local warlords as in Somalia and Afghanistan. Only with a U.S. security presence throughout the country could we be certain that the U.N. inspectors could enter the country and search it for weapons of mass destruction. Only with a new Iraqi government that respects international law and abides by its international obligations could we have confidence that Iraq would not revert to the path laid out by Saddam Hussein.

Over the longer term, the United States could transform its reputation in the Arab world. By building a stable, inclusive new Iraqi political system coupled with a prosperous new economic system, the United States would demonstrate its commitment to the future of the Arab world. Similarly, if Iraq could, with U.S. assistance, create a new Arab-style democracy and an Arab-style market economy, these could serve as models for the rest of the Arab world. Last, by investing the time and resources needed to build a new Iraq, the United States would ensure that it would not be intervening in Iraq again in the near future and would create a new ally in the Arab world that could help bring further stability and progress to the region, rather than contributing to its backwardness and instability—as a new dictatorship or an Iraq torn by civil war or warlordism would.

The critics of the Reconstruction Approach raise several objections. First, they argue that it may not work, that there has never been a functional Arab democracy nor anything close to it. They argue that Iraqi political society is entirely unprepared for representative government and that it would therefore take many false starts to make it work—if it ever could. The critics contend that during this long period of transformation, the United States would have to remain in the country in force and would inevitably become a target for Iraqi grievances, leading to attacks on American forces. They believe that the United States would be seen as an imperialist occupying power that would stir up Iraqi nationalism, feeding such animosities and creating concomitant security problems.

The critics also believe that the costs of such a transformation for the United States would be well beyond what the American people would be willing to pay—that transforming Iraq's political and economic systems would cost tens (if not hundreds) of billions of dollars and last many years.

Other critics argue that it would cripple the U.S. military—that such an occupation would require hundreds of thousands of U.S. ground troops for a decade or more. They claim that the U.S. Army and Marines would have to deploy three to six of their twelve (combined) combat divisions in Iraq during this period, gravely weakening our ability to mount military operations elsewhere in the world—especially when coupled with other ongoing missions such as Bosnia, the Sinai peninsula, drug interdiction, and counterterrorism. Alternatively, we would have to call up National Guard formations for occupation duty in Iraq, which would be politically unpopular in the United States, and which, because National Guard units are not as well trained to handle force protection problems, could potentially result in more American deaths in Iraq.

U.S. FORCE LEVELS AND IRAQ AFTER SADDAM

It is also important to recognize that our decisions about the overthrow of Saddam's regime would have important ramifications for our actions and opportunities once the regime had fallen. This is particularly the case with regard to the size of the ground forces the United States would employ in the operation.

It would be somewhat easier for the United States to adopt the Pragmatic Approach to post-Saddam Iraq if we were to employ only small ground forces. The larger the ground forces we employed, the more damage we would be likely to do to the regime's military forces, thereby further weakening the post-Saddam power bases and making it harder for them to secure their own ethnic and religious regions of the country. (Of course, the greater their forces and the less the U.S. military presence throughout the country, the more likely the postwar groupings would perpetrate atrocities and wage war against one another.) Likewise, the more forces we employed, the harder it would be to extract them from Iraq and the more likely that U.S. troops would become enmeshed in local difficulties. Since the goal of the Pragmatic Approach is to get rid of Saddam and then get out of the country, this approach would be easier with a smaller ground contingent.

In contrast, the Reconstruction Approach would require the United States to employ large ground forces. Since the goal would be for the United States to take over the security mission completely, and since we would want to prevent all Iraqis from using force against one another—either to seek vengeance or to advance their political agendas—the United States would require a large enough force to fulfill the basic security function throughout the country.[1] Likewise, we would want such a security presence throughout the country to provide security for the U.N. weapons inspectors as well as U.N. and nongovernmental organization personnel handling humanitarian aid distribution, and later political and economic reform. With only a small force, the United States would not have the strength to assume the security function throughout the country (and therefore would not be able to allow the United Nations to handle the economic functions) and so would be heavily reliant on local Iraqi leaders and the forces under their control to handle those tasks. This would produce the warlordism this approach seeks to prevent, thereby making the creation of a unified and reformed Iraqi political and economic system impossible.

RECONSTRUCTING IRAQ

I believe that the United States will have to adopt the Reconstruction Approach to post-Saddam Iraq. The Pragmatic Approach would almost certainly produce chaos in Iraq—civil war or warlordism—that would destabilize the other countries of the region and breed new terrorism. This is what we are allowing to happen in Afghanistan by sticking with the Pragmatic Approach there. Hamid Qarzai barely rules in Kabul. His ministers are being knocked off one by one, and he may be next. The warlords control the country beyond Kabul, and the central government has little ability to control or even coordinate their actions. Afghanistan is sliding back into the state it was in during the early 1990s, which produced civil war, the rise of the Taliban, and then the entry of al-Qa'eda.[2] The Pragmatic Approach would almost certainly produce the same effects in Iraq. It would be a shame if the United States were to allow Afghanistan to slip back into chaos, but it would be a disaster if we were to allow Iraq to do the same. Iraq is too important a country in too important a region of the world. The reason that we must eliminate Saddam Hussein's regime is because of the threat it poses to the economic and political stability of this crucial region of the world. It would be madness for the United States to eliminate one threat only to create the conditions for another, different but equally dangerous, threat to those same interests.

Nor is the prospect of the rise of a new dictatorship much more appealing. First, it is unlikely given how weak the different power brokers will be after Saddam's fall; thus their attempts to make themselves dictator are more likely to spark a civil war. If the effort were successful, it would mean tremendous bloodshed in Iraq. What's more, *at best* it would leave Iraq no better than the other regional autocracies. For many Iraqis, living in a system like Mubarak's Egypt would be a significant improvement in their lot, but only in relative terms. The Egyptian people are deeply unhappy with their current state of affairs. There is good reason why we are concerned about the future stability of Egypt and the other Middle East autocracies. Yet the best outcome the Pragmatic Approach could offer would be to create another important Middle Eastern state with all of the same problems as Egypt, Syria, Saudi Arabia, and the rest. A new Iraqi dictatorship could also mean the resurrection of many of the problems the United States experienced with Saddam: massive human rights abuses, pursuit of weapons of mass destruction, flouting of the U.N. resolutions, support for terrorism, and aggression against Iraq's neighbors. None of these outcomes would enhance the stability of the region or advance U.S. interests.

In contrast, rebuilding Iraq politically and economically holds out the greatest likelihood for stability in Iraq and the region. Instead of an invasion of Iraq resulting in merely the removal of a negative, it would also be the creation of a positive. Consequently, it is the approach that would be most likely to improve the overall strategic situation of the United States. Whenever we embark on a major military operation, our intent should not be just to cauterize the immediate problem and then withdraw. If the United States is going to employ major military force, it should seek to create an end-state that is significantly more positive than what existed beforehand, and only the Reconstruction Approach offers that prospect in the case of Iraq.

Moreover, the critics tend to exaggerate the likely costs to the United States of pursuing the Reconstruction Approach. In purely economic terms, Iraq itself, with its vast oil wealth, would pay for most of its reconstruction. It might take some time to bring the oil back online, depending on how much destruction Saddam's minions were able to do to the oil infrastructure, but it is hard to imagine that it would take more than two to three years to have Iraq back to 2000 or 2001 production levels, and to have some lesser level of production and exports much sooner. The Saudis and other Gulf states would be equally concerned about creating a stable Iraq, so we would undoubtedly be able to elicit significant contributions from them. Likewise, by building a coalition for the war against Saddam, we should be able to count on contributions from the European Union, Japan, and other wealthy U.S. allies around the world. Consequently, in purely economic terms, it is unimaginable that the United States would have to contribute hundreds of billions of dollars and highly unlikely that we would have to contribute even tens of billions of dollars. The United States probably would have to provide $5 billion to $10 billion over the first three years to help get Iraq's oil industry back on its feet, initiate the reconstruction of Iraq's economy, and support the Iraqi people in the meantime—including providing food and other humanitarian goods, paying salaries for Iraq's large public sector, redeveloping infrastructure, and other basic costs.[3] However, the need for direct U.S. aid should decline steeply thereafter.

Iraq is also the best endowed of any of the Arab states. In addition to its vast oil wealth, it also has some of the best agricultural conditions in the Middle East. Likewise, prior to the Gulf War, it had probably the best-educated, most secular, and most progressive population of all of the Arab states. In other words, Iraq has all of the raw materials to be a prosperous state and to make an economic transformation viable. It is not as if we would be trying to transform a virtually resourceless state. Instead, we (and hopefully the international community) would be hoping to harness existing Iraqi resources to create a moderately wealthy and stable society.

The same is likely to hold true regarding the presence of U.S. forces. In Bosnia, NATO initially deployed roughly 60,000 troops to provide security for a population one fifth the size of Iraq's.[4] This suggests that, initially, a force of about 250,000 to 300,000 troops would be necessary to provide security for Iraq—essentially the size of the U.S. invasion force envisioned in Chapter 11. In Bosnia, the initial force deployment was reduced to 30,000 troops within three years and cut to 20,000 troops two years after that.[5] This suggests that within five years, foreign forces in Iraq could be cut to 100,000 troops or less, and the number could keep declining over time. What's more, there is no reason why all of the troops need to be American. Although initially U.S. forces would make up the vast majority of the security forces, fairly quickly we could transition to a more multinational force by bringing in contingents from our European, Asian, and regional allies. Indeed, it is entirely realistic to believe that within five years, if Washington handled the diplomatic aspects of coalition building properly, U.S. forces in Iraq could amount to roughly a reinforced division. Such a requirement would be little more onerous than the initial U.S. deployment to Bosnia itself, which certainly did not break the U.S. Army. If we chose to provide National Guard units for this role, it is worth pointing out that we did so in Bosnia with little political stir at home. Of course, maintaining U.S. troops in Iraq will also add to the costs of rebuilding the country— possibly by as much as $5 billion to $15 billion per year at first, but declining quickly as U.S. forces are drawn down. In this case as well, we should be able to diminish these costs significantly by securing commitments of both troops and funding from our allies.

Likewise, we should not exaggerate the danger of casualties among American troops. U.S. forces in Bosnia have not suffered a single casualty from hostile action because they have become so attentive and skillful at force protection. Although the United States may not enjoy such incredible success in Iraq, neither should we assume that we would suffer large numbers of casualties. Those who argue that the United States would inevitably become the target of unhappy Iraqis generally also assume that the Iraqi population would be hostile to U.S. forces from the outset. However, the best evidence we have suggests that the Iraqi people would be pleased to be liberated, and over the longer term, their acceptance of U.S. forces would likely be determined by the efforts the United States undertook. If the United States ensured their security, provided substantial economic support, and assisted in the creation of a stable, inclusive, and pluralist Iraqi political system, it seems quite likely that the Iraqi people would approve of the U.S. presence—especially if the United States were to reduce that presence over time, making clear its intention to eventually depart. In fact, what we have found in the Balkans, Afghanistan, Haiti, and elsewhere in recent years is that local populations generally welcome U.S. forces and instead resent other contingents, whom they often regard as their inferiors, making the Americans the best-suited security forces.

With regard to Iraq's neighbors, it is no doubt true that they would have reservations if the United States were to embrace the Reconstruction Approach, but these should not be insurmountable. Iran and Syria would dislike any large U.S. military presence next door to them. The Turks would dislike any form of government that gave Iraq's Kurds greater control over their own destiny, even if it were within a federal, pluralist system. And the Jordanians, Saudis, and other Gulf monarchies might be uncomfortable with such an Iraqi government simply because of its democratic attributes. With the Iranians and Syrians, the United States could make it clear that if they attempted to create problems for us in Iraq, we could create problems for them too. We would have to work closely with the new Iraqi government to take Turkey's concerns into account and to ensure that the territorial integrity of Iraq was maintained, while convincing Ankara that a federal system did not present a significant threat to Turkish interests (and perhaps pointing out that American support on other issues of importance to Turkey could suffer if Turkey did not acquiesce to the new Iraqi political structure).[6]

Even with the Jordanians, Saudis, and other Gulf states, there is reason for considerable optimism. All of the Arab monarchies recognize the need for democratization (and economic reform) in their countries. As a result, all have taken some steps to make their governments more inclusive, to give their people a greater voice in policy making, and to ensure that their policies are not too out of step with the sentiments of their populations. Kuwait, Jordan, Bahrain, and Qatar all have lively parliaments, which, though possessing little actual power, allow for popular participation in the process of government—and whose sentiments are not lightly dismissed by the true policy makers. In Saudi Arabia, Crown Prince 'Abdallah has spoken frequently of the need for the Kingdom's government to be more transparent and inclusive as well as the need to establish the rule of law. His frequent Majlises—where any Saudi can walk in and question the crown prince—are a remarkable form of direct democracy. Consequently, we should be able to make the case to the Saudis that the establishment of an Arab-style democracy (or quasi democracy) in Iraq is merely a manifestation of the future they already know is fast approaching and could serve as a model for their own inevitable democratic reforms. Moreover, we should work hard to persuade them that the alternative is probably not a Sunni strongman in Baghdad, as they would like, but chaos, civil war, and warlordism. This may be the most persuasive argument of all in Amman, Riyadh, and the Gulf capitals.

Finally, I reject the notion that Iraq is incapable of establishing a democratic form of government. The fact that Iraq has never had a functional democracy suggests that it will not be easy but does not preclude it.[7] There are countless countries around the world today that had no democratic tradition in the past but within the last twenty years have developed into functioning democracies, albeit not without their problems. It has frequently been the case that critics claimed that this country or that was culturally, psychologically, or even racially unsuited to democracy.[8] After World War II, many Americans and Europeans believed that the Germans were unsuited to democracy and pointed to the failure of the Weimar Republic as proof. The same claim was made about the Japanese—that they were culturally incapable of creating a functioning democracy. White South Africans regularly claimed that their black compatriots were somehow unequipped to participate in the democratic process. Many British said the same about India before independence. Since the fall of the Soviet Union, we have seen democracy break out across Eastern Europe; in some cases it has been a relatively quick success—as in Poland, Estonia, the Czech Republic, and Hungary—and in others more of a disappointment—as in Belarus. In virtually all these countries, however, and in dozens of others around the world, democracy is a work in progress, but it is not hopeless.

Across the Middle East, there are stirrings of democracy that at least indicate that the people of the region desire it. Within the strict parameters of Syrian control, Lebanon has a fairly vibrant pluralistic system. Jordan, Kuwait, Qatar, Bahrain, and Yemen have instituted democratic changes that appear to be building momentum for greater reforms.[9] In Iraq, no one has ever attempted to create a modern pluralistic system that would be backed by the resources of the United States and its allies, and, hopefully, with the assistance of the United Nations and other international organizations that have proven instrumental elsewhere around the world.[10]

It is difficult to imagine a government that could represent the will of the Iraqi people without being at least quasi-democratic and that would ensure the basic rights of Iraq's different ethnic and religious groups without being federal in structure. Because Saddam has ruthlessly eliminated any potential leaders in the country, there are no national figures such as Nelson Mandela or Lech Wałesa in whom the people would willingly invest their trust. Nor are there really lesser figures who could run the country as a "Council of Notables" of some sort. Such a government would probably represent less than half of the population of Iraq. The Kurdish leaders might well represent their population, but they would be the exception. The Shi'ite clergy could represent the small percentage of Shi'ites who favor an Islamic form of government, but they probably constitute less than 15 percent of the Shi'ite population. Shi'ite shaykhs could represent their own small tribal constituencies, just as Sunni shaykhs could represent their followers. However, tribal Iraqis living in tribal circumstances (Sunni or Shi'ah) now comprise a fraction of the population, probably less than 15 percent. On the other hand, 70 percent of the population is urban, and even those city dwellers who retain some links to their tribes probably would not want to be represented by shaykhs who know nothing about life in Iraq's cities. So who would represent the mostly secular urban lower and middle classes that constitute the bulk of Iraq's population? Not the former magistrates of Iraq's cities—these would all be appointees of Saddam's regime who owed their positions to loyalty and service to him. In short, without democratic elections of some kind, there would be no way to give voice to the majority of the populace.

Nevertheless, there is no reason that Iraq must adopt a full-blown Western system of democracy, rather than creating a new Arab-style pluralist state. Pursuing the Reconstruction Approach does not mean insisting on a Western-style democracy for Iraq. Our goal should be to see the establishment of a government representative of the Iraqi people's will, respectful of their rights, responsive to their aspirations, transparent in its operations, committed to the rule of law, and inclusive of the entire Iraqi populace. While such a government would inevitably have many democratic aspects, it does not necessarily have to adopt the U.S. Constitution.

The Limits of Knowledge and Planning

It is vital that before we embark on an invasion of Iraq (or any effort to bring about regime change, for that matter) we have a clear idea of what we would like Iraq to look like in the post-Saddam era, a strategy to achieve that goal, and plans to implement such a strategy. Once U.S. forces enter Iraq, situations would be likely to arise that would require quick U.S. decisions, and we would want to take actions that would be consistent with our long-term goals and move us toward them, rather than taking us in a completely different direction that could make it difficult (or even impossible) to achieve what we had intended.

We should be under no illusions that we could precisely map out all of the details of such an effort. Much will depend on the conduct of the war, conditions on the ground, and other unforeseeable circumstances. Consequently our planning should incorporate significant room for flexibility and large margins of error.[11] There are four reasons for this:

- Our information about the situation in Iraq is poor. Once we arrive in the country, we might discover that the reality was quite different from what we had expected, requiring us to reformulate plans, strategies, and possibly even goals to conform to what we encounter.
- Past efforts at nation building have generally worked best when they were conducted flexibly. For example, the distribution of new resources generally works best when it can be tied into local cultural traditions, and we might not fully understand how that could work until we were on the ground in Iraq.
- The United States should not impose a new government or a new economy ready-made on the people of Iraq. We will need to move in with a framework for a market-style economy and a pluralistic political structure, but the Iraqis themselves must ultimately build their own system of government, choose their own leaders, and create their

own economy consistent with their past, their cultural traditions, and their aspirations. The United States can help them to do so, but principally by creating the proper security and economic circumstances—not by drafting a constitution ourselves, designating the new leaders, or crafting the new economy. That is likely to cause the Iraqis to reject our efforts and the U.S. presence altogether.

- An enormous issue for Iraq would be how to handle the regime's misdeeds, crimes against humanity, truth and reconciliation, and amnesties. Iraqi civil society has been traumatized, and the reconstruction of Iraq must deal with this issue as well. Every country that has experienced severe repression and human suffering as Iraq has, has had to make decisions about how to deal with these issues as part of a reconstruction process. And every country has devised a unique approach. It would be a grave mistake for the United States to attempt to dictate an approach to Iraq on this extremely volatile issue, and until the Iraqis have decided on such an approach, their overall emotional recovery will go only so far.

First Things First: Security and Humanitarian Considerations

In the wake of a U.S. invasion, our first priority must be establishing security throughout the country. American and allied forces would have to be able to fulfill two goals: to ensure that force was not used against Iraqis and that no Iraqi group would be able to use force to advance its political agenda. Obviously, the United States could not prevent all petty crime in Iraq, but we could, and should, prevent all systematic violence. This means no reprisal killings, no repression, no ethnic or religious cleansing, no civil war, no bids for dictatorship. While this may sound daunting, it is likely to be the least challenging task we face and one that is well within demonstrated U.S. capabilities—as long as we have the troop strength needed to do the job. The surviving Iraqi military forces should be confined to garrisons and guarded by U.S. military personnel to ensure they stay put. Security would also have to be extended to protect U.N. arms inspectors and humanitarian aid personnel, who should move into Iraq promptly. In addition, U.S. and allied forces would have to ensure Iraq's territorial integrity by preventing foreign incursions.

American and allied forces would also have to meet the immediate humanitarian needs of the Iraqi people, at least until the United Nations and personnel from nongovernmental organizations could move in and take over these tasks, which likely would take only a few weeks, given past experiences. This would mean the provision of food, medical care, and other basic necessities on a large scale. It would also mean that American personnel would have to attend to the provision of basic services around the country—including water, power, and sanitation, to name only the most obvious. In most cities, the basic utilities would likely remain intact, but where they had been disrupted by the invasion, as a result of either physical destruction or the loss of key manpower, the United States would have to make basic repairs and organize replacement personnel in conjunction with the United Nations. Again, with adequate manpower and resources, this would be well within the capabilities of the U.S. armed forces and their civil affairs and engineer arms.

The Importance of the United Nations

The reconstruction of Iraq would be infinitely easier, in both the short term and the long, with the participation of the United Nations. Indeed, it is hard to imagine the United States attempting to tackle such a task without the United Nations, and it is hard to imagine the United Nations not agreeing to take an active role. It would be far better for the United States and for Iraq if we allowed the United Nations and NGOs to handle the nuts and bolts of nation building. Our greatest contributions should be the creation of the security and economic conditions to enable nation building by providing military forces and extensive financial and other assistance. However, both we and the Iraqis would likely be much better off if we left the details of economic and political reform to the United Nations and the vast community of international organizations that are more experienced in these tasks and more politically neutral than we are.

Allowing the United Nations to take the lead in coordinating the economic and political reconstruction of Iraq (and relying primarily on nongovernmental organizations to perform most functions at local levels) would have benefits other than simply being the best way to achieve our goals. Many more countries are likely to be willing to participate under U.N. auspices than under an American aegis. In addition, such an approach would allow for the rapid conversion of the oil-for-food program into a humanitarian/reconstruction program for Iraq. The oil-for-food program is the largest program in U.N. history and already is deeply interwoven with the Iraqi economy. Conducting the reconstruction efforts under U.N. auspices would probably allow for an easy shift in which the United Nations would temporarily take over the Iraqi end of the oil-for-food program, the contracting and distribution of goods. A new Security Council resolution could grant the Office of the Iraq Program, or whatever body the Security Council deemed appropriate to handle the coordination of the reconstruction effort, full control over oil-for-food monies. In fact, the existence of the oil-for-food program provides a source of immediate resources for humanitarian assistance and reconstruction, as well as an obvious foundation for the administration of such efforts.

Following the Bosnia Model

In 1996, after the Dayton Peace Accords, NATO and the United Nations created an extensive new program to rebuild Bosnia. Although few would actually use the words, this was an attempt at nation building. It got off to a very rocky start, in large part because the international organizations that did most of the work on the ground were not used to the United Nations' coordinating their efforts and were often reluctant to accept the United Nations' authority. As a result, early efforts were badly disjointed. In addition, the deep-seated ethnic resentments—hardened by the recent war—left Bosnians suspicious of one another and unwilling to cooperate fully. However, over time the effort has improved, and although Bosnia is hardly a model democracy, by as early as 1998 the U.S. State Department could brag that the country's GDP had doubled, unemployment was falling, basic services had been restored throughout the country, an independent media was thriving, and public elections had been held for all levels of government.[12] After the cessation of hostilities in Kosovo in 1999, the Bosnia model was refined and reemployed there, where it worked better as a result of the experiences in Bosnia. In particular, the efforts of the international organizations were better planned and coordinated by the U.N. Interim Administration Mission in Kosovo.[13] The lessons of Bosnia and Kosovo also played an important role in guiding the United Nations and international organizations after the fall of the Taliban in Afghanistan, although there the scope of the effort has been quite different.

The Bosnia model features simultaneous efforts to reform the political, economic, and military spheres over time. In Bosnia, these efforts included modernizing agriculture, reviving and reforming education, restoring health care (including by rebuilding hospitals and modernizing equipment and practices), repairing infrastructure, building and repairing housing, restoring sanitation and sewage services, restructuring and reforming the police force, establishing the rule of law, training lawyers and judges, building political parties, promoting transparency and accountability in governance, restoring and modernizing the energy sector, promoting the adoption of international standards of accounting, developing a regulatory banking system, privatizing industry, creating capital markets for investment, providing loans for the start-up of new companies, and building an independent media and other political institutions. Iraq would probably require a similar program.

However, in many ways, rebuilding Iraq would have advantages that have not been present in most other situations.[14] Of greatest importance, Iraq's vast oil wealth means both that it would have a ready source of cash to finance reconstruction and that many foreign countries would be looking to play an active role in rebuilding Iraq. Likewise, Iraq has a viable agriculture sector, established financial markets, and a reasonably developed infrastructure base. Prior to the imposition of the sanctions and the rationing that followed, Iraq was a largely market-based economy, and even after the Gulf War there was still a heavier market component in Iraq than had been the case behind the Iron Curtain. Afghanistan is one of the most underdeveloped countries in the world, whereas Iraq was one of the most modern in the Arab world—a relative statement but still a significant one. Finally, because of the oil-for-food program, the United Nations and many international organizations already have considerable experience in Iraq and a good understanding of where the problems lie and how they could be addressed.

Administering the Country and Building a New Polity

At the most basic level, until a new Iraqi government is formed and can take over the administration of the country, the job should probably be performed by tripartite coordinating bodies operating at a variety of levels. These tripartite bodies should each consist of an American or allied military officer in command of the forces providing security for the locality; a U.N. or senior NGO official responsible for coordinating the humanitarian assistance, economic reconstruction, and political education efforts; and either a local Iraqi leader or a committee of local Iraqi notables to work with the United States and the United Nations and advise them on all aspects of security and reconstruction. In some areas, the Iraqi component will be obvious—a local shaykh acknowledged by all, for instance—in other places it may not be so obvious, and councils of elders or committees of professionals and notables might be necessary. Such tripartite coordinating bodies would be necessary at local (township and neighborhood) levels but probably would also be useful at the provincial and national levels. Indeed, at the national level, it would be extremely helpful to form some sort of advisory council early on (preferably designated by the United Nations) to assist in decision making. Since none of the Iraqis on any of these coordinating bodies would be elected (and therefore legitimate) representatives, we would have to be careful to limit their authority. However, it would be invaluable to have Iraqis actively participating in day-to-day administration of the country as well as in building the processes that would eventually produce a new Iraqi government.

Creating a new Iraqi government that represented the will of the Iraqi people would take some time. There are at least two basic paths that Iraq could follow. A top-down approach would focus on convening an Iraqi constitutional convention (probably within six to twelve months of the end of combat operations), followed by legislative and executive elections (probably twelve to twenty-four months later) to create the central government. The central government would then be responsible for holding elections for lower-level positions and appointing personnel to the central bureaucracy. A bottom-up approach would begin with local municipal elections to put in place lower-level officials and perhaps local legislative bodies of some kind. This would be followed by the election of officials at the provincial level, ultimately building to national-level elections. The top-down approach would put a central government into place faster, allowing a more rapid turnover of political authority to the Iraqis themselves. The bottom-up approach would be more stable and would allow the Iraqis to gradually acquire experience with democratic processes before making the most important decisions. Either way, the United States and United Nations must focus on constructing brand-new Iraqi political institutions and bringing new people into the government. The old institutions and most of the officials would probably be tainted by the regime, and relying on them would inevitably mean a creeping return to old, corrupt practices and inefficient notions of administration.

Over time, U.N. officials should increasingly turn over the administration of the country to Iraqi officials as elections are held and Iraqis are legitimately brought into office. The goal should be a gradual process of transferring power back to the Iraqi people as represented by their new government. This is effectively the model that the United Nations has em-

ployed in Bosnia and Kosovo, and, given the similarly radical transformation required in Iraq, it would appear to be the best model to employ there
as well.

Military Reform

At some point after the invasion and the start of reconstruction, Iraq would
need a new army. The United States would probably welcome this development as providing us with the opportunity either to withdraw forces from the
country completely or at least to reduce them to a minimum. The key would
be to reform the Iraqi military thoroughly, to depoliticize it and inculcate
professional values and a commitment to civilian rule. This would require
everything from minor fixes—such as instituting something like the Israeli
system, whereby no serving military officer may run for political office or
occupy any other government post (such as prime minister, president, or defense minister)—to farther-reaching changes—such as revamping military
education to teach the principle that the army must be committed to defending the system of government against all foes, whether foreign or domestic
(just as American military personnel swear allegiance to the Constitution,
not the president).

The Iraqis would no doubt want a strong new military, both for reasons
of national pride and to defend themselves against their external enemies,
particularly Iran. However, the United States and its allies would want to
make sure that Iraq does not again become an overmilitarized society that
would threaten the region. In addition, we would want Iraq to honor its
obligations to the United Nations not to develop weapons of mass destruction. Consequently, the experience of West Germany after World War II
might furnish a model for Iraq's security development amenable both to the
Iraqis and to the international community. In particular, we might work to
embed a rearmed Iraq within a regional alliance system including the Gulf
states, the United States, and possibly Jordan and Egypt as well. Such a
structure would reduce Iraq's sense of threat (encouraging it to keep its military forces to modest levels) while providing a mechanism to tie the new
Iraqi armed forces in with the United States' military and with those of its
GCC neighbors to the south. If the new government in Baghdad wanted it,
the United States might retain a military presence in Iraq to ensure Iraq's
external security, even after it was no longer needed for internal security, as
we did in Europe after World War II. Obviously, such a presence would
also be reassuring to the Gulf states, without the political cost of housing it
on their own territory.

Truth and Reconciliation

Every nation that has suffered the kind of repression that Iraq has over the last thirty years has had to establish some process to deal with the crimes of its past. In some cases, this has taken the form of a general amnesty for all but a small number of the very top leaders, under the practical assumption that the society cannot withstand a long and far-reaching effort to punish every person with blood on his or her hands. Other societies have instituted only limited amnesties, believing that victims must be able to seek justice within the new political and legal system or they will pursue it outside of the system. South Africa developed the unique approach of granting individual amnesty to anyone who simply confessed to his or her crimes in full, asked forgiveness, and demonstrated genuine remorse. Although the case of South Africa is exceptional, it has the most important lesson to teach: that every nation must create a process of reconciliation that suits its unique history, cultural traditions, and political needs. In that sense, the United States should not attempt to impose any such process on Iraq and should do no more than help the Iraqis to find the process that will fit their own history, culture, and political needs.[15]

A NECESSARY TASK

If the United States is determined to overthrow Saddam Hussein's regime, we must also be determined to rebuild Iraq as a stable, functioning nation. This will not be quick; it will not be easy; and it will not be cheap. Indeed, to attempt only a minimal effort toward rebuilding post-Saddam Iraq would be to court disaster. Whenever we have taken the easy way out, the result has been chaos, civil war, and dictatorship that have only created new problems. All signs indicate that the same would hold true in Iraq, and Iraq is not a country where the United States can afford to have chaos, civil war, or another dictator like Saddam. In contrast, whenever the United States has made a long-term commitment to help rebuild a conquered state, the result has been to create a powerful new ally of the United States that has increased our own prosperity and security. One need only look to Germany, Japan, and South Korea for examples of this phenomenon.

So once again, the choice is between short-term and long-term benefits. The Pragmatic Approach offers a short-term fix but one that comes with steep risks over the long term (and the long term may only be a matter of months). The Reconstruction Approach offers a long-term solution, but only if we are willing to pay considerable costs in the short term. Although those costs should not be prohibitive and the evidence suggests that they would probably be considerably less than critics contend, they would still be considerable. American troops would have to remain in Iraq for five to ten years. The United States probably would have to spend $5 billion to $10 billion on reconstruction over that same period of time, plus as much as another $10 billion to $20 billion to maintain a military presence in the country—perhaps more if our allies are unwilling to contribute to the effort. In addition, the U.S. government would be fairly absorbed in the reconstruction effort, although there too, the examples of Bosnia and Kosovo suggest that the burden would lighten fairly quickly as the program overcame its initial difficulties.

The United States has a compelling strategic incentive to mount a full-scale military campaign to overturn Saddam Hussein's regime in the near future. Doing so would eliminate an intolerable threat to our vital national interests. Only the willingness to build a new Iraq—stable, prosperous, and pacific—would ensure that we do not simply trade one threat for another. How can any responsible American leadership tear down Saddam's regime and then leave it to fate to decide what follows? This is the crux of the security of the Persian Gulf region: it is too important to both the United States and the world to be left to chance. Where the stability and security of the Persian Gulf are concerned, we cannot afford to pinch pennies.

Not Whether, but When

At the end of the Gulf War in 1991, the international community undertook a commitment to Kuwait, Saudi Arabia, Israel, and the other nations of the Middle East. This commitment was to prevent Saddam Hussein from ever again threatening them as he had in the past. Nor was this commitment wholly altruistic; it was also motivated by a consensus that the combination of Saddam Hussein's clearly demonstrated goals, his past behavior, and his determination to acquire the most powerful weapons of mass destruction constituted a threat to the oil exports of the Persian Gulf, which were (and are) vital to the economic stability of the entire world. The international community, acting under the auspices of the U.N. Security Council, attempted to honor that commitment by imposing a demanding set of disarmament and political requirements on Iraq backed by draconian sanctions and the implicit threat of additional military operations. For the first few years after the Gulf War, this policy worked. The inspectors went in and the sanctions stayed on, and whenever Iraq attempted to renege on its commitments or challenge the authority of the international community, the Security Council sanctioned military action by the United States, the United Kingdom, and sometimes France.

However, a few more years later, this policy began to fall apart. It did not fall apart because Iraq repented of its past behavior, stopped trying to acquire weapons of mass destruction, or abandoned its aggressive goals. Remarkably, the first and most important moves by members of the international community to abandon the commitments they had made to the countries of the Middle East and to one another followed the revelations regarding Iraq's secret WMD programs by Hussein Kamel, Wafiq al-Samarra'i, and Khidhir Hamza in 1994 and 1995. They followed immediately after the Iraqi military threat to Kuwait in 1994 and after the Iraqi attack (and massacre) at Arbil in 1996. They followed immediately after Iraq began to ratchet up the pressure on the U.N. inspectors, hindering them more blatantly and in some cases even endangering their lives. Initially, the claim of the recidivists was that they wanted to loosen the containment of Iraq to aid the suffering Iraqi people—a self-evidently noble goal. However, even after the Security Council created the oil-for-food program, more and more nations walked away from their commitment to contain Iraq. Indeed, the more the Security Council liberalized the oil-for-food deal, the less support there was for containment and the more countries ignored the sanctions altogether.

Americans like to blame themselves, or their domestic opponents, for the failure of containment of Iraq. Republicans like to blame the Clinton administration for misplaying the hand left to it by the first Bush administration. Democrats like to blame the first Bush administration for leaving them a weak hand. Certainly, both claims have merit: the sanctions left in place at the end of the Gulf War were too severe to last long and lacked adequate enforcement mechanisms, while U.S. policy in the years thereafter often did not make enough of an effort to shore up diplomatic support against Iraq and push back hard against Saddam's challenges. If we had it to do all over again, the United States might well have done better with containment by dealing itself a better hand and playing it with greater determination. We probably could have made containment last many years longer.

However, to say that the United States could have handled containment better than we did is not to suggest that we were responsible for its demise. We weren't. Indeed, we and a handful of other countries—Saudi Arabia, Kuwait, Great Britain, Holland, Japan, and Australia come immediately to mind—are the only ones that are blameless in this tragedy. The culprits are the French, Chinese, Russians, and every other country that not only walked away from the commitments they joined the international community in making in 1990–91 but actively worked to undermine them. The reason that we are now faced with such unpleasant choices regarding Iraq is not so much because of our own failures but because of the perfidy of others. The fault was not in ourselves but in our stars.

The United States made a good-faith effort to try to handle the problem of Saddam Hussein and his pursuit of weapons of mass destruction through multilateral containment.[1] We tried arduously for eleven years, fighting and being repeatedly slandered by Saddam Hussein and his allies for our efforts. The United Nations' effort at collective security with regard to Iraq has failed despite our labors; but because we are the world's only remaining superpower and the only country with the capability to prevent Saddam from again threatening the region and its oil supplies, we are the ones who will have to clean up the mess we tried to prevent others from making. There is a lesson here beyond Iraq—that the members of the international community who bleat about the importance of collective security, multilateral diplomacy, and international law have gravely weakened all three (not to mention the U.N. Security Council) by allowing Iraq to flout them while chastising the United States (and our handful of allies) when we objected and attempted to hold Iraq accountable for its actions. Why would the United States, or any other country, turn to the United Nations for a multilateral solution to another difficult security problem after the experience of Iraq?

HALF MEASURES WILL NO LONGER WORK

So now, once again, we are confronting the threat of Saddam Hussein, his determination to dominate the Persian Gulf region and its oil resources, and his quest for nuclear weapons in pursuit of that goal. And the choices we face are much starker today because we have already tried so many of the "middle options"—those policies lying between the extremes of deterrence and invasion—only to see them founder on the faithlessness of our allies or be overtaken by the events that have transpired since the end of the Gulf War.

For the same reasons that containment failed, it is unrealistic to imagine that it can be revived. The international community has forgotten its commitment to the countries of the region and its past concerns about Saddam Hussein. Even if some of these countries could be persuaded to support new containment measures as the only alternative to a U.S. invasion, they would not last. How long would Russia, China, Syria, Iran, Jordan, Turkey, or six dozen other countries actually respect such new measures? Would we measure their adherence to a new containment regime in months, weeks, or just days? Their behavior gives no reason to expect them to make good on new pledges, nor is it even clear what kind of pledges we could get from them. In a world that has simply decided that the Iraq sanctions are evil and have caused the death of millions of Iraqis, how could the United States get the Security Council to enact new, stricter sanctions with explicit punitive measures for those who violate them? In a world that has decided that Saddam is "qualitatively disarmed," how would the United States convince the Security Council to impose a new inspections regime capable of doing what the original inspections regime could not and actually root out Saddam's clandestine programs? Moreover, how could we convince the international community to sustain such measures over time?

Even if the United States could convince the international community and Iraq to accept these new measures because the gun of a U.S. invasion force massed in Kuwait and Saudi Arabia were held to their heads, how long would they abide by what they inevitably would consider a form of extortion by Washington? Especially having seen us fail to pull the trigger so many times and knowing that we could not hold that gun in place for more than a few months, Iraq's advocates might not even give us a "decent interval" before they started abandoning their own promises. And let us not delude ourselves that we will get another chance to invade if we pass this one up. In the wake of 9/11 and with the Iraqis as far along on their nuclear program as the former inspectors and knowledgeable defectors believe them to be, a window is open now that will close in the near future. When it does, it will not open again.

Nor should we think that there is a "silver bullet"—a CIA assassin or the magic of air power—that would allow us to solve the problem of Saddam without exerting ourselves. We, and other countries, have tried the covert action route and failed. We have failed because protecting himself against assassins, coups, and popular revolts is the one thing Saddam is good at. Likewise, the conditions that made victory possible in Afghanistan using only air power, special forces, and opposition ground forces are not the conditions we would encounter in Iraq, making it unlikely that this strategy could work against Saddam. The Iraqi opposition is a shambles, and its main groups will not support the Afghan Approach, nor will the allies in the region that would be crucial to its success. We tried a far more punishing air campaign against Iraq in 1991, yet the tattered army that emerged from Operation Desert Storm was still able to crush the two largest opposition revolts in Iraqi history in just a few weeks. Even if we could somehow solve all these problems, we would still have to find ways to deal with Saddam's counteroffensive options while we were trying out our "theories of air power."

To try to topple Saddam with halfway measures would be to court disaster. In the case of regime change in Iraq, we will get what we pay for. If the United States is unwilling to commit the forces necessary to ensure success and the resources necessary to rebuild a stable, prosperous Iraq afterward, it has no business trying to bring about Saddam's overthrow.

RISKS AND COSTS

So there are two paths now left open to the United States. We can decide that we are never going to try to make an all-out effort to remove Saddam before he acquires nuclear weapons but rather will simply try to deter him once he has acquired them, or we can embark on an invasion. These two options could be likened to two paths, one flat and easily traversed but laced with land mines, the other steep and rocky, but without land mines and with little risk of falling off the edge because we are surefooted and possess the best mountain-climbing tools.

This is the difference between deterrence and invasion as policy options, the difference between risks and costs. Deterrence is very low cost (at least for the United States), although it is not "no cost." We would have to maintain combat-ready forces in the Gulf region and the capability to reinforce them quickly, we would continue to pay a political price for their presence in Saudi Arabia and the problem of "linkage" with the Arab-Israeli confrontation, and we would have to work hard to convince Saddam that we really would be willing to fight a nuclear war amid the oil fields of the Persian Gulf region to defend Kuwait. But these requirements are still relatively cheap, at least in economic and military terms. The operational costs would be a tiny portion of the massive Pentagon budget, and on any given day the likelihood that Saudi public opinion would cause a real problem is small. However, we should not forget the terrible price that the people of Iraq, and especially the Kurds, would pay once the last vestiges of their American protection were removed. Shifting to deterrence might mean enabling genocide.

The trade-off deterrence makes to get those low costs is running very high risks. The lesser of those risks—just because it seems less likely—is that our continued presence in the Gulf region for many years to come (as long as this Iraqi regime remains in power) could help create real instability in Saudi Arabia or some of the other Gulf states. The greater and much more ominous risk is that we will find out that Saddam cannot be deterred once he acquires a nuclear weapon. The central assumption of deterrence is that once Saddam acquires nuclear weapons, he will suddenly behave in a manner completely different from (in fact, diametrically opposed to) how he has acted since he first came to power in the early 1970s. Saddam's decision making has been characterized by miscalculation, extreme risk taking, a total disregard for human life, a willingness to suffer tremendous damage in pursuit of his goals, and a terrifying willingness to interpret reality in fantastic ways to suit the needs of the moment. He has consistently taken actions that could have proven suicidal—and which many of his aides seem to have recognized as potentially fatal—but that he convinced himself were certain to turn out in his favor.

Indeed, there is nothing about Saddam's track record or personality profile to suggest that he will behave in a conservative, risk-averse manner once he obtains nuclear weapons. And this is the fundamental risk of deterrence: that we have to trust Saddam Hussein to behave like a reasonable, conservative leader who will not even start down the road to miscalculation. For anyone willing to live with these risks, deterrence undoubtedly makes great sense. But ask yourself if you truly are willing to bet your savings, your job, or your life that Saddam Hussein will not use a nuclear weapon or embark on some new aggression in the belief that his nuclear weapons will deter the United States. That is the risk of deterrence.

An invasion of Iraq promises to minimize the risks, but it does so at potentially high costs. Just as deterrence is not cost-free, so an invasion would not be risk-free—in particular, there is the risk that a U.S.-led invasion would provoke widespread unrest in the Arab world and possibly even lead to the overthrow of one or more of the moderate Arab states. However, this seems highly unlikely, and the moderate Arab states themselves (which tend to exaggerate their own internal problems) do not seem to be overly worried about such a development. It seems reasonable not to be "more Catholic than the Pope" on this issue and to believe that if the moderate Arab states believe they can handle any popular backlash from an invasion, so too can we.

Strangely, then, an invasion is actually the *conservative* course of action in the sense that it accepts higher costs to minimize risks. It is the one policy that would give us the greatest certainty that Saddam Hussein will never be able to threaten the region, the United States, or the world with nuclear weapons. It is the one strategy that would guarantee that the problem of Saddam will be solved. It is the one policy that would guarantee us that we will not have to endure multiple nuclear crises with Saddam or fight a war against a nuclear-armed Iraq.

Of course, these certainties (or near certainties) come with significant price tags attached. The United States would have to be willing to mount a full-scale invasion of Iraq that would be costly in terms of both dollars and missed opportunities elsewhere in the world. An invasion of Iraq would be our highest foreign policy priority for a considerable period of time, during which we might well have to forgo other initiatives. It is also certain that some American soldiers and some Iraqi civilians would die in an invasion. Although it is likely that deaths from an invasion would number in the high hundreds for U.S. military personnel and the high thousands for Iraqi civilians, if things did not work out the way we expected them to (a not infrequent occurrence in war), we might suffer several thousand American military personnel killed and several tens of thousands of Iraqi civilians killed. Of course, we could end up with a virtually painless victory if things worked out better than we expected, but we should go into this with our eyes open to the worst-case possibilities and be willing to pay those costs before committing ourselves to this course of action.

Even a low-cost invasion would require a potentially expensive nation-building effort to create a new, stable, prosperous, and legitimate Iraqi state thereafter. Even with considerable help from our allies in Europe, Asia, and the Middle East and the expectation that Iraqi oil and the abilities of a reasonably gifted Iraqi populace would limit our own contribution to reconstruction, the United States would have to be willing to make a major commitment to Iraq for years to come. We would have to be there to keep the peace, to help build a new political and economic system, to help mend the wounds Saddam has inflicted on Iraqi society, to defend Iraq against predatory neighbors, and to institutionalize all of these changes. We would undoubtedly have to contribute financially to Iraq's recovery as well, and this could easily amount to several billion dollars per year for as long as a decade. And because Iraq is too important a country in too fragile a part of the world, we could not afford not to make such a commitment if we were to lead an invasion that pulled down the current Iraqi political system.

If we are not willing to bear these costs, we should not embark on an invasion. But if we are reluctant to bear these costs, we should also consider the potential costs of not invading—the costs we will have to pay if, as seems likely, we had to fight Iraq at some point after Saddam Hussein has acquired nuclear weapons. From that vantage point, I suspect that the costs of an invasion and reconstruction of Iraq would look paltry and we would seem tragically shortsighted if we refused to pay them. How many would die in a war against a nuclear-armed Saddam? And how much would it cost to repair the damage to the whole world if the oil infrastructure of the Persian Gulf region were obliterated in such a war? In this case, an ounce of prevention would likely be worth a ton of cure.

SOONER OR LATER?

Looked at purely from the narrow perspective of U.S. policy toward Iraq, the sooner we undertake the invasion of Iraq the better. Saddam is working to reconstitute his weapons of mass destruction programs, and the more time he has, the more lethal that arsenal will become. Of greatest importance, the more time we give him, the more likely he will be able to acquire one or more nuclear weapons. To return to the assessments of Western intelligence agencies, if Saddam began a crash program in 1998, as recent sources have indicated, the most pessimistic assessments suggest he could have a nuclear weapon by 2004, while the more optimistic ones predict that he will have one by 2008. Since the whole point is to prevent Saddam from acquiring nuclear weapons, we may not have to move immediately, but we cannot tarry for very long.

The sooner we move against Iraq, the weaker Saddam will be in terms of both his conventional and nonconventional capabilities and therefore the lower the potential costs of an invasion. Some have argued that the weakness of Iraq's current arsenal means that it is unnecessary to invade at this point—because Saddam does not constitute an immediate threat.[2] This claim effectively suggests that we should wait until Saddam acquires the capacity to inflict massive damage before we take action against him. This is the problem we face: by the time Saddam truly is threatening, it will be too late to do anything about it. We act either before he has acquired these capabilities or not at all. It is the relative weakness of Iraq's current weapons of mass destruction that makes an invasion feasible. Given that Saddam's motives are well established and that every other multilateral or unilateral approach to stopping him has failed, it would be madness to wait until he has developed the capabilities to cause grievous damage to us and to the region before we decided to take action against him. At least those who advocate a policy of deterrence recognize that once Saddam has acquired nuclear weapons, we cannot try to remove him and instead will then have to try to find a way to live with him.

In addition, we need to keep in mind that what makes any of this discussion possible is the shock to the American populace as a result of the terrorist attacks of September 11, 2001, and the public's willingness to make sacrifices and take forceful action to eliminate other such threats. This willingness may not last forever. Especially given the administration's bizarre determination not to engage the American public in the war on terrorism and instead to urge Americans to go back to their normal lives, the sense of threat may dissipate quickly. Indeed, the polls demonstrate that with each passing month, the willingness of Americans to use force to remove Saddam from power declines a bit further. Once this willingness disappears, it will be difficult for the administration to motivate the American public to make the sacrifices necessary to remove Saddam from power.

However, there are also some important countervailing pressures with regard to timing. Even within the parameters of the Iraq policy, the United States would have to do a lot of work before it would be ready to invade. Not only would there be military preparations that could take anywhere from three to five months from a decision to go, but there would be a range of diplomatic and political tasks as well. The administration would have to make its case to the American people and their representatives in the Congress and secure popular support for both the military campaign and the subsequent occupation and reconstruction efforts. Washington would have to line up the support of the Gulf states, Egypt, and Turkey, at the very least, just to be able to make the operation happen. Beyond that, we would do well to work hard to try to bring as many European, Asian, and other allies on board as possible. Some could provide military help; others could provide economic assistance; all would provide important diplomatic support. A larger coalition would reduce the strains on the moderate Arab states; generate greater legitimacy for the operation in the United States, Iraq, and around the world; and greatly ease the burden of the rebuilding of Iraq afterward.

We also have some unfinished business at the moment that should take precedence over invading Iraq. Namely, we first need to deal with the threat of terrorism. Although Saddam Hussein's acquisition of nuclear weapons may ultimately constitute a greater threat to the United States and the world than al-Qa'eda terrorism, it is also a somewhat more distant threat. Even if Iraq is only a few years from acquiring a nuclear weapon, the fact is that al-Qa'eda is attacking us right now and has demonstrated a capability that Saddam never has—the ability to reach into the U.S. homeland and kill three thousand American civilians. We don't necessarily have to finish the war against al-Qa'eda before taking up arms against Saddam—that is likely to be a very long fight because of the amorphous nature of bin Ladin's terrorist network. However, we certainly need to be at a point where we do not have monthly government warnings of possible terrorist attacks. In the immediate wake of 9/11, we rightly devoted all of the United States' diplomatic, intelligence, and military attention to eradicating the threat from al-Qa'eda, and as long as that remains the case we should not indulge in a distraction as great as toppling Saddam. We cannot afford to alienate our allies over our policy toward Iraq and convince them to drag their feet in helping us against al-Qa'eda in return.

When al-Qa'eda will be defanged enough for us to undertake an invasion of Iraq is going to be a judgment call. No matter how successful we are, because of the nature of our open society and the terrorist threats, we will probably still suffer occasional terrorist attacks in the future. Likewise, we are unlikely ever to eradicate all of the al-Qa'eda cells or capture all of the al-Qa'eda personnel in the world. Hence that cannot be the standard either. However, we can cause the organization as a whole to wither—just as the West did with some of the worst terrorist organizations of the 1970s, such as the Baader-Meinhof Gang and the Japanese Red Army Faction. Of course, in those cases, only in retrospect did we realize that these groups had essentially disappeared years before.

The best way to think about sorting out the priorities between Iraq and al-Qa'eda is to imagine that the United States invades Iraq and that while we are doing so, al-Qa'eda conducts another terrorist attack that results in the death of several hundred Americans. In this hypothetical scenario, the president should be able to honestly tell the relatives of the victims killed in such a new terrorist attack that there was nothing else the U.S. government could have done to prevent the attack and there was nothing about the operations in Iraq that distracted or diminished the nation's vigilance against al-Qa'eda. Only when the administration can meet this standard should we embark upon so large an additional endeavor as invading Iraq.

Another factor arguing for a somewhat longer timeline is the need to cool the tensions of the region, especially the Israeli-Palestinian violence. Much as we may or may not like it, the simple fact is that we must have the Gulf states, Egypt, and Turkey on board to be able to conduct an invasion. Only when those countries believe that their internal stability can withstand any potential unrest triggered by an invasion will they be willing to act. We certainly should hold their feet to the fire and make clear that the threat from a nuclear-armed Saddam—which they fear as much as we do—is not one that will wait, nor will U.S. public opinion remain energized forever. But by the same token, it is reasonable for them to expect us to take a more active role in attempting to mollify the problems of the region, particularly the Israeli-Palestinian violence. Much as we may not like mediating between Israel and the Palestinians, if we are going to deal with the problem of Saddam Hussein, it is necessary that we do so.

So this is the choice that confronts us: not whether, but when. And "When?" is a hard question to answer. We cannot postpone an invasion for too long, or it will become impossible and the very event we seek to prevent will come to pass. What's more, we simply do not know when Saddam will have a nuclear weapon, and we cannot afford to be wrong. The conservative course of action would be to invade as soon as possible to guard against the uncertainty in our assessments of Iraq's nuclear program. However, we have a lot of work to do in terms of political, military, and diplomatic preparations; the need to get the more immediate threat from al-Qa'eda under better control; and the need to reduce the bedlam in the Middle East to lower levels. Unless and until we have done that preparatory work, an invasion of Iraq itself would be the risky option.

LOOKING BACK ON THE FUTURE

At the beginning of this book, I raised the analogous situation confronting Britain and France as they faced Germany in 1938. Despite the fact that the balance of power lay in their favor, London and Paris decided against war in 1938 because of the potential costs of a war at that time, even one they expected to be victorious. Those costs seemed so high that they concluded that there had to be another way and so opted for appeasement. In addition, many people in Britain and France were certain that Hitler would be satisfied with the Czechoslovakian Sudetenland and would change his ways after that. Imagine going to those same decision makers in 1945, after the graves of tens of millions had been dug, hundreds of cities had burned to the ground, and the smoke from London, Rotterdam, Dresden, and Berlin had started to clear. Imagine asking them then if, knowing what they did in 1945, they might have felt differently about the costs of going to war on their terms in 1938 rather than allowing Hitler to start the war on his terms in 1939.

We face a similar choice with Iraq today. No one can say for certain that we will have to fight a war with a nuclear-armed Saddam, but based on all of his history and all of the evidence we have about his thinking, it seems very likely. If we go to war today on our terms, we can be as confident in victory as it is possible to be in an undertaking as inherently uncertain as warfare. On the other hand, we can wait till tomorrow and risk the death of millions and the ruin of the global economy in the hope that Saddam will defy the evidence and the odds and become a man of peace.

It is wrong to claim that Saddam Hussein is irrational. However, it is equally wrong to believe that because he coldly and rationally calculates the odds, he gets those calculations correct. For more than thirty years, Saddam's pattern has been to coldly miscalculate the odds, with disastrous results for Iraq and its neighbors. Where the lives and livelihoods of so many are at stake, it would be reckless and irresponsible to gamble with the future by betting on Saddam's sudden conversion to prudence and restraint.

What's more, it is also important to consider the two futures of the Middle East and the world. The status quo means more of the same: more crises with Iraq, someday with the added incendiary of nuclear weapons; more disputes with our Gulf allies over our policies, our military presence, and everything else under the sun; more Arab-Israeli crises; more instability; more stagnation; more autocracy, anti-Americanism, and terrorism. The Middle East has bred nothing but trouble for decades. A U.S. invasion of Iraq probably wouldn't suddenly transform the entire region any more than Saddam's acquisition of nuclear weapons is likely to transform his decision making. However, it would present an opportunity to rebuild Iraq—to create a stable, prosperous, inclusive new Arab state that could serve as a model for the region. It would give us an opportunity to turn Iraq from a malignant growth helping to poison the Middle East into an engine for change for the entire region. It would allow us to harness the human and material resources of what is probably the most richly endowed of all of the Arab states and try to make it a force that could help start to bring the Arab world out of the miasma into which it has sunk.

We are at an important moment in the history of the United States. We know that we face a grave problem with Saddam Hussein, and we have good evidence that it is going to be a much bigger problem in the future than it is today. We can ignore the problem and hope it will just go away, or we can take the steps needed to solve it. Those steps will not be easy, and we should not downplay them. But they also will not be excessively onerous, and we should not exaggerate them—we will not have to mount World War II and the Marshall Plan again. The question that we need to ask ourselves today is, ten years from now, when we look back on this moment which choice will we most regret not having made?

We faced an identical moment in 1941. We like to tell ourselves that the reason we fought World War II in Europe was because Hitler declared war on us. Nonsense. We went looking for that fight, and we welcomed it when it came. If we had not felt threatened by Hitler long before Pearl Harbor, there would have been no aid to Britain and Russia, no Lend-Lease, no Churchill-Roosevelt conversations, no staff discussions, no destroyers-for-bases deals. And had we not been open supporters of Germany's adversaries, there is little reason to think Hitler would have declared war on us when he did. Instead, we could have remained in isolation and embraced a policy of deterrence against Hitler, just as we are being urged to do against Saddam. After all, the threat we felt from Hitler was also not immediate— it was the vague notion that if Germany possessed all of the wealth of continental Europe, it would inevitably pose some kind of threat to the United States. We knew that joining the war against Germany would not be easy, but we believed that the costs were worth bearing because the alternative was to fight a much worse war in the future. Fighting Germany in World War II was one of the best things this country ever did. It did cost us a great deal, but it saved us from having to fight that much worse war, and it allowed us to remake the world.

Saddam Hussein is not Adolf Hitler, mostly because Iraq is not as powerful as Germany was. And defeating Saddam Hussein will not require the same sacrifices as defeating Hitler did. But the threat that Saddam presents to the United States and to the world is just as real, and the one we have today is no less pressing than those we faced in 1941. Franklin Delano Roosevelt defended the provision of aid to Great Britain against Nazi Germany under the Lend-Lease Act by arguing that if your neighbor's house were on fire and you had a hose, wouldn't you lend it to him—if only to put the fire out before your house caught too? Today another house is burning, and we are the only ones strong enough to douse the blaze. An invasion of Iraq may not be cost-free, but it is unlikely to be horrific and it is the only sensible course of action left to us. We would do well to remember John Stuart Mill's remark that "war is an ugly thing, but it is not the ugliest of things." In our case, the ugliest of things would be to hide our heads in the sand while Saddam Hussein acquires the capability to kill millions of people and hold the economy of the world in the palm of his cruel hand.

ACKNOWLEDGMENTS

This book would have been impossible without the assistance of a number of people. Pride of place, however, should be given to my two researchers, Lauren Cook and Dafna Hochman, who proved invaluable to the entire endeavor. Lauren and Dafna performed above and beyond the call of duty under tremendous time constraints. Their work was outstanding, and on several occasions the information they uncovered opened up entirely new paths for me. They carried much of the burden of this book, and they did it with grace, cheer, and intelligence. In the midst of this process, we also received welcome reinforcement in the form of Ari Varon, who pitched in immediately and made an instant contribution.

Leslie Gelb, Larry Korb, Patricia Dorff, and the Council on Foreign Relations have my deepest thanks for their support, encouragement, and assistance throughout the writing of this book. Les and Larry quite simply made the book possible by giving me the time to write with minimal distractions and the resources to get it done. More than that, Les Gelb's strategy sessions on Iraq and our constant discussions on the subject provided important opportunities for me to develop my thinking and pursue alternative approaches. Les forever stirred my thinking and forced me to defend my positions. In addition, Les's constant prodding to take advantage of the full resources of the Council, and particularly its world-class experts, made this a much better book than it otherwise would have been. I am very proud to have this work carry the imprimatur of a Council on Foreign Relations book, because without the Council's support it would have been a far poorer effort. In addition, my work on this book was made possible by a generous grant from the John M. Olin Foundation to the Council, and having been a beneficiary of its support before, I continue to be grateful to them for making my work possible.

I have always believed that the more comments and criticism a book or article receives, the better it turns out. This book was no exception, and I have many friends and colleagues to thank for their assistance. Bart Aronson, Dan Byman, Martin Indyk, Ben Miller, Andrew Parasiliti, Mark Parris, Bruce Riedel, Gideon Rose, Joe Siegle, Steve Ward, and Michael Weinstein all read parts or all of the manuscript and provided a wealth of good advice. It is a much better work for their efforts, and any remaining flaws are mine alone. Jeff Wichman and Jamie Renner also pitched in with important advice on key issues. In addition, as always when I write on Iraq, Amatzia Baram was generous with his wealth of knowledge and wisdom on things Iraqi, and he once again has my sincere thanks.

On several occasions, Admiral John Sigler (USN, Ret.), Lieutenant General Bernard Trainor (USMC, Ret.), Colonel Phillip Rudder (USMC), Colonel Chris Miller (USAF), Colonel Robert McClure (USA), Captain Jeffrey Niner (USN), Dr. John Hillen (USA, Res.), and Guillermo Christensen helped me (wittingly or unwittingly) to work through some of the complicated issues regarding the use of force against Iraq. In addition, there are a number of other U.S. military officers who provided advice and guidance on these matters but who requested anonymity, and I am happy to comply with their wishes while thanking them for their assistance.

This book was vetted by both the National Security Council and the Central Intelligence Agency, my former employers, according to the requirements of my security clearance agreements with them. They did request that I delete or rephrase several minor passages in the interest of national security. I do not believe that these changes detract from the book in any meaningful way. Scott Koch and Rod Soubers have my gratitude for handling these procedures quickly and efficiently. In addition, Jane Green and Jeff Wichman also have my thanks for allowing me latitude on a prior commitment to make it possible to produce this volume.

Jonathan Karp, my remarkable editor at Random House, also deserves thanks for several reasons. First and foremost, for thinking to ask me if I would like to do some writing for him. I will never forget the day I got a blind e-mail from Jon asking me if I wanted to turn my *Foreign Affairs* article on Iraq policy into a book. Second, for helping me to write a book that would be useful to people beyond my narrow world of Middle East policy experts. Jon frequently gave the most important advice of all: pointing out when I was getting too deep into the weeds of Iraqi military history or U.S. diplomatic affairs for anyone else to care. For someone who had never written anything other than policy memos and academic articles, I am grateful to have had Jon play a much needed Virgil to my uncertain Dante.

Random House virtually turned itself inside out to help me get this book written, published, and sold. I'm particularly grateful to publisher Ann Godoff, deputy publisher Howard Weill, and associate publisher Ivan Held for believing in this project and making the process so easy. Production editor Steve Messina, designer Casey Hampton, production manager Kathy Rosenbloom, and managing editor Amy Edelman did superb work, with flexibility and attentiveness I will always appreciate. Thanks also to Libby McGuire, Carol Schneider, Tom Perry, Todd Doughty, and Elizabeth Fogarty for their marketing and publicity savvy. Jake Greenberg did most of the heavy lifting for all of the details that have to get done to publish a book, and he too has my gratitude. Dan Rembert did a magnificent job with the book cover, and Lynn Anderson accomplished the Sisyphean task of copyediting my prose with such skill that she seems to have actually gotten the boulder over the hill.

And last, I'd like to thank my wife, Andrea, to whom this work is dedicated. She is my inspiration and my salvation. She is also the best thing to have come from fifteen years of wrestling with Saddam. For what I know seemed like a lifetime, she put up with me and the writing of this book. Without her support, encouragement, affection, and patience, I don't think I could have gotten through it. And for this, and for so much more, she has my undying love and gratitude.

NOTES

Introduction: The Problem of Iraq

1. Doyle McManus and Robin Wright, "After Kabul, Should Iraq be Next?" *Los Angeles Times,* November 22, 2001.
2. There is some confusion about the proper shorthand for Saddam Hussein's name. The correct shorthand is "Saddam." It is not "Hussein," which is merely Saddam's father's first name, not Saddam's family name. Indeed, the insistence of many American newspapers in referring to Saddam as "Mr. Hussein" is even more ridiculous than calling Mao Zedong "Mr. Zedong." In Iraqi tribal society, most people do not have family names. Instead they are called by their own first name and their father's first name, and sometimes add their grandfather's first name, and even their great-grandfather's first name. Thus Saddam Hussein essentially means "Saddam, son of Hussein." Saddam's father's name was Hussein 'Abd al-Majid—'Abd al-Majid being Saddam's grandfather's name. Saddam's sons' names are Udayy Saddam and Qusayy Saddam—their own first names followed by their father's first name. Sometimes, the patriarch of a family will give his name (his first name) to his entire clan, which then becomes a family name. This is not the case for Saddam: he reportedly hates the memory of his father and refuses to allow his father's name to become a clan name for his near relatives.
3. See the conflicting versions in Michael Isikoff, "The Phantom Link to Iraq," *Newsweek,* May 6, 2002, p. 36; and Radio Free Europe/Radio Liberty, "Hijacker Met with Iraqi Agent, Czech Official Says," *Iraq Report,* vol. 5, no. 17, June 7, 2002.
4. Jeffrey Goldberg, "The Great Terror," *The New Yorker,* March 25, 2002, pp. 69–70; Scott Peterson, "Iraqi Funds, Training Fuel Islamic Terror Group," *The Christian Science Monitor,* April 2, 2002.

5. Paul Pillar, *Terrorism and U.S. Foreign Policy* (Washington, D.C.: Brookings Institution, 2001), p. 160.

6. Pew Research Center, "Americans and Europeans Differ Widely on Foreign Policy Issues," April 20, 2002, http://peoplepress.org/reports/display.php3?PageID=453, downloaded on May 14, 2002.

7. Andrea Stone, "Poll: 59% Say U.S. Should Take Military Action in Iraq," *USA Today,* June 21, 2002.

8. Technically, these should be referred to as "chemical warfare weapons" and "biological warfare weapons," and the acronyms CW and BW actually stand for "chemical warfare" and "biological warfare," but I have adopted the colloquialisms for this book.

9. The six GCC states are Saudi Arabia, Kuwait, Bahrain, Qatar, the United Arab Emirates, and Oman.

10. Susan Blaustein and John Fawcett, "Sources of Revenue for Saddam & Sons, Inc.," Coalition for International Justice, draft manuscript, pp. 16–29; David Butter, "Dancing on Sanctions' Grave," *Middle East Economic Digest,* December 8, 2000; David Butter, "The Baghdad Dilemma," *Middle East Economic Digest,* January 18, 2002; "Can Sanctions Be Smarter?" *The Economist,* May 24, 2001; *The Economist* Intelligence Unit, "EIU Country Report Iraq," March 2002; "Iraq Accused of Smuggling Illegal Oil," *Los Angeles Times,* October 26, 2001; "Lebanon, Iraq Sign Oil Pact," United Press International, July 11, 2002; Colum Lynch, "Iraq Caught Smuggling Oil, UN Official Says," *The Washington Post,* October 26, 2001; William Orme, "The World: Syria Faces Pressure to Halt Alleged Iraqi Oil Flows," *Los Angeles Times,* January 29, 2002; "Iraq Seeks to Torpedo New Sanctions Resolution," *Middle East Economic Digest,* June 1, 2001; Nicole Pope, "Sanctions 'Leaking all Over the Place,' " MSNBC, available at www.msnbc.com, downloaded April 2002; Charles Rechnagel, "Turkey: Iraqi Diesel Trade Seen as Too Valuable to Stop," *Radio Free Europe/Radio Liberty,* August 4, 2000.

11. Sarah Graham-Brown, *Sanctioning Saddam* (London: I. B. Tauris, 1999), p. 174, n. 48.

12. Nicholas Berry, "China, Fiber-Optics and Iraq," Center for Defense Information, February 26, 2001.

PART I: IRAQ AND THE UNITED STATES

Chapter 1: From Sumer to Saddam

1. The best overview of the Islamic era remains Albert Hourani, *A History of the Arab Peoples* (Cambridge, Mass.: Harvard University Press, 1991).

2. The Sunni are the mainstream Islamic sect, representing the majority of Muslims in the Middle East, except in Iraq, Iran, and Bahrain. The Kurds are a non-Arab people believed to be an amalgam of Semitic and Central Asian groups.

3. On the Ottoman era, see Lord Kinross, *The Ottoman Centuries* (New York: Morrow Quill, 1977).

4. On the origins of the Iraqi state, see David Fromkin, *A Peace to End All Peace* (New York: Avon, 1989).

5. He may have been born in 1939. See Said K. Aburish, *Saddam Hussein: The Politics of Revenge* (New York: Bloomsbury, 2000), p. 10.

6. Although none of the biographies of Saddam available in English is without problems, the two best known are Said K. Aburish, ibid.; and Efraim Karsh and Inari Rautsi, *Saddam Hussein: A Political Biography* (New York: Free Press, 1991).

7. Karsh and Rautsi, ibid., p. 37.

8. On Iraqi history since World War I, the best sources are Hanna Batatu, *The Old Social Classes and the Revolutionary Movements of Iraq* (Princeton, N.J.: Princeton University Press, 1978); Phebe Marr, *The Modern History of Iraq* (Boulder, Colo.: Westview, 1985); Marion Farouk-Sluglett and Peter Sluglett, *Iraq Since 1958* (New York: I. B. Tauris, 1990); Charles Tripp, *A History of Iraq* (Cambridge, England: Cambridge University Press, 2000). Marr is currently writing an updated version of her work. A good recent popular history is Sandra Mackey, *The Reckoning: Iraq and the Legacy of Saddam Hussein* (New York: W. W. Norton, 2002).

9. Kanan Makiya, *Republic of Fear,* 1998 paperback edition (Berkeley: University of California Press, 1998), p. 72.

10. Michael A. Palmer, *The Guardians of the Gulf: A History of America's Expanding Role in the Persian Gulf, 1833–1992* (New York: Free Press, 1993), pp. 1–12.

11. Palmer, ibid., pp. 13–14; Daniel Yergin, *The Prize* (New York: Simon and Schuster, 1991), pp. 135–139.

12. Palmer, ibid., p. 22; Yergin, ibid., pp. 305–388.

13. Quoted in Yergin, ibid., p. 393.

14. Quoted in Palmer, *Guardians of the Gulf,* p. 42.

15. Ibid., p. 269, n. 5.

16. Ibid., pp. 85–96.

17. Anthony Cordesman, *The Gulf and the Search for Strategic Stability* (Boulder, Colo.: Westview, 1984), p. 160.

18. John Ranelagh, *The Agency: The Rise and Decline of the CIA* (New York: Simon and Schuster, 1986), pp. 607–608.

19. Palmer, *Guardians of the Gulf,* pp. 102–103.

20. Bruce W. Jentleson, *With Friends like These: Reagan, Bush, and Saddam, 1982–1990* (New York: W. W. Norton, 1994), p. 41.

21. On Iraq's war aims, see, e.g., Phebe Marr, "The Iran-Iraq War: The View from Iraq," in Christopher C. Joyner, ed., *The Persian Gulf War: Lessons for Strategy, Law, and Diplomacy* (Westport, Conn.: Greenwood Press, 1990), pp. 59–74.

22. On the military conduct of the Iran-Iraq War, see Kenneth M. Pollack, *Arabs at War: Military Effectiveness, 1948–1991* (Lincoln: University of Nebraska Press, 2002), pp. 183–235.

23. The name Osiraq comes from combining the name of the French reactor, "Osiris," and the name "Iraq." In French, it is spelled "Osirak" since the French spell Iraq "Irak."

24. On the Iraqi military in the 1973 Arab-Israeli War, see Pollack, *Arabs at War,* pp. 168–175.

25. Jentleson, *With Friends like These,* pp. 52–53; Dilip Hiro, *The Longest War: The Iran-Iraq Military Conflict* (New York: Routledge, 1991), p. 63; Ze'ev Schiff and Ehud Ya'ari, *Israel's Lebanon War* (New York: Simon and Schuster, 1984), pp. 99–100.

26. Jentleson, ibid., p. 33; Jeffrey T. Richelson, *The U.S. Intelligence Community,* 4th ed. (Boulder, Colo.: Westview, 1999), p. 352.

27. Aburish, *Saddam Hussein,* p. 228; Rick Francona, *Ally to Adversary: An Eyewitness Account of Iraq's Fall from Grace* (Annapolis, Md.: U.S. Naval Institute Press, 1999), pp. 5–6; Jentleson, ibid., pp. 42–55; Richelson, *The U.S. Intelligence Community,* p. 352.

28. Jentleson, ibid., p. 45.

29. Khidhir Hamza with Jeff Stein, *Saddam's Bombmaker* (New York: Scribner, 2000), pp. 196–197, 209–210.

30. There are some who contend that Saddam struck the *Stark* on purpose. Although it is possible, this strikes me as unlikely. There are claims of secret signals intelligence reports or Israeli spy reports proving Iraq's malice, but I have never seen any of them. Such an Iraqi move would have required a fairly elaborate conspiracy theory to make sense, and none has the ring of truth. What's more, the Iraqi pilot did nothing out of the ordinary: he flew down the Saudi coastline until he could see Farsi Island, swung east, turned on his radar, and fired at the first ship he saw. U.S. intelligence and military personnel saw this time and again during the Iran-Iraq War, and many had been saying for years that given how poor the Iraqi pilots were and how bad their mission planning was, it was only a matter of time before there was a nasty accident.

31. Jentleson, *With Friends like These,* pp. 48–49.

32. Interview with Wafiq al-Samarra'i, "Former Military Intelligence Chief Interviewed," Voice of the People of Kurdistan, December 18, 1994, in FBIS-NES-94-243, December 19, 1994, p. 33; Hamza, *Saddam's Bombmaker,* pp. 200–202; David McDowall, *A Modern History of the Kurds* (London: I. B. Tauris, 1996), pp. 349–360.

33. Jentleson, *With Friends like These,* pp. 68–93; McDowall, ibid., p. 363.

34. Jentleson, ibid., p. 81.

35. Aburish, *Saddam Hussein,* p. 216.

36. Ibid., pp. 228–229; Jentleson, *With Friends like These,* pp. 47–48.

37. Lawrence Freedman and Efraim Karsh, *The Gulf Conflict, 1990–1991* (Princeton, N.J.: Princeton University Press, 1993), p. 21.

38. Ibid., p. 22.

39. Anthony Cordesman and Abraham Wagner, *The Lessons of Modern War,* vol. 2: *The Iran-Iraq War* (Boulder, Colo.: Westview, 1990), p. 389.

40. Ibid., pp. 395–399; Gary Sick, "Trial by Error: Reflections on the Iran-Iraq War," *Middle East Journal,* vol. 43, no. 2 (Spring 1989), pp. 239–242.

41. Sinan al-Shabibi, "Prospects for Iraq's Economy: Facing the New Reality," in John Calabrese, ed., *The Future of Iraq* (Washington, D.C.: Middle East Institute, 1997), p. 57.

42. Amatzia Baram, "The Iraqi Invasion of Kuwait: Decision-Making in Baghdad," in Amatzia Baram and Barry Rubin, eds., *Iraq's Road to War* (New York: St. Martin's Press, 1993), p. 7; Freedman and Karsh, *The Gulf Conflict,* p. 39; Dilip Hiro, *Neighbors, Not Friends: Iraq and Iran after the Gulf Wars* (New York: Routledge, 2001), p. 20; Palmer, *Guardians of the Gulf,* p. 154.

Chapter 2: The Worm Turns

1. On the use of the term "constructive engagement" to describe the Bush administration's policy, see Zachary Karabell, "Backfire: U.S. Policy Toward Iraq, 1988—2 August 1990," *Middle East Journal,* vol. 49, no. 1 (Winter 1995), p. 31, n. 14.

2. Baram, "The Iraqi Invasion of Kuwait," pp. 7–8; Francona, *Ally to Adversary*, pp. 31–32; Hiro, *Neighbors, Not Friends*, p. 20; Palmer, *Guardians of the Gulf*, p. 154.

3. Baram, "The Iraqi Invasion of Kuwait," p. 8; Amatzia Baram, *Building Toward Crisis: Saddam Hussein's Strategy for Survival*, Policy Paper no. 47 (Washington, D.C.: Washington Institute for Near East Policy, 1998), pp. 27, 51; Freedman and Karsh, *The Gulf Conflict*, pp. 29–30; interview with Karim al-Juburi, "Exclusive Confessions of an Iraqi Refugee: I, Captain Karim, Was Saddam Hussein's Bodyguard," *Le Nouvel Observateur*, December 12, 1990, pp. 56–57; "Saddam's Former Bodyguard Profiled: al-Juburi Interviewed," *al-Majallah*, January 9, 1991, in JPRS-NEA-91-012, February 12, 1991, pp. 13–14.

4. Jentleson, *With Friends like These*, p. 103.

5. Laurie Mylroie, "The Baghdad Alternative," *Orbis*, Summer 1988, pp. 340, 350. See also Laurie Mylroie and Daniel Pipes, "Back Iraq: It's Time for a U.S. 'Tilt,' " *The New Republic*, April 27, 1987, pp. 14–15.

6. Jeffrey T. Richelson, *The Wizards of Langley* (Boulder, Colo.: Westview, 2001), p. 245.

7. Karabell, "Backfire," p. 33.

8. Jentleson, *With Friends like These*, pp. 134–137; Karabell, ibid., pp. 32–34.

9. Ofra Bengio, *Saddam Speaks on the Gulf Crisis* (Tel Aviv: Tel Aviv University, 1992), pp. 16–17; Marr, *The Modern History of Iraq*, p. 245.

10. Baram, "The Iraqi Invasion of Kuwait," p. 12.

11. Francona, *Ally to Adversary*, p. 36; Jentleson, *With Friends like These*, pp. 139–140; David Makovsky, "Rabin: Huge Iraq Missile Advances," *The Jerusalem Post*, December 21, 1989.

12. Baram, "The Iraqi Invasion of Kuwait," p. 12; Freedman and Karsh, *The Gulf Conflict*, p. 32.

13. Baram, ibid., p. 8; Jentleson, *With Friends like These*, pp. 145–147.

14. Francona, *Ally to Adversary*, p. 37; Jentleson, ibid., p. 151.

15. Amatzia Baram notes that Saddam's threat was a variation on a common Baghdad street thug threat, "I shall burn half your house"; Baram, "The Iraqi Invasion of Kuwait," p. 12.

16. Ibid., pp. 11–13; Jentleson, *With Friends like These*, pp. 155–156; Freedman and Karsh, *The Gulf Conflict*, p. 32; "Saad al-Bazzaz: An Insider's View of Iraq," *Middle East Quarterly*, December 1995, pp. 68–69.

17. Baram, ibid., p. 11.

18. Ibid., p. 13.

19. Ibid., pp. 8, 10–14; Bengio, *Saddam Speaks*, pp. 14–17.

20. "Oral History: Wafic al-Samarrai," *PBS Frontline: The Gulf War*, available at www.pbs.org/wgbh/pages/frontline/gulf/oral/samarrai/1.html, downloaded May 2, 2002; Eliot A. Cohen and Thomas A. Keaney, general eds., *Gulf War Air Power Survey*, vol. 1, part 1: *Planning* (Washington, D.C.: GPO, 1993), p. 59. (Hereafter, all volumes in this series are referred to as *"GWAPS,"* followed by the name of the appropriate volume).

21. Freedman and Karsh, *The Gulf Conflict*, p. 39; Hiro, *Neighbors, Not Friends*, p. 20; Palmer, *Guardians of the Gulf*, p. 154; William C. Ramsey, "Oil in the 1990s: The Gulf Dominant," in Phebe Marr and William Lewis, eds., *Riding the Tiger: The Middle East Challenge After the Cold War* (Boulder, Colo.: Westview, 1993), pp. 51–52.

22. *GWAPS,* vol. 1, part 1: *Planning,* pp. 59–60.

23. Baram, "The Iraqi Invasion of Kuwait," p. 16.

24. *GWAPS,* vol. 1, part 1: *Planning,* p. 58.

25. Karabell, "Backfire," pp. 40–42; interview with Sandra Charles, Washington, D.C., June 10, 2002.

26. The text can be found in a variety of places, including Micah L. Sifry and Christopher Cerf, *The Gulf War Reader* (New York: Times Books, 1991), pp. 122–133.

27. Karabell, "Backfire," p. 44.

28. See George Bush and Brent Scowcroft, *A World Transformed* (New York: Alfred A. Knopf, 1998), pp. 311–314; interview with Sandra Charles, Washington, D.C., June 10, 2002.

29. For a concurring view, see John Olsen, "Interview with Iraqi General," unpublished report, August 7, 1998.

30. For a description of the military operations in the Iraqi invasion of Kuwait, see Pollack, *Arabs at War,* pp. 235–237.

31. Janice Gross Stein contends that Iraq's aggressive moves on August 5 were intended to intimidate the Saudis into keeping the Saudi-Iraqi oil pipeline open, "or else." Although possible, this seems unlikely and there is no evidence to back up this supposition. Janice Gross Stein, "Deterrence and Compellence in the Gulf, 1990–91," *International Security,* vol. 17, no. 2 (Fall 1992), pp. 168–169.

32. Interview with Sandra Charles, Washington, D.C., June 10, 2002; Bruce O. Riedel, personal correspondence, June 2002.

33. Samarrai interview, *Frontline.*

34. Norman Cigar, "Iraq's Strategic Mindset and the Gulf War," *Journal of Strategic Studies,* March 1992, pp. 9–11; Norman Friedman, *Desert Victory* (Annapolis, Md.: Naval Institute Press, 1991), pp. 66, 108–111.

35. Public Statement by Saddam Hussein on September 5, 1990, Baghdad Domestic Service in Arabic, September 5, 1990; Samarrai interview, *Frontline;* Sifry and Cerf, *Gulf War Reader,* pp. 122–133; Cigar, "Iraq's Strategic Mindset," pp. 2–5.

36. See, e.g., the account given by Soviet envoy Yevgeny Primakov of his meetings with Saddam Hussein in FBIS-SOV 91-083, April 28, 1991. Also see Cigar, "Iraq's Strategic Mindset," pp. 14–18.

37. *GWAPS,* vol. 1, part 1: *Planning,* p. 65. Also see "Saddam Hussein's Message to President Bush, 16 January 1991," in Bengio, *Saddam Speaks,* pp. 164–171; Saddam, "Speech to the Islamic Conference," *Baghdad Voice of the Masses,* January 11, 1991, FBIS-NES 91-009; and the Primakov interview, April 28, 1991, FBIS-SOV 91-083.

38. Many commentators now claim that Iraq never had more than about 300,000 troops in the KTO prior to the Gulf War. This is simply wrong. It is based on a mistaken understanding of the number of units Iraq deployed in the KTO and a misappreciation of Iraqi army structure. Most of these accounts assume incorrectly that Iraq deployed only forty-two divisions to the KTO. In fact, it deployed fifty-one. [For sources citing fifty-one divisions, see Central Intelligence Agency, *Operation Desert Storm: A Snapshot of the Battlefield* (Washington, D.C.: CIA, September 1993; *GWAPS,* vol. 1, part 1: *Planning,* p. 74; Barry D. Watts, "Friction in the Gulf War," *Naval War College Review,* vol. 48, no. 4, Sequence 352 (Autumn 1995), pp. 94 and 106, n. 5.] In addition, these mistaken calculations

(including some in volumes of the U.S. Air Force's Gulf War Air Power Survey) simply multiplied the number of Iraqi divisions by their authorized personnel strength and then factored in rough estimates of desertions to arrive at the total numbers of Iraqi personnel in the theater. This completely fails to take into account the large numbers of corps-level and army-level assets that were also present. For example, the fifty-one divisions in the KTO were commanded by eight corps headquarters, each of which also fielded independent armored brigades, commando brigades, and artillery battalions, not to mention all of the logistical formations that the Iraqi Army concentrated at corps level. Watts, "Friction in the Gulf War," has the best discussion of Iraqi manpower issues.

39. Since the Gulf War, it has become clear that the success of the Patriots against the Scuds was apocryphal, as few, if any, al-Husseins were actually intercepted by Patriots. The best analysis of this subject is Theodore A. Postol, "Lessons of the Gulf War Experience with Patriot," *International Security,* vol. 16, no. 3 (Winter 1991–1992), pp. 119–171.

40. Pillar, *Terrorism and U.S. Foreign Policy,* p. 57.

41. Interview with Taha Yasin Ramadan, Cairo al-Sha'b, in Arabic, May 28, 1991, FBIS-NES-91-108, June 5, 1991; "Saddam says Allies 'Lost' War Against Iraq," Baghdad al-Thawrah, in Arabic, March 11, 1992, FBIS-NES-92-053, March 18, 1992; Cigar, "Iraq's Strategic Mindset," p. 18.

42. Lawrence Freedman and Efraim Karsh, "How Kuwait Was Won: Strategy in the Gulf War," *International Security,* Fall 1991, p. 32; John Olsen, "Interview with Iraqi General," unpublished report, August 7, 1998.

43. Using comprehensive U-2 imagery of the entire theater, CIA photoanalysts counted 3,475 Iraqi tanks and 3,080 armored personnel carriers in the Kuwaiti Theater of Operations. They also determined that roughly one third of those armored vehicles did not move or fight during the coalition ground offensive. There were at least three common reasons that these vehicles did nothing during the ground war: they had been destroyed or immobilized by air strikes before the ground war began, they were inoperable because the Iraqis had largely stopped performing routine maintenance, or their crews had fled during either the air campaign or the ground campaign. Based on accounts from Iraqi defectors and POWs, the distribution among these three problems appears about even, but it is difficult to say. Consequently, the best we can say is that air strikes probably destroyed at least 600 Iraqi armored vehicles and no more than about 1,800, although the right number is probably around 1,200. CIA, *Snapshot of the Battlefield; GWAPS,* vol. 2, part 2: *Effects and Effectiveness,* pp. 207–220.

44. Army Component, United States Central Command (ARCENT), *Battlefield Reconstruction Study: The 100 Hour Ground War,* April 20, 1991, declassified version, pp. 58–59; *GWAPS,* vol. 2, part 2: *Effects and Effectiveness,* pp. 165–169, 220; U.S. Department of Defense (DOD), *Conduct of the Persian Gulf War* (Washington, D.C.: GPO, 1992), p. 159; Watts, "Friction in the Gulf War," p. 94. The Watts article contains the most accurate statistics regarding Iraqi formations, equipment, and manpower in the KTO. As noted by *GWAPS,* desertion rates varied widely among Iraqi units in the KTO. The frontline infantry divisions were the most heavily depleted by desertions. The regular army armored and mechanized divisions suffered fewer desertions than the infantry. The Republican Guards suffered least from desertions and were closest to their authorized

strength when the ground war began. Memorandum for Record, Document no. NA-22, "The Gulf War: An Iraqi General Officer's Perspective," March 11, 1991, declassified 1998, provides a useful snapshot of desertions from selected Iraqi divisions. Some of the figures provided are remarkably accurate, others (such as for the Hammurabi Armored Division) are laughably inaccurate, concocted by an officer who spent most of his time trying (unsuccessfully) to desert the army.

45. Ofra Bengio, "Baghdad Between Shi'a and Kurds," Policy Focus no. 18, Washington Institute for Near East Policy, February 1992, p. 7.

46. Primakov interview, p. 11; "INA Reports 'Aziz' Moscow News Conference," Iraqi News Agency, February 23, 1991, in FBIS-NES-91-037, February 25, 1991, p. 35; "Saddam Addresses Nation on Initiative 21 Feb," *Baghdad Domestic Service,* February 21, 1991, in FBIS-NES-91-035, February 21, 1991, p. 21; and Freedman and Karsh, *The Gulf Conflict,* pp. 377–381. For the texts of the various Iraqi initiatives, see Sifry and Cerf, eds., *The Gulf War Reader,* pp. 337–345.

47. Although it is fairly clear that by February 22 Baghdad was trying to throw in the towel, it would be a mistake to see this as reflecting a genuine willingness to accede to all of the United Nations' demands. The Iraqi regime had a long history of reneging on agreements, finding or fabricating loopholes in treaties, delaying the implementation of unpleasant accords, and trying to find other ways around distasteful obligations. The pervasive duplicity and deceit in Iraq's dealings with the outside world had left the U.S.-led coalition entirely unwilling to trust Baghdad. Moreover, Iraqi dealings with the international community after the Gulf War, including the U.N. inspection regime, leave little doubt that Iraq would have attempted to manipulate the terms of a peaceful withdrawal from Kuwait to the maximum extent possible. The aerial bombardment and the threat of a ground offensive had forced Iraq into a corner, but it is a virtual certainty that once the bombing stopped, Iraq would have worked tirelessly to evade its commitments.

48. On Iraq's military performance during the Gulf War, see Pollack, *Arabs at War,* pp. 235–264.

49. On the battles on February 26 and 27, 1991, see ibid., pp. 252–256.

50. On U.S. decision making at the end of the war, see Rick Atkinson, *Crusade* (New York: Houghton Mifflin, 1993), pp. 469–481; Ann Devroy and Molly Moore, "Winning the War and Struggling with Peace; U.S. Unprepared for Iraqi Retribution, Extent of Exodus in Conflict's Aftermath," *The Washington Post,* April 14, 1991; Michael R. Gordon and General Bernard E. Trainor, *The Generals' War: The Inside Story of the Conflict in the Gulf* (Boston: Little, Brown, 1995), pp. 400–432. For the perspective of some key participants, also see Bush and Scowcroft, *A World Transformed,* pp. 483–492; General H. Norman Schwarzkopf, *It Doesn't Take a Hero* (New York: Bantam, 1992), pp. 465–478.

51. As only one example, see the account of the Iraqi retreat from Kuwait by the chief of staff of the Iraqi Sixth Armored Division in Staff Brigadier General Najib al-Salihi, *al-Zilzal (The Earthquake): What Happened in Iraq After the Withdrawal from Kuwait? Secrets of the Bloody Days!* (London: al-Rafid Distribution and Publishing, 1998), trans. by FBIS, May 1999, pp. 24–47. For a more authoritative account, see CIA, *Operation Desert Storm: A Snapshot of the Battlefield.*

52. CIA, ibid.

53. Bush and Scowcroft, *A World Transformed,* pp. 488–490.

54. Interview with Sandra Charles, Washington, D.C., June 10, 2002; "Interview: Richard Haass," *PBS Frontline,* available at www.pbs.org/wgbh/pages/ frontline/shows/unscom/interviews/haass.html, downloaded May 25, 2002; Bruce Riedel, personal correspondence, June 2002; author's interviews with former senior administration officials, May 2002.

55. al-Salihi, *al-Zilzal,* pp. 50–51.

56. Mackey, *The Reckoning,* pp. 287–288; Yitzhak Nakash, *The Shi'is of Iraq* (Princeton, N.J.: Princeton University Press, 1994), pp. 276–277.

57. Andrew and Patrick Cockburn, *Out of the Ashes: The Resurrection of Saddam Hussein* (New York: HarperCollins, 1999), pp. 12–13.

58. Bengio, "Baghdad Between Shi'a and Kurds," p. 26, n. 44.

59. Gordon and Trainor, *The Generals' War,* pp. 454–456.

60. James A. Baker, III, *The Politics of Diplomacy* (New York: Putnam, 1995), p. 439.

61. Bush and Scowcroft, *A World Transformed,* p. 489. Also see the exchange between General Scowcroft and Peter Jennings of ABC News reprinted in Makiya, *Republic of Fear,* p. xx.

62. Nora Boustany, "Violence Reported Spreading in Iraq; Army Units Clash," *The Washington Post,* March 6, 1991.

63. Bengio, "Baghdad Between Shi'a and Kurds," p. 9; interview with Wafiq al-Samarra'i, "Former Military Intelligence Chief Interviewed," p. 34.

64. See the firsthand account of the *intifadah* in al-Salihi, *al-Zilzal,* pp. 63–227.

65. Amatzia Baram, *Building Toward Crisis,* p. 27.

66. Bengio, "Baghdad Between Shi'a and Kurds," pp. 10–11; al-Salihi, *al-Zilzal,* pp. 90–91.

67. Amatzia Baram, "The Effect of Iraqi Sanctions: Statistical Pitfalls and Responsibility," *Middle East Journal,* vol. 54, no. 2 (Spring 2000), p. 199, n. 13.

68. On the course of the *intifadah,* see Nora Boustany, "Guard's Brutal 'Harvest'–Troops Slaughtering Civilians, Say Refugees," *The Seattle Times,* March 26, 1991; Ann Devroy and Molly Moore, "Winning the War and Struggling with Peace: US Unprepared for Iraqi Retribution, Extent of Exodus in Conflict's Aftermath," *The Washington Post,* April 14, 1991; Brian Donovan, "Iraq Rebels Claim Major Wins; Many Deaths Reported," *Newsday,* March 11, 1991; Mackey, *The Reckoning,* pp. 285–298; McDowall, *History of the Kurds,* pp. 371–373; "Last Rebel Stronghold Falls to Saddam's Onslaught," *Jerusalem Post* (compiled from news agencies), April 4, 1991; Neil MacFarquhar, "Iraq Says Uprising's End Is Near, Collapse of Kurdish Resistance in 3 Cities Is Cited as Sign of Failing Revolt," *The Boston Globe,* April 3, 1991; Kanan Makiya, *Cruelty and Silence: War, Tyranny, Uprising, and the Arab World* (New York: Norton, 1993), pp. 15–104; al-Salihi, *al-Zilzal,* pp. 88–204.

69. Sarah Graham-Brown, *Sanctioning Saddam* (London: I. B. Tauris, 1999), p. 23.

70. See for example, U.S. House of Representatives, Committee on Armed Services, "Intelligence Successes and Failures in Operations Desert Shield/Storm," August 1993, pp. 35–38.

71. Hamza, *Saddam's Bombmaker,* p. 258.

Chapter 3: Containment and Beyond

1. My thanks to Gideon Rose for first making this comparison. Gideon Rose, personal correspondence, July 7, 2002.
2. This is not to say that every Middle East regionalist was a hawk on Iraq. Many were old-school Arabists who abhorred the use of force against Iraq and generally disliked even the sanctions and inspections. As can be imagined, there were serious debates among the Iraq hawks and the Arabists at lower levels of the government too. However, for the purposes of this book, it seems unnecessary to delve into those battles.
3. As quoted in Cockburn and Cockburn, *Out of the Ashes,* p. 43.
4. Cockburn and Cockburn cite an interview with former CIA officer (and then chief of Near East Operations Division) Frank Anderson. Cockburn and Cockburn, *Out of the Ashes,* p. 31; Robert S. Litwak, *Rogue States and U.S. Foreign Policy* (Washington, D.C.: Woodrow Wilson Center Press, 1999), p. 126; Jeffrey T. Richelson, *The U.S. Intelligence Community,* 4th ed. (Boulder, Colo.: Westview, 1999), p. 353.
5. Hiro, *Neighbors, Not Friends,* p. 52; Richelson, ibid., p. 354.
6. Hiro, ibid., p. 46.
7. Ibid., p. 60.
8. Phil Davison, "Trapped in Saddam's Triangle of Death: Thousands Die in Southern Marshes," *The Independent,* June 16, 1991, p. 11; Leonard Doyle, "Iraq 'Trying to Wipe Out Marsh Arabs,' " *The Independent,* August 1, 1992, p. 13; Andrew Finkel and Michael Theodolou, "Saddam's Victims Fear Backlash over Downed Warplane," *The Times* (London), December 29, 1992; Robert Fisk, "Iraqi Drainage Scheme Cripples Marsh Arabs," *The Independent,* February 27, 1993, p. 10; Ron Howell, "Iraq Attacking Shiites, UN Told," *Newsday,* August 12, 1992, p. 5; Michael Littlejohns, "Iraq Keeps Up Shelling of Marsh Arabs," *The Financial Times,* November 24, 1993, p. 4; Julia Preston, "UN Reports Iraq Attacks Against Marshland Arabs," *Chicago Sun-Times,* November 24, 1993, p. 42; Julia Preston, "UN Report Describes Iraq as 'Regime of Terror,' " *The Washington Post,* November 24, 1993, p. A12; "SAIRI Radio Reports 'Large-Scale' Attack on Government Offices, Forces in Fuhud," Voice of the Islamic Revolution in Iraq, December 6, 1993, in *BBC Summary of World Broadcasts,* December 8, 1993.
9. Nuha al-Radi, *Baghdad Diaries* (London: Saqi Books, 1998), p. 51.
10. Hiro, *Neighbors, Not Friends,* pp. 34, 41–42.
11. Sarah Graham-Brown, "War and Sanctions: Cost to Society and Toll on Development," in John Calabrese, ed., *The Future of Iraq* (Washington, D.C.: Middle East Institute, 1997), p. 34; Graham-Brown, *Sanctioning Saddam,* pp. 157–158; Mackey, *The Reckoning,* pp. 302–303.
12. Hiro, *Neighbors, Not Friends,* pp. 50–51.
13. Khidhir Hamza, on-the-record Remarks at the Council on Foreign Relations, April 17, 2002.
14. Cockburn and Cockburn, *Out of the Ashes,* pp. 96–102.
15. On Iraqi efforts to penetrate and intimidate UNSCOM, see Baram, *Building Toward Crisis,* pp. 75–76; Cockburn and Cockburn, ibid., p. 198.
16. Cockburn and Cockburn, ibid., p. 102; Hiro, *Neighbors, Not Friends,* pp. 63–64.
17. Cockburn and Cockburn, ibid., pp. 51–52; Kenneth Katzman, "Iraq: U.S. Efforts to Change the Regime," Congressional Research Service Report RL31339,

March 22, 2002, pp. 2–3; Richelson, *The U.S. Intelligence Community,*
pp. 353–354.

18. Ann Devroy and Julia Preston, "Iraq Given Ultimatum on Missiles," *The Washington Post,* January 7, 1993, p. A1; Ann Devroy and Barton Gellman, "U.S. Attacks Industrial Site Near Baghdad; MiG Downed as Gulf Allies Display Might," *The Washington Post,* January 18, 1993, p. A1; Michael R. Gordon, "Iraq Apparently Rebuffs Allies on Missiles Deployed in South," *The New York Times,* January 8, 1993, p. A1.

19. Martin Indyk, "The Clinton Administration's Approach to the Middle East," speech to the Soref Symposium, May 18, 1993, Washington Institute for Near East Policy, available at www.washingtoninstitute.org/pubs/indyk.htm, downloaded July 13, 2002.

20. Martin Indyk, "Back to the Bazaar," *Foreign Affairs,* January–February 2002, pp. 76–77.

21. Litwak, *Rogue States,* pp. 127–128.

22. On the strike and events surrounding it, see Alfred B. Prados, "Iraq: Post-War Challenges and U.S. Responses, 1991–1998," Congressional Research Service Report 98-386F, March 31, 1999, pp. 9–10.

23. Interview with Martin Indyk, Washington, D.C., May 23, 2002; interview with Mark R. Parris, Washington, D.C., May 15, 2002; Bruce O. Riedel, personal correspondence, June 2002.

24. Baram, *Building Toward Crisis,* pp. 27, 57–58; Cockburn and Cockburn, *Out of the Ashes,* pp. 211–212.

25. Graham-Brown, "War and Sanctions," pp. 34–36.

26. GlobalSecurity, "Hammurabi Division (Armored)," available at www.globalsecurity.org/military/world/iraq/hammurabi.htm, and "Al Nida (Armored)," available at www.globalsecurity.org/military/world/iraq/al-nida.htm, both downloaded July 13, 2002; Michael R. Gordon, "Threats in the Gulf: The Military Build-up," *The New York Times,* October 10, 1994, p. A1; Michael R. Gordon, "Kuwait Is Allowing U.S. to Station Squadron of Warplanes," *The New York Times,* October 28, 1994, p. A3; Hiro, *Neighbors, Not Friends,* pp. 80–81; Thomas W. Lippman and Bradley Graham, "Iraqi Troops Move Near Kuwait Border," *The Washington Post,* October 8, 1994, p. A1.

27. After his defection, Hussein Kamel argued vociferously that Saddam did intend to invade Kuwait to force the United Nations to lift the sanctions. As a defector looking to mobilize international opinion against Saddam, Hussein Kamel had an incentive to portray Saddam in as bad a light as he could. However, Hussein Kamel was one of the very few people in the Iraqi regime who may have been privy to Saddam's thinking on this matter, and many of the U.S. intelligence personnel who debriefed him after his defection believe he was telling the truth on this matter. See "Hussein Kamel on Army Strength, Saddam Fedayeen," *al-Watan al-'Arabi,* in FBIS-NES, November 27, 1995, p. 33.

28. On the October 1994 crisis, see Prados, "Iraq: Post-War Challenges," pp. 11–13.

29. Interview with Martin Indyk, Washington, D.C., May 2002.

30. Cockburn and Cockburn, *Out of the Ashes,* p. 162.

31. Ibid., p. 111.

32. During the early years of containment, the Russian leadership was determined to placate the United States and so supported Washington fully on Iraq. In the mid-1990s, there was a turnover in Moscow, bringing in more traditional Russian na-

tionalists who hoped to regain the position they had enjoyed as part of the USSR. In particular, Yevgeny Primakov, who became the Russian foreign minister in 1996, was a former Soviet ambassador to Baghdad and was disgustingly subservient to Iraq.

33. Interview with Martin Indyk, Washington, D.C., May 2002; interview with Mark R. Parris, Washington, D.C., May 2002.

34. On the CIA's role in the March 1995 Kurdish offensive, see Robert Baer, *See No Evil: The True Story of a Ground Soldier in the CIA's War on Terrorism* (New York: Crown Publishers, 2002), pp. 171–213; Alan Cooperman, "Rolling Up in Iraq: Hussein Backs Down for the Moment, but a CIA Operation Is Destroyed," *US News and World Report,* September 23, 1996, pp. 50–54; Christopher Dickey and Gregory L. Vistica, "Mission Impossible: How Saddam Foiled the CIA's Ambitious Effort to Drive Him from Power," *Newsweek,* September 23, 1996, pp. 38–39; Kevin Fedarko, "Saddam's CIA Coup," *Time,* September 23, 1996, p. 42; Katzman, "Iraq: U.S. Efforts," p. 3; John Jacob Nutter, *The CIA's Black Ops: Covert Action, Foreign Policy, and Democracy* (Amherst, N.Y.: Prometheus Books, 2000), pp. 67–69; Richelson, *The U.S. Intelligence Community,* pp. 354–355; Elaine Sciolino, "Purged General 'Attempted Coup,' " *The Guardian,* March 15, 1995, p. 15; Evan Thomas, Christopher Dickey, and Gregory L. Vistica, "Bay of Pigs Redux," *Newsweek,* March 23, 1998, pp. 36–44; Richard Leiby, "Spy Writer; After a Career Spent in Shadow, Ex–CIA Man Bob Baer Has Found the Limelight," *The Washington Post,* April 8, 2002; Martin Walker, "Clinton 'Blew Iraq Coup,' " *The Guardian,* June 27, 1997, pp. 1, 14; interview with Martin Indyk, Washington, D.C., May 2002; interview with Mark R. Parris, Washington, D.C., May 2002.

35. The main text of the cable is reproduced in Baer, *See No Evil,* p. 173.

36. On the military aspects of the March 1995 Kurdish offensive at Arbil, see "Army Defectors on Defeat of Government Forces," Iraqi Broadcasting Corporation, March 21, 1995, in FBIS-NES-95-055, March 22, 1995, p. 39; "Attack on 2nd Division Forces Reported," Iraqi Broadcasting Corporation Press Release, in FBIS-NES-95-054, March 21, 1995, pp. 32–33; Baram, *Building Toward Crisis,* pp. 55–56; "Battle Situation in North Updated," Iraqi Broadcasting Corporation, March 8, 1995, in FBIS-NES-95-046, March 9, 1995, pp. 12–13; "Capture of 53 'Enemy' Troops Reported," Voice of the People of Kurdistan, March 8, 1995, in FBIS-NES-95-046, March 9, 1995, p. 14; Cockburn and Cockburn, *Out of the Ashes,* pp. 189–190; "100 Iraqi Army Elements Said Killed," *al-Sharq al-Awsat,* March 16, 1995, in FBIS-NES-95-052, March 17, 1995, p. 51; "Kurdish Forces Attack Regime Post in North," Voice of Iraqi Islamic Revolution, March 13, 1995, in FBIS-NES-95-049, March 14, 1995, p. 30; Regis W. Matlak, "Inside Saddam's Grip," *National Security Studies Quarterly,* Spring 1999, p. 10; "PUK Claims Brigade Commander Killed," *al-Hayat,* March 13, 1995, in FBIS-NES-95-049, March 14, 1995, p. 29; "PUK Claims Major Victory over Government Troops," Voice of the People of Kurdistan, March 22, 1995, in FBIS-NES-95-056, March 23, 1995, p. 33; "PUK Rounds Up Battle Situation," Voice of the People of Kurdistan, March 12, 1995, in FBIS-NES-095-048, March 13, 1995, pp. 24–25; interview with Mark R. Parris, Washington, D.C., May 2002.

37. Interview with Martin Indyk, Washington, D.C., May 2002.

38. Baram, *Building Toward Crisis,* p. 70.

39. Ibid., p. 27.

40. Ibid., pp. 12–13.

41. Prados, "Iraq: Post-War Challenges," pp. 13–14; Bruce O. Riedel, personal correspondence, June 2002.

42. Hamza, *Saddam's Bombmaker*, p. 237.

43. Hiro, *Neighbors, Not Friends*, pp. 96–97.

44. Baram, *Building Toward Crisis*, pp. 70–71; Hiro, *Neighbors, Not Friends*, p. 10; Latif Yahia and Karl Wendl, *I Was Saddam's Son* (New York: Arcade Publishing, 1997), p. 281.

45. In purely financial terms, the U.S. military commitment to the Gulf region that was the key to the containment strategy cost on average $1.2 billion per year—a minuscule amount of the annual defense budget, especially given the importance of the region. In late November 1998, the Pentagon reported that the military operations and force buildup in the Gulf region since the Gulf War had cost a total of $6.9 billion. In addition, the DoD reported that they had cost $1.6 billion in FY 1998, $1.3 billion in FY 1999, $1.1 billion in FY 2000, and $1.1 billion in FY 2001, for a grand total of $12 billion from 1991 to 2001. See Alfred B. Prados and Kenneth Katzman, "Iraq-U.S. Confrontation," CRS Issue Brief for Congress IB94049, updated March 28, 2002, pp. 9–10.

46. Cockburn and Cockburn, *Out of the Ashes*, pp. 218–219; Marie Colvin, "Revealed: CIA's Bungled Iraqi Coup," *The Sunday Times* (London), April 2, 2000; Katzman, "Iraq: U.S. Efforts," p. 4; Eric Margolis, "The Bay of Camels," syndicated column, August 25, 1997; interview with Mark R. Parris, Washington, D.C., May 2002; Bruce O. Riedel, personal correspondence, June 2002; Richelson, *The U.S. Intelligence Community*, p. 355.

47. Bruce O. Riedel, personal correspondence, June 2002.

48. Barton Gellman, "U.S. Spied on Iraqi Military Via U.N.," *The Washington Post*, March 2, 1999, p. A1; Seymour M. Hersh, "Saddam's Best Friend," *The New Yorker*, April 5, 1999, pp. 32–41; Philip Shenon, "Former UN Arms Inspector Is Criticized by State Department," *The New York Times*, February 24, 1999.

49. Hiro, *Neighbors, Not Friends*, p. 108.

50. On the failed June 1996 coup and the CIA's role in it, see Baram, *Building Toward Crisis*, p. 51; Cockburn and Cockburn, *Out of the Ashes*, pp. 219–230; Dickey and Vistica, "Mission Impossible," pp. 38–39; Hiro, *Neighbors, Not Friends*, p. 107; Colvin, "Revealed: CIA's Bungled Iraqi Coup"; Katzman, "Iraq: U.S. Efforts," p. 4; Nutter, *The CIA's Black Ops*, pp. 67–69; Richelson, *The U.S. Intelligence Community*, p. 355; "U.S. Reports Purging of Army in Iraq: Officers Apparently Paying for Coup Against Saddam," *San Francisco Chronicle*, July 6, 1992, p. A7.

51. Hiro, *Neighbors, Not Friends*, p. 109.

52. Baram, *Building Toward Crisis*, p. 53; Cockburn and Cockburn, *Out of the Ashes*, pp. 231–237; Hiro, *Neighbors, Not Friends*, pp. 109–110; interview with Mark R. Parris, Washington, D.C., May 2002.

53. "Army, Republican Guard Officers Decorated," Iraq Television Network, November 18, 1996, in FBIS-NES-96-225, November 21, 1996.

54. Baram, *Building Toward Crisis*, pp. 128–129; Daniel Byman, Kenneth Pollack, and Matthew Waxman, "Coercing Saddam: Lessons from the Past," *Survival*, Autumn 1998, pp. 138–139; Cockburn and Cockburn, *Out of the Ashes*, p. 243;

Hiro, *Neighbors, Not Friends,* p. 112; Prados, "Iraq: Post-War Challenges,"
pp. 14–15; Bruce O. Riedel, personal correspondence, June 2002.

55. Baram, *Building Toward Crisis,* pp. 51–52.

56. Hiro, *Neighbors, Not Friends,* p. 116.

57. Cockburn and Cockburn, *Out of the Ashes,* p. 249; Katzman, "Iraq: U.S. Efforts,"
p. 4; Prados, "Iraq: Post-War Challenges," pp. 15–16.

58. For concurring opinions, see Baram, *Building Toward Crisis,* pp. 51–52; Kanan
Makiya, *Republic of Fear,* 1998 paperback edition (Berkeley: University of California Press, 1998), pp. xvi–xvii.

59. Baram, ibid., p. 130.

60. Ibid., pp. 18–19; Cockburn and Cockburn, *Out of the Ashes,* pp. 255–259.

61. For a discussion of the impact of sanctions, see Chapter 5.

62. These are my suppositions of Berger's thinking based on numerous conversations during my time working for him as his director for Persian Gulf affairs.

63. Richard Butler, *The Greatest Threat* (New York: Public Affairs, 2000), p. 3.

64. Prados, "Iraq: U.S. Challenges," p. 21.

65. Interview with Martin Indyk, Washington, D.C., June 2002.

66. Steven Lee Myers, "U.S. Will Not Ask to Use Saudi Bases for Raid on Iraq," *The
New York Times,* February 9, 1998, p. A1; Prados, "Iraq: U.S. Challenges," p. 22.

67. Baram, *Building Toward Crisis,* p. 1.

68. Butler, *The Greatest Threat,* pp. 6–11.

69. Bruce O. Riedel, personal correspondence, June 2002.

70. See Byman, Pollack, and Waxman, "Coercing Saddam," pp. 127–152. Also see
Kenneth M. Pollack, "Responding to Iraq: Crises and Opportunities," Policy-
Watch 274, Washington Institute for Near East Policy, October 31, 1997.

71. Interview with Martin Indyk, Washington, D.C., June 2002; Bruce O. Riedel,
personal correspondence, June 2002.

72. Prados and Katzman, "Iraq-U.S. Confrontation," p. 4.

73. Anthony H. Cordesman, "The Military Effectiveness of Desert Fox," Center for
Strategic and International Studies, December 23, 1998, pp. 6–14; Prados and
Katzman, ibid., p. 4.

74. Byman, Pollack, and Waxman, "Coercing Saddam," pp. 127–152; Pollack, "Responding to Iraq"; Michael Eisenstadt, "Target Iraq's Republican Guard," *Middle
East Quarterly,* December 1996, pp. 11–16.

75. Hiro, *Neighbors, Not Friends,* pp. 165–173; Regis W. Matlak, "Inside Saddam's
Grip," *National Security Studies Quarterly,* Spring 1999, pp. 8–9.

76. "Firing Blanks: The Plot to Oust Saddam and the Constant Pounding from US
Jets Are Going Nowhere," *Time,* November 8, 1999.

77. My own support for the Iraqi opposition was based not on any change of heart
regarding the INC's foolish plan for a military campaign but on the fact that I did
believe that a cohesive Iraqi opposition could play a role in a larger program of
regime change that employed a range of other levers to bring pressure against
Saddam's grip on power.

78. See, e.g., the interviews with Ivo Daalder on "Frontline: War in Europe," available at www.pbs.org/wgbh/pages/frontline/shows/kosovo/interviews/daalder.html,
downloaded May 18, 2002.

79. For a clever account of other compromises the United States made to secure
French support for the resolution, see David Albright and Corey Hinderstein,
"Comparison of Drafts of Comprehensive Security Council Resolution on Iraq,"

Institute for Science and International Security, December 14, 1999, available at www.isis-online.org/publications/iraq/unnscrescomp.html, downloaded May 2002.

80. See for example, Christopher S. Wren, "Hussein's Enemies Meet, But with Little Meeting of the Minds," *The New York Times,* November 1, 1999, p. A6.

81. In fact, I had written a piece in 1997 that had argued for a radical revision of containment at that time, warning that if the United States did not reform containment then, it would soon face an unpleasant choice between deterrence and all-out regime change. See Kenneth M. Pollack, "Contain Narrowly," in Patrick Clawson, ed., *Iraq Strategy Review* (Washington, D.C.: Washington Institute for Near East Policy, 1998), pp. 35–58.

82. Leon Barkho, "Saddam Says Iraqi Army Ready to Fight Israel," Associated Press, November 10, 2000; GlobalSecurity, "Hammurabi Division (Armored)"; David Zeev Harris, "Iraq Moves Troops West," Jerusalem Post Radio, October 12, 2000, available at http://wander.co.il/samples/, downloaded July 13, 2002; "Israeli Chief of Staff Warns of 'Regional Deterioration': Arafat plane 'Smuggling Arms,' " *BBC Summary of World Broadcasts,* November 9, 2000; Radio Free Europe/Radio Liberty, "Iraqi Armored Units in Western Iraq Withdrawing," *Iraq Report,* vol. 3, no. 36 (November 3, 2000).

83. See, e.g., Johanna McGeary, "Odd Man Out," *Time,* September 10, 2001, p. 24; Alan Sipress, "Presidential Pressure Point: Arab-Israeli Conflict Could Undercut Policy on Mideast, Iraq," *The Washington Post,* August 6, 2001, p. A1; Robin Wright, "Colin Powell: At the Policy Helm," *Los Angeles Times,* September 9, 2001, p. 3. Also see Federal News Service, "Media Roundtable with Douglas J. Feith, Undersecretary of Defense for Policy," September 4, 2001, especially pp. 2–3.

84. Katzman, "Iraq: U.S. Efforts," pp. 6–8.

85. Peter Grier, "Bush Relearns Lessons of Mideast," *The Christian Science Monitor,* June 16, 2001, p. 1; Katzman, ibid., pp. 7–8.

PART II: IRAQ TODAY

Chapter 4: Iraqi State and Society

1. Regis W. Matlak, "Inside Saddam's Grip," *National Security Studies Quarterly,* Spring 1999, p. 2.

2. On the role of Iraq's tribes in Saddam's rule, see Baram, *Building Toward Crisis,* pp. 7–31; Amatzia Baram, "Neo-Tribalism in Iraq: Saddam Hussein's Tribal Policies, 1991–96," *International Journal of Middle East Studies,* vol. 29 (1997), pp. 1–31; Judith Yaphe, "Tribalism in Iraq, The Old and the New," *Middle East Policy,* vol. 7, no. 3 (June 2000), pp. 51–58.

3. Baram, *Building Toward Crisis,* p. 26.

4. Amatzia Baram, "The Iraqi Armed Forces and Security Apparatus," *Conflict, Security and Development,* vol. 1, no. 2 (2001), p. 113.

5. See Baram, *Building Toward Crisis,* pp. 7–44.

6. Efraim Karsh and Inari Rautsi, *Saddam Hussein: A Political Biography* (New York: Free Press, 1991), p. 2.

7. Ibid., pp. 26, 89.

8. Baram, *Building Toward Crisis,* pp. 2–3.

9. Baram, "The Iraqi Armed Forces and Security Apparatus," p. 114.

10. "Saddam's Former Bodyguard Profiled: al-Juburi Interviewed," p. 11.

11. On the Iraqi internal security services, see Aburish, *Saddam Hussein,* p. 233; Baram, "The Iraqi Armed Forces and Security Apparatus," pp. 113–123; Hiro, *Neighbors, Not Friends,* pp. 54–57; Michael Eisenstadt, *Like a Phoenix from the Ashes: The Future of Iraqi Military Power* (Washington, D.C.: WINEP, 1993), pp. 9–16; interview with Karim al-Juburi, "Exclusive Confessions of an Iraqi Refugee: I, Captain Karim, Was Saddam Hussein's Bodyguard," *Le Nouvel Observateur,* December 12, 1990, pp. 45–59; Makiya, *Republic of Fear,* pp. 11–16; Matlak, "Inside Saddam's Grip"; "Saddam's Former Bodyguard Profiled: al-Juburi Interviewed," pp. 10–19; al-Salihi, *al-Zilzal,* p. 232.

12. Makiya, *Republic of Fear,* p. 14.

13. The two best books on the subject remain Makiya, ibid., and Makiya, *Cruelty and Silence.*

14. United Nations Commission on Human Rights, "Resolution on Human Rights Abuses in Iraq," April 11, 2002.

15. John Sweeney, "Iraq's Tortured Children," BBC News, June 22, 2002.

16. Quoted in Makiya, *Republic of Fear,* p. xiii.

17. The annual reports of Amnesty International (available at www.amnesty.org) and the works of Kanan Makiya provide a good introduction for those wishing further elaboration on the Iraqi regime's methods of torture and other human rights violations. See also Amnesty International, "Iraq: Systematic Torture of Political Prisoners," August 15, 2001, available at http://web.amnesty.org/ai.nsf/Index/ MDE140082001?OpenDocument&of=COUNTRIES\IRAQ, downloaded May 27, 2002.

18. "European Report on the Situation in Iraq," International Alliance for Justice News Service, April 29, 2002.

19. U.S. Department of State, "Iraq," *Country Reports on Human Rights Practices, 2001,* available at www.state.gov/g/drl/rls/hrppt/2001/nea/8257.htm, downloaded May 28, 2002.

20. Central Intelligence Agency, "The Destruction of Iraq's Southern Marshes," IA 94-10020, August 1994; Graham-Brown, *Sanctioning Saddam,* pp. 202–204; Mackey, *The Reckoning,* pp. 313–315.

21. "Millions Dead from Starvation says North Korean Defector," BBC News, February 18, 1998, available at http://news6.thdo.bbc.co.uk/hi/english/world/asia-pacific/newsid_57000/57740.stm, downloaded June 7, 2002; "UNICEF, The State of the World's Children, 1996," available at www.unicef.org/sowc96/ 5famdis.htm, downloaded May 30, 2002; Food for the Hungry, "Factsheet: Hunger and Famine," available at www.fh.org/findout/faminefacts.shtml, downloaded May 30, 2002.

22. World Health Organization, "Epidemiological Fact Sheets on HIV/AIDS and Sexually Transmitted Diseases: Ethiopia," 2000 Update (Revised), p. 3; World Health Organization, "Epidemiological Fact Sheets on HIV/AIDS and Sexually Transmitted Diseases: Kenya," 2000 Update (revised), p. 3.

23. Amatzia Baram, "The Effect of Iraqi Sanctions: Statistical Pitfalls and Responsibility," *Middle East Journal,* vol. 54, no. 2 (Spring 2000), pp. 199–202.

24. Graham-Brown, *Sanctioning Saddam,* p. 316.

25. Hamza, *Saddam's Bombmaker,* p. 189.

26. Graham-Brown, *Sanctioning Saddam,* pp. 163–166.

27. Sarah Graham-Brown, "War and Sanctions: Cost to Society and Toll on Development," in John Calabrese, ed., *The Future of Iraq* (Washington, D.C.: Middle East Institute, 1997), pp. 32–33.

28. Central Intelligence Agency, *The World Factbook, 1991* (Washington, D.C.: GPO, 1991), p. 149.

29. Graham-Brown, "War and Sanctions," pp. 32–33.

30. Graham-Brown, *Sanctioning Saddam*, p. 157.

31. Hiro, *Neighbors, Not Friends*, pp. 74, 115.

32. Graham-Brown, *Sanctioning Saddam*, pp. 180, 317.

33. Ibid., p. 181.

34. Graham-Brown, "War and Sanctions," p. 36.

35. Amatzia Baram, "The Effect of Iraqi Sanctions," p. 215. Also see Cockburn and Cockburn, *Out of the Ashes*, pp. 121–123; Graham-Brown, "War and Sanctions," p. 35; Graham-Brown, *Sanctioning Saddam*, pp. 167–168; Hiro, *Neighbors, Not Friends*, p. 145.

36. Graham-Brown, *Sanctioning Saddam*, p. 188; ibid., p. 115. My thanks to Joseph Siegle for clarifying this important point.

37. al-Radi, *Baghdad Diaries*, 1998), p. 61.

38. Richard Garfield, *Morbidity and Mortality Among Iraqi Children from 1990 to 1998: Assessing the Impact of Economic Sanctions* (Goshen, Ind.: Institute for International Peace Studies, University of Notre Dame, 1999), Executive Summary; Hiro, *Neighbors, Not Friends*, p. 130.

39. Sinan al-Shabibi, "Prospects for Iraq's Economy: Facing the New Reality," in Calabrese, ed., *The Future of Iraq*, pp. 54–80.

40. Graham-Brown, *Sanctioning Saddam*, p. 162.

41. Baram, *Building Toward Crisis*, p. 72; Amatzia Baram, "The Iraqi Invasion of Kuwait: Decision-Making in Baghdad," in Amatzia Baram and Barry Rubin, eds., *Iraq's Road to War* (New York: St. Martin's Press, 1993), p. 8.

42. Graham-Brown, *Sanctioning Saddam*, pp. 165–167; Hiro, *Neighbors, Not Friends*, p. 74.

43. Graham-Brown, ibid., p. 165.

44. Ibid., pp. 185–188.

45. Cockburn and Cockburn, *Out of the Ashes*, pp. 121–123; Graham-Brown, *Sanctioning Saddam*, pp. 179–187; Youssef Ibrahim, "Iraq Is Near Economic Ruin," *The New York Times*, October 25, 1994.

46. Graham-Brown, ibid., p. 182; Hiro, *Neighbors, Not Friends*, pp. 130, 145.

47. For concurring opinions, see Graham-Brown, "War and Sanctions," p. 32; Graham-Brown, ibid., p. 161.

48. Graham-Brown, *Sanctioning Saddam*, pp. 169, 185.

49. Ibid., p. 184.

50. Baram, "The Effect of Iraqi Sanctions," p. 211; Graham-Brown, ibid., pp. 169, 180.

51. Baram, ibid., pp. 204–207; Garfield, "Executive Summary."

52. U.S. Department of State, "Saddam Hussein's Iraq," September 1999, p. 12.

53. Graham-Brown, *Sanctioning Saddam*, p. 181.

54. U.S. Department of State, "Saddam Hussein's Iraq," September 1999, p. 12.

55. Richard Butler, *The Greatest Threat* (New York: Public Affairs, 2000), p. 45.

56. Hamza, *Saddam's Bombmaker*, pp. 253–254.

57. Graham-Brown, *Sanctioning Saddam,* p. 170.
58. Graham-Brown, "War and Sanctions," pp. 35–36; Graham-Brown, ibid., pp. 169, 185.
59. U.S. Department of State, "Saddam Hussein's Iraq," September 1999, p. 10.
60. Graham-Brown, *Sanctioning Saddam,* p. 169; Kenneth Katzman, "Iraq: Oil-for-Food Program and International Sanctions," CRS Report RL30472, July 10, 2001, p. 5.
61. Baram, "The Effect of Iraqi Sanctions," pp. 205–206.
62. Butler, *The Greatest Threat,* p. 45. On the critical shortage of tires prior to oil-for-food, see Graham-Brown, *Sanctioning Saddam,* p. 164.
63. Baram, "The Effect of Iraqi Sanctions," pp. 204–207.
64. Evelyn Leopold, "UN Complains Iraq Neglecting Health, Oil Sectors," Reuters, January 17.
65. Baram, "The Effect of Iraqi Sanctions," p. 216.
66. U.S. Department of State, "Saddam Hussein's Iraq," September 1999, p. 8.
67. Baram, "The Effect of Iraqi Sanctions," p. 218.
68. U.S. Department of State, "Saddam Hussein's Iraq," September 1999, p. 3.
69. For World Health Organization, UNICEF, and the UN FAO repeating or arbitrarily modifying Iraq's made-up numbers, see Cockburn and Cockburn, *Out of the Ashes,* p. 137; Hiro, *Neighbors, Not Friends,* pp. 129, 177.
70. Baram, "The Effect of Iraqi Sanctions," pp. 195–196.
71. Ibid., pp. 196–198.
72. Ibid., pp. 197–198.
73. Garfield, "Executive Summary," pp. 1–2.
74. Ibid., p. 17.
75. Baram, *Building Toward Crisis,* p. 72; Baram, "The Iraqi Invasion of Kuwait," p. 8; Graham-Brown, *Sanctioning Saddam,* p. 180.
76. Ofra Bengio, "Baghdad Between Shi'a and Kurds," Policy Focus no. 18, Washington Institute for Near East Policy, February 1992, p. 2.
77. Baram, "The Effect of Iraqi Sanctions," pp. 204–207; Garfield, "Executive Summary."
78. Ofra Bengio, "Iraq's Shi'a and Kurdish Communities: From Resentment to Revolt," Baram and Rubin, eds., *Iraq's Road to War,* pp. 52–53; Bengio, "Baghdad Between Shi'a and Kurds," p. 1; Yitzhak Nakash, *The Shi'is of Iraq* (Princeton, N.J.: Princeton University Press, 1994), pp. 109–140, 277.
79. Bengio, "Iraq's Shi'a and Kurdish Communities," pp. 52–53.
80. On the Kurds and their history, see Mehrdad R. Izady, *The Kurds: A Concise Handbook* (Washington, D.C.: Crane Russak, 1992); David McDowall, *A Modern History of the Kurds* (New York: I. B. Tauris, 1996).
81. For instance, see Amberin Zaman, "Thriving Kurdish Enclave Fears Saddam Strike," *The Daily Telegraph,* May 25, 2002; Amberin Zaman, "Iraq's Wary Kurds Wonder What Washington Has in Mind," *Los Angeles Times,* June 3, 2002.
82. Graham-Brown, *Sanctioning Saddam,* p. 314.
83. See, e.g., Nicholas Birch, "Iraq's Kurds Aren't Looking for a Fight," *The Washington Post,* May 5, 2002, p. B3; John F. Burns, "Kurds, Secure in North Iraq, Are Cool to a U.S. Offensive," *The New York Times,* July 8, 2002; Sally Buzbee, "Iraqi Kurds Worry That U.S. Invasion Could Lead to Backlash from Saddam," Associated Press, May 27, 2002.

Chapter 5: The Threat

1. Jerrold M. Post, "The Defining Moment of Saddam's Life: A Political Psychology Perspective on the Leadership and Decision-Making of Saddam Hussein During the Gulf Crisis," in Stanley A. Renshon, ed., *The Political Psychology of the Gulf War* (Pittsburgh: University of Pittsburgh Press, 1993), pp. 52–53.

2. Ofra Bengio, *Saddam's Word: Political Discourse in Iraq* (London: Oxford University Press, 1998), p. 73.

3. Ibid., p. 82.

4. Post, "The Defining Moment," pp. 54–55.

5. Amatzia Baram, *Culture, History and Ideology in the Formation of Ba'thist Iraq, 1968–89* (New York: St. Martin's Press, 1991), p. xv.

6. Bengio, *Saddam's Word,* p. 74. The "long days" also refers to Saddam's early political activities and assassination attempt against Qasim, which were the foundation of his political rise. His biography and a television miniseries about this period of his life—suitably mythologized—both bear the name *The Long Days.*

7. Quoted in ibid., p. 155.

8. Post, "The Defining Moment," p. 53.

9. Quoted in Bengio, *Saddam's Word,* p. 146.

10. Ibid., p. 147.

11. Amatzia Baram, "An Analysis of Iraqi WMD Strategy," *The Nonproliferation Review* (Summer 2001), p. 35; Charles A. Duelfer, "Weapons of Mass Destruction Programs in Iraq," Testimony before the Subcommittee on Emerging Threats and Capabilities, Armed Services Committee of the United States Senate, February 27, 2002; Scott Ritter, *Endgame: Solving the Iraq Problem—Once and For All* (New York: Simon and Schuster, 1999), p. 102.

12. Ofra Bengio, *Saddam Speaks on the Gulf Crisis* (Tel Aviv: Moshe Dayan Center for Middle Eastern and African Studies, 1992), p. 15.

13. Alix M. Freedman and Steve Stecklow, "How Iraq Reaps Illegal Oil Profits," *The Wall Street Journal,* May 2, 2002, p. A1.

14. Aburish, *Saddam Hussein,* p. 116; Karsh and Rautsi, *Saddam Hussein,* pp. 101–102.

15. Jentleson, *With Friends like These,* pp. 52–53; Hiro, *The Longest War,* p. 63; Schiff and Ya'ari, *Israel's Lebanon War,* pp. 99–100.

16. "Saad al-Bazzaz: An Insider's View of Iraq," *Middle East Quarterly,* December 1995, p. 69.

17. Pillar, *Terrorism and U.S. Foreign Policy,* p. 170.

18. Quoted in Jentleson, *With Friends like These,* p. 54.

19. Aburish, *Saddam Hussein,* p. 255; Jentleson, *With Friends like These,* p. 53; "Saddam's Former Bodyguard Profiled: al-Juburi Interviewed," pp. 11, 16–17; U.S. Department of State, "Fact Sheet: Iraq's Support for Terrorists," U.S. Department of State Dispatch, November 5, 1990.

20. Butler, *The Greatest Threat,* p. 35; Patrick Cockburn, "Interview with Wafiq al-Samarra'i: Saddam Has Missiles and Will Use Them," *The Independent,* July 5, 1996, p. 11.

21. Norman Cigar, "Iraq's Strategic Mindset and the Gulf War: Blueprint for Defeat," *The Journal of Strategic Studies,* vol. 15, no. 1 (March 1992), pp. 5–6 (Cigar was the head of the U.S. Army Intelligence division responsible for the Persian Gulf

during the Gulf War); William Drozdiak, "Security Officials Foresee Saddam Turning to Proxy Terrorists," *The Washington Post,* August 14, 1990; Norman Kempster, "U.S. Reports Decline in Terrorism Worldwide Violence: The Drop Comes
Despite Iraq's Threat to Attack Western Targets," *Los Angeles Times,* May 1, 1991;
"Iraq Puts Out Call for Terrorism," *Chicago Sun-Times,* January 20, 1991.

22. Pillar, *Terrorism and U.S. Foreign Policy,* p. 104.

23. Ibid., p. 57.

24. Ibid., p. 100.

25. U.S. Department of State, "Patterns of Global Terrorism, 2001," pp. 65–67.

26. The Council on Foreign Relations, "Terrorism: Questions and Answers," available at www.terrorismanswers.com/sponsors/iraq.html, downloaded June 7,
2002; "Iraqi Influence in West Bank, Gaza on the Rise," *Middle East Intelligence
Bulletin,* January 2001.

27. Doyle McManus and Robin Wright, "After Kabul, Should Iraq Be Next?" *Los
Angeles Times,* November 22, 2001; James Risen, "Terror Acts by Baghdad Have
Waned, U.S. Aides Say," *The New York Times,* February 6, 2002, p. A10.

28. "Interview: Sabah Khodada," *PBS Frontline,* available at
www.pbs.org/wgbh/pages/frontline/shows/gunning/interviews/khodada.html,
downloaded May 25, 2002; "Interview: An Iraqi Lt. General," *PBS Frontline,*
available at www.pbs.org/wgbh/pages/frontline/shows/gunning/interviews/
general.html, downloaded May 25, 2002.

29. Pillar, *Terrorism and U.S. Foreign Policy,* p. 104.

30. Raymond Bonner, "Experts Doubt Iraq Had Role in Latest Terror Attacks," *The
New York Times,* October 11, 2001, p. B7; Risen, "Terror Acts by Baghdad Have
Waned, U.S. Aides Say."

31. Bill Gertz, "CIA Won't Rule Out Iraq, Iran," *The Washington Times,* March 20,
2002.

32. An Iraqi armored division consists of seven tank battalions and five mechanized
infantry battalions, fielding roughly 200 to 250 tanks and 150 to 180 armored
personnel carriers. An Iraqi mechanized infantry division consists of the opposite: five tank battalions and seven mechanized infantry battalions, comprising
150 to 180 tanks and 200 to 250 armored personnel carriers.

33. Anthony Cordesman, "If We Fight Iraq: Iraq and the Conventional Military Balance," Center for Strategic and International Studies, February 27, 2002, pp. 3–6,
7–17; Michael Eisenstadt, *Like A Phoenix from the Ashes: The Future of Iraqi Military Power,* Policy Paper no. 36 (Washington, D.C.: WINEP, 1993), pp. 49–52;
Kenneth M. Pollack, "Conventional Military Capabilities," in Patrick L. Clawson,
ed., *Iraq Strategy Review* (Washington, D.C.: WINEP, 1998), pp. 175–177.

34. Pollack, *Arabs at War,* pp. 243–246, 248–255.

35. Cordesman, "If We Fight Iraq: Iraq and the Conventional Military Balance,"
pp. 3–6; Eisenstadt, *Like a Phoenix,* pp. 50–51; Pollack, "Conventional Military
Capabilities," pp. 175–177.

36. Cordesman, ibid., pp. 3–6, 18–25; Eisenstadt, ibid., pp. 53–57; Pollack, ibid.,
pp. 177–178.

37. Cordesman, ibid., pp. 3–6, 26; Pollack, ibid.

38. On the causes of these patterns of military effectiveness, see Kenneth M. Pollack,
"The Influence of Arab Culture on Arab Military Effectiveness," Ph.D. thesis,
Massachusetts Institute of Technology, February 1996.

39. For a more detailed analysis of Iraqi military history and capabilities, see Pollack, *Arabs at War,* pp. 148–266.

40. On Iraqi politicization and its depoliticization during the Iran-Iraq War, see Pollack, "The Influence of Arab Culture on Arab Military Effectiveness," pp. 263–351, 662–664.

41. Pollack, *Arabs at War,* pp. 218–228.

42. Ibid., pp. 148–266.

43. *GWAPS,* vol. II, part 1: *Operations,* p. 77.

44. Pollack, *Arabs at War,* pp. 184–266.

45. Eisentadt, *Like a Phoenix,* pp. 49–52; Pollack, ibid., pp. 184–266.

46. Cordesman, "If We Fight Iraq: Iraq and the Conventional Military Balance," pp. 38–41; Eisenstadt, ibid., pp. 54–55; Pollack, "Conventional Military Capabilities," pp. 176–178.

47. Pollack, *Arabs at War,* pp. 235–237.

48. Radio Free Europe/Radio Liberty, "Iraqi Armored Units in Western Iraq Withdrawing," *Iraq Report,* vol. 3, no. 36, November 3, 2000.

49. Eisenstadt, *Like a Phoenix,* pp. 8–9, 50; Pollack, "Conventional Military Capabilities," p. 177.

50. The United States reportedly has already detected indications of such activity. William Orme, "U.S. Alleges Iraqi Army Is Rebuilding," *Los Angeles Times,* March 7, 2002.

51. "Interview with Wafiq Samarrai," *Der Spiegel,* February 9, 1998, pp. 138–140, in FBIS-NES-98-40.

52. Federation of American Scientists, "UNSCOM and Iraqi Missiles," available at www.fas.org/nuke/guide/iraq/missile/unscom.htm, downloaded June 2, 2002.

53. Actually, two of the al-Husseins launched at Israel were called "al-Hijarahs"—al-Husseins with solid warheads intended to try to penetrate into the core of Israel's Dimona nuclear reactor.

54. Office of the Special Assistant to the Deputy Secretary of Defense for Gulf War Illnesses, "Information Paper: Iraq's Scud Ballistic Missiles," July 25, 2000, p. 11; Timothy V. McCarthy and Jonathan B. Tucker, "Saddam's Toxic Arsenal: Chemical and Biological Weapons and Missiles in the Gulf War," in Peter Lavoy, Scott D. Sagan, and James J. Wirtz, eds., *Planning for the Unthinkable* (Ithaca, N.Y.: Cornell University Press, 2000), p. 56.

55. Robert J. Einhorn, "Addressing the Iraqi WMD Threat," Testimony before the Subcommittee on International Security, Proliferation, and Federal Services, Senate Government Affairs Committee, March 1, 2002.

56. Duelfer, "Weapons of Mass Destruction Programs in Iraq"; "Interview with Wafiq Samarrai," pp. 138–140.

57. Central Intelligence Agency, "Unclassified Report to Congress on the Acquisition of Technology Relating to Weapons of Mass Destruction."

58. CIA, "Unclassified Report to Congress on the Acquisition of Technology Relating to Weapons of Mass Destruction"; Cordesman, "If We Fight Iraq: Iraq and Its Weapons of Mass Destruction," p. 1; Federation of American Scientists, "Iraq: Ababil-100/al-Samoud," available at www.fas.org/nuke/guide/iraq/missile/ababil.htm, downloaded June 2, 2002.

59. Cited in Cordesman, "If We Fight Iraq: Iraq and Its Weapons of Mass Destruction," p. 18.

60. Duelfer, "Weapons of Mass Destruction Programs in Iraq."
61. Central Intelligence Agency, "Iran-Iraq Chemical Warfare Continues," November 1986, declassified version, available at www.gulflink.osd.mil, downloaded May 25, 2002; McCarthy and Tucker, "Saddam's Toxic Arsenal," pp. 69–70.
62. Cordesman, "If We Fight Iraq: Iraq and Its Weapons of Mass Destruction," p. 16.
63. CIA, "Unclassified Report to Congress on the Acquisition of Technology Relating to Weapons of Mass Destruction"; Carl W. Ford, "Statement by Carl W. Ford, Jr., Assistant Secretary of State for Intelligence and Research," Senate Committee on Foreign Relations, Hearing on Reducing the Threat of Chemical and Biological Weapons, March 19, 2002.
64. Ford, ibid.; Duelfer, "Weapons of Mass Destruction Programs in Iraq."
65. Duelfer, ibid.
66. Ibid.
67. Office of the Special Assistant to the Deputy Secretary of Defense for Gulf War Illnesses, "Information Paper: Iraq's Scud Ballistic Missiles," July 25, 2000, p. 11.
68. Central Intelligence Agency, "Iraqi BW Mission Planning," 1992, GulfLink document no. 062596_cia_74624_74624_01.txt, available at www.gulflink.osd.mil, downloaded June 2, 2002.
69. CIA, "Unclassified Report to Congress on the Acquisition of Technology Relating to Weapons of Mass Destruction"; Ford, "Statement by Carl W. Ford, Jr., Assistant Secretary of State for Intelligence and Research."
70. Einhorn, "Addressing the Iraqi WMD Threat."
71. Duelfer, "Weapons of Mass Destruction Programs in Iraq."
72. Ibid.
73. Hamza, *Saddam's Bombmaker,* pp. 53–83.
74. Ibid., pp. 81–83.
75. Ibid., pp. 237–239, 334.
76. Ibid., pp. 333–334.
77. Duelfer, "Weapons of Mass Destruction Programs in Iraq."
78. Hamza, *Saddam's Bombmaker,* pp. 335–336.
79. Einhorn, "Addressing the Iraqi WMD Threat."
80. Cordesman, "If We Fight Iraq: Iraq and its Weapons of Mass Destruction," p. 5; Einhorn, ibid.
81. "German Intelligence: Iraq May Have Nuke in 3 Years," Reuters, February 24, 2002; Reuven Pedatzur, "German Intelligence and the Iraqi Threat," *Ha'aretz,* February 27, 2002.
82. Duelfer, "Weapons of Mass Destruction Programs in Iraq."
83. "Interview with Wafiq Samarrai," pp. 138–140.
84. Duelfer, "Weapons of Mass Destruction Programs in Iraq."
85. Amatzia Baram, "An Analysis of Iraqi WMD Strategy," *The Nonproliferation Review,* Summer 2001, pp. 25–27; Amatzia Baram, "The Iraqi Armed Forces and Security Apparatus," *Conflict, Security and Development,* vol. 1, no. 2 (2001), p. 120.
86. Baram, "An Analysis of Iraqi WMD Strategy," p. 28.
87. McCarthy and Tucker, "Saddam's Toxic Arsenal," p. 60.
88. Central Intelligence Agency, "Extract from VII Corps Report," GulfLink document no. 970613_7_corps_ext_txt_0001.txt, available at www.gulflink.osd.mil, downloaded June 2, 2002.

Chapter 6: The Regional Perspective

1. Much of this chapter is based on countless conversations over the last twelve years with officials, diplomats, businessmen, academics, and members of the ruling families of the different countries whose views are summarized. Unfortunately, there is no way to source these conversations.
2. Palmer, *Guardians of the Gulf,* p. 55.
3. Ibid., p. 77.
4. Ibid., pp. 83, 98–99.
5. For some thoughtful pieces on the issue of Arab popular opinion and its relationship to U.S. policy, see Augustus Richard Norton, "America's Approach to the Middle East: Legacies, Questions, and Possibilities," *Current History,* vol. 101, no. 651 (January 2002), pp. 3–7; Dale F. Eickelman, "Bin Laden, the Arab 'Street,' and the Middle East Democracy Deficit," *Current History,* vol. 101, no. 651 (January 2002), pp. 36–39.
6. Neil MacFarquhar, "Baghdad-Kuwait Accord—Support Is Rebuff to Bush's Efforts," *The New York Times,* March 29, 2002; Bassem Mroue, "Senior Iraqi Embraces Saudi Crown Prince, Arabs Oppose Use of Force Against Iraq," Associated Press, March 28, 2002; Sue Pleming, "U.S. Skeptical of Deal Between Iraq and Kuwait," Reuters, March 28, 2002.
7. Basim Sakkijha, "Uday Discusses War 'Facts,' Saddam's Decisions," *Akhir Khabar,* December 2, 1991, in FBIS-NES, December 4, 1991, p. 24; Patrick J. Garrity, "Why the Gulf War Still Matters: Foreign Perspectives on the War and the Future of International Security," Center for National Security Studies, Los Alamos National Laboratory, Report no. 16, July 1993, p. 34.
8. Cockburn and Cockburn, *Out of the Ashes,* pp. 40–41.
9. For a summary, see Alfred B. Prados, "Iraq: Post-War Challenges and U.S. Responses, 1991–1998," CRS Report 98-386F, March 31, 1999, pp. 20–23.
10. Hiro, *Neighbors, Not Friends,* pp. 137–138; Myers, "U.S. Will Not Ask to Use Saudi Bases for Raid on Iraq," p. A1. See also Prados, "Iraq: Post-War Challenges," p. 21.
11. Prados, ibid., pp. 22–23.
12. Zogby International, "The Ten Nation Impressions of America Poll," Utica, N.Y., April 11, 2002.
13. Radio Free Europe/Radio Liberty, "Iraq's Rapproachment with Arab World Continues . . . ," *Iraq Report,* vol. 5, no. 17 (June 7, 2002), p. 2.
14. For concurring opinions, see Douglas Jehl, "On the Record, Arab Leaders Oppose U.S. Attacks on Iraq," *The New York Times,* January 29, 1998, p. A6; Prados, "Iraq: Post-War Challenges," p. 23.
15. Zogby International, "The Ten Nation Impressions."
16. Prados, "Iraq: Post-War Challenges," pp. 20–23.
17. See for example, Heidi Kingstone, "Sibling Rivalry, Baghdad Style," *The Jerusalem Report,* June 18, 2001, p. 28.
18. Energy Information Administration, "Iraq Country Analysis Brief," March 2002, p. 2.
19. Conversations with Kuwaiti businessmen, July 2001 and March 2002.
20. Zogby International, "The Ten Nation Impressions."
21. Hiro, *Neighbors, Not Friends,* pp. 86, 115.

22. All statistics from Central Intelligence Agency, *The World Factbook, 2001* (Washington, D.C.: GPO, 2001).

23. Rana Awad, "Trade Deficit Stands at JD124 Million in January 2002," *Jordan Times,* March 12, 2002; Graham-Brown, *Sanctioning Saddam,* p. 67; International Monetary Fund, *Direction of Trade Statistics Yearbook, 2001* (Washington, D.C.: IMF, 2001); "Millions of Dollars in Jordan-Iraq Contracts Pushed to This Year," *The Wall Street Journal,* April 25, 2002.

24. "Jordan King Opposes U.S. Action in Iraq," Associated Press, May 12, 2002.

25. CIA, *World Factbook, 2001.*

26. See for example, Charles Rechnagel, "Iraq: Syria Considering End to Oil Smuggling," *Radio Free Europe/Radio Liberty,* March 7, 2001.

27. "Syrian-Iraqi Trade Reached $2 Billion in 2001," Middle East News Agency, May 27, 2002, available at www.menareport.com, downloaded May 27, 2002.

28. Radio Free Europe/Radio Liberty, "Iraq's Rapproachment with Arab World Continues . . . ," p. 2.

29. Conversations with Kurdish officials, Washington, D.C., May 2002.

30. John Ward Anderson, "Iraq's Neighbors Feel Pain of Sanctions," *The Washington Post,* July 1, 2001, p. A14; Kenneth Katzman, "Iraq: Oil-for-Food Program and International Sanctions," Congressional Research Service, CRS Report RL30472, July 10, 2001, p. 11; Graham-Brown, *Sanctioning Saddam,* p. 68; Chris Morris, "Sanctions on Iraq Stir Neighbors," *The Christian Science Monitor,* July 2, 2001, p. 1; "Turkey's Trade Volume with Iraq to Increase," *Turkishpress.com,* March 30, 2002.

31. Ayad Ahmed, "Iraq's Neighbors Seek Assurances Before Supporting a U.S.-Led Invasion," *Radio Free Europe,* May 18, 2002.

32. Mohammad Noureddine, "Turkey Will Be There When America Batters Iraq," *Daily Star,* March 28, 2002; interview with Mark R. Parris, Washington, D.C., May 15, 2002; Alan Makovsky, personal correspondence, June 2002.

33. Zogby International, "The Ten Nation Impressions."

34. Joyce Howard Price, "Peres Encourages U.S. Action on Iraq," *The Washington Times,* May 12, 2002.

35. Katzman, "Iraq: Oil-for-Food Program," p. 11.

36. "Iraq Disappointed in Ties with Iran," *Middle East Intelligence Bulletin,* vol. 2, no. 11, December 2000, p. 2.

37. See, e.g., Kamal Ahmed, "Blair to Back U.S. War on Iraq," *The Guardian,* April 7, 2002; Al Webb, "Blair Girds Britons to Strike Iraq," *The Washington Times,* March 11, 2002.

38. Philip H. Gordon and Michael O'Hanlon, "Tony Blair Has a Chance to Bridge the Gap on Iraq," *International Herald Tribune,* April 5, 2002; Andrew Grice and David Usborne, "Blair Says No Attack on Iraq Without UN Assent," *The Independent,* May 10, 2002.

39. Hiro, *Neighbors, Not Friends,* p. 75.

40. Ibid., p. 76.

41. See, e.g., Judy Dempsey and Brian Groom, "Action on Iraq Must Not Bypass UN, Says Russia," *The Financial Times,* March 20, 2002; "Russian Parliamentary Chairman for International Affairs: 'We Will Not Accept Military Force Against Iraq,' " *al-Sharq al-Awsat,* February 2, 2002, in MEMRI, Special Dispatch Series, no. 342.

42. David M. Shribman, "Russia, France Offer Gauge for Iraq Policy," *The Boston Globe,* March 12, 2002.

43. Nicholas Berry, "China, Fiber-Optics and Iraq," Center for Defense Information, February 26, 2001.

PART III: THE OPTIONS

Chapter 7: The Erosion of Containment

1. My thanks to Andrew Parasiliti for making this point.

2. Susan Blaustein and John Fawcett, "Sources of Revenue for Saddam & Sons, Inc.," Coalition for International Justice, draft manuscript, June 28, 2002, pp. 24–45.

3. John Ward Anderson, "Iraq's Neighbors Feel Pain of Sanctions," *The Washington Post,* July 1, 2001, p. A14; Blaustein and Fawcett, "Sources of Revenue," pp. 24–45; David Butter, "Dancing on Sanctions' Grave," *Middle East Economic Digest,* December 8, 2000; David Butter, "The Baghdad Dilemma," *Middle East Economic Digest,* January 18, 2002; "Can Sanctions Be Smarter?" *The Economist,* May 24, 2001; Harry Dunphy, "Iraq Earned $6 Billion Illegally," Associated Press, May 29, 2002; The *Economist* Intelligence Unit, "EIU Country Report: Iraq," March 2002; "Iraq Accused of Smuggling Illegal Oil," *Los Angeles Times,* October 26, 2001; Graham-Brown, *Sanctioning Saddam,* p. 163; Katzman, "Iraq: Oil-for-Food Program," pp. 10–11; Colum Lynch, "Iraq Caught Smuggling Oil, UN Official Says," *The Washington Post,* October 26, 2001; William Orme, "The World: Syria Faces Pressure to Halt Alleged Iraqi Oil Flows," *Los Angeles Times,* January 29, 2002; "Iraq Seeks to Torpedo New Sanctions Resolution," *Middle East Economic Digest,* June 1, 2001; Nicole Pope, "Sanctions 'Leaking All Over the Place,' " MSNBC, available at www.msnbc.com, downloaded April 2002; "Syrian-Iraqi Trade Reached $2 Billion in 2001," Middle East News Agency, May 27, 2002, available at www.menareport.com, downloaded May 27, 2002.

4. Anderson, "Iraq's Neighbors Feel Pain"; Blaustein and Fawcett, "Sources of Revenue," pp. 24–31; Butter, "Dancing on Sanctions' Grave"; Butter, "The Baghdad Dilemma"; "Can Sanctions Be Smarter?" *The Economist;* Dunphy, "Iraq Earned $6 Billion Illegally"; "EIU Country Report: Iraq," March 2002; Graham-Brown, *Sanctioning Saddam,* p. 163; Katzman, "Iraq: Oil-for-Food Program and International Sanctions"; Lynch, "Iraq Caught Smuggling Oil"; "Iraq Seeks to Torpedo New Sanctions Resolution," *Middle East Economic Digest;* Pope, "Sanctions 'Leaking All Over the Place' "; Charles Rechnagel, "Turkey: Iraqi Diesel Trade Seen as Too Valuable to Stop," *Radio Free Europe/Radio Liberty,* August 4, 2000.

5. Anderson, ibid.; Blaustein and Fawcett, ibid., pp. 32–36; Butter, "Dancing on Sanctions' Grave"; Butter, "The Baghdad Dilemma"; "Can Sanctions Be Smarter?" *The Economist;* Dunphy, ibid.; "EIU Country Report: Iraq," March 2002; Graham-Brown, ibid.; Katzman, ibid.; Lynch, ibid.; "Iraq Seeks to Torpedo New Sanctions Resolution," *Middle East Economic Digest;* Pope, ibid.

6. Anderson, ibid.; Blaustein and Fawcett, ibid., pp. 40–45; Butter, "Dancing on Sanctions' Grave"; Butter, "The Baghdad Dilemma"; "Can Sanctions Be

Smarter?" *The Economist;* Dunphy, ibid.; "EIU Country Report: Iraq," March 2002; Alix M. Freedman and Steve Stecklow, "The Oil 'Top-Off': Another Way Iraq Cheats UN," *The Wall Street Journal,* May 2, 2002, p. A10; Graham-Brown, ibid.; Katzman, ibid.; Lynch, ibid.; "Iraq Seeks to Torpedo New Sanctions Resolution," *Middle East Economic Digest;* Pope, ibid.

7. *Petroleum Intelligence Weekly,* reprinted in "Iraq Seeks to Torpedo New Sanctions Resolution," *Middle East Economic Digest,* June 1, 2001.

8. "Can Sanctions Be Smarter?" *The Economist,* May 24, 2001; Energy Information Administration, "Iraq," available at www.eia.doe.gov, downloaded March 2002; Katzman, ibid., p. 10; Iraqi oil-for-food revenue figures available from the U.N.'s Office of the Iraq Program at www.un.org/Depts/oip/background/basicfigures.html, downloaded June 8, 2002.

9. Freedman and Stecklow, "How Iraq Reaps Illegal Oil Profits," p. A1; Simon Henderson, "Illegal Oil Surcharges Earn Baghdad Extra $300 Million," *Radio Free Europe/Radio Liberty,* May 10, 2002; "Iraq Seeks to Torpedo New Sanctions Resolution," *Middle East Economic Digest;* David Ignatius, ". . . And Your Oil," *The Washington Post,* February 18, 2001; David Nissman, "Iraq Demands an Oil Kickback from India," *Radio Free Europe/Radio Liberty,* vol. 5, no. 6, February 15, 2002; Alan Sipress, "US Shifts Attack on Iraq Trade; Border States Seen as Key to Enforcing Sanctions," *The Washington Post,* March 26, 2001.

10. Peg Mackey, "Iraq Cuts Kickbacks to Boost UN Oil Sales," Reuters, June 6, 2002.

11. Freedman and Stecklow, "How Iraq Reaps Illegal Oil Profits."

12. "Delhi Company Fuelled Iraq's Weapons System," *Daily IRNA,* June 6, 2002; Ashok Sharma, "Indian Arrested for Allegedly Exporting Arms Material to Iraq," Associated Press, June 6, 2002.

13. Nicholas Berry, "China, Fiber-Optics and Iraq," Center for Defense Information, February 26, 2001.

14. The text of Resolution 670 is available at www.un.org/Docs/scres/1990/670e.pdf.

15. "Russians Flout Iraq Air Ban," CBSNews.com, August 19, 2000, available at www.cbsnews.com/stories/2000/08/19/world/main226342.shtml, downloaded on June 9, 2002.

16. "French Plane Heads for Iraq Despite Sanctions," CNN.com, September 22, 2000, available at http://europe.cnn.com/2000/WORLD/meast/09/22/iraq.france.reut/, downloaded June 9, 2002; Gary C. Gambill, "Iraq Returns to the Regional Stage," *Middle East Intelligence Bulletin,* vol. 2, no. 9 (October 5, 2000).

17. See, e.g., Michael Slackman, "Oil Barrels Fuel Baghdad's Clout in the Region," *Los Angeles Times,* May 8, 2002.

18. Katzman, "Iraq: Oil-for-Food Program," pp. 11–13; Robin Wright, "Bush's Foreign Policy Team Is Split on How to Handle Hussein," *Los Angeles Times,* February 14, 2001.

19. Neil King, Jr., "New Iraq Sanctions Are Short on Support—Strategy's Success Depends on Neighboring Lands, Which Rely on Iraqi Oil," *The Wall Street Journal,* June 18, 2001, p. A15; "Millions of Dollars in Jordan-Iraq Contracts Pushed to This Year," *The Wall Street Journal,* April 25, 2002.

20. Butter, "Dancing on Sanctions' Grave"; Gary C. Gambill, "Syria's Foreign Relations: Iraq," *Middle East Intelligence Bulletin,* March 2001; William Orme, "The World: Syria Faces Pressure to Halt Alleged Iraqi Oil Flows," *Los Angeles Times,*

January 29, 2002; Charles Recknagel, "Iraq: Syria Considering End to Oil Smuggling," *Middle East News Online,* March 7, 2001; Secretary of State Colin L. Powell, "Briefing for the Press Aboard Aircraft En Route to Brussels, February 26, 2001," U.S. Department of State, February 27, 2001.

21. "Turkey's Trade Volume with Iraq to Increase," *Turkishpress.com,* March 30, 2002.

22. Pope, "Sanctions 'Leaking All Over the Place.' "

23. Blaustein and Fawcett, "Sources of Revenue," pp. 26–29; Iranian Customs Department, available at www.irantpcnet.com/economy_business/foreigntrade/imports.htm, downloaded June 6, 2002.

24. Deputy Director, DCI Nonproliferation Center, A. Norman Schindler, "Iran's Weapons of Mass Destruction Programs," Statement to the International Security, Proliferation and Federal Services Subcommittee of the Senate Governmental Affairs Committee, September 21, 2000; U.S. Department of State, "Iran Is Still Seeking WMD Capabilities," *Washington File: International Information Programs,* October 5, 2000.

25. Neil King, Jr., "New Iraq Sanctions Are Short on Support"; U.S. Department of State, "Iraq: Rebuff of Revised Sanctions Regime Seen as U.S. Policy Setback," *Office of Research: Foreign Media Reaction,* July 13, 2001.

26. Peter Baker, "U.S. and Russia Agree to Overhaul Sanctions on Iraq," *The Washington Post,* March 29, 2002; Ben Barber, "Russia OKs Plan to Ease Iraq Sanctions," *The Washington Times,* March 29, 2002; Somini Sengupta, "UN Broadens List of Products Iraq Can Import," *The New York Times,* May 15, 2002; Patrick E. Tyler, "U.S., Russia Deal Revises Iraq Penalties," *The New York Times,* March 29, 2002.

27. Deborah Seward, "Russia Criticizes UN Oil Pricing Policy for Iraq," Associated Press, June 18, 2002.

28. For those interested in the topic, former UNSCOM Chairman Richard Butler has a number of excellent stories about outrageous Russian, French, and Chinese devotion to Iraq regardless of the Iraqi regime's lies, obfuscation, or noncompliance. See Butler, *The Greatest Threat,* esp. pp. 93–232.

29. Ibid., p. 216.

30. Alfred B. Prados and Kenneth Katzman, "Iraq-U.S. Confrontation," Congressional Research Service, Report No. IB94049, March 28, 2002, p. 10.

31. Michael Isherwood, "U.S. Strategic Options for Iraq: Easier Said Than Done," *The Washington Quarterly,* vol. 25, no. 2 (Spring 2002), pp. 148–149; Joshua Marshall, "Bomb Saddam?" *The Washington Monthly,* June 2002; Jessica Matthews, "The Wrong Target," *The Washington Post,* March 4, 2002, p. A19.

32. For an excellent early treatment of this problem, see Daniel L. Byman, "A Farewell to Arms Control," *Foreign Affairs,* January–February 2000, pp. 119–132.

33. Charles Duelfer, On the Record Remarks at the Council on Foreign Relations, April 17, 2002.

34. Robert J. Einhorn, "Addressing the Iraqi WMD Threat," Testimony before the International Security, Proliferation, and Federal Services Subcommittee of the Senate Government Affairs Committee, March 1, 2002.

35. Again, see Butler, *The Greatest Threat,* esp. pp. 93–232, for some examples of this behavior.

36. Robert J. Einhorn, "Addressing the Iraqi WMD Threat."
37. As one example, see Gregg Easterbrook, "Smart Bomb: The Case for an Ameri-can Osirak," *The New Republic,* February 25, 2002. The author, who is not a government official and holds no security clearances, claims to know the location of Iraq's WMD sites and argues that striking them would eliminate the threat from Saddam's WMD. The three facilities he mentions were well known to the United States and the U.N. inspectors. The author leaves out the inconvenient but crucial fact that Saddam has other facilities that we cannot locate and may not even know exist.
38. Prados and Katzman, "Iraq-U.S. Confrontation," p. 4.

Chapter 8: The Dangers of Deterrence

1. For an excellent early argument regarding deterrence as a policy option, see An-drew Parasiliti, "Deter," in Patrick Clawson, ed., *Iraq Strategy Review* (Washing-ton, D.C.: WINEP, 1998), pp. 101–116. For a more recent argument in favor of deterrence, see Philip H. Gordon and Michael E. O'Hanlon, "Should the War on Terrorism Target Iraq?" Brookings Institution, Analysis Paper No. 11, December 3, 2001, esp. pp. 6–7.
2. Bruce O. Riedel, personal correspondence, June 2002.
3. Amatzia Baram, "The Iraqi Invasion of Kuwait: Decision-Making in Baghdad," in Amatzia Baram and Barry Rubin, eds., *Iraq's Road to War* (New York: St. Martin's Press, 1993), pp. 11–13; Jentleson, *With Friends like These,* pp. 155–156; Lawrence Freedman and Efraim Karsh, *The Gulf Conflict, 1990–1991* (Princeton, N.J.: Princeton University Press, 1993), p. 32; "Saad al-Bazzaz: An Insider's View of Iraq," *Middle East Quarterly,* December 1995, pp. 68–69.
4. Amatzia Baram, "Israeli Deterrence, Iraqi Responses," *Orbis,* Summer 1992, pp. 397–409; Bazzaz, ibid., p. 69.
5. Richard K. Betts, "Universal Deterrence or Conceptual Collapse? Liberal Pes-simism and Utopian Realism," in Victor A. Utgoff, ed., *The Coming Crisis: Nu-clear Proliferation, U.S. Interests, and World Order* (Cambridge, Mass.: MIT Press and the Belfer Center for Science and International Affairs, 2000), p. 71.
6. Aleksandr Fursenko and Timothy Naftali, *"One Hell of a Gamble": The Secret History of the Cuban Missile Crisis* (New York: Norton, 1997), p. 242.
7. Patrick Morgan, "The Impact of the Revolution in Military Affairs," *The Journal of Strategic Studies,* vol. 23, no. 1 (March 2000), p. 160, n. 1.
8. Ibid., p. 146.
9. For a critique of the assumption that what made Cold War deterrence work is universally applicable, see Keith B. Payne, *The Fallacies of Cold War Deterrence and a New Direction* (Lexington: University Press of Kentucky, 2001).
10. Roger C. Molander and Peter A. Wilson, "On Dealing with the Prospect of Nu-clear Chaos," *The Washington Quarterly,* vol. 17, no. 3 (Summer 1994), p. 21.
11. See, e.g., Barry R. Posen, "U.S. Security Policy in a Nuclear-Armed World, or What If Iraq Had Had Nuclear Weapons?" in Victor A. Utgoff, ed., *The Coming Crisis: Nuclear Proliferation, U.S. Interests, and World Order* (Cambridge, Mass.: MIT Press and the Belfer Center for Science and International Affairs, 2000), p. 184.
12. Aharon Levran, *Israeli Strategy After Desert Storm: Lessons of the Second Gulf War* (London: Frank Cass, 1997), pp. 68–71.

13. My thanks to Hope Harrison for helping me stumble onto this important exception that proves the rule.

14. Jerrold M. Post, "Saddam Hussein of Iraq: A Political Psychology Profile," *Political Psychology,* vol. 12, no. 2 (1991), p. 284.

15. Kenneth Kaplan, "Iraq Holds the Key," *The Jerusalem Post,* September 24, 1989, p. 4.

16. Post, "Saddam Hussein of Iraq," p. 284.

17. Norman Cigar, "Iraq's Strategic Mindset and the Gulf War: Blueprint for Defeat," *The Journal of Strategic Studies,* vol. 15, no. 1 (March 1992), p. 1.

18. Baram, "Israeli Deterrence, Iraqi Responses," p. 401.

19. Jerrold M. Post, "The Defining Moment of Saddam's Life: A Political Psychology Perspective on the Leadership and Decision-Making of Saddam Hussein During the Gulf Crisis," in Stanley A. Renshon, ed., *The Political Psychology of the Gulf War* (Pittsburgh, Pa.: University of Pittsburgh Press, 1993), p. 50.

20. See, e.g., the story of the death of Minister of Health Riyad Ibrahim, who questioned one of Saddam's purges. Saddam pulled out a gun and unloaded the entire magazine into Ibrahim in front of his bodyguards and others. "Saddam's Former Bodyguard Profiled: al-Juburi Interviewed," *al-Majallah,* January 9, 1991, in JPRS-NEA-91-012, February 12, 1991, p. 18.

21. On this latter charge, see Butler, *The Greatest Threat,* p. 106.

22. "Interview with Yevgenni Primakov," *Paris Europe Number One,* April 28, 1991, in FBIS-SOV 91-083, p. 11.

23. See, e.g., "Saad al-Bazzaz: An Insider's View of Iraq," *Middle East Quarterly,* December 1995, p. 71.

24. Saddam Hussein interview with Diane Sawyer, "Saddam Speaks," *Primetime live,* ABC News, June 28, 1990.

25. Hamza, *Saddam's Bombmaker,* p. 235.

26. Anthony Cordesman and Abraham Wagner, *The Lessons of Modern War,* vol. 2: *The Iran-Iraq War* (Boulder, Colo.: Westview, 1990), pp. 78–79. On Saddam's reliance on soothsayers, see "Oral History: Wafic al Samarrai," *PBS Frontline: The Gulf War,* available at www.pbs.org/wgbh/pages/frontline/gulf/oral/samarrai/1.html, downloaded May 2, 2002.

27. See Memorandum for the Record, Document No. NA-22, "The Gulf War: An Iraqi General Officer's Perspective," March 11, 1991, declassified 1998; Army Component, United States Central Command (ARCENT), *Battlefield Reconstruction Study: The 100 Hour Ground War,* April 20, 1991, declassified version, pp. 23–24, 30–36; *GWAPS,* volume 1, part 1: *Planning,* p. 77.

28. Hamza, *Saddam's Bombmaker,* p. 150.

29. Cigar, "Iraq's Strategic Mindset," pp. 24–25; Post, "The Defining Moment of Saddam's Life," p. 50.

30. Cordesman and Wagner, *The Lessons of Modern War,* pp. 78–80; Edgar O'Ballance, *The Gulf War* (London: Brassey's, 1988), pp. 30–48; John S. Wagner, "Iraq," in Richard Gabriel, ed., *Fighting Armies: Antagonists in the Middle East* (Westport, Conn.: Greenwood Press, 1983), p. 68.

31. Post, "The Defining Moment of Saddam's Life," p. 52.

32. Sifry and Cerf, *The Gulf War Reader,* pp. 122–133.

33. Baram, *Building Toward Crisis,* p. 70.

34. Karsh and Rautsi, *Saddam Hussein,* p. 84.

35. On Iraqi military effectiveness in 1973 and 1980, see Pollack, *Arabs at War,* pp. 167–176, 183–193. On Syrian military effectiveness in 1973 and 1976, see Pollack, *Arabs at War,* pp. 481–523.

36. Karsh and Rautsi, *Saddam Hussein,* p. 104.

37. Author's interview with former Iraqi senior military officer, November 1998; Cordesman and Wagner, *The Lessons of Modern War,* pp. 64–79; Phebe Marr, "The Iran-Iraq War: The View from Iraq," in Christopher C. Joyner, ed., *The Persian Gulf War: Lessons for Strategy, Law, and Diplomacy* (Westport, Conn.: Greenwood Press, 1990), pp. 59–74; O'Ballance, *The Gulf War,* pp. 30–48; Arthur C. Turner, "Nationalism and Religion: Iran and Iraq at War," in James Brown and William Snyder, eds., *The Regionalization of Warfare* (New Brunswick, N.J.: Transaction Books, 1990), p. 157; Wagner, "Iraq," p. 68.

38. Central Intelligence Agency, "Iran-Iraq Chemical Warfare Continues," November 1986, declassified version, available at www.gulflink.osd.mil, downloaded May 25, 2002; Cordesman and Wagner, ibid., pp. 506–518; Timothy V. McCarthy and Jonathan B. Tucker, "Saddam's Toxic Arsenal: Chemical and Biological Weapons and Missiles in the Gulf War," in Peter Lavoy, Scott D. Sagan, and James J. Wirtz, eds., *Planning for the Unthinkable* (Ithaca, N.Y.: Cornell University Press, 2000), pp. 63–65.

39. Cordesman and Wagner, ibid., pp. 157–158, 191, 205–206, 255–256, 279–280, 310–311.

40. Amatzia Baram, "An Analysis of Iraqi WMD Strategy," *The Nonproliferation Review,* Summer 2001, pp. 29–30.

41. Ofra Bengio, *Saddam Speaks on the Gulf Crisis* (Tel Aviv: Moshe Dayan Center for Middle Eastern and African Studies, 1992), p. 14.

42. Jeffrey T. Richelson, *The Wizards of Langley* (Boulder, Colo.: Westview, 2001), p. 245.

43. Cockburn and Cockburn, *Out of the Ashes,* p. 7.

44. See, e.g., the interview with Tariq Aziz by Milton Viorst, "Report from Baghdad," *The New Yorker,* June 24, 1991, pp. 66–67; "Aziz Denies Glaspie Gave Green Light," *The Washington Times,* May 31, 1991, p. A2.

45. Pierre Salinger and Eric Laurent, *Secret Dossier* (New York: Penguin, 1991), pp. 82–83; Freedman and Karsh, *The Gulf Conflict,* p. 203; Jean Edward Smith, *George Bush's War* (New York: Henry Holt, 1992), p. 14.

46. U.S. News and World Report, *Triumph Without Victory* (New York: Times Books, 1992), pp. 8–13.

47. On Saddam's expectations, see "Interview with Yevgenni Primakov," *Paris Europe Number One,* April 28, 1991, in FBIS-SOV 91-083, p. 11.

48. Even if the United States had dispatched greater military force to the region in late July, because these forces inevitably would have been small and light, they probably would have looked to Saddam like what he had already decided he was likely to face and thought he could defeat. Only if the United States could somehow have convinced Saddam that it would respond to an Iraqi invasion with a massive military campaign employing America's full arsenal would this have changed Saddam's thinking. It is very hard to imagine how the United States might have convinced Saddam of this. It would have required a very large and very rapid buildup of U.S. forces in the Persian Gulf region. Such a move would have been very difficult in 1990 because the United States lacked the infrastruc-

ture and forward bases to suddenly deploy large, heavy forces to the region on short notice (as it now can). About the best Washington could have done would have been to move a brigade or two of the Eighty-second Airborne Division, a Marine Expeditionary unit, an aircraft carrier, and maybe a few fighter squadrons—precisely what Saddam seems to have expected to face. Moreover, given their thinking at the time, it is highly dubious that any of the Arab states would have given the United States permission to start such a deployment prior to the Iraqi invasion.

49. Stockholm International Peace Research Institute, *Armaments, Disarmament, and International Security, 1992* (London: Oxford University Press, 1992); U.S. Department of Defense (DOD), *Conduct of the Persian Gulf War* (Washington, D.C.: GPO, 1992), p. 86.

50. On Iraqi elite attitudes before the Gulf War that Iraq should negotiate its way out of Kuwait rather than fight the U.S.-led coalition, see Cockburn and Cockburn, *Out of the Ashes,* pp. 9–14; Hamza, *Saddam's Bombmaker,* pp. 237–251; Memorandum for the Record, Document No. NA-22, "The Gulf War: An Iraqi General Officer's Perspective," March 11, 1991, declassified 1998; al-Salihi, *al-Zilzal,* pp. 11, 15–17; *Frontline* interview with Samarra'i, May 2, 2002.

51. "Interview with Yevgenni Primakov," *Paris Europe Number One,* April 28, 1991, in FBIS-SOV 91-083, p. 11.

52. *Frontline* interview with Samarra'i, May 2, 2002. It seems a reasonable assumption that Samarra'i and his colleagues were far more respectful when they actually raised this question with Saddam than his postwar interview would suggest.

53. "Interview with Yevgenni Primakov," *Paris Europe Number One,* April 28, 1991, in FBIS-SOV 91-083, p. 11.

54. Post, "The Defining Moment of Saddam's Life," pp. 58–59.

55. Baram, "Israeli Deterrence, Iraqi Responses"; *Frontline* interview with Samarra'i, May 2, 2002. Also see Shai Feldman, "Israeli Deterrence and the Gulf War," in Joseph Alpher, ed., *War in the Gulf: Implications for Israel* (Jerusalem: Jerusalem Post Press, 1992).

56. "No Chem Scuds?" *Armed Forces Journal International,* March 1991, p. 23; McCarthy and Tucker, "Saddam's Toxic Arsenal," pp. 55–56, 59; Gerald M. Steinberg, "Parameters of Stable Deterrence in a Proliferated Middle East: Lessons from the 1991 Gulf War," *The Nonproliferation Review,* Fall–Winter 2000, p. 55.

57. For Israeli experts who suspect that this may be the case, see Amatzia Baram, "Israeli Deterrence, Iraqi Responses," p. 400; Steinberg, ibid., p. 55.

58. Central Intelligence Agency, "Iraqi BW Mission Planning," 1992, GulfLink document no. 062596_cia_74624_74624_01.txt, available at www.gulflink.osd.mil, downloaded June 2, 2002.

59. Rick Francona, *Ally to Adversary: An Eyewitness Account of Iraq's Fall from Grace* (Annapolis, Md.: U.S. Naval Institute Press, 1999), p. 137; McCarthy and Tucker, "Saddam's Toxic Arsenal," pp. 69–70. Francona was a former DIA analyst and Defense attaché with long experience on the Iraq account, including during the Gulf War. McCarthy and Tucker are former UNSCOM inspectors.

60. Although before the war Saddam boasted of having "binary" CW rounds, these claims were not entirely accurate. In U.S. military parlance, binary rounds con-

tain two chemicals separated by a buffer that shatters when the round is launched, allowing the chemicals to mix to form the lethal agent. Because the precursor chemicals independently are not dangerous, binary rounds are much safer to handle. Iraq did not have such binary munitions. Instead, what it had were munitions that were partially filled—they contained one of the precursor chemicals and so were easily handled. However, the other chemical had to be added before firing, making the process no less time-consuming, cumbersome, or dangerous than filling an ordinary CW munition.

61. Baram, "Israeli Deterrence, Iraqi Responses," p. 400; Thomas Houlahan, *Gulf War: The Complete History* (New London, N.H.: Schrenker Military Publishing, 1999), pp. 436–437; McCarthy and Tucker, "Saddam's Toxic Arsenal," pp. 69–70.

62. My thanks to Steve Ward for raising this important point. On Baker's warning to Aziz, see Freedman and Karsh, *The Gulf Conflict,* p. 257; Gordon and Trainor, *The Generals' War,* p. 197.

63. *Frontline* interview with Samarra'i, May 2, 2002.

64. Hamza, *Saddam's Bombmaker,* p. 237.

65. *Frontline* interview with Samarra'i, May 2, 2002.

66. Amatzia Baram, "An Analysis of Iraqi WMD Strategy," *The Nonproliferation Review,* Summer 2001, p. 35; Baram, *Building Toward Crisis,* p. 81; Charles A. Duelfer, "Weapons of Mass Destruction Programs in Iraq," Testimony before the Subcommittee on Emerging Threats and Capabilities, Armed Services Committee of the United States Senate, February 27, 2002; Hamza, ibid., p. 244; Scott Ritter, *Endgame: Solving the Iraq Problem—Once and for All* (New York: Simon and Schuster, 1999), p. 102.

67. See, e.g., Patrick J. Garrity, "Why the Gulf War Still Matters: Foreign Perspectives on the War and the Future of International Security," Center for National Security Studies, Los Alamos National Laboratory, Report No. 16, July 1993, pp. 34–35; Basim Sakkijha, "Uday Discusses War 'Facts,' Saddam's Decisions," *Akhir Khabar,* December 2, 1991, in FBIS-NES, December 4, 1991, p. 24; "Oral History: Wafic al Samarrai," *PBS Frontline: The Gulf War,* available at www.pbs.org/wgbh/pages/frontline/gulf/oral/samarrai/1.html, downloaded May 2, 2002.

68. "Hussein Kamel on Army Strength, Saddam Fedayeen," *al-Watan al-'Arabi,* in FBIS-NES, November 27, 1995, p. 33.

69. Barry R. Posen, "U.S. Security Policy in a Nuclear-Armed World," p. 159.

70. For a similar, lengthier exposition of this argument, see Janice Gross Stein, "Deterrence and Compellence in the Gulf, 1990–91," *International Security,* vol. 17, no. 2 (Fall 1992), pp. 147–179.

71. Baram, "Israeli Deterrence, Iraqi Responses," p. 405; Baram, "An Analysis of Iraqi WMD Strategy," pp. 25, 29–30.

72. For oil production and consumption figures, see the Energy Intelligence Agency's statistics, available at www.eia.doe.gov.

73. Office of Technology Assessment, *U.S. Oil Import Vulnerability* (Washington, D.C.: GPO, 1991), p. 39.

74. James M. Kendell, "Measures of Oil Import Dependence," Energy Information Agency, 1998, available at www.eia.doe.gov/oiaf/archive/issues98/oimport.html, downloaded May 2, 2002; interview with James Placke, Washington, D.C.,

March 2002; telephone interview with Phillip Verleger, April 2002; interview with Michael Weinstein, New York, N.Y., March 2002.

75. *Frontline* interview with Samarra'i, May 2, 2002.

76. Something that, by the way, would increase the value of the Iraqi (and Kuwaiti) oil fields enormously.

77. Human Rights Watch, *Iraq's Crime of Genocide: The Anfal Campaign Against the Kurds* (New Haven, Conn.: Yale University Press, 1995).

78. Morgan, "The Impact of the Revolution," p. 145.

Chapter 9: The Difficulty of Covert Action

1. On Aidid, see John L. Hirsch and Robert B. Oakley, *Somalia and Operation Restore Hope* (Washington, D.C.: USIP Press, 1995), p. 121, n. 17. Ambassador Oakley was the president's special envoy to Somalia. On Saddam, General Schwarzkopf notes in his autobiography that assertions that the United States was not trying to kill Saddam were "true, to a point." H. Norman Schwarzkopf, *It Doesn't Take a Hero* (New York: Bantam, 1992), pp. 318–319; former National Security Adviser Brent Scowcroft was asked about assassinating Saddam in an ABC News interview: "So you deliberately set out to kill him if you possibly could?" To which he replied, "Yes, that's fair enough." Transcript, ABC News, Peter Jennings Reporting, "Unfinished Business: The CIA and Saddam Hussein," June 26, 1997. Also see George Bush and Brent Scowcroft, *A World Transformed* (New York: Alfred A. Knopf, 1998), p. 433. On bin Ladin, see Barton Gellman, "Broad Effort Launched After '98 Attacks," *The Washington Post,* December 19, 2001, p. A1. On Qadhafi, see Charles G. Cogan, "The Response of the Strong to the Weak: The American Raid on Libya, 1986," *Intelligence and National Security,* vol. 6, no. 3, 1991, pp. 615–616; Brian L. Davis, *Qaddafi, Terrorism, and the Origins of the US Attack on Libya* (Westport, Conn.: Praeger, 1990), pp. 137–141; David C. Martin and John Walcott, *Best Laid Plans: The Inside Story of America's War Against Terrorism* (New York: Harper and Row, 1988), pp. 309–311.

2. See Duane R. Clarridge, *A Spy for All Seasons: My Life in the CIA* (New York: Scribner's, 1997), pp. 174–175.

3. James A. Baker III, *The Politics of Diplomacy* (New York: Putnam's, 1995), pp. 183–187; Stephen Engleberg, "CIA Seeks Looser Rules on Killings During Coups," *The New York Times,* October 17, 1989, p. A8; Stephen Engleberg, "Reagan Agreed to Prevent Noriega Death," *The New York Times,* October 23, 1989, p. A10.

4. Cockburn and Cockburn cite an interview with former CIA officer (and then chief of Near East Operations Division) Frank Anderson. See Cockburn and Cockburn, *Out of the Ashes,* p. 31; also see Jeffrey T. Richelson, *The U.S. Intelligence Community,* 4th ed. (Boulder, Colo.: Westview, 1999), p. 353.

5. "Clinton Had Plan to Arrest or Kill bin Laden," CNN.com, September 23, 2001; "Clinton: I Tried to Kill Bin Laden," Agence France-Presse, September 24, 2001.

6. Hiro, *Neighbors, Not Friends,* p. 61.

7. For accounts of the security surrounding Saddam and his sons, see Latif Yahia and Karl Wendl, *I Was Saddam's Son* (New York: Arcade Publishing, 1997); Major Karim Abdallah al-Jubburi, in *al-Majallah,* January 9, 1991, in JPRS-NEA, February 12, 1991, pp. 10–19.

8. William H. Arkin, "Baghdad: The Urban Sanctuary in Desert Storm?" *Airpower Journal,* vol. 11, no. 1 (Spring 1997), pp. 4–20.

9. *Frontline* interview with Samarra'i, May 2, 2002.

10. Baram, *Building Toward Crisis,* pp. 18–19; Cockburn and Cockburn, *Out of the Ashes,* pp. 255–259.

11. Franklin L. Ford, *Political Murder: From Tyrannicide to Terrorism* (Cambridge, Mass.: Harvard University Press, 1985), p. 387.

12. Stephen T. Hosmer, *Psychological Effects of U.S. Air Operations in Four Wars, 1941–1991* (Santa Monica, Calif.: RAND, 1996), pp. 44–45, 49–55.

13. Bush and Scowcroft, *A World Transformed,* p. 433.

14. Hiro, *Neighbors, Not Friends,* p. 61; Karsh and Rautsi, *Saddam Hussein,* pp. 43–45.

15. Bob Woodward, "President Broadens Anti-Hussein Order," *The Washington Post,* June 16, 2002, pp. A1, A8.

16. Quoted in Cockburn and Cockburn, *Out of the Ashes,* pp. 31–32.

Chapter 10: The Risks of the Afghan Approach

1. For a fuller critique, see Daniel L. Byman, Kenneth M. Pollack, and Gideon G. Rose, "The Rollback Fantasy," *Foreign Affairs,* January–February 1999, pp. 24–41.

2. See, e.g., Seymour M. Hersh, "The Debate Within," *The New Yorker,* March 11, 2002, pp. 34–39; Nicholas Lemann, "The Iraq Factor," *The New Yorker,* January 22, 2001, pp. 34–38; Nicholas Lemann, "The Next World Order," *The New Yorker,* April 1, 2002, pp. 42–48; Rowan Scarborough, "Size of Force on Ground Key in Plan for Iraq War," *The Washington Times,* April 26, 2002, p. 1.

3. See, e.g., James S. Robbins, "War in the Shadows: Covert Operations in Iraq," *National Review Online,* February 21, 2002, available at www.nationalreview. com/contributors/robbinsprint022102.html, downloaded June 23, 2002.

4. Steven Kosiak, "Estimated Cost of Operation Enduring Freedom: The First Two Months," Center for Strategic and Budgetary Assessments, December 6, 2001, available at www.csbaonline.org/4Publications/Archive/B.20011207.Estimated_ Cost_of_/B.20011207.Estimated_Cost_of_htm, downloaded June 29, 2002.

5. Eliot A. Cohen, "Kosovo and the New American Way of War," in Eliot A. Cohen and Andrew J. Bacevich, eds., *War over Kosovo* (New York: Columbia University Press, 2001), p. 54.

6. Kenneth M. Pollack, "How to Win a War Against Al Qaeda," *The Wall Street Journal,* September 18, 2001, p. A22.

7. Daniel L. Byman, Kenneth M. Pollack, and Gideon G. Rose, "Beef Up the Taliban's Enemies," *Los Angeles Times,* September 20, 2001.

8. Patricia Cohen, "Getting It Right: Strategy Angst," *The New York Times,* October 27, 2001, p. 11; Carl Conetta, "Strange Victory: A Critical Appraisal of Operation Enduring Freedom and the Afghanistan War," Project on Defense Alternatives Research Monograph No. 6, January 30, 2002, p. 10; Colonel James E. Miller, USAF (ret.), "Cities Fall. What Next?" *National Review Online,* November 13, 2001, available at www.nationalreview.com/comment/comment-miller111301.shtml, downloaded June 21, 2002; "Secretary Rumsfeld Press Conference with Tajikistan Foreign Minister," U.S. Department of Defense, November 3, 2001, available on DefenseLink at www.defenselink.mil/news/

Nov2001/t11032001_t1103sd2.html, downloaded June 21, 2002; "U.S. Counters War Cynics: Military Chief Says Campaign on Track, a Win Will Take Time," *Detroit Free Press,* November 9, 2001.

9. For example, only days before the fall of Mazar-i-Sharif, Secretary of Defense Rumsfeld cautioned reporters that the war in Afghanistan was "a new kind of war" and that they should not expect "instant victory or instant success." Likewise, CENTCOM Commander General Tommy Franks argued that while the campaign was going according to plan, it might take some time to achieve victory. According to *The Washington Post,* before the war, "top-ranking U.S. military officials cautioned that it would take until summer to break the Taliban's five-year hold on power." See Gerry J. Gilmore, "Rumsfeld: Don't Expect 'Instant Victory' in Anti-Terror War," *American Forces Information Service: News Articles,* November 1, 2001; Dana Priest, " 'Team 555' Shaped a New Way of War," *The Washington Post,* April 3, 2002, p. A1; "U.S. Counters War Cynics." For other U.S. government predictions that defeating the Taliban would require many months more, see Peter Pae, "U.S. Predicting Fight Will Last Well into Spring," *Los Angeles Times,* October 22, 2001, p. 1; Robin Wright and Doyle McManus, "U.S. Shifts Gears After a Week of Setbacks," *Los Angeles Times,* October 28, 2001, p. 1.

10. My track record on Iraq has also been quite good. For example, I was one of only three U.S. government analysts to predict the Iraqi invasion of Kuwait. I also predicted that the Iraqi Army would prove far less capable than many in the U.S. military (let alone outside experts) were claiming at the time of the Gulf War. In fact, I told a congressional committee that I expected the United States would more than likely smash the Iraqis because our strengths matched up well against Iraq's weaknesses. I predicted that the post–Gulf War *intifadah* would fail and that without U.S. intervention Saddam would survive. I also predicted that Saddam would not cooperate with the U.N. inspectors, that he would make tactical concessions only, and that he would increasingly obstruct the inspectors' activities over time. At the very start of the oil-for-food program, I predicted that Saddam would use Iraq's contracts to manipulate foreign countries by insisting they support his efforts to erode the sanctions. I predicted that Operation Desert Fox would destabilize Saddam's regime but that the effect would be only temporary if it was shut down after a few days. To be honest, I did miss two fairly significant calls on Iraq. First, on August 5, 1990, I was pretty convinced I was looking at the start of an Iraqi invasion of Saudi Arabia. Second, during the Gulf War, I was certain that Saddam would employ chemical weapons to prevent the destruction of his armed forces. Both of these calls were proven wrong. That said, there is mitigating evidence in both cases. In the first instance, bad information we received (overestimating the size of the Iraqi armored forces moving toward Saudi Arabia), unintended actions by Iraq (the "friction" of war carrying Iraq's logistical units and artillery batteries to the Saudi border, where they were not meant to be), and threatening Iraqi actions that were designed to deter us from intervening in Kuwait (uploading chemical weapons onto Iraqi aircraft), were all reasonable indicators of such an attack. Likewise, as noted in Chapters 5 and 8, there is good evidence that Saddam had not ruled out using CW in the event that the ground war did not go as he planned, but he was prevented from doing so by the speed and scope of the coalition victory.

11. "The Taliban's Military Forces (Prior to Hostilities)," available at
    www.janes.com/defence/news/misc/jwa011008_2_n.shtml, downloaded June 24,
    2002.

12. On the formation and early victories of the Taliban, see in particular Michael
    Griffin, *Reaping the Whirlwind: The Taliban Movement in Afghanistan* (London:
    Pluto Press, 2001); Ahmed Rashid, *Taliban* (New Haven, Conn.: Yale University
    Press, 2000); Barnett Rubin, *The Fragmentation of Afghanistan* (New Haven,
    Conn.: Yale University Press, 1995).

13. Conetta, "Strange Victory," p. 3.

14. Ibid., p. 31; Anthony H. Cordesman, "If We Fight Iraq: The Lessons of the Fight-
    ing in Afghanistan," Center for Strategic and International Studies, December 7,
    2001, p. 2; David Lamb, "Missteps Toppled Taliban, Analysts Say," *Los Angeles
    Times,* December 27, 2001.

15. Cordesman, ibid., p. 2; Michael E. O'Hanlon, "A Flawed Masterpiece," *Foreign
    Affairs,* vol. 81, no. 3 (May–June 2002), p. 49.

16. Lamb, "Missteps Toppled Taliban"; Cordesman, ibid.

17. Edward Cody, "Taliban's 'Hide-and-Wait' Strategy Failed," *The Washington
    Post,* December 23, 2001, p. 12; Anthony H. Cordesman, "The Lessons of
    Afghanistan: Warfighting, Intelligence, Force Transformation, Counterprolifera-
    tion, and Arms Control," Center for Strategic and International Studies, February
    21, 2002, p. 8; Priest, " 'Team 555.' "

18. Conetta, "Strange Victory," p. 3. For reports that bombing killed far fewer Tal-
    iban troops and equipment than had been claimed, see Priest, " 'Team 555.' "

19. Jon Lee Anderson, "The Surrender," *The New Yorker,* December 10, 2001; Cody,
    "Taliban's 'Hide-and-Wait' Strategy Failed," p. 12; Conetta, ibid., pp. 3, 31; An-
    thony H. Cordesman, "Sending in the Marines: What Happens Next," Center for
    Strategic and International Studies, November 27, 2001, p. 1; Cordesman, "The
    Lessons of the Fighting in Afghanistan," p. 4; Anthony H. Cordesman, "The Old-
    New Lessons of Afghanistan," Center for Strategic and International Studies,
    March 4, 2002, p. 1; Cordesman, "The Lessons of Afghanistan," p. 8; Lamb,
    "Missteps Toppled Taliban"; O'Hanlon, "A Flawed Masterpiece," p. 49.

20. Cody, ibid., p. 12; Conetta, ibid., p. 32; Anthony H. Cordesman, "Why the Tal-
    iban Collapsed So Quickly," Center for Strategic and International Studies, No-
    vember 13, 2001, p. 2; Cordesman, "The Lessons of Afghanistan," p. 8;
    Cordesman, "The Old-New Lessons of Afghanistan," p. 1; O'Hanlon, ibid., p.
    49.

21. Anderson, "The Surrender"; Cody, ibid., p. 12; Conetta, ibid., pp. 32–33; Lamb,
    "Missteps Toppled Taliban."

22. Conetta, ibid.

23. Initially, NATO claimed that there had been little cooperation between its air
    forces and the KLA units on the ground. However, since then, it has come to
    light that cooperation between NATO and KLA was much greater than admitted.
    In particular, NATO aircraft provided on-call close air support for KLA forces as
    needed. See, e.g., Benjamin S. Lambeth, *NATO's Air War for Kosovo* (Santa
    Monica, Calif.: RAND, 2001), pp. 54–55.

24. Ivo H. Daalder and Michael E. O'Hanlon, *Winning Ugly: NATO's War to Save
    Kosovo* (Washington, D.C.: Brookings Institution, 2000), p. 152; Paul C. Forage,
    "The Battle for Mount Pastrik: A Preliminary Study," *The Journal of Slavic Mili-*

tary Studies, vol. 14, no. 4 (December 2001), pp. 63–64; Lambeth, ibid., pp. 54–55.

25. Arkin, "Operation Allied Force," pp. 5–7; Stephen T. Hosmer, *Why Milosevic Decided to Settle When He Did* (Santa Monica, Calif.: RAND, 2001), pp. 77–78; Lambeth, ibid., pp. 25, 28.

26. Stephen Biddle, "The New Way of War?" *Foreign Affairs,* vol. 81, no. 3 (May–June 2002), pp. 140–142; Hosmer, ibid., entire; Lambeth, ibid., pp. 67–86.

27. On the inability of NATO air forces to do any significant harm to the Serbian ground forces, see Hosmer, ibid., pp. 77–90; Lambeth, ibid., pp. 53–59, 120–136.

28. Arkin, "Operation Allied Force," p. 14.

29. Lambeth, *NATO's Air War for Kosovo,* p. 62.

30. Arkin, "Operation Allied Force," p. 25; Daalder and O'Hanlon, *Winning Ugly,* pp. 153–154; Lambeth, ibid., pp. 130–131. Although NATO assumes that the other 67 tanks, 135 APCs, and 369 artillery and mortar tubes were either repaired and returned to duty or transported back to Serbia for repair, there is no evidence of this. In fact, most of the armored vehicles NATO believed it had destroyed turned out to be decoys.

31. Lambeth, ibid., p. 61.

32. Arkin, "Operation Allied Force," pp. 8–9, 11, 13–15, 19; Hosmer, *Why Milosevic Decided to Settle,* p. 87; Lambeth, ibid., pp. 28–29, 37.

33. Arkin, ibid., p. 19; Hosmer, ibid., p. 88; Lambeth, ibid., pp. 28–29, 121, 132.

34. Arkin, ibid., pp. 8–9, 11, 13; Daalder and O'Hanlon, *Winning Ugly,* pp. 239–240; Hosmer, ibid., pp. 85–86.

35. Forage, "The Battle for Mount Pastrik," pp. 60–63; Hosmer, ibid., p. 89; Lambeth, *NATO's Air War for Kosovo,* pp. 53–54.

36. Hosmer, ibid., p. 89. Also see Forage, ibid., p. 67; Lambeth, ibid., p. 59.

37. Lambeth, ibid., p. 62.

38. Army Component, United States Central Command (ARCENT), *Battlefield Reconstruction Study: The 100 Hour Ground War,* April 20, 1991, declassified version, pp. 58–59; Watts et al., *GWAPS,* vol. 2, part 2: *Effects and Effectiveness,* pp. 94, 165–169, 220; U.S. Department of Defense, *Conduct of the Persian Gulf War* (Washington, D.C.: GPO, 1992), p. 159. Watts, "Friction in the Gulf War," p. 94. The Watts article contains the most accurate statistics regarding Iraqi formations, equipment, and manpower in the KTO.

39. Watts et al., ibid., p. 199.

40. Stephen T. Hosmer, *Psychological Effects of U.S. Air Operations in Four Wars, 1941–1991* (Santa Monica, Calif.: RAND, 1996), pp. xxvi–xxviii, 168–169, 181–188; Watts et al., ibid., 187–202.

41. Hosmer, ibid., pp. 141–169, 196; Memorandum for the Record, Document No. NA-22, "The Gulf War: An Iraqi General Officer's Perspective," March 11, 1991, declassified 1998.

42. An accurate count of Iraqi equipment destroyed by air strikes during the Gulf War remains elusive. We may never know precisely how many vehicles were destroyed in the air campaign because the Iraqis themselves did not keep accurate records (debriefs of unit commanders and records captured during the Gulf War are extremely spotty: some units kept very accurate counts of destroyed equipment; others did not). I arrived at these numbers in the following manner. First,

according to the most accurate assessment of Iraqi strength—a CIA equipment count using U-2 imagery of the entire theater taken immediately after the war—the Iraqis had 3,475 tanks and 3,080 APCs in theater at the start of the war (*GWAPS,* vol. 2, part 1: *Operations,* p. 254). Second, the CIA found that of the 2,665 tanks in the twelve heavy divisions Iraq deployed to the KTO, 1,135 (43 percent) did not move to fight or flee during the ground war. Likewise, of the 2,624 APCs in these same twelve divisions, 827 (32 percent) did not move during the ground war (see Central Intelligence Agency, *Operation Desert Storm: A Snapshot of the Battlefield* [Washington, D.C.: GPO, September 1993]). These 1,135 tanks and 827 APCs represent the upper end of the number of tanks and APCs in these twelve divisions that might have been destroyed by the air campaign. However, the actual number is probably considerably lower because many of these tanks did not move not because they were destroyed by air strikes, but because they had been abandoned by frightened crews or were inoperable because of maintenance problems. Postwar inspections of Iraqi equipment found that as many as 50 percent of tanks and APCs in some units had simply been abandoned in this fashion. Debriefings of Iraqi prisoners of war revealed that large numbers of vehicle crews had abandoned their tanks and APCs and surrendered or fled rather than try to stop the coalition ground offensive. Similarly, the Iraqis have always had abysmal maintenance practices, and an operational readiness rate of 65 percent is the norm in many combat units. Indeed, during the Iran-Iraq War, readiness rates of around 50 percent for tanks and APCs were commonplace in Iraqi line formations. Consequently, the actual number of tanks and APCs in the twelve heavy divisions that were destroyed by air strikes during the Gulf War was probably, at most, half of those that the CIA study found did not move during the ground war—or 568 tanks (21 percent) and 414 APCs (16 percent). A more likely estimate is that only one third of the armored vehicles that did not move to fight or flee were actually destroyed by air strikes—or 375 tanks (14 percent) and 273 APCs (10 percent).

In addition to the tanks and APCs in the twelve armored and mechanized divisions in the KTO, the Iraqis deployed 810 tanks and 456 APCs in independent brigades and battalions, as well as battalions attached to some of the thirty-nine infantry divisions deployed in the KTO (CIA, *Operation Desert Storm*). The air campaign clearly destroyed some of these too. In fact, air power probably destroyed a greater percentage of these vehicles than those in the Iraqi heavy divisions. The coalition flew more sorties and had much longer loiter times with its deadliest tank-killing aircraft—the A-10 Thunderbolts—against the frontline infantry divisions and their supporting armor in the south of the KTO than against the heavy divisions farther north (*GWAPS,* vol. 2, part 1: *Operations,* pp. 268–282). Moreover, both the CIA study and anecdotal accounts from Iraqi personnel captured during the war indicate that tanks and APCs attached to frontline infantry divisions suffered more than those in the heavy divisions (CIA, *Operation Desert Storm;* U.S. DOD, *Conduct of the Persian Gulf War,* pp. 158–160). Consequently, it seems reasonable to believe that these units had a greater percentage of tanks and APCs destroyed than the heavy divisions, perhaps as much as 50 percent tank losses and 40 percent APC losses, which would equate to another 405 tanks and 182 APCs. (I would not go higher than this because many of these armored vehicles were deployed along the Kuwaiti and Iraqi coasts and in the northern KTO, where they did not suffer the same pounding as the units along the Iraqi front lines.)

These rough estimates produce a range of total numbers of armored vehicles probably destroyed by the coalition air campaign of 780 to 983 tanks (22 to 28 percent) and 455 to 596 APCs (15 to 19 percent). As a final note, the largest U.S. survey of Iraqi armor captured during the war found that only 10 to 20 percent had been destroyed by air attack. Although this survey examined only 6 percent of all Iraqi tanks destroyed during the war, and then only those in a small part of the KTO, it nonetheless indicates that while my numbers may not be precise, they are probably not off by much but may slightly overstate the amount of physical destruction caused by the air strikes. (See U.S. General Accounting Office, *Operation Desert Storm: Evaluation of the Air Campaign,* Report to the Ranking Minority Member, Committee on Commerce, House of Representatives [Washington, D.C.: GPO, June 1997].)

43. CIA, *Operation Desert Storm.*
44. See Hosmer, *Psychological Effects of U.S. Air Operations,* pp. 179–180.
45. For instance, see Ian Gooderson, "Allied Fighter-Bombers Versus German Armour in North-West Europe, 1944–1945: Myths and Realities," *Journal of Strategic Studies,* vol. 14, no. 2 (June 1991), pp. 210–231; Ian Gooderson, "Heavy and Medium Bombers: How Successful Were They in the Tactical Close Air Support Role During World War II?" *Journal of Strategic Studies,* vol. 15, no. 3 (September 1992), pp. 367–399; and Hosmer, ibid.
46. Debriefings of Iraqi personnel after the Gulf War were instructive on this point. Senior Iraqi officers tended to be equally concerned by American B-52 heavy bombers and A-10 attack aircraft. They hated the B-52s because they were terrifying and destroyed the morale of their men even though they generally did not kill anyone or destroy much equipment. They hated the A-10s because the A-10s employed PGMs (in the form of Maverick antitank missiles) that actually did destroy their tanks and artillery pieces, thus reducing the ability of the units under their command to execute their missions. For Iraqi troops and junior officers, however, who cared much less about executing their missions and much more about staying alive, really only the B-52s mattered. They were terrified of the B-52s, and it was clear that the heavy bomber strikes played the greatest role in breaking their morale, while the ability of the A-10s to destroy their equipment was almost irrelevant, especially when compared to their fear of the B-52s. Hosmer, ibid., pp. 165, 196.
47. For accounts of the tenacious resistance of the Republican Guards at the 73 Easting, see ARCENT, pp. 117–121; Vince Crawley, "Ghost Troop's Battle at the 73 Easting," *Armor,* May–June 1991, pp. 7–12; Colonel Gregory Fontenot, "Fright Night: Task Force 2/34 Armor," *Military Review,* January 1993, pp. 38–51; Michael J. Mazarr, Don M. Snider, and James A. Blackwell, Jr., *Desert Storm* (Boulder, Colo.: Westview, 1993), p. 147; Jim Tice, "Coming Through: The Big Red Raid," *Army Times,* August 26, 1991, pp. 13–20; Steve Vogel, "A Swift Kick: 2nd ACR's Taming of the Guard," *Army Times,* August 5, 1991, pp. 28–61; Steve Vogel, "Metal Rain: 'Old Ironsides' and Iraqis Who Wouldn't Back Down," *Army Times,* September 16, 1991, p. 16; Steve Vogel, "The Tip of the Spear," *Army Times,* January 13, 1992, pp. 13–54; and U.S. News and World Report, *Triumph Without Victory* (New York: Random House, 1992), pp. 336–342, 351–370.

48. Lambeth, *NATO's Air War for Kosovo,* p. 18.

49. Eliot A. Cohen and Thomas A. Keaney, *Gulf War Air Power Survey Summary Report* (Washington, D.C.: GPO, 1993), p. 200.

50. Michael G. Vickers, "Revolution Deferred: Kosovo and the Transformation of War," in Eliot A. Cohen and Andrew J. Bacevich, eds., *War over Kosovo* (New York: Columbia University Press, 2001), p. 193.

51. On the ability of the Iraqis to surprise U.S. Central Command at R'as al-Khafji, the subsequent air effort against them, and their losses, see Central Intelligence Agency, *Operation Desert Storm;* Major Daniel R. Clevenger, "Battle of Khafji, Air Power Effectiveness in the Desert," vol. 1, Air Force Studies and Analyses Agency, July 1996; Michael R. Gordon and General Bernard E. Trainor, *The Generals' War: The Inside Story of the Conflict in the Gulf* (Boston: Little, Brown, 1995), pp. 267–288.

52. Lieutenant Colonel Charles H. Cureton, *US Marines in the Persian Gulf, 1990–1991: With the 1st Marine Division in Desert Shield and Desert Storm* (Washington, D.C.: Headquarters, USMC, 1993); interview with Lieutenant General William M. Keyes, "Rolling with the 2nd Marine Division," in Major Charles D. Melson, Evelyn A. Englander, and Captain David A. Dawson, *US Marines in the Persian Gulf: Anthology and Annotated Bibliography* (Washington, D.C.: Headquarters, USMC, 1992), p. 153; Lieutenant Colonel Dennis P. Mroczkowski, *US Marines in the Persian Gulf, 1990–1991: With the 2nd Marine Division in Desert Shield and Desert Storm* (Washington, D.C.: Headquarters, USMC, 1993), pp. 52–53; U.S. DOD, *Conduct of the Persian Gulf War,* p. 258; U.S. News and World Report, *Triumph Without Victory,* pp. 294–312, 322–324; Lieutenant Colonel J. G. Zumwalt, USMCR, "Tanks! Tanks! Direct Front!" *Proceedings,* vol. 118, no. 7 (July 1992), pp. 74–80.

53. This is based on the discussion in Forage, "The Battle for Mount Pastrik," pp. 66–67, which is not clear cut but notes that the air strikes only "slowed" the Serbian advance, which was ultimately stopped by KLA positions *inside Albania,* i.e., at the KLA's start positions.

54. One of the reasons that some members of the extreme right wing favor the Afghan Approach is that they want to overturn the governments of many of our Arab allies in the region. For example, in a recent article in *The Washington Monthly,* Joshua Marshall noted that many of the neoconservatives believe that "it would be a *good thing* if the repressive governments of Egypt or Saudi Arabia fell" (emphasis in original). He quotes former Assistant Secretary of Defense Richard Perle commenting on the threat to Egyptian stability in a new war with Iraq that "Mubarak is no great shakes" and "Surely we can do better than Mubarak." Marshall goes on to say, "I put the same question to Perle's colleague from the Reagan administration and fellow hawk, Ken Adelman. Did he think wobbly or upended regimes in Egypt and Saudi Arabia were worth the price of removing Saddam? 'All the better if you ask me.' " Joshua Micah Marshall, "Bomb Saddam?" *The Washington Monthly,* June 2002, available at www.washingtonmonthly.com/features/2001/0206.marshall.html, downloaded July 2, 2002.

55. Vernon Loeb, "U.S. Gains in Attacking Mobile Arms," *The Washington Post,* July 5, 2002, p. A14.

56. Nicholas Birch, "Iraq's Kurds Aren't Looking for a Fight," *The Washington Post,* May 5, 2002, p. B3; John F. Burns, "Kurds, Secure in North Iraq, Are Cool to a

U.S. Offensive," *The New York Times,* July 8, 2002; Sally Buzbee, "Iraqi Kurds Worry That U.S. Invasion Could Lead to Backlash from Saddam," Associated Press, May 27, 2002.

57. Amnon Barzilai, "Believe It or Not," *Ha'aretz,* June 22, 2002, available at www.haaretzdaily.com/hasen/pages/ShArt.jhtml?itemNo=178598, downloaded June 30, 2002.

58. Andrew Parasiliti, "Deter," in Patrick Clawson, ed., *Iraq Strategy Review* (Washington, D.C.: WINEP, 1998), p. 111.

59. See, e.g., Hersh, "The Debate Within," pp. 34–39; Dave Moniz and Jonathan Weisman, "Military Questions Iraq Plan," *USA Today,* May 23, 2002; Thomas E. Ricks, "Military Bids to Postpone Iraq Invasion," *The Washington Post,* May 24, 2002, p. A1; Rowan Scarborough, "Size of Force on Ground Key in Plan for Iraq War," *The Washington Times,* April 26, 2002, p. 1; Thom Shanker and David E. Sanger, "U.S. Blueprint to Topple Hussein Envisions Big Invasion Next Year," *The New York Times,* April 28, 2002, p. A1; Eric Schmitt, "U.S. Plan for Iraq Is Said to Include Attack on 3 Sides," *The New York Times,* July 5, 2002, p. A1.

60. Birch, "Iraq's Kurds Aren't Looking for a Fight"; Burns, "Kurds, Secure in North Iraq, Are Cool to a U.S. Offensive"; Buzbee, "Iraqi Kurds Worry That U.S. Invasion Could Lead to Backlash from Saddam"; Scott Peterson, "As U.S. Targets Iraq, Key Rebels Balk," *The Christian Science Monitor,* February 15, 2002.

Chapter 11: The Case for an Invasion

1. A U.S. ground division consists of roughly 20,000 troops. U.S. armored and mechanized divisions (heavy divisions) normally field more than 300 tanks and a similar number of armored personnel carriers.

2. For similar assessments, see John Hillen, "Invade," in Patrick Clawson, ed., *Iraq Strategy Review* (Washington, D.C.: WINEP, 1998), pp. 117–147; Eliot A. Cohen, "Iraq Can't Resist Us," *The Wall Street Journal,* December 18, 2001. Hillen is a decorated veteran of the Persian Gulf War. Cohen is a highly respected military analyst. Cohen argues that a single U.S. ground corps should be adequate to defeat the Iraqi armed forces. I agree with Cohen's assessment but believe that the United States will inevitably require more troops both to take on additional missions beyond simply defeating the Iraqi Army (e.g., preventing Scud launches against Israel) and to have enough forces to guard against unforeseen developments.

3. U.S. Department of Defense, "National Guard and Reserve Mobilized as of June 26," Press Release No. 329-02, June 26, 2002; U.S. Department of Defense, *Conduct of the Persian Gulf War,* Final Report to Congress (Washington, D.C.: GPO, 1992), p. 471. Admittedly, some of the 85,000 troops called up in 2001–02 were for operations in support of the war on terrorism not closely linked to the campaign in Afghanistan. However, the vast majority were called up to support the Afghan operation, and a significant number of those called up in 1990–91 also performed security, intelligence, and other functions to secure the United States and its interests elsewhere around the world against Iraqi-motivated terrorism similarly unrelated to the operations in Iraq. Indeed, only 106,000 of the 245,000 reservists mobilized actually deployed to the Persian Gulf.

4. See Michael R. Gordon and General Bernard E. Trainor, *The Generals' War: The Inside Story of the Conflict in the Gulf* (Boston: Little, Brown, 1995), pp. 123–158.

5. Eliot Cohen makes this point nicely in his essay "Kosovo and the New American Way of War," in Andrew J. Bacevich and Eliot A. Cohen, eds., *War over Kosovo* (New York: Columbia University Press, 2001). See especially pp. 53–56.

6. Daryl G. Press, "The Myth of Air Power in the Persian Gulf War and the Future of Warfare," *International Security,* vol. 26, no. 2 (Fall 2001), p. 39.

7. In support of this, see the various comments in Staff Brigadier General Najib al-Salihi, *al-Zilzal (The Earthquake): What Happened in Iraq After the Withdrawal from Kuwait? Secrets of the Bloody Days!* (London: al-Rafid Distribution and Publishing, 1998), trans. by FBIS, May 1999, esp. pp. 11–12, 23.

8. Amatzia Baram, *Building Toward Crisis: Saddam Hussein's Strategy for Survival,* Policy Paper No. 47, (Washington, D.C.: WINEP, 1998), p. 43.

9. Author's interviews with U.S. military officers, February–April and October–December 1997.

10. See, e.g., Andrea Stone, "Poll: 59% Say U.S. Should Take Military Action in Iraq," *USA Today,* June 21, 2002.

11. Barbara Crossette, "Little Support for Iraq Attack in Group's Poll," *The New York Times,* December 30, 2001; Steven Thomma, Jack Koszczuk, and Jonathan S. Landay, "Bush Faces Many Hurdles Before Any Iraq War," *The Philadelphia Inquirer,* March 27, 2002.

12. Anthony Clark Arend, "Iraq: First Make the Case," *The Washington Post,* April 17, 2002, p. A15; Lee A. Casey and David B. Rivkin, Jr., " 'Anticipatory' Self-Defense Against Terrorism Is Legal," *Legal Opinion Letter,* vol. 11, no. 19 (December 14, 2001), available at www.wlf.org/upload/casey.pdf, downloaded July 7, 2002; Craig Gilbert, "Can U.S. Be First to Attack Enemy?" *Milwaukee Journal Sentinel,* March 31, 2002; Norman Kempster, "Leaders and Scholars Clash over Legality," *Los Angeles Times,* March 26, 1999.

13. See Louis Rene Beres, "Twenty Years Later: Israel, Osiraq and Anticipatory Self Defense," Tzemach Institute, June 7, 2001; Louis Rene Beres and Colonel Yoash Tsiddon-Chatto (IDF Res.), "In Support of Anticipatory Self-Defense: Israel, Osiraq, and International Law," Freeman Center for Strategic Studies, 1997, available at www.freeman.org/m_online/jun97/beres1.htm, downloaded July 7, 2002; Casey and Rivkin, ibid.

14. "Saad al-Bazzaz: An Insider's View of Iraq," *Middle East Quarterly,* December 1995, p. 73.

15. "Oral History: Wafic al Samarrai," *PBS Frontline: The Gulf War,* available at www.pbs.org/wgbh/pages/frontline/gulf/oral/samarrai/1.html, downloaded May 2, 2002.

16. Nuha al-Radi, *Baghdad Diaries* (London: Saqi Books, 1998), p. 53.

17. Ibid., p. 67.

18. Ibid., p. 99.

Chapter 12: Rebuilding Iraq

1. For a similar view of the Afghan situation, see Richard Holbrooke, "Rebuilding Nations . . . ," *The Washington Post,* April 1, 2002.

2. For concurring views, see Roberta Cohen and Michael O'Hanlon, "Send Stronger 'Stability Force' to Afghanistan," *The Baltimore Sun,* June 14, 2002; Editorial Desk, "Afghanistan at Risk," *The New York Times,* March 27, 2002, p. A22; Michael Elliott, "The Battle over Peacekeeping," *Time,* March 4, 2002,

pp. 31–32; Richard Holbrooke, "Rebuilding Nations . . ."; International Crisis Group, "Securing Afghanistan: The Need for More International Action," *Afghanistan Briefing,* March 15, 2002; Sarah Sewall, "Confronting the Warlord Culture," *The Boston Globe,* June 6, 2002.

3. The likely U.S. aid level was arrived at as follows: U.S. aid to Europe under the Marshall Plan amounted to $200 to $300 per person per year; U.S. aid to Japan and Korea in the 1950s and 1960s amounted to $50 to $75 per person per year; and international aid to the Balkan countries and the Palestinians in the 1990s amounted to about $300 per person per year. (All figures from Michael E. O'Hanlon, "The Aid and Reconstruction Agenda for Afghanistan," Brookings Institution, Analysis Paper No. 13, December 19, 2001.) With a population of 23 million, Iraq would therefore need somewhere between $1 billion and $7 billion per year, depending on the aid level required. Even if we assume the high end of $7 billion per year, Iraq's own oil production should be able to defray at least $1 billion during the first year of reconstruction, and this figure should mount steadily thereafter. As soon as Iraq's oil production can be restored to preinvasion numbers, it should be earning $12 billion to $25 billion per year (depending on prices), which ought to account for virtually all reconstruction costs. Given our recent experience restoring Kuwaiti oil production, it is difficult to imagine that it would take more than three years to restore Iraqi oil production to its preinvasion levels. Even during the first one to three years, we should be able to count on at least several billion dollars in aid from the Gulf states (since it is unrealistic to believe that we could launch the invasion without their support). Thus, between Iraq's own oil production and contributions from the Gulf states, the United States would probably have to put up no more than an average of about $3 billion per year for the first three years, or a total of $9 billion to $10 billion. However, if we put together an international coalition that included European and Asian states as well, aid from those states ought to allow us to cut our own contributions in half, to $5 billion, spread out over the first three years.

4. U.S. Department of Defense, "Fact Sheet: Operation Joint Endeavor," December 11, 1995, available at www.dtic.mil/bosnia/fs/fs006b.html, downloaded July 20, 2002.

5. On the reduction of U.S. forces in Bosnia, see the sections regarding Operations Joint Endeavor, Joint Guard, and Joint Forge at Global Security.org, available at www.globalsecurity.org/military/ops/yugo-ops.htm, downloaded July 20, 2002.

6. On creating a federal system in an Arab state, see Gabriel Ben-Dor, "Federalism in the Arab World," in Daniel J. Elazar, ed., *Federalism and Political Integration* (Ramat Gan, Israel: Turtledove Publishing, 1979), pp. 191–203; and Gabriel Ben-Dor and Ofra Bengio, "The State and Minorities Toward the Twenty-First Century: An Overview," in Ofra Bengio and Gabriel Ben-Dor, eds., *Minorities and the State in the Arab World* (Boulder, Colo.: Lynne Rienner, 1999).

7. For a description of Iraq's early experience with "sham democracy" and an argument that it is unready for true democracy, see Elie Kedourie, *Democracy and Arab Political Culture* (Washington, D.C.: WINEP, 1992).

8. Lisa Anderson dispels the notion that democracy has not taken hold in the Arab world for cultural reasons and instead points to political and structural problems—problems that would not exist in Iraq if Saddam's regime were overthrown by a U.S.-led invasion followed by an international reconstruction effort.

See Lisa Anderson, "Arab Democracy: Dismal Prospects," *World Policy Journal,* vol. 18, no. 3 (Fall 2001), pp. 53–60. For another account of the problems facing democracies in the Islamic world (which the author does not believe to be insurmountable), see Fatima Mernissi, *Islam and Democracy: Fear of the Modern World,* trans. by Mary Jo Lakeland (Reading, Mass.: Addison-Wesley, 1992).

9. On democratic stirrings in the Arab world, see Saad Eddin Ibrahim, "Crises, Elites, and Democratization in the Arab World," *The Middle East Journal,* vol. 47, no. 2 (Spring 1993), pp. 292–305; Augustus Richard Norton, "The Future of Civil Society in the Middle East," *The Middle East Journal,* vol. 47, no. 2 (Spring 1993), pp. 205–216; Alan Richards, "Economic Imperatives and Political Systems," *The Middle East Journal,* vol. 47, no. 2 (Spring 1993), pp. 217–227; Larbi Sadiki, *The Search for Arab Democracy* (New York: Columbia University Press, 2002).

10. On political reform and transitions to democracy, see Thomas Carrothers, *Aiding Democracy Abroad: The Learning Curve* (Washington, D.C.: Carnegie Endowment, 1999).

11. My thanks to Joe Siegle on these various points. Joseph Siegle, personal correspondence, July 2002.

12. For detailed accounts of the effort to rebuild Bosnia, see, e.g., "Bosnia Minority Refugee/Displaced Persons Returns 2000," U.S. Department of State, fact sheet released by the Bureau of European Affairs, January 10, 2001; Marcus Cox, "State Building and Post-Conflict Reconstruction: Lessons from Bosnia," The Rehabilitation of War-Torn Societies, a Project Coordinated by the Centre for Applied Studies in International Negotiations, January 2001; "Economic Reform Programs," United States Agency for International Development, July 2001, available at www.usaid.ba.information/sheets/econjul011.htm, downloaded June 24, 2002; "Europe: Central and Eastern: Bosnia-Herzegovina," National Democratic Institute for International Affairs, updated June 2002, available at www.ndi.org/worldwide/cee/bosnia/bosnia_pf.asp, downloaded June 24, 2002; "Lessons for Rebuilding Southeast Europe, the Bosnia and Herzegovina Experience," World Bank Press Backgrounder, 1999, available at www.worldbank. org/html/extdr/kosovo/kosovo-pb.2.htm, downloaded June 24, 2002; "Reconstruction of Bosnia and Herzegovina: Priorities for Recovery and Growth," World Bank press release, undated; "Summary of US Government Policy on Bosnia," U.S. Department of State, released by the Bureau of European and Canadian Affairs, July 16, 1998, available at www.state.gov/www/regions/eur/ fs_980716_bosqanda.html, downloaded June 24, 2002.

13. For detailed accounts of the effort to rebuild Kosovo, see, e.g., Curt Tarnoff, "Kosovo: Reconstruction and Development Assistance," CRS Report for Congress, updated June 7, 2001; "Fact Sheet: Winning the Peace in Kosovo: A Progress Report," White House Office of the Press Secretary, November 23, 1999, available at www.clinton3.nara.gov/WH/New/Europe-9911/facts/ 1999-11-23b.html, downloaded June 25, 2002; National Democratic Institute, "Europe: Central and Eastern: Yugoslavia: Kosovo," June 2002, available at www.ndi.org/worldwide/cee/kosovo/kosovo_pf.asp, downloaded June 25, 2002; Organization for Security and Co-operation in Europe, "Mission in Kosovo," available at www.osce.org/kosovo, downloaded June 25, 2002; Hansjörg Strohmeyer, "Collapse and Reconstruction of a Judicial System: The United Na-

tions in Kosovo and East Timor," *The American Journal of International Law,*
vol. 95 (January 2001), pp. 46–63; "US Efforts to Promote Human Rights and
Democracy in Kosovo," fact sheet released by the Office of the Special Advisor
to the President and the Secretary of State for Kosovo and Dayton Implementation, July 26, 1999, available at www.state.gov/www/regions/eur/kosovo/
fs_990726_kosovo_drl.html, downloaded June 25, 2002; Steven J. Woehrel and
Julie Kim, "Kosovo and US Policy," CRS report for Congress, updated December 4, 2001; United Nations, "UN Interim Administration Mission in Kosovo:
UNMIK at a Glance," available at www.unmikonline.org/intro.htm, downloaded
June 25, 2002.

14. I am indebted to Joe Siegle for making these points to me. Joseph Siegle, personal correspondence, July 2002.

15. For an excellent discussion of these issues using the South African case as a
model, see Lorna McGregor, "Individual Accountability in South Africa: Cultural Optimum or Political Façade?" *The American Journal of International Law,*
vol. 95 (January 2001), pp. 32–45.

Conclusions: Not Whether, but When

1. The editors of *The Economist* deserve credit for first making this point. See
"Saddam and His Sort," *The Economist,* June 29, 2002.

2. See, e.g., "War on Iraq Is Wrong," *The Nation,* July 8, 2002, available at
www.thenation.com, downloaded June 25, 2002.

ABOUT THE AUTHOR

KENNETH M. POLLACK wrote this book as Olin Senior Fellow and Director of National Security Studies for the Council on Foreign Relations. From 1995 to 1996 and from 1999 to 2001, he served as director for Gulf affairs at the National Security Council, where he was the principal working-level official responsible for implementation of U.S. policy toward Iraq. Prior to his time in the Clinton administration, he spent seven years in the CIA as a Persian Gulf military analyst. He is also the author of *Arabs at War: Arab Military Effectiveness, 1948–1991* (University of Nebraska Press). He is a graduate of Yale University and received a Ph.D. in political science from the Massachusetts Institute of Technology. He lives in Washington, D.C., with his wife and is director of research at the Saban Center for Middle East Policy at the Brookings Institution.

ABOUT THE TYPE

This book was set in Times Roman, designed by Stanley Morison specifically for *The Times* of London. The typeface was introduced in the newspaper in 1932. Times Roman has had its greatest success in the United States as a book and commercial typeface, rather than one used in newspapers.